CW00802981

The publisher gratefull ...ᴋᴄᴜges the generous contribution to this book provided by the Humanities Endowment Fund of the University of California Press Foundation.

THE FIRE

THE FIRE

Collected Essays
of Robin Blaser

Edited and with a commentary
by Miriam Nichols

University of California Press
Berkeley Los Angeles London

University of California Press, one of the most distinguished
university presses in the United States, enriches lives around
the world by advancing scholarship in the humanities, social
sciences, and natural sciences. Its activities are supported by
the UC Press Foundation and by philanthropic contributions
from individuals and institutions. For more information, visit
www.ucpress.edu.

For acknowledgments of permissions, please see page 481.
The photograph used as a frontispiece is reproduced courtesy
of Christos Dikeakos. Photographs that appear in the illustration
section (following page 410), except for the last one, are
reproduced courtesy of Robin Blaser.

University of California Press
Berkeley and Los Angeles, California

University of California Press, Ltd.
London, England

Library of Congress Cataloging-in-Publication Data

Blaser, Robin.
    The fire : collected essays of Robin Blaser / Robin Blaser ;
edited and with a commentary by Miriam Nichols.
        p. cm.
    Includes bibliographical references and index.
    ISBN-13 978-0-520-24510-5 (alk. paper),
ISBN-10 0-520-24510-5 (alk. paper) — ISBN-13 978-0-520-
24511-2 (pbk. : alk. paper), ISBN-10 0-520-24511-3 (pbk. :
alk. paper)
    1. Poetics.   2. Poetry—History and criticism.   I. Nichols,
Miriam.   II. Title.
    PS3552.L37F57 2006
    808.1—dc22   2005025772

Manufactured in the United States of America

15   14   13   12   11   10   09   08   07   06
10   9   8   7   6   5   4   3   2   1

This book is printed on New Leaf EcoBook 50, a 100% recycled
fiber of which 50% is de-inked post-consumer waste, processed
chlorine-free. EcoBook 50 is acid-free and meets the minimum
requirements of ANSI/ASTM D5634–01 (Permanence of Paper).

nothing simpler than what I have said because
I didn't say it, nothing simpler than what
I have said, because I said it—

Robin Blaser, "The Art of Combinations,"
The Holy Forest

CONTENTS

ILLUSTRATIONS

PREFACE

Since the 1960s Robin Blaser's essays on poetry and poetics have appeared in small press publications, anthologies, and the "Selected Poems" of other poets. This volume gathers them for the first time. Best known for his participation with Robert Duncan and Jack Spicer in the San Francisco Renaissance of the 1950s, Blaser is unique among his companions of that period: not only is he belated, publishing his first, distinguishing statement of poetics only in 1967 in "The Fire," but his writing life extends much beyond the New American moment so famously anthologized in Donald Allen's *The New American Poetry* of 1960 and includes the distance of a cross-border perspective. In 1966 Blaser moved from Berkeley to Vancouver, British Columbia; he became a dual citizen of Canada and the United States in 1974. He has been a professor in the Departments of English and Fine Arts at Simon Fraser University for twenty years. He has sustained literary friendships across national and generational boundaries with the poets Charles Bernstein, George Bowering, Robert Creeley, Rachel Blau DuPlessis, Kevin Killian, Daphne Marlatt, Steve McCaffery, Erin Mouré, bp Nichol, Michael Ondaatje, Sharon Thesen, Phyllis Webb, and many others. This collection of essays is a virtual conversation about poetics with such personal writer-friends as well as philosophers and artists, living and dead, whom Blaser has found companionable. It is also an intense reading of the postmodern that winds its way through fifty years of cultural history to arrive at an alternative view of the arts.

Blaser's version of the postmodern develops out of a sense of cultural crisis. The failure of Anglo-American moderns such as William Butler Yeats, Ezra Pound, or T.S. Eliot to salvage the master narratives, followed by a suspicion of culture in the deconstructive 1970s and 1980s, has produced a long-lasting skepticism in the humanities that was a catastrophe before it became postmodern theory and finally the unremarked wallpaper of our contemporary condition.

Before Jacques Derrida, Jacques Lacan, Jean-François Lyotard, Julia Kristeva, Gilles Deleuze, and Homi Bhaba took their turns as passwords in university English departments, however, Charles Olson wrestled with the problems of cultural identity and aesthetic representation posed by heterogeneity. This notion is clear in his notes on the visits to Ezra Pound at St. Elizabeths Hospital, 1946–48, where Pound was awaiting trial for treason after his pro-fascist radio broadcasts during the war. In a prescient passage, Olson describes Pound's embrace of Italian fascism as nostalgia for a nation of small farmers and petty patricians. A "200 year *political lag*," Olson says, blinded Pound to "the single most important fact of the last 100 years, the most important human fact between Newton and the Atomic Bomb—the sudden multiple increase of the earth's population, the coming into existence of the MASSES" (*Olson and Pound* 53). This crucial fact, which Olson notices at the very beginning of the postwar era, is telling for poets because it instantly troubles their place in the world. If the "makers," as Spicer called them (*Collected Books* 113), cannot assume a common tradition among their readers—if they cannot identify a "tribe" to tell the tale of, as Pound thought possible—then they must either reinvent the concept of community or talk to themselves. Blaser's keen awareness of this problem shows in his remark in "The Fire" that poets are often accused of writing for a coterie, but the thought haunts his work everywhere in the shape of an absent *polis* and a sustained effort after renewal.

"The Fire" thus marks Blaser's entry into an ongoing conversation about public meaning among poets from the midcentury avant-garde to the contemporary. Charles Olson, with whom Blaser corresponded in the 1950s, had proposed a new "human universe" in the first *Maximus* poems, "The Human Universe," and "Projective Verse." In the aftermath of Auschwitz and the reduction of persons to so much "fat for soap" ("The Resistance," *Collected Prose* 174), Olson argued the need for a serious reassessment of humanity at the species level, especially the Western portion of it. Metaphysical abstraction, in his view, stood behind a traditional Euro-American disdain for life that had turned a nightmarish face outward in the Holocaust. As Blaser would say later in "The Stadium of the Mirror," "the thought of totals [is] the original totalitarianism." What a *poet* might do about such matters, Olson suggested, was to rewrite the human as a historical creature rather than a metaphysical one. This revision of the human was to become a major generational push. What Olson does with history, Duncan does with myth. With his invocation of a *grand collage* (*Bending the Bow* vii), or virtual archive of cultural narratives, Duncan opens up the whole of human self-fashioning to exploration and reassessment. In both cases, the implied community exceeds national, linguistic, and ethnic boundaries to include all of humanity. Among Blaser's closest companions, Jack Spicer as well begins at this same level of inclusion, pulling his defining terms from linguistics, however, rather than history or myth. Anticipating next-generation language poets and deconstructionists, Spicer took language as the common ground of the human universe, but for him it posed the question of how to achieve lyric expressivity in an impersonal medium rather than how to reshape the *imago mundi*. Robert Creeley is the other lyricist crucial to Blaser, and, like Spicer, Creeley was acutely conscious of the loss of a realist epistemology and the consequent difficulty of writing lyric. But rather than focus on an impossible desire for unmediated expression, he works at creating a place to live from the welter of a life-world come loose from meaningful narration. The local is "not a place but a place in a given man" (*Collected Essays* 479), he says, and his "auto-bio-graphy" is a poetics of the small step. Unstructured human space, traversed on foot, may slowly become place—if one is lucky and can find the leisure to live for it.

What these poets share is a problem rather than a solution, and this is what keeps the virtual conversation going between them, as well as what carries over into subsequent generations. Bereft of a world made homely by shared traditions, subjected to intractable linguistic mechanisms and social mediation, the lyric bird sharpens his tongue on the cage of language, while the epic bard struggles with the unwieldiness of a "tribe" that has spilled over any and all defining boundaries. Here is the "'*cultural orphanhood*'" (preface to "Syntax," *Holy Forest*; original emphasis) that Blaser begins to address in "The Fire." In this essay and those that follow, he restates the problem of the common as a struggle for the real, meaning, if I read him rightly, a struggle for what is to count as public reality. Dante is a cherished model because he confronted a Christian world that had not yet found its image, just as poets of the postwar era had to face an epoch still moiling. In the postwar period, however, the task of the poet as witness of deeds and shaper of meaning had to be performed in a postfoundational context that left only the empirical sciences relatively unscathed by skepticism. In such a climate, any claim to a world image becomes suspect because it can be exposed as mediated or exclusive in some way. (As Roland Barthes would say, "the content of the word 'Order' always indicates repression" [*WDZ* 26]). The poet is allowed to amuse, but he or she has no public voice except, perhaps, that of the critic of ideology. Hence the need to defend a big poetry that reaches for meaning, relationship, and shapeliness in the lived world. This is Blaser's polemical push. In "The Violets" (1981), for instance:

> Poets have repeatedly in this century turned philosophers, so to speak, in order to argue the value of poetry and its practice within the disturbed meanings of our time. These arguments are fascinating because they have everything to do with the poet's sense of reality in which imagery is entangled with thought. Often, they

reflect Pound's sense of "make it new" or the modernist notion that this century and its art are simultaneously the end of something and the beginning of something else, a new consciousness, and so forth. It is not one argument or another for or against tradition, nor is it the complex renewal of the imaginary which our arts witness, for, as I take it, the enlightened mind does not undervalue the imaginary, which is the most striking matter of these poetics; what is laid out before us finally is the fundamental struggle for the nature of the real. And this, in my view, is a spiritual struggle, both philosophical and poetic. Old spiritual forms, along with positivisms and materialisms, which "held" the real together have come loose. This is a cliché of our recognitions and condition. But we need only look at the energy of the struggle in philosophy and poetry to make it alive and central to our private and public lives. (197)

Here and elsewhere, Blaser argues that what has come to be the dominant reading of perceptual experience as untrustworthy is a misapplication of the scientific criteria for knowledge and a form of positivism as well because it disguises the unsupportable assumption that rational and empirical modes of knowledge are closer to some objective reality than the *mere* subjectivity of perception. Yet the lived world, more overtly than the discourses of science or philosophy, is a matter of relationships among persons, places, things, and events: as such it is neither true nor false. The New American experiment began as a search for methods through which human relations might be reimagined with fidelity to the times. In the work of poets such as Duncan and Olson, this search for an adequate vision of the human universe takes shape as a phenomenology of belief—not to be confused with a philosophy bound still to the rubric of truth and falsehood if only by its Husserlian brackets. Blaser is at his most polemical when he speaks against the dismissal of this poetic project and urges the necessity of a "'perceptual relation to the universe'" ("The Fire" 6).

In many side-by-side readings of poetry with philosophy and the other arts, Blaser tracks the contest for the really real over fifty years of unfoldings. His unique contribution to the conversation is first evident in two important features of "The Fire" that return in different forms throughout the essays. The most immediately noticeable of these is the copious quotation. As Blaser notes in "Mind Canaries" and "'Here Lies the Woodpecker Who Was Zeus,'" the essays read like anthologies. There are several reasons for this. First, the situated voice is crucial to Blaser: his first-person singular always appears among others. Representation thus gives place to conversation, and the real as permanent condition to the real as ongoing project. Second, Blaser chooses memory as both trope and method for his poetics, rather than history (Olson), myth (Duncan), or language (Spicer). In contrast to public histories or archetypal renderings of culture, personal memory evokes the past as a multitude of little stories, most of them hidden from public view. From this lowercase perspective, what can be held in common is simply the perspectival nature of experience as such: as Blaser argues in "Particles," what we share is our particularity. The "particles," however, may become a powerful wellspring of unpredictability and challenge to official narratives. In personal memory, the past opens out to myriad alternative constructions and the future, consequently, to possible new directions. Memory is the virtual plentitude of history, and Blaser's passion for salvaging it is a means of reclaiming the power of the makers against historical and social determinations as well as philosophical skepticism. Translated into genre, this poetic stance means lyric historicized. In Blaser's version of the serial poem, lyric is made reflexive and open to historical content as well as personal expression. The poem unfolds as a personal view of public matters—rather like "a large, crowded reception / in a private house" in Blaser's phrasing ("à cet ultime instant," *Holy Forest*).

Alongside personal memory, however, Blaser emphasizes the importance of cultural remembering as essential to understanding where we have come from. In conversation, he jokes that a professor from his Berkeley student days dubbed him and Spicer and Duncan "the museum poets," but he calls on the museum, nonetheless, to speak against postmodernisms that have too often expressed a collective amnesia. Because secular societies think they do not believe, because the Western cultural heritage is considered by many to be ideologically tainted, and because the heterogeneity of current populations coupled with technological revolution in communications brings a welter of traditions and historical trajectories to the world stage, the unspoken tendency of the postmodern has been to forget. So in "The Recovery of the Public World," this passage:

> There is no possibility of understanding, appreciating, enjoying or of participating in the modern, artistic project of being in the world, except by familiarity with traditional art and its thought. . . . The inability to understand the modern project . . . turns into a cultural forgetting. Some years ago, during one of my lectures on modernism—Picasso's *Les demoiselles d'Avignon* large on the wall behind me— a hand went up. The student asked, "Sir, did you make this up?" After a puzzled moment, I burst into laughter. The student replied, "Well, you're talking about things seventy years old. Why haven't I ever heard of them?" This, it turned out, was no dumbbell, nor was he a country bumpkin. His resentment was real and thoughtful. A victim of educational effacement. But, then, one whispers, his parents, his teachers, the system that tutors him, none of them could fill the emptiness. Charges of elitism become silly and dangerous under such cultural circumstances. (82)

Blaser's many citations urge conversation against the "financial surface" of our culture ("Recovery" 82), and to that end they create on the page a forum of past and present voices. At once an offering, exhortation, curriculum, and vir-

tual community, the voices Blaser summons also propose an art of memory—
"[i]n order to gain 'an attitude that knows how to take care and preserve and
admire the things of the world'" ("Recovery" 86).

I have divided the essays into writings on poetics and commentaries on other
poets—this to draw out the shapeliness of the oeuvre. "The Fire" (1967) is a
foundational first statement that Blaser then elaborates as politics in "Particles"
(1969) and as aesthetics in "The Stadium of the Mirror" (1974). "Poetry and
Positivism" (1989), "The Recovery of the Public World" (1993), and "The
Irreparable" (2003) set the poetics to work in the crucial contexts of contem-
porary philosophy, politics, and current events. These six pieces, along with the
brief "out of the velvet" on the repressive nature of nationalism and other
"isms," constitute the theoretical core of Blaser's prose work to date. The com-
mentaries offer explications and expansions. In particular, "The Practice of Out-
side" (1975) and "'My Vocabulary Did This to Me'" (1986) on Spicer and the
Olson-Whitehead meditation in "The Violets" (1981) stand out as essential elab-
orations of Blaser's pursuit of the real and his rereading of poetic history. To
follow Blaser in these and in all his engagements is to remember another way
back to the future.

The texts here have been taken from the publications in which they first ap-
peared with the following minor alterations. Quotations have been checked
against original sources, and the various documentation styles have been made
uniform. In some cases, where permissions have not been forthcoming, quo-
tations have been edited. Italicized phrases in the body of the text not other-
wise marked as quotations are Blaser's; they occur primarily in the earlier es-
says and denote words or phrases cited from memory. References to poems in
The Holy Forest are by title, rather than page number, to avoid confusion between
the 1993 Coach House edition of these collected poems and the University of
California release of the revised edition in 2006. I have preserved variations be-
tween American and Canadian spellings, as well as Blaser's dates when he has
given them in the originals, at the end of each essay; these latter are dates of
completion, not the publication dates I have used in the table of contents. Blaser's
notes, other than simple citations and page references, appear as footnotes. My
editorial annotations are grouped as endnotes at the back of the book

This collection has been made possible through the hard work of my research
assistants, Maureen Donatelli, Leif Einarson, and Melanie Hughes. I owe spe-
cial thanks to Leif for his scholarly work on the references and documentation.
I am also indebted to Meredith Quartermain for her assistance in tracking sources
for "The Fire," "Particles," "The Stadium of the Mirror," and "The Practice of

Outside" and to Meredith and Peter Quartermain for editorial advice. Staff at the Contemporary Literature Collection, Bennett Library, Simon Fraser University, have been unfailingly helpful in supplying rare materials for my annotations. The University College of the Fraser Valley provided course releases and funding for my assistants through the Work Study program, the research program, and a Social Sciences and Humanities Research Council of Canada (SSHRC) Aid to Small Universities grant. Thanks are due as well to my editors at the University of California Press, Laura Cerruti and Rachel Berchten, who saw this project through the production process with sensitivity and attention. I am especially grateful to Robin Blaser for his patience and good humor in responding to my many requests for information.

Miriam Nichols

PART I

Poetics

The Fire

especially for Ebbe Borregaard[1]

I am here writing about my poetry in relation to poetry. The writing had an occasion: for a few in San Francisco, where I read it last March 8th [1967].[2] I want to talk about the personalism and the so-called obscurity of my poems in relation to the *sight, sound,* and *intellect* that compose them. "The test of poetry," in Zukofsky's words, "is the range of pleasure it affords as sight, sound, and intellection."[3]

One difficulty I want to describe is that I'm haunted by a sense of the invisibility of everything that comes into me (aware that nothing is more invisible than emotion—by emotion, I mean the heat of one's sense of the war, or a place, or a body, or of the extensions of these, the earth, the existence of gods, and so forth—the I-have-seen-what-I-have-seen, recorded by Pound in "Canto II"). I believe there is a reality, which, given the leisure to live for it, is neither conceptual and systemized in the ordinary sense of these words—nor imageless. There are many times when, forced by exhaustion, I take the lazy way of the conceptual and imageless, but it is a kind of desire which leads me to write of that other, outside world. Because the personal stake in companionship becomes so great in the way I live, I am sometimes lost when a reader finds me uninteresting or too obscure, his interest too soon exhausted to come to any meeting. I am literal about that other reality. It is, I think, the purest storytelling to try to catch that light—and the difficulty of it, the loss of it, is personal. If I see the light, even fragmentarily, and lose it, that too is subject matter, and leads to a kind of heartless poem, for it is not the elegiac loss which interests me, but the difficulty, the activity, of holding on to it. Burning up myself, I would leave fire behind me.[4]

To hold an image within the line by sound and heat is to have caught something that passed out there. The psychological accuracy of this perception is not enough; the sculptural imagistic quality is not enough; and the very aesthetic quality of taking the one image, or even three images as a whole, the beauty of the idea that you can write a single poem, is a lie. The processional aspect of the world has to be caught in the language also. The body hears the world, and the power of the earth over the body, the city over the body, is in terms of rhythms, meters, phrasing, picked up—the body's own rhythms compose those or it would shake to pieces.—The music of the spheres is quite real, but the sound of the earth must meet it. I suppose I want to say that the real business of poetry is cosmology, and I'm claiming my own stake in this. And this is the activity of telling the story—the necessity is chemical—it is *not* invented, but it is original, personal, singular, and even domestic. If one man gives up his life for the world, the energy of it is not symbolical: it is the story of one man tied to the heaven and hell he recognizes. No symbols.

My friend Stan Persky[5] was reading to me one night when a passage turned up that is so much to my purpose, slightly re-worded, that I won't give the author credit: it is in that meeting entirely mine: "What we describe as imagination is no free play of the soul, but a real meeting with real elements that are outside of us, and what matters is not the surrender to the images of fantasy that appear, but to redeem those elements themselves. What we suppose we effect merely in our souls, in reality we effect on the destiny of the world."[6]— Here, I wish to say that it is not language which is the source: it is the record of the meeting, and the magical structure of sight, sound, and intellect is indeed a personal responsibility. Language is given to us and in the most insidious way it controls sight, sound, and intellect, but it is also the medium which can be shaped.—Metaphor as a focus is an immediate escape from the ordinary focus, which rots for some reason I can't explain, and keeps me always from using the word *we*, though there is a kind of we that I hope to earn the right to use. But the poem offers a field of energy and activity—to be met by whatever companion can be found. If you imagine, as I do, that, at any waking moment, you are a corpuscle in the left wrist of god, then any reality is precisely to be found in the flow of corpuscles in that vast body.

In the constant interruption that it is to go to work every day, to talk in generalities of things that can only be known in specifics, this time guiding others through American writing, I'm struck by this thing called cosmology: Poe wanders off into a long prose piece, *Eureka*, which he calls a poem, and it is, drawing on all the contemporary science he can digest to record a cosmology; Emerson drops poetry and heads into poetically structured essays, wherein he can describe a cosmology; Thoreau drops poetry to write two strangely structured books,[7] where, as in *Walden*, the detailed attention given to the seasons is cosmological; Melville goes about it backwards—in *Moby-Dick*, myths had to be reset so that they could say what they should say about origins, where he is, then later the poetry clanks along unable to hold on to what he wants; Whitman comes in with a new line, as open as he could make it; Henry Adams moves from the well-formed novel to the work on the great Virgin of the 13th century to tell in detail the story of a unified world;[8] Pound puts it in the *Cantos* when he says the first thing was to break the iambic pentameter. It seems to me that the whole marvelous thing of open form is a traditional and an American problem—"hung up" on form because it was so difficult to open it. The whole thing came in a geography where the traditional forms would no longer hold our purposes. I was very moved when, some years ago, I was reading a scholarly book by Jo Miles[9] in which she is making an argument for the sublime poem, which oddly has something to do with the public poem, and she begins to talk about the narrative of the spirit. I think the key word here is narrative— the story of persons, events, activities, images, which tell the tale of the spirit.

I'm interested in a particular kind of narrative—what Jack Spicer and I agreed to call in our own work the serial poem—this is a narrative which refuses to adopt an imposed story line, and completes itself only in the sequence of poems, if, in fact, a reader insists upon a definition of completion which is separate from the activity of the poems themselves. The poems tend to act as a sequence of energies which run out when so much of a tale is told. I like to describe this in Ovidian terms, as a *carmen perpetuum*, a continuous song in which the fragmented subject matter is only apparently disconnected. Ovid's words are:

> to tell of bodies
> transformed
> into new shapes
> you gods, whose power
> worked all transformations,
> help the poet's breathing,
> lead my continuous song
> from the beginning to the present world

> In nova fert animus mutatas dicere formas
> corpora: di, coeptis (nam vos mutastis et illas)
> adspirate meis, primaque ab origine mundi
> ad meo perpetuum deducite tempora carmen![10]

The sequence of energies may involve all kinds of things—anger may open a window, a sound from another world may completely reshape the present moment, the destruction of a friendship may destroy a whole realm of language or the ability to use it—each piece is in effect an extended metaphor (another word is probably needed), because in the serial poem the effort is to hold both the correspondence and the focus that an image is, and the process of those things coming together—so that the light from a white linen tablecloth reflects on the face of one's companion, becomes light, fire, and the white moth which happens to be in the room is also light in the dark around the table, and is thus both the light and the element of light that destroys it. I ask you to remember that every metaphor involves at least four elements—which are a story, and the bringing them together is an activity, a glowing energy if stopped over, if entered. If the joy one feels in the sunny morning comes out as: the boat on the fire of the sea moves slowly to burn out—the story is of a boat on the sea— the fire is the sun on the water and the movement is of the boat, of the flow of the sun, and of the passing of the sun toward night. The joy of the movement is held a moment, then unfolds the story of the four elements, the boat and where it is, and the sun and what it is doing.

I wish now to extend these remarks by referring to some sources, which, in this case, were brought to me by Stan Persky, who has turned anthropologist, and who offers the pleasures of a real discourse. The gift is a passage in Edith Cobb. She says, "I became acutely aware that what a child wanted to do most of all was to make a world in which to find a place to discover a self. This ordering reverses the general position that self-exploration produces a knowledge of the world" (540). Furthermore, while observing the "*passionate world-making behavior* of the child," she noted that "accompanied by a population of toys, fauna and flora, and artifacts that do duty as 'figures of speech,'" she became "keenly aware of those processes which the genius in particular in later life seeks to recall" (540, my emphasis).[11] Edith Cobb in her interest in biological psychology moves to describe what she names a "cosmic sense," which in a separate essay, Margaret Mead describes as "a human instinctual need for a perceptual relation to the universe."[12] This is the scientific basis for the proprioceptive process which Charles Olson speaks of. In this context, I am arguing not for my pretensions as a poet, but for what the poetry reflects, if it is entered. That the poet does the job of entering this world and continues through his life to record that entrance is a fact, not pretense—that it is personal, original, and singular is also a fact. And here I want to quote the ethnologist Frank Speck on the Naskapi Indians (Labrador). He says that among them the form of the earth is like a hill and floats upon the water. He calls this a general concept, which is not true; it is a well-known image among them, and his informant, Charley Metowe'cic, said that the earth's form comes to be known only from the testimony of a man about to die. "In the vision that comes at this time the mind can view the universe and sees all around the earth as it rises above the water. And he feels it rocking" (58).[13] This is a statement which draws my attention because it is my own belief that any vision of the world is not complete until a man dies.[14] I mean here that imagination is more a power to take in and hold than it is a power of making up, though it must in its activity take responsibilty for the uncreated.

I want now to describe some very personal matters—as indications of the singularity—the personalness of language and form. I want here to create the image of a field which is true history, and autobiography, as well as land, place, and presence. I come to poetry with a definite sense of foreignness. Spicer once said that I was the only person he had ever met who could speak quotation marks, and these always appeared around the slang words I used. Now that given thing, language, comes to me through a combination of settled Americans on the one hand and from immigrants on the other. On the paternal side, a grandfather, born in the south of France, and a grandmother born in Wales, who was deeply ashamed of any non-English elements. That grandfather, Augustus Frederick Blaser, arrived in New York in the 1880s and came west to Sage, Wyoming, as a laborer for the railroad, and he was to work his way up to the exalted position of roadmaster and bishop of the Church of the Latter-day Saints. On the maternal side, a great-grandmother, whom I knew, from Springfield, Mass., who came west with the Mormons, and who had been secretary to Brigham Young. My own Roman Catholic thing comes from that great-grandmother's hatred of Mormons, so that my mother and I were in turn sent to the Catholics— with whom we were both to learn "The Star-Spangled Banner" in Latin.[15] In the midst of this interplay of talk about revelation of God here on the American continent, somewhere on the Great Plains was my sense of it, and of the ritual mystery of the Catholic Church, performed for kneeling and rising men and women, we lived in houses that were always by the railroad tracks, sometimes between two railbeds—the houses were remodeled railway cars, sometimes dining cars—with window after window where the tables had been. These were painted yellow and placed upon cement foundations. There was always a vast desert of sagebrush, and in one's place a small garden, watered from a well—of poplar trees, goldenrod, and—the garden was one's own population. Shoshone and Blackfoot passed at a distance walking beside their wagons or dragloads. The people who lived and worked in this land were largely foreign— Greeks, Italians, Mexicans, and so on. Their hold on the land, the houses, the work, and the language was like that of migratory birds. Cities were dreams— I have never forgotten the early morning hum of the city waking up in the first city I had ever seen—Boise, Idaho. Towns I lived in had populations of 8 persons, 14, seldom 20—Kimima, Wapai, Orchard. Cities were imaginary— like oceans.[16] The name of a man would be a town. Blaser, Idaho, has, according to the current Rand McNally Commercial Atlas, no population. In this setting, that force to be English and American, settled, not migratory, forced that paternal grandfather to whisper any French words he wished to remember. And so far as I know, in this, I was his only companion. If we were alone listening to the radio, we would play at translating the words of popular songs:

Tu es la crème de mon café
Tu es le pois de ma soupe

Outwardly, to others, he was not foreign; the long southern a's and trilled r's of his French were secrets between us. He sported a goatee, and told me with increasing detail the strange tale that he was the lost Dauphin of France. This story and this language are fragmentarily preserved by me. None of his children knew it; my father denies his father was foreign born. When that grandfather was dying, riddled with cancer, I was called home from college to speak with him because the only words he knew were a childish French. And no member of the family knew enough to keep him company. That English and American thing had such force that the other English which most people spoke, more like Woody Guthrie's, was also forbidden sound and thought:

I been doin' some hard travelin'
I thought you knowed

There was a step-grandfather besides, who was German, with one eye, and could not hide his accent.[17] Because of his talk of the Kaiser, though the war was long over, they painted the house yellow, which was funny because the house was already yellow. But this was a bright yellow and when they threw a bucket of it over a window, the beautiful color was there, though it killed the verbenas in the window box. But the deer would have come to eat them anyway. Around this, like a circle with two circumferences, the house was surrounded by talk of Joseph Smith's golden tablets, and the hatred of that talk. The laughter that a prophet could be named Smith still rings in my head.

I think every poet has a favorite imagery which helps him to explain the preoccupations of his work. I have repeatedly chosen the Orphic, and in so doing, I will remind you of certain elements of Orpheus's story. Unfortunately, the usual reference to him covers his power in song over animals and rocks, and this has become thoroughly sentimentalized—the magic that it represents cheapened by the view that one wants power over rather than entrance to. There is fairly good evidence that Orpheus was a man, another Greek hero, of early date, pre-Homeric, and that his life is closely attached to the realm of Dionysus, who precedes Apollo at Delphi and later shares the oracle with him. Orpheus's death is recorded in the story, his journey to hell, which he was able to complete only once, though at least four entrances to hell were well known in ancient Greece.

One part of his story has to do with the power of death over love and the power of death over the dead. The other part has to do with his death at the hands of the Bacchantes, when he is torn to pieces. His head floats down a river or over a stretch of Ocean and continues to speak in prophecies, but this is stopped by jealous Apollo, when he becomes really dead. Clearly, the Orphic Dionysus is being edited. In some peculiar sense, Orpheus is really repeating the life of Dionysus, the god who is both joyous and terrible, who is bringer of wine, who can be defeated, thrown into the sea by a mortal, locked in a chest, torn to pieces by giants, and who dies. That he holds within himself all the contradictions, the change and process of the world as it is known, and the terror that goes with that process, as Orpheus contradicts his power, has the power to charm with his music, but cannot charm the Bacchantes, has the power to bring Eurydice back from the dead, at least metaphorically, but cannot look at her. It is precisely in the image of the scattered body and mind of Orpheus that I place whatever I know about the poetic process—that scattering is a living reflection of the world.

I am thirty years old before I begin even tentatively to accept the title of poet. In San Francisco, I was tied to two other poets[18] who, it was my superstition, wrote my poems for me. When that notion became sentimental, I dropped it, and became another poet. I have worked since 1955[19] to find a line which will hold what I see and hear, and which will tie a reader to the poems, not to me. This fascination precedes my great debt to Charles Olson, for it is in a school-book problem, Plato's description of the power of music over the body and the dangers of poetry in *The Republic*, and it was the fantastic pull of hearing [Arthur] Brodeur[20] read *Beowulf*, a hundred lines at a whack on a good day, which led Spicer and me to compete in our translations to bring over the heat of that story. I am greatly moved by what is received and held with force in a poet's work. And sometimes that work promises that a great deal more will be held. In 1945, August, when Jack Spicer came to Berkeley from Los Angeles, and wound up living with me, I had read little philosophy, and Jack soon led me into that mess (though he later turned violently against it). He was soon reading Leibnitz and Spinoza. I can't say that a very great deal of this came over to me, nor did it seem to stick in detail with Jack, but I do remember discussions of monads and reflections. Recently, reading an exciting book by Frances Yates, *The Art of Memory*, I ran into a passage which brought back part of those dialogues with Jack: " . . . the monads, when they are human souls having memory, have as their chief function the representation of reflections of the universe of which they are living mirrors."[21] Her book contains a description of the Memory Theater, a box with tiers, where the initiate would take the place of the stage and look out on the tiers, which in an ordinary theater would hold the audience—

here there are images upon images, so that a man could hold the whole world in view. The idea is that the best means of memory is by image, and the image will hold best when it is given a place. Here the place itself is built to hold the images.[22] Were I in this theater, and before I could take responsibility for the images of the whole universe or hold them, I would have to hold on to those images first, to dwell upon them, which hold the nature of two stars eminently important in my life:

Taurus: *A man ploughing, a man bearing a key, a man holding a serpent and a spear.* This is almost clear, but I can't say in which hand he holds the snake and spear, so the memory is incomplete, or uncreated.

and Saturn: *A man with a stag's head on a dragon, with an owl which is eating a snake in his right hand.* It is my view that the nature of this star cannot be held in a poem until the uncreated dragon is created.[23]

I am trying to describe the foreignness, the outsideness, as a kind of metaphor for the sense I have of the process that leads to a poem, which again is outside, when made, and it is akin to translation, a word which in its parts holds the meaning of the word *metaphor*, the bringing over. This is here a problem of describing the process of inclusions, which as a man's work extends, enlarges and must take in both earth and sky. The heat I'm after is not simply the personal heat of the meeting, the recognition, but a heat and a passion which are of the nature of existence itself. The personal, yes, but then the translation of the personal to correspond with larger and larger elements, images of earth, is a process of inclusion—a growth of sensibility, in Valéry's phrase, but also a making which is not self-expressive. To be included, to be caught, to be brought over. Though I consider most of my work as a kind of translation, I have moved toward translation in the ordinary sense. My Nerval is an effort to bring over the chimeras of another poet, because the recognition was word for word. In doing so, I spent months trying to find words in English to carry the heat of the Nerval world, which is cosmic, but also most personal. And it is this content which must be translated—not the word-for-word crib, but the actual heat of the process which gave form to the poems.[24] Nerval begins in a real image of loss— the women of his world who disappear into the earth, and if they continue to exist, the realms of death have to be seen in terms of change and in images which hold that change. All this is most clear in one of Nerval's dreams, from which I took my lead:

The lady I followed, displaying her slender form in a movement that caused the folds in her dress of changing taffeta to glisten, gracefully placed her bare arm around a long stalk of hollyhock, then under a clear ray of light, she began to grow in such a manner that little by little the garden took her form, and the flowerbeds and the trees became the roses and garlands of her garment, while her figure and her arms printed their contours on the violet clouds in the sky. In this way I lost sight of her in a process of transfiguration, for she seemed to disappear into her own grandeur. "Oh!, do not leave me! I cried . . . for nature dies with you." (Nerval, *Selected* 131)

Nerval took the ultimate responsibility for the other side of the world, like the old idea, before it was photographed, of the other side of the moon. He saw and recorded a world in which the sun is black, the alchemical sol niger, under the earth yes, but in addition an in FORM ing vision. How personal the first vision of this was is seen in an early poem, which Nerval had adapted from a poem by Bürger, and which I translated:

THE BLACK SPOT

whoever has stared directly into the sun
thinks he sees before him,   unyielding,
flying around in the air an ashen spot

really young once and a lot braver,
I dared to fix my eyes on glory
for an instant:
what my eyes craved left a black point

since then, mingling with everything
like a token of grief,   everywhere,
in places where my eyes rest
I see it perch also,   a black spot

ask me if this is always true   it is
between me and fortune constantly
this bad luck and shared sorrow
if only an eagle looks in the Sun
and the Glory   without punishment[25]

Here, I wish to point to the responsibility of the poet for the experience of power as it is seen and felt in the world. And no more ultimate vision is possible than the one which tells the tale and holds the cost of the vision of the other side, the way down, sometimes the way up, the realms of deadness both in and out of the world—held in image, not a tract full of wisdom, but a reality created, held by image and sound. This is seen in the first poem of Nerval's sequence, Les Chimères, a serial poem, in his use of myth, original in his recognition—the tale behind the sirens—that they are indeed cursed muses, forced to be birds of the sea, which is the realm of love and eros. The siren is a sea bird from her origin in this very ancient story. The image holds it absolutely. When I come to a work, like *The Moth Poem*, which is not a translation in this sense, it is, however, a translation of the record of the burning light and death of certain presences. I believe that all men live in this realm, the serious, intense kingdom, funny as it is at times, with its passionate thought.

And it is just here that an accusation is leveled at many poets. "He writes for a coterie, the poets talk only among themselves. They live in a world of flattery and selfhood." It is my belief that it is somewhere in this messy denial of the thought of poetry that an explanation can be found for the importance of community. That poets do band together. I am demonstrably bad at the kind of communism one dreams of, yet I have repeatedly worked in and added to a community of that sort. The reason is that only in such communities is the necessary talk of this high, serious realm possible. Such communities tend to build a structure for men who wish to keep, hold, and record the passionate relation with the outside that the world, the nation, need. This is the only place where such talk goes on. That we have reached a point now here where such discourse must include the nation, our politics, the scholarship in which we tend to lay down the images of poetic thought—is obvious. This is a kind of memory theater in which the poet with his craft is after not some thing or place remembered, but present. Nothing would be more painful or more costly to the mind, and ugly in a sense that great poetry may be very ugly, than a poetry in which the present war[26] was present, held in sight and sound and intellect. Not opinion or reflection or dialectic about the presence. Few poets have caught the terror, which is the other side of the world. Those who have, Spicer, Pound, and Olson, for example, took a long time to burn—and their lives are of different lengths.

Particles

The relation of poetry to politics has received too little attention. Often, those who have made this matter their business have desired poetry's service and they wove nets of slavery around her activity. Before I lead you into my argument, I want to point to my dependence upon two scholars who act as masters in my life and thought: Ernst Kantorowicz, who taught me to read history in terms of events, actions, and men in relation to ideas, rather than as a process and generality;[1] and Hannah Arendt, whose work has clarified the partnership of politics and society for me.[2] I remain their dependent in political concern because I am trained in a world where that thought is either sublimated or opinionated. This is not to say they would always approve of my use of them.

The usual definition of the problem, poetry and politics, is the obvious one found in critical descriptions of that poetry which has politics for its content. This approach is exemplified by an uninteresting little book published two years ago by Sir Maurice Bowra, entitled *Poetry and Politics*. In this case, one gets nowhere. The activity which spells poetry's sure relation to life is ignored. Poetry is seen as an opinionated sponge. Bowra gives us little more than a list of poets, Mayakovsky, Neruda, etc., who have written poems with political content. This we could more usefully do ourselves, since his definition of politics is largely a matter of current events.

A second approach is to choose an historical instance, a war or revolution, which has drawn numerous poets to write what we take to be poems by their shape. For example, the Spanish Civil War, and this has been done in Hugh Ford's *A Poet's War* (1965).

(In these direct references to books on the subject, I am outlining methods, which, I think, you will have expected me to follow, and since I'm not going to, I thought it would clear the air, if I dismissed them, for reason, one by one. I am, in fact, leading you into a corner where a particle of land is all you've got.)

One advantage of Ford's book is that one gets a clear record of C. Day Lewis's efforts to argue for a Marxist poetry, while fighting, as all poets do, the attempt "to palm off the didactic or propagandistic, at the expense of the poetic" (Ford 91). The trouble is that the political record is dismal. And the "poetic"? We are pushed to study Day Lewis's taste. It would probably have been more to the point to have studied Day Lewis's hidden argument for the rational structure of the poem, an absolute in terms of his taste, so as to find a balance between reason and passion as they relate to politics. That is, if one cared about the poetry of C. Day Lewis.

Another approach is found in Ernst Fischer's *The Necessity of Art: A Marxist Approach*. This book was published in East Germany in 1959 and in an English translation in 1963; it is a highly sophisticated rendering of the Marxist view of art. In many ways, it does away with 40 years of argument about the social, not to say political, uses of art. I am vulgarizing only a little when I summarize the argument:—the hand in its relation to tools formed the mind; art was originally magic, and magic has power over things. Fischer says, "Clearly the decisive function of art was to exert power—power over nature, an enemy, a sexual partner, power over reality, power to strengthen the human collective. Art in the dawn of humanity had little to do with 'beauty' and nothing at all to do with aesthetic desire: it was a magic tool or weapon of the human collective in its struggle for survival" (35–36). The difficulty with such a view is this: the evolution of mind is so little understood that Fischer's discussion amounts to misinformation for the sake of his dialectical concerns,—simplicity's trick. Also, the relationship of art and magic—poetry and magic—is arguable. Basically, magic is a kind of knowledge, not power, and when the author chooses to put it just that way, we are again tricked. Knowledge involves discipline and a seeing. Fischer gives us relations but no participation. It isn't my purpose here to argue in detail the problems of this book, but the author's discussion of mythology indicates that he knows little about thought of that kind. And that he is a poet satisfied with his own statement shows up in the pie-in-the-sky final chapter, where with the state withered away, art will be free: " . . . the artist's experience will no longer be a privilege but the normal gift of free and active man; we shall achieve, as it were, social genius" (225). And he continues, "Man, who became man through work, who stepped out of the animal kingdom as transformer of the natural into the artificial, who became therefore the magician, man the creator of social reality, will always stay the great magician, will always be Prometheus bringing fire from heaven to earth, will always be Orpheus enthralling nature with his music. Not until humanity itself dies will art die" (225). Need I point out that Prometheus was not a magician, but a thief—the created world, whatever its shape, is not artificial but alive—Orpheus, according to the story was not responsible, was not a magician, enchanted nature without taking power over her, unless, of course, by nature we mean death, and even there he failed. I am disturbed by the lack of attention to the kind of knowledge in poetry and by the whole implication that the content of human life is drawn up into something called collective will.

One final method you might have expected me to follow is found in John R. Harrison's *The Reactionaries: A Study of the Anti-democratic Intelligensia* (1966), introduction by William Empson, who, as someone said, is that man who has rewritten Milton for us. From Harrison's discussion of Yeats, Wyndham Lewis, Pound, Eliot, and Lawrence, I choose only one example to indicate the mess of the approach described in his title—the defense of a slogan. To dismiss as this author has done, these writers for their political concern is not acceptable. Near the end of the book, the author tells us these writers are old-fashioned, of no interest to the "young." Fortunately, it is not likely that the young will bother to read this book. The concern of every author discussed is with political and social integrity. Harrison's concern is with a defense of liberal, 20th century democratic tradition. He nowhere makes it clear what elements of this tradition remain with us, nor for that matter does he ever say what it is we have, had, or haven't, but he is quite clear that all these authors were soft on fascism. Again, little or no information is given about the nature of fascism, and since whatever it is, is directly involved with modern revolutionary thought, one would expect better scholarship. For example, with Yeats, the author tells us that there is a tendency toward fascism and he will describe for us the relation of this tendency of Yeats's thought to his poetic style. We are then entertained by the notion that the "hardness" of Yeats's later style has something to do with the "hardness" of fascism, implying, I suppose, that softness is democratic (33, 57–59).[3] More to the point is the fact that all these authors were concerned with the problem of authority. And I am dismissing Mr. Harrison who does not understand the questions or the ground from which they were asked. In 1946, when Pound was to stand trial for treason, Charles Olson imagined a letter from Yeats in the other world to his friends in America. In that letter, Yeats said, " . . . it is for you to hold the mirror up to authority, behind our respect for which lay a disrespect for democracy as we were acquainted with it. A slogan will not suffice."[4] It is curious that Harrison nowhere indicates that he understands the importance of authority as a political question. Perhaps, he should be excused. The book seems to settle for its commercial occasion.

It is a peculiar circumstance that in the discussion of politics and poetry, we are faced on the one hand with the view that poets are removed, delicately so, from public events and on the other with the view that poets may be used by wiser men to propagandize and support either the status quo, which the poet by the nature of his work will know to be a lie, or the revolution, which the poet by the nature of his work will try to understand. Harrison closes his considerations with this statement: "The advance of science, not democracy, has created the mass society, and also the means to destroy it. This is the real problem; whether the kind of sensibility necessary to the writing of good literature can survive the pressures exerted on the individual by the continual threat of mass destruction, together with other insecurities which seem inherent in the new mass society" (210). I make no comment except to say that security is not one of the defining qualities of art. Mr. Harrison dismisses thought in poetry— unless he agrees with what he understands. His approach implies that thought in poetry is something less than an original activity developing meaning. Again, I turn to Olson's letter from Yeats—". . . perhaps some consideration of descents and metamorphosis, form and the elimination of intellect" (*Human Universe* 102; *Collected Prose* 143). So Yeats writes:

> It is a simple thing I ask as I might question a beggar who stopped me for a coin. It is the use, the use you make of us.
>
> Are you a court to accept and/or reject JEFFERSON AND/OR MUSSOLINI, indict GUIDE TO KULCHUR and write a better, brief me contrary ABCs, charge why 100 CANTOS betrays your country, that poem which concerns itself so much with the men who made your Revolution for you? I have said I often found there brightly painted kings, queens, knaves but have never discovered why all the suits could not be dealt out in some quite different order. What do you find, a traitor?
>
> Dean Swift says in a meditation on a woman who paints a dying face.
>
>> Matter as wise logicians say
>> Cannot without a form subsist;
>> And form, say I as well as they,
>> Must fail, if matter bring no grist.
>
> What have you to help you hold in a single thought reality and justice?* (Olson, *Human Universe* 102; *Collected Prose* 144)

Now, having dismissed those approaches, for reason, let me turn to my own considerations. And since I am a poet, I'll begin by repeating a couple of stories,

---

* Charles Olson, "This Is Yeats Speaking," published in *Human Universe and Other Essays* (1967). Compare the Rapallo section of *A Packet for Ezra Pound.*

a story being a basic poetic concern, and the stuff of metaphor itself. The first, also cited by our friend Fischer, from Novalis, I'll take as an epigraph:

> The organs of thought are the sexual organs of nature, the world's genitals.[5]

And the second is a tale of the Spanish Civil War. The story involves [Miguel de] Unamuno, who was at the time Rector of the University of Salamanca:

You must imagine a great hall at the University. The walls are covered with tapestries. The grandeur can only be remade with words. There is a dais where the learned and their guests are seated—a bejeweled Bishop, whose ring of office glitters, the Provincial governor, one of Franco's important generals, and Madame Franco surround the Rector, Miguel de Unamuno. And above them is a large photograph-banner of Franco. A packed audience faced the dais waiting for the speakers. The date is October 12, 1936. According to my source, a Professor of Literature spoke first, expressing his sincere hope for the future. Then, a visitor from Saragossa spoke of the "energies of Spain at white heat in a crucible of passion—and like gold from the crucible . . . " etc. (Portillo 398). But the man they were waiting to hear was General Millan Astray—thin, emaciated, one eye and one arm. My source uses the words "mutilations" and "gashes" to describe him (398). This general was known for his iron discipline, his campaigns in Africa, and his battle cry, "Viva la Muerte!" As he stood to speak, someone in the audience shouted, "Viva la Muerte!" According to my source, the General opened his speech with the statement that "'more than one half of all Spaniards were criminals, guilty of armed rebellion and high treason'" (399). He said, "'Catalonia and the Basque country—the Basque country and Catalonia—are two cancers in the body of the nation. Fascism, which is Spain's health-bringer, will know how to exterminate them both, cutting into the live, healthy flesh like a resolute surgeon free from false sentimentality. And since the healthy flesh is the soil, the diseased flesh, the people who dwell on it, Fascism and the Army will eradicate the people and restore the soil to the sacred national realm . . . '"(399).

He said, "'Every Socialist, every Republican, every one of them without exception—and needless to say every Communist—is a rebel against the National Government which will very soon be recognized by the totalitarian States who are aiding us, in spite of France . . . '" etc. General Millan Astray's speech ended with the audience shouting, "Franco, Franco, Franco!" (399, 400).

When Unamuno rose, the crowd became silent, and this, according to my source, is what he said:

> "All of you are hanging on my words. You all know me, and are aware that I
> am unable to remain silent. I have not learnt to do so in seventy-three years of my

life. And now I do not wish to learn it any more. At times, to be silent is to lie. For silence can be interpreted as acquiescence. I could not survive a divorce between my conscience and my word, always well-mated partners.

"I will be brief. Truth is most true when naked, free of embellishments and verbiage.

"I want to comment on the speech—to give it that name—of General Millan Astray who is here among us

"Let us waive the personal affront implied in the sudden outburst of vituperation against Basques and Catalans in general. I was born in Bilbao, in the midst of the bombardments of the Second Carlist War. Later, I wedded myself to this city of Salamanca which I love deeply, yet never forgetting my native town. The Bishop, whether he likes it or not, is a Catalan from Barcelona. . . .

"Just now I heard a necrophilous and senseless cry: 'Long live Death.'" To me it sounds the equivalent of "Muera la Vida" "To Death with Life!" And I, who have spent my life shaping paradoxes which aroused the uncomprehending anger of others, I must tell you, as an expert authority, that this outlandish paradox is repellent to me. Since it was proclaimed in homage to the last speaker, I can only explain it to myself by supposing that it was addressed to him, though in an excessively strange and tortuous form, as a testimonial to his being himself a symbol of death.

"And now, another matter. General Millan Astray is a cripple. Let it be said without any slighting undertone. He is a war invalid. So was Cervantes. But extremes do not make the rule: they escape it. Unfortunately, there are all too many cripples in Spain now. And soon, there will be even more of them, if God does not come to our aid. It pains me to think that General Millan Astray should dictate the pattern of mass-psychology.

"That would be appalling. A cripple who lacks the spiritual greatness of a Cervantes—a man, not superman, virile and complete, in spite of his mutilations—a cripple, I said, who lacks that loftiness of mind, is wont to seek ominous relief in seeing mutilation around him." (401–2)

The audience was very quiet, but their feelings of unease and confusion filled the air. The General could no longer stand it, and interrupting Unamuno, he shouted, "'Muera la Inteligencia!'"—"'To death with Intelligence!'" "'To death with bad intellectuals!'" a journalist from Cadiz yelled, something prompting him to correct the General's statement, if only a little (402).

Unamuno's presence had such authority, he was able to make himself heard again:

"This is the temple of intellect. And I am its high priest. It is you who are profaning its sacred precincts.

"I have always, whatever the proverb may say, been a prophet in my own land. You will win, but you will not convince. You will win, because you possess more than enough brute force, but you will not convince, because to convince means to persuade. And in order to persuade you need what you lack—reason and right

in the struggle. I consider it futile to exhort you to think of Spain. I have finished."
(402–3)

According to my source, Unamuno's life was in danger on the spot, where they could have shot him down in the excitement, but a Professor of Common Law, whose name should be once again recorded, Don Esteban Madruga, took Unamuno by the arm and offered the other to Madame Franco, who was stunned enough to take it. And the three of them left the dais. Unamuno remained a prisoner in his house until he died, December 31 of the same year.[*]

With these stories hovering over our heads, I want now to turn to a kind of statement. I have thus far made it clear that the relation of poetry to politics should not be defined so simply as a poetry with political content or as a poetry which is to be used in the service of an ideology. My insistence upon the serious ground of poetic thought is what is at stake.

Many of us share the view that the political structures which rule us must be questioned, remade, or changed. The Vietnam War and the Black Power Movement stand in my mind as indictments of our government. It is seen to be far removed from large sections of the constituency. Its concerns in Vietnam are not public. And there is something afoot in the U.S. which I can only describe as political anguish. I think we need to remind ourselves frequently that the American government was founded by a Revolution. In fact, it is the only revolution in modern times which founded a government on a basis of freedom. This government was originally intended to be public. And as Hannah Arendt describes it, the public realm is the only realm in which men can be free, since freedom is by definition not a private concern. The other great revolutions of our time, the French Revolution and the Russian Revolution, were quickly lost. The Cuban and Chinese Revolutions are still going on, and we cannot read them. I can myself only support these revolutions because they have overthrown governments whose contempt for the freedom and economic well-being of their people is fully documented.

Freedom in a shared world is an activity difficult for us to understand because we take freedom to be attached to our private necessities only. "In my house, I am free." Freedom here is not apparent because the house and your efforts to keep it are tied to the society of job-holders. "I am free in my choice of jobs." This is not true, because there one is not free of one's own limitations or of the market. "I am free in my mind. They cannot touch me." (That *they* which in a more meaningful time would have been your own creation.)

* The details of this story and all the direct quotations are taken from Luis Portillo's moving memorial, "Unamuno's Last Lecture," published in Cyril Connolly's *The Golden Horizon*, pp. 397–403.

This is not freedom if one considers that one's own mind is an empty physiological and chemical concern until it shares with an object a feeling or an activity.* And, here, unless the record of poetry tells me nothing, the World enters and our concerns are public.

Now this public realm: here I want to spell out my propositions:

First: the public realm is necessarily political, having to do with our lives in our cities, provinces, and federations.

Second: though we live in what appears to be a settled body politic, our political thought is dominated by modern revolutions beginning with the American and continuing with involvement in the Chinese Revolution.

Third: our thoughtful concern about revolutionary purposes always revolves around the problem of authority—the way in which institutions are set up to guide and protect the public realm.

Fourth: the purpose of a revolution is to destroy a rotting body politic in order to replace it with another in which the foundations are laid for freedom, but not for happiness. The impossibility of government-instituted happiness is seen in the Marat-Sade movie, that amazing scene in which Charlotte Corday knocks at the gate to see Marat, and she says, "I am unhappy, and therefore have a right to his aid."[6] She does not say I am poor and have a right to his aid; she says I am unhappy.

Fifth: freedom is an activity involving deeds and words in a shared public realm—it is not necessary to life, though there can be no freedom when the necessities of existence are lacking—or when every definition of value is tied to the idea that work and the necessities of life, enlarged to include the insatiable desires of the consumer, constitute the geography of our world.

And sixth: the idea, current everywhere that life is the highest good is not understood for the enclosure it is, when it becomes, as ideas do, active in the world. The assumption it hides is that the satisfaction of our biological needs constitutes the map of the world. That satisfaction of either needs or desires is a map ignores the activity of meaning and the nature of human exchange. When a man says he cares only for his family, he is little different from another man who sits in complete darkness expecting to receive a vision, when that man has no capacity for vision at all, had not seen an image in the world that was not himself or his biological extensions.†

* I am too brief. The issue of freedom should be checked out in Hannah Arendt's two books, *The Human Condition* and *On Revolution*. No single page reference is adequate—it's the whole argument, but especially, see *The Human Condition* (Doubleday, 1958), pp. 285–87, where it is said the cosmos holds immortality—we do not.

† Hannah Arendt, *On Revolution* (New York: Viking, 1963; reprint, 1965), pp. 111 ff., especially pp. 135–37.

The political world of the U.S. once reflected a shared public activity, but it has removed itself further and further from us—in part due to our lack of knowledge about the tendency of representational institutions to act only in terms of generalizations and in response to those invisibilities, power groups. My distrust of the very men who represent me grows because their authority was invested in an earlier founding revolution whose leaders, at least Jefferson and John Adams, believed knowledge was what men would hold in common. And it is my contention that knowledge (*logos*) is an activity, a revelation of content, requiring the specific, the particular, the place. If this seems dangerously close to the argument that there can be no public world which is not an immediate situation—no city, no province, no federation, then you have misunderstood me. Greek and Roman political experience argues that to act intelligently in the public realm requires a *vision of things*. The words themselves, vision and things, are telling. Vision, full of that sense of seeing and image, which are basic to knowing—and things—even bits and pieces. There is no vision of things without the emotions of particularity.

It has been the peculiar burden of serious modern art to defend particularity in the public realm. Poetry has moved since early in the century to the inclusion of political content, not because the relevance of poetry can be defined by its political or ideological content, but because the public world is sick and has in many places disappeared for lack of particularity. Nothing is shared and no vision of a shared world is possible. The particularity of the poet is considered irrelevant, egotistical. And the future is seen, without a vision including the particular, to entail the modern superstitions—that we are given up to general, impersonal forces—"'history,' 'necessity,' 'World-Spirit,' 'laws of nature,' . . . 'society,'"* or the will of the people. I use the passive with consideration, *we are given up to,* for, as verbs always do, the passive here denotes the intellectual condition of great parts of the world. For most men, if they recognize the interdependence of heart and mind on the world, know that there is no such thing as "the will of the people" or "Society" except as they describe the common denominators of biological necessity. With heart and mind we return to emotion and thought, and thus to particularity. Those generalities become the modern means of asserting political authority without regard to heart or mind. (Check out this notion of a "general will" or "a will of the people" in Rousseau, rather than in Marx, where the *volonté générale* requires one particularity always ignored, an enemy.)†

* I have taken this list of "impersonal forces" from Sheldon S. Wolin, *Politics and Vision* (1960), pp. 373–74. See also his discussion, pp. 362–73. The intellectual condition these forces bring us to now is clearly developed in an essay on American sociologists: Noam Chomsky, "Intellectuals & Vietnam," *New York Review of Books* (January 2, 1969).

† Hannah Arendt discusses this issue in detail, Rousseau in particular, *On Revolution*, pp. 72–75.

Obviously, I am arguing the ancient view that politics is a public activity, for which space and freedom are guaranteed, and I want further to say that this activity is *discourse*,—in which words grasp whatever we know of meaning. Twentieth-century poetry and the poetic theory inscribed by its poets have repeatedly worked out the ground of this activity. What has to be understood is that form and content combine in an activity which reveals meaning, grasps the mind of the reader, so that he is forever changed, because, if he has understood, there has been a meeting. And that meeting has permanence since it is held in public words. Now, it is objected that the particularity of modern poetry, its concern with deeds, thoughts, place, make it private and irrelevant. This is not so much ignorance as it is disrespect for particularity. Which is to say that men share not their place, their time, and those invisible activities called emotions,—to which poets give permanence—, but only generality. That poem is about love, the man says. And it is forgotten that love does not exist, even in thought, without its particularity. I love one, and with the peculiar virtue words have of attaching sound to the name I give away, each man can grasp that love. Even if we are drawn into the love of god. Words are instruments. The sounds are so important; it is as if something outside oneself called. We loan our clothes to the World. We have clothed the world and god in our clothes. How particular the image is. This too is part of the activity of discourse. It is simply not true that we share only our generalities. Sharing required discrimination and recognition, once upon a time.

We have to face the meaninglessness which destroys the minds of whole areas of the North American populations. I have blamed it upon absence of thought in this giving up to large generalities. If we consider that our personal relationship to such large value systems as Societies—whatever groups of interest we divide them into—is one of uncommitted definition, and it means that our understanding of ourselves, as well as the way we are understood, is not an activity of intelligence, but a measuring by large numbers, everyday behavior, and automatic trends. The proof that freedom and its substance, passion and thought, are not required for life is that whole peoples may function without regard for them.

In the social realm, tied as it is to the necessities of biological life, we can be measured by our function, and our outward behavior is the direct result of our social function. The disaster comes when everything is defined as behavior or as an expression of society. In the history of societies, everything has been claimed as an expression of society—art, literature, and religion—(the wonderful phrase "God is 'only society transfigured and symbolically expressed'" turns up—I think it's Durkheim[7]).* The difficulty is in the word *express*. Art, lit-

* Sheldon S. Wolin again, p. 362.

erature, and religion are none of them expressions of either society or the self. They are activities of content—passion and thought—the relation of a man to the world as the world calls to him, and the activity is not simply relational. I will for this occasion stick to poetry. No serious poetry can be described as self-expression. This is to confuse the strictly private with what is defined as public and permanent. (I am not here concerned with bad art.) The strictly private can only be read in terms of behavior and generality. Otherwise the private is invisible. Behavior becomes a substitute for the public, knowledgeable "inter-est"— what is between us—and we wind up with problems in our cities.

Abundance and consumption dominate politics in the U.S. The foreign policy never works on the basis that free and independent people are only capable of sharing a world with the North Americans if they have escaped the terrible needs of poverty. The many who now question this have begun to test the authority invested in that government; that government had best begin to study and renew the grounds of its authority. If men "no longer feel at home politically," "if they no longer believe in the authority of those who rule," their government is no longer public and its authority rests on forces hidden from the public, like those of the military-industrial complex of the U.S. The tradition of discourse, wherein public concerns are tied to thought and persuasion, is lost.

I think all men interested in politics should restudy the American Revolution— fully aware that Paine and Jefferson knew that the business of government is not to guarantee happiness, which is impossible, but freedom. Paine and Jefferson both insisted that it was the right of every generation to recreate society as it saw fit.* Late in life, Jefferson recognized a problem basic to American government: the importance of the small community, the town hall, to the building of a public, shared realm had not been built into the constitution (Arendt, *Revolution* 253). Government was removed by representation. A man's knowledge could only be represented, and we know what this has come to. But the problem was recognized early and stated most clearly by Thoreau in his manifesto on Civil Disobedience, delivered to the Concord Lyceum on January 20, 1848: "This American government—what is it but a tradition, though a recent one, endeavouring to transmit itself unimpaired to posterity, but each instant losing some of its integrity?" (356). It is this integrity which is at stake. And it is in the specific and the particular that integrity resides. What happens to emotion when it is not tied to the particular is that it becomes as large as Society and as dangerous as "the will of the people," which according to modern history is not recognizable ex-

---

* The complicated problems of a continuing revolution are discussed by Arendt, *On Revolution*, pp. 234 ff.

cept by one man at the top. And it is in this realm of integrity that poetry has its political base. It is in the concrete nature of poetic speech that integrity remains and endures as a permanence in human affairs.

My seventh proposition is this: what we share is our particularity. In our natures, we share the activity which is the beginning of intelligence, a direct and lonely meeting with particulars of a world which is outside us. The dead-end singularity this could be is resolved in poetry, where the recurrence of that meeting is made visible and we re-enact it. This requires a sense of speech that does not emphasize the current notion that the only shared meaning is a generality. In a profound sense, poetry always remains at the beginning, where the body is involved in thought—the passion that a man reaches for the world before he has any sense whatever of an uncreated thing like happiness. This involves the "process of image" and the "rhythm of it."[8] The reading of a poem is the re-enactment of the images of contact with the world. In this sense, as Charles Olson puts it, "art is the only twin life has—its only valid metaphysic" (*Human Universe* 10; *Collected Prose* 162). We return again and again to the importance of language in its activity of holding on to the world and life in that world.

I am asked why I write—and the answer lies in the statement that the life process is not the highest good. Poets are men who have grasped the essential relationship between invisible passions and invisible thought to the real. They objectify in a form which is an *activity*. Art is charged with irrelevance because of its particularity, which is exactly what makes it most relevant to the human side of things. The real in which one wishes to find a place has an "undisclosed character." We are after "meaning and thing,"[9] and the intensity of that activity is what is at stake.* The charge of irrelevancy comes from outside, and from those generalizations about the life process, and it should be translated into the crap it is,—art in that view is irrelevant because it is not a true commodity, no "disinterested use of language" is;[10] it cannot be consumed as no activity can.

I think we need a new beginning. Back to Paine's and Jefferson's notion that every generation has a birthright to recreate society as it sees fit. Even an enemy of poetry tells us about the special virtue of beginnings: from Plato we get this, paraphrased from the Laws: "For the beginning, because it contains its own principle, is also a god who, as long as he dwells among men, as long as he inspires their deeds, saves everything."† This is a principle of revolution. And all men necessarily share this sense of beginning unless it is destroyed. When

* See Charles Olson, "Quantity in Verse and Shakespeare's Late Plays," published in *Human Universe and Other Essays.*

† This is Hannah Arendt's paraphrase, taken from her discussion of this issue of beginnings, *On Revolution*, p. 214.

Whitman thought America a beginning, his poetry, that public activity, which can be entered, providing you want action of that kind, drew a map in which Body, Comradeship, and World took a journey—he gave lists of rivers and cities. Only in poetry can such maps be found.

"Let me bring this to a close—I pronounce openly for a new distribution of roles."[11]

The Stadium of the Mirror

Unless the *Image-Nations* are read by image, there is no saving grace. They will be stopped by a diminished and interruptive present, a misreading of the one here that is flowing in every direction. Their effort to recover the primary language in which the world and the sacred are alive will go unrecognized. The reader will be pushed into an argumentative unknown, which he will not believe because he has separated it out, as he wants to do with what he knows. The fragmentary angelology of the poems will look like gilt. Unless. When I have moved out to speak with the languageless men, their phrases coil—"Fuck the verbal shit"—"It isn't there"—"What am I to do with that?" Suddenly one is turned backward. "Those who have lost the good of the intellect!"[1] "God is day night, winter summer, war peace, satiety hunger . . . and undergoes alteration in the way that fire, when it is mixed with spices, is named according to the scent of each of them" (Kirk 189). The names are alive, out of jars (H.D.) "The e of Eros closes and reopens the rose."[2]

Here, at the back of the book, I ask permission to read the counsel of my own poems, rather than simply to go back to them. Here, I've drawn all the *Image-Nations* to date together, 1962–1973. This arrangement changes the way they voice themselves. In their original context, they are intermittent events in the narrative of *The Holy Forest*. Noises in the forest. Forests are where one is lost, and sometimes found. For any man, they are very dense in the West where the mind goes. I see the first 5 poems poised in a disorder—syntactically incomplete. And so, would bring forward their troublesomeness. Syntax is the order of a man's words, the arrangement he makes in a work. It may be largely unconscious and tied to the invisible violence of the Language we enter. That the order of our words is not our discourse is plain enough, even sure-footed, in nursery rhymes. It belongs to a permanence in language that surrounds the impermanence of our words. It is older than we are and seated elsewhere. It is a misapprehension to enter this movement, empowered to order it, and then not recognize that the order of your will is only yourself. And an aggrandizement. If we take the order of language to be the arrangement of words without noting the silence between words and at the beginning and end of sentences, we have lost the protagonist language is,—to make of it a totality of wisdom that does not compose the real, but imposes upon it. A transcendent or "creative" language, which is true only to itself. All language is musical, even idle talk, but the rhythm of poetry brings forward the silence and tension of words—rhymes and older metered patterns did not originally close lines, but open their silence, as if the words burst into flame out of an absence of words. The Language is not a consciousness of ourselves, but rather an inherence in the world. The first Image-Nations began a movement that became a consciousness. A reversal of the consciousness I did not believe, but had been taught—the ownership of the poet, the transparency of the language, the imposition of form upon the real, the cogito. Form is alive, not a completion of the heart or of the mind. The first tentative effort was to remove that syntax which had been a misapprehension—in order to let the image speak out of the absence the Other had become.

I am not, there where I am the plaything of my thought, I think about what I am there where I do not think I am thinking. (Lacan)[3]

Before these poems—around 1957—Charles Olson, in one of those wild conversations—wild because they were a composition of a world and not an imposition of himself—commented that he'd trust me anywhere with image, but I had no syntax. As if the world spoke a sentence and I had not caught it. I could then hardly articulate my disbelief in the cogito of most poetics. Jack Spicer was working it out inside a costly and necessary dictation ("Song for Bird and Myself" and "A Poem to the Reader of the Poem," 1956). I did not miss Charles's meaning or the stake of it in his work. I'd read him a poem. In it, I wore one of those huge pumpkin flowers on my head that grow in the White Mountains, big as a hat, and I'd whirled out of the patch into the trees. That was all there was to it, yet I'd added this and that so the laughter of the poem disappeared into a significance. The arrangement of words, as I had learned it along with everybody else, offered a logic from the self, which perjures, or a transparent knowledge, which imposes, removes the real, and turns out to be ourselves on a power trip. Under the furniture, the floors become mirrors. (I won't become obscene about it.) Feeling and the thought that is said to be without feeling may both overlay the real and steal it. There is a visibility in such language, comfortable and apparently complete without the risk of the invisibility that surrounds it—of whatever order. This visibility ends up seated in a high-minded garden or by a swimming pool, where an ideality makes up for the real or rocks the wreckage of my visibility as it is invaded by whatever is invisible to it. In grand matters—for example, the 2/3rds of the world's population that lives at the edge of starvation and the man, woman, or child that dies of it just a little under every 6 seconds—my pity could drink the death up into my feeling, which is hardly their terror, or my thought could make it transparent like gossip. No wonder there are men who prefer deeds without words, who hate the utopianism of a certain kind of art, as if the spiritual were a day-dream rather than active in the composition of the real. They are, whether they know it or not, against the language that is only ourselves speaking. They err in the imposition of a language which promises a redeemed manhood, but in it the words are devoured by his needs. At the end of those deeds which will "fix" it, he will have been spoken, his visibility unattached to the sentence that is speaking. Ptolomaic language. Anthropomorphic dead ends.

It is my purpose to make it difficult for the first *Image-Nations*. Their small lighted words seem very distant in this composing context. Their fragmentation and lack of syntax disturb, as if the poems wished to stop. Helpless. Five has been erased—it moved so negligent, uneasy, inarticulate. I wish in this way to suggest what it is that haunted their composition. I could have wound up there inside the lyric logic of the disappearance—of myself, a syntax, the whole damn cultural grid. While then the image would have remained the possibility of an entrance, magically, still the danger was that the I, the poet, and the manhood of the poems in the distance of the work would become only a spectator. Like the naïveté of trying to gain outwardness, or rather its semblance, by erasing all the I's of a poem and substituting other pronouns. Or like the tendency of some to dress up a simple love lyric, sexually viable perhaps, to look like a cosmology by adornment. The Other is not an object, but acts chiasmatically (Merleau-Ponty's word).[4] Not a stillness. Not a rest. Always the opposite and companion of any man's sudden form. This is the unrest given to thought. And to our invisibility. Perhaps this is also the life of Beauty whose companion is Terror or a coldness.

> The wild-logos
> the reversability of experience and language
> neither experience nor language is a reality that
> will suffice to itself alone
> two aspects of the reversability which is ultimate
> truth
> there is no frontier between language and world
> A wild-logos   to recognize the movement that

prevents the fixing of the meaning of the thing,
visible or invisible, and makes arise indefinitely,
beyond the present given, the latent content of the
world

(Lefort, Merleau-Ponty)[5]

The work is always the passage of a wildness. The suddenness of the man I watch is both visible and invisibly continuous. At an edge. At the edge of his thought and feeling. I am reminded of a passage:

He is free to go or not to go onto that terrifying
promontory of thought from which darkness is per-
ceived—if he goes on that peak he is caught.
The profound waves of the marvelous have appeared
to him.

(Hugo)[6]

But just now he is not free not to go there. The whole culture has brought him there at the edge of himself. It seems odd to me that it is not the most public language. The great public Greek drama is difficult to understand. They watched, not, as we do, the characteristics of a humanism, but the images of an action— there for the sake of the action, not in the art vice-versa (Aristotle).[7] I speak entering what is speaking—at an edge. I enter many directions, the synchron or coming together of time, in order to find words which are not alone. The humanism, which destroys our thought, must know what it has said. The beloved suddenness, the body, is polar to language and not absent from it, as one is polar to happiness but not absent from it. A wildness. The edge is absence which meets any presence.

Poetry always has to do with consciousness. Its restlessness is what we have called the unconscious, expecting the past and future from the present. The man I watch with all my heart is both visible, a stop, and invisibly continuous. The static is oneself alone or translated into the mass where we are all alike.

The true is the Bacchantic frenzy in which no friend is not drunken; and because each as soon as it differ-
entiates itself, immediately dissolves—the frenzy is as if transparent and simple repose. (Hegel)[8]

Poetry, for all its snazz, reverses into the simple birthright—that one does step into a cosmos.

Those small lighted words I look back on are posed in an absence. They are meant to act into present form—their presence, a nexus of what is absent. The body of them—their lyric sound—discloses an old awareness,—that the body is polar. It is easy to recognize the fundamental dialectic of thought and feeling in a dynamic between the known and the unknown. These now reverse terribly out of a misappropriated language into experience. As if the unthought suddenly sought to reach our forms.

This desire of the extreme duplicity of language is not mine because I am inside it. It has led me repeatedly here to go beyond the occasion of the Image-Nations. Such desire is perhaps the frisson of the poems which has been said to be missing. By extension in the series, the absence of syntax becomes polar to another language—of presences alongside absences, of speech alongside a silence of words, of a visibility tensed alongside a love which traces its invisible open-work. But I wish to let the reader loose in the invisibility where the text leads him. He is after all a perception of the text. He may find himself inside a distaste or disgust. He may be terrified to find himself an image of the action of a world-text where he is dispossessed. It is always possible "the Master," whom the centuries have come to know as ourselves, as Mallarmé noticed, may disappear from the language, but then the language goes on speaking news of his translation. *We are never in possession of ourselves, yet passion is ourselves* (Merleau-Ponty).[9] Here, in an endless narration, you, dear reader, are visible in a nexus.

Looking back eleven years over a few pages of poetry, I notice what I was not thinking. The lack of syntax—the disorder and the poetic illiteracy—was expert. The disadvantage—a stupefying refusal to accept feeling, personality, or discourse for the real—became a discipline of that which does not enter any language reduced to what men are—socratic, final, and bound by a language that is only between ourselves. Such language is worldless. The Language on the other hand may be relearned as guardian and primary—an immense, untapped laughter. There is a bitter laughter inside the "unprejudiced view" of dialectic, so that the sky walks around in a raincoat just like mine. The "deified History" of it looks so much like Him, whose name is Foreclusion (Lacan's word), we are all gone for a sex change. When He came to the cities, he was known as He-who-is-the-break-in-the-chain-of-mountains. Just there, She must also enter our hearts. He, as *Foreclusion, would be a sort of "original hole," never capable of finding its own substance again since it has never been anything other than "hole substance"* (Leclaire).[10] The wreckage of prenouns is a great deal of fun.

From the first, the Image-Nations questioned syntax. I don't know now that they adequately hold on to the terror that was there—as in the broken crust of the earth in the 4th poem, where the feet slip into the fire. The movement there had barely begun that turns into the volcano of the mind in the 10th poem. The Sublime, the Beautiful, the Terror are not exactly human (Arendt),[11] and that is the reason the Image-Nations are not devoted to my logic of desire, but to a nation invaded by what is other than itself—a continuous forming. An original precision of meaning may then enter the word desire: "Perhaps (like *con-siderare*) allied to *sidus*, a star, as if to turn the eyes from the stars" (Skeat).[12] The body in the suddenness of its form stands there like the period at the end of a sentence. This off-spring of the universe then refurls. Dis-aster—the reversal of an act—dis—to turn from aster—star. Dis-stars.

My poems have been dismissed for obscurity, crazyness, and personalism,— even for the grandeur of a "mysticism which means nothing to anybody."[13] They were once viewed as the productions of a Marlon Brando of poetry. I think the reviewer had a speech defect in mind. So, back of the first *Image-Nations* was the old comfort—a discourse which I could have substituted for the holes in intelligence, and thus, have closed the poems inside a formality of what my mind constituted,—an anthropomorphism in tatters. And a tantalizing misuse of poetry, making of it a removed, unearned transcendence. Poets do often turn up at masquerades dressed as Tantalus. One finds then the tiresome voices of themselves. In my terms, what frisson would free a reader from misreading what he took to be style or surface hardness—the punch-old-Blanche-in-the-mouth routine? That he had only a passion for himself in his words? That they would empty so fearsomely at the end of his sentence? That the manifold synchronism of Language went on in all directions around the words where he had died— talking to himself—buried in the salt of his visions? The movement back of the great poets is not to a tradition—a golden time or wisdom behind us that places thought in the past and kills it—but it is toward a reopening of words—toward the violence and dynamism of Language—the work of it is in Pound's return to Homer, Egypt, Na-Khi and in Olson's ultimate return to Pleistocene,—his curriculum. A beginning again with everything. This reopening of words lets us see their solidifications—the crystals FORMing in the work—(a crust, akin to *cruror*—blood, *Kryos*—icy-cold, a coagulation that is the "external expression of a definite internal structure."[14] An open language is not a wise-doom. I have come to know *how unpleasant it is to reveal the limitations and necessities of a practice in language where one is used to seeing . . . the expression of genius and freedom in all its transparency* (Foucault).[15] I would not take it away from you, if it had not become the mirror of our deadness. *Half under its breath, amid the murmuring of things,*[16] all experience is interiorized language. I (we) lose the words because the structure of what I (we) thought closed. There is nonetheless a speaking that *lodges within my own speech.*[17] I would not give you the *malicious grace of an esprit libre,* if the interior life were not an interiorized language (Lacan).[18] The mind is only the body's invisibility (Merleau-Ponty).[19] *The language regards the guilty man as he who it was* (Curtius).[20]

A courage breaks into its syllables—cor—heart and the suffix "age," which denotes an aggregation of contents and functions around the heart. But the heart is invisible. The arrangement. The taxis. The arrangement of words. Under the arrangement of words (hypotaxis), the hierarchies come into a stasis. A standing still. The system of it, from Gk. *histánai*, I halt. Ek—out of stasis.[21] Ecstasy. Stretching back in the web-graph of his speech, a man may see the song close into his own visibility—half of his manhood, speaking, perhaps, half-words. The Other that is the place of his desire is absent, or, as in the sciences, present without him. The murmur of things interrupts the logic of his arrangement An old speech notices the delayed subordinations—allows the I to ride inside the action: "that way was I carried, for on it did much-attending horses carry me, pulling the chariot; and the maidens led the way" (Parmenides, quoted from Mourelatos).[22] Through the arrangement of words (parataxis), there is a speech alongside my speech, which allows a double-speech. A placement. The Other is present and primary to our speaking. There is no public realm without such polarity of language. The operation of its duplicity is the poetic job. A peril and an ecstasy. The traffic around a heart which is heartless. The characters do not speak only of themselves, since they are images of an action. Transcendence is not a position somewhere else, but the manner of our being to any other (Merleau-Ponty).[23] A co-existence.

So, an operational Language[24]—just where I (we) had thought to find the stable forms, the recognition that it is only ourselves. These closed words stop and become empty. They are then, where we were thinking, unstable and invaded, as if the known and thought had by a metamorphosis become the unknown and unthought. Just there, the visibility of men died. Against this, the operational Language begins again—allowing very little anthropomorphism. There where he does not think he is thinking. The astonishment of these reopened shapes in lives and poems. But then I (we) move back, for I (we) have been taught there is no operation in language. The poetic langauge is said to be apart—a wisdom—transcendent to it and not its composing intelligence. Is it in order to protect our eyes from some terrible finitude that has already happened? Or is it simply a mistake that takes on the proportions of the species?— as it is true to say the buffalo still doesn't know what a gun is. And I (we) have been taught always to translate the field of Language into a highwire—creative, transcendent, fictive to the terror the culture has been speaking. It is comforting to love nitrogen balloons. A discourse must return without transparency, but it cannot compose itself of closed words—the "spatial capture" of our words—in the stadium of the mirror (Lacan's *le stade du miroir*, translated for the metaphor).[25]

We have on our hands then an instability of forms, an instability of ourselves and an unthought manhood. This proposes simultaneously a death of forms, a return of past form, and a disclosure of unknown forms of thought and experience. They are like Jake Spicer's inescapable diamond in the Runcible Mountains, which has bases and players inside it.[26] Like Shelley, his greatest gift was to know this instability and work with it. I think of the marvelous instability, the breathing breathlessness, of the triads in *West Wind* and *The Triumph of Life*, which, not unlike the flow of Jack's serial poems, disclose life.[27] The golden section inside a west wind [in] Shelley comes to mind because he is perhaps the first modern, dumped out of determination, preceding Poe, whose life is drunk up into the acts of language. To read him as an idealist is understandable but mistaken. He polarized the ideal and its invisibility, thus making it a compositional factor in the real, not a separated meaning. He is gnostic in the perilous polarization of himself to an absent reality. What happened to his personality is in the books: he was, according to Rossetti, seen to be walking in opposite directions simultaneously, and there is the cloaked and hooded figure at his bedside who when the hood fell back turned out to be himself. These curious stories:[28] the first witnessed by his friends, the Williamses, and the second told by himself after he stopped screaming. The style of his work is entirely operational, doubled over, and the personality of the man in the work can only be read in terms of the distance travelled. Style is initially a loss of personality or personality at stake. The Muses remain the missing absolutes of Language, alive and acting, however much we have wished to stop them at one place or another. We also have an instability of words— the big ones that come at the ends of our sentences—gods, loves, lives, laughter, jokes—where something is composed on one tongue or another and doesn't stop for a name.[29]

Difficult voices speak to us. "We have now reached the point we had to reach in order to discover from it the reason for this oversight . . . we must completely reorganize the idea we have of knowledge, we must abandon the mirror myths of immediate vision and reading, and conceive knowledge as a production" (Althusser and Balibar).[30] So that thinking poetically will not always, inside what the culture thinks, idle the heart away—*Gerede* (just talk)—*parole vide* (empty words).[31] It may be one dies into another language. Certainly, a manhood is at stake. The empty words that were once situated in logos. There, I find the appearance of the Word defined as the act of words acting in a world-sentence.

But this enlargement of my poetics—does it punish the poems I have asked you to read? I think not, if serial structure is understood. An actual directive of all serial poems is that the series is other than, not simply more than, its parts— "ah, so," says the aesthetical Charlie Chan, "like stepping into the same visibility twice, which I demonstrate here is impossible."[32] That is, the particularity, the singular voice and condition of "Image-Nation 5," say, does not quite complete itself—here it is erased and and what it was haunted by replaces the instability with something else—the singularity imposes itself and then ceases to be "visible as particular" in the next poem (Merleau-Ponty on serial music).[33] The serial field is honest, if dangerous ground. "Meaning is a kind of movement" never disrespectful of the indeterminate which is its musical, inescapable ground.[34] The serial poem constantly circumscribes an absence that brings its presences to life. An indefiniteness that is one of the providing aspects of the world. The reader is disclosed in an act of such worldliness, or rather, he is open to it, and has not constituted the real himself. He may enter a disclosed obedience, different from the polis imposed upon our time. He—there—then—comes to a gate. And as he steps through, he becomes invisible—suddenly to begin his visibility again.

The distance between the first and last poems of the *Image-Nations:*—I did not want to face the disembodiment. The map of a language that appears and disappears. Incredible silence and inability in speech. As if, faced by those who have no language, whose "talk" empties into their limit, the language-man had no words either to fit our condition. The image now and again could replace empty words like a mandala. I knew from Mallarmé that the language went on speaking—older and other than ourselves.[35] There was also the sudden discovery that silence is not the contrary of speech (Merleau-Ponty), but its violent opposite, by which we pull words out of the world.[36] The ontological necessity of what we are speaking is our invisibility, the companion of our visibility. One may offer another only a world, not oneself. The silence behind and in front of us, horizons of the heart, by a tension between words and their absence "discloses a world-thesis" (Merleau-Ponty's phrase).[37] "At least such is the speech that . . . does not cede to the vertigo of eloquence, does not wish to suffice to itself or close in upon itself and upon its sense, but opens upon and leads to the outside" (Lefort xxix). The "dissimulation of our inherence in the world, history and language" (Lefort) may go on.[38]

we cannot find an origin in God, in nature, or in man such   attempts converge in the misapprehension of a total explication of the world (Lefort)[39]

Stops. The thought of totals, the original totalitarianism, is a rooted dissimulation and turns the present into the past or into the already thought. A poetics of this allows a poet to dominate his own work, an ownership that results in the disaster of anthropomorphism, which in modern terms becomes the substitute for all other totals. A substitute coherence, it is not an inherence. Mirror, mirror, on the wall? The seat of the language in the Other is the necessary exploration.

This "freedom from the sense of root" (Lefort on Merleau-Ponty)[40] is both terrible and beautiful, giving us entrance to the unthought and to an immanent new form of thought (Foucault).[41]

in the interior labyrinth where the frontiers of the visible fade[42]

the oldest labor of poetry is still *an installation.*[43]

The map of language ties us to time, but such time, the life of the visible, is synchronous. There is the arche out of which the language spoke—its necessity and its continuing to begin. There's the pre-chronic, before men, when the things murmured, and this continued when men moved from the ice-edge by their ability to make fire and left only their garbage dumps. The poor still live there, murmuring under the closed language, where we do not see them because their words are devoured by their need. Where the work of language drinks us up, their need swallows the words. The terrible lie of the language of totals—that it is transparent to life—drinks them up, who are left out of the life of the invisible by a crime in language. The dia-chronic, phonemic, worded time of the earth, of one's own steps, of American words, of English words, which must not be resolved into one's own, remains virtual discourse with the Other. Diachronic—linear, unidirectional words of a time that has become only ourselves. The act of words throned in the Other is missing. The synchronic—the sentence moving in every direction—a reversable time-sentence reenters our words (see Lévi-Strauss on these terms):

the grammatical could come to fruition in the heart of what is alone (Lévi-Strauss on Freud)[44]

we must ground the notion of the Other with a big O as being the ground of the deployment of the Word (Lacan)[45]

"It must be posited that, as a facet of an animal at the mercy of Language, man's desire is desire of the Other" (Lacan).[46] You are inside out.

In the poems I have asked you to read, Naught appears now and again in the sequence. He is the first drunkenness of the poems—always there at the point of the pencil. He is like a zero-phoneme—first in opposition to all other phonemes—I can't hear–I can't see—then he is in opposition to the absence of phonemes (Jakobson via Wilden).[47] In their original context, these poems are like squawking birds, events of the peril of the narration. Their devotion is to the unthought and the unknown as they are technical to my (our) experience. The method, which is the same thing as belief (Olson),[48] composes a language before and at the end of our discourse, primary and penultimate. The ultimate language is absent,—that is to say, it is alive at the edge of mine or yours. The ultimate of my languages or yours—or the culture's—is missing.[49] The terror that I am *spoken rather than speaking* (Lacan's phrase) is present in their heartlessness.[50] Their broken voice is not meant to be another comfortable grief. Instead,

The Magus Zoroaster, my dead child,
Met his own image walking in the garden[51]

If we have found the father-pronoun of the universe trembling, it is perhaps necessary. *It is enough to have seen in the present epidemic a blinded rabbit in the middle of the road, lifting the emptiness of his vision changed into a look toward the setting sun* (Lacan).[52] Penultimate. The last syllable, silent and golden, always belongs to another poet. The duplicity of my (our) language blends a child's thought with the risks of the "perilous act"[53] thought is—and permits no luxurious ownership of language or of a consequent knowledge. All true language is thought and so reverses into experience.[54] A breath-boundary, where it is a natural art. The dictation is natural. Things and words are not separate. Such language is not representational of a meaning backward or forward, occulted, lost or unfound, secret to a beginning or an end. It is not a manipulation of words, as in discourse, to refer transparently to a real significance. The operational language reposes the *profound kinship of language with the world* (Foucault).[55] The dissolution of that binding and entangling has turned out to be ourselves or our discourse. The poetic left to an ideality or transcendence is not a poetic at all—but merely a substitute for the limitation my (our) thought has become. The operational language is conjunctive and reties the heart. The retied heart is an Other Heart. Who is speaking?— (Nietzsche's profound and original question, asked again by Foucault)—reopens the language into its natural speech,—a double voice of a projective real whose harmony and disharmony are my (our) job.[56] *The Other Language.*

The finitude of my language, its childishness and foreignness, its means and music, fills with its masters and is meant to reopen into what is older and other than itself. What works without me may disclose a graph of the epic Eros, who includes the smallness of my love. The *Image-Nations* will have no formal end, no completion of what they feel or know. They are too adventurous for that. And too nearly overwhelmed by the *intentionless and non-communicative utterances of a world* (Arendt).[57] If ever we "cross our celestial legs in the celestial grass,"[58] I may be forgiven this reading of the intention of my poems. I have endeavoured to make this essay absolutely dialectical between my smallness and the largeness that is at stake. I make a wish that the young may be able to write again. I merely leaned over the flow of the work to see the "ungraspable phantom of life that is the key to it all."[59] "How curious," Colin said, "that all poets have bent shoulders!"[60] I borrow in order to reword a directive of what I saw—that *in these great times, which I knew long before they had grown up, you should not here and now expect any word of my own from me* (Kraus)[61]

flesh composed of suns   how can that be?[62]

a book for Edgar Allan Poe

May 30, 1973
West Vancouver
British Columbia

Poetry and Positivisms

High-Muck-a-Muck or "Spiritual Ketchup"[1]

Except for us, Vesuvius might consume
In solid fire the utmost earth and know
No pain (ignoring the cocks that crow us up
To die). This is part of the sublime
From which we shrink. And yet, except for us,
The total past felt nothing when destroyed

. . . .

His firm stanzas hang like hives in hell
Or what hell was, since both heaven and hell
Are one, and here, O terra infidel.

The fault lies with an over-human god,
Who by sympathy has made himself a man
And is not to be distinguished, when we cry

. . . .

The death of Satan was a tragedy
For the imagination. A capital
Negation destroyed him in his tenement
And, with him, many blue phenomena.

Wallace Stevens, "Esthétique du mal," 1947[2]

Silence, the Word and the Sacred. There is to my mind
a bird-like swiftness in the relations of these three terms—a there and a not-
there on the highest branch of a topless tree. Yet, each is also a field of distur-
bance, an expanse for which "Map is not territory" (Korzybski).[3] And so, earth
and sky are not disposable humanisms, but aspects of the Sacred. My sense of
my own time is that the Word and all its words disappear into Silence. Thus,

the vast field of Silence becomes the Sacred. This wondrous *Silentium*, then, becomes worded, for that is our noise and our effort at meaning. I am here trying to suggest the territory, the largeness, in which we try to live and think. The Western tradition since Socrates has worked this otherness by reduction— whether through logic or its companion, humanism—until the great sciences of *phusis* and *bios* have claimed all such thought. Poetry, however, has never let go of a "discourse of cosmos"[4] that keeps the attention of the old vocabulary of God, gods, and goddesses intelligent at least.* The subject of our greatest poetry remains this manifold otherness, which is too little remarked, or it is dismissed as idiosyncrasy. It is, I think, fair to say that the fundamental push of twentieth-century poetry has been to break out of "the confines of the lyric voice and sensibility."[5] Yeats and Pound are the founders of such possibility for our time—the former by way of a quarrel with himself and an obsession with the sacred and the latter by way of an opposition to the tradition of self-knowledge. In a recent study, Thomas Grieve notes: "Self-knowledge, for Pound, could not be an end in itself. It is pursued only so that the object of study can be displaced to let the world in" (278).

I think also of Rilke writing to explain his *Elegies*:

> *Affirmation of life-AND-death appears as one in the "Elegies."* To grant one without the other is, so it is here learned and celebrated, a limitation which in the end shuts out all that is infinite. *Death is the side of life averted from us, unshone upon by us:* we must try to achieve the greatest consciousness of our existence which is at home in *both unbounded realms, inexhaustibly nourished from both.* . . . The true figure of life extends through *both* spheres, the blood of the mightiest circulation flows through *both: there is neither a here nor a beyond, but the great unity in which the beings that surpass us,* the "angels", are at home. . . .
>
> *We are the bees of the invisible. Nous butinons éperdument le miel du visible, pour l'accumuler dans la grande ruche d'or de l'Invisible. (Letters,* vol. 2: 373, 374; original emphasis)

And I would like to place his sense of those "beings that surpass us" here at the beginning of my remarks, because whatever experience of the sacred I have includes them:

Wer, wenn ich schriee, hörte mich denn aus der Engel
Ordnungen?
und gesetzt selbst, es nähme
einer mich plötzlich ans Herz: ich verginge von seinem
stärkeren Dasein.

---

* Michel de Certeau, *Heterologies: Discourse on the Other.* I have freely adapted the phrase.

Who, if I cried out, would hear me among the angels'
hierarchies?
and even if one of them pressed me
suddenly against his heart: I
would be consumed
in that overwhelming existence.

(*Selected Poetry*, "First Duino Elegy," 151)

It seems necessary to say that I am not writing about religion in the ordinary sense. That institutionalization of imaginary forms has become an immobility of foregone conclusions, for all the current return to religion, which should be studied with greater care than ever before, especially in the face of René Girard's challenge in *Violence and the Sacred*. I am not writing about the other world, but only about this one in which the relation to the complexity of the other is fundamental and should not be understood as the realm of the dead. This is a particularism—not ideology—in which the poet presumes, without letting go of an extraordinary sense of the materiality of language, "a continuum between the linguistic and the psychological" (Godzich) depth and surfaces.[6] The materiality of language brings us into its presence-absence provocation. My insistence is that we take our poets seriously—their "lived experience—of the other" (Godzich xvi)[7]—their sense that we cannot appropriate the other into a realm of knowledge, their continuous argument that there is no autonomy of poetic language, even as language itself can be experienced as other. I am aware of the theoretical unease with such concerns in academic circles, best stated by Edward Said in *The World, the Text and the Critic*. For him, the intellectual is secular and exclusive; the other and the sacred somehow are not secular. The problem is, of course, with the word secular—"Of or pertaining to the worldly or temporal as distinguished from the spiritual or eternal" (*Webster's*). To quarrel with such gnosticism—dualism—is precisely my undertaking in pointing to the entangling of discourses in modern poetry. This gnosticism has its parallel from the other side of the *duo* in Catholic Jacques Maritain's *Creative Intuition in Art and Poetry* in which poets since Baudelaire should beware of an improper handling of the sacred. As the contemporary return to religion demonstrates, the public and the social (Said's admirable concerns) are not separate from the ruins of the spiritual. Nor do body and soul so easily separate in the contemporary mind. Nor is this a matter of privacies and hermeticisms outside the social and public, because they are—*fortune, infortune, fortune*[8]—entangled. Wlad Godzich's discussion of this, in his "Foreword" to Michel de Certeau's *Heterologies: Discourse of the Other*, while sympathetic to Said, is most useful in delineating the problematical equation of "unthinkability, undecidability, paradox" with "magic, divine ordinance, sacred texts" (xvii). Magic is not so easily put away because it involves an ancient psychology which is not epistemological; divine providence is gone and need not be argued with, except in its current political manifestations; and texts of the sacred should be discovered. There is an uncertainty of the real that always opposes "the 'tyranny of the whole.'"* What had been imaginings of the whole, whether philosophical or historical, now become an imagination of holes. If there is an end of history—that armchair portent—it is of parts, and we are still working with the operation of it.

Michel de Certeau notices the "humiliation of the Christian tradition" which began in the sixteenth and seventeenth centuries and a "fundamental decline" of the "institutions of meaning" involved in "the disintegration of a sacred world" (*Heterologies* 86). The Word in ruins—that is to say, become historical—results in "a 'wound' inseparable from the social ill" (86). I move forward to remember Melville writing to Hawthorne in April of 1851:

> We incline to think that the Problem of the Universe is like the Freemason's mighty secret, so terrible to all children. It turns out, at last, to consist in a triangle, a mallet, and an apron,—nothing more! We incline to think that God cannot explain His own secrets, and that He would like a little information upon certain points Himself. We mortals astonish Him as much as He us. But it is this *Being* of the matter; there lies the knot with which we choke ourselves. As soon as you say *Me*, a *God*, a *Nature*, so soon you jump off from your stool and hang from the beam. Yes, that word is the hangman. Take God out of the dictionary, and you would have Him in the street. (*Correspondence*, Letter 83, 186)

I think of Girard's challenge. In this context, Michel de Certeau is also useful in the care he takes with "practices and discourse," as Godzich emphasizes, "that are either on the wane or in the making, or that even do not quite manage to constitute themselves" (xiv).

Alongside the modern experience of the materiality of language, there is also afoot a materiality of soul. But first to insist on the nature of that language—poetic language—with the help of Godzich's reflections on de Certeau. I avoid, as he does, the words literature and literary, just now, because they are institutional terms and carry all the weaknesses of that source—the positivisms—which have led to an extreme form of deconstruction with at one end of it an end of history that is largely an end of literature. ("Such positivism!" someone said from a great height.) The quality of poetic language, Godzich suggests,

---

* The phrase is Ron Silliman's on Spicer. [Editor's note: "the 'tyranny of the whole'" occurs in Ron Silliman's essay, "Spicer's Language," where it appears as an undocumented quotation: it is not Silliman's phrase (*New Sentence* 153).]

does not come from the fact that it is a special mode of language, but rather from the fact that it is a part of language, a mode of language use, that is a discourse. *Unlike language, which, as an object of knowledge, is a construct of philosophers and linguists, discourses constitute forms of actual social interaction and practice.* As such, they are not irrational, but they are subject to the pulls and pressures of the situation in which they are used as well as to the weights of their own tradition. They must always handle the complex interplay of that which is of the order of representation and the nonrepresentable part which is just as much constitutive of them, their own other. (xx; my emphasis)

Thus, every realism—the subjective, the social, the psychological—doubles over, and requires an interpretative vocabulary that keeps such fundamental contrariety alive. Alongside this, then, set a materiality of soul, the poetic version of which was first given us by Blake in what was a Satanic voice: "Man has no Body distinct from his Soul . . . " (*The Marriage of Heaven and Hell* Plate 4). But I am concerned with those discourses, as I said, which claim the real in repeated positivisms, so allow me to make use of one who knows them well and who, in his own words, does not forget "that the economic and the hierarchical can be toppled from their throne, the functioning of the society made more intelligible to everyone, and a new and different *paideia* made possible for men and women" (Castoriadis 330)—Cornelius Castoriadis in *Crossroads in the Labyrinth*:

> . . . meaning and content exist only in and through the life of a body, to which nonetheless they cannot be reduced, and . . . their manifestations differ in level, in quality, in intensity and in time, so that we are referred irresistibly to an organization, to forces or tendencies, and to identifiable regularities. An organization of what, forces acting where, regularities connected with what? Something— namely, the soul—is presupposed by or implied in this, and the frankest way of speaking of it is to speak of it as a thing. Certain philosophers grow annoyed and complain about realism. But the realism is to be found in their camp. Never having been able to think except in the realist perspective, they believe that realism is identical with the thing. In fact, naive philosophical pre-emptions aside, we do not know what a thing is; we only know what the idea of a thing is in a realist philosophy—an idea whose real referent has never been found. (30)

And he returns us to the problem of metaphorical language, especially by way of Freud. Metaphorical language has to do with the complexity of image, and by way of knowing it, we come better to understand both the play and the peril of language.

We have, then, in the twentieth century, poetry that is unable and unwilling to depend upon the direct and simplifying clarity of the ego at the centre, a concern with the arrangement of words which both renews and disturbs our relation to words and to the rhythm of form—so to compose the representable alongside the nonrepresentable. Though modern insistence upon this begins as far back as Hölderlin and Blake, critical theory increasingly reflects upon its relation to words. This, in my view, is the fundamental gift of contemporary theory, when it does not resolve itself in various positivisms of knowledge—psychologism, sociologism, anthropologism, historicism, scientism of matter or spirit. This theory, when it is most vital, is an interrogation of our relation to words—more a questioning of our history-in-words than a knowledge of solutions. In poetic terms, there are no solutions to or resolutions of language on the horizon, because the depths of language are found in a creative relation to words. In the broadest terms, contemporary theory—out of its extraordinary debt to Mallarmé—delineates with clarity the two traditions of language and text that mix, at times mystifyingly, in our writing: the contrasting relations to the word, on the one hand, in the Hebraic tradition and, on the other, in the Greek. Susan Handelman draws this to our attention most usefully in *The Slayers of Moses: The Emergence of Rabbinic Interpretation in Modern Literary Theory*. I emphasize, in this context, only her early consideration of our relation to words in the two traditions—the conflict between them outlined in her chapter titles: "Greek Philosophy and the Overcoming of the Word" and "Rabbinic Thought: The Divinity of the Text."

> Though *davar* means both *thing* and *word* in Hebrew, it is crucial to point out that *thing* did not have the Greek connotation of *substance*. As I. Rabinowitz puts it [in "'Word' and Literature in Ancient Israel"], "the word is the reality in its most concentrated, compacted, essential form." *Reality* is a far more appropriate word to use than *thing*, for it does not evoke the same connotations as do *substance* and *being*. Of course, the physical object itself was not considered to be identical to the word which designated it, but for the Hebrew mind, the essential reality of the table was the word of God, not any idea of the table as in the Platonic view, or some *ousia*.
>
> The Hebrew word was not an arbitrary designation, but an aspect of the continuous divine creative force itself. Each word, as Rabinowitz puts it, was the inner specific character or essence of its respective reality. Names are not conventional, but intrinsically connected to their referents; the name, indeed, is the real referent of the thing, its essential character—not the reverse, as in Greek thought. One does not pass beyond the name as an arbitrary sign towards a non verbal vision of the thing, but rather *from the thing to the word*, which creates, characterizes, and sustains it. Hence, *davar*, is not simply *thing* but also *action, efficacious fact, event, matter, process*. (32; original emphasis)

This describes an originative—not original—relation to language.

Handelman's consequent discussion of Christian developments is important, and I hope I am doing little damage in offering pieces of it:

In Christianity, the Hebrew Scriptures . . . acquired the status which words had in Greek thought—mere signs, figures, shadows pointing to the true word, the word of flesh. True reality became again for Christianity substantial being, not verbal pattern; the text was supplanted. (32)

I note that to understand "verbal pattern" as mere verbal pattern is to misunderstand the process and, certainly, any poiesis

> In the first verses of the Gospel of John, where the word-become-flesh idea is most fully articulated, the Greek term *logos* is used for *word*. Thorlief Boman devoted considerable attention to the contrast between *davar* and *logos* in his book *Hebrew Thought Compared with Greek*. Boman points out that the root of *logos* in Greek means *to gather, to put together in order, arrange*, and only gradually did *logos* come to designate *word, reckoning*. Originally, it had nothing to do with the function of speaking [for which *mythos* would be the correct term]. *Logos*, the concept of *gathering together in an order* then came to be defined as *reasonable content, rational principle, or knowable governing law.* . . .
> The tendency to *gather various meanings into a one* is . . . characteristic of Greek thought in general: its movement towards the universal, the general, the univocal. The Rabbinic tendency, by contrast, is toward differentiation, metaphorical multiplicity, multiple meaning. One needs to search the forms, the shapes, patterns of words, and their varying connections within an expansive text; there is no confinement of meaning within the ontology of substance. (32–33; original emphasis)

Handelman notes that this "liberation from the ontology of substance" is "Derrida's intent" (33).*

The relevance of this to the poetry which interests me is important for an understanding of its constant, forceful renewal of our relation to words and of its sensitivity to the presence and absence that is the *poiesis*. Handelman notes: "This tension between presence and absence is expressed more readily through voice than vision. Vision, appearance, is fullness, complete presence of the thing [I interrupt to say that "complete presence" is a possible condition of the real that the twentieth-century mind cannot have]; sound is a more subtle mode of presence, a moving vibration that both is and is not there [again, I interrupt to say that all studies of modern prosody must account for this]" (35). Her reflection on our literature follows from her thoughtful engagement with Auerbach's brilliant and focal essay "Odysseus' Scar":

---

* [Handelman's] bibliography is useful. For the cited passages: Thorlief Boman, *Hebrew Thought Compared with Greek* (Philadelphia: Westminster Press, 1954); and Isaac Rabinowitz, "'Word' and Literature in Ancient Israel," in *New Literary History* 4 (1972), 119–30.

Perhaps it could be said that Western literature has always been plagued by the appearance-reality conundrum because of the conflict between the foundational world view of Greek philosophy and the insights of art. The delusions of appearance, the ambiguities of being, the contradictory rather than solidly logical and substantial nature of being and time, are issues in art from its earliest beginnings to the present. . . . One of the reasons, no doubt, why we are at present witnessing the coronation of metaphor as the new philosophical idol is because the metaphorical view of reality . . . celebrates ambiguity, contradiction, and occurs precisely on the borderlines of ontology when something simultaneously both is and is not. Metaphor is alternative metaphysics. (35)

I would prefer to say an alternative to any positivism. The language of poetry, as Blake so brilliantly recognized, remains closer to the biblical process than to the Greek of Socrates and Plato. A creative process. An "expansive text." Unconfined meanings.

We men and women of literature—of poetics I would prefer to say—now enter a period that is rich in possibility. But we also come upon a pallor in the face of twentieth-century experience of art. Jean-François Lyotard noted in 1982:

This is a period of slackening—I refer to the color of the times. From every direction we are being urged to put an end to experimentation, in the arts and elsewhere. I have read an art historian who extols realism and is militant for the advent of a new subjectivity. I have read an art critic who packages and sells "Transavantgardism" in the marketplace of painting. . . . I have read that a new philosopher is discovering what he drolly calls Judaeo-Christianism, and intends by it to put an end to the impiety which we are supposed to have spread. . . . I have read from the pen of a reputable historian that writers and thinkers of the 1960 and 1970 avant-gardes spread a reign of terror in the use of language, and that the conditions for a fruitful exchange must be restored by imposing on the intellectuals a common way of speaking, that of historians. I have been reading a young philosopher of language who complains that Continental thinking, under the challenge of speaking machines, has surrendered to the machines the concern for reality, that it has substituted for the referential paradigm that of "adlinguisticity," . . . and who thinks that the time has now come to restore a solid anchorage of language in the referent. (Postmodern Condition 71–72)

Et cetera. I could extend Lyotard's examples with my own into pages, as they become furniture of the houseless. One turns for relief, respect, and laughter to

Imagine the twelve deaferended dumbbawls of the whowl abovebeugled to be the contonuation through regeneration of the urutteration of the word in pregross. (Joyce, Finnegans Wake 284)

Ullhodturdenweirmudgaardgringnirurdrmolnirfenrirlukkilokkibaugimandodr-
rerinsurtkrinmgernrackinarockar! Thor's for yo!
—The hundredlettered name again, last word of perfect language. (424)*

Though this is not the place to consider in detail Lyotard's important argu-
ment with this "slackening," certain aspects of it relate directly to my purpose:

> Eclectism is the degree zero of contemporary general culture: one listens to reggae,
> watches a western, eats McDonald's food for lunch and local cuisine for dinner,
> wears Paris perfume in Tokyo and "retro" clothes in Hong Kong: knowledge is a
> matter for TV games. (Postmodern Condition 76)

The problem, he argues, is to avoid a narrow "sociologizing and historicizing":

> Stepping over Benjamin's and Adorno's reticences, it must be recalled that science
> and industry are no more free of the suspicion which concerns reality than are art
> and writing. To believe otherwise would be to entertain an excessively humanis-
> tic notion of the mephistophelian functionalism of sciences and technologies. (Post-
> modern Condition 76)

Both scientist and capitalist in their politics and sociology, the argument goes,
are "imprinted" by "a kind of flight of reality out of the metaphysical, reli-
gious, and political certainties that the mind believed it held" (Postmodern Condi-
tion 77). This is the one aspect of our modernity, whether we name it indus-
trialism or post-industrialism. Neither science nor industry is much given to
reflection on the "flight" to which they are indebted and out of which they
claim reality. Modernity—the just-now (modo, originally the ablative of modus,
by measure, plus hodiernus, of today)—the sense of it is not something un-
precedented in history, but historicizing it removes the process of the flight as
well as its flowing content. Lyotard writes:

> Modernity, in whatever age it appears, cannot exist without a shattering of belief
> and without discovery of the "lack of reality" of reality, together with the inven-
> tion of other realities.
>   What does this "lack of reality" signify if one tries to free it from a narrowly
> historicized interpretation? The phrase is of course akin to what Nietzsche calls
> nihilism. But I see a much earlier modulation of Nietzschean perspectivism in the
> Kantian theme of the sublime. I think in particular that it is in the aesthetic of the
> sublime that modern art (including literature) finds its impetus and the logic of
> avant-gardes finds its axioms. (Postmodern Condition 77)

* See Norman O. Brown's use of these passages in Closing Time (New York: Random House, 1972),
p. 95.

The sublime, it seems to me, is that aspect of our poetry and art which is let go, passed over, dropped into the subjective by so much academic criticism, perhaps because of a lack of vocabulary or, more likely, because other discourses—though they too are a dis-currere, a running to and fro to arrange things—cannot contain such largeness. In the dictionary definition of the sublime, based on Kant, it is an "intimation of a capacity of the mind to apprehend the limitless or indeterminable" (Flew, *Dictionary*, "Sublime" 344).

The movement, the flight, of our condition amidst shattering beliefs has been the concern of modern poetry—indeed of all the arts—when the writing is not self-addressed to the "dead letter office" (Spicer, *Collected Books* 149). In this context, Lyotard's definitions are worth working with:

> I shall call modern the art which devotes its "little technical expertise" . . . to present the fact that the unpresentable exists. To make visible that there is something which can be conceived and which can neither be seen nor made visible: this is what is at stake in modern painting. But how to make visible that there is something which cannot be seen? Kant himself shows the way when he names "formlessness, the absence of form," as a possible index to the unpresentable. He also says of the empty "abstraction" which the imagination experiences when in search for a presentation of the infinite (another unpresentable): this abstraction itself is like a presentation of the infinite, its "negative presentation." He cites the commandment, "Thou shalt not make graven images" (Exodus), as the most sublime passage in the Bible in that it forbids all presentation of the Absolute. (*Postmodern Condition* 78)

Lyotard's view that "modern aesthetics is an aesthetic of the sublime" (81) is convincing. I am, however, uneasy when he remarks that it is a "nostalgic one" in order to differentiate the modern from the post-modern—that the former "allows the unpresentable to be put forward only as the missing contents" (81). This seems true only in patches and retrogressions. He writes then of the post-modern:

> The postmodern would be that which, in the modern, puts forward the unpresentable in presentation itself; that which denies itself the solace of good forms [traditional, harmonious], the consensus of a taste which would make it possible to share collectively the nostalgia for the unattainable. (81)

This is useful, if we consider that part of the flight involves us in a changed view of ourselves and of the range in recognitions of the other. The imagination of wholeness is being undone and displaced by a poetics which approaches that of Paz, having to do with movement and change. The post-modern moves to correct modernism, especially the political horror that manifests itself in many of its greatest writers. Lyotard closes his essay with what amounts to an admonition:

> Finally, it must be clear that it is our business not to supply reality but to invent allusions to the conceivable which cannot be presented. And it is not to be expected that this task will effect the last reconciliation between language games [discourses?] (which under the name of faculties, Kant knew to be separated by a chasm), and that only the transcendental illusion (that of Hegel) can hope to totalize them into a real unity. But Kant also knew that the price to pay for such an illusion is terror. The nineteenth and twentieth centuries have given us as much terror as we can take. We have paid a high enough price for the nostalgia of the whole and the one, for the reconciliation of the concept and the sensible, of the transparent and the communicable experience. Under the general demand for slackening and for appeasement, we can hear the mutterings of the desire for a return of terror, for the realization of the fantasy to seize reality. The answer is: Let us wage a war on totality; let us be witnesses to the unpresentable; let us activate the differences and save the honor of the name. (81–82)

For all the "chasm" "between language games," an entangling of them will make them all subtler and less positive in their closures.

One measures the flight of this condition, as poet or anyone who loves persons, things, and places, it seems to me, by knowing precisely one's relation to the tradition. Relation is not "relative to," but relation, an activity, both intellectual and emotional. The terms are not necessarily religious, but, rather, belief, disbelief, and unbelief to be gauged by the sense, which Olson pointed out long ago, that all method is belief.[9] Silence, the Word and the Sacred, then, on one's own experience, while noting that one's own experience is always a reduction, a corner of a very large room, at times a pie with a plum in it, and so on: I am brought up a Roman Catholic—the Mass in English, French, and Latin—some careful training in Church Latin—an unsuccessful attempt that became ridiculous to make a priest of me. All of this in the territory of the Latter-Day Saints—my great-grandmother was, for a time, an unhappy "secretary" to Brigham Young, and I never heard the end of it. Recently, on a visit to UCLA, I looked out of my hotel window at a handsome art-deco building with a shining gold figure, trumpet in hand, on its roof. No one in the hotel could tell me who it was, so I walked to the building and recognized that "heretical" angel, Moroni of the American revelation. I brush-stroke this to suggest that I have some experience with both the European and the American entrance to *sacer, sacra, sacrum,* from Greek *saos, soos,* which becomes Latin *sanus, -a, -um,* and I have often thought how comfortable and sane it was—*Je crois en un seul Dieu, Le Père tout puissant qui a fait le ciel et la terre, toutes les choses visible et invisible.*[10] Here, the twentieth-century experience enters, never allowing me to forget that *sacer* also means the accursed, the criminal, the destructive.

But, out of Idaho, I did not come into the twentieth century until it was nearly half-way over. As it has been for so many, the door only opened by way of University and the gathering of minds that offered neither comfort nor convention. Could one have continued to wander in that transcendental happiness and its promises without the art, the historical knowledge, the political-social concern of one's own time?[11] Without assurance, one hopes not. A few names come to mind as I continue to stumble, read, quote, write: the great poets, Jack Spicer and Robert Duncan, who were students with me and friends, and later Charles Olson and Robert Creeley; one historian, Ernst Kantorowicz; and a philosopher, Hannah Arendt.

Jack Spicer, Presbyterian-Methodist-Wobbly when we met in 1945, asked first off, "Just what are you?" and he commented, "Oh, you're one of those who eat your God." Jocular but truly *protestant*. He died in 1965, leaving a major poetry, which began in a reading of Rilke in the late 1940s and in his own *Imaginary Elegies*:

God's other eye is good and gold. So bright
The shine blinds. His eye is accurate. His eye
Observes the goodness of the light it shines
Then, pouncing like a cat, devours
Each golden trace of light
It saw and shined.
Cat feeds on mouse. God feeds on God. God's goodness is
A black and blinding cannibal with sunny teeth
That only eats itself.

(Imaginary Elegy III, *Collected Books* 335)

The words take us to a depth of opposition.

Robert Duncan came out of what he called the "hermetic muck of his grandmother," a sense of an older, less imperial, sacred, and he distrusted Roman Catholics deeply. I offer lines from a poem of the late 1950s:

OFTEN I AM PERMITTED TO RETURN
TO A MEADOW
as if it were a scene made-up by the mind,
that is not mine, but is a made place,

that is mine, it is so near to the heart,
an eternal pasture folded in all thought
so that there is a hall therein

that is a made place, created by light
wherefrom the shadows that are forms fall.

(Opening 7)

His poetics move across the years and continue to shape them.

Charles Olson, who died in 1970, left an astounding work. Let us hear him around 1956 in a lecture:

> We were able, I take it, to establish a cosmology *without letting God in* as creator in the old sense, in the old static sense of the universe. I believe we are equally enabled today to establish a mythology *without letting God in* as a primordial nature in the old static sense, but only an image of Primordial Nature in the prospective sense of the absolute which is included in the relative. (*Special View* 55; original emphasis)

This is from his *The Special View of History* with its play on Einstein's famous title. Over the years of his labour on the *Maximus Poems* from 1940 until his death, Olson made Alfred North Whitehead's cosmology a companion of his work— the "philosophy of organism" that was to abolish the detached mind. A passage from Whitehead's *Process and Reality* can usefully, in this context, be placed alongside Olson's:

> The secularization of the concept of God's functions in the world is at least as urgent a requisite of thought as is the secularization of other elements in experience. The concept of God is certainly one essential element in religious feeling. But the converse is not true; the concept of religious feeling is not an essential element in the concept of God's function in the universe. In this respect religious literature has been sadly misleading to philosophic theory, partly by attraction and partly by repulsion. (II.IX.VIII 315–16)

In the complex development of Whitehead's argument, this secularization leads to the final opposites of his cosmology: "joy and sorrow, good and evil, disjunction and conjunction . . . the many in one," ending in God and the World. Whitehead allows the opposites "a certain ultimate directness of intuition," except God and the World, which "introduce[s] the note of interpretation" (V.I.IV 518). Which is exactly where we are—in interpretation with interpenetrating discourses of the entirely physical, still not complete, becoming of things.

Robert Creeley, whom I read as a companion in poetry—that is, a guide to my need to have a direct relation to language—shows no unease with what is broken. The word sacred does not sit easily beside him, unless my determination to take the word away from religion and positivisms works. He tells us:

The simplest way I have found to make clear my own sense of writing . . . is to use the analogy of driving. The road, as it were, is creating itself momently in one's attention to it, there, visibly, in front of the car. There is no reason it should go on forever, and if one does so assume it, it very often disappears all too actually. When Pound says, "we must understand what is happening," one sense of his meaning I take to be this necessary attention to what is happening in the writing (the road) one is, in the sense suggested, following. In that way there is nothing mindless about the procedure. It is, rather, a respect for the possibilities of such attention that brings Allen Ginsberg to say, "Mind is shapely." Mind, thus engaged, permits experience of "order" far more various and intensive than habituated and programmed limits of its subtleties can recognize. (*A Quick Graph* 58)

Harald Mesch in an important essay on Creeley—one of the few that goes to the depths where Creeley goes—takes up the significance of this:

Creeley's abandonment of the metaphysical view and the renunciation of the transcendental, atemporal shelter it offers—accessible only to the mind—his "overcoming of the metaphysical," is the desperate consequence of his acute sensitivity to the dangers of solipsism, but should not be construed as a step towards the acceptance of a desperately hopeless temporality. The subject that adheres nonintentionally to the law of temporal "occasion" falls from atemporal transcendence into an atemporal presence rather than a one-dimensional temporality, or, as Wittgenstein has it, into "timelessness": "If we take eternity to mean not infinite temporal duration but timelessness [*Unzeitlichkeit*], then eternal life belongs to those who live in the present." (81–82)*

This reflects an aspect of Wittgenstein's thought, which positivisms tend to ignore to their detriment, as I shall note later. Here, I cannot over-emphasize the importance of what the poet is doing.

Ernst Kantorowicz, medievalist and historian of Byzantium, first gave me a sense of history as the record of human action and human consciousness. His two great books, *Frederick the Second*—Holy Roman Emperor, German King, King of Sicily and Jerusalem—and *The King's Two Bodies*, on medieval political theology, summarize much of what Spicer, Duncan, and I studied with him. I did not learn what little Greek I have in order to read the classics or even the *New Testament*. Those came later. First, it was to prepare for a course which studied a single document, *Constantine Porphyrigentius*,—how to approach the Emperor, crawling on your belly, nose and eyes to the floor. It was available in a French translation, but that was not good enough for Kantorowicz. By the time I was

---

* [Mesch] cites Ludwig Wittgenstein, *Prototractatus: An Early Version of Tractatus Logico-Philosophicus*, ed. and trans. B. F. McGuiness et al. (Ithaca, N.Y.: Cornell University Press, 1971), 6.4422.

prepared, he had left Berkeley in protest over the loyalty oath, which, in 1950, must have struck him as a repetition of one aspect of his German experience. The study with him of the early Christian centuries still strikes me as important: all the arguments over *Homoiousian* (essential likeness of Son to Father), *Homoousian* (the same substance of Son and Father), *Heteroousian* (other than the same substance as the Father)—in other words, the history of all the trouble to overcome the Word with all the political and social consequences. And, of course, the thirteenth century with Dante at the centre was formative of what I thought poetry should be:

> It remained . . . to the poet to visualize the very tension of the "Two Bodies" in man himself, to make *humanitas* (according to Roman Law the medium of God-imitation) the sovereign of *homo*, and to find for all those intricate cross-relations and interrelations the most complex, terse, and simple, because most human, formula: "I crown and mitre you over yourself." (Kantorowicz, *King's Two Bodies* 495)

Hannah Arendt, another refugee from the dominations and powers of the twentieth century, was at Berkeley briefly, always surrounded by crowds of students, the largest I had ever seen, except for those drawn by Robert Oppenheimer. She brought forward a political consciousness that was also a consciousness of the history of political forms. She was in the midst of her work on *The Origins of Totalitarianism*, and that book remains, for me, one that must be thought through again and again. A paragraph from the Preface to the first edition of 1950 stops the heart and mind that are not historical:

> We can no longer afford to take that which was good in the past and simply call it our heritage, to discard the bad and simply think of it as a dead load which by itself time will bury in oblivion. The subterranean stream of Western history has finally come to the surface and usurped the dignity of our tradition. This is the reality in which we live. And this is why all efforts to escape from the grimness of the present into nostalgia for a still intact past, or into the anticipated oblivion of a better future, are vain. (ix)[12]

"The subterranean stream of Western history," at once religious and political, as Blake in poetic thought and Marx in political analysis so clearly argue, repeatedly involves us in a search for the domination of the whole, prepared for in "manifest destiny," given by Providence. The one blesses the other, though neither redeems us in Nature or in our own natures. Their meaningless relation, it turns out, does not lead to *humanitas* or community. Hannah Arendt's thought, after she left Berkeley, had to be tracked over the years in her books which were so watchful of men and women in "dark times." She could spot what was not taught elsewhere: in Lessing, for example, "the possible antagonism between truth and humanity" (*Dark Times* 28). In later years, her essay on Walter Benjamin became central; not only did it first draw my attention to that brilliant voice and the problematic of the "theological-metaphysical" element that haunts his thought—which in my view haunts the whole of the twentieth-century effort—but also I was brought to attend to Benjamin's "concentration on the philosophy of language" and Mallarmé's powerful example therein. In this context, Arendt writes:

> Any period to which its own past has become as questionable as it has to us must eventually come up against the phenomenon of language, for in it the past is contained ineradicably, thwarting all attempts to get rid of it once and for all. (*Dark Times* 204)

Our work, then, with the past becomes our labour with words.

These instances of my own entrance into the twentieth century, breaking, as they do, into the continuity of this discussion—in which I am uneasily assuming a knowledge of the lifetime works of Spicer, Duncan, Olson, and Creeley—are perhaps more events in my mind than they are in the minds of others. I can only recommend them to the attentive. I have wished to say that our cultural condition has a great deal to do with the nature of the sacred and that poetry of a certain order returns again and again to a discourse of cosmos with new attentions and cares. Jack Spicer:

> God is a big baseball that has nothing to do but go in a
>   curve or straight line. I studied geometry in highschool
>   and know that this is true.
> Given these facts the pitcher, the batter, and the catcher all look
>   pretty silly. No Hail Mary's
> Are going to get you out of a position with the bases loaded and
>   no outs, or when you're 0 and 2, or when the ball bounces
>   out to the screen wildly. Off seasons.
> I often thought of praying to him but could not stand the
>   thought of that big, white, round, omnipotent bastard.
> Yet he's there. As the game follows rules he makes them.
> I know
> I was not the only one who felt these things.
>
>   (*Collected Books* 258)

That is one measure that I know well. Nothing in the twentieth century allows me to sit still with the old definition of the soul, nor am I free to take an armchair on the matter of the *Logos* (Word), which for Spicer becomes the "low-ghost." Logos, whether it is The Word—"the actively expressed, creative, revelatory thought and will of God," as the dictionary says—or the rational principle in the universe, Newtonian, apart and complete, leaves the soul as it is, a "fleeting" and "flitting thing."

We may approach the theological-metaphysical past with justifiable and personal rage, as Weston La Barre has done in *The Ghost Dance: The Origins of Religion* (1970); its dedication "to Jean François Lefebvre, Chevalier de La Barre, burned at the stake in Abbeville, 1 July 1766 at the age of eighteen," is a reminder of much. We may, indeed, begin with his notice that

> Many metaphysical problems arise because we do not understand the logic of language (as Socrates did not) or what language itself is (Plato did not), and consequently such philosophical "problems" are no problems at all. They are only quibbles over what we do not know or understand: our linguistic behavior. For example, if (behavioristically) "God" be our term for the Unknown, then we cannot assert anything, whatever about it—not even to predicate its "unknowability" for this is to claim knowledge that is unknowable. (1)

This Wittgensteinian point is only agreeable if we are talking about knowledge—which is what the theologians claim—but our poetic context involves relation to an unknown, not a knowledge or method of it. We may again join La Barre on the absolute "omniscient, omnipotent and omnibenevolent" something in which the "three Absolutes immediately collide and have grave logical trouble coexisting. *Si Deus Bonum, unde malum?*" (La Barre 5). The word "absolute" (past participle of Latin *absolvere*—to free from imperfection) whether post-Kantian, Hegelian, or F. H. Bradleyan, is, perforce, a problem: "the totality of what really exists"; "a unitary system"; reality as "spiritual, and . . . unanthropomorphic"; or with Bradley, as the dictionary tells us, "quality and relation, substance and cause, subject and object, time and space, are all equally irredeemable" (Flew, "absolute" 2). Oh ho! We may agree with La Barre that "'Absolute' is an absurd word" (6)—*absurdus* originally meant simply "out of tune"—even as the use of it suggests an effort to get around Plato's *eidos* with its derivation from *idein* (to see) and all the visionary difficulties that tossed the poets out of the *Republic*.

Poets may be on firmer ground with La Barre and, in good part, hostile to Plato and Hegel in the following:

> The "ground of being" theologians talk about is, of course, one's own physical body, temporarily on loan from the material universe. . . . In this context, theology is really, ignorantly and unwittingly, discussing human biology under the pretense of discussing a grandiose cosmology—actually discussing the "facts of life" after having quite illegitimately identified two distinct Others, father and cosmos, as One. . . .

> Of course, since the body is the physical locus or psychological focus of pain, frustration, anxiety and guilt, one can mislearn to hate and fear the body, and to lay the emotional ground for world-hating Platonism. (La Barre 97n)

The slip here is not to notice that cosmos has been the traditional concern of poetry before it is made religion. La Barre, then, turns to the deadnesses:

> each dead society has bequeathed to us its historical sickness—the Greeks, Platonism as the Great Tradition in western philosophy; the Hebrews, the fallen temple of their ancient tribalism and their lost Davidic messiah; and the Romans, the ghost of Rome, the Church and western patterns of political and intellectual despotism. (635)

He cites Stephen Dedalus' struggle to awake from the "nightmare" of history (635). I would turn with greater assurance to Joyce's version of this in *Finnegans Wake* where the Finnegans wake in the language. There is so much agreeable in La Barre that one is tempted not to notice that his anger settles for a psychological and anthropological positivism that shirks the problem of "sacred discontent." Out of such positivism, one can hardly read the human nature that may appear.

In the long run of his learned argument, La Barre also cites Rilke's letter to Ilse Jahr (Feb. 22, 1923): "As Rilke knew, God, the-no-longer-sayable, is stripped of his attributes: eternity, omnipotence, infallibility return to the dead universe without a father" (19). The dead universe! Instead of belabouring this misstep, let us consider a larger share of that letter:

> So I *named* him at that time too, the God who had broken in upon me, and lived a long time in the anteroom of his name, on my knees . . . Now you would scarcely ever hear me name him, there is an indescribable discretion between us, and where once nearness was and penetration, there stretch new distances, as in the atom, which the new science also conceives as a universe in the small. The comprehensible escapes us, is transformed, instead of possession one learns relation, and there arises a namelessness that must begin again with God in order to be complete and without evasion. The experience of feeling recedes behind an endless longing for all that can be felt . . . attributes are taken away from God, the no longer expressible, fall back to creation, to love and death. (*Letters*, vol. 2: 324)

The tone of this letter, a response to the young woman's "affection" for what Rilke calls his "onetime heart," is gentle, but firm:

> The mysteries are greater than you can yet surmise, but you already know much about them since you could write that on your "beloved God's earth," all was beautiful, only all was just "differently beautiful." Take that conception very broadly and don't let yourself be frightened or confused. (*Letters*, vol. 2: 325)

The "sometime heart" of the letter has changed into what Rilke called his "Herzwerk," which, as Erich Heller tells us in his beautiful essay, "Rilke and Nietzsche," became the work of "God is dead." Nietzsche's *ewige Wiederkehr* (eternal recurrence) corresponds to Rilke's *Ein Mal und nichtmehr* (Once and no more) in the "Ninth Elegy" (Heller 159, 161):

Ein Mal

jedes, nur *ein* Mal. Ein Mal und nichtmehr. Und wir auch
ein Mal. Nie wieder. Aber dieses
ein Mal gewesen zu sein, wenn auch nur *ein* Mal:
irdisch gewesen zu sein, scheint nicht widerrufbar.

Once for each thing. Just once; no more. And we too,
just once. And never again. But to have been
this once, completely, even if only once:
to have been at one with the earth, seems beyond undoing.

(*Selected Poetry* 198–99)

The "Seventh Elegy" had prepared this extraordinary acceptance and celebration:

Jede dumpfe Umkehr der Welt had solche Enterbte,
denen das Frühere nicht und noch nicht das Nächste gehört.

Each torpid turn of the world has such disinherited ones,
to whom neither the past belongs, nor yet what has nearly arrived.

(*Selected Poetry* 188–89)

Thus, the cultural condition that is changing is being answered everywhere in our writing. It is not merely a subjectivity. Cultural deprivation, the vast forgetting, is a furtherance of the problem for readers and teachers. The tendency is to throw the weight of our effort on content—to bring back what's missing or disappearing. This sets the full relation of content and form aside, a relationship that finally must come down to the arrangement of words and our creative relation to those words. Here, I take careful note of one a/theologian's insight: "God, self, history, and book are . . . bound in an intricate relationship in which each mirrors the other. No single concept can be changed without altering all the others" (Taylor 7). Each of these four terms represents a category of discourse and each involves a poetics, even if in one instance it may be the history of poetics. This in turn draws us into what I have called a "discourse of cosmos," the complex poetics of the other, large and small. It is only a truism to say that the humiliation of Christianity that began in the Renaissance continues with increasing acerbity and retrenchment in our own time. The poets have worked radically with this shifting relation of God, self, history, and book, again and again.

I think a focal point in our measurement of this is to be found in Mallarmé:

> Quand les souffles de ses ancêtres veulent souffler la bougie . . . ("Igitur," 1869)
>
> When the breath of his ancestors wants to blow out the candle (thanks to which, perhaps, the characters continue to exist in the *grimoire*)—he says "Not yet!"[13] (*Selected Poetry and Prose* 91)

I note the careful image of cultural change in the ancestor's desire to blow the candle out, which leads directly to the problematic of the "reality" in the *book of spells* that keeps our human character intact.

Igitur, a very young child, reads his assignment to his ancestors. The problematic becomes the assignment. Earlier than this and in preparation for it, we come upon a letter to Henri Cazalis, May 14, 1867:

> And yet how infinitely more impossible it was a few months ago when I struggled with that creature of ancient and evil plumage—God—whom I fortunately defeated and threw to earth. But I had waged that battle on His boney wing, and in a final burst of agony greater than I should have expected from Him, He bore me off again among the Shadows; then victoriously, ecstatically, infinitely, I floated downward until finally one day I looked again in my Venetian mirror and saw the person I had been several months before—the person I had forgotten. I should add . . . that the price of my victory is so high that I still need to see myself in this mirror in order to think; and that if it were not in front of me here on the table as I write you, I would become Nothingness again. Which means that I am impersonal now: not the Stéphane you once knew, but one of the ways the Spiritual Universe has found to see Itself, unfold Itself through what used to be me. (*Selected Poetry and Prose* 87)

Mallarmé's Nothingness in this letter offers the sharpest sense of a materiality without a discourse of cosmos—what Blake had called a negation. God, self, and book (our traditional relation to words) all begin to shift in an historical condition of terror. Mallarmé's poetic courage is admirable, as it manifests itself in disturbed syntax and in the duplicity and multiplicity of meaning in words— the famous suggestiveness of his poetics. To my reading, Mallarmé is a guide to what Olson called the "Western box," to get out of which Olson went outward and backward to find a wealth of other relations. Mallarmé's approach, as I understand him, was to test the *logos* (the word) itself.

And what fascinates me is that Mallarmé's art is a kind of distillate of so many intellectual challenges to art. For all the arguments on one side or the other, which have gone on since his death in 1898, there can be no doubt that Mallarmé had a considerable knowledge of Hegel. Janine Langan's *Hegel and Mallarmé* (1986) seems to me to settle the issue of what he knew, and, indeed, she offers an interesting, if laboured, Hegelian reading of *Un Coup de Dés*. But a very great deal depends upon the way one reads the relation of the poet to the philosopher. Langan favours Hegel's "spiritual reality" in order to demonstrate a celebratory and redemptive reading of Mallarmé, thus to counter the critics who argue that he knew little philosophy and that his work ended in defeat, sense drowned in Chance. Hers is an admirable effort, but I do not believe that Mallarmé's concrete experience of words can be equated with Hegel's abstract use of them. Certainly, one does follow the Hegelian possibility in one of the most famous passages from "Crisis in Poetry":

> I say: a flower! and outside the oblivion to which my voice relegates any shape, insofar as it is something other than the calyx, there arises musically, as the very idea and delicate, the one absent from every bouquet. (*Selected Poetry and Prose* 76)

The *Idea* is the resolving possibility throughout the essay, even as Mallarmé distinguishes between the imperfection of languages and the "verse [that] makes up for what languages lack" (75). "The very idea and delicate." Delicate, indeed, as one goes back again and again to the activity of the words in his poems—their arrangement and expansiveness. On the other side of an Hegelian reading of the work as a whole, we have Jean Hyppolite and Derrida against the criticism that has been "massively idealist," for whom reading Mallarmé can be neither Platonist nor Hegelian: "'within this materialism of the idea [Mallarmé] imagines the diverse possibilities for reading the text'" (Hyppolite, cited in Derrida, *Dissemination* 207n).

Here, we must stop briefly to understand the crisis. One way to read the essay is to recognize that Hegel's "spiritual reality" represents a crisis in poetry—which, then, has consequences in the Marxist attitude toward the literary text as ideology or propaganda—language as a system of ideas with which to push the "real" around. As we enter Hegel's "phases of spirit," art, religion and philosophy, we will include art by overcoming it, just as we had done with the Word:

> We are beyond the stage of reverence for works of art as divine and objects deserving our worship. . . . Art is no longer able to discover that satisfaction of spiritual wants, which previous epochs and nations have sought for in it and exclusively found in it. . . . (Hegel, quoted in Hazard Adams, *Philosophy of the Literary Symbolic* 96)

As Hazard Adams notices, the fundamental issue here is not entirely a matter of belief transformed into "pure self-thinking thought, absolute spirit" (96). Our relation to language is primary:

Hegel believes that language produces "signs," which are arbitrary in their relation to matter and phenomena and thus in his view purely intellectual and universal. . . . Thus language cannot embody particulars and always moves to the universal and ultimately to the pure idea. (Adams 96)

He cites Croce to the effect that "'Hegel always abstracts every language act from its context, which is always particular'" (96). On the basis of this view of language, Hegel could predicate the end of art. From the poetic point of view, this is a negation of the activity of language in the particular. We should, perhaps, remember Blake:

> They take the Two Contraries which are calld Qualities,
> with which
> Every Substance is clothèd, they name them Good & Evil.
> From them they make an Abstract, which is a Negation
> Not only of the Substance from which it is derived,
> A murderer of its own Body: but also a murderer
> Of every Divine Member: it is the Reasoning Power
> An Abstract objecting power, that Negatives every thing
> This is the Spectre of Man: the Holy Reasoning Power
> And in its Holiness is closed the Abomination of Desolation.
>
> (*Jerusalem* 1, Plate 10)

Blake's notion of a dictated language is not a superstition; it posits an activity of language among things, including the genius of language in metaphor and symbol, which are things in activity of relation. The point may be made that reason outside relation is Blake's "Negation" and "Abomination," the latter which brings on desolation, comes, of course, from what we know as the pseudepigraphical Daniel (ix.27, xi.31, xiii.12) by way of Jesus' direct reference to Daniel in Matthew (24.15) and Mark (13.14). Blake knew that the abomination was an idol, whether or not he knew the apocryphal Maccabees (1.54), wherein it is made clear that it is a Greek idol placed in the temple by Antiochus IV Epiphanes in 168 B.C.[14] For Blake, the abomination was also informed by the idol of Reason at the center of the French Revolution.

But to return to the problematic of Mallarmé's poetics: his *Nothingness*, out of which he will recover words without an assured referent, brings us into silence. Hazard Adams has most usefully discussed the magnificence of his problematic— magnificent as experience, rather than theory, for all that Mallarmé did not solve the problem of an absent reality or world:

Mallarmé's linguistic creativity is cut off from the world. His choice is that of a temperament and an experience different from Blake's and under greater cultural stress. While Blake will invade the world he sees and compel it to become material for his poem, Mallarmé will withdraw from that world by invoking the magicality of annihilation into a poem which is self-mirroring object. "Silence" becomes a word to describe not only the annihilation but also the whole formal structure of the work as well as the nothingness displaced by the work. . . .

Mallarmé's self-reflexive language in its silent space is not, in most of his moods at least, a vehicle by which to copy a realm of ideas or archetypes either above or within. The poem, examined from this point of view, is purely creative of and out of "nothingness." But the problem of referentiality still dogs Mallarmé's critical language. If "silence" is meaningful as a term, there must be noise somewhere. There is simply no solution to this problem as long as his vocabulary is either rooted (albeit by negation) in the epistemological assumptions of positivism, which do not allow for a theory of mind as creative in its facing "outward" to the manifold of sensation, or is so negative as to force the disappearance of the world. . . .

. . . If Mallarmé could rid himself of . . . the "obsession" of positivist premises he would also rid himself of the solipcism that threatens him, and he would reconstitute the whole relation of mind and of poem to the world. (138–39)

In this difficulty, we need to remind ourselves that there is, now and again, the Mallarmé who knew what it means "to perceive oneself, simple, infinitely on the earth"—"se percevoir, simple, infiniment sur la terre" (Bucolique).[15]

Among the writers I am studying today, wrapped round by their richness, Mallarmé is not alone in his problematical poetics. Hermann Broch, with the "welling fountain of the middle"[16] and his imagination that Virgil had wished to burn the Aeneid, records a profound challenge to art itself. Throughout The Death of Virgil, this destructive desire stuns our traditional—not necessarily twentieth-century—sense of the value of the text. When Augustus wins the text from Virgil, it is only that the poet has given up the argument. What is beyond words takes over the direction of Virgil's mind. Hannah Arendt in her essay on Broch notices that in this prose-poem "the dubiousness of art in general became the thematic content of a work of art itself"—that, for Broch, "literature, knowledge, and action" come into conflict (Dark Times 112, 113). After the knowledge of the death camps became clear, he stopped writing:

He demanded of literature that it possess the same compelling validity as science, that science summon into being the "totality of the world" as does the work of art whose "task is the constant recreation of the world," and that both together, art impregnated with knowledge and knowledge that has acquired vision, should comprehend and include all the practical, everyday activities of man. (Dark Times 112)

The demand here, that we have all felt, becomes an intolerable tension. Where Broch began with a hope for a "new mythos" (Dark Times 120), understood as "'totality of the world'" (112), he turned finally to argue that "literature . . . lacks the cogency of *logos*" (119). Hannah Arendt, who has been able to study the essays, philosophical works and the *Mass Psychology*, as I have not, tells us that "during the last years of his life [he was] completely convinced of the primacy of knowledge over literature, of science over art" (*Dark Times* 115). He began, she writes, with a youthful question, which involves the problem that art seems to do nothing—"What then shall we do?"—and he continued throughout his life to try to find the answer in the face of what he knew about the twentieth century. An "unwearied search for an absolute," finally became an argument for "an 'earthly absolute,'" based upon positivistic, epistemological grounds (116). In detail, as Arendt demonstrates, this philosophical direction was complex and sophisticated, but it had come full circle to the search for the wholeness that haunts twentieth-century thought and poetry. Nevertheless, we are told, Broch left an unfinished novel which in Arendt's judgment returns to the poetic quality of *The Death of Virgil*, the conflict, I take it, unresolved. But the exceedingly long, flowing, poetic sentences with their careful repetitions try again, or so one hopes. Of his practice in language, Arendt writes, quoting him:

> For him, what is essential about language is that it syntactically indicates an abrogation of time "within the sentence" because it necessarily "places subject and object in a relationship of simultaneity." The "assignment" which is imposed on the speaker is "to make cognitive units audible and visible," and this is "the sole task of language." Whatever is frozen into the simultaneity of the sentence—to wit, thought, which "in a single moment can comprehend wholes of extraordinary extent"—is wrenched out of the passages of time. (*Dark Times* 133)

The transposition of time into a relation with space, as alive and alert as earth and sky, has been a long effort in modern poetry.

The "reconstitution of the whole relation of mind and of poem to the world"[17] is foundational to modern and contemporary poetics—of a certain order, one needs always to say. Positivisms of right, left and centre, grasping for reality, have dissipated respect for *poiesis*. A passage from Herbert Schneidau's *Sacred Discontent*, the section called "The Epistle to the Highbrows," will bring me back to Rilke's "affirmation of life-AND-death," with which I began:

> Positivism is discourse containing an implicit assumption that we have an easily accessible standard of "external reality" against which to measure any of our utterances. Usually it tends to assume, also, that only the thinking of the most recent epoch (variously defined) has been usefully guided by the application of this standard, and that all previous discourse is tainted with superstition. From technology it borrows the assurance that the latest "state of the art" is the best, for-

getting the tendency of all eras to take their own ways of thinking for granted. We might do well to ask if the bulk of modern discourse which assumes its own enlightenment has not compounded hubris with complacency. Will not much of our thought seem quaint and fatuous in the next century? We have no doubt corrected certain errors. But anyone who has ever dealt with printed texts knows that to correct one error is to invite others.

Twentieth-century positivism is not more benighted than others, but its special errors are indicative. Typically it congratulates itself on being liberated from theologization, while its very notions of "reality" and "truth" are, fairly obviously, covert theologizations. Positivism is associated with the discrediting of metaphysics in our time, but often it simply borrows a naïve version of what it denounces. In the medieval view, if you weren't worshiping the true God you were surely worshiping some false one: to be human, they thought, was to worship, to elevate some principle into the realm of the sacred. Those who worship success, or money, are hardly even worth pointing to, especially since the once-almighty dollar has declined; but consider how many votaries "the natural" has today. It would not be difficult to delineate more devious and complex fetishes in modern discourse. Relevant here would be that sacralization of methodology in the sciences and pseudosciences. Many practitioners of specialties seem to assume that asking the proper questions, in the proper order, as in a quest ritual or Ali Baba story, will magically open doors to stunning new knowledge. . . . To question methodology we need not subscribe to Romantic myths of "inspiration"; rigor remains a value, but to face the possibilities of the future we need more heuristic means. For one thing, we need to be able to skew our visions of "reality." (248–49)*

This "reality" is and will remain labyrinthine among discourses.

Which returns us to the "Tutelar of Place" whom George Whalley cited in his defense of the *nisus formativus*, "the formative impulse" (*Studies* 230), of social men and women:

> When they sit in Consilium
> to liquidate the holy diversities
>> mother of particular perfections
>> queen of otherness
>> mistress of asymmetry
> patroness of things counter, parti, pied, several
> protectress of things known and handled
> help of things familiar and small
>> wardress of the secret crevices
>> of things wrapped and hidden . . .

* See also Eric Voegelin's history of positivism in *From Enlightenment to Revolution*, ed. John H. Hallowell (Durham, N.C.: Duke University Press, 1975).

empress of the labyrinth
                    receive our prayers. . . .
When the technicians manipulate the dead limbs of our culture as
though it yet had life, have mercy on us.
                    (David Jones, quoted in Whalley, *Studies* 248)[*]

[*] The complete poem is available in *Introducing David Jones,* ed. John Matthias (London: Faber and
Faber, 1980).

The Recovery
of the Public World[1]

The idiot Reasoner laughs at the Man of Imagination
And from laughter proceeds to murder by
undervaluing calumny

William Blake, Milton

And only the "idiot Reasoner" so forgets that reason
is far more complex and natural than a logic or a factuality of this and that. The
range of this murder of human nature I shall discuss as I go along. My work-
ing title is taken from Hannah Arendt, whose life-long meditation on the vital
relationship between public and private worlds of men and women—a funda-
mental happiness, if truly alive—informs my own. Her work begins with a ma-
jor effort to understand the totalitarianism that dogs the political, social, and
artistic life of the twentieth century and of our modernity. In the 1950 preface
to The Origins of Totalitarianism—a date close to the one usually assigned to the be-
ginning of the postmodern condition—she reminds us:

> Two world wars in one generation, separated by an uninterrupted chain of lo-
> cal wars and revolutions, followed by no peace treaty for the vanquished and no
> respite for the victor, have ended in the anticipation of a third World War between
> the two remaining world powers. This moment of anticipation is like the calm that
> settles after all hopes have died. We no longer hope for an eventual restoration of the
> old world order with all its traditions, or for the reintegration of the masses of five
> continents who have been thrown into a chaos produced by the violence of wars
> and revolutions and the growing decay of all that has still been spared . . . home-
> lessness on an unprecedented scale, rootlessness to an unprecedented depth. (vii)

She argues that we deal with an unpredictable future, with "forces that look
like sheer insanity," and with "those for whom powerlessness has become the
major experience of their lives" (vii).

It has been noted by some critics of her work that the whole of it is caught—
implying an important limitation—in her personal experience of European Naz-
ism, as if our North American cultural condition with all its differences, whether
we think of Canada or the United States, were not embedded in the common
European and Christian fate. The reduction of Arendt's world-experience to
the merely personal is, of course, silly, and it results from a darkling percep-
tion of the place of individual experience within cultural conditions. Or, per-
haps, it is simply North American where one's homestead has not been di-
rectly touched by war and revolution. Yet wars and revolutions tattoo our
modernity. Cultural condition is not a picket fence or a yuppy Safeway. Cul-
tural condition always approaches what we mean by the word world or the
process of composing one. (Later, I will take up my view that artistic discourse
of the last two hundred years has been at work composing not a privacy but
a world. Obviously, I'm avoiding the awkward clichés of the term worldview.)
The world is never separately—by simplicity's trick—social, political, artistic,
or sacred, but, rather, it is made up of an entanglement of discourses having
to do with men, women, earth, and heaven. Religions have long won hearts—
from the beginning, one might say, when cities were first built for the gods—
because they speak of earth and heaven and of many different immortalities.
The largeness to which we respond in the world should not be underestimated,
nor should we forget the ricketiness of the circles that the cultural condition
draws around largeness. Death is the boundary of all our thought, and such a
bounded condition is worth the thought given it everywhere, inside and out-
side religions. But religion must not be allowed to cover over, invade, and so
delimit the social, political, and artistic discourses of our condition. Relation
to the Other is multi-dimensional and multi-logical. History, which is an ex-
traordinary Other in relation to the individual and to present social reality, is
nevertheless our own activity—not God's or Providence's—for which we have
responsibility according to our talents. The realisms of those separate dis-
courses, each in turn, claims the whole reality, and thus the world is maimed.
Thinking and emotion are irreclaimably individual whereby a man or a
woman repeatedly falls out of any group into a solitude that may be won-
drous, banal or defeated, according, I believe, to one's sense of the world. "Civ-
ilization is an individual task" to which nation, state, or social body does not
answer. I think from premises which derive in part from reading Hannah Arendt
over the years and which I must simplify here.

For one, I find it useful to discriminate among discourses—of the social, of
the political, of the artistic, and of the sacred—in order to understand the claim
that any one of those arrangements of things and purposes may have on reality—
since reality, whatever we mean by the word, is also multi-dimensional and
multi-logical. The social is not my dinner table: that is a personal matter of

friendship and conversation, and as infrequently as possible professional or official. The social has to do with the problems of large numbers of people: food, shelter, clothing, sanitation—in a word, necessity. To solve necessity, we draw together in reasoning, logic, and syntax—a discourse concerning these needs. This, it seems to me, is reality enough for social discourse to claim. Ideologies of social reality are built on this basis, and then in a little-understood and decadent Platonic fashion, whichever ideology is said to comprise reality. Only for the mass subjected to such ideology, out of which, as I've said, every man and woman drops repeatedly, even hourly, certainly daily. I am simplifying, indeed, but I have so stated this matter of social reality in order to insist that socio-economic reality, profound as it is, is not all of reality. At the risk of appearing impertinent, I mean to extend this limitation of the reality claims to the whole range of humanistic studies—sociologism, anthropologism, and psychologism—which tend to become closures of our thought of reality: for example, the utilitarian claim, along with its historical development in socialism, that reality, physical and cultural, is entirely determined by the social; or, for example, going the other way around, the apparent psychological defence of the individual, which defines the real by way of a self that becomes ahistorical, like the traditional soul, but otherless—and "therapeutically triumphant." This version of humanism collapses into itself, wordless, and leaves the large numbers of people who define it moiling.

The disaster and danger of such total claims to reality, in which the complex discourses of a world and their relation to one another disappear in the hegemony of one of them, spread far and wide in modernity. I choose as example revolution because that process of change colors and stains all of our modernity since the American and French Revolutions: the latter, to the dismay of the tradition, resulted in the modern discovery of poverty, when the masses poured into the streets of Paris, and of the Enlightenment. Before the French Revolution, society did not include the masses: as historians have evidenced, though recent new techniques of detail begin to give us a sight of the "structure of everyday life" back then; as Marx argued when he privileged not the masses but the proletariat of the cities; as Hannah Arendt interpreted this vast modern discovery of the social (Arendt, Human Condition 7 1).[2] Since I have assigned the social to a pre-eminent concern with necessity, let me stop briefly over the word. It means that-which-does-not-go-away. I have been flummoxed—which is worse than perplexed—when talking to a wide range of people, that they were stupefied by the word, as if it were a technical or philosophical term of rare provenance. I can only assume that in the comfort of our own society, we have forgotten that our strength of heart and mind—an aspect of freedom—is based upon ever-varying solutions to the problems of food, shelter, clothing, and sanitation. When the masses, from whom most of us derive, burst into history, their experience was circumscribed by those very problems. A direct sense of NECESSITY, named by the Greeks *Ananke* to which even the gods of the physical world, born as they were from it, had to yield, is to understand the fate of the body and its maw, if that is all there is—Russian and German labor camps knew the use of starvation for the control of human nature, at the edge of which even the sexual drive disappears. It seems beside the point to say that emotional needs here at home, however much they imprison us, require a different ordering of the real and a different discourse because neither society nor its projection, the State—even when they are benevolent—can offer happiness.

Revolutions dream and act to solve the problems of necessity. That is their virtue and their spell. Again and again, they turn into tyrannies in the name of what goodness. When I think of Engels's "orthodox Marxism" with its "universal science of nature and history"—which, in the vulgate of practice, evinced neither science nor nature, only historicism and a misreading of human nature—I stumble, hurting all ten toes, over that bugaboo, the "universal" and its resultant "oppressive dogma." In *History and Class Consciousness* (1923), Georg Lukacs noted the oppression and the intended liberation it stultifies, along with his discovery of Marx's Hegelian dialectic. But the problem compounds itself in both Lukacs and Lenin, as Lee Congdon notices:

> The class consciousness of the proletariat was what it would be—Lukacs spoke of its "objective possibility"—if it were fully *conscious* of its, and hence humanity's, true interests and historic mission. Until consciousness arrived at that point, it could only be *imputed* to the proletariat, as Lenin had maintained in *What Is To Be Done?*
>
> This was an important point, for with the positing of an ideal consciousness known only to the initiated, Lukacs was preparing the ideological ground of tryanny. (552)

Such tryanny—we have come to know it well in this century—results from an improper use of the discourse of social reality, unmeasured by other discourses of the real, in which wholeness is claimed or, rather, imposed, and social reality is consequently dehumanized. I am not now concerned to offer the other side by way of a consideration of what is Marx's powerful and fundamental gift—certainly not the "Marxist-Leninist" reality, but the recognition of our own responsibility for human actions and for human processes in the world. (I want to have no part in vulgar and reactionary anti-Marxism.) Michel Foucault has, it seems to me, given us a start on a vocabulary to correct the hegemony of the social: that twentieth-century men and women enter upon and articulate themselves into three great othernesses, Life, Labour, and Language.* The otherness of each of them is a subject in itself and very difficult to think in our culture of ownership. Such thinking probably requires a *poiesis* alongside the discourse that belongs strictly to the social.

Life, Labour, and Language, understood as othernesses always older than any of us, are not God or His attributes, since in the Western tradition, He—the anthropomorphic marvel becomes increasingly puzzling—is outside the world. The tradition is severely challenged by such a sense of otherness, but the Western atheism that answers to this seems to me beside the point. "Western atheism is," as Octavio Paz has argued, "only a negative and exasperated form of our monotheism" (*Duchamp* 69). We need be neither religious nor anti-religious in the discourse having to do with food, shelter, clothing, and sanitation, though we may be thankful. The de-mythologizers have a crust like burned toast. Twentieth-century poetic versions of this have wisely moved Hell from the centre of the earth, directly beneath Jerusalem, and out of Eternity, to find it on the surface of the earth where we have created it.

Many have noticed something like a theodicy at work within the claims of a total reality—God and Justice supplied with other names—among them, Steven B. Smith in his recent discussion of G. A. Cohen's *Karl Marx's Theory of History: A Defence* (1978) and Jon Elster's *Making Sense of Marx* (1985). We have Cohen's "technological determinism" which becomes a "transcendental cause." We have Elster's better society which would, should, could, etc., in the midst of a devastating reading of Marx, the mind of modern revolutionary concern, to wit:

> [Marx's] philosophy, based on an amalgam of Leibnizian and Hegelian theodicy, is largely unempirical and speculative, especially the belief that history has a goal independent of intentional agents. . . . He borrowed from Hegel the belief that history represents the unfolding and development of Humanity. Humanity in the idiom of German idealism is a technical term referring not merely to the aggregate of human beings existing at any one time but to a normative conception of a fully developed, somewhat protean, species capable of realizing simultaneously all human capacities and attributes. History is the story of the emergence of this collective actor whose spiritual principle Hegel once defined as "the sum total of all perspectives."
>
> The concept of a gradually emerging Humanity carries with it the corollary that history is a "slaughter bench" and that until its end is reached, there are no absolute constraints on the sacrifices the present generation can be expected to bear for the sake of the future. (Quoted in Smith, "Analytical Marxism" 572)

* See Michel Foucault, *The Order of Things* (New York: Pantheon, 1970), better titled in French, *Les Mots et les choses*.

In this line-up along the linearity of historical reality, how many gods (wholenesses) there are! With and without attributes. I need only capitalize them to notice the abstracted, indeed distracted, anthropomorphism. Technology. History. Humanity. Collective Actor. Sum Total. All Perspectives. Future. The pack of them involves a superstition of wholeness. None of them implies a relation to a world—in fact, any world disappears in a truncated wholeness that is only one-half of whatever. Technology is especially interesting because it is, with its mesmerizing intelligence, the human will projected without measure of the care of relation with the world. These divinities are shadows of what the twentieth-century mind means when it calls itself humanist, bounded as that mind-set is, by our great, human disciplines—anthropology, psychology, and sociology. Within a knowledge of the finest uses of these methods—method has all the characteristics of a belief system[3]—I would hold onto Proteus, the shape-changer. Science, as distinguished from technology, is, of course, another matter in that it approaches a world—mathematically, which it expresses popularly in images and in a *dynameis* of opposites, the very ground of our experience— though, until recently, it left us out (Schrödinger).[4]

Humanism, it seems necessary to point out, is an aspect of our Roman inheritance, wherein it had to do with the integrity of the person. As Hannah Arendt suggests, it identifies "one who knows how to choose his company among men, among things, among thoughts, in the present as well as in the past," and "it was the study of art and literature rather than of philosophy which was supposed to result in 'humanity'" (*Between Past and Future* 226, 241, n. 17). "The discovery of antiquity in the Renaissance," she notes, "was a first attempt to break the fetters of tradition, and by going to the sources themselves to establish a past over which tradition would have no hold" (*Between Past and Future* 25–26). This breaking of the fetters was also the reopening of the Romanized, Christian, other-worldly tradition that had defined, codified, and displaced many of the interesting questions surrounding the qualities of being human. Ancient humanism and Renaissance humanism were not merely a matter of "polite studies." The Renaissance version—in spite of Michelangelo's anti-perspectival rebellion against it, which was stunningly inherited by Blake—set the pattern of human perspective in the arts for something like four hundred years. Modern humanism becomes confused and confusing within itself: "polite" and useless studies, especially literature and languages; anthropology, psychology, sociology—the "realisms"; and often modern humanism implies a remedy, unstated and unthought, for the displaced centre, which was successively Adam, the earth, the sun. Ah, Ptolemy, Copernicus, Galileo. As Melville's sentimental narrator and misconceiver in *Bartleby* says, "Ah, humanity!"[5] One hears abroad, especially among artists, the refutation, "I am not a humanist." This is not a misanthropy, but rather a call to order a world that is not a closure into human finitude or into a skeddaddled, absent humanity—*humanitas abscondita*.

I find it useful, now and again, to stop over the word *humanity* itself, close to the ground and to the earth, especially in the face of twentieth-century experience, which brings its meaning into question, but not for the first time. We are, if we attend to the long labour of our culture, prepared for the question, Marx, Kierkegaard, and Nietzsche, read as thinkers rather than as ideologues, all question "what the specifically human quality of man is"—thus, Hannah Arendt draws our attention to such a reading of them (*Between Past and Future* 39). We take the word from Latin *humanitas*, for which there is no equivalent in Greek. When the Latins used the word to translate, uneasily, the Greek *philanthropia*, they were concerned with the care of the gods and rulers, not with this curious speculation about human nature (*Between Past and Future* 224–26). (With Greek *philia* and *philos*, love and the beloved, we enter a different melody, having to do with the "fragility" of relations, social and individual, whereby, in philosophy, we find Plato's anguished desire for permanence and Aristotle's stringent "practical reason," which describe conflicting aspects of the good in human nature and in the public world.)* The Roman sense of *humanitas*, as the quality and feeling of being human, had, as I've noted, to do with the "integrity of the person," with his and her "worth" and "rank," and with "friendship," which were not to be "sacrificed . . . to the primacy of an absolute truth." Hannah Arendt cites Cicero, for whom the "mind is like a field" which must be cultivated:

> This Roman *humanitas* applied to men who were free in every respect, for whom the question of freedom, of not being coerced, was the decisive one—even in philosophy, even in science, even in the arts. Cicero says: In what concerns my association with men and things, I refuse to be coerced even by truth, even by beauty.
>
> This humanism is the result of the *cultura animi*, of an attitude that knows how to take care and perserve and admire the things of the world. (*Between Past and Future* 224)

More directly, our modern sense of humanity develops out of the Renaissance, and it may be seen in essential texts by Ficino and Pico della Mirandola; I say more directly, though our relation to the Renaissance has swerved and in many circles is nearly deceased or become a mere specialization. To take only the one example, Pico's *Oration on the Dignity of Man* (1486), with its denunciation of astrology because Pico brooked no determinism over the freedom that was allowed

---

* See Martha C. Nussbaum's recent and brilliant discussion of this in *The Fragility of Goodness* (Cambridge: Cambridge University Press, 1986).

human nature, is memorable. Pope Innocent VIII stopped the public disputation for which this oration was to be the introduction, and the search for heresy among Pico's nine hundred theses began. One, so to speak, stands before this argued vision of freedom in wonder and, then, in alarm, for its freedom is always beyond necessity, poverty, and terror—alarm because of its ideality and lack of relations in the world—and titillation that such freedom would challenge the hierarchies of church and state. The closing argument of the *Oration* leads from this freedom, characteristic of a transcendent human dignity, to a desired unity of truth, which, for Pico, meant the reconciliation of the philosophies of Plato and Aristotle—the project which, some have noted, Hegel developed and left in modern hands.

Pico's *Oration*, wonderful and erudite, is, to my mind, a paradigm of our problem in thinking of human nature. As a voice of the Renaissance, it gathers up the proud recovery of human size, shape, and activity out of antiquity and molds it with that sense of the whole-business that Plato so dangerously assigned to philosophers alone. Curiously, the complete text was not available in English translation until the 1940s, and I think it is important, in this context, to note the place of its publication: the important, surrealist magazine *View*, out of New York in war-time, 1944.* Doubtless, surrealist interest gave Pico a very special reading which was based upon not the high-flying idealism of his text, but upon the indeterminateness of human nature implied therein. The not-determined aspect of human nature is the important point against the behaviourism of modern social thought. It was this not-determined characteristic of human nature that also brought the work of Giambattista Vico into such prominence in modern thought. Surrealism, I must stop to say, continues to be a major twentieth-century effort to renovate human consciousness (which accounts for their early, abortive attempts to join with Marxism, when it was still possible to believe that the latter had to do with a revolution in consciousness, whereas capitalism with its utilitarian base cares little for consciousness as cultural form). Surrealism's emphasis upon irrationality—more properly "the marvelous"—is meant to return reason from the absence of "absolute truth" to an activity of thinking a world.

I look back over this notion of *humanitas* in order to find something—what was meant by the word. The forgetfulness of our cultural condition destroys our ability to think. Since the meaning of the term has become questionable in one discourse after another—indeed, murdered by way of some of them— I think our sense of our humanity is central to whatever we may believe. We began, I'm told, in conversation with God; we've come to converse, if we con-

---

* Noted by Paul Oskar Kristeller, in *The Renaissance Philosophy of Man*, ed. Ernst Cassirer (216, note 4).

verse at all, only with ourselves. God, someone said, should, perhaps, be considered the name of human limit—outside the world and without a world. The trouble is that both inside and outside the universities, each discourse approaches the "unity" (truth) of its method and, then, claims the real in modern terms as the intellectual scientist Michael Polanyi has pointed out, by deductivism, reductivism, positivism, and determinism. These become the cultural modus operandi. Until recently, the arts were defended by arguing that they composed a discourse apart, autonomous, and high. Religious studies, so fundamental to the history of human consciousness, scattered to a few enclaves. Languages, those friends of the mind's heart, became Language, "an object of knowledge," not discourses of a world (Godzich xx). With such "knowledge" one can do without the greater part of the contents of all of these examples, and, in so doing, history, the last bastion of knowing anything about ourselves, is gutted. The scientism of it is the shadowy reason of that absolute truth which haunts our tradition, now increasingly become a materialism: materiality or spirituality, neither of which separately holds any meaning without the other, or so the tradition tells us. Now and again the intellectual scientists remind us of their stake in the world and of the "humanness of science," Michael Polanyi for one: "We undertake the task of attaining the universe in spite of our admitted infirmity, which should render the task hopeless, because we hope to be visited by powers for which we cannot account in terms of our specifiable capabilities" (quoted in William Scott 624, 625). That we may turn again to an understanding of ourselves, Czeslaw Milosz is surely right that an "anti-Hegelian vaccine" be useful (Milosz 153). The wholeness or completeness derived from such thought, whether it is called material or spiritual, is careless of relations in the world and tends to become a dreadful, fun-house, mirrored image of humanity.

"The opalescent notion [of] humanitas," then, will lead us to the problematics of our political discourse (Kantorowicz, King's Two Bodies 451). I turn to a text older than Pico's, which doubtless informs his, Dante's De Monarchia (1309?). I draw attention to it here because it is a first investment in what I take to be our own predicament, the conversation, or lack of it, between the discourses of the political and of the sacred. It is little read, I suppose, because Dante's vocabulary is that of his time, imperial in the conflicting claims and powers of Pope and Emperor, whereas ours is a purée of mixed-masters, the two Super Powers. But, first, I need to set the perspective. We talk of secular humanism, derived from John Dewey most directly, often without acknowledgement—our culture dislikes memory—and we fail to notice a curious aspect of the belief system it creates, the tendency to roam the precincts of a sacred humanity. I need to remember, and I am aided by another intellectual scientist, Alfred North Whitehead:

The notion of God as the "unmoved mover" is derived from Aristotle, at least so far as Western thought is concerned. The notion of God as "eminently real" is a favourite doctrine of Christian theology. The combination of the two into the doctrine of an aboriginal, eminently real, transcendent creator, at whose fiat the world came into being, and whose imposed will it obeys, is the fallacy which has infused tragedy into the histories of Christianity and Mahometanism.

When the Western world accepted Christianity, Caesar conquered; and the received text of Western theology was edited by his lawyers. (PR V.II.I. 519)

Whitehead then outlines "three strains of thought" which "fashion God" in theistic philosophy: "God in the image of an imperial ruler"; "God in the image of a personification of moral energy"; "God in the image of an ultimate philosophical principle" (PR V.II.I. 519–20). Humanisms. His notice that "Hume's *Dialogues* criticize unanswerably these modes of explaining the system of the world" reminds us of an important argument that our public culture has forgotten (PR V.II.I. 520). Each of these fashionings remains with us and each involves an unnoted humanism of discourse in which human limit is transmogrified—transformed in an absurd way—though transmigration was intended. Whitehead also draws up, as from a well, that aspect of the tradition which "dwells upon the tender elements in the world" (PR V.II.I. 520). But the attendant transmogrifications stupefy. One current example: "I felt an overwhelming holy presence all around me. When I opened my eyes, there He stood . . . some 900 feet tall, looking at me. . . . He stood a full 300 feet taller than the 600 foot tall City of Faith [Oral Roberts in Tulsa, Oklahoma]" (quoted in Martin Gardner, "Giving" 18). I watch the cant steaming in the pots of the helpless—is it death, illness, lack of wealth, or cultural forgetting that composes such grammars of the real—such worldlessness and individual futility? Opalescent humanity.

Dante, then, in order to think again. The great poet opens his discussion in *Monarchy* with his sense of "debt to posterity" (127) that is also a use of the past. The standard English translation (Wicksteed, 1904) catches the writer toiling, "enriched by the toil of those who have gone before" (127). Dante was a toiler in discourses in the full range of thought, not in what the modern mind takes to be the merely personal voice of poetry. His *Monarchy* is a political companion to the vision of the *Comedy*, which posterity dubbed "divine," as if the political dimension of the Italian poem needed a prose extention in international Latin. He moves quickly to consider the nature of the "public good":

For he who, himself imbued with public teachings, yet cares not to contribute aught to the public good, may be well assured that he has fallen far from duty; for he is not "a tree by the streams of waters, bearing his fruit in due season," but rather a devouring whirlpool, ever sucking in, and never pouring back what it has swallowed. (127)

(Our contemporary problem in terms of the public good is perhaps more exactly described as a drying-up, from which there is little to swallow except the dangerous swamp of public manipulation.) For my purposes, the importance of Dante's document on the public good, imbedded, as it is, in the turmoil of the 1300s, is underscored by the medievalist Ernst Kantorowicz:

> It remained to the poet to establish an image of kingship which was merely human and of which MAN, pure and simple, was the center and standard—MAN, to be sure, in all his relations to God and the universe, to law, society, and city, to nature, knowledge, and faith. *Homo instrumentum humanitatis* . . . provided that the opalescent notion *humanitas* be perceived in all its numerous hues. (451)

Here, the exemplary significance for us—if we had time or memory to reread Dante's *Monarchy* along with his *Comedy* and if we made more artful our sense that democracy, so recent a political form, has entirely solved the problems of power and authority—is to be found in those relations and in the discourses that properly and publicly arrange them to create a human community, not a transmogrified humanity. Kantorowicz also draws attention to Dante's concept "of a purely human *Dignitas* which without Dante would be lacking, and would have been lacking most certainly in that age" (453). Dante's is a primary document in our effort to imagine and measure a human community worthy of our words—and in which we hold only a "middle place."

Dante:

> Two ends have been set by Providence, that ineffable, before man to be contemplated by him: the blessedness, to wit, of this life, which consists in the exercise of man's proper power and is figured by the terrestrial paradise; and the blessedness of eternal life, which consists in the fruition of the divine aspect, to which his power may not ascend unless assisted by the divine light. And this blessedness is given to be understood by the celestial paradise. (Quoted in Kantorowicz, *King's Two Bodies* 457–58)[6]

"Those were," Kantorowicz observes, "two utterly different goals of the human race" (458). Opposition to Dante was powerful, and strong enough to place his *Comedy* on the *Index Librorum Prohibitorum* for a time. Dante's peccability was compounded; not only had he so valued the "merely human," he had imagined the celestial paradise guided by his uninvented Beatrice. That we have lost faith in the celestial paradise in spite of its popular, ever-anxious resurgence—the ups and downs of its exchange value and its cupidity of all sorts—does not

dismiss the gift of Dante's thought and its humanity measured by those rela-
tions to God, universe, law, society, city, nature, knowledge, and faith (of these,
God and faith are notably and currently under erasure, as the jargon goes). Those
relations define *humanitas* at any given time—relations, not relativism. I like to
remember that Dante's human community—*humanitas* exists only in these rela-
tions which become community—enfolded all the "mortal human beings" of
the world, not just Christians. Kantorowicz reminds us of Dante's care for "the
totality of that by which man became Man" (474). The unlearned, modern *hu-
manitas*, implying an innate, rather than a created, human goodness, has no re-
liable witness.

Our humanism is strangely out of line and unthought because we do not
know or honor in a public way that by which man and woman became Man
and Woman. The humanities—arts, languages, literatures, mathematics, history,
and philosophy—are not culture in modern society. Consider the metaphor the
word *culture* carries; it tells us a lot. The humanities are creative nodes and op-
erations of human nature inside a world, which I wish we cultivated in order
to have a conversation about the world. One that is not reductively simply our-
selves. The humanities hold the record of our relations with innumerable oth-
ernesses, small and large. To name the humanities culture in the face of what
modern society cultivates confuses matters. We have to ask what it is that our
social reality cultivates in order to have any sense of the meaning of the word.
The answer tells me that the humanities ought, perhaps, to change their name.
The humanism I'm writing about has become, in cultural terms, a snark and a
boojum,[7] a non-sense of ourselves. Humanism, separated from what we called
the humanities, becomes an organized system which spreads through all our
disciplines, like a crazy-quilt, but it creates no human community. In fact, I fear
such a supernumerary humanity in politics, ideology, and religion.

The contemporary humanism that troubles me, whether in the guise of God,
Man, or Woman, lacks a world. Its forms still reflect those fashionings as "ruler,"
as "moral energy," as "ultimate philosophical principle," each of which has a
history of its dangerous propensity. I think of David Hume's moving remarks
in *A Treatise on Human Nature* (1740): "Fain wou'd I run into the crowd for shel-
ter and warmth; but I cannot prevail with myself to mix with such deformity. . . .
I have declar'd my dis-approbation of their systems" (92). His point, as I un-
derstand it, is the self-deception of such systems. The humanism which con-
fronts us now, it should be understood, is a twentieth-century arrogation of the
term made current in the early Renaissance in order to name a renewed inter-
est in human nature after centuries of concern with divine nature. (My own
favourite examples of this are Dante and Donatello.) David Ehrenfeld takes up
the self-deception in *The Arrogance of Humanism* (1978):

. . . the idea of using a nature created for us, the idea of control, and the idea of human superiority became associated early in our history.

It only remained to diminish the role of God, and we arrived at full-fledged humanism. This was achieved in the Renaissance and afterwards, coincident with the great flowering of the doctrine of final causes in the religious sphere. The transition to humanism was an easy one; it could occur in steps. One only had to start with the belief that humans were created in God's image. God could then be retired on half-pension, still trotted out at the appropriate ceremonies wearing the old medals, until bit by bit He was demystified, emasculated, and abandoned. (8)

Ehrenfeld cautions that the "better parts of humanism are not in question here" (5). Those better parts have to do with Whitehead's "tender elements in the world" and with what I am calling relations (PR V.II.I. 520). The bitter part has to do with the wholeness that is merely a closure into the human centre, a boundary that becomes mirror and overwhelms. I quote Ehrenfeld at length because I have made him a companion of my concern and because he is clear and very useful:

The paradox of humanism, the religion of humanity, leading to machine worship has another and deeper explanation. We must worship the machine if we wish to maintain the fiction that the myth of control is true. For in all of us there is the lurking awareness that the arrogance and brag are unjustified; this is continuously being confirmed by ordinary experience. Humans are not gods, despite the occasional god-like quality that crops up to astonish us for a while. The evidence of our technology, alone, tells us this. Yet technology is our major godly output, our flow of miracles. . . .

Many avowed humanists profess to be strongly anti-machine and anti-technical. I do not think this is a pose. Having abstracted many of the finest qualities of humanism for their own philosophies, these humanists fail to see what humanism in toto has done to everybody else. . . . The idea of separating the good and evil consequences of humanism, with the result that the latter are rarely traced to their source, may have been facilitated by Christianity, which has never felt at ease with the Judaic view that good and evil are the normal portions of humanity and are inextricably mixed in every person, albeit not necessarily in the same ratio. In any case the confusion, the ambivalence, and the weakness of the perceptive humanists [are] understandable and tragic; they are unaware that the source of the immense damage which they so clearly recognize is the central dogma of their own philosophy. (102–3)

The "techniques of self-deception," Ehrenfeld gives us notice, comprise an immense field for discovery:

The overwhelming trend of the humanist-dominated present is towards more ruined soils, more deserts, more children with anomie, more shattered, violent societies, more weapons whose horror surpasses imagination, more techniques of autocratic suppression, and more mechanisms for isolating human beings from one another. (127)

The mirror on the wall does not tell us who is most beautiful, but it does tell of an ugliness for which there is no make-up. *Humanitas*, which can know itself only in the measures of community, has become a golden idolatry whose commerce controls form in thought and feeling.*

There are broadly two laws that we must attend: one of the human will and another of the world around us. The humanist clichés—such as "voice of doom" or "apocalyptical," often dated to the 1960s—which are used to dismiss this view, are careless of what is asked for: a knowledge of human measure and the good it can compose in measured relations. There is wide confusion about relations—relationability as fundamental condition—that dates from the 1920s when humanists tried to understand the concept of relativity. As the concept shifted from physics and its magnificent, objective model of the universe, which does not include us, to an imagination of the real, which does include us, the point was lost: that we are implicated in the "whole" (scare marks are again called for). Humanism with its Cartesian syntactical genius has divided this "whole" between the subjective and objective modes of being in the world (the former means thrown under, the latter thrown against, like being bumped into).† The subjective and the objective are better understood as active relations in the world. Relativism—the merely related to, rather than joined with, something or other—is a misunderstanding which imposes upon any man's or woman's stance in the world a dualism, now clearly demonic in the separation of the human and the other—all value and privilege given to the former. This is an irreligion built into Western religious and secular cultural tradition alike, a psychopathy enlarged from one to many, if not all.

Our political discourse does not, of course, stand apart from these concerns. I have already noted its uses in our accommodation of dominations and powers. It is also the arena of our running to and fro trying to imagine a public world. And it is there that we may make the effort to discover our human form, since we are not born with one, but with an animality that we share with all creatures,

* See Jean Clay, *Modern Art, 1890–1918* (New York: Vendome Press, 1978): his introduction offers a remarkable discussion of this problem.

† I am, of course, thinking with the following in mind: Erwin Schrödinger, *What Is Life & Mind and Matter* (Cambridge: Cambridge University Press, 1967); David Bohm, *Wholeness and the Implicate Order* (London: Routledge & Kegan Paul, 1980); and Bernard Lovell, *Emerging Cosmology* (New York: Columbia University Press, 1981). The last is one of a series of monographs, called *Convergence*, founded and edited by Ruth Nanda Anshen, which should be followed closely.

whatever their size. Like everyone else, I repeatedly fall back from this public possibility to lean on the intimacy and limited reality of family, lover, or friends, there to meet the conflict, indeed contradiction, between the private and the public. The public world is an enlargement of relations—a worldliness—not simply a matter of the behaviour that increasingly defines *humanitas*. Hannah Arendt:

> . . . the term "public" signifies the world itself, in so far as it is common to all of us and distinguished from our privately owned place in it. This world, however, is not identical with the earth or with nature, as the limited space for the movement of men and the general condition of organic life. It is related, rather, to the human artifact, the fabrication of human hands, as well as to affairs which go on among those who inhabit the man-made world together. To live together in the world means essentially that a world of things is between those who have it in common, as a table is located between those who sit around it; the world, like every in-between, relates and separates men at the same time.
>
> The public realm, as the common world, gathers us together and yet prevents our falling over each other, so to speak. What makes mass society so difficult to bear is not the number of people involved, or at least not primarily, but the fact that the world between them has lost its power to gather them together, to relate and to separate them. (*Human Condition* 48)

This definition of the "public" as a worldliness has also to be distinguished from the strictly social. "Society," Hannah Arendt observes, "when it first entered the public realm, assumed the disguise of an organization of property-owners who, instead of claiming access to the public realm because of their wealth, demanded protection from it for the accumulation of more wealth" and "private possessions—which are essentially much less permanent and much more vulnerable to the mortality of their owners than the common world, which always grows out of the past and is intended to last for future generations— began to undermine the durability of the world" (*Human Condition* 60).

The durability of the world. We can hardly understand it, even though it has only changed technologically. Where the durability of the world is our primary concern, we uncover, alongside the discourses of the social and the political, the related—or should-be related—discourses of the arts and of the sacred. But durability has become unattractive with built-in obsolescence, and our culture sets the latter discourses aside, unless they can become an exchange value. What was the durable in-between of the world is now an abstraction, or series of them, drawn from the characteristics of large numbers of people. Hannah Arendt, to my reading, clarifies this matter unequivocally:

> Large numbers of people, crowded together, develop an almost irresistible inclination toward despotism, be this the despotism of a person or of majority rule; and although statistics, that is, the mathematical treatment of reality, was

unknown prior to the modern age, the social phenomena which make such treatment possible . . . [are] great numbers, accounting for conformism, behaviorism, and automatism in human affairs. (*Human Condition* 39–40)

This leveling is fundamental to our modern culture; it is, indeed, what we cultivate: "Statistical uniformity is by no means a harmless scientific ideal; it is the no longer secret political ideal of a society which, entirely submerged in the routine of everyday living, is at peace with the scientific outlook inherent in its very existence" (40). This is not, of course, all of the science that we may know; rather, it is, as René Girard names it, "scientism,"[8] really another humanism, and its outlook involves us deeply, as, by it, we become objective to ourselves, a condition the poets—initially and most importantly, William Blake—recognize as largely dangerous (Blake's term is "Eternal Death," which, I know, strikes the ear of the current reality principle as "poetic" and unreal).

I look again to insist that Hannah Arendt be present to these considerations:

> To gauge the extent of society's victory in the modern age, its early substitution of behavior for action and its eventual substitution of bureaucracy, the rule of nobody, for personal rulership, it may be well to recall that its initial science of economics, which substitutes patterns of behavior only in this rather limited field of human activity, was finally followed by the all-comprehensive pretension of the social sciences which, as "behavioral sciences," aim to reduce man as a whole, in all his activities, to the level of a conditioned and behaving animal. If economics is the science of society in its early stages, when it could impose its rules of behavior only on sections of the population and on parts of their activities, the rise of the "behavioral sciences" indicates clearly the final stage of this development, when mass society has devoured all strata of the nation and "social behavior" has become the standard for all regions of life. (*Human Condition* 41–42)

That is, we become "massified."

The political consequences of this interest me, especially in terms of the obvious frustration and truncation of human capabilities. The dream of a public space founded on human excellence was brief and was lost somewhere around 430 B.C.—even then it was based upon slavery and the exclusion of women. Peter Fuss reflects: "Pericles' faith in the power of the Athenian *polis* to actualize and to sustain human greatness was, for understandable reasons, so short-lived that political thought and political decision from Plato to the present day might well be regarded as an escape from 'politics' altogether" (Fuss 157). A second highly political consequence is the solipsism of the "massified" experience:

> When solipsism is experienced, rather than speculated on, it is not the case that only one's self is real. Nothing is real, one's self included.
> However, the loss of reality does not occur only when men are radically iso-

lated from one another! It occurs just as readily when men become massified, when they behave as though they were all but numerically indistinguishable, when each merely multiplies and prolongs his neighbor's perspective. (Fuss 166)

This one-point perspective has little or nothing to do with the Renaissance discovery of the human centre.

Massified in "a wilderness of monies" (Arendt's phrase). The violent oneness of massified populations, whether monarchical, democratic-bureaucratic or authoritarian, has a long history in the West, Christian, Muslim, and modern, which tells me that it is inherent in our cultural possibilities—according, that is, to what we cultivate or form in our minds. The public world, compounded of thought and feeling, flows from the past into the present, leaving the human future to a human creation, since the world out there and the world in here are equally an on-going creation or violation according to our pursuits.

Finally, I come to the discourses of art and of the sacred. I have kept them together throughout these remarks because they are both, as active elements in the world, ejected by our cultural condition and by the humanism that directs it. I also have another reason which interests me even more: they both belong to our worldly project in language. They are discourses, like those of the social and political, in that they, too, run about arranging things—this time by perceptions in words, colors, musical tones, and carved objects. The discourses of art and of the sacred are not exactly the same, because the latter always claims that large Otherness, so contrary to ourselves that we have called it God and misunderstood the biology of language. Still, the texts of the sacred, acknowledged apart from the historical hierarchies of churches, mosques, and statehoods, are activities of artistic discourse. (I do not mean the Bible as literature; it would be more accurate to turn the sentence around.) I have in mind Hazard Adams's argument—I avoid for this occasion his term, "'the secular' symbolic," fearing those who do not know his argument might confuse it with secular humanism—that "creation need not be what Heidegger laments as 'mastery'":

> In this mode of thought language is fundamentally poetic, out of which culture is built. Man projects his gods vertically into the sky and his nature horizontally into an other; but both the gods and nature are his, and to abuse them is to abuse himself. If man abandons contrariety and declares the absolute domination of any single form, he condemns himself to a Hell he has made. By the same token, he corrupts truth by claiming to discover the one truth that he declares transcends them all. (Adams 393)

This contrariety is what I have understood as relationship to the otherness of persons, things, and the world. This process of relationship in contrariety and otherness is the fundamental activity of artistic discourse throughout its history. It is that activity which gives art its strange and wonderful permanence, unlike any other discourse.

Thus, we come upon the "cultural crisis," the cries of it everywhere. Our modern, critical disciplines—sociology, psychology, and anthropology—should, and sometimes do, lead us to confront this condition, provided they do not claim a reality beyond their competencies and so enter the positivism of modern thought. Arnold Hauser's *The Social History of Art* is a case in point; it is helpful because the author knows as much about art as he does about social reality, the one does not disappear into the other. He also reaffirms the importance of "aesthetic judgment"—that is, judgment by perception. And he is clear on that cheap-shot, elitism. When art was no longer a public art, "marked [by] the beginning of the dissolution of the great Greco-Christian Idea of divinity" in the Renaissance (Paz, *Duchamp* 75), it became a matter of ownership and privilege during the Bourgeois Revolution. It is this period that overshadows our sense of art, that it belongs to "society," but not to the masses of such recent appearance in our thought. We need, it seems to me, only to know this—to talk and think it out—in order to return artistic discourse to its cultural place. Arnold Hauser:

> There is today hardly any practicable way leading to a primitive and yet valuable art. Genuine, progressive, creative art can only mean a complicated art today. It will never be possible for everyone to enjoy and appreciate it in equal measure, but the share of the broader masses in it can be increased and deepened. (Vol. 2: 959)

Not a chance inside the mercantilism we actually cultivate. Hauser's concern with the economic and social monopoly of culture, by which he means art, seems to me to be overwhelmed by the cultural mercantilism that, I repeat, controls form and excludes the process of being in the world, which requires art and imagination.

The brief quotation from Arnold Hauser approaches another matter that is crucial: the project of modernism in the arts. It is not an overstatement to say that modernism undertook from the beginning to answer to that "dissolution of the great Greco-Christian Idea of divinity, the last universal faith" of "the community of European and Slavic peoples," in Octavio Paz's words (*Duchamp* 75). There is no possibility of understanding, appreciating, enjoying or of participating in the modern, artistic project of being in the world, except by familiarity with traditional art and its thought. This becomes extremely difficult in our cultural circumstances, and the difficulty is compounded by provincialism—at least in North America where traditional art is not around us. The problem for modern art can be all the greater where it is unknown, or bits and pieces of it are understood as a mere expression of the self. As I have repeatedly inferred, culture and art are not the same thing—at least, for us—yet I cannot think of a culture that is not recognized by its arts, as they are fundamental to its thought. We now must think of a dire possibility: "art's radical effacement," replaced by the "financial surface" of things (Clay, *Modern Art* 23). The inability to understand the modern project of being in the world turns into a cultural forgetting. Some years ago, during one of my lectures on modernism—Picasso's *Les demoiselles d' Avignon* large on the wall behind me—a hand went up. The student asked, "Sir, did you make this up?" After a puzzled moment, I burst into laughter. The student replied, "Well, you're talking about things seventy years old. Why haven't I ever heard of them?" This, it turned out, was no dumbbell, nor was he a country bumpkin. His resentment was real and thoughtful. A victim of educational effacement. But, then, one whispers, his parents, his teachers, the system that tutors him, none of them could fill the emptiness. Charges of elitism become silly and dangerous under such cultural circumstances.

But the cultural crisis needs to be plumbed beneath this financial surface on which we can, at least, float, one by one, toward a civilization. We need to consider why it is that the tradition of our culture has come into question. In simpleminded moments, I think that the financial surface is our answer to the pain of the question. I began these thoughts with notice of a midway book—that is, midway in our experience of this century—Hannah Arendt's *The Origins of Totalitarianism*. In the preface to the first edition (Summer 1950), she writes of the twentieth-century challenge to our tradition:

> Antisemitism (not merely the hatred of Jews), imperialism (not merely conquest), totalitarianism (not merely dictatorship)—one after the other, one more brutally than the other, have demonstrated that human dignity needs a new guarantee which can only be found in a new political principle, in a new law on earth, whose validity this time must comprehend the whole of humanity while its power must remain strictly limited. . . .
>
> We can no longer afford to take that which was good in the past and simply call it our heritage, to discard the bad and simply think of it as a dead load which by itself time will bury in oblivion. The subterranean stream of Western history has finally come to the surface and usurpt the dignity of our tradition. This is the reality in which we live. (ix)

A civilization devoted to production and consumption and a tradition that is in ruins, partly forgotten or in sentiment alone come together in a shapelessness difficult to fathom.

The story of how human became human is told by the arts and religion, the latter understood outside dogmatic definitions and entrenchments. Here, our most powerful, current belief system, technology and its moony progress, steps in. I have no regrets—what with kitchen fixtures, furnaces, hot water, plumbing, etc.—but as a belief system, it does trouble my sleep. Technology offers no image of the world, nor is it a guide to vital relations therein. It is projective of the human will let loose upon the world. Where form should be alive, an activity of relations in the world, it is consumed. Technology is an ultimate humanism and it promises a further "gap between past and future." Out of his reading of Hannah Arendt, Stan Spyros Draenos takes up this troubling concern:

> With the loss of tradition and the ground from which it alone might be rebuilt, the mind becomes embattled and loses its freedom of movement—its ability to move with confidence through and across reality. And, under the stress of battle, the thinker is in danger of being overrun by the blind march of time—that is, of succumbing thoughtlessly to whatever the course of things might be. The intention of Arendt's location of being in time is to regain this freedom of movement for the mind by restoring the capacity of thought to literally remember a past we are forgetting. (221–22)

Draenos stresses that this literal remembering of the past is not a "need for authority" and certainly not a "longing for a dead past," but something more akin to what he finds in these lines from the great twentieth-century Greek poet George Seferis:

> As pines
> keep the shape of the wind
> even when the wind has fled and is no longer there
> so words
> guard the shape of man
> even when man has fled and is no longer there.
>   (Seferis, quoted in Draenos 223)

Technology, in which we currently put our faith, "aspires to substitute a universe of machinery for the real reality," as Octavio Paz has argued, hiding the human will that is its secret (*Bow* 241).

I close with the virtues, not values, of the discourses of the arts and of the sacred, fully aware that they tangle with the discourses of the political and the social, and must in order to allay the latter's hegemonic power over the real. The discourses of the arts and of the sacred have to do with the othernesses of the world, of being in the world. Otherness is the *fandango* itself and not the *fanfaronade* we have thought it—the flow of persons, places, things, and cosmos in relation. Concerning the sacred, I keep one of William Blake's "Principles" (1788) in mind: "The Religions of all Nations are derived from each Nation's different reception of the Poetic Genius" (1). And in terms of our modernity, I call to mind Gregory Bateson:

> I claim not uniqueness but membership in a small minority who believe that there are strong and clear arguments for the *necessity* of the sacred, and that these arguments have their base in an epistemology rooted in improved science and in the obvious. I believe that these arguments are important at the present time of widespread skepticism—even that they are today as important as the testimony of those whose religious faith is based on inner light and "cosmic" experience. Indeed, the steadfast faith of an Einstein or a Whitehead is worth a thousand sanctimonious utterances from traditional pulpits. (Bateson and Bateson 11)

The quarrel is not with science, but, as I have already indicated, with "scientism." I noted earlier that the discourse of science always approaches a world; now that discourse tells us that "The realms of the subjective and of the objective are no longer at odds," according to Michel Serres (82). In the matter of worldliness, we are all poetic thinkers of love, laughter, grief, and cosmos, which are not materialities of the subjective, the objective or the abjective— that is, of the thrown under, the thrown against or the thrown out.

A few reminders:

1. "Mass society . . . wants not culture but entertainment, and the wares offered by the entertainment industry are indeed consumed by society just like any other consumer goods" (Arendt, *Between Past and Future* 205). The *Globe and Mail*,[9] for example, doesn't know the difference; books, music, painting, and sculpture are all in the "Entertainment" section. Only sports, which are not simply entertainment, properly receive a separate section. "*Panis et circenses* [bread and fun] truly belong together; both are necessary for life, for its preservation and recuperation, and both vanish in the course of the life process—that is, both must constantly be produced anew and offered anew, lest this process cease entirely" (Arendt, *Between Past and Future* 206).

2. "It has always been the mark of educated philistinism to despise entertainment and amusement, because no 'value' could be derived from it. The truth is we all stand in need of entertainment and amusement in some form or other, because we are all subject to life's great cycle." Watch for the "sheer hypocrisy" and its dear companion, "social snobbery" (Arendt, *Between Past and Future* 206).

3. The arts belong to the continuous vitality of thinking again and again. They are "thought things," like the *Pentateuch* and the *Aeneid* (Arendt, *Life* II: 207). They belong to the world as we must imagine and re-imagine it. They have this in common with political discourse: that both work for a common world. But the political passes in the currency of accommodations and powers. Artistic discourse turns into a form in the world, which can be thought and experienced

again. " . . . the conflict between art and politics . . . cannot and must not be solved" (Arendt, *Between Past and Future* 218).

4. William H. Gass: *It is simply not enough to live and to be honey-happy, to hump and holler, to reproduce. Bees achieve it, and they still sting, still buzz. To seek the truth (which requires method), to endeavor to be just (which depends on process), to create and serve beauty (which is the formal object of style), these old "ha-has," like peace and freedom and respect for persons, are seldom aims or states of the world these days, but only words most likely found in Sunday schools, or adrift like booze on the breath of cheapjacks, preachers, politicians, teachers, popes; nevertheless, they can still be sweet on the right tongue, and name our ends and our most honorable dreams.*

There is, then, meaning contemplated, meaning we repeatedly return to, meaning it is as good to hold in the mouth as good wine; and there is also its opposite, and here the analogy with language may help us find the enemies of culture which culture itself creates, because language allows anonymity as well as distinction; it has its signs which say GENTS, *its fast foods, its wetting dolls, its drively little verses which sentimental sogs send as sops to other sogs, endless paragraphs and pages and entire books which anyone could have written and probably did: guidelines and directions and directories and handbooks and all sorts of reports and memos and factual entries and puffy bios of politicians and punks, stars of stage, screen, field, and whorehouse, and petty lies and dreary chat and insinuating gossip and the flatterous tittle-tattle of TV talk shows, with their relentless cheery hosts, and vomitous film scenarios and wretched radio gabble and self-serving memoirs and stilted forms and humiliating applications, contracts, agreements, subpoenas, creditors' threats, and private eye/romantic/western/spy and sci-fi/fantasy films and fictions, and dozens of dirty gumshoe did-him-ins and wise guy all-abouts, how-tos, and why-nots, and fan mags and digests and Hardy Boys and Nancy Drews and clubby hobby gun and body beautiful books and the whole copiously illustrated pulp and porno scandal pushers from the hard-core soft-on press; and indeed machines might have made them, and one day will, with the same successful sameness as sheets of toilet tissue, similarly daisied, similarly scented, similarly soft, are presented to the uniformly smiling crack of all those similar consumers.*

Even that is not the triumph of our culture's bottom end: it is the glassy plastic drinking cup. Scarcely an object, it is so superbly universal Hegel might have halloed at it (203–4; emphasis added).

5. Stanley Cavell: *But everyone stands in need of the power of poetry, so long as anyone does. Society merely limits who may have it. This is one measure of the disorder of the world* (Claim 461; emphasis added).

Ah, the recovery of the public world, then. How can we uncover its disappearance in the tawdry? Culture-mongering will hardly answer. And the worrisome matter of public support for contemporary arts and artists barely touches the issues. From my point of view, an answer can only be found in a cultural policy that is also an educational policy. We need to know how old we are in the events of human consciousness. The Venus of Laussel (Dordogne) and Artemis Ephesia should not be secrets or, even, surprises of our common effort.

Nor should the passageways of the great temples of the New Kingdom in Egypt, "which accepted no stand-still in life and death," be silent.* The Mahābhārata and The Rgveda, like Gilgamesh and the Odyssey, are events in human consciousness which accompany the teachings of the biblical prophets, Zoroaster, Kung Fu-tse, Gautama Buddha, Christ, and Mohammed. These move us as events in the history of consciousness; of how it is that men and women became human. I mean by these to suggest the tradition, along with those historical processes which derive from them, that created a world or worlds. We need to know how old we are. We need to trace the consciousness of that ageing. In order to gain "an attitude that knows how to take care and preserve and admire the things of the world" (Arendt, Between Past and Future 225). Perhaps, then, we could turn with greater assurance and finer judgment to the modern project which is devoted to change. Good grief! And flights of angels see thee to thy restlessness.[10]

* See S. Giedion, The Eternal Present: The Beginnings of Art (New York: Bollingen Foundation, 1962) and The Beginnings of Architecture (New York: Bollingen Foundation, 1964).

Among Afterthoughts
on This Occasion

I begin as is my wont with scholarly company.

What has become of the concept of imagination in the postmodern era? In our Civilization of the Image might we not expect to find imagination accorded a privileged place by contemporary philosophers? The very opposite is the case. Right across the spectrum of structuralist, post-structuralist and deconstructionist thinking, one notes a common concern to dismantle the very notion of imagination. Where it is spoken of at all, it is subjected to suspicion or denigrated as an outdated humanist illusion spawned by the modern movements of Romantic idealism and existentialism. The philosophical category of imagination, like that of "man" himself, appears to be dissolving into an anonymous play of language. For many postmodern thinkers, it has become little more than the surface signifier of a linguistic system. . . .

Seduced by the summary ideologies of the latest media cult or craze, we seem to have entered an age where reality is inseparable from the image, where the original has been replaced by its imitation, where our understanding of the world is preconditioned by the electronically reproducible media of television, cinema, video and radio—media in which every "live" event or performance is capable of being mechanically recorded and retransmitted *ad infinitum*. (Kearney, *Wake of Imagination* 251–52)

So, to think my way out of a box with a closed lid—or is it a pit with a manhole cover?—and to awake from the passivity of rock-a-byes that we call culture, I ponder these reflections from Richard Kearney's *The Wake of Imagination*. His is a learned and approachable book, meant to guide us through complex historical changes in our understanding of imaginative activity from the biblical and Platonic/Aristotelian foundation onward to our own predicament. These changes are reason enough for cultural concern because we are inside them and because there is increasingly the problem of cultural forgetting.

I do not mean by cultural forgetting merely to confirm the on-going fissure between "high" art and thought on the one hand and the "murmuring anonymity" of beloved everyday life on the other (de Certeau, *Practice of Everyday Life*). The word "high" itself gives the operative nature of imagination away to the order of an other above and beyond our stake in the ordinary. But it is the everyday and the ordinary that have come into question. Imaginative activity, by which we usually characterize the arts and their pertinence in cultural terms, is under attack—and by more than the cliché that you only imagined that. Or should I say, politely, that the arts are under consideration? Which is to say, determined. Determinations are, indeed, under way—by those who "think" these matters through and by those who don't (non-philosophers and all kinds of people). *Terminus ad quem* or *terminus a quo?* I don't know. "Viewed from the postmodern perspective," Kearney summarizes, "the demise of imagination would be deemed inseparable from the demise of man. And neither would be regretted" (248).

Astonishment is, it seems to me, a likely and correct response, even for those who have undertaken the necessary labour of following modern thought from the Enlightenment to postmodernism. An aroma of post-toasties may remind us of how we came to this. The promise of transcendence. The promises of progress. Of social justice. Of reason. And then, our disappointments. Even in ourselves, as the twentieth century puts the questions to tradition and to the time-space of our own being and becoming. Thought of these matters is as much indebted to the arts as to philosophy and the human sciences. Or, indeed, to the sciences, unless it is true that they have left us out. Deconstruction, for example, seems to me to be almost unthinkable without that primary imaginer/ laborer of the materiality of language—Mallarmé. Thus, the arts and cultural concern are intertwined—even in the everyday. But it is the everyday that has come into question.

This occasion[1] drew together a group of scholars and writers to discuss cultural concern with the arts in different times and places. It was not, as I understood it, another effort to propose a cultural policy. Nevertheless, it was, so to speak, to consider a wide range of what has to be there before cultural policy can be anything more than an entrapment in our present predicament. Such entrapment is a kind of unconsciouness—social, economic, political, religious: all of them systems of power, which control content and form. One of them— even in our unconsciousness of its power—takes precedence over another now and again and consequently asserts peeves and positivisms about everybody's reality. Peeves and positivisms are, perhaps, the same thing. I think of art as a fundamental record of human consciousness, alongside traditional systems and totalities, seldom redemptive, but always a tale of the effort and luxury of meaning, close to home.

The purely operative aspect of our thoughtful experience is most accessible in the arts. For that reason alone, we should know them—not to say love them—historically and currently. I note the manner in which twentieth-century arts—particularly poetry—are being buried faster than youth can discover them as he/she comes from "home" into his/her responsibility for operative thought. But and then, we have long been subject to the Hegelian pronouncement of the end of art—continuing, with changed logical means, Plato's republican dismissal. Ah, things-public! Hegel accorded his fifteen minutes of fame. Or was it seconds? The where-are-we, the what-are-we, the why-are-we, the how-are-we play in the havoc—of public thought. It is the arts in the exits and entrances of their form/content issues that respond to this with questions and commotion. The arts, in an old word, commove. Even the lyric voice, in which we had lost faith, only to find it returned (in desperation? in reaction?), is at its best as a commoter—the person who handles commotion.

> Often I am permitted to return to a meadow
> as if it were a given property of the mind
> that certain bounds hold against chaos, . . .
> (Duncan, *Opening* 7)

Or take the Bard's voice from a time when the imaginative was not merely bardy.

> There is a Negation, & there is a Contrary
> The Negation must be destroyd to redeem the Contraries
> (Blake, *Milton* 2, Plate 40, ll. 32–33)

. . . .

> They take the Two Contraries which are calld Qualities, with which
> Every substance is clothed, they name them Good & Evil
> From them they make an Abstract, which is a Negation
> Not only of the Substance from which it is derived. . . .
> (Blake, *Jerusalem* 1, Plate 10, ll. 8–11)

Or go back even further, where we need a scholar's help to read aright, because we have forgotten.

> When Odysseus returns to his obscure little island to create *homophrosyne* ["like-mindedness"—a human sense of mindedness] there, he has already begun to recreate *homophrosyne* between his mind and the heavenly paradigms. Thus he enters into a courtship, which he had performed many years before, in phase now with the courtship of sun and moon. The courtship on earth coincides precisely with the courtship in heaven. Such is the *Odyssey*'s definition of *hora*, the right season, and its definition too of mind, a definition vaster than that bequeathed to us by our

tradition of the individual body housing an isolated soul, man set in an adversary position towards the universe. (Norman Austin, *Archery* 252–53)

The words strike us in the cities of our mind's doing. Perhaps.

The arts bring us into a secularity of concern that is our own doing and that may still pummel the public world with its careless dividing line between the sacred and profane into an astonishment. An astonishment as moving, I think, as that to be faced in contemporary philosophy and theory. It may be, by way of the arts, that many could hear the thunder characteristic of important thought: one obvious example from our imaginative past is in the devolving lightning of the change from the Christian-Byzantine, symbolic icon of wholeness triumphant to the human centring attendant upon the slow-motion closing of Christ's eyes, over decades, on the great crucifixes, piteous, labouring, and sometimes naked. All within a public art. This centring—a re-placement of the centre before Copernicus and Galileo—became our standpoint for something like four hundred years of art and thought. Now, perhaps, a prospect rather than a perspective. And modernism and postmodernism—however the beauties and uglinesses of their complexity go—put the questions. This secular—of-this-world—must necessarily remind itself, in Geoffrey Hartman's words, that "The secular is the sacred integrated, rather than degraded or displaced" (*Beyond Formalism* 22).

This gathering of work by scholars and writers leads to afterthoughts. The occasion was a pleasure even with its moments of what I can only call agreeable disagreements. It has long seemed to me that the making of art (*poiesis*) should attend to its own history in order to correct a likely simple-mindedness before its own ideologies and mere expressiveness. Scholarship and the arts, given the current public world of cultural forgetting, should find a way of companionship. It is in the democracy of scholarship that the information of its disciplines is needed as always and, perhaps, as never before. At least in a different way. I make these remarks in the context of overheard challenges: one by a young arts administrator who found no reason to listen to "all this stuff—just tell us what to do"; and by another to the effect that it was all middle-class rummaging.

Such challenges have to be listened to and they ought, perhaps, to have been presented at the table among the participants. The first example is clearly a call for help out of helplessness to which a bureaucratic answer is sought. The second is impatient and political according to uneasy class relations, and implies a preference for action over this scholarly return to the arts and their not so manifest destiny. Neither implies an interest in or experience with the historical, strange, and changing consciousness of art. Nor would I trust either of them in the "management," as the "bottom-line" argues, of the unmediated, ongoing consciousness of contemporary art. What does the first do with anti-art as it becomes repetitious within the parts and parcels of the contemporary scene and is increasingly and ironically institutionalized? And what does the second do with the obvious uses of an anti-stance? Nowadays, the arts are cards. From which I deduce that we are all cards. But someone threw the deck into the air and the cards are still settling in corners. And this leads me back to that fundamental record of human consciousness and the forgotten.

Whatever this coming together of scholars and writers accomplished—and Evan Alderson's introduction[2] is very useful in leading the reader in—one hopes readers will find some pleasure in their intelligence and continue the task. As one of those readers, I notice certain homes on the range,[3] though the range may, at times, seem unrecognizable. And so, what has imaginative activity (the arts confounded) "fallen" from—be wary of the metaphor—in order to have "fallen" into something-or-another and possible effacement?

> By the time Sartre and his contemporaries were grappling with the meaning of existence, the "affirmative" dreams of the enlightenment and idealist thinkers had degenerated into the nightmare of a global warfare which shook European civilization to its very foundations. The belief in the inevitable progress of history, or indeed of human consciousness, was no longer tenable after the holocaust and the barbaric consequences of modern totalitarianism. (Kearney 218)

Some part of thought—and the best art is, of course, thoughtful, not merely expressive—seems always to be symptomatic (even its methodologies largely a matter of belief) alongside the marvelous effort to have come through. Kearney also reminds us that Adorno and Sartre both questioned the possibility of poetry after what the twentieth century has seen of itself. (Paul Celan, Anna Akhmatova, and many another answer.) It's fair to say that, for many of us, the "fall" is directionless into our own history. Everyday creatures of becoming, facing with our backsides the being that had once been so beautifully explained. What a crick in the neck!

Out of the Enlightenment with its promises of social justice—promises of food, shelter, clothing, sanitation, of sexual and religious freedom, which go hand in hand, and of a commonality in liberty and beauty, all under the aegis of human reason—came the work of the Enlightenment and sadly another story that the twentieth century tells. And amidst this, in Kearney's words: "The discovery of an autonomous imagination which creates meaning out of itself is a modern event. Only with Kant and the German idealists would Western philosophy officially and explicitly proclaim the existence of an imagination prior to, and independent of, both sensation and reason" (111).

And behind this affirmation, Kearney reminds us, a preparatory and protesting view that seems to have returned: "All men who participate in human culture are, Hume sardonically admits, liars; and poets and artists are unique only in that they are 'liars by profession'" (166). The story of the efficacy of imaginative activity repeats itself, but more and more drastically. Out of the Enlightenment comes the ubiquity of Marxisms in humanistic studies and in contemporary poiesis. We might demand an accounting by way of the history of its practices, including the hatred and banality that go beyond biographical explanations of Mao and Stalin. We may turn to current Marxism reconsidered (say, Anthony Giddens and Leszek Kolakowski) and to its refurbishment (say, Terry Eagleton, David Harvey, and Fredric Jameson).* These have reason to question, though I remain guarded as they posit their "realism." It is piffle to say that imaginative activity has nothing to do with capitalism or whatever Marxism is now. It is one or the other's grasping hold on an "essential reality"—an ideality in spite of their competitive materialities—that has proven neither true nor false. Ah, realism! Just here, we need to enter upon the arts as participants in moral vision (ethos of our behaviour toward one another) against the grain of current silliness and reaction.

In these remarks, I have, yes, fooled around with the notion of a consciousness of the human record in art—not meaning to lay the whole blame on certain lacks in education, but to ask something of that process—in order to shift consciousness of away from the conventional authority of the realm of clear and systematic ideas over consciousness. The imperium of that authority and its enormous usefulness dismiss the intelligence of the arts that, so to speak, goes on before and behind that imperium, in the midst of it, and after its quaking. The arts are not simply commodities of either of these mind-sets—however much, like everybody, everyday, they are implicated. The arts do not very often teach boys and girls to be good, but they do teach the undulating way toward meaning.

We are, indeed, in the midst of "a radical readjustment in the sense of time and space in economic, political and cultural life."† The trouble is that our culture is so commodified—all desire with a price on the pieces of it (perhaps, a new thigh or rump awaits my aging selfhood on the department store shelves)— that the readjustment is covered over and unthought in public life except as it

---

* Anthony Giddens, A Contemporary Critique of Historical Materialism, vol. 1: Power, Property and the State (London & Basingstoke: Macmillan, 1981); Leszek Kolakowski, Main Currents of Marxism, 3 vols. (Oxford: Clarendon Press, 1978); Terry Eagleton, The Ideology of the Aesthetic (Oxford: Basil Blackwell, 1990); David Harvey, The Condition of Postmodernity (Oxford: Basil Blackwell, 1989); Fredric Jameson, "Postmodernism and Consumer Society," Postmodern Culture, ed. H. Foster (New York: Pluto Press, 1985). The last of these is interestingly cited in Kearney, Wake.

† The phrase is David Harvey's, Condition of Postmodernity, a little out of context.

is specialized and expertized. This is perhaps a good part of the reason that administrations, commissions, and conferences about the arts (including their travelling mongers) are so blinded: their arguments in favour of the arts as a cultural industry are persuasive only on the surface of art—its successes in commodity terms. Jean Clay has made my point mercilessly: "a mercantilism that controls distribution and hence form . . . result[s] little by little in art's radical effacement" (23).[4] "Art has no vocation for eternity" (Clay 23), and we now read the Bible and all our books in that estranging light. "The romantic imagination could not possibly deliver on its promises," I am reminded (Kearney 185). And modernism? Do we understand that project, full of mistakes and marvels? And postmodernism. Do we understand that its real job is the correction of the modern project, not an apocalypse, which traditional desperation leaves us awaiting at any door? Though the desirous mind may hold such violations of things-as-they-are in a *poiesis*.

It is strikingly odd that our commodified culture brings the arts to the edge of effacement just as certain aspects of postmodernism would deliver them to an ending. The maw of it, either effacement or ending, startles one or another of us into an extraordinary attention—because it leaves everybody outside the creation of meaning. Oh, so alone and, at the same time, massified. I turn to Stanley Cavell's *In Quest of the Ordinary*:

> Philosophical and literary [imaginative] issues of, let us say, encountering, meet in Emerson's question, in the second paragraph of "Experience": "How many individuals can we count in society?"—meet, I mean, if we listen to Emerson's question, as I urge in "Being Odd, Getting Even," as a re-asking, or recounting of Descartes's question, "Am I alone in the world?"; listen to the edge Descartes's question gives to the Pascalian question of cosmic isolation: Am I *so much as* alone? Without providing an answer to this question of skepticism you do not know whether the world has become a plenum, that is, a statistical crowd, or else a void of others. (xi)*

Our problem is in "deflecting attention, as rushing too quickly away, from the act or encounter entailed in the historical and individual process of inheriting" (Cavell 131). Though I let go of much of the subtlety of Cavell's discussion, his reminder is worth quoting here: "So the ordinary is always the subject of a quest and the object of an inquest" (Cavell 149).

Without the discourse of the arts—whether "high" or "pop," having to do with the everyday—it may be that we enter a daymare, disguised for All Hallows

---

* Stanley Cavell's important essay "Being Odd, Getting Even" is published in *In Quest of the Ordinary*.

as complacencies in the shop-windows passing by. Still our fall into historical materiality—social, economic, political, and cosmological—is to be considered. "The fall (bababadalgharaghtakamminarronnkonnbronntonnerronntuonn-thunntrovarrhounawnskawntoohoohoordenenthurnuk!)" is evidence of God as Joyce tells us, waking (*Finnegans Wake* 3).

And it may be that our materiality changes—or so the arts tell me—and the great paradigms of what we're always talking about—"God, self, history, and book" (Taylor 7) all of them discourses, including the discourse of art—shift. A contemporary a/theologian argues that they are "bound in an intricate relationship in which each mirrors the other. No single concept can be changed without altering all the others" (Taylor 7). Such a condition is not commercially available.

If, then, we imagine a culture in which many of us are increasingly outsiders—without, so to speak, the price of the pieces, which is so to say something or other is priceless—what is to be done? I'll put the charge in John Berger's words:

> Those who rule are today legitimatised by manufactured "popularity," while the aspirations of the majority of the ruled are temporarily smothered by manipulated consumerist fears and promises. It is here that advertising achieves its political, as distinct from economic, purpose: politics have become management. ("Intellectuals" 37)

I interrupt to recall that I heard a man on CBC, whose name I've thoughtfully misplaced, explaining to national Canada: "Advertising tells us who we are . . . and presents a completely integrated culture." Believe it!

> It is not only the survival of nature which is threatened, but also the survival of politics and culture—which is to say the survival of human self-respect. . . .
>   Collective nostalgia is always a form of privileged decay. . . . Modern technology is essential to the modern world. The danger is that the instantaneity of its techniques defines its aims. Instant profit. Instant greed. Instant prestige. The instant future. This is why a sense of history has become a condition of our survival. (Berger, "Intellectuals" 37)

Slowly but surely, as the many become outsiders—in this "virtual matter of outsiderdom" (Mayer xix)[5]—everywoman and everyman and everyday come to renew our attention. And here, I'll adapt Michel de Certeau's disclosures to my purpose: on an ordinary day, we meet "a common hero, an ubiquitous character walking in countless thousands on the streets," and "dedicate to him the writing that one formerly offered in praise of the gods or the inspiring muses" to the "very ancient . . . murmuring voice of societies" (*Practice of Everyday Life* v).
    Thus,

We witness the advent of the number. It comes along with democracy, the large city, administrations, cybernetics. It is a flexible and continuous mass, woven tight like a fabric with neither rips nor darned patches, a multitude of quantified heroes who lose names and faces as they become the ciphered river of the streets, a mobile language of computations and rationalities that belong to no one. (de Certeau, *Practice of Everyday Life* v)

The numbers do not want art. That was a primary value of their invention. The autonomy of the "reality" of large numbers of people—important as it is to our political and social thought—meets the anonymity of singularities, "being odd, getting even," whose "reality" can't be approached except in art. That is, if we try to approach "the fleeting and massive reality of a social activity at play with the order that contains it" (de Certeau, *Practice of Everyday Life* xxiv).* Everyday.

* Michel de Certeau's phrase (*Practice of Everyday Life* [xxiv]) occurs in the context of acknowledging the importance of Freud's *Civilization and Its Discontents*.

out of the velvet—
the denim—the straw
of my mind

I look into my poems, especially those I've not yet written—just now, *the affection of crows or a marvelous conversation with birds*—and I know I'm a "word-child" (Amos Oz).[1] I do not see my work in the context of a national state, though I hold, with conscience, dual citizenship by birth in the United States and by responsibility to Canada, where I have lived and earned my living during the last thirty-two years. Oh, yes, I worry about nationalisms, their mythic destinies borrowed from religion, and the endangered democracies here and abroad. I also think about what Christopher Hitchens[2] calls their "styrofoam Round Tables." I watch their fake wars over the Islas Malivinas, Grenada, and Panama, apparent successes in pulling out of the air a popularity for nationhoods—their salvos. I protest the corruption of U.S. Cuban and Latin American policies. I marched and read with others against the War in Vietnam. I've stood in daylight and nightlight before Maya Lin's[3] black granite rampart—between the whitenesses of the Washington Monument and the Lincoln Memorial—the shimmering meaning of 60,000, whom we may name according to the day each one died. "The piece itself is apolitical," she tells us, "in the sense that it doesn't comment directly on the war." This is, of course, political *poiesis*, which the pernicious, political right recognizes and moves to curtail. I turned to look up the hillock where Ross Perot placed his traditional, bronze soldiers, whose uniforms and weapons are mute in the shadows beyond Lin's shimmering thought. No, the serious or ramshackle poet in us hasn't a chance at being apolitical, even if the elf of his or her language wishes to be.[4] (There is no real quarrel between popular culture and "high"—only commercialism says there is, according to the amount it can sell, whereas both have always entwined in human consciousness.) My sense of democracy—so new and little understood, so fragile—is that it is first devoted to social justice in matters of food, shelter, clothing, and health for large numbers (Hannah Arendt).[5] On the record, governments are vicious manipulators of matters imperial, religious, moral, and philosophical—we wind up with, for example, a call for the death penalty for homosexuals in Texas, another bush-whacker, or with, say, the degradation of the philosophical notion of an end to history in Francis Fukuyama,[6] whereas Hegel actually argued that a culture is a judgment on itself. (The current culture had best take some care with its down-at-the-heel sense of élitism, lest it lose the ability to think through the vast effort of human consciousness to find meaning here and about.) I listen to our governments whine that they do not know how to manage global capitalism, all the while joining the gobble of that reality. No government devoted to social justice is allowed to live under its capitalism or its privatization. Someone said, "Advertising tells us who we are and presents a completely integrated culture." How true! For my part, I do not understand how it is possible to come to terms with democracy and the government of it, while teaching Lordship, Mastery, and Love that sacrifices mortality for someplace else, a Totality that forgives us. The cost of these Totalities—of Christianism, of Marxisms, of Capitalism—are on the public record—forgiving themselves again and again for the terror of this century. I reject the apocalyptics of modernism and of postmodernism—these are borrowed from Daniel and Revelation, religious under their skins. Our language has other work to do. Admiring the vast human effort of it and living within the "vast exhaustion" of it, I founder in the bitterness of Western metaphysics. I have chosen a poetic practice of entangling discourses, including the running about of my lyric voice. A companionship of seeing through "the lack of meaning in our time and the lack of a world at the centre of meanings we try to impose."[7] The challenge of *syntaxis*, the actuality of *parataxis*. I continue to write *Exody*, my necessary exit from all that which denies the "existentially given"[8] in the heart of things:

> The world of the happy and that of the unhappy, the world of the good and that of the evil contain the same states of things; with respect to their being-thus they are perfectly identical. The just person does not reside in another world. The one who is saved and the one who is lost have the same arms and legs. The glorious body cannot but be the mortal body itself. What changes are not the things but their limits. It is as if there hovered over them something like a halo, a glory. (Agamben, *Coming Community* 92)

Working the materiality of language—

1999

The Irreparable

In the long run of our talking-reading-writing lives, now and again we come upon language—that dear, homemade music—as utter shock, even collision. Recently, out of my reading of the Italian philosopher Giorgio Agamben, I stopped over two careful propositions in *Infancy and History*:

> . . . the pure exteriority of language. (6)

and

> The unprecedented violence of human power has its deepest roots in [the] structure of language. (7)

Language is not our own—no more than our life or death is in our ownership—historically or now. We have only to honor them. The notion that we have a god-spoken "sacred book" derives, I think, from that ancient strange recognition. And how awesome it is that the word *God* tumbles within it through the centuries of cultural wondering—effervescent and turgid.

I watch words wander in our arrangement of them, on top of them, across the mirrors that things thereby become. The marvel of our delicate, pronominal *I* needs also to be honored. It stands or sleeps alongside things, in fact, alongside the whole world of its garnering. The statement *I drive the car* is much less interesting than what the car is doing. *A key, silver-silk, gas, burns, gears, motion, outer parts, wheels, hubs, spokes, fellies, tires, Fortuna, distances: I drive.* Perhaps Amor hitches a ride. The first example is arranged according to hypotaxis, the "subordinative expression" of what is going on in the sentence—I'm in charge. The second is arranged according to a kind of parataxis, one thing beside another without "expression of their syntactic relation."

Now, let us consider this current, world-wide war with its stunned vocabulary of sorrow (September 11) mixed with appetites for vengeance, oil, and money, and try to find the soldier who's been sent there. First off, we run into a manipulation of language that is meant to shape a herd, an amalgamated voice, answered from the other side by a violent refusal to be subordinated. Whiffs of god on both sides of this "manifest destiny" to found the good. The shepherds are many in this intermeddling tradition—Hebrew, Christian, Muslim—a clangor of splendors. The herds are obedient, especially since the media have been instructed not to show the mutual brutality and barbarism. Then the appropriation of this war and its leaders to God, verified predominantly in English, needs to be reminded that the words god and good are not etymologically related. So, what of the one who stands and sleeps alongside things, even you and me? Inside all of this? This war with its eyes out. *Air clear, hot in the sand, zing, scream, blood, terror, a man, a woman, a child, a whatnot: I shot.* Words become tears. We enter a territory of what-to-do except weep. There is of course the task of it—personal, social, political. Ethos and dwelling. I think of Hélène Cixous's primary "task of bridging the immeasurable distance between love and language" in The Book of Promethea:

> I do not believe in magic or in parapsychology, as I have said elsewhere. But I do believe in poetry. I believe that there are creatures endowed with the power to put things together and bring them back to life: I do not know what these powers consist of but I am not alone in feeling their effects. Travel and you will see cities covered with dust, and you will see cities as shining and resonant as crystal glasses. Someone is there. This was something acknowledged in The Bible. We want to forget it, but God, or whatever replaces god, is never wrong. (103)

This is the "I" of a loving book speaking—of "physical presence"—of "a sense of infinity"—between two women (back cover). I too believe in the affirmation in this passage, then take note of the irony with which it closes—especially now, here, entangled as we are in the impropriety of claims of divine guidance and its concomitant power and cruelty, also acknowledged in the Bible—the circumambient, "immeasurable distance between love and language"[1]—love that is life itself and the gift of it.

We are overwhelmed by what Giorgio Agamben calls "the destruction of experience." I quote in extenso:

> When humankind is deprived of effective experience and becomes subjected to the imposition of a form of experience as controlled and manipulated as a laboratory maze for rats—in other words, when the only possible experience is horror or lies—then the rejection of experience can provisionally embody a legitimate defense. (16)

Is there a human voice, a voice that is the voice of man as the chirp is the voice of the cricket or the bray is the voice of the donkey? (3)

The singularity which language must signify is not something ineffable but something superlatively sayable: the thing of language. (4)

One of the most urgent tasks for contemporary thought is, without doubt, to redefine the concept of the transcendental in terms of its relation with language. . . . [H]ere "transcendental" must instead indicate an experience which is undergone only within language. (4)

These observations and urgencies are drawn from Agamben's *Infancy and History: The Destruction of Experience*, which he proposes as a "review" and a "philological project." For our purposes this involves a new relation to time and the voice of it.

> The moment has come to end the identification of history with a vulgar concept of time as a continuous linear and infinite process, and thereby to take cognizance of the fact that historical categories and temporal categories are not necessarily the same thing. It is a precondition of the review's proposed undertaking to reach a new point in the relationship between time and history—that is, first and foremost, a new and more primary experience of time and history. There must be a critical demolition of the ideas of process, development, and progress whereby historicism seeks to reinsert the pseudo-meanings of the Christian "history of salvation" into a history which it has itself reduced to a pure chronology. Against the empty, continuous, quantified, infinite time of vulgar historicism must be set the full, broken, indivisible and perfect time of concrete human experience; instead of the chronological time of pseudo-history, the cairologicial time of authentic history; in place of the total social process of a dialectic lost in time, the interruption and immediacy of a dialectic at a standstill. (148)

"Cairological time" would unfold a sense of the due-measure (Gr. *kairós*) of time, the poetic quest streaming alongside each of us. This, our secular task, was initiated by the Troubadours during the eleventh, twelfth, and thirteenth centuries and triumphant in Dante's Beatrice. His original title was simply *La Commedia*—the word *comedy* carrying down the centuries its Greek root *komos*, a festal procession—in Dante's instance, a festal procession of life. This is the territory of the other language. By way of it, one finds a repopulation of emptiness—political, social, religious.

This other language holds hands, so to speak, with our otherness and imagination. Giorgio Agamben offers a map of the "reversal of the status of imagination":

> Nothing can convey the extent of the change that has taken place in the meaning of experience so much as the resulting reversal of the status of the imagination.

For Antiquity, the imagination, which is now expunged from knowledge as "unreal," was the supreme medium of knowledge. (Infancy 24)

This expunging results in "the destruction of experience" all around us and in the tattered hearts and minds of it. The joy of the action of language prepares for the imagination to act. According to Agamben:

As the intermediary between the senses and the intellect, enabling . . . the union between the sensible form and the potential intellect, it occupies in ancient and medieval culture exactly the same role that our culture assigns to experience. Far from being something unreal, the mundus imaginabilis has its full reality between the mundus sensibilis and the mundus intellegibilis, and is, indeed, the condition of their communication—that is to say of knowledge. (Infancy 24)

Necessarily abbreviating the breadth and depth of his analysis, for this occasion, I turn to his remark on Descartes and modern science, when the work of imagination

is assumed by the new subject of knowledge: the ego cogito. . . . Between the new ego and the corporeal world, between res cogitans and the res extensa, there is no need for any mediation. The resulting expropriation of the imagination is made evident in the new way of characterizing its nature: while in the past it was not a "subjective" thing, but was rather the coincidence of subjective and objective, of internal and external, of the sensible and the intelligible, now it is its combinatory and hallucinatory character. . . . From having been the subject of experience . . . [imagination] becomes the subject of mental alienation, visions and magical phenomena—in other words, everything that is excluded by real experience. (25)

Given over to the "unreal," "real experience" here amounts to an irremediable shrinkage of human nature and a vulnerable, manipulated "reality" lacking in "truth value" of any kind. Such a "reality" in its overwhelming empowerment endangers democracy and junks us into the midst of "the destruction of experience." Agamben:

The removal of imagination from the realm of experience . . . casts a shadow on the latter. This shadow is desire, the idea of experience as fugitive and inexhaustible. (25)

Further in his discussion we meet "the mediating nature of imagination"— "love has its only site in imagination" (25). Later, he cites Rilke's poetics which evokes "the things in which individuals 'accumulated the human' . . . which were thereby made 'liveable' . . . and 'sayable,' in contrast to the 'appearances of things' which 'bear down from America' and have now transposed their existence 'within the vibration of money'" (43). How long ago did that voice speak out of "Old Europe"?

Our poetic quest has no Grail and that is our story of the Grail: its disappearance. Agamben observes that "the Grail . . . is simply what constitutes the matter of human experience as an aporia, literally as the absence of a road [a-poria]. Thus the quest is . . . the recognition that the absence of a road (the aporia) is the only experience possible for man" (28–29).

Here, the other language folds into whatever it was we were meant to be. It can feel like a dictation of otherness while it remains a return to where we are and have never been.

We do have the marvel of language—the voices of time and place that are so much at stake—its lucens that may or may not wind up in an off-rhyme with loose-ends. What is it? Where does it come from? Indo-European roots? And behind those? "[L]inguists tell us," says Agamben, that "the baby forms the phonemes [the smallest unit of speech in any language] of every language in the world" (53). Thus, mysteriously the arguments for "human invention" or "divine gift."

> We never find man [or woman] separated from language, and we never see him [or her] in the act of inventing it. (Humboldt, quoted in Infancy 49)

Linguistics, "however far back it goes in time, never arrives at a chronological beginning of language, an 'anterior' of language" (49). It is "itself constitutive of the human" (Infancy 49).

Early in this invaluable book, Agamben leads us to Wittgenstein's experience with language:

> if the most appropriate expression of wonderment at the existence of the world is the existence of language, what then is the correct expression for the existence of language? (9)

His reply:

> The only possible answer to this question is: human life, as ethos, as ethical way. The search for a polis and an oikìa [home, dwelling] befitting this void and unpresupposable community is the infantile task of future generations. (9–10)

Oh! The ergon of the other language—the other mind that so suits "the immensity of here and now"—"the rustling of the past" "the present moment": I was sleepless and it took some time before I realized that I was picking up phrases in a mental swim through Hermann Broch's astonishing Death of Virgil.

It was after 1:00 A.M. so I decided to get up and start a rereading of that wonderful, long prose-poem. Instead, I was suddenly walking again over the Volantic footbridge across that startling river in Bilbao—just around the corner from Frank Gehry's Guggenheim where Jeff Koon's giant, wire, flowering dog says hi! and invites entrance—and here all white, suspended flight, Santiago Calatrava's bridge, a maze-like exit at one end meets Old Living Europe at both ends—very beautiful contemporary mind—Oh! minds in contrast to "brains" arranging the consumption of existence. Then, as suddenly, I was in Berlin wandering through Daniel Liebeskind's beautiful, sharp-edged Jewish Museum— before it was made into another Holocaust museum and that horror overcame the other mind of the architect—my enchanted guide and interpreter making sure that I understood every word of the ambience of the metal walls still speaking out of the best of twentieth-century Jewish thought. I followed a corridor that became narrower and narrower to a point of complete darkness, utter lonely silence, even the screams had gone. I climbed the stairway that came to a dead end near the ceiling, turned and, so it was designed, I could not see the same staircase going back down. I went into the garden of steles, stumbling over stones in the pathways, shaded by Russian olives, silver-grey leaves, growing from the top of each stele, substitutes for the fruit olives which cannot weather the winters in Berlin. I imagined I had beauty in my hands. I wept. And then I slept.

In this essay I have wished to draw attention in detail to the invaluable work of Giorgio Agamben and particularly to those "most urgent tasks for contemporary thought": "to redefine the concept of the transcendental in terms of its relation with language" (Infancy 4)—to take it back into our experience of language. I've called this the other language and will turn to examples of it. But first, to note certain characteristics of the transcendental: the Absolute, the abstract, the high-as-the-sky-and-beyond insistence of the time and place of truth, reality, death, and meaning. This is not a proposal of atheism; its practices in Nazi Germany and in Communist Russia prove it to be simple-minded negation with horrifying consequences. The place of negativity is a philosophical question in our lives and within language, not simply a negation of one toppling transcendental for another, such as the famous "promise of a thousand years." In a later book, Language and Death: The Place of Negativity, Agamben opens, by way of analysis and poetics, the possibility for "humankind when negativity is overcome" (back cover blurb). "A completed foundation of humanity in itself should, however, signify the definitive elimination of the sacrificial mythogeme" (106) and accompanying transcendentals.

Just now I've come across five pages of interviews by the British journalist Graham Turner who had spent five weeks travelling around America "talking

to members of the administration, university presidents, military command-
ers, CEO's of giant corporations and banks—and ordinary citizens"—published
in the *Vancouver Sun*, August 16, 2003. Among the interviewees are a few thought-
ful critics, but the weight is on the aggressive side. Without names, I'll give a
few examples.

> "If we pull out of the Kyoto Protocol, it's a dead letter. If we're not part of the In-
> ternational Criminal Court, it's a sham court." (C1)

> "There is nothing more frightening than American innocence. It's a fearsome,
> sometimes murderous innocence. Our inability to question our own motives is
> truly alarming." (C2)

> "The American empire is ideological, not territorial. We are the most ideological
> people in the world, and we are so united in our view that we don't understand
> there can be other views." (C2)

> "We are not a nation which prays in its closet. We expect the president to be our
> principal preacher, to express constantly the idea that God has showered us with
> special blessings and that we, therefore, have a special identity, a special mission
> in the world. It is a mission which is realized in part just by being who we are,
> but which also requires us to encourage others to be just like us." (C2)

> "The president is now the great Pope. He's not infallible yet, but he's coming close."
> (C4)

> "America, after all, believes that its world view is omniscient, omnipotent, omni-
> present. Just like Marxism, it's a globalizing system. Just like Marxism, it is highly
> intolerant of other ideas and brooks no opposition." (C4)

> "This is a seminary which trains the clergy of global capitalism." (C4)

> "You could say we're promoting American values, but these are universal values."
> (C4)

> "On a global scale, the dominant phenomenon of our time is not the growth of
> secularization but its collapse." (C5)

> "The war turned our TV journalists into shills, patsies. They weren't providing
> news—they were cheerleaders." (C6)

> "The reaction to how this country has responded militarily in Afghanistan and Iraq
> is a case of whistling past the graveyard." (C6)

> "The absence of meaning will catch up with America unless we are careful." (C6)

Therein, a record of the wreckage of the Transcendental—Absolutism—God—
Ideology—dangerous drivers of these Powers along the aporia of Heaven. Can
it be that we are all forced to walk the aporia of spreading miasmata? Well, one

needs to ask—perhaps to answer or begin again—in the midst of delirium, dishonesty, and the theft of meaning—with the cry of Flaubert's Anthony— *être la matière!*

> O happiness! happiness! I have seen the birth of life, I have seen the beginning of movement. The blood in my veins is beating so hard that it will burst them. I feel like flying, swimming, yelping, bellowing, howling. I'd like to have wings, a carapace, a rind, to breathe out smoke, wave my trunk, twist my body, divide myself up, to be inside everything, to drift away with odours, develop as plants do, flow like water, vibrate like sound, gleam like light, to curl myself into every shape, to penetrate each atom, to get down to the depth of matter—to be matter![2] (232)

Perhaps to challenge this irreparable wreckage of where we are.

Talking, reading, writing lives—companionship of thought—the pleasures of civilization—the *there*, the *here*, the *where* of lives in languages.

I've come upon this passage from Oz Shelach's novel *Picnic Grounds*:

> Having since boarded an airplane and left Israel full of bitter disappointment and hope for the future, I now yearn for a time not very long ago, but which I have never known, before ever I existed, or preferably, before we did. (14)

There, where your first thoughtfulness began, even before you could read or write, an image, a sound, a texture, perhaps some luck, as in my case—the fierce face of Dante by Gustave Doré in a book that seemed half my height.[3]

Here, where you find a lifetime of talking, reading, writing—it has a kind of body. In whose hands. . . . !

Where—when suddenly you must look up and down and around from your talking, reading, writing life and ask "where are we?" Just now this question has an immeasurable urgency.

John Berger, novelist, painter, essayist, approaches this urgency—emergency— in his essay "Where Are We?" I offer excerpts:

> . . . the present pain of living in the world is perhaps in some ways unprecedented. Consumerist ideology, which has become the most powerful and invasive on the planet, sets out to persuade us that pain is an accident, something we can insure against. This is the logical basis for the ideology's pitilessness. (13)

> To the anguished question of Where are we? the experts murmur: Nowhere. Might it not be better to see and declare that we are living through the most tyrannical— because the most pervasive—chaos that has ever existed. . . . Its ideological strat- egy, beside which Bin Laden's is a fairy tale, is to undermine the existent so that everything collapses into its special version of the virtual, from the realm of

which—and this is the tyranny's credo—there will be a never-ending source of profit. (13–14)

The precondition for thinking politically on a global scale is to see the unity of the unnecessary suffering taking place. This is the starting point. (14)

The next step is to reject all the tyranny's discourse. Its terms are crap . . . the re-current terms are: Democracy, Justice, Human Rights, Terrorism. Each word in the context signifies the opposite of what it was once meant to. Each has been trafficked; each has become a gang's code word, stolen from humanity. (14–15)

Today the power of the same country that inspired such hopes has fallen into the hands of a coterie of fanatical (wanting to limit everything except the power of capital), ignorant (recognizing only the reality of their own firepower), hypo-critical (two measures for all ethical judgments, one for us and another for them), and ruthless B-52 plotters. How did this happen? The question is rhetorical, for there is no single answer, and it is idle, for no answers will dent their power yet. But to ask it in this way in the night reveals the enormity of what has happened. (16)

And eliminate every opposition by calling it terrorist. (16)

No, I have not forgotten the couple who threw themselves from one of the twin towers instead of being burned to death separately. (16)

Hand in hand.

Another version of Berger's essay appears as "Introduction" to David Levi Strauss's *Between the Eyes: Essays on Photography and Politics*—another voice that we must call to our urgency. Berger catches him exactly: "This is written in the night. In the night by the light of his intelligence and compassion. David Levi Strauss talks about "what has been forgotten, what is being systematically erased, and what we need to remember tomorrow" (xv). How does the sacred remain—how to look upon the "Epiphany of the Other"—how can we work in the dark. A brilliant book to map where we are and where we might be. Strauss:

> I tell him when we look at images we're like Orpheus looking back. Like him, we're looking back out of love and doubt—love for the subject we've left behind, and doubt in the laws of consequence—so our gaze is always both faithful and illicit. (195)

John Berger closes this version of his essay: "In war, the dark is on nobody's side, in love the dark confirms that we are together" (xv). Thus, we must call back and forth in this darkness—writing in the pain of the world, where. . . .

I have not forgotten September 11: sorrow for those who died there, sorrow for New York, sorrow for America.

I have received a letter from a young woman, a "Human Shield" in Iraq—her witnessing of both sides.

I have read of a proposal to include the "unborn" in the Pledge of Allegiance. The spreading popularity of the death sentence and its perpetrators are a disease in the social body. Only life has the right to death.

I have read about the shipment of red heifers to Israel in preparation for the rebuilding of the temple after the destruction of the Mosque there on the Mount. A TV minister said the sacrifices would begin again—"this time in the name of Christ."

The rumbling tradition of the West is embedded in ancient Hebrew, Christian, Muslim urgencies. The religions of it forgive themselves with the speed of slot machines.

So, I have tried to track The Irreparable—the destruction of experience, the shattered transcendentals, the current enormity—in the recognition of these for what they are—as if by chance[4] to discover an opening into our contemporary task: "to redefine the concept of the transcendental in terms of its relation with language" (Agamben, Infancy 4). I call this the poiesis of thought—or more simply the honest work of language—never an afterthought, for we are inside The Irreparable. We are as we are implications of it. Infants of the task. Infants in the language of it. I have studied and loved the footsteps (yes, you can love footsteps—think of your own—these footprints are news of us)—into the poiesis of The Irreparable—thus, in Jean Paul, Nerval, Baudelaire, Mallarmé, Rimbaud and Jarry—in the currents and cross-currents of modernism and in the missaid post-modernism—the poiesis of these footprints in the poetry since 1945, Jack Spicer pressing the shifting sands of this irreparable aporia—the sundered, risky, refounding language of so many—the astonishment of such honesty that transforms the poiesis into beauty out for this walk with ugliness.

I turn again to Giorgio Agamben, this time to his book *The Coming Community* of which Jean-Luc Nancy has written:

> *The Coming Community* tries to designate a community beyond any conception available under this name; not a community of *essence*, a being-together of existences; that is to say: precisely what political as well as religious identities can no longer grasp. Nothing less. (Inside back cover)

Agamben:

> The Irreparable is that things are just as they are, in this or that mode, consigned without remedy to their way of being. States of things are irreparable, whatever they may be: sad or happy, or atrocious or blessed. How you are, how the world is—this is the Irreparable.
>
> Revelation does not mean revelation of the sacredness of the world, but only revelation of its irreparably profane character. . . . Revelation consigns the world to profanation and thingness—and isn't this precisely what has happened? The possibility of salvation begins only at this point; it is the salvation of the profanity of the world, of its being-thus.
>
> (This is why those who try to make the world and life sacred again are just as impious as those who despair about its profanation).
>
> The world—insofar as it is absolutely, irreparably profane—is God. (Coming Community 90)

> The proposition that God is not revealed in the world could also be expressed by the following statement: What is properly divine is that the world does not reveal God. (Coming Community 91)

> The world of the happy and that of the unhappy, the world of the good and that of the evil contain the same states of things; with respect to their being-thus they are perfectly identical. The just person does not reside in another world. The one who is saved and the one who is lost have the same arms and legs. The glorious body cannot but be the mortal body itself. What changes are not the things but their limits. It is as if there hovered over them something like a halo, a glory. (Coming Community 92)

> Thus means not otherwise. (Coming Community 93)

> "So be it" means "let the thus be." In other words, it means "yes."
>
> (This is the meaning of Nietzsche's yes. . . . The thus is eternal.) (Coming Community 103)

It is the limits that stand out for study and love in the exposure of being. One of them is death, but many are political, social and religious injustices.

I turn now to two poems that Giorgio Agamben drew to my attention in *Language and Death*. The first is by Paul Klee, "a poet who claimed to dwell among the unborn" (97) and titled *Elend* (misery or desolation). It is an extraordinary instance of imagining "another land"—another geography and politics—outside the pain of the world in which we are writing. The poem is not an escape but a geography of an imaginary moment:

Land ohne Band,	Land without chains,
neues Land,	new land
ohne Hauch	without the breath
der Erinnerung,	of memory,
mit dem Rauch	with the smoke
von fremden Herd.	of a strange hearth.
Zügellos!	Reinless!
wo mich trug	Where I was brought
keiner Mutter Schoss.	by no mother's womb. (97)

One notices the weight of *ohne* (without) twice over, the rhyme of *Hauch* (breath) with *Rauch* (smoke) and the assonance in *Zügellos* (reinless) and *Schoss* (womb), which carry us into a geography without pain. But the title "Misery" haunts this new land where the poet cannot have been, domestic and familiar as the hearth suggests. Nevertheless, the hearth is strange, as the place is not-before-known. This is the shine of the poem, its gift.

The second poem, so smartly placed next to it by Agamben, is by the great contemporary Italian poet Giorgio Caproni, titled *Ritorno* (Return)—to the shine of life:

Sono tornato là	I returned there
dove non ero mai stato.	where I have never been.
Nulla, da come non fu, è mutato.	Nothing has changed from how it was not.
Sul tavalo (sull'incerato	On the table (on the checkered
a quadretti) ammezzato	tablecloth) half-full
ho ritrovato il bicchiere	I found the glass
mai riempito. Tutto	which was never filled. All
è ancora rimasto quale	has remained just as
mai l'avevo lasciato.	I never left it. (97–98)

The beauty, the marvel of this poem are the work of language—an otherness to hang onto. Here, as Agamben observes in both poems, "language . . . returns to that which never was and to that which it never left, and thus it takes the simple form of a habit" (*Language and Death* 97)—the simple form of a habit holding the shine of our "being-thus." The heart of it.

I close with Giorgio Agamben's summons at the end of *The Coming Community*:

Seeing something simply in its being-thus—irreparable, but not for that reason necessary; thus, but not for that reason contingent—is love.

At the point you perceive the irreparability of the world, at that point it is transcendent.

How the world is—this is outside the world. (106)

Return.

2003

PART II

Commentaries

The Practice of Outside

for *Jack Spicer*
January 30, 1925–August 17, 1965

> With fifteen cents and that I could get a
>   subway ride in New York. My heart
> Is completely broken. Only an enemy
> Could pick up the pieces.
> "Fragments of what," the man asked, "what?"
> A disordered devotion towards the real
> A death note. With fifteen cents and real
> Estate I could ride a subway in New York. No
> Poet starved. They died of it.
>
>   From a Spicer notebook, late 1964

At first this essay was short and simple—about Jack. But that became a reduction which every twist and turn of the work denied— a biography without the world the poet earned or a split between the man and the work which drank him up and left him behind. I fell into the experience of another poet's request: *"until you understand a writer's ignorance, presume yourself ig- norant of his understanding"* (Coleridge, *Biographia* 1:12, 160). It is difficult, out of friendship and care, to find details disappearing into details rather than into meanings. My essay then became watchful of the context of the poetry and of the composing "real" that is Jack's concern. His ignorance is not one of lack of assurance. He knew the good and size of his work and he had assurance to give away to others. His ignorance seems to have been of the cost of this venture which he turned into a narrative. It is part of his notion that poetry is neces- sary to the composition or knowledge of the "real" and this drew him into a combat for the context of poetry—that it was an act or event of the real, rather than a discourse true only to itself. He had said early on in conversation with a young poet that one had first to learn to use the I and then to lose it. This becomes an attack on the "subjective aim" and assurance of a whole culture. And it cuts the ground from under a poetry that ceaselessly returns to wrap itself around a personality. It was especially costly to a poet who refused those resolving images of the writer as victim or hero. In the face of this work, both hero and victim are humanisms which do not measure up. In an extreme move to gain what he variously called a dictation, the unknown, an outside, Jack's work contradicts them as resolutions or explanations of anything. They became names rather than acts, as in the last poem he wrote at the end of the *Book of Magazine Verse*. In an earlier poem on heroes, he laughs at them and at the same time puts them back into a mystery.

> Heros eat soup like anyone else. Sometimes the kitchen is so far away
> That there is no soup. No kitchen. An open space of ground recovered by
> The sky.
> Heros eat soup like anyone else. False ground.
> Soup
> Of the evening
> Beautiful soup.
> And the sky stays there not an image
> But the heros
> Like the image of an image
> (What is made of soup from)
> Zooms.
>
> (*Collected Books* 220–21)[1]

In *The Collected Books*, it is as if the reader and the poet had to begin again—not with a false ground—perhaps with a ground that is simultaneously true and false—where a composition begins again. In *Admonitions* he took it up in a poem for himself, "For Jack":

> Tell everyone to have guts
> Do it yourself
> Have guts until the guts
> Come through the margins
> Clear and pure
> Like love is. (63)

And in "A Postscript for Charles Olson" at the end of the same book:

> If nothing happens it is possible
> To make things happen.
> Human history shows this
> And an ape
> Is likely (presently) to be an angel. (65)

Simply and almost childishly expressed, this opens into the ranging care of his work and into its extremity, where the poems carry "messages" and the poet tends to disappear from his work. There may be, in this sense, an "angel of the work."

The poetry of *The Collected Books* begins in 1957, when that composing factor— the dictation, the unknown, or the outside—enters the work, and Jack began to construct a poetry that was not lyric but narrative. This narrative, he came— "jokingly," he said—to call "the serial poem."[2] It had to hold on to a motivation that was not strictly his own. Since I will be following this motivation through and translating it into other terms, it is useful at the outset to hear Jack's description of it. The harsh and beautiful words of his poetry are discoveries of it. Here, he is speaking to a group of poets, June 13, 1965, in Vancouver, British Columbia, and it was, he said, the 100th anniversary of Yeats's birth. Yeats's proposition of a poetry by dictation

was the first thing since Blake on the business of taking poetry as coming from the outside rather than from the inside. In other words, instead of the poet being a beautiful machine which manufactured the current for itself, did everything for itself, almost a perpetual motion machine, of emotion, until the poet's heart broke, or was burned on the beach like Shelley's. Instead there was something from the outside coming in.

Now, the difference between, "We have come to bring metaphors for your poetry," and what I think most poets—who I consider good poets—today believe— and this would include people as opposite in their own ways as, say, Eliot on one hand, and Duncan on the other—is essentially that there is an outside to the poet— now what the outside is like is described differently by different poets, and some of them believe that there's a welling up of the subconscious or the racial memory, or the this or that, and they try to put it inside the poet. Others take it from the outside—Olson's idea of energy in *Projective Verse*—something that comes from the outside. I think that the source is unimportant, but I think that for the poet writing poetry, the idea of just what the poet is, in relationship to this outside— whether it's an id down in the cortex—which you can't reach anyway, it's just as far outside as Mars—or whether it is as far away as those galaxies that seem to be sending radio messages to us with the whole galaxy blowing up just to say something to us, which are in the papers all the time now. . . . But at any rate, the first step is reached, I think, with Yeats getting the thing—But the way that it works— "We have come to bring metaphors for your poetry"—this is like "We have come to bring fertilizer for your fields"—that kind of thing. You know, "Well, you've had such nice poetry, Mr. Yeats, the spooks have come down from above to give you metaphors to hang it onto."

Now this is not really what happens—in my own experience—and I'll be talking about my own experience most of the time, but I think I can say for other people's experiences too, of those that I know—in dictated poetry—I think that the first kind of hint one has as a poet, and I must confess I was, as Karen would say, a "retard" in this respect, is—after you have written poems for a while and struggled with them, and everything else, a poem comes through just in about one-eighth of the time that a poem normally does, and you say, "Well, gee, it's going to be much easier if I can just have this happen very often." And so then you write 17 or 18 different things which are just what you're thinking about at the moment—and are lousy.

It isn't simply the matter of being able to get a fast take—It's something else— But the fast take is a good sign that you're hooked up with some source of power, some source of energy. Then, the next thing is you suddenly figure out, well, gee, when I've been wanting something, I've been, ah—say, I'm in love, and I want to sleep with this person, and, you know, the normal thing is with the fast take you write all these things down—with an idea of—essentially a way of selling a used car. And this doesn't work.

So one day, after you have this first experience, which was just something that you couldn't imagine, and the poems haven't come this clean, this fast—and they don't usually in dictated poetry anyway—suddenly there comes a poem that you just hate and would like to get rid of, that says just exactly the opposite of what you mean, of what you have to say—to use Olson's thing in one of its two meanings. Olson talks about the poet is a poet when he says what he has to say. Now, you can read that in two ways. What he HAS to say, namely, "I want to sleep with you, honey." Or, "I think that the Vietnam crisis is terrible," or "Some of my best friends are dying in loony bins," or whatever you want to say that you think is a particular message—that's the bad thing. But what you WANT to say—the business of the wanting comes from the outside, like it wants five dollars—being ten dollars—that kind of want is the kind of thing which is the real thing—the thing that you didn't want to say in terms of your own ego—in terms of your image, in terms of your life, in terms of everything. And I think the second step for a poet who's going on to the poetry of dictation is when he finds out that these poems which say just exactly the opposite of what he wants himself, per se, poet, to say, the poems that say just exactly the opposite—if you want to say something about your beloved's eyebrows and the poem says, the eyes should fall out—and you don't really want the eyes to fall out, or have any even vague connection—or you're trying to write a poem on Vietnam and you write a poem about skating in Vermont— these things, again, begin to show you just exactly where the road of dictation leads. But then you—just like when you wrote the first poem which came easily and yet was a good poem, a poem beyond you, the second stage—you then say, "Oh, well then, you know, I'll just write this thing, and I'll take a line from someplace or an- other, or use a Dada or Surrealist thing . . . taking the arbitrary and all of that . . . and that won't be what I want to say—and so that'll be great, that'll be hunky- dory." Unfortunately, that doesn't work terribly well either. You have to—not re- ally want—not what you don't want to say. It's a very complicated kind of thing. You can't play tricks on it. That's the second stage.

The third stage, I think, comes when you get some idea that there is a differ- ence between you and the outside of you which is writing poetry—where you feel less proud of the poem that you've written, and you know damn well that it belongs to somebody else . . . the poem then, and for a poem sometimes it's a twelve-hour struggle to get a ten-line poem, not changing a single word of it as you're writing, but just as it goes along—trying to distinguish between you and the poem—the absolute distinction between the outside and the inside—and here the analogy of the medium comes in, which Yeats started out, and which Cocteau in his *Orphée*—both the play and the picture—used a car radio for, but which is essentially the same thing. . . . And the more that you clear the mind away from yourself. . . . Now, if you have a cleft palate and are trying to speak with the tongue of men and angels, you're gonna still speak through a cleft palate. And things which are in you, the poem comes distorted through. Your tongue is exactly the kind of tongue you're born with, and the source of energy, whatever it is, can take advantage of your tongue, can make it do things that you didn't think it could—but your tongue will want to return to the same normal position of ordinary cleft palate speech of your own dialect, and this is the kind of thing you have to avoid. There are a great many things you can't avoid. It's impossible for the source of energy to come to you in Martian or North Korean or Tamil or any language you don't know—it's impossible for the source of energy to use images you don't have— or, at least, don't have something of. It's as if a Martian comes into a room with children's blocks—with ABCDE, which are in English—and he tries to convey a message—this is the way the source of energy goes—but the blocks on the other hand are always resisting it.

Now, the third step in dictated poetry is to try to keep all of yourself that is possible out of the poem. . . . The more you know, the more languages you know . . . the more building blocks the Martians have to play with. (Vancouver Lecture 1)[3]

Jack's lively and storied language pushes us into a polarity and experienced dialectic with something other than ourselves. It involves a reversal of language into experience, which is not a dialexis between ourselves or a discourse true only to itself, but a broken and reforming language which composes a "real." The doubleness of a man and a world are recovered to operate in the language. Where, so to speak, a public language has closed itself in order to hold meaning, it becomes less than the composition of meaning. It stops and relegates both the language and its hold on the "real" to the past. The place of language in the social, as a performance of the "real," is displaced to a transparency and becomes an imposition rather than a disclosure. In Jack's work, a fundamental quarrel with a discourse that does not hold a present or a future possibility is apparent from the visibility and invisibility of *After Lorca*, through the *logos* and low-ghost[4] of *Heads of the Town up to the Aether* and the dissonant noisy voices of *The Holy Grail* to a culminating argument in the pieces of language in the book *Language*. The last poems of the *Book of Magazine Verse* turn repeatedly from an anger and rage to a simple love that flows from and composes out of the real. A *reopened language* lets the unknown, the Other, the outside in again as a voice in the language. Thus, the reversal is not a reduction, but an openness. The safety of a closed language is gone and its tendency to reduce thought to a reasonableness and definiteness is disturbed. Poetry has always kept the unreasonable voice, but it is said to be true only in a poetic discourse and, of course, peripheral to the reason our lives are referred to. Here in the insistence of Jack's outside, an other than the reasonable is said to enter the real. The real doubles in the experience and in the language. The voice arguing the necessity of an outside may strike a reader as odd since the outside, in whatever sense one takes it, is usually assumed. It belongs then to a discourse or to a science. Its placement here as a composing factor in the poem disturbs our sense of a settled relation to language. It does, as I hope the ensuing argument makes clear, insist that language is not so simply relational, but rather a knowing, an event in men's lives, as words are important to hold on to whatever it is that composes us.

From *After Lorca* on, Jack works in a poetry that is a "compound of the visible and the invisible."[5] These words are not so difficult once one realized that the visibility of men in speech opens on an invisibility he has not spoken or thought. The fundamental polarity extends into a space that is not recognized. The movement of Jack's work is to retie language and experience as they are composed in the exchange of visibility and invisibility. Perhaps, it was his knowledge as a professional linguist that brought him to this point in an understanding of a composing "real,"—as a "sense" seems visible and a "nonsense" seems fallen out of the visible or about to enter it.

Following a lecture on his own work, he was accused of being more interested in truth than in poetry and he replied, "Well, I'm interested in being a conveyor of messages" (Vancouver Lecture 2).[6] This insistence upon an outside becomes an intricate argument for a transcendence—both a distance and a verticality. This verticality—and the looseness of any discourse we have at hand to hold on to it—is caught exactly in the rope trick of "A Textbook of Poetry":

> The Indian rope trick. And a little Indian boy climbs up it.
> And the Jungians and the Freudians and the Social Reformers all
> leave satisfied. Knowing how the trick was played.
>
> There is nothing to stop the top of the rope though. (173)

Jack was not much given to explaining his work, for it seemed to him that was the reader's job as much as his own, but one of his observations draws attention here. "A Textbook of Poetry," he says, takes the divine in relation to the human and *The Holy Grail* turns this around to take the human in relation to the divine (Vancouver Lecture 2).[7] As I note here in the essay, the word divine is among the ruins of a discourse, broken in thought and experience into belief and disbelief. In Jack's work, the divine is resituated in a composition where belief and disbelief are composing elements of its meaning. The dictation of the outside brings us up against a number of words that float in and out of a meaning. It is not, for Jack, any ordinary supernaturalism, but literal to a condition that may be called a "polar logic" of experience. A meaning is constantly playing within the poetry because the poetry in its openness is more than a meaning and in the composition less than a meaning. Unfixed. A meaning in the poems is also constantly doubling back to meet the manhood and the ghostly, silver voices of it ("A Textbook"),[8] where death is an interrogation close to the world because it is not ourselves. Death and ghostliness in this work must be seen, not as a choice against life or even a helplessness within it, but as a literal pole, where life is present to a point and then suddenly absent from an articulation.[9] The curious thing about language and experience, which haunts Jack's work, is that they are so immediately reversible.[10] And as a friend said, discussing this essay with me, if you don't have knowledge of that reversal, then you don't have the heart of it. This goes for translation, as in *After Lorca*, and for all directnesses of language. Suddenly, in the contemporary experience, the formal, public language does not hold and our language in the midst of a recomposition has to account for what is stopped, lost, loose, and silent. I am reminded of Merleau-Ponty's "wild-meaning" and "wild-logos" which include an experience of a "birth of meaning."[11]

It was for this reason Jack refused to accept a language for poetry that is a poetic discourse true only to itself and as such, simply another discourse patterned on the language system we have lived in, and though it is heightened, it has remained equally peripheral, an addition to the real. The "infinitely small vocabulary,"[12] the purity and pointing of *After Lorca* comes into a literal condition, where the meaning plays and composes before our eyes. This comes to be an essential aspect of the narration or serial poem. According to Jack, "you have to go into a serial poem not knowing what the hell you're doing." "You have to be tricked into it, it has to be some path that you've never seen on a map before."[13] It has to be a renewed language and information that becomes a kind of map. Ideally, Jack worked in that long form without looking back and without thought of the previous poem, so that the poet could be led by what was composing. The serial poem is often like a series of rooms where lights go on and off. It is also a sequence of energies which burn out, and it may, by the path it takes, include the constellated. There is further a special analogy with serial music: the voice or tongue, the tone, of the poem sounds individually, as alone and small as the poet is (the cleft palate of Jack's example), but sounded in series, it enters a field.* In this way the dictation and the serial form join to bring the poet, his voice, tone, and stance into a dimension where he is either lost or found. A "necessary world" is composed in the serial poem.

For this occasion, which is Jack's, I have chosen to follow this polarity through. Our words for it may lead to confusion: a dualism, a dialectic, a contrarium. The point is to take the doubleness out of statement and return the process to experience where the language composes. This man, now silent, leaves us to face his work. The darkness, the torn shapes and ghosts of Jack's poems are an admission and they are also an openness, where thought and feeling begin again. They shadow the laughter, the jokes and the naturalness of his language. Such polarity is not reductive to a simple-minded authenticity or to a signature that is only one's self. The "only-feeling" of so much bad and helpless verse. Where I have found the public language removed from a real, or only, by an irony Jack's ghosts laugh at, an expression of ourselves, I have also found Jack's work returning the language to us. It brings us close to "what must be thought" and to what has been under or outside our discourse (Foucault).[14] Merleau-Ponty again comes to mind in his remarks on dialectic become a statement, "'embalmed' dialectic," and the edge we have reached where we must "recommence perception" and a "thinking speech" (*Visible* 175). Such speech will account for the other that opens before us. It amazes me that Jack Spicer's work moves us to this point, which contemporary philosophers, especially Foucault and Merleau-Ponty, have argued. Though they inform my essay in the effort I am making to say that this is a fundamental poetic concern, Jack did not know their work or care. He moved from the necessity. His fascination with the "unknown" including the complex experience of the contents of an invisibility led him to emphasize the silence around and between poems. This renewed speech, in another man's words, "teaches us a necessity that is not logical but ontological" (Lefort xxviii):

> Thus we were to understand that speech is between two silences: it gives expression to an experience that is mute and ignorant of its own meaning, but only in order to make that experience appear in its purity; it does not break our contact with the things, but it draws us from our state of confusion with all things in order to awaken us to the truth of their presence and to render palpable their relief and the tie that binds us to them. At least such is the speech that speaks in conformity with its essence and . . . does not cede to the vertigo of eloquence, does

* The possibility of this analogy was drawn to my attention in Alphonso Lingis's preface to Merleau-Ponty's *The Visible and the Invisible*: "Serial music, Merleau-Ponty points out . . . discovers the ability of any tone in a series to function as an individual sounded in a field and as the dominant, the field tone, the level at which the melody plays" (xlix–l).

not wish to suffice to itself or close in upon itself and upon its sense, but opens upon and leads to the outside. (Lefort xxviii–xxix)

To trace this is difficult. I begin with Jack's visibility and invisibility in *After Lorca*, with the life and death of one poet flowing into another. But I wish to give this a context in a more than personal challenge to the visibility we understand ourselves to be speaking in our language. Or, I wish to take it back to the composition, the ontology, the beginning of a language that is full of the world. It is within language that the world speaks to us with a voice that is not our own. This is, I believe, a first and fundamental experience of dictation and correspondence—the dead speaking to us in language is only one level of the outside that ceaselessly invades our thought. In this way, I mean to suggest Jack's effort to trace the vectors of a composing real in his "disordered devotion." In his books, we begin in an exchange of life and death, visibility and invisibility, known and unknown, human and divine. In the reversal of language into experience,[15] these fold into one another and unfold, composing as voices in our language. They are elemental and also ultimate at either end of a narration. To understand the "outside," that curiously naive-sounding insistence of this work, it will not do to take off on those supernaturalisms which precondition and explain the experience. The dictation remains persistently of the world, and as it is unknown, it moves into the language as the imageless moves into image. Jack's discipline of emptying himself in order to allow his language to receive an other than himself may be traced back to his tradition and sources, but he works there independently and fiercely. The discipline is intended to re-open the discourse. (Here I would place him among his direct peers—Poe, Mallarmé, Artaud, and Duchamp in their emphasis upon loss of meaning turning into necessity of meaning.) There is a dangerous factor in such work, for it removes the manhood or the image of it, which the settled discourse gathered and held together in a stoppage or finitude that spoke only of itself. My companions in this thought, which Jack's work forces me to articulate, will help clarify this openness later. Just now, I need only say that Jack's "outside" implies a world and a cosmology without an image. It is unknown and entering the time of language again.

If, along with my sources, I am right that a discourse, a language system, has ended in a "transparency" of descriptions and relations (Foucault),[16] which set the imaginative apart from the real and give it up to the ideal or by a twist, dump the whole business into a sadly limited personality, then I may take seriously the profound consequences of the strangeness and estrangement that enter Jack's work. That "transparency" leaves entire realms unacknowledged. They become unknown, unimaged, and unthought. Such "transparency" reverses itself into a lie. And the unknown comes forward without visibility—outside oneself and outside one's language, but it begins to compose itself within language. This brings us to a "recommencement of perception"[17] that has barely begun, and within it, we re-enter a composition of the real.

MAGIC

Strange, I had words for dinner
Stranger, I had words for dinner
Stranger, strange, do you believe me?

Honestly, I had your heart for supper
Honesty has had your heart for supper
Honesty honestly are your pain

I burned the bones of it
And the letters of it
And the numbers of it
That go 1,2,3,4,5,6,7
And so far.

Stranger, I had bones for dinner
Stranger, I had bones for dinner
Stranger, stranger, strange, did you believe me? (132)

In this poem, the movement from words to bones is an exact expression of a condition. The words disappear into the bones and even those are eaten by the strange voice of the poem. The Orphic explanatory note to the poem makes it clear that in the telling, the voice of the poem is a ghostly other and outside of meaning.

Orpheus was never really threatened by the Underworld during his visits there. In this poem they present him with a diplomatic note.

Honesty does not occur again in the poem.

The numbers do. (132)

The poem and the note both return us to time, a running of the numbers and a traversal. This poem is from the first section of the book *Heads of the Town up to the Aether*, a hell of meaning, a playing out of sense and nonsense, which precedes the concern for paradise in the final section.[18]

The entrance of strangeness to the work takes many forms—most obviously in the ghosts, who are "not the same as the dead"[19] but who are voices and shadows that enter life. This haunted meaning wanders in and out of the poems. And it is a proposal of the wildness of meaning—a lost and found, a going and coming. It is harsh and beautiful—and, as Jack would say, "scary." It takes the question—who is speaking in a poem?—and changes it into a question of where he is speaking—from what place—in what order—in what composition—a shadowy participant in a folding with something outside himself. I may attach this to traditional motifs and to common experience—the sense of a "cosmic crypt," [Oswald] Spengler's dread, gnostic dualism, and so forth, but Jack's work does not stop in fear. It summons. It brings again into the present a beginning of a man and a world.*

The largest, most difficult proposal of this work is then to be found in the stake of Jack's poetics. The outside as it becomes technical to our experience re-poses a tense discourse, which interrogates the humanism and anthropomorphism of what is usually thought to be the poem's expression. The guide here is not the poet of a limited biographical occasion because he is guided toward the disclosure of a tied and retied heart, a manhood entangled with the world. This disclosure must not be reduced to psyche, however much we find it in a time of one man or in the disfigurations of our own time. It is more likely that the limited, psychic man, pushed in this direction, will find another, still unfigured manhood. For this reason, Jack would remove himself, as that which is expressed, from his language in order to reopen the worldliness of language. An old story comes to mind that once when Pythagoras was asked what Chronos is, he answered that it is the psyche of the universe. His answer implies a differently posed intelligence. As for the disclosure of the retied heart, that veiled thing that is so mixed with thought, I am reminded of Pound's lovely Latin citation in Canto XC: *the human soul is not love, but from it love proceeds, and therefore, the soul does not delight in itself, but in the love which proceeds from it.*[20] I know these are difficult elements that bring us into a love composed within a commotion of belief and disbelief, but I am after the public love in these poems and the magic of disturbance Jack used among his friends, as if nothing could rest, not even friendship. The love tends to manifest itself as a folding and unfolding of a real which composes out of North Beach and Berkeley and then leads to an outward of contents which are unspoken, unthought and unknown, like the possible diamond in *Book of Magazine Verse.*[21] Why there is this flowing kind of genesis that one either dams up, forgets and gives up to a dead discourse or participates in, is difficult to put into words because it is process and names pop out of it and are never up to date. It may be recognized as elemental. The genesis

* Here, I am informed by Henry Corbin's discussion of the stranger and the guide in *Avicenna and the Visionary Recital* (16 ff.).

changes the lyric question, who is speaking, into a double voice. This double voice, as it accounts for the "dictation" opens into speech and begins a redefinition of the heart. I put it back, so to speak, in an ancient sense into the thought that it is participant in intelligence. By way of the poetics, the constant elemental aspect of the poetic thought, we "recommence the perception."[22] As perceptions are veils of the heart, at the edge of them there folds an other than oneself. We reach, especially in Jack's work, the poem's real business, an "exhibition of world" (Heidegger).[23] I have, I think, said enough to foreground this extravagant outside, its presence and absence, the edge of its necessity. To be without a discourse, or rather to be within "a disappearance of Discourse" (Foucault, *Order* 307), as this essay argues, is something like being in a space ship. The outside invades and doubles over us.

A poetry that composes that meeting is tied to the event in the language. One is, to Jack's sporting language, batting or pitching or catching one's life. This is the terrible meaning of

> God is a big white baseball that has nothing to do but go in a
>   curve or a straight line, I studied geometry in highschool
>   and know that this is true.
> Given these facts the pitcher, the batter, and the catcher all look
>   pretty silly. (258)

To live in a discourse, to use a discourse, which does not hold on to this composition is, as Jack says in *Language*, to "have the ground cut from under us."[24] In such circumstances the language of the real appears to belong to an imposed order rather than to a disclosed order that is performed in public speech. Just here, poetry may become a necessary function of the real, not something added to it. It can best handle thought that is a disclosure. In his last years, Jack talked about "the fix." He meant by that both a political and an economic fix that stops us. He also meant the language of it—a fix of the language that is not true to its own structure and that tends to stop the real in something one can only refer to. This brings forward in Jack's work both an explanation and a performance of all that poetry talking about itself, which has haunted contemporary poetry and annoyed a lot of readers. It does confuse when it is only a young man's desire to be a poet that is being expressed or an older one's failure to get through. In Jack's work, it is a renewal of language and an interrogation of it in terms of our inward and outward life—dangerous because the manhood in the language comes close to a disappearance. I think of Mallarmé's "master" who disappears from the "ceremony of his book" (Foucault).[25]

Jack's oppositions and contrariness look destructive, even despairing, but they tend to bring forward a language that holds. We may read this as an aspect of

his sure-footed Americanness—a Puritanism, a Calvinism at the heart of his ex-
perience. And certainly, his life-long interest in Hawthorne comes to mind. Such
a reading could be useful, but it would, I think, lead to a misreading. Here, it
is the holding power and what I have called the commotion of his work that I
wish to describe. His last work, *Book of Magazine Verse,* is an example of this. The
idea behind the title is an old one with Jack and it is meant to challenge the
public place of poetry. The poems were written in order to prove that the mag-
azines for which he wrote them would not publish them. It is a set-up, of course,
but that does not spoil the point he is making. Some of them are for magazines
which cannot be expected to publish poetry, though Jack's point is that poetry
belongs to the real of them, whether that real is of sports, jazz, or politics. The
only poems he actually submitted were for the *Nation* and they were predictably
rejected. Jack commented that it would have spoiled everything if they'd been
accepted. He seemed to want the bitter laughter I heard when the space where
his poetry belonged turned out not to be there. The *Book of Magazine Verse* is an
unfair interrogation of the public place of poetry. The poems of it combine an
anger and an affirmation that unravels the real the magazines talk about:

> I can't stand to see them shimmering in the impossible music of
>   the Star Spangled Banner. No
> One accepts this system better than poets. Their hurts healed
>   for a few dollars.
> Hunt
> The right animals. I can't. The poetry
> Of the absurd comes through San Francisco television. Directly
>   connected with moon-rockets.
> If this is dictation, it is driving
> Me wild. (265)

The poem is dedicated to a young poet, Huntz, and in the poem, his name is
changed into the act and event of the "Hunt" as a directive. The hunt for the
right animals takes place in an absurd of the shimmering astronauts landing on
the moon. The rage at the center of the poem is caught in this lifting of the Star
Spangled Banner into space, a shimmering there as false as it is here. It is not,
so to speak, a real landing on the moon, a movement beyond the walls, but an
extension of the same discourse and its resulting social form. The landing on
the moon would perhaps be real if it were not an extension into space of the
same conditions. We have landed ourselves on the moon. As the work moves
in those last poems from the imagination of a city on a "baseball diamond
high / In the Runcible Mountain wilderness" (*Collected Books* 259) toward a de-
parture, "Things desert him" (*Collected Books* 265), the shimmer is not true. The

shimmering image of the astronauts suggests a beauty one would like to hold just there, but the words, "I can't stand to see them" (*Collected Books* 265), turn that beauty back to what it covers. In a stunning refusal, Jack reverses language into experience, where it must begin again. The moon in the poem disappears or is returned to what we will make of it. And the wildness of the poem is a loosened meaning. If one follows the contents of the serial narrative in this book and looks back on the field of its composition, the city on a diamond stands there on a Lewis Carroll mountain—a nonsense fundamental to the sense. This duplicity or commotion is remarkable in his thought and it was both terrible and joyous in his life, as a long list of friends, poets, and enemies may testify. He was so alive in the commotion he made around him. The condition of that beginning again in language and meaning is between our manhood, the anthropology of our thought, and everything outside its orders. It is, at times, almost a *divestment* of the memory of words. Undressed words. Jack shares the profound issue of this divestment in modern poetics, in its lack of wisdom and in its thought and feeling at the edge of a disclosure, with Mallarmé and Artaud.

In the movement of the whole of Jack's work toward the imagination of that city, which remains where he left it, only a possibility, there is also an *investment* of words. An installation.[26] This is the "spiritual discipline" he says a poem must be—out of the dictation. For this Jack used an Orphic methodology, as if the cosmos or love had fallen into hell. The experience is tropic—in the turn, hell is discovered and the true and the false begin to play. And, unfortunately, as Jack says, the dictation will be true and false,[27] because as a proposition of an ultimate duplicity in the real itself, the dictation will be wild and playful, a disappearance and an appearance, an invisibility and a visibility exchanging their powers in the heart. The looking into something as it composes in the poem, especially as it is of our own time, is to see what is on the other side, but not separate from this side or its terror. One can't see without meaning and this is the momentary interruption of the "I can't" in the poem for Huntz. As these last poems move to an open end,

> The poem begins to mirror itself.
> The identity of the poet gets more obvious. (265)

The poems reflect this reversal of language into experience. This is a costly recovery of an "operative language" (Merleau-Ponty's phrase),[28]

> which possesses meaning less than it is possessed by it, does not speak of it, but speaks it, or speaks *according to it*, or lets it speak and be spoken within us, breaks through our present. (Lingis liii)

This language is then "'open upon.'"[29] In the last poems, the "identity of the poet" returns almost nakedly, driven by the wildness, just at the point where the poet is to disappear from his work. This insistence of the dictation that an outside, an other than ourselves, speaks to us notices first a disappearance or emptying out of a manhood from his language, and then watchfully approaches "a field" including the other and a "topography" that is a folding and unfolding of a real that contains us.* Such language may disclose a new manhood and a new visibility along with another courage.

The poet is in the field of his work. He becomes a voice sounded in series that is also another voice, a doubling in the heart of an intelligence. Jack's voice remained to the end outside the paradise or city of its concern because such a city is outside our time or at the edge of it. As his language is open upon an outside, whose meaning disturbs and changes, his poetry becomes a profound interrogation, an operation of language, because it is a meeting.

> You flicker,
> If I move my finger through a candleflame, I know that there
>   is nothing there. But if I hold my finger there a few minutes
>   longer,
> It blisters.
> This is an act of will and the flame is not really there for the
>   candle, I
> Am writing my own will.
> Or does the flame cast shadows?
>   At Hiroshima, I hear, the shadows of the victims were as if
>   photographed into concrete building blocks.
> Or does it flicker? Or are we both candles and fingers?
> Or do they both point us to the grapheme on the concrete
>   wall—
> The space between it
> Where the shadow and the flame are one? (241)

Morphemics, Phonemics, Graphemics, as his book Language follows them through, will be "words" and "loves" in a composing real.

This is an extraordinary poetry for us to take on. It was, of course, for the most part not taken on at all, though it opened language again and again to the young who drifted across the country to meet Jack at his table in the bar. San Francisco became a loved habit of friends, bars, streets, the Broadway Tunnel, and Aquatic Park. His hours were pretty much set. If it became too quiet, Jack

---

* See Merleau-Ponty's sense of visibility as it is discussed by Lingis (xlvi–l).

would disturb it and "make things happen." San Francisco is an odd place. With all the beauty and comfort of its landscape, it is the end of the land. It seems to be at the edge of something, a gated place, an end which opens again. And so one finds it in Jack's poems where the imagery of the sea carries an openness, strangeness and endlessness. This edge becomes a literal quality of his work.

It is this edginess which leads me to speak of Jack's poetic argument. It involves the place and context of poetry in a composition of the real, which I have already touched upon and now wish to tie down. This argumentativeness about poetics, as it is widely reflected in contemporary poetry, has been dismissed by the criticism as the weakness of poetry talking about itself. The helplessness of poetry mirroring itself. On the contrary, it is indicative of a new consciousness of the power and violence of language, and in Jack's work, it becomes an insistent argument for the performance of the real by way of poetry. I am reminded of Vico's far away argument that all thought and experience begin in poetry and of Heidegger's that we end there too.[30] I do not wish to be long-winded, slap-dash, or pretentious here at the end of a distinguished work, but it is in this issue of the context of poetry that I find a way to tell you the cost of what Jack tried to do.

Wherever I go I hear the question—what killed Jack Spicer? Some offer the comfortable explanation that it was booze. But most who knew him well say poetry. This is the hidden issue of what I wish to say. It's interesting that the question always takes the same form, as in a detective story, except they ask what rather than who. Jack collapsed in an elevator. Two days later I found him in a hospital. No one had been notified. His body had given way and his speech become a garble—just the other side of what he meant to say. Listening to him, I thought of Artaud's special language, another language that seems to begin again.[31] And I thought of the "Martian" Jack sometimes spoke with his friends—full of laughter, catching us in what he was doing. One day I leaned over his bed and asked him to repeat the words or phrases he wanted to say because I would, I said, figure the pattern of the nonsense. The garble of his speech was the shadow of his sense and equally real. With extreme physical effort, he somehow retied his head and his speech to speak clearly. What he said, I've relegated to the end of this essay where I think it will be understood— just as I have had so much trouble understanding it. In between what I have already written and his last words, I wish to take on the context of the poetry. This is my way of explaining what he meant when he said language is "the furniture in the room"[32] through which the world speaks. He was not in the final poetics speaking only of himself. The "disordered devotion towards the real" of the poem with which I opened is no naive realism, and what it leads to requires come meditation. Here, I return to the ignorance I spoke of. Jack did not, it seems, know how far he had to go. In that emptying out in order to free the language, which is part of his care, he found a discipline which suggests that we are free to think again.

🖎

The Collected Books of Jack Spicer draws together all the work in books of the years 1957–1965. My purpose in following this division between an earlier and a later poetry, which originates in Jack's own sense of his work, is to foreground the special value the poet gave to composition by book. In this, I am trying to account for the long run of twenty years of conversation with him on poetry—"there's no such thing as a single poem"—"a book isn't a collection of poems." The division emphasizes the long form of the poems and the movement of his thought which led to this discovery of a new narrative. Further, the collection presents what Jack thought of as his poetic task—complete. To be sure, there are marvelous letters, four lectures, and a few separate poems from the same years. Some of these will be quoted here, but most of them are set apart for another occasion. The early work also is set apart, the poems, letters, and plays of 1946–1956, following the instruction given me by letter in *Admonitions* (1957). The point is to keep intact the separation he made between his early poems and the poetry he wanted. I am guided by his reasons and by the work of another order printed here. His reasons are operative in the worlds of this poetry and in its voices. I am taking the occasion of Jack's book to speak of the battle for the real of poetry in which all important contemporary poetry in America is engaged. It began with Pound and continues. For me, it moves West and becomes an imagination in the fateful meeting of three men—Jack Spicer, Robert Duncan, and myself in 1946. That imagination is complex and the poetics of it is made out of the dissonant companionship in poetry. Jack's division of his work is precise to the difference he saw and earned in his own work between a peripheral and a directive poetics. One hears the vulgarization roundabout that poetry and life are the same thing. They are not, of course, but such a misreading may be taken from either Jack or Olson. Both insist upon the closeness and necessity of a poetic meaning. Jack in particular is clear on the part language plays in the composition of what we call real. Thus, the poetics becomes directive to perception and stance, a way rather than a fictive transcendence. From 1957, following the narrative of *After Lorca*, Jack tended to write in books. The propositions of his practice move us toward long and open forms. I call this openness worldly because it measures the I of the poetry and includes the poet in a world.

This is the public Jack Spicer. The best preface is his own *After Lorca*, which opens the book and begins the new poetry—a preparation beyond, as he said, the expression of his hatreds and desires. Where this poetry leads is one of my questions. The pieces of an answer draw me into a discussion of the oppositions and contraries, which are reflected in the poetry. I will be arguing that oppositions and polarities are basic to intelligence and that they reopen the entire range of the aesthetic as perception relating directly to the formation of public, political, and social life. A heavy hand to lay on poetry, that delicate, pretty thing that has cost some poets their lives and sanity. The public, the political, the social are all forms of thought and experience, and according to Jack's argument, these forms must begin again because we are inside the death of these forms, the "fix" of them. Here, the operative, performing nature of poetic language comes into play. Jack's poetry takes on the experience, so exact to our present condition, that where we are is equally an experience of not being there at all—of disappearing and destroyed men—of fallen hierarchies and broken honesties, like towers, that once were governments. The men themselves, when one could see them in their acts, were horizons. Their acts remain in language where we join them. When the language breaks up into disbelief, their images disappear and we are, as now, invisible to one another. Left alone inside our needs and desires. We may all be the same there, but it is a levelling and a disappearance into an invisibility called necessity. The curious thing about language is that it holds and makes visible. It performs one's manhood. But it is so much older than oneself, so much a speaking beyond and outside oneself, that a man's entrance to it becomes at once new and old, spoken and speaking, a self and some other. The hierarchies of thought were found in combat and became quietnesses. They proposed, whatever our vocabulary for them, an interplay of earth, men, and world. "They sort of drifted up like clouds—what we're getting now is the rain—like fallout," a friend said. Disbelief and invisibility are as real to experience as belief and visibility. They are technical issues of our method of moving along. The increasing invisibility of where a man is brings forward every question of what is prior to him. This priorness is sometimes called god, as in Jack's work, or meaning, an assumed complete intelligence, as in philosophy. The extraordinary nature of language is that it attaches to the prior, to the before one, and to the after one. It is determinedly polar to one's presence in it. If our visibility falls out of language, the language comes back to talk by itself. For such extravagance, see Mallarmé's Un Coup de Dés and Jack's Language—"Sable arrested a fine comb" (227), a computer language, a language speaking by itself. Such language may seem obscure because it is double—that is, holds a duplicity—it is a language bound to the breadth and distance of what it perceives. On the one hand, a belief is met by a disbelief, on the other, a visibility, a piece of ourselves, by an invisibility. In the doubling, there is an unreason that is half the form of reason—its reason—and a non-sense in conjunction with sense. Among these interchangeable contents of experience, the sublime returns to a public place—the terror, the uncanny, the bestial and the beautiful—Jack's ghosts and the shimmering of his thought.

The duplicity. We have been taught to dislike any suggestion of a dualism, essential as it is to our experience of the inward and outward pieces of the real, of a man and a world, that it composes wherever we are—in fact, composes the visibility we have called manhood. We are busy studying the synthesis, the lie that belief has become. The "subjective aim" of most men is an escape from the thought of something so alive they can't stop it. The worldly models of our sciences read a marvelous duplicity in the world, but we are absent from it. Contemporary poetics has repeatedly moved toward field theory, the physics of energy and process, to find the real where manhood takes place or is contained. Some have done this by a system of analogies and wind up in an allegory of divine manhood, a resolution that makes a man the same as everything else. It was at least a religion or a binding. Others have said it is the stretch of our perception and wind up inside that from which we are separated. The duplicity is especially the business of poetry because it is a primary aspect of thought and poetry is primary thought before it is vision, fiction, or transcendence. Poetry is also perhaps at the end of thought or reason, where a finite manhood doubles back, reverses, and is invisible or silent, except for his part in language. The modern stance becomes increasingly poetic, but it is a poetic which is a disclosure, a ceremony, a performance, rather than an imposition.

I am here entering that combat for language which was Jack's. And I'm having a hell of a time with the description of the process which he performed. I feel my language thicken and become more abstract. I lean on the linguistic necessity of invisibility to give meaning to visibility or vice-versa, entangled in the oppositions which are natural in our words. Jack knew we were inside a performance of language. The issue here is *discourse.* A discourse is the language system in which one lives—the use of language each of us agrees to. During all the years I knew him, Jack liked to disturb this agreement. His repeated instruction to young poets that they should read "far-out stuff," the strangest they could find, comes to mind here. His purpose had affinities with Rimbaud's *dérè-glement* and it was a continuous interrogation. For us, outside the strangeness of poetry, discourse has been accepted as an act of language between ourselves, an agreement of logical structure that turns out to be our imposition of an order. This amounts to a closure of language, which brings it into our own limit, and ultimately that discourse will die as a man does. It does not entangle us with the world. The death at the center of such discourse is extraordinary and begins to let us see the extremity of our condition. This brings forward the combat for the "real" in contemporary poetry—Pound's "I have brought the great ball of crystal; / who can lift it?"—Olson's "my drum fell / where the dead are, who / will bring it up, my lute / who will bring it up"—Jack's "We shall clear the trees back, the lumber of our pasts and / futures back, because we are on a diamond" (259).[33] Where the *poiesis* reopens the real and follows its contents, the presuming discourse imposes form and closes it, leaving us at the mercy of our own limit. The already-formed discourse has disappeared and become a reversal of its order into a disorder and disbelief, though it does remain official, where it protects the worst social forms or what Jack called "the fix." Jack notices both the extremity and the necessity:

> the kind of thing which you have in modern poetry, the fact that most poets from say 19 to 27, that I know, who are good, in San Francisco, are really against education because they can't resist—that if they have all of these benches and chairs in the room—not to arrange them themselves, instead of letting them be arranged by whatever is the source of the poem.
>
> Creeley talks about poems following the dictation of language. It seems to me that's nonsense—language is part of the furniture in the room. Language isn't anything of itself—it's something which is in the mind of the host, the parasite that the poem is invading—five languages just make the room structure more difficult and also possibly, more usable. It certainly doesn't have anything to do with any mystique of English or anything else. Duncan's business of words and their shadows, and sounds and their shadows seems to me again, taking things which are in the room, rather than things which are coming into the room, and it seems to me essentially that you arrange—when you get a beautiful thing which uses the words and shadows of words, and the fact silly once meant blessed instead of silly as it now does—you ought to be distrustful—although at the same time, the thing which invades you from outside can use it. Now, the other kind of thing, other than Olson's "energy," which, I think, Olson looks on as a sort of—energy to him, it's something you plug in the wall—and it's really the machine which is the convertor of the electricity which makes another machine work, and so forth. And I don't agree with that either, but I'd go nearer to that. And then there's finally [Williams] who sees in objects, essentially, a kind of energy which radiates from them, the fact that this chair has a chairness, a nimbus around it, a kind of electrical thing, which gives energy enough so that it can be transformed almost directly, if the thing that chair in its chairness radiates—into poetry—and all these things I think are perfectly useful explanations of it. I prefer more the unknown. (Vancouver Lecture 1, *Caterpillar* 179; *House* 9–10)

The extremity of our condition and experience is apparent in the use of the word parasite and in the insistence upon the unknown, which is invisible and imageless. As it enters the poetic language, it is piecemeal, disturbing, strange and unsettled. The emphasis upon an invasion from outside is striking and exact to the experience of the world's absence, which suddenly, frighteningly, nonsensically, becomes a presence. I shall return to the darkness of this experience apace. The use of it takes us back to the *poiesis* which includes a direct, disclosed knowledge of a doubling.

In order to establish the context of this argument and fuss about language, it's useful to remember Charles Olson's long-standing effort alongside Jack's. "One wants therefore," he says, writing in 1964, "to enter this ring on a different footing: it isn't true, and has left the universe out, substituting for it a prune or wrinkled grape, the social" (*Collected Prose* 357). In this essay, his attack is on the dialectical and, not unlike Foucault, he watches the large movement of method in language, in order to say that the key to our social forms is in the use we make of language. He argues that "an immediate discharge of mental engagement in which the will and the mind are like aggressive motor actions" is the direct inheritance of Socratic, Platonic, and Aristotelian discourse.

> we don't even know what it does mean to change society comparably to how they did engage to do it, so much of our own discourse is in fact theirs. . . .

> There is a discourse. There is a grammar. There is a sentence you do have. It happens also to be a motive of things that you are not, but which you do . . . attend to. You are not free than otherwise to perceive.
>   This, then, would be the conversation.[34]

It may be argued that the push of contemporary poetics towards locus, ground, and particularity is a remaking of where we are. In this sense, the poem becomes an extraordinary field of forces which measure and contain the I of men and poets. From Pound's hierophanies and Williams's ground to Olson's cosmology and Spicer's narrative of the unknown, a remaking of the real is at stake. One needs only to notice how much of it is a common experience and also something regained, rather than an invention. The vocabulary to talk about it slips and slides. In the old discourse, the real as it is claimed for poetry becomes a pretentious word or it denotes an ideality without the field out of which it was drawn. This is the peripheral and utopian poetry I've already noted. It amounts to a thought which gives up the actual to needs, materiality, and immediacy of the skin without enjoinment. We are now in a curious downward journey of ideas, which brings every man into their forming. I am reminded of Octavio Paz's complaint in his essay on Duchamp that "Our only idea, in the proper sense of that term, is Criticism" (*Duchamp* 75). The danger is, he points out, that we will become "obsessed by sensation"—that we will be unable to join it to anything other than ourselves. Other phrases from that fine essay suggest the predicament: "Vision is not only what we see; it is a stance taken, an

idea, a geometry" (7)—"a beauty free at last from the notion of beauty" (10)—
and, drinking up a whole range of contemporary concern with our method in
language, he notes "the conception of language as a structure in movement"
(11). This last is challenge enough, if thought about, to the dead discourse. It
is also our experience as well as our conception. In the wreckage of our dis-
course, as Jack's work draws my attention to it here, I notice first how alive the
language is, how new and messaged. And in it are the presences and absences
with which our thought tries to deal. I notice the love-hate thematics of our
writing as it meets the public space. It is an absent America whose presence is
at stake.

The doubling is where the public space begins. Where our words become
uneasy as to meaning and designation, it is just there that a life in language be-
gins again. The uneasiest of all in this context is imagination, and I shall return
to it. I also notice that the word intellect is in as much trouble. I take seriously
the enraged intelligence of such phrases as "Fuck the verbal shit"—(when it
was thrown at that most public messenger, Allen Ginsberg). Its anger is an ex-
pression of the acceptance of an absent discourse—of being unbound and un-
narrated. Words which once contained a cosmology or at least implied a worldly
stance—god, soul, spirit, angel, ghost—now bring forward disbelief and have
for a long time. They belong to religious forms, which have become periph-
eral, or they are tolerated in the unreality of imagination. They are used with
embarrassment. There is a sloppiness around the public use of the words "soul"
and "spirit" which is evidence of their disappearance. These words are odd now
and it is perhaps only their oddness that charges them. They draw attention to
the angelology which once confronted anthropology as a world view. They are
words, like "world," which propose an essential dualism or polarity. That is,
their vitality is precise in the degree to which they point to an other than the
manhood. We need not return to them, and cannot in any sense that we now
understand, but they haunt us. And they are, so to speak, tossed up by our task
in language. They propose a binding and an entangling with the essential un-
known that is part of the life of the known. Since I mean nothing here that is
not common to experience, that is, open experience, I bring to mind Merleau-
Ponty's term, chiasma—a crossing, an "intertwining."[35] It is necessary, I know,
to stop over the known, which like one's body, closes form, but then I move
again to the edge of it. It is this entangling—out of poetics—that is the source
of public love.

The loss of the entangling—art's job—has become a broken structure in the
public realm. It is what Michel Foucault in his book The Order of Things calls the
"disappearance of Discourse" (307). I choose a passage near the end of his ar-
gument, which is both a dedication and a defiance:

To all those who still wish to talk about man, about his reign or his liberation, to all those who still ask themselves questions about what man is in his essence, to all those who wish to take him as their starting-point in their attempts to reach the truth, to all those who, on the other hand, refer all knowledge back to the truths of man himself, to all those who refuse to formalize without anthropologizing, who refuse to mythologize without demystifying, who refuse to think without immediately thinking that it is man who is thinking, to all these warped and twisted forms of reflection we can answer only with a philosophical laugh—which means, to a certain extent, a silent one. (342–43)

I think we can answer as well with the laughter of poetry.

Foucault's description of the "disappearance of Discourse" moves us from the density of one kind of language to the representational clarity and dichotomy of another, which he designates as neo-classical. The words of the latter sort fit exactly as we throw them onto a table or into a picture. The trouble is that poetry under such criticism or reading exists only by reference to that picture, that completion. This is the language with which literature is talked about, and it leaves the mass of it unread in its density. It is by way of the transparency of this reference that the poetic density and enactment, what I have called the performance in language, are lost. For a vast readership, poetry becomes a bore, a soft philosophy, a feeling. Just here, I remember Jack's often repeated phrase, "Nobody listens to poetry."[36] The present "dispersion of language," Foucault argues, is linked to the "disappearance of Discourse" (Order 307). Where the language exists only "in the form of natural discourse, the accumulation of truth, description of things, a body of exact knowledge, or an encyclopedic dictionary,"

> It exists, therefore, only in order to be transparent; it has lost that secret consistency which, in the sixteenth century, inspissated it into a word to be deciphered, and interwove it with all the things of the world. (Order 311)

Again a key to my having placed Jack's work in this broad context and inside the dilemma his poetry so brilliantly performs: from the time I first knew him, 1945, he was fascinated by Renaissance thought. Among the few books he owned, characteristic of the way he seemed to perch among us, mixed with paperback mystery stories, a Skeat, a volume or two on chess and bridge, was Cassirer's *The Renaissance Philosophy of Man*. His sense of language and his magical use of it move us back there. "A wonderful book," he said to me, when he brought it over and presented it as a real discovery: Petrarca, Valla, Ficino, Pico della Mirandola, Pomponazzi, Vives. I would have to add to this his special interest in John Dee. Perhaps from these, one could reconstruct the beginning of his contrary sense of language and its task. This is fundamental to Jack's sense of magic as form and entrance, as he taught it in the Magic Workshop, 1957.[37] Language is always tied to magic with its renaming, secret names and powers which translate in and out of language to become a blasphemy or something found or disclosed. This edge of language always enters the peculiar experience that the real is not what it seems and yet is there in the language.

Foucault's thought meets mine and aids me in this delineation of Jack's importance to poetic thought. With the disappearance of that discourse—(students at the universities, where poetry is guarded over, may smile that in their experience that discourse has not disappeared or rage that it is madly imposed upon them)—there is discovered a new figuration—a manhood that is entirely tied to its finitude. In ordinary thought, the presence of the outward begins to totter. One is, so to speak, within one's own skin. The nexus of inward and outward is now tied to the specific and the particular and we get a "motive of a new presence" and a "new relation . . . between words, things and their order" (Order 312). We are thrown into "an order that now belongs to things themselves and to their interior law" (313). Man is then governed by "labor, life, and language" (313), not god, soul, or angels, and these are all of them also an "exteriority," larger than any one man or many men, unmastered and unclosed. The finitude we are drawn to is "marked by the spatiality of the body," "the yawning of desire," "the time of language," yet these constitute "a finitude which is radically other" (315).[38]

> Far from leading back . . . towards a peak . . . of identity, far from indicating the moment of the Same at which the dispersion of the Other has not yet come into play, the original in man is that which articulates him from the very outset upon something other than himself. (Order 331)

In this, which is so clearly a part of Jack's sense of the Unknown, there is a terrible consequence for our understanding if the other is left out or reduced to a kind of embodiment. Among other consequences, there is a despair of language, if we are led to a "psychologism" of all knowledge or to a "sociologism" which defines the "real" as simply consequent to the experience of large numbers. This is not to say one turns from the socialism that discovers the constant growth of poverty and proposes its solutions, but rather that the "real" of need, however worldwide and covered up by Western fixed political forms, articulates only a first visibility. Witness the lonely voices of Jack's revolutionaries in The Holy Grail, imprisoned and singing of the absent Heimat. The imprisonment of needs is the antithesis of world. My purpose in drawing the polarity and experience of poetry forward is to oppose a giving up to that terrible simplicity.

Foucault has noticed outside the dead discourse, the discovery of a double manhood:

Man and the unthought are, at the archaeological level, contemporaries. Man has not been able to describe himself as a configuration in the *episteme* without thought at the same time discovering, both in itself and outside itself, at its borders yet also in its very warp and woof, an element of darkness, an apparently inert density in which it is embedded, an unthought which it contains entirely, yet in which it is also caught. The unthought (whatever name we give it) is not lodged in man like a shrivelled-up nature or a stratified history; it is, in relation to man, the Other: the Other that is not only a brother but a twin, born, not of man, nor in man, but beside him and at the same time, in an identical newness, in an unavoidable duality. (*Order* 326)

To this duality, duplicity, polarity, we again direct our attention. It has always been the issue of poetry involved in the "exhibition of a world" (Heidegger's phrase).[39] Its newness is perhaps due to a different consciousness of our mortality and finitude. That I think of poetry as an interrogation, rooted in the experience that any true question must be, particularly as I find such care and unease in Jack's work, leads me to make a claim for poetry as the deepest involvement in life. Its positioning as a thought tied to a manhood gives it special responsibility in the long-run of the thought we enter by habit and training. Foucault traces this long-run. "Where," he says,

at the end of the eighteenth century, it was a matter of fixing the frontiers of knowledge, it will now be one of seeking to destroy syntax, to shatter tyrannical modes of speech. . . . God is perhaps not so much a region beyond knowledge as something prior to the sentences we speak; and if Western man is inseparable from him, it is not because of some invisible propensity to go beyond the frontiers of experience, but because his language ceaselessly foments him in the shadow of his laws. (*Order* 298)

I have already cited Jack's image of God as a big white baseball, somehow other than, but entering the game our lives are. I notice the laughter at the edge of the image, but also its harshness. The cutting thought of it. At the dead-end, at the in-ourselves, the words collect strangely. To this unease, Foucault has brought the question I have wished to ask: *who is speaking?*[40] He cites the overwhelming experience of Mallarmé, who, in the effort of the question, "was constantly effacing himself from his own language, to the point of not wishing to figure in it except as an executant in a pure ceremony of the Book in which the discourse would compose itself" (*Order* 306). Here, I am reminded first of Mallarmé's "The sky is dead" ("L'Azur," *Selected Poetry and Prose* 15) and then of another passage:

the "'terrible fight with that old and perverse plumage—brought down, fortu-
nately, God! But as the struggle took place on his bony wing, which, in a death-
agony more vigorous than I would have expected of him, transported me into
the shadows, I fell, victorious—abandonedly and infinite . . . '" (Michaud 47).
"Nothingness," he found, "was not an end but a point of departure" (Michaud 53; original
emphasis).[41] It is this profound sense of departure I wish to call attention to. It
informs the whole of Jack's work. It is fundamental to our thought and experi-
ence and Jack's effort is a performance and interrogation of it. By it, we head di-
rectly into the ghosts and deaths of his work. Foucault has called this a freed
sense of origin and a "ceaseless rending open" (Order 334).

It comes as an extremity of experience that the image of man himself has
become invisible. As public manhood goes, one either covers one's eyes or dis-
believes. I'm told that there is too much grief here for thought to handle. But
I have already spoken of a new and different courage, which I believe Jack's
work reflects. If a truer discourse, re-forming in our hearts, does not so sim-
ply belong to our poet or to the man in the street, perhaps it composes another
to which he is tied:

> . . . rejecting not only psychologism and historicism, but all concrete forms of the
> anthropological prejudice, we attempt to question afresh the limits of thought. . . .
> Perhaps we should see the first attempt at this uprooting of Anthropology . . . in
> the Nietzschean experience: by means of a philological critique, by means of a
> certain form of biologism, Nietzsche rediscovered the point at which man and
> God belong to one another, at which the death of the second is synonymous with
> the disappearance of the first, and at which the promise of the superman signifies
> first and foremost the imminence of the death of man. . . . It is no longer possi-
> ble to think in our day other than in the void left by man's disappearance. For this
> void does not create a deficiency; it does not constitute a lacuna that must be filled.
> It is nothing more, and nothing less, than the unfolding of a space in which it is
> once more possible to think. (Foucault, Order 342)

In this effort to follow the pattern of Jack's concern and to throw it out there,
so to speak, among the thinkers and writers of our time, as Jack ultimately
wanted it in his last years, after the San Francisco scene no longer nourished
his work, the passage above helps me articulate the qualities of independence,
separateness and renewed thought, which belong to this work. It also brings
me to think over the importance of Nietzsche to his thoughtfulness. Jack pored
over Nietzsche during his first years in Berkeley and referred to him often in
conversation. He was amused by it and drawn to it, though it was not his way
to become theoretical. There he found the fundamental description of the lyric
voice, which had defined the extent of the poem's concern, and his dissatis-

faction with it, and he also found the extreme question, who or what is speaking? I think it was Yeats's interest that first drew him to Nietzsche. Certainly the duplicity of *A Vision* holds a special place in his poetic learning. Or it was part of that natural erudition which Jack used without wearing it like too much jewelry. Or there was something in Nietzsche that met his recognitions—that the apocalyptic in modern thought has already happened. In this sense, we have been spoken and begin to speak again. The insistence of Jack's work that the closed "real" of our thought is invaded draws all my attention. Another passage from Foucault lets us see the extremity, the extraordinary, the strangeness and ghostliness of it:

> . . . it becomes apparent, then, that the death of God and the last man are engaged in a contest with more than one round: is it not the last man who announces that he has killed God, thus situating his language, his thought, his laughter in the space of that already dead God, yet positing himself also as he who has killed God and whose existence includes the freedom and the decision of that murder? . . . [I]t is in the death of God that he speaks, thinks, and exists. (*Order* 385)

This is most particularly difficult when, as Foucault has been at pains to show, it is also the death of himself, where he stops. This is an edge of thought and it is perilous[42]—just where Jack worked. How odd! No American poet, as a friend said, was more at home with America—its laughter, its baseball, its ordinariness, its quick, turning language. If we follow the whole of Jack's narrative through, we are led to the last poem he wrote at the end of *Book of Magazine Verse*. Addressed to Allen Ginsberg, it ends in the image of a combining heart followed by a line of multiple meanings—"People are starving" (267). The North Beach story of the meeting behind the poem is this: Allen arrived at Jack's table in Gino & Carlo's Bar and said he'd come to save Jack's soul. Jack replied that he'd better watch it or he'd become a cult leader rather than a poet. This is a very limited view of Allen, doubtless. But the key to it is given in the poem— "One hundred thousand university / students marching with you. Toward / A necessity which is not love but is a name" (267). The final aspect of Jack's work is in this—that the reader participates in the meaning of the poem—that the poet is only one voice alongside another—that the poetic reopens words into an action. As readers we may move back into the work to find the structure of paradise in *Heads of the Town up to the Aether*, the noise of the god-language in *The Holy Grail* with some sense of a reopened language. It is curious that the contents of the word god, whatever they were, come alive in an unmediated way— the place and power of evil, the shit of the world, the manliness perched in it, and finally the universe as an aspect of that which is so other than oneself, unknown and entering the heart.

At the center of a poetry of this order, there is a *perilous act*, which is of the nature of thought itself.* The man in the poem becomes an incident in his own narrative—an image within the action. Poetry, as a beginner's thought, is elemental to this by modes of image. Poetry is also at the end of thought as description and logical structure, where it proposes a dynamism of thought and experience, which I can only place in the largest terms as a commotion between the visible and the invisible. I have looked everywhere for a description of this dynamism and found little outside the philosophers I've used here and the texts of a few poets. Yet, I don't think I'm wrong in saying that our time has brought many into the necessary watchfulness. An affirmation of what I wish to say is going on comes oddly, against the grain, out of the 18th century with Vico. It is in Vico that I found an argument for the relation of poetry to "the qualitative and dynamic structure of the primordial moment," to which we inevitably return (Caponigri 164). It is Vico who points to the "unemployment of aesthetics" and to language as a focus of inner and outer experience. One scholar of his thought summarizes it for us neatly. Vico attaches a dialectic or dynamic of language to the indefinite and indeterminate, which shadow our sense of the definite and determinate. The "finite spirit" becomes "only as it generates concrete and specified forms of presence" (Caponigri 151).

> This open or indeterminate presence, the indefinite nature of man, in Vico's words, is not to be thought of as in any way actual or pre-existent with reference to the concrete process of the life of finite spirit; it is wholly immanent to that concrete process and, in itself, without form. Under this aspect, it bears the character of absence rather than of presence, but absence which is pregnant with presence. . . . Thought is the active generation of presence; it is speech. (Caponigri 150–51)

Vico bases an entire theory of poetry and myth upon this, and in so doing, brings us back into the density and commotion of our words. Words are the curious foundation of all nameless, active possibilities—friendship, love, and public space. It was Vico's proposition to recover logos by considering it fable or myth and he defined this logos as "'true narrative'" (Caponigri 178).[43] This issue is basic to contemporary poetics and within our troubled sense of what a narration is, Jack's serial form is a major contribution. At the edge of the map.

As a poetry of this order had to face the displacement of poetry and imagination from the "real" in everyday thought, the peril of it reties the heart and the mind and this begins in strangeness and a near madness. I do not mean to

---

* Foucault: "thought, at the level of its existence, in its very dawning, is in itself an action—a perilous act" (*Order* 328).

say that Jack was mad, one could depend on his intellectual reasonableness to the end, but he did know a dynamism of thought and feeling that is at the edge. It is worth reminding ourselves of the job every poet faces to replace imagination in public thought where it means the invented, the made-up, the idealized, the untrue. "You just made that up!" Perhaps this context can best be summarized by a passage from a leading critic, so that by contrast the crisis in Jack's work and its closeness to life may sit there to challenge us. I take this passage from a good book on Jack's favorite master, Yeats. (Jack repeatedly said during his last year that nobody read Yeats right.)

> Think of modern aesthetics, with politics half in mind. The single article of faith which goes undisputed in the Babel of modern criticism is the primacy of the creative imagination. It bloweth where it listeth, indisputable and imperious, it gives no quarter. In extreme versions, it concedes no rights to nature, history, other people, the world of natural forms is grist to its mill. It is strange that we have accepted such an authoritarian notion in aesthetics while professing to be scandalized by its equivalent in politics. The poet is free to deal with nature as he wishes, whatever form the imposition takes. The point is not answered by saying that a political act has immediate consequences in the lives of ordinary people, while an aesthetic act is merely virtual, and affects nobody. What is in question is an attitude to life, whatever we wish to say further about the relation between attitude and act. The freedom conceded to the poet's imagination is fundamental in European Romanticism, represented accurately enough by Coleridge. The modern understanding of imagination assumes that order is imposed upon experience by those exceptional men, the few, capable of doing so: that it is natural for such men to do so, as an act issues from prior capacity. It would be possible, I suppose, to devise an aesthetic which would consort with a democratic politics, but no such aesthetic has flourished in modern literature. If you start with the imagination, you propose an élite of exceptional men; their special quality is power of vision. The relation between this élite and the masses is bound to be a critical relation, and it is likely to proceed by authority. (Donoghue 121–22)

I won't stop to express my amazement. I recognize it as the common teaching and it is reflected in some contemporary poetics. It has been true since Coleridge, rather than because of him. It is not true to the imaginative structures of those poets, Pound, Yeats and Lawrence, whose social authoritarianism does trouble us. For criticism, it is a kind of counter to that discourse which made a peripherality of the poetic act. A let's-make-up-for-it routine. The notion goes something like this. The poetic can only be a persuasive dressing-up of a system or a grid of meanings. It is then only a disguised discourse. The poetic, where it breaks out of the ordinary discourse and is either too elemental or too visionary, will have a life of its own and be true to itself. This transcendentalism has not been built out of a "coexistence of man and world." The aesthetic, which has everything to do with the consciousness of perception, then becomes an untied beauty. We're up there! On the contrary, Coleridge in "On Poesy or Art" is clear that the poem is a "proceeding" (262). And, to name only one other from the "guilty" period, Keats's negative capability is suggestive of a discipline which contradicts such imposition.

The view that Coleridge sits behind this mess must be reconsidered and we can better do it now with Owen Barfield's brilliant book, *What Coleridge Thought*, in hand. He makes it clear that Coleridge argued two forces which "took the place of the exclusively physical base presumed by the educated opinion of his day, and of our own, to lie at the foundation of the world." These "'contrary forces' . . . are 'real' and not mere logical opposites. . . . They are "'two conflicting principles of the FREE LIFE and the CONFINING FORM'" (30). They can be "grounded neither in a thing nor in an *abstraction*" (31).

Every power in nature and in spirit must evolve an opposite

> as the sole means and condition of its manifestation: and all opposition is a tendency to re-union. This is the universal law of polarity or essential dualism promulgated by Heraclitus, 2000 years afterwards re-published and made the foundation of both logic, of physics, and of meta-physics by Giordano Bruno. (Coleridge's *The Friend*, quoted in Barfield 31)

To which I add the passage from "On Poesy or Art":

> Remember that there is a difference between form as proceeding, and shape as superinduced;—the latter is either the death or the imprisonment of the thing;—the former is its self-witnessing and self-effected sphere of agency. (Coleridge 262)

Coleridge's tracing backward is not unlike the contemporary poetic effort. Blake in his practice can take us further than Coleridge, but my point is nearly made. Coleridge's argument then in a few phrases: "[p]olarity is dynamic, not abstract"—"'a living and generative interpenetration'"—"[w]here logical opposites are contradictory, polar opposites are generative of each other"—"the apprehension of polarity is itself the *basic act of imagination*" (Barfield 36)—it is not a matter of "a picture of bodies already formed" (Barfield 43). Out of this polar structure comes Coleridge's argument for the imagination. The dynamic or process of it contrasts sharply with the authoritarian imagination credited to him. In fact, that authoritarian imagination is a fabrication of a discourse that doesn't believe a word poetry has spoken. There is, however, a true authority in the handling of the process and the performance of the intelligence of it in public space. One finds Coleridge extending the dynamic to argue the conditional aspect of nature and spirit, that they are antitheses and so tied in thought and experience. In such a dynamic, neither nature nor spirit is consumed in one's needs, but they do act into another manhood or courage. This "'lost Dynameis'" (Barfield 11) turns, as Barfield notices, toward modern field theory and a physics of energy (138). The poetic practice in these terms opposes the view that the life one leads is "a mere *ens rationis* or 'creature of discourse'" (Barfield 41). It is more likely that Jack came upon this "flowing boundary"[44] in Poe rather than in Coleridge, but the state of American reading of Poe is so bad, except for the breakthroughs of William Carlos Williams and Richard Wilbur, that it is easier to establish the point in Coleridge, where Poe found it.

With this discussion of the displacement and replacement of poetry in the public space, I have meant to draw attention to the political aspect of Jack's work and to its cost.

> In the modern age, literature is that which compensates for (and not that which confirms) the signifying function of language. Through literature, the being of language shines once more on the frontiers of Western culture—and at its center— for it is what has been most foreign to that culture since the sixteenth century; but it has also, since this same century, been at the center of what western culture has overlain. This is why literature is appearing more and more as that which must be thought. (Foucault, *Order* 44)

As Jack worked to build the poetic, he found no rest. Nothing held firm. The flowing life of that work drank him up and left us with the text to face. This, I think, is the key to our care. The work without the author. We cannot turn back to the author, but to his work which is full of care and nearly overwhelmed.

> At least we both know how shitty the world is. (Spicer, *Collected Books* 267)

I find his work rends something open. A coexistence begins again. This is the work of a "new morphology," a new consciousness of form, our own included. It is close to the chiasma, the entwining, I have already borrowed from Merleau-Ponty, which, he says, "must subtilize the sense of polarity," "of western dualism" and "of revolutionary contraries." This is part of his view that the "sense of bipolarity" does not return us to anthropomorphism, which has clothed the real. And I suppose it is only the clothing that is worn out. This accounts for his "anti-psychologism," which translates the "coexistence of man and world" into only a "psychic reality." "And the Jungians and the Freudians and the Social Reformers all / leave satisfied. Knowing how the trick was played" (Spicer, *Collected Books* 173). Nothing, Merleau-Ponty's friend and editor points out, will "deliver us from the necessity of thinking the world as if it had to be thought for the first time" (Lefort xviii). As I read Jack, the presence and absence of this coexistence haunt my thought. His care is stunning and stands against the aesthetics of only-feeling or ideality. Here, Merleau-Ponty's suggestion of a wild-*logos* is useful (Lingis liii). I have already called attention to the wildness in Jack. This wildness is "not opacity, but dimensionality" (Lingis xlix). We study the operative in language which "open[s] upon the things" (Lingis liii). The imaginary in this philosopher's admonition and recovery of its place is "not simply the production of mental images, but the 'baroque' proliferation of generating axes for visibility in the duplicity of the real" (Lingis liii; original emphasis).

> Perception is not first a perception of *things*, but a perception of *elements* (water, air . . .) of *rays of the world*, of things which are dimensions, which are worlds, I slip on these "elements" and here I am in the *world*, I slip from the "subjective" to Being. (Merleau-Ponty, *Visible* 218; original emphasis)

Alongside this realism of the world and its presence, I place a passage from another of Jack's key authors, Rilke:

> *We are the bees of the invisible. Nous butinons éperdument le miel du visible, pour l'accumuler dans la grande ruche d'or de l'Invisible* . . . at the work of these continual conversions of the beloved visible and tangible into the invisible vibrations and excitation of our own nature, which introduces new vibration-frequencies into the vibration-spheres of the universe. (Since different elements in the cosmos are only different vibration-exponents, we prepare for ourselves in this way not only intensities of a spiritual nature but also, who knows, new bodies, metals, nebulae and constellations.) (*Letters*, vol. 2: 374; original emphasis)

Which returns us to the invisible interchange of *After Lorca*. This book is, as I have said, the preface to the whole of the final work. The details of it propose a special relationship with Garcia Lorca and then move without warning beyond the strictly relational. Lorca's introduction, posted from his grave outside Granada, tells the reader there is a mix here, translations which are not translations, poems which are not Lorca's, dependent upon a sense of the game. The challenge may be accepted to search through Lorca to know what is Lorca's, what is Jack's, what is translated or changed, which is which. I've done this and wind up in the joining. The book proposes, instead, the lack of separation, that one poet is the other. These poems and this poet continue the recognitions of the other poet and his poems. The game may be reopened and played by the reader. I notice the final letter from Jack to Lorca:

> It was a game, I shout to myself. A game. There are no angels, ghosts, or even shadows. It was a game made out of summer and freedom and a need for a po-

etry that would be more than the expression of my hatreds and desires. It was a game like Yeats' spooks or Blake's sexless seraphim. (*Collected Books* 51)

The game had been the original idea of the book—translations to learn by and a trick of composition which would leave one wondering. But it is clear that Jack found another order in the book, as though the game were life itself. It is a profound turn of Jack's thought that the real proposed by the poems is always possibly unreal. In *After Lorca*, there is a single poet composed simultaneously of the live Jack and the dead Lorca. They stream into one another.

This streaming, in its particularity, is the subject of his book. What I have called the "flowing boundary." The active, vital order of the poems is directive to those first terms which designate the elemental, invisible flowing of what men are. And one measure of its importance lies in the fact that neither bios nor spirit is turned over to sentimentalities or dogmas. These first terms are concomitants of that necessary loneliness Jack points to late in the narrative of *After Lorca*. It is not simply his loneliness. In this sense the book is not about life and death; it is a narrative of events in which lives appear and disappear. And the reader's stake in this is known only in re-enactment. If it is a game, that is because games like chess and baseball always propose a seeing of the terms. The rules are invisible and the images on the board or diamond move in a gradually tightening sequence of events, until the skill and courage of one man is at stake. Images from chess and baseball run like a theme through Jack's poetry. His point is most clear in *The Holy Grail*, where in the second poem of the Gawain sequence:

> . . . George
> Said to me that the only thing he thought was important in
>   chess was the killing of the other king. I had accused him of lack of
>   imagination.
> I talked of fun and imagination but I wondered about the nature
>   of poetry . . . (187)

As a young friend wrote me, "when George [Stanley] said he thought the object of chess was to get the king, that is of course, end game. And what kind of objective is that? It's a given. What really counts is the quality of the play, of the thought, which is the texture of the game. That's where the ecstasy is. It has to do with consciousness and skill, a board and pieces, a beginning and an end." In the conversation a few weeks before his death, when he was accused of being more interested in truth than in poetry and replied, "I'm more interested in messages," he then added that poetry, baseball, and chess aren't for pleasure.[45] In another context, Jack commented that the poet is more like a catcher, but likes to believe he's a pitcher. "The batter is the Martian, spook, or ghost."[46] The determined assertion of Jack's poetry, that it is among the powers, forces, and events of an outside that we live, begins in *After Lorca*. Poetry becomes an active record of that outside which draws into itself the man, the poet, and his landscape—as in the sounding of the cosmos, which poets have called the music of the spheres, which becomes in this work: "A noise in the head of the prince" (Spicer, *Collected Books* 2 1 3). The grief, the dark, and the dying, which give measure to the joyous and the celebratory, and shadow them, are held in this poetry with courage—face into the intelligence of their action, as we act into and are acted upon.

So much of that action in *After Lorca* and the following poetry is held pointedly in the use of the word "ghost." In the early poems, the word is frequently attached to the ghoulish or spooky, funny and strange, but even then, it is suggestive of a special haunting. Here, Garcia Lorca is a ghost, a haunting, but the book and its images bring a man and his shadow together, and the paradox is set—the inseparability of life and death, or on another level, past and present. The act of translation emphasizes the bringing over of the Lorcan world; an entrance to that world then turns into Jack's world. Or to follow the metaphor of entrance, one goes into the book of this poet, only to go out to the book of another poet. Traditional elements in Jack's work are consistently seen in terms of information, and thus he avoids that easier accuracy, the imitation of a model. As a trained linguist and philologist, Jack was aware of the uncertain origin of the word *ghost*, in tearing, in rage (like fire), and in terror, and he was drawn by the currency of the word to the ambiguity of its meaning. Our sense of the word always plays around that fineness and depth of English meaning which gives the word its traditional place as a translation of *sanctus spiritus*. And part of the usage of the word in Jack's work reflects the battle of the highest contemporary poetry to recognize spirit.[47] In *After Lorca* the power of the ghost is that it prepares a simultaneous appearance and disappearance, as with Lorca who appears and disappears, time and again in the musical movement of Jack's words, until he is finally gone at the end of summer. Indeed the word's meaning tears at a sense of life, and it is the nature of such tearing that it may lead to rage and terror, as it does throughout Jack's poetry. The ghost gives actuality to the other face of the game and to the other faces of the players, as it attaches to appearance or manifestation it points to life, and as it attaches past to present it affirms two worlds: the afterlife, which draws out part of the significance of the title *After Lorca*. This life is somehow perched in the disturbance of language without giving it up to language. This significance, which is taken up again in a different way in *Heads of the Town up to the Aether* lends substance to the view that Jack's poetry is a "pot-of-disturbance," and while in *After Lorca*, the reader first notices the presence of this disturbance, it remains at issue in all the poetry, wherein every affirmation accounts for its own destruction and all elements of order and resolution draw to themselves a fragmentation of meaning. This is the actuality of either order or non-order. And whatever one may see in the meaning of the word, ghost, it always proposes an image of life which holds on to the fragmentation. I think of that careful use of the word in Donne's poems, which early on drew Jack's attention. It is curious that nothing, not even Hallowe'en cuteness, has destroyed its strength. This is not to say that the storied laughter of all those teasing, noisy ghosts does not also fill our sense of the word. The joke or trick of it is the turn of meaning, where meaning does not rise above us, but is alive:

> The jokes
> Are ghosts
> The joke
> Is a ghost
> How can you love that mortal creature
> Everytime he speaks
> He makes
> Mistakes (148)

Jack's dictation, which develops from a "spiritual discipline," as I have noted, or from what he described as an emptying out in order to let something speak through his language is not difficult to follow. It is at times frightening. The possibility of it, he derives from Yeats, who derived his from Blake. It is not the derivation that makes it alive, but the practice. His language appears to speak by itself or it is used by another order. The poet's voice reappears in a polarity that forwards the entire range of what is not exactly himself. The landscape is not then a picture postcard, but the narration of an action in which the poet and reader are imaged. The visibility of it is measured against the vast other that language also holds. As the "perilous act" begins at the gates of existence, the measuring is all important. The result is to push the reader to undertake another order of interpretation in which the double is caught and a measurement of that doubleness followed: so

> In art the construction of a work out of earth creates a world; "the work grasps and holds earth itself in the openness of a world." The building up of earth and the exhibition of world are . . . the two basic tendencies of the work of art. (Palmer 160)

The openness then is the problem. It is near a madness as we learn to live in it, renewed and changed. Contemporary poetics has called this open-form and it has meant by this the necessity of world and the re-opening of discourse. The openness may well be a joy or a terror. It has cost a few poets their lives. Jack argues this in *After Lorca* before he knew where he was going: "A really perfect poem has an infinitely small vocabulary," rather than a discourse:

> It is very difficult. We want to transfer the immediate object, the immediate emotion to the poem—and yet the immediate always has hundreds of its own words clinging to it, short-lived and tenacious as barnacles. And it is wrong to scrape them off and substitute others. A poet is a time mechanic not an embalmer. The words around the immediate shrivel and decay like flesh around the body. No mummy-sheet of tradition can be used to stop the process. Objects, words must be led across time not preserved against it. . . .

> Most of my friends like words too well. They set them under the blinding light of the poem and try to extract every possible connotation from each of them, every temporary pun, every direct or indirect connection—as if a word could become an object by mere addition of consequences. Others pick up words from the streets, from their bars, from their offices and display them proudly in their poems as if they were shouting, "See what I have collected from the American language. Look at my butterflies, my stamps, my old shoes!" What does one do with all this crap?

> Words are what sticks to the real. . . . They are what we hold on with, nothing else. They are as valuable in themselves as rope with nothing to be tied to. (25)

Nothing could be clearer or more tensed. The principle of translation in *After Lorca* proposes that one must reenact life again, that it is the same as it was, but with a difference. Lorca's poetry corresponds to and with Jack's. When the poems are translations, there are subtle shifts—as in the first poem in the book, where Lorca's "infinity" is translated to endlessness and his "spikenard" to seaweed. The extraordinary issue of that first poem, that the imagination wounds or cuts holes in a white and endless invisibility, that the image is a piece, but not the whole of it, begins the large dimension of *The Collected Books*. The doubleness. A friend has noted that the book ends with a Postscript, rather than a translation, a radar which signals appearance and disappearance. I note that the death in these poems is an imageless point at which the acted visibility meets and enters the other which articulated it. It is part of an extreme ghostliness in language itself. It includes the sublime, the terrible and the uncanny, as these enter the work to measure and guide the work's real. This dimension is an aspect of the *where* of this work, which I have tried to follow—where the body will not and cannot stop, even in its desires—where the false manhood of the old discourse does not hold the conversation. There is here an experience of *dictation*, now opening to all of us, beginning where the manhood leaves off—at the open end of what we are. This is, I think, a beloved that may begin in sexuality, but it will end in the world—a vocabulary for it, a task, and a chemical necessity.

The dictation or emptying out allows the unknown, as it is experientially and technically present to what we know, to enter and use the words, where it has been all along—strangely. The dictation resides not in the shambles of a life, or in a pathology, or even in an unhappiness, but in the heart. It is as if the old mythologies were right that said the mind resided in the heart because it is so tied to speech and breath. An opening of the mouth. It is also true that the heart will unwind off the spool. That is part of our openness and our invisibility. The curiosity will remain, and in one sense, the Work is always incomplete, because it contains the double men once again have met. The context I have drawn was meant to show this as a task and a reparation. How difficult and costly that the double should have been forwarded in just this way—the discovery of a finitude, where a man or a poet thought he found only himself, the displacement of language to a dead picture that turned out to be only his discourse—and there, just there, in the double of his disappearance and appearance, the form opened again. I don't think we know exactly what is there. The form is in this sense ghostly—a past that moves to a point and reopens. But then our sense of form will perhaps never close again, but rather a discourse compose itself to hold a disclosure.

There is a madness at the center of it. It is not a mental illness, that inability to get through and to last in the midst of the shit. It is not a biographical defeat, where a man gives up or makes the wrong choice.

> . . . a work that seems to drown in the world, to reveal there its non-sense, and to transfigure itself with features of pathology alone, actually engages within itself the world's time, masters it, and leads it; by the madness which interrupts it, a work of art opens a void, a moment of silence, a question without answer, provokes a breach without reconciliation where the world is forced to question itself. . . . The madness in which the work of art is engulfed is the space of our enterprise, it is the endless path to fulfillment, it is our mixed vocation of apostle and exegete. . . . Henceforth, and through the mediation of madness, it is the world that becomes culpable (for the first time in the Western world) in relation to the work of art; it is now arraigned by the work of art, obliged to order itself by its language, compelled by it to a task of recognition, of reparation, to the task of restoring reason from that unreason and to that unreason. (Foucault, *Madness* 288)

Here I have tried to speak of a poetry at the gates of existence, like Nerval leaning over the silence of the young soldier, so that "suddenly the mouth is simply a capability, as well as words are a capability, they are not the ultimate back of it all" (Olson, *Poetry and Truth* 47) Olson comes to mind in his little book which argues that poetry and truth flow together—I suppose because both are alive—"the life that one lives is practically the condition of the poetry, rather than the poetic life being a thing in itself" (12).

an actual earth of value to
construct one, from rhythm to
image, and image is knowing, and
knowing, Confucius says, brings one
to the goal: nothing is possible without
doing it. (12)

In Whitehead's sense, we have only the Event of the real.[48]

Jack's work so carefully brings us into time—an appearance and a disap-
pearance, as in Billy the Kid or Fifteen False Propositions Against God, where one finds
the terrible, joyful mysteries—where we enter into dissolutions and proposi-
tions of their meaning in order to reopen the real. I think the rage of it drank
him up. The beautiful book Language opens with an argument which I've already
noticed: "No / One listens to poetry" (217). A few weeks before he died, in a
lecture entitled "Poetry and Politics," he argued that no poem had ever influ-
enced the political realm.[49] This was an old subject with him and was the title
of the course he wished to give in the college he planned with Robert Duncan
and myself—White Rabbit College to counter all other colleges. We didn't. There
was a kind of despair in his voice that day, which expressed the truth of our
condition. Suddenly, I remember a conversation following a reading. A young
man commented, "It's beautiful, Jack." And Jack replied sharply, "I know it's
beautiful, what does it mean?" Here, at the end of an argument for his context
and for the size of the reparation in his work, I notice the fundamental "trans-
formation" he proposes—it is reflected in the simple love of his final poems
and the warning of them in Language:

> We make up a different language for poetry
> And for the heart—ungrammatical. (233)

We may, I think, take from his work what he gave his heart to.

> But dream is not enough. We waking hear the call of the
> In-
> Visible world
> Not seen. Hinted at only. By some vorpals, some sea-lions,
>   some scraggs.
> Almost too big to get used to, its dimensions amaze us, who are
>   blind to Whatever
> Is rising and falling with us. (223–24)

This suggestion of the constellated forms in his work comes forward again and
again. I have tried to situate it in the conditions of contemporary thought, where

Jack was proudly at work. Thus, I have thrown the balance to the conditions of his poetics. Whatever my purpose, his language is re-situated in the being of language. It is the primary language and in this sense ungrammatical. Here I am reminded of what seem useful phrases from a source I do not remember—his proud sense and restless thought are "mosaics of the same elemental particles that compose the dark, drifting clouds of interstellar space"—a "conformation of the primordial space-time field."[50] I have not forgotten the interplay or game of the temporary and the permanent with which Jack's book opens (*After Lorca*). And I move to his sense of a "perfect poem" in that initial book:

> A really perfect poem (no one yet has written one) could be perfectly translated by a person who did not know one word of the language it was written in. A really perfect poem has an infinitely small vocabulary. (25)

This is a statement of a re-situated language. And I recall one of Jack's favorite poems, Lewis Carroll's *The Hunting of the Snark*. In that exaggeration used when one means it, he said it was the greatest metaphysical poem in the language and so pointed to its laughter, its wariness and scariness, the language always at the edge of a meaning.

> In the midst of the word he was trying to say,
>   In the midst of his laughter and glee,
> He had softly and suddenly vanished away—
>   For the Snark *was* a Boojum, you see.
>
>   (Hunting 63)

Jack "no longer speaks of identity but of correspondence."[51] I may take this backward into his by no means haphazard erudition—to his love of Virgil's 4th *Georgic* (Orpheus and bee-keeping) which he willfully confused with Ovid's *Art of Love*, book I, on the basis of a single phrase, "et e medio flumine mella petat," and let him seek honey in the middle of a river, turned by Jack in an early poem, which plays on the name of a young man, into "Mela, Mela peto / In medio flumine,"[52] I seek honey in the middle of a river—or to his fascination with St. Augustine's definition of a sacrament as a "verbum visible" or the early time he spent over Calvin's *Institutes* in which God is entirely Other, or to his general reading in the Renaissance, his notice of Poe's *Eureka* and Baudelaire, his care for Rimbaud and Cocteau. This only suggests his reading and will not help much. The positioning of his language, however full of strangeness, is at home where he was. The "spiritual discipline" he proposed as part of the practice of poetry is involved in the "purely spiritual world of images." Jack's funny instruction to the young, "read the far-out-stuff," has been true since the crisis in Shelley's work. It is rereading meant to resituate. In this meandering paragraph, I am reminded of a scientist's remarks in a similar range.

> . . . it is a definite religious attitude toward the universe that finds expression in reserving for the earth, the dwelling place of mankind, an absolute prerogative among all other bodies of reference. It is the attempt to uphold within the realm of objective reality the idealistic position, according to which I am the center of the world disclosed to me. But here where the recognition of the thou is required of the ego and the ego has to be extended so as to include the whole of mankind, the idealistic position of necessity takes on a historical and cosmo-theo-logical character. This is the reason why the book of Copernicus became a turning point of world conception; and in this direction Bruno drew the conclusions with stormy enthusiasm. The supreme act of redemption by the Son of God, crucifixion and resurrection, no longer the unique pivot of world history but the hurried small-town performance of a road show repeated from star to star—this blasphemy displays perhaps in the most pregnant manner the religiously precarious aspect of a theory which dislodges the earth from the center of the world. (Bruno had to pay for it at the stake.) "The statement, found equally with Kepler, Galileo, and Descartes, that it be foolish to think of the purpose of the universe as lying in man," says Dilthey[,] . . . "consummates a complete change in the interpretation of the world. As these thinkers were led to an immanent teleology finding its expression in the harmony and beauty of the universe, the character of the hitherto prevailing Christian religiosity was changed." And Goethe . . . "Perhaps never before has a greater demand on mankind been made; for what did not go up in smoke with this acknowledgement: a second paradise, a world of innocence, of poetry and piety, the testimony of the senses, the conviction of a poetical-religious faith. Small wonder then that one did not want to let go of all this, that one opposed in every conceivable manner a theory which involved for him who accepted it the right and the challenge of a hitherto unknown, now undreamed-of, freedom of thought and elevation of mind." (Weyl 98–99)

This, if I may ask a reader to play it back among the considerations of a context in this essay, will go far to explain why I have simultaneously quarrelled with a naive realism, the reduction of experience, and the idealism of a certain poetics. And it will, perhaps, help clarify the reason I have not fallen back on the history of mysticism, however much we are reminded of it, or on such explanations of the tradition of dictation as Gwendolyn Bays' *The Orphic Vision*. I do not mean that Jack knew Bruno—the translations and the obvious scholarly sources are too recent. But certainly he had followed through the challenge and disturbance of the others. He had a poet's entrance to science, professional in the computer methods of studying language (see his article published with David Reed, *Language*, July–September 1952, which becomes the cover of Jack's *Language*) and otherwise broad and taken in terms of its implications for experience. One of his last projects, of which there is no record, involved a fascination with Pythagorean numbers. I have wished to establish the context of the polarity in his work.

I wanted to go at the size of Jack's work rather than leave it to the simple statement that this is a high poetry. I also wanted to go against the grain of what we have usually meant by aesthetic concern. In so doing, I have departed from Jack's simple, marvelous language.

> Dear Lorca,
> These letters are to be as temporary as our poetry is to be permanent. They will establish the bulk, the wastage that my sour-stomached contemporaries demand to help them swallow and digest the pure word. We will use up our rhetoric here so that it will not appear in our poems. Let it be consumed paragraph by paragraph, day by day, until nothing of it is left in our poetry and nothing of our poetry is left in it. It is precisely because these letters are unnecessary that they must be written. (15)

It is difficult to insist upon the truth of poetry. There are simpler reasons perhaps. He was always sitting in the midst of poetry. An ungrammatical disturbance. At his table in the bar—night after night—predictable only in that. Most of us noticed the way he wove poetry in and out of what we were. In The Place on Grant Street, 1957, he set up a "blabbermouth night." It was, when I heard it, a kind of wonderful, funny jabberwocky that was spoken, full of a language alive to the tongue of anyone ready to stand up there. Later, at Gino & Carlo's on Green Street, things changed. George Stanley[53] once commented that it was the Beatles that did him in. There is some truth in this. Another sound entered. You could not be heard at the table. The language game that was played was partly destroyed. Even in Vancouver, B.C., which had given him a brief sense of beginning again,

> The Beatles devoid of form and color, but full of images play
>   outside in the living room.
> Vancouver parties. Too late
> Too late
> For a nice exit. (261)

And what of the heart? Returning to my point earlier of the fallen words, that word too is part of the ruin. It is only-feeling, a need, a privacy, a hole in the earth without volcanoes. It is also that broken thing at the center of our poetry, where it discovers courage or some other shape of its acts.

> It then becomes a matter of not
> Only not knowing but not feeling. (262)

The body, as a friend said, is continually mistaken for the heart. My friend called this the "occultation of the heart." There is a struggle to pull the words back out of definitions and sentiments that stop them. One has the peculiar sense that the body is neither material nor spiritual. That it is the alembic itself. Any unity or disunity takes place there. For now, one may take the curious entangling I've argued apart and make it elemental. The issue then is a meeting of the elementals and intelligence. I borrow a Blakean word to say they fold. I seek here to draw attention to a poetry at the gates of existence because it is there that the polarity begins, elemental and inescapable. This is the necessary laying of oneself alongside another content, which brings form and keeps it alive—the double of language, where it holds to both reason and unreason, thought and unthought. Jack seems so important here among the poets who have moved to find what is also there at the gates—a discourse, recomposing, which also happens to be a "motive of things that we are not." And that begins a retying of intelligence, the folding, which is not an imposition of a discourse, fixed or silent. The folding contains that constellation which commands us. The ceremony or composition of it is the disclosure of a new discourse, and it is the public poem.

I place here the visionary range in Jack's work. It is so tied or caught in the web, there is a chance some might forget or miss it. He never quite allows it to float out of his hands, or rather he keeps it so tied to the doubles out of which it was formed that it is more expected than there. There is a long preparation for its possibility, which the reader may follow in the *ceremony* of these books, from *After Lorca*,

> The universe falls apart and discloses a diamond
> Two words called seagull are peacefully floating out where the
> waves are
> The dog is dead there with the moon, with the branches, with
> my nakedness
> And there is nothing in the universe like diamond
> Nothing in the whole mind. (23)

to the *Book of Magazine Verse*:

> Start with a baseball diamond high
> In the Runcible Mountain wilderness. (259)

This is one of that last run of poems, written in the spring of 1965. The diamond has come to be part of the skill of the game. It relates to Jack's view that neither baseball nor poetry are for amusement. They disclose something— perhaps only a virtuality. The rules are invisible, the players a visibility. They are commitments to that "disordered devotion to the real," with which I began. Here the heart comes into play. It may be lost there, given up to the disorder, or it may lift. The traditional word for this lifting, this first outward, is love.[54] It is a reason that physical love and its opposite repeatedly suggest to us another fold of what we know. It may indeed take the intricate structure of books like Jack's *Language* to remind us that love is a function of knowledge, a word we have used for its process, and never simply a designation of an acceptance or convention of seeing one another or of looking privately out at the world. The structure of *Language* is an interleaving of his life with a belovèd and a world. The hold or discovery of meaning is a tension of the alphabet from the opening section, "Thing Language" to the closing "Graphemics." These enclose the "Love Poems."

> But that the syntax changes. This is older than towns.
> Troy was a baby when Greek sentence structure emerged. This
>   was the real Trojan Horse.
> The order changes. The Trojans
> Having no idea of true or false syntax and having no recorded
>   language
> Never knew what hit them. (233)

The deadness of the discourse haunts that book and the indefiniteness of a missing discourse begins a partial definition of the ghosts in the poetry:

> Two consonants (floating in the sea of some truth together)
> Immediately preceded and/or followed by a vowel. (238)

One notices the voice of the poet in that book is promissory of a composition:

> For you I would build a whole new universe but you obviously
>   find it cheaper to rent one. Eurydice did too. She went back
>   to hell unsure of what kind of other house Orpheus would
>   build. "I call it death-in-life and life-in-death." (229)

The cost of a language. Perhaps the clearest expression of this may be found in the angry words from *Language*, unfairly addressed to Robert Duncan and George Stanley. Now, these words leave the personalities of that occasion behind and are addressed to our constantly retreating sense of the origin of our language means:

> "If you don't believe in god, don't quote him," Valery once
>   said when he was about ready to give up poetry. The
>   purposeful suspension of disbelief has about the chance of
>   a snowball in hell.
> Lamias maybe, or succubi but they are about as real in

California as night-crawlers
Gods or stars or totems are not game-animals. Snark-hunting is
     not like discussing baseball.
Against wisdom as such. Such
Tired wisdoms as the game-hunters develop
Shooting Zeus, Alpha Centauri, wolf with the same toy gun.
It is deadly hard to worship god, star, and totem. Deadly easy
To use them like worn-out condoms spattered by your own
     gleeful, crass and unworshiping
Wisdom (226)

"Which," he then says, "explains poetry." "Distances / Impossible to be mea-
sured or walked over" (227). The "toy gun" suggests the dead discourse and
the "distance" an experience in the depths of a discourse which recomposes and
is not behind us in the complex metaphor of a god-language of original wis-
dom. The poetry at the gates of existence is then a poetry involved in the com-
position of the real. Following this suggestion of a folding real, one does not
stop the love of the final poems. That would too easily turn back to the test of
the physical event, its success or frustration, and become either an attribution
of oneself or of the desired belovèd, a relation and a behavior, just where this
love involves us in the profound interdependence of visibility and invisibility.
For Jack's work, as for all others in which love is a commotion of the real, love
includes an anticipation of "something that is still absent" (Corbin 155).

At the end of *Language*, we wind up in "The dark / forest of words" and finally
in what is left—"Words, loves" (243). At the end of *Book of Magazine Verse*, the
final poem takes issue with love—that it is not oneself—that it is a commotion
and information of the real, and an enlargement that has political consequences.
The poems often, and I leave the detailed recognition to the reader, question
and play out the distance between divine and human love. The word love, which
may be taken softly and personally or as the difficult understanding that it is in
Jack's work, proposes an entangling that is the mode of the real. This is curi-
ously reflected, for example, in *The Holy Grail*.

The grail is the opposite of poetry
Fills us up instead of using us as a cup the dead drink from. (188)

This is perhaps Jack's harshest statement of the poetic issue—that the poetic is
fundamental to our sense of meaning and to our recognition as we perform
the real with which this essay began in the poem of the broken heart. In that
book, the storied imprisonment of Merlin for a foolish love is jammed with
voices of the prisoners of our own time, as the words of *Die Moorsoldaten*,[55] which

Jack remembers with a mistake in the German, rise out of the text.[*] At the end of the "Book of Merlin," the magician is called to the phone: "Carefully now will there be a Grail or a Bomb which tears the / heart out of things?" (205). Merlin is followed by Galahad, who, as Jack said in conversation, when he found

[*]   Die Moorsoldaten
     Wohin auf das Auge blicket*
     Moor und Heide rings herum
     Vogelsang uns nicht erquicket*
     Eichen stehen kahl und krumm*

        Wir sind die Moorsoldaten
        Und ziehen mit dem Spaten
        Ins Moor

     Auf und nieder gehen die Posten
     Keiner, keiner kann hindurch
     Flucht wird nur das Leben kosten
     Vielfach ist umsäunt die Burg

     Chorus: (same)

     Doch für uns gibt es keine Klage
     Ewig kann nicht Winter sein
     Einmal werden wir froh sagen
     Heimat du bist wieder mein*

        Dann ziehen die Moorsoldaten
        Nicht mehr mit dem Spaten
        Ins Moor

(Lines followed by asterisks are those picked up in *The Holy Grail*.)

     Wherever the eye looks
     Moor and heath all around
     No bird-song quickens us
     Oak-trees stand bare and crooked.

        We are the Moor-soldiers
        And dig with spades
        Into the Moor

     Back and forth the guards go
     No one, no one, can get thru
     Flight would only cost one's life
     Many times is the fortress surrounded

     Chorus

     Yet we do not complain
     Winter cannot be forever
     One day we will joyfully say
     Homeland you are mine again

        Then the Moor-soldiers will dig
        No more with spades
        Into the Moor.

(Jim Herndon's version and translation of the song as Jack would have learned it.)

the Grail in all his purity, took it away with him. In Jack's book, he "[c]asually, ghostlessly" leaves the story (208). The book opens with the fool and the fool killer, a figure Jack claimed was present in the folklore of Southern California, but as he used it, the figure is also informed by the sharp fear of Helen Eustis's mystery story, *The Fool Killer*. The double nature of the fool fascinated Jack and one could hear it when he talked about the nature of the Fool in the Tarot pack— the man at center of the commotion of the higher arcana and yet also outside it. *The Holy Grail* ends with the "Book of Arthur":

> A noise in the head of the prince. Something in God-language.
> In spite of all this horseshit, this uncomfortable music. (213)

In the poem, even a word doubles to move from one meaning to another: "A / noise. / It annoys me to look at this country" (213). The voice of the golden head there strikes one—it is as if we had come to the edge of something— "Time future," the golden head said, / "Time present. Time past" (213). The movement of all time into a past draws attention, stops there and then reopens. It is useful, but not necessary in the way Jack uses and renews his sources, to recognize the original mixture of laughter and the uncanny which goes with the story of the magical head. In Robert Greene's play, the alchemist, Friar Bacon, has labored seven years to make the brazen head that will give him impossible knowledge—notice that each of the sections of *The Holy Grail* has seven parts, whatever you wish to do with that. On the day the head is ready to speak, the Friar, worn-out, has to rest and he asks his apprentice, Miles, to wake him if anything, anything at all, happens. Miles does not wake him in time, thus in some sense becoming every one of us:

> [*A great noise is heard*]
> *The Brazen Head:* Time is!
> *Miles:* "Time is"! Why, Master Brazen-head, have you such a capital nose, and answer you with syllables, "Time is"? Is this all my master's cunning, to spend seven years' study about "Time is"? Well, sir, it may be we shall have some better orations of it anon. Well, I'll watch you as narrowly as ever you were watched, and I'll play with you as the nightingale with the slow-worm; I'll set a prick against my breast. ["Nightingales were supposed to lean against a thorn when they sang."]
> [*Again a great noise*] . . .
> *The Brazen Head:* Time was!
> *Miles:* Well, Friar Bacon, you spent your seven-years' study well, that can make your head speak but two words at once. "Time was." Yea, marry, time was when my master was a wise man, but that was before he began to make the Brazen Head. You shall lie while your arse ache, an [sic] your head speak no better. Well,

I will watch, and walk up and down, and be a peripatetian and a philosopher
of Aristotle's stamp. What, a fresh noise? Take thy pistols in hand, Miles. . . .
The Brazen Head: Time is past!
[*Lightning flashes, and a hand appears that breaks down the Head with a hammer*] (Greene 149)

This destruction of what we might have seen informs the whole of Jack's book.

But there is at the edge of this work, as I have already suggested, another fold-
ing of the intelligence of the real. It is, where it occurs, the public performance
in words of the composition and disclosure of what is traditionally called para-
dise. It is not without tension because it is a fold of the known and the unknown,
and has the sense that in thought and experience hell is only the outside of heaven.
I think of Pound's paradise which is not artificial.[56] Heaven and paradise—more
words among the ruins. Jack's suggestion that he is dealing with paradise comes
from his long standing description of *Heads of the Town up to the Aether,* the book in
which the principle of dictation is first fully and consciously articulated. The parts
of it, he said, have the structure of Hell, Purgatory, and Paradise. "Homage to
Creeley" becomes a hell of meanings, everything slips or slides into nonsense
and is haunted by meaning and laughter. "A Fake Novel about the Life of Arthur
Rimbaud" becomes a book about visibility or time and its messages issue from
a strange post-office, the dead letter and the dead letter officer. "A Textbook of
Poetry" is, he said, a kind of paradiso. This will strike any reader as odd unless
he catches the point that Paradise is always held in the presence and absence of
paradise. That is to say it is alive and virtual.

> St. Elmo's Fire. Or why this will be a textbook concerning
> poetry for 20,999 years. Almost a lifetime.
>
> I chicken out at the edges of it and what doesn't come
> through to me at the edges of it isn't as if angels met singing or
> any of that business.
>
> We are all alone and we do not need poetry to tell us how
> alone we are. Time's winged chariot is as near as the next
> landmark or busstation. We need a lamp (a lump, spoken or
> unspoken) that is even above love.
>
> St. Elmo's Fire was what was above the ships as they sailed
> the unspoken seas. It was a fire that was neither a glow or a
> direction. But the business of it was fire. (181)

That book closes with the voice that will be a ghost and with the voices of
ghosts—at the deep-end that is the outward of paradise. The "I" becomes a
"we" among ghostly voices:

What I am, I want, asks everything of everyone, is by
degrees a ghost. Steps down to the first metaphor they invented
in the underworld (pure and clear like a river) the in-sight. As a
place to step further.

It was the first metaphor they invented when they were too
tired to invent a universe. The steps. The way down. The
source of a river. (182)

We do not hate the human beings that listen to it, read it,
make comments on it. They are like you. (183)

I know no poet who more clearly brings the doubleness forward and at great
cost because it is experienced as a simultaneity of life and death. It is seen not
as his alone, but as a large and cultural extremity in which meanings fall to be
remade again. I have described this as the disappearance of manhood and wish
to draw attention to Jack's concern for a flowing, incomplete sense of form.
The basic question—who is speaking?—turns of the gossip, the baseball fore-
casts and the meannesses—turns into a world.

There are aspects of memoir and problems of exegesis in this work, which have
not been the concern of this essay. Indeed, they suggest another occasion. For
example, the first reading of the completed *Heads of the Town up to the Aether* began
with Johnny Horton's rendition of "The Battle of New Orleans," Jack seated for-
ward with a chair directly behind him. Jack in a baseball cap. And from the chair
behind him, I read the "Explanatory Notes." Jack's erudition was very great, but
it is so tied to the life of his language and experience one hardly notices. The ti-
tle, *Heads of the Town up to the Aether*, becomes a direct image, but it is taken from a
book on the Egyptian gnostics and is the title of a Gnostic work (Doresse 50).[57]
The words found or discovered in a book are one level of a dictation. Here they
rang a bell, though there is no systematic relation in Jack's poem to what we
know about the contents of that mysterious book. However, the source and the
title open for us Jack's concern with the extremity of thought common to all
gnosticism, an opposition of light and dark and extensions of these in metaphor
and experience. Jack's *Heads of the Town* also draws attention to what he called the
surrealism of the poet, the under-the-real which comes forward when the fixed-
real dissolves. In Jack's work, this is, of course, the mode of an operational lan-
guage distinct from a language which stops the world. And it is attached to an
Orphic methodology of great complexity, which the book keys by way of ded-
ications to the figures of Cocteau's *Orpheus*, which Jack knew from the film and
from the Poet's Theater production of the play in Cambridge. These are subjects

in themselves. They could be made academic, but they do involve the reader. I think also of Jack's use of the phrase attributed to Tertullian and of his interest in St. Anselm's ontology in *Book of Magazine Verse*—*Credo quia absurdum* (I believe because it is absurd, drawn from the long tradition of Tertullian's thought in *De Carne Christi, Certum est quia impossibile est,* it is certain because it is impossible) and *Cur Deus Homo?* (why God became man?) in which Anselm's *credo ut intelligam* (I believe in order to understand) is hidden. In Jack's terms, I might play with this last phrase and say, I disbelieve in order to understand. Belief and disbelief. They are aspects of the narrative of a composition of the real which begins in the presence-absence and known-unknown flowing around us in a basic duplicity of the real. "Take a step back and view the / sentence" (227). It is as if Jack too had said,

> I don't want to eat my poem but I want to give my heart to my poem. And what is my heart to my poem? My heart is what isn't my ego. To give one's self to one's poem is also to risk being violated by it. (Artaud, *Anthology* 101)

Thus, I have gone to the ranging of this work. I have also put aside for now the beginning of it all in Berkeley, 1945/46. What I called the fateful meeting of Jack, Robert Duncan, and myself. That fatefulness is not simply a reading from my own desk. Jack sometimes gave his birthdate as 1946. In order to speak of this I would have to go at the respect and distance between Jack and Robert. It still seems to me important that, having met Duncan at an anarchist's meeting, Jack brought three typescripts of Duncan's poems, a present of something really found. Then we all met. For both Jack and me, Duncan was a man of knowledge in poetry. He was older and certainly surer. He offered information, ground, and belief. Out there, as Duncan once said, we made a poetry up out of wholecloth. I would have to account for the ground of Duncan's poetics in the idea of the poet as hero and in Emerson's *Representative Men.* Jack is closer to Poe. I think of *Eureka* where the universe is an invisible heart that is also your heart, where you begin again each time. Jack knew Poe's work well: I notice the one piece of direct evidence in *A Book of Music* in which the opening poem picks up a line from Poe's *Marginalia* on the indefinite.[58] McLuhan has noticed the importance of Poe, who, in contrast to Emerson, "first worked out the rationale of this ultimate awareness of the poetic process and who saw that instead of directing the work to the reader, it was necessary to incorporate the reader in the work" (McLuhan 276). It is Poe "who solves crimes by a method of artistic perception" (McLuhan 277). When the distance and dissonance between Duncan and Jack appears, it involves what I have described as the context and purpose of language. I don't think the debt to Duncan for the ground of poetic belief he gave ever disappears in the work of either Jack or myself. But that is another occasion. Once years ago, full of laughter, Jack said we were three immortals. I think he had Tu Fu's wonderful poem, "Eight Immortals of the Wine Cup," in mind:

Ho Chih-chang rides his horse as though he were sculling a boat, And is quite willing to tumble into a well asleep.

The Prince of Ju-yang had his three gallons before going to Court; Yet a passing brewer's cart makes his mouth water And his heart long for a transfer as Prince of Wine Spring.

Ten thousand coins a day our Second Minister spends On the drinks he takes as a whale the waters of the sea; Yet says he, "I like the unmingled and avoid the split."

Ts'ui Tsung-chih—a young man handsome and carefree—With bland eyes lifts his cup to the blue skies. And stands like a sparkling jade tree in the wind.

Honoring an embroidered Buddha, Su Chin is a vowed vegetarian; But how he enjoys his lapses whenever he is drunk with wine!

A hundred poems Li Po will write for a gallon And will sleep in a wine shop in the market of Ch'ang-an. Disobeying the Imperial command to board the barge, He says, "Your Majesty's servant is an immortal of the cup."

Give three cupfuls to Calligrapher Chang Hsü, Even before dignitaries he will throw off his cap And draw clouds on paper with his brush.

Chiao Sui will need at least five gallons to be awake—To startle the company with eloquence in discussion or debate. (Hung 51–52)

Jack was so West a man. Whatever we may say of the wise symbolic East, it is from this shore West of us.

I have left in suspense, hoping to lead my reader through to this point, Jack's last words. I return to the scene in the hospital, the alcoholic ward of the San Francisco General Hospital one afternoon during the two weeks he was there before he died. I have already said his speech was a garble. He could manage a name once in a while. Otherwise there were long-runs of nonsense sounds. No words, no sentences. That afternoon, there were something like a dozen friends around his bed, when it became clear that he wished to say something to me. By some magic I can't explain, everyone left to let it be between us. It was odd because I didn't ask them to leave and Jack couldn't be understood. Their affection simply accounted for something inexplicable. Jack struggled to tie his speech to words. I leaned over and asked him to repeat a word at a time. I would, I said, discover the pattern. Suddenly, he wrenched his body up from the pillow and said,

My vocabulary did this to me. Your love will let you go on.

The strain was so great that he shat into the plastic bag they'd wrapped him in. He blushed and I saw the shock on his face. That funny apology he always made for his body. "(When I saw you in the morning / My arms were full of paper.)" (*Collected Books* 37). What he wished to say seemed incomplete. He tried again. He saw something in the empty corner. I suppose I will never stop going over those two sentences. I dream about them and grind my teeth. The first is so succinct to what I've said in all these pages at the end of his work. The second is not, as has been said, a recantation, but rather, I think, an admonition and a notice of danger. It is true that one could just go on in a love that rides over the consequences of this art. I have not.

At the end of a twenty-year friendship, it is endless. That is how I wind up here. If you ask me why I loved him—

Si on me presse de dire pourquoy je l'aymois, je sens que cela ne se peut exprimer, qu'en respondant: Par ce que c'estoit luy; par ce que c'estoit moy.[59]

There is a continuing recognition here that I share with others.

Imaginary Letters by Mary Butts

Afterword

Mary Butts, 1890–1937

"Mais comme tu taquines éternité."
(*Armed with Madness* 81)

"Up, then, Melpomene! the mournefulst Muse of Nyne—

Dido, my deare, alas! is dead,
Dead and lyeth wrapt in lead—

All musick sleepes, where death doth leade the daunce,
And shepherds wonted solace is extinct,
The blew is black, the greene is grey in tinct—
The knotted rush-ringes, and gilte Rosemaree—

Ah! they bene all y-clad in clay;
One bitter blast blew all away.
O heavie herse!

Thereof nought remaynes but the memoree
O carefull verse!

(Lines from the "November Eclogue,"
recomposed by Mary Butts [*Crystal Cabinet* 219])

Thy lovers were all untrue,
Thy chase had a beast in view,
Thy lovers were all untrue.

(Song quoted in her story,
"From Altar to Chimney-
Piece," *Selected Stories* 251)

Am I to go through all my life looking for the lover whose pace equals mine?
("Lettres Imaginaires," *Selected Stories* 1 6 1)

fifteen ways of looking at a finch
mica glittered like sweat
But she had turned the corner where love sees
the lover of a bird
                    (Phrases from *Armed with Madness* 7 7–7 9)

They wanted to live and to know. These people wanted nothing so exhausting.
(*Death of Felicity Taverner* 99)

I was to know myself, and remember the counterpoises attached to every action under heaven. I had said I loved the mind. Now I had to trust it. In the hope that, in the end, the mind would come to no dishonour through me. (*Crystal Cabinet* 267)

"Without God there is no man; without supernature there is no nature; without philosophy there is no psychology; without theology there is no science; without mysticism there is no common sense."
All this is truth and all the truth; but truth that our age has chosen, clause by clause, to reverse. (*Crystal Cabinet* 2 7 5)

Give bread and drink
To soap: even to prayers.
For the surprise it prepares.
                    (*Imaginary Letters* 26)

These quotations, passages, and phrases come to mind from Mary Butts's work. They are given here without regard to her chronology—though the Spenser comes from her reminiscences of school days; rather, I hope they will suggest both the size and the fragmentation of her concern. A worldly author and a very modern one. The bits and pieces with which I've begun suggest a prose-poem, and so indeed does her work in whole and in part. Here is a serious, high language and a composition out of which her laughter, the songs and jazz of her days, rings true. The work of her text, offering a polish and a labour, belongs to those who care about writing. I don't mean that she's simply a writer's writer—suspense, tension and the elements of a detective story, out of Poe, perhaps, suggest a possible popularity—but it is the writers who have remembered her. During more than thirty years, I've returned now and again to this exceptional, startling art. So to speak, Mary Butts smiles out of the depth of a wing chair, a shadow across her puzzled face—a little frantic, large in body, commanding. In a recent rereading, I set myself the task of stopping over whatever caused impatience—political naïveté, a very English allegiance to her class, the country-gentry, an elegiac stance toward that very modern condition of loss of "meaning" and "belief." In her books, lives interweave a good and an evil which is their own enchantment and their own composition of a world. Belief and disbelief are, she knew, for us, the same condition. When I first read her, searching for titles which few libraries have, I felt no impatience. Even now, those elements settle out like static in a very good radio set. Nor did I notice then that she clearly belongs to the thought of the freedom of women, her constant struggle with the admonition that men should not know that she knew—she would not be attractive—described in her autobiography, *The Crystal Cabinet* (1937). It takes us only to her twentieth year. She died, March 5th, 1937, in her forties (victim, I'm told, of an incompetent diagnosis), recognized by some of the best readers, and little read.

The novelist and gossip Douglas Goldring knew her for something like sixteen years, having met her first in 1919. Annoying and fascinating information about her can be found in his autobiographical *Odd Man Out* (1935) and *South Lodge* (1943). What he gives us in both books is sometimes word for word the same, yet, curiously, spite and grudging admiration in the later volume color an earlier pleasure and generosity. She was a

> natural surrealist, with a flair for everything queer in art and life, a tremendous zest for parties and a child-like delight in all the more exotic forms of naughtiness. She had a fine "presence," and when she took trouble with herself, with her red-gold hair, fair skin and glittering "boot-button" eyes, she was a gorgeous apparition at a party. (*Odd Man* 281)

Yes, a book is badly needed. I first found out about her red hair in a conversation with E. M. Forster, 1949, who found her "flashing," but seemed to know little of her work. Goldring had originally a taste for her vitality, her power with people, her tendency to transform relationships, to make them unstable in order to keep them alive—what she might have called the magic of persons. In the end, he seems not to have understood the work, though it was he who encouraged her to collect the early stories in her first book, *Speed the Plough* (1923). Of course, it is difficult to understand the passionate. They are seldom safe in their own hearts, let alone in their relations with others. On the evidence of the books, she adored men and, I think, frightened them. Somehow, her life threw her among homosexual and bisexual men. She understood their distance from women, the underworld of their thought, even to madness. She understood the unrequited, the youthfulness of all sexuality and its terror. A world folds round her characters and sometimes the lack of one unfolds around them in desperation. From Goldring we learn that she was first married to John Rodker (*South Lodge* 147), a fine translator, whose excellent Lautréamont should be reprinted, and a poet; that after 1919, she lived with the painter and Joyce critic, Cecil

Maitland, with whom she "dabbled" in the occult (*South Lodge* 148); that in her last years, she married Gabriel Park-Aitkin, an artist known in London for his personal beauty, and settled with him in Sennen (Cornwall) (*South Lodge* 149). So little. I note that her fine historical novel, *The Macedonian* (1933), is dedicated "To Gabriel, χαριστήριον," an offering of thanks. Mary Butts's work manifests no important relation to surrealism in image or structure. Apparently, Goldring refers to the way she organized her life around the marvelous, the search for it and the structure of it. This she shares with the great surrealists, but her language is very different. Her novels do have some affinity with French writing she knew well—Radiguet and Cocteau wherein, neglecting any profound disturbance of language, the style reaches for nameless events of experience and sudden recognitions. In Goldring again, we glimpse Alec Waugh's party given in Mary Butts's flat, 43 Belsize Park Gardens, September, 1923, and we glimpse Evelyn Waugh, G. B. Stern and Rebecca West there (*Odd Man* 282). Again, we catch her in Paris, welcome in Ford Madox Ford's circle (*Odd Man* 299)—and later at Sennen, the vicar has come to tea and after a few pleasantries he falls asleep in his chair (*South Lodge* 149). But neither her life nor her art is banal, she knows too well its dangers.

Recognition of her work came by way of publication in the *Little Review*, and Louis Zukofsky was to include her in *An "Objectivists" Anthology* (1932). The poems need collecting, even if there is only a pamphlet of them. In 1919, she was reading poems on the Greek mysteries to visitors, Goldring tells us. She had a fine imagination for the classical as both her historical novels, *The Macedonian*, on Alexander, and *Scenes from the Life of Cleopatra* (1935), demonstrate. They are really brilliant books, the tales well told. With that sure sense of what mattered in the new writing, Ford Madox Ford announced the contributors he would depend upon in the *Transatlantic Review* ("Purposes," Paris, November, 1923)—among others, H. G. Wells, Conrad, Joyce, Cummings, Pound, Eliot, Mina Loy, Robert McAlmon and Mary Butts. She should be measured and understood from this centre.

Mary Butts has always had a band of readers. They turn up, here and there—in San Francisco, New York, London, Paris, and now in Vancouver with this new 1979 edition of the *Imaginary Letters* [1924]. Years ago in Berkeley, her books informed three young poets—Robert Duncan, Jack Spicer, and myself. My first copy of *Imaginary Letters* is a photocopy, handbound with an ink-drawn cover by Robert Duncan of an imaginary Mary Butts, backed by a splendid tapestry rather like a paisley shawl. And when I found a poorly bound copy of *Speed the Plough*, Duncan added an ink-drawn cover with another image of Mary Butts in 1920s high fashion standing before a decorated wall, a yellow sun in crayon above her head. Later, in *The Crystal Cabinet* we found Cocteau's sharply focused drawing of her, head high, arms folded, a cigarette between her fingers. Mary Butts was one of many introductions Duncan prepared for us in those young days—William Carlos Williams, Stein, Joyce and H. D. Brilliant young Jack Spicer gave his first lecture on *Armed with Madness* (1928) during the Fall term, 1949, even then interested in the "sacred game" or an excuse for it such as the Grail. Thus, Mary Butts became a figure inside the imagination of what was later to be called the "Berkeley Renaissance," and then, with important changes of emphasis, the "San Francisco Renaissance." Initially, or so I read the work of Duncan and Spicer, an imaginary landscape was at stake, a map that would not leave the world out. A principle of transformation is at work in all the art we knew, and present to our own thereby, without utopian ignorance of meanness, desperation or the contemporary revelation of human affairs. The "real" in this sense is both possible and impossible. Certainly a composition and a task. A writing. In *Death of Felicity Taverner* (1932), her last novel, excepting the two on classical subjects, the landscape saved, its magical orders intact, requires a murder that is both a gift to the protagonists and their damnation. Mary Butts's work stops just where splendor begins. Repeatedly, she writes, "Brightness falls from the air," taking the line from Thomas Nashe.[1] Here is the working model of an art, and so we read her. In *Armed with Madness*, the interplay—the magic that meaning is, when it is alive and a task of lives—among one woman and five men is a tale of a possible Grail. We never know whether the jade cup found in a well, planted there by the character named Picus, is the Sanc-Grail, an old English altar vessel, an ashtray, as it is used in the novel, a spitting cup, so used by Picus's father's mistress before her death, or a poison cup out of the East—jade is said to detect poison. It is, of course, all of these simultaneously. The lives of the men and the women shape a spiritual condition that is both frightening and an "enormous lark," like our own. "There was," she wrote, "something in their lives spoiled and inconclusive like the Grail story." Picus could "whistle up a mystery,"—so could we all.

> And I hope when you get it you'll like it. Looking for the Sanc-Grail. It's always the same story. The Golden Fleece or the philosopher's stone, or perpetual motion, or Atlantis or the lost tribes or God. All ways of walking into the same trap. (*Armed with Madness* 121)

And, also, as Mary Butts points out, we go about our sex lives. Along with Henry James in, say, *The Spoils of Poynton* and Laura Riding in that extraordinary book, *Progress of Stories*, no one else spoke of these matters so well.

We found Mary Butts's writing holding its own in the main stream with distinguishing marks of its special intelligence. She has an outstanding ability to portray madness and extremity, as with Clarence in *Armed with Madness*. This man creates elegance and order within the country cottage he shares with Picus, of jade-green walls, a grey-silver couch with scarlet pillows. When the love his order depends upon breaks, in a startling scene of innocence gone wild and vicious, he ties the woman, whom he sees as his rival, to the tall sculpture he's made of his friend, and shoots her with arrows fashioned out of wooden shingles. Next day, he doesn't remember. She is not badly injured, but his spiritual failure is mapped, and he begins to carve a punch bowl for her. Instability of feeling, betrayal of trust and lost purposes inform many of her characters, spectacularly mixed in the character of Boris who is introduced in *Imaginary Letters* and whose capacity for good and evil haunts both *Armed with Madness* and *Felicity Taverner*, though his surname is changed. Her work is dazzling with natural scenes, of Dorset and Cornwall, exact images. "The first thing that I remember," she writes in the opening of *The Crystal Cabinet*,

> is a puddle of yellow mud. Outside the front door, on the drive, after rain; when the new gravel had been put down and the gardeners had gone over it with a round thing that groaned. (My father said they were fools, because they would not think when to put on and take off the weights that were inside the thing: the thing called the garden-roller that would not move for one, however hard one tried. That memory comes later.) The mud in the shallow puddle was lovely, like something you could eat. It happened when the ivy on the porch and on the walls was smooth and glossy and shiny and dripped. You ought to be able to eat it—like cream or the yellow out of the paint-box; you ought to spoon it up. Perhaps something that wasn't food and looked as if it ought to be food would taste all right this time. Nurse was a few steps ahead. Perhaps if it wasn't sweet, it was like the yellow of egg. I had my best green coat on and a bonnet to match with fur round its edge that came off a beaver in the picture book. Dark green. With the gravel it would look like egg and spinach. (1)

But the most striking characteristic of the work is Mary Butts's fascination with the magic of persons and things, an enchantment, and the loss of it that is no less real than banality. This is sometimes described directly in the vocabulary of magic, her sense of the ancient, ritual rings of the British landscape or a search for the Grail. The word *magic* is difficult because it is loaded with the squabbles of the ignoble and the charlatans. For Mary Butts, it is not the practice of abracadabra, but a kind of awareness, a primary condition of seeing men and things, a loosening of the connections defined by the banal and the ordinary. This is a *dérèglement* or misrule of the senses that belongs to modern art and writing—that effort to turn to a primary operation of meaning because writers do not like what they see or what they are told. I will not argue the usefulness of a vocabulary of magic, only its appeal for many modern writers in order to begin again. It is part of the vast modern vocabulary which decomposes a culture which is dead in heart and mind.

Magic has not yet been properly defined. In its *practice* it is, of course, very largely primitive science, misunderstandings by false analogy of the way things work, of natural law. But behind that there seems to remain a very peculiar kind of awareness, an awareness modified and sometimes lost by people whose life has been passed in towns. It is most difficult to describe. It has something to do with a sense of the invisible, the non-existent in a scientific sense, relations between things of a different order: the moon and a stone, the sea and a piece of wood, women and fish. (*Traps for Unbelievers* 25)

True to her times and to the excitement of questions her days asked, Mary Butts investigated the occult tradition. Since, with the exception of *Ashe of Rings* (1926), her books know more about disbelief than about belief, I take it she remained a detective of her times. We know from Goldring that pentagrams and circles were drawn on the floor of Cecil Maitland's bedroom, Belsize Park gardens, also Mary Butts's address. No information is given about the placement of the designs, but Goldring foolishly assumes a black art operation (*South Lodge* 158). Maitland is clearly not seriously communicative when questioned. We know also from Goldring that Cecil Maitland and Mary Butts were invited to join an eminent mage in Italy.[2] This mage was, of course, Aleister Crowley, and his reflections on their first visit are recorded in his *Confessions*, first published in 1969. Crowley's *Confessions* are themselves a magical operation with words by which he could transform anyone who came to him, students of vision, into swine or angels. In the language of his hatred, there are a tremendous number of swine. The passage dealing with Mary Butts viciously transforms Maitland and John Rodker, and Crowley finds a particularly unpleasant image of her.

Few jewels in my collection of freaks are more precious than Cecil Maitland. From his birth, he aroused the liveliest hopes among students of entomology; for his father, a distinguished Anglican controversialist, followed Newman and Manning into apostasy. His projects for attaining the papacy were, however, thwarted by the unscrupulous action of a charming lady, who insisted upon dragging him from the very foot of the altar to a rival sacrament pedlar, who promptly conjoined them in wedlock at the regular rates. This escapade did not escape the notice of the Vatican. The Pope was surprised into the exclamation "Tut," or its Latin equivalent. He scratched his head and muttered, "Martin Luther!" After a moment's reflection he dispatched his chamberlain for bell, book and candle; and proceeded to the magical operation against this occasion made and provided. As in the case of the Jackdaw of Rheims, the effect of the curse was to ruffle the feathers of the audacious follower after the false god Hymen. A touch of rheumatism brought matters to a climax. He rang up Harrod's and ordered a supply of sackcloth and ashes. Receiving, like Job, visits of condolence from various righteous friends he besought them to intercede with the Almighty on his behalf; and as they numbered not a few influential people, with strings on the College of Cardinals, the Pope was eventually persuaded to "silence that dreadful bell," return the book to its shelf and snuff the comminatory candle. The Rev. Mr. Maitland was restored to the bosom of the Harlot of the Seven Hills; though not to the priesthood; and on the strict condition that for the future he should regard his wife as tabu. Things thus satisfactorily settled, she brought forth a man child and called his name Cecil James Alexander, rejecting with contumacy the suggested alternative Caoutchouc. He grew in stature and in favour of God and man, so far as research has hitherto been able to determine. But he was subject to amiable delusions, one of which took the sinister shape of *Cacoethes Scribendi*. In the Great War he joined the army and became a real "capting." Advised of this fact, the Germans wisely refrained from entering Edinburgh. His next step was to become a dipsomaniac and lose his teeth. During this period he suffered from hydrophobia and did not wash for eighteen months. This romantic situation enflamed the virgin heart of a large, white, red-haired maggot named Mary Butts, or rather Rodker.

In a previous spasm she had rushed to the registrar the most nauseating colopter that ever came under my microscope. It was a Whitechapel Jew who proclaimed himself a poet on the strength of a few ungrammatical and incoherent ramblings, strung together and chopped at irregular intervals into lines. He used to hang about studios in the hope of cadging cigarettes and drinks. He even got into mine on one occasion, owing to a defect in the draught excluder. Luckily the plumbing was perfect. One tug on the chain, a gush and a squeal, and I saw him no more. But somehow he squirmed out of the sewers and, as I said, obtained the official position, louse pediculosis, with Mary Butts. She washed him and dressed him, which naturally led to disenchantment, and Cecil reigned in his stead.

In 1922, they were paying the price of their outrage on morality. They were both in very bad health and very hard-pressed for money. One of their favourite amusements was playing at Magick. (878–81)[3]

And so, Crowley tells us, they came to him. He invited them to the Abbey of Thelema at Cefalu. The visit seems not to have lasted long. The remarks on Rodker make it clear, however, that acquaintance was made in London before Cecil and Mary had moved to Paris. Meticulous, thoughtful Rodker, whose poems are indeed free in form, gentle and elegiac—aristocratic, Scottish Catholic, scholarly Maitland—the Mary Butts of her books—all made over by Crowley. I can only speculate that they crossed him, perhaps refusing his "word," the total vision he was composing in *The Book of the Law*. Crowley's fault as a man and as an occultist was messianic and authoritarian. Perhaps they rejected the sexual emphasis in his art and his interest in pain. Whatever. Goldring tells us that they would not talk about it on their return from Italy. Unfortunately, the language of praise is not so exciting or so amusing. A few pages later, near the end of the *Confessions*, Crowley tells us that he showed the manuscript of *Magick* (1929) to Mary Butts and his tone changes.

I showed the manuscripts to Soror Rhodon (Mary Butts) and asked her to criticize it thoroughly. I am extremely grateful to her for her help, especially in indicating a large number of subjects which I had not discussed. At her suggestion, I wrote essay upon essay to cover every phase of the subject. (922)

Had Mary Butts seen the earlier description, she could only have told us what really happened, and that, I suppose, would have taken some of the laughter out of his prose.

Mary Butts came to this interest in the strange and marvelous through her father and William Blake. In *The Crystal Cabinet*, named for Blake's poem of a desire so grasping that it broke the crystalline vision and left the poet a weeping babe, she describes the Blake room at her family home, Salterns (Dorset). The important collection of paintings, including some of the illuminated texts, is now for the most part in the Tate. It was inherited from her great-grandfather, Thomas Butts, friend and patron of Blake. Her knowledge of Blake is perhaps not profound, but it is fundamental—the beautiful room, the glowing books, and one notices her grief when, after her father's death, her mother had to sell them. Now and again, in her work, I find her struggling with the notion of opposites, which she would first have drawn from Blake. How different from Crowley's, Blake's prophetic concerns must have seemed. Perhaps she knew:

> There is a limit of opaqueness, & a limit of contraction
> In every individual man, & the limit of opaqueness
> Is named Satan, and the limit of contraction is named Adam.
> (*Jerusalem* Plate 42, 29–31)

In *Ashe of Rings*, one finds a conversation between Anthony, transparently like her father, an older man who is soon to die, and Melitta, his younger, second wife—Mary Butts was the daughter of a second wife who was considerably younger than her father—who will somehow not understand.

> "What is this place about? What has the house to do with the Rings, and what have the Rings to do with me, now I've married you?"
> He considered and said stiffly: "We are a priestly house, like the Eumolpidae."
> "You know I know nothing about your classics."
> "I'm sorry, but what I've said is the answer. If you really want to know more you will find out for yourself."
> "Anthony, you pretend that there are ways of looking at things which have nothing to do with Christianity."
> "Little Melitta, Christianity is a way, a set of symbols, in part to explain, and to make men endure the unutterable pain that is the world. There are other sets, like chessmen. But only one game."

"Do you believe in the heathen Gods?"

"Yes."

"And not that Christ died for us?"

"Yes." (*Ashe of Rings* 24)

Eumolpus was regarded as the founder of the Eleusinian mysteries and the first priest of Demeter and Dionysius. The family inherited the position to the latest times.

Imaginary Letters begins Mary Butts's major work in fiction, though it appears very close to her life, and may be autobiographical. Here we meet Boris for the first time, a white Russian émigré who will not stay still. Goldring tells us that Mary Butts had a special sympathy for these Russians, princes who had lost their world and were down and out in Paris.[4] Boris is beautiful— Mary Butts seems to seek the beautiful in men rather than the handsome— underhanded, unstable, lost, homosexual, unavailable. It is Boris, more fully imagined, who commits murder as a gift to save the land from a real estate development, parking lots and tourists in *Felicity Taverner*. In *Imaginary Letters*, we find the first care that brought him into her art, and there also we find anger, womanly, direct, puzzled. He somehow starts the imaginary process. Though they will never be sent, these letters are addressed to Boris's mother. Back there, at the beginning, she would understand him. What happened that formed him so? These letters are, in fact, addressed to the imagination where love usually has his seat. In what appears to be a companion piece, "Lettres Imaginaires" (*Little Review*, 1919; *Last Stories*, 1938), there are also letters that will not be sent—they are written by someone named Varya in order to see her way through the end of a relationship, the strangeness, the emptiness and the tearing thought,

> Faint white world,
> I stand at my door.

> There are only masses and spears of light, coloured, interchangeable. All things are dissolved into their elements, all things dance.
> Athis . . . (*Selected Stories* 170–71)[5]

In *Imaginary Letters*, Boris, she writes, leads us "a pretty dance." "Capricious, selfish, insensitive." "Lecherous, drunken, bold and chaste" (10). The qualities build in the first pages—someone shapeless and changing. "He arouses equally unconquerable affection and despair" (10). "A monster of vanity and pride" (10). "He is cruel, devoted, jealous" (10), this "black and green boy" (59). The words create this figure, whom, in kind, most of us meet sometime in our lives. Protean love. He or she may be only ourselves, a desire, or perhaps that figure is out there, as Mary Butts says, "the cause of art in others" (9).

I would like to close my remarks with the poem, on Corfe Castle (Dorset), that Louis Zukofsky chose to include in An "Objectivists" Anthology.

CORFE

Corfe, the hub of a wheel
Where the green down-spokes turning
Embrace an earth-cup of smoke and ghosts and stone.
The sea orchestrates
The still dance in the cup
Danced for ever, the same intricate sobriety
Equivocal, adored.

But when I remember you Corfe, I remember Delphi
Because your history also is a mystery of God.

"And God is no blind man and God is our father":
But like lovers
Your cup is full of the courts of other princes
Disputing you.

Very sweet is the Sacred Wood
In the gold clearing, in the mustard patch;
But at night comes a change
Like a gold ball thrown out
And a black ball thrown in
(Not sunset behind Tyneham Cap
On a night without a moon.)
But a shift of potencies
Like a black ball thrown in
And a gold ball thrown out
And the players are princes
Of the turf and the weed
And the wind-moulded trees
And the hazel thicket
And the red blackberry thorn.

Never trust a hemlock
An inch above your mouth.
An ice-green hemlock
Is a lover
In the wood.
Now every way the wind blows this sweetie goes
In the south

Where goes the leaf of the rose
And the evergreen tree.

II
Inside the house, above the wood
Look out of the tall windows squared
With wood-strips painted white.
The wild grass runs up the wild hill
The wild hill runs up the wild sky
The wild sky runs over itself
And goes nowhere.

A man crosses the rough grass
Up the wild hill;
Strong graceless kharki legs in sihouette
Tired and tough, treading the hill down.

He will not wear it down
Let him try!
He is here only because this place is
A button on the bodies of the green hills.

III
God keep the Hollow Land from all wrong!
God keep the Hollow Land going strong!
A song a boy made in a girl
Brother and sister in a car
Over the flints, upon the turf
Beside the crook-backed angry thorn
Under the gulls, above the dead
To where the light made the grass glass.

Until they came to the world's end
The sea below and under them
The gulls above and over them
And through the thunder and the wailing
Sun full of wings was over them
In a glass world made out of grass.
"God keep the Hollow Land from all wrong!
God keep the Hollow Land going strong!
Curl horns and fleeces, straighten trees,
Multiply lobsters, assemble bees.

Give it to us for ever, take our hints
Knot up its roads for us, sharpen its flints,
Pour the wind into it, the thick sea rain.
Blot out the landscape and destroy the train.
Turn back our folk from it, we hate the lot

Turn the American and turn the Scot;
Take unpropitious the turf, the dust
If the sea doesn't get 'em then the cattle must.

Make many slugs where the stranger goes
Better than barbed wire the briar rose;
Swarm on the down-tops the flint men's hosts
Taboo the barrows, encourage ghosts.

Arm the rabbits with tigers teeth
Serpents shoot from the soil beneath
By pain in belly and foot and mouth
Keep them out of our sacred south." (36–39)

August 1978

George Bowering's
Plain Song

"Why, what do I ever find him but awfully clever?"

Well, what's that but silly? What on earth does
"awfully clever" mean? For God's sake try to get *at*
him. Don't let him suffer by our arrangement. Speak
of him, you know, if you can, as I should have
spoken of him.

I wondered an instant. "You mean as far and away
the biggest of the lot—that sort of thing?"

. . . "Oh, you know, I don't put them back to back
that way; it's the infancy of art! But he gives me a
pleasure so rare; the sense of"—he mused a little—
"something or other."

I wondered again. "The sense, pray, of what?"

"My dear man, that's just what I want you to say!"

Henry James, "The Figure in the Carpet" (358–59)

Some readers quickly lay this brilliant poetry aside—
on a bedside table and put the lights out. And that is serious. They say, "It is
too fragmentary"; or "It is stricken with problems—of where we are, just now";
or "It's a game, it isn't complete and restful in thought." Ah, their expectations
have been disappointed. So many are devoted to form as rest. Bowering's work
is restless. One difficulty with a selection from the size of it is that the process
of selection may formulate and anthologize what is alive and delicate in the po-
ems. The imaginative expanse—both a project of spirituality and a project of
form—which Bowering's work as a whole is developing, like a responsibility,
would then be truncated. I have tried to avoid such maiming by reading again
and again to select parts of the work, which lead piece by piece to fundamen-
tal qualities of the writer's thought and feeling. These qualities gather to them-

selves a strange and fine reality—the strangeness as natural as the laughter in many of the poems, quiet and loud.

Such qualities also draw attention to certain strategies of this poetic practice. One of these is restlessness of meaning which becomes in the poems a processional of mind and heart. Form, then, in this practice is alive[1] and difficult of access because it is not before or after the fact of the writing, but within it. That is to say, the movement of life into language—a marvel that begins childishly where we all begin—is not formulaic or expected. It is perhaps a surprise.

Another quality which becomes a strategy of Bowering's practice is the naturalness of the poet in these poems. He lacks absolutes and is not superstitious about the artist's activity.[*] This poet insists upon a naturalness of stance and consequently of language, seeming to say poetry is after all day by day, night by night. But the day and night are not simply repetitions of the self as one finds them often in lesser poets. And the formal, superior stance of the poet in some great part of the modern literary movement seems ever so slightly unbuttoned. Readers can be taken off-guard by what appears to be an off-handedness. This is, instead, characteristic of Bowering's commitment, in his own words, to "[m]aking beauty out of very very plain language" (Bayard and David, Out-Posts 83). A very difficult beauty because the sense of beauty for many has changed. The lovely older sense of beauty as a harmony and order of perception and thought, heart and mind, has for many been difficult to gather to oneself since, say, Shelley watched the swan.[†] Beauty now for many is found through solitude, terror, the sublime or the naturalness of plainest song, which, as qualities of unreduced experience in certain works, mix and fragment like crystals. Reflections of a carefully sought beauty, which, as in Poe or Lampman, require a descent to the ground, are found throughout Bowering's work. In the poem "The Descent" "he descends, remembers, lives again,"[2] ascending from a basement. I take beauty in Bowering's poems to belong to the phenomena of self and other. This mixing with the outside—personal and public, barbarous and civilized—is neither philosophical nor formal in a traditional sense, but rather something like a shining among fragments of the day and night, a virtuality. In an interview (1979), David McFadden asks this pointed question: "There's a tradition in Canadian poetry for most dedicated poets to be—let me boil it down—to be dedicated to their own egos and reputations and things like that, and, what are you dedicated to?" ("14 Plums" 100). Bowering answers: "The first thing I think of is that I wouldn't want to shame the language. That sounds

* Compare Susan Sontag, *Styles of Radical Will* (4).
† Remember *Alastor*, lines 276–95?

very pretentious but it's true. Literally I don't want to bring shame down on the language and I feel the same way about other people's poetry. That involves abrogating its space, using language as a tool" (100). The abrogation here is of the personal ownership of language, the self-expression, in order to enter a context of imaginative form. To simplify overmuch, language as a tool of thought and feeling is always in part the contrary of the self and its companion. Bowering, by the immediacy of his language, emphasizes this. To be in the language is a profound pleasure of writing and reading—the old word for this is enchantment—and it is not the same as an appropriation of the language to the self or a formality.

Bowering himself has said, "The language is burning" (Bayard and David, Out-Posts 95), to explain his extraordinary sense of language. The distinction here is between the authentic and the conventional in the language and the result is a forbidding honesty and irreducible simplicity. This leads to a third, much misunderstood, strategy of his work: constantly to be vulnerable to the condition of writing. He is not a poet simply of the fallen condition of contemporary meaning, the strictly personal, but of the wounded status of writing today. What exactly can writing say beyond or in spite of oneself? Bowering's ground rule for the handling of this wounded "reality" is to follow the indeterminacy of himself as a writer, the looseness or doubt of who or what the writer actually is in contemporary terms. This is not doubt of himself as writer—he has that assurance—but, accepting the unease of the contemporary writer's identity, he turns to process and searches out *the state of being in the language*, a passage in and out of words and syntaxes. It is a remade significance in the writing. This is a marvel in Bowering's work, which I have tried to follow in this selection. And this art of the passage from one state of being in language to another is a major concern in serious contemporary Canadian writing. Alongside Bowering, I think of the large imaginative structures built over the years by bp Nichol in *Martyrology* and Fred Wah in *Breathin' My Name with a Sigh*. Bowering seems always to be telling the truth. Sometimes he laughs with it and sometimes at it. "It is difficult," some of us remember, "to speak the truth, for although there is only one truth, it is alive and therefore has a live and changing face" (Kafka, quoted in Arendt, *Dark Times* 28).

It is this strategy which has led to the charge that Bowering never shows "'the results of his thinking,'" but only "'the barren chess game of the mind itself'" (Purdy, quoted in Bayard and David 87). To which, Bowering has replied tellingly: "I'm not interested in the results of thinking—I'm interested in the process of thinking itself" (Bayard and David 87). Here, Bowering throws the emphasis in the artistic act on a kind of thinking and thus upon a careful consciousness of language. The charge itself implies a lack of objectivity which the result of thinking is assumed to be. Other charges have been of a self-indulgence and an unevenness. The unwitting demand is that Bowering give us a unity—this is the word for a nostalgia or sentiment of form in so many writers and readers—which in his work is not lacking, but is relentlessly questioned. The lack of objectivity in Bowering's work has "nothing whatsoever to do with subjectivity because it is always framed not in terms of the self but in terms of the relationship" to the world and consequently to language.[*] "It is important not to be deceived," Geoffrey Hartman writes, "by the sophisticated vagueness of such terms as unity, complexity, maturity, coherence, which enter criticism at this point. They are code words shored against the ruins. They express a highly neoclassical and acculturated attitude; a quiet nostalgia for the ordered life; and a secret recoil from aggressive ideologies, substitute religions and dogmatic concepts of order" (Beyond Formalism 365). The nostalgia and sentiment of form are no answer to the conditions in which we live.

This selection is drawn from twenty years and twenty-nine volumes of Bowering's work, opening with a key poem of 1961, "Radio Jazz," and closing with three selections from a poem of 1978, "Old Standards," in which one hears, metrically exact and startlingly extended, pennies from heaven, moonlight becomes you, and singing in the rain. The work of the last two years is best left in place—easily available in Another Mouth (1979) and Burning Water (ms. "The Dead Sailors") (1980). The poems here are arranged according to the month and year in which they were written. My purpose in this arrangement is to follow the continuous development of Bowering's imaginative purpose, at least to suggest the fullness of it, year by year, book by book. One advantage of this chronology is that it allows one to see the push in the work toward larger forms, a contest and a narrative of the state of being in the language.

A short poem in prose, "E," from Another Mouth is clear:

This writing, it is a life done in secret, that
is its charm. It's charm, the stolen (yeah, trickster)
moments, stolen E motion. Nobody but nobody can
stop you at that moment & say hey you're holding
that wrong let me show you.

(Another Mouth 80)

The oldest rebellion of all, which in writing is not a privacy but a recognition of the solitude and secrecy of our entrance to the otherness of language, older

---

[*] I think this is a useful distinction to make in reading contemporary poetry. I've adapted it from H. Arendt, Men in Dark Times (29).

and other than ourselves[3] again and again. With Bowering, the immediate and un-mediated entrance to language is fundamental, a natural, unmystical magic. This is part of the amazement and exactness to that amazement in his lyrics with all their musical competence. Beyond that self-consciousness comes the transition to imagination which I have tried to follow in the selection. Bowering has said that he is no longer a lyric poet—he did not wish to write the same poem over and over again—and he has dated that point in his work from the writing of the poem-sequence *Genève* (1970) (Bayard and David, *Out-Posts* 92). There is no finer statement of his point than "I Never Felt Such Love," dated March, 1972:

Nearly all the poems I have written in the past few years have been a book long. When I'm kidding around I refer to this present as my symphonic period. But not really kidding—you know that.

So what of that period just before the long poems. At about the time I turned thirty I moved from the West to southern Ontario. I found it difficult to keep on writing lyrics. I found it difficult but I did it, I kept on writing lyrics. But the poems were different from those that had come before. In my twenties in the West I'd been learning to write lyrics by finding my voice as it sounded according to my sense of place, in Vancouver, by the sea, the mountain valleys of B.C., the snows of Alberta's crumpled plains. But in southern Ontario there is no place. At least not the kind you can get lost in & find your way in. So I didn't quite know what I was doing, but I began to look elsewhere, inward, as they say, & into my personal time, around me in dreams, over my shoulder at the approach of the dentist & his friend the man in alligator shoes.

In your twenties, I was saying, you are a cell, interacting. In your thirties you enter time, that is not only yours. In your thirties you become all ways aware of your life as a drama, of the cycle, the place in the pattern your life is now taking, who's been there & who's coming. You see that where you are is where Gilgamesh was. The passion takes over, & in art the passion takes over from mere worship, what you were doing in your lyrical twenties. To think that for thirteen years I was completely convinced that I'd die at twenty-nine!

As it shows up in the art, it makes itself known in the emotions. My experience is that I feel things more deeply since turning thirty. Sometimes I think, my god, can this growth in feeling go on forever? There were feelings in the previous decade, obviously, but the senses were so busy taking in details that I was always saying or learning to say, oh, there it is out there. After thirty I said, oh, here it is in here. It was as if the language was not going out to meet the objects, but was being said by them from inside up to my larynx & out there.

I used to say, as I was on the verge of thirty, that if I survived I wanted nothing more in the future than I wanted wisdom, though it is mixt with despair, etc. I got pain & tears & cosmic laughter that promised to bring on wisdom. I now feel that it will come, & am immediately aware of the work involved, whereas earlier I merely hoped for the promise. That makes little lyrics while waiting. I have learned to agree with Robert Creeley, who wrote:

How wise age is—
how desirous!

though it hurts that it keeps on happening. (*In the Flesh* 8–9)

The point is not that he will never write lyrics again—while waiting they will
return with loves, sorrows and occasions—but rather to think into the world.
Thus Bowering has moved further than ever before in the splendid adventures
of *Autobiology* (1971), *Curious* (1972), *Αλλοφανεs* (1975), and *A Short Sad Book*
(1976). These are all extended forms, books, composed of fragment-structures.
I must admit the awkwardness of selecting from them, even the danger of mis-
representing the accomplishment of them. I believe my selection remains true
to the fundamental structures of his imagination, the most obvious of which
are the doubling vision and the multiplied voices of those narratives: in *Auto-
biology*, an ever changing three-year-old narrator meets and mixes with the puz-
zled and puzzling mind of George Bowering-writer; in *Curious*, the writer, very
conscious of his own stake in the art, writes forty-eight portraits of writers he's
known, which, drawn together, become a strange portrait of the artist in his and
our time; in *Αλλοφανεs* St. Arte makes a funny, startling appearance, twisting
in and out of our lives with many voices—is she the real itself, like a pun, ap-
pearing and disappearing from underfoot—"Do you believe all this stuff?"—;
in *A Short Sad Book*, a deliciously Canadian book, the writer enters Canadian his-
tory and art, and screws them up, much as he received them, with a narrator
who is, we are told, eight years old, who is to change fifteen years later, in love
with Canada, who is, of course, also George Bowering who is the forty-one-
year-old writer of the book meeting the wounded reality of himself and of
his Canada. How brilliant they are, made of thought fragments which crys-
tallize and return us to the *essential poetic phenomenon of language*, as if we had lost it.
I think we have. "And this thinking, fed by the present, works with the 'thought
fragments' . . . ."*—to answer to my own sense of art as out of the "darkness
of the lived instant" into form. I turn back to Bowering's lonely, truthful be-
ginnings in "Radio Jazz"; to the Canadian prairie of "Grandfather" Jabez Harry
Bowering; to the universal question of "Moon Shadow"; to *Baseball*, a memo-
rial poem for Jack Spicer, which makes the skill of baseball analogous to the
skill of poetry—that real; to the visionary love of *The Sensible*; to *George, Vancouver,
a discovery poem*, documentary and map of the northwest passage toward poetry,
the extraordinary Strait of Anian. And thence, once again, to the long poems
and books of the last ten years.

* Arendt discussing Walter Benjamin in *Men in Dark Times* (205).

Autobiology and *A Short Sad Book* appear to be prose. They are, however, anti-prosaic and are written against the unconsciousness or innocence of ordinary prose. The style of them—and style is a great pleasure in this work, presenting a distance moved in the depth of the language and a freed verbal imagination—stands in extreme contrast to the "straight" prose of Bowering's novel, *Mirror on the Floor* (1967), and the short stories in *Flycatcher* (1974). Both *Autobiology* and *A Short Sad Book* have to do with transformations of self and place into imaginative structures, which derive from the discovery poems in prose. Both are shaped by discontinuous, short chapters which Bowering has derived from a finely thought use of William Carlos Williams (*The Great American Novel*), Beckett, Jack Spicer and Gertrude Stein—use being, of course, the finest offering an author can make to the writers he respects.

A few remarks on *A Short Sad Book*, since it is the book most disturbed in [its] order by selection from it. It opens with an epigraph from Robbe-Grillet:

> "Under our gaze, the simple gesture of holding out our hand becomes bizarre, clumsy; the words we hear ourselves speaking suddenly sound false; the time of our minds is no longer that of the clocks; & the style of a novel, in its turn, can no longer be innocent." (Epigraph n.p.)

A Short Sad Book is then a novel without innocence or realism of plot, character and action. Thus, it enters concernedly the long modern meditation on anti-forms—the anti-novel and anti-poem—which by a paradox becomes a renewal of form in consciousness. The author then asks:

> Dear Reader Reading:
> 1. Please take your time.
> 2. Also there is one dream in the following pages.
>   You should be able to find it. (Epigraph n.p.)

The text begins with an apparent naïveté of surface and brief, simple sentences that stop and start as if the "novel" itself were talking back, and it is. This is the beginning of a lost innocence in writing, which is our own, the reader's loss, and of a regained language and imaginative form. A marvellous, raucous laughter works on us throughout. *A Short Sad Book* is divided into six parts: "Canadian Geography," "The Exile of Evangeline," "Canadian History," "The Black Mountain Influence," "The Pretty Good Canadian Novel" and "The Return of Evangeline." It is then a "history" of Canada with a plot—will Evangeline be brought back, out of "women's heaven" (*Short Sad Book* 172), to be a Canadian posthumously and spiritually? And the book has another plot: that of writing writing itself into Canadian history. At one point in the book, Evangeline and Sir John A.

Macdonald have come west on the CPR [Canadian Pacific Railroad]. We note, by the way, that Evangeline's story was written by the American Longfellow and that the CPR was built by the American Van Horne. Evangeline and Sir John climb a mountain, which turns out to be Black Mountain on Vancouver's north shore, and make love. It is a very funny breaking-down of time by which culture is given back to its indeterminate parts, just as one receives it according to one's place, condition and labor. We have a detective, Al, who is Al Purdy, searching out what is truly Canadian and how much of it has been defoliated by the Black Mountain influence of Charles Olson, etc. This is an amusing playing around with an important poet whom Bowering has elsewhere respectfully named "the world's most Canadian poet" (*Al Purdy* 1). Near the end of the book, Evangeline returns to put her case for "repatriation" before the Prime Minister, Robert Fulford on *Saturday Night,* and the nationalist Sparrow, who is Robin Mathews,[4] so called because robins migrate and sparrows never leave.

> The others watcht as she stood on tiptoe momentarily to kiss me in front of my brain, then walkt swiftly to her craft & disappeared from her audience.
> I swore on the spot to do the same. (*Short Sad Book* 185)

When in Ottawa at the National Gallery, he meets art, the shapes change—"I saw a human shape slumpt against the wall . . . & I wondered is he alive or is he art" (35).

> The shape lay with his feet straight out & his hat tipt over his chest not a hat but a parka hood. He was a figure on the ground.
> So he must have been art all right. (35)

The shape turns out to be Gabriel Dumont, both Louis Riel's lieutenant and Evangeline's separated lover; then he changes to David McFadden, and then again to the wonderful painter of "Indians," Paul Kane. Somewhere, Al the Canadian "was smiling because he knew the Canadian mystery would be solved in the west" (118).

The book is funny, its title playing off Gertrude Stein's *A Long Gay Book* of 1912, and it is sad before an audience that would culturally determine the author without regard for his conscious and caring task. This writing is a new condition and it may be seen as an affirmation of a primary innocent language that is exactly north and west. The result is a finely sophisticated art. On this occasion, I can only note the importance of Stein. *A Long Gay Book* is fundamental to an understanding of her "incongruous" and "discontinuous" method. It was to be about her sexuality, that is to say, about her identity. It is a record of the famous change of style that leads to the later work. In a fine essay on her 1940 book, *Ida,* Bowering writes of the most difficult issue, "the conflict between identity, which is to do with nouns, & entity, which is to do with verbs" ("That Was Ida" 37). "Ida spends the first part of her life trying to fashion an identity & the second part trying to survive it" (37). This, he argues, leads to two kinds of birth in her writing, very like, I note, the births in *Autobiology* and *A Short Sad Book*: "Inside where the continuous verb is, & outside, where the noun is" (38). "More conventional fiction uses climax & denouement to assert an unproven greater significance for man's fate. Stein didnt want to tell such tall stories; she wanted to write lives" (39).

> There is no final real identity at the end of the rainbow, & the end of the rainbow anyway continues receding over yonder hills the self walks toward. No resolution, no solution, the story of Ida is not over till the *reader* dies. We put up with our own identities, & theirs, till then. ("That Was Ida" 46)

Bowering has been moved by the "liberation of her verbal imagination" and has found his own.[*]

I want now to reflect briefly on the context and vocation of this poet, George Bowering. Looking back and speaking of himself and young poet friends, "[W]e were people who had been deracinated—we didn't get any Canadian writing at school in B.C." (Bayard and David 81). Checked out, Stephen Leacock turns out to be the one exception in Bowering's early experience. I can guess at the school-book romanticism he must have been given, the deracinated curriculum of culture in which every romantic author is misread and sentimentalized. From it, one can only learn never to cover and distort the world by sentiment. Later, Bowering will turn around in recognition and reparation to face Blake and Shelley (superbly in "Mars" and *The Sensible*).[5] In 1966 and 1967, he undertook, but did not complete, a Ph.D. on Shelley. Bowering has often described that deracination. He answered it first with a love of Hemingway and James T. Farrell. They were, so to speak, in the air, like jazz on the radio from Salt Lake City. The extraordinary naturalism of Frederick Philip Grove was not. Out of realism and naturalism, Bowering built his faith in plain and natural language— to be in touch with the daily life and ordinary language. Later, he will turn to the anti-realism I have described to escape the limitations of form they induce. He has credited Kenneth Rexroth, Kenneth Patchen and William Carlos Williams with a part in his finding his own voice—the plain song of it. Particularly Williams taught him, by example, to start with the ground, but the ground from the beginning is Bowering's own, as in the beautiful poem "Grandfather."[6] Bow-

---

[*] See Richard Bridgman, *Gertrude Stein in Pieces* on *A Long Gay Book* (102–3).

ering has been blamed for this first language; it is said to be American in a critical rejection of what this poet is and what he witnesses. I think of the academic who remarked: "George would know there's a Canadian tradition if only he'd been born in Toronto." Apart from the difficulty of the way the gods cheat one or another of us, tradition is a modernist problem, not simply a provincial one. Neither provincialism nor regionalism qualifies Bowering's work. Still, Bowering had to begin with the "sticks and stones"[7] of his own conditions. Acculturation weakens in the small towns and in relation to the distance from the "establishment," largely, these days, academic. The young man, born in Penticton in 1935, would inevitably think he had to make "it" out of whole cloth.[8] During his years in the Royal Canadian Air Force,[*] 1954–1957, the pleasures and assurances of realism were challenged by his reading what he calls writers of "odd character," Henry Miller and e.e. cummings, writers who work against the grain of the accepted or expected. In 1957, at the University of British Columbia, he had a whole library to search through. Here it was that the works of Rexroth, Patchen and Williams turned up. I think Williams's "The Desert Music" was a key discovery. It opens with the poem "The Descent" and moves from the "formerly / unsuspected" (Pictures 73) place to affirm a music, a dance, a verb:

I am, a poet! I
am. I am. I am a poet, I reaffirmed, ashamed
                    (Pictures 120)

I think of Bowering's poem of 1973, "Desert Elm": "I had never said the word / poetry without a funny accent."[9] The discovery here is of locus, of, in Bowering's words, "trying to find out where you are—not a literary device."[10] The location of the self in a place is a primitivism in poetry, perhaps its only constant, certainly its first purpose. This brings every writer initially into conflict with the abstractions of a tradition. The understanding of the individual voice inside the enormity and chaos of meaning in this century is difficult. Via the individuality that all poetry discloses—without any necessary theory of genius— in the persistence of its song, the lyric base-note or fragment, the poet perforce does love his time—celebrates it—in order to stop its fall. Nowadays, the condition of the artist and the identity of the artist, his portrait, fall "within the twentieth-century conflict marked by realism and naturalism on one hand, and stream of consciousness, surrealism, and archetypal literature on the other—a minute faithfulness to accepted categories of meaning versus a direct chroni-

---

[*] George Bowering and his buddies joked that RCAF means, "Red Cock After Fucking."

cling of mental process, in whatever guise that process is understood to exist" (Wendy Steiner 2). Thus, Bowering's art of process—"the process of thinking itself"—answers first to that deracination and then to a condition that is abroad, modern and contemporary.

Within the university context, Bowering met the poet Lionel Kearns in 1959, recently returned from Montréal with news of Louis Dudek, Irving Layton and Raymond Souster. The enjoinment of these Canadian models to those of his earlier discoveries in the art of language was crucial. The voices of Dudek, Layton and Souster were protesting, direct and natural. They not only drew a Canadian poetry forward for recognition, they drew attention to a deep division in Canadian poetic concern. This division has been described as a difference in poetic taste and function between the "cultivated" and the "uncultivated" and as a "crude-fine" paradox in all North American writing.* These are useful distinctions up to a point and they do not cloud the issues by hazardously adopting the Russian term "formalist" to distinguish one poetic direction from another. I will for my part save the word form to describe the active work of those who love form and seek its possibilities—what Bowering calls his "love of form." The profound nature of the division was made clear in the now famous essay by John Sutherland, "Mr. Smith and the 'Tradition,'" (1947).† Louis Dudek and Michael Gnarowski have noted that for Sutherland, "The 'modern' school was not 'metaphysical' or 'cosmopolitan,'" as A. J. M. Smith had argued, "but essentially local and particular" (46). Eli Mandel summarizes: Sutherland "simply identified 'cosmopolitan' with British poetry and consequently with social reaction. . . . Smith is constructing a rationale for his own poetry and the poetry of A. M. Klein, F. R. Scott, and Leo Kennedy; Sutherland, for Irving Layton, Louis Dudek, and Raymond Souster" (Mandel 12). The distinction to be noted is between what used to be called a "high art" and language which stood apart from circumstance and another art which is intimate with circumstance. This will have extraordinary consequences in Canadian writing because it emphasizes the "intimate relationship of form and circumstance" (Bacigalupo 124).

It was that emphasis that led to the foundation of TISH: A Poetry Newsletter, 1961–1969, in Vancouver and to the mingling recognitions of George Bowering, Frank Davey, David Dawson, Jamie Reid and Fred Wah in those early years. The gathering purposes of form and circumstance make TISH still very readable and lead one to follow the work of Bowering, Davey and Wah as each

* See Eli Mandel, "Introduction" to Contexts of Canadian Criticism (12 ff.), citing Warren Tallman. And Louis Dudek and Michael Gnarowski, eds., The Making of Modern Poetry in Canada (46 ff.).

† The important documents of this division are available in Dudek and Gnarowski, The Making of Modern Poetry in Canada.

enters, now separately, upon large imaginative assertions. Of course, the line-up of poets indicative of that division in the Canadian imagination did not remain so simple. Looking back in 1971, Frank Davey writes:

> . . . in the overall tradition of Canadian poetry TISH and its poets belong to the "universist" line of Lampman, Carman, W. W. E. Ross, Klein, Souster, Layton and Purdy, rather than to the humanist and rationalist one of Goldsmith, Sangster, Pratt, Smith, F. R. Scott, Finch, LePan, Reaney, Mandel and Gustafson. The distinction between these lines is not a firm one.[11] ("Introduction," TISH 10)

Indeed, it is not, but the point of an anti-humanism is fundamental. The term must not be misunderstood or reduced. It indicates a profound implication of the intimacy of form and circumstance. Bowering has repeatedly felt called upon in interviews to say he is not a humanist. Davey, the most responsible theorist of this renewal of form, tries some definitions:

> The differences lie primarily in world-view and concepts of form. The universist writers tend to see the universe as vast, divine, mysteriously structured, and essentially ungraspable by human reason. The humanists see it as finite, orderly, and manageable by man. The universists regard form as active and alive; the humanists as a manipulated showplace for the human mind. To the universists the poem involves the poet in recognition and surprise, it leads him to more than he knew or planned. To the humanist it is a culture-object, moulded and chiseled [sic] to a shape preconceived by its author's intelligence and will—expressing his ideas, bearing the stamp of his style. ("Introduction," TISH 10)

This is anti-perspectival. The humanism, out of the Renaissance, with its idealism of reason does not answer to the terror and chaos of this century; a humanism, without measure, which ended in human limits spelled out plainly, has long made poets impatient. I think of Margaret Avison writing years ago:

> Your law of optics is a quarrel
> Of chickenfeet on paper. Does a train
> Run pigeon-toed?
>
> I took a train from here to Ottawa
> On tracks that did not meet. We swelled and roared
> Mile upon mightier mile, and when we clanged
> Into the vasty station we were indeed
> Brave company for giants.
>
> ("Perspective")[12]

The anti-humanism and the anti-perspectival aspects of this poetry are against the negation that human reason has become and for a changed vision of the world with a measured sense of the humane. Such vision does not precede the work of the poem. The forms of it may work by displacements, dissociations and fragments, but the world the poet witnesses is not small. This is a Blakean critique of human reason as limit and fall and is present without having been derived from Blake in some very important Canadian writing.

The "TISH poets" have been in Canada identified with an Americanism, an injudicious freedom, the "Black Mountain influence"—all based on Robert Duncan's having set off the idea for a magazine and on the famous Vancouver Poetry Conference of 1963—visitors were Duncan, Olson, Ginsberg, Creeley, Levertov, Whalen and Avison. It is time to reread this with some subtlety. Unfortunately, the proceedings of the Conference are largely unpublished.* Therein can be found the clearest evidence for what I have said of this gathering purpose, originally Canadian, of the intimacy of form with circumstance. Those "wonder merchants"[13] (Warren Tallman's name for them) had similar concerns and a similar struggle to undergo.

I have been careful in tracing thus briefly Bowering's entrance into poetry in order to say his poetry is not foreign here. From 1959 on, Bowering seems to have worked with and through that division in Canadian poetic concern. The work of Dudek, Layton and Souster first offered a Canadian model in which an intimacy of form is strict and demanding. When later, Bowering comes to measure his place in Canadian poetry, he does so with two careful studies, a book on Al Purdy (1970), and a fine essay on Margaret Avison, 1971.[14] But to begin with, it was those three with all their particulars. Bowering has said that ultimately he probably got most from Souster—the short, inimitable lyric. Souster, Davey writes, "demands . . . that we sing 'when there's really no reason why.' He asks that we face the impermanent and tawdry modern world, if not hopefully, at least (like the last patch of April snow) 'dirty-white/but defiant.' . . . He sings of the minimal, the familiar, the easily overlooked" (From There to Here 244). The notion of what poetry is becomes familiar, unspectacular, never heightened. This naturalness of poetry is a kind of courage, though it can undercut all larger imaginative structures, as if modern, urban man must go on without them. "If you look at the 1950s stuff those guys were doing and the contentions they were making in their magazine," Bowering has said, "—it was really exciting. I was getting it about five years out of date. But I read every one of those. I read Laughter in the Mind—oh, a great book, and I was reading Dudek's East of the City—fantastic" (Bayard and David, Out-Posts 81).

* The one exception is the limited and private edition of Charles Olson's remarks at the Conference, edited by Ralph Maud. The proceedings were taped and the tapes are available in the Simon Fraser University Library, Contemporary Literature Collection.

Irving Layton's *A Laughter in the Mind* (1958) is a brilliant book: "my favourite image is Fire; my favourite word, *Blaze*" (*Laughter* 11). Not yet, as later, dependent upon a repeated personal aggression, the poems of this book are made of air and the objects of attention, thus, the fire. The primary condition of the poet is made clear in a wonderful opening "note":

> Each day the world must be created anew. Otherwise the symbolic volcano is forgotten and people build their lives of slag. More, they spread the heresy that the universe is composed only of slag, the more impudent among them—the so-called "cultured"—displaying proudly the ashflecks on the lapels of their grey flannel suits. When I meet someone for the first time, I ask: "Does he know he is a burning taper?" For if he does, he burns evenly and there is a sweet light in his countenance; otherwise his eyes gutter and his skin and hair have a rancid smell. (*Laughter* 11)

Layton, with such a book, is central to the imagination of poet and poetry in Canada. Within the divided interests of Canadian poetry, his demand is that the form hold energy rather than distance and polish. From this, the larger structures of imagination are possible and promissory. But Layton has not accomplished this in his later work; I take the reason to be that for him the poet's identity must not be shaken. The larger imaginative work seems to require a transformation of the poet's state in his text, a disappearance and reappearance of whatever he considers himself to be therein. A rebellion of the language and the poet. Louis Dudek seems to me to be of extraordinary importance. It is strange that he has been out of sympathy with so much Canadian poetry since the late 1950's. Frank Davey notes: "In recent statements he has asserted the 'hard' austere values of the modernist tradition against the post-modern fragment-structures of such writers as George Bowering and bp Nichol" (*From There to Here* 93). But Bowering has long remembered the sharp realism of *East of the City* (1946). This book is throughout a call for intelligence:

> So that someday we may go, and see the sun rise
> Outside this world of rubble. . . .
>
> (Dudek, *East of the City* 49)

For Dudek, the solution is a meditative poem-structure on the dark of the modern condition. His honesty is such that he allows no stop to the fallen condition. Beauty seems trapped or lost. Where he would seem to be headed for a transformation of self and society, he falters. Unlike Souster and Layton, Dudek has worked for large imaginative structures in *Europe* (1954), *En México* (1958), and *Atlantis* (1967). A long meditative form, *Atlantis*, free in movement between hope and despair, is Dudek's finest achievement. It is fragmented, which makes one wonder that he has disliked the later "fragment-structure" poets. It is a terrifying poem. In it, reality is lost. "The real, or the unreal— / beginning where you are" falls into the sea (*Atlantis* 151).

Try to change the world . . .
Not to change, but to break through the glut of bad change,
to "the power and the glory" that is always there.

(Atlantis 95)

One could whisper of the pure spirit
but the pure spirit is smoke.
It was to set fire to the real it came among us.

What I hold against Jesus
            is that he ascended again into heaven
and left us here to "believe." (96)

Nothing—is always true.
In any crisis, it's the best thing to do.
Nothing—is what it comes to.
It's where we begin.
Nothing—is what we like to do. (150)

Belief is only a quotation. The magnificent formal possibilities of *Atlantis* will turn up again and again in the work of later poets. Davey has noticed this currency in Bowering, Coleman, Marlatt, bp Nichol, Dennis Lee, and himself (*From There to Here* 95). The trouble with Dudek is in the moral and humanistic solution he offers. It is one of the greatest problems of imagination, as it differs from ordinary logical discourse, not to resolve form into an order, a nostalgia, beyond its actuality.

I have stopped over these important writers because they are central to the Canadian imagination. They have stood for qualities of the imagination that backed Bowering up. I have tried to spot the problematics of their work because Bowering has had to depart from them. In his measured portraits of poets in the book *Curious*—like Stein, he is interested in the literary portrait—we find Souster:

        His photographs are in the right place &
he is always looking at the camera & it does not make
him smile.
        It does not make him smile but it does
not make him strike a pose. He is nobody else.

("Raymond Souster")

and Layton:

> I cant imagine him actually
> I cant imagine him————a woman or a
> boy or even an animal. I cant imagine it.
>
> ("Irving Layton")

and Dudek:

> He says it over &
> over & this year there must be still some poets
> who hear it & remember when he was not alone &
> said so & wrote & was a publisher & started to
> make us all famous.
>
> ("Louis Dudek" n.p.)

"So that these exercises exhaust the average mind" (Dudek, *Atlantis* 150). Modernism has been naturalized in Canada for a long time. I use the word modernism here, not to point to a style, experiment or manner, but to designate the twentieth century condition—loosened meaning, distrust of tradition, dark times. In poetry, there have been many answers to this condition—a reconstituted relation to tradition often ironic of the present, an aesthetic purity, a deconstructive dadaism, a transformational surrealism,* and so forth. Many threads of wisdom and despair for the writer. Every young writer enters upon this condition to answer as best he can. Looking back over the "modernity" of this century's writing, Frank Davey has chosen to argue a "post-modern" stance. This term, adapted from Charles Olson and by Olson from the American painters of the 1950's, is slippery, but the intentions it names are clear. On the one hand, I want to place Bowering's work within the modern condition—that is, to see its significance within "the enormity of present experience" (Hartman, *Beyond Formalism* 367). On the other, I am concerned with his contemporaneity. The term "post-modern" so conscientiously inserted into Canadian criticism by Frank Davey—and supported by Bowering's own literary essays—signals a strong movement among important Canadian writers to separate themselves from certain characteristics of modernism. Their emphasis is upon the democratic and against the authoritarian, upon naturalness of language, and upon fragment-structures of thought and feeling without undue anxiety about the absence of reconciliatory and conservative structures of meaning. Modernism is identified with "hard, austere values" and authoritarianism. "Modernism," Davey writes, "was essentially

---

* See André-G. Bourassa, *Surréalisme et Littérature Québécoise.*

an elitist, formulaic, anti-democratic, and anti-terrestrial movement" (*From There to Here* 19). The push is to shake off the structural hierarchies in modernism even as these are seen in Eliot, Pound and Yeats, forefathers. Davey, in the same context, notes that "[p]olitics and art have become interwoven as never before" (*From There to Here* 14), and argues to solve this by a diminished central authority. This then translates into counter-structures against form as completion or conclusion. Such counter-structures with their infinite variety must be witnessed again and again. Davey's views, which are close to Bowering's—out of an old camaraderie—then come to suggest a large arena of concern. "Canada," he writes, "has struggled to become itself a significant counter-structure" (*From There to Here* 15) the key event of which is the Canada-U.S. struggle, with George Grant's *Lament for a Nation* (1965) central to the thought of that struggle. Significant contemporary Canadian writing reflects this as a *contest* of form in the strategies of art, though George Grant cannot acknowledge more than a "hectic" and "shallow" art, oddly citing Burroughs as typical. In *Technology and Empire* (1969), he draws the sorts which no living writer, even a toady, fails to contemplate:

> . . . the events in Vietnam must help to push them toward that divide where one can no longer love one's own—where indeed it almost ceases to be one's own. (74–75)

And three pages later:

> . . . what lies behind the small practical question of Canadian nationalism is the larger context of the fate of western civilization. . . . What is worth doing in the midst of this barren twilight is the incredibly difficult question. (78)

I want to emphasize that today the writer writing is within that condition. But it is not as new as Vietnam, which finally made it crucial here and south of the border. Pushed back to the lyric voice, out of honesty, the poet takes a chance of repeating during his whole career, a tiresome whine, a tiresome joy. In the context of the "incredibly difficult question," the beautiful lyric tradition is profoundly questioned by writer and reader. The personal poem does not answer. Thus Bowering and others of his peers like Davey and bp Nichol have moved to build larger imaginative structures, narratives that are not simply a desire for identity. True poetic form may well begin and end in lyric, the poet is after all only the poet. Still, there is a way of working in the world that is "poetic thinking." One of the pleasures of Bowering's work is the devolvement in it year by year of an extended imaginative range. Imaginative order is a lifetime task, even for the non-literary man, never still or complete. I have wanted to talk of the condition in which it is made. Geoffrey Hartman writes:

Take the contemporary situation. Many artists, today, doubt art to the point of be-coming incapable of it. . . . The artist has a bad conscience because of the idea that forms, structures, etc. always reconcile or integrate, that they are conservative de-spite themselves. To create a truly iconoclastic art, a structure-breaking art; to change the function of form from reconciliation and conservation to rebellion, and so to participate in the enormity of present experience—this is one Promethean aim still fiery enough to inspire. It is the psychic state of art today. (*Beyond Formalism* 367)

Of Bowering's imagination, it is fair to say with the help of Guy Davenport:

The imagination is like the drunk man who lost his watch, and must get drunk again to find it. It is as intimate as speech and custom, and to trace its ways we need to re-educate our eyes. (*Geography* 5)

And we may learn to read again the romance to which poetic thinking always returns us. Bowering:

As I get older, I come more to realize that my activity as a poet composing is an extension of my desirous childhood Christianity. I want like crazy to get here alone and hear God's voice, I mean it. If I hear the gods instead, I am acknowl-edging, like it or not, my adulthood.*

In Chapter 48 of *Autobiology*, the marvellous birth imagery gives us a body which is a stream that is not muddy:

If this is the stream & I am still to float what is the boat.
What is the boat. (102)

One hears the loss of Shelley's "My soul is an enchanted boat," only to find it again in the question. The word soul remains in the wreckage of our modern minds and hearts. We may, however, heed Geoffrey Hartman once again:

Only one myth, perhaps, proves inexhaustible. A poet, says Keats, "has no Iden-tity; he is continually in for—and filling—some other Body." There will always be an Other, or the dream of Otherness. Literature is the form that dream takes in an enlightened mind.† (*Beyond Formalism* x)

Bastille Day, 1980

---

* Bowering's statement on Ἀλλοφανες, "Look into your Ear and Write: Allophanes," in Michael Ondaatje, ed., *The Long Poem Anthology* (329).

† The essays of this volume are excellent companions for those concerned with poetic think-ing. Late in the volume, Hartman offers a splendid discussion of Apollo, "the god of art by tradi-tional equation," in the third book of *Hyperion*. "We have only to look at the crisis point in Keats's

Hyperion," he writes, "to see this struggle for 'appearance' accompanied by all the suggestiveness that hidden frontiers bestow. . . . While attempting to dawn, Apollo suffers pangs like those accompanying childbirth or sexual climax or the biomorphic passage from one state of being to another" (*Beyond Formalism* 369). With Bowering's *Autobiology,* Wah's *Breathin' My Name with a Sigh* and bp Nichol's *Journal* and *Martyrology* in mind, I would like to bring together that "biomorphic passage from one state of being to another" and my own sense of "the state of being in the language, a passage in and out of words and syntaxes." Hartman:

> To understand the "art" in art is always essential. But it is even more essential today, for we have clearly entered an "era of suspicion" in which art seems arty to the artist himself. The artist, indeed, is often the severest critic of his own medium, which turns against itself in his relentless drive for self-criticism. Artistic form and aesthetic illusion are today treated as ideologies to be exposed and demystified—this has long been true on the Continent, where Marxism is part of the intellectual milieu, but it is becoming true also of America [and Canada]. If literary history is to provide a new defense of art it must now defend the artist against himself as well as against his other detractors. It must help to restore his faith in two things: in form, and in his historical vocation. (*Beyond Formalism* 358)

The Violets

Charles Olson and Alfred North Whitehead

"a cosmological reading of a cosmology"*

The American poet who has made the most profound use of Whitehead's thought is Charles Olson. On this occasion, when I am to mull over the interchange between them, I am reminded of John Russell's remark as he begins his book on the meanings of modern art: "in art, as in the sciences, ours is one of the big centuries" (9).† Out of the gloom, so to speak. Olson and Whitehead are not, of course, alone, but they stand there among the most important figures. And I like to note that Olson many times expressed his view that the finest compliment one can pay to another mind and work is in the use made of them. When he died in 1970, just turned sixty and by his own reckoning ten years short of the time he needed to complete his work (Boer 137), he was well into the third volume of a major verse epic, *The Maximus Poems*, which stands alongside Pound's *Cantos* and Williams's *Paterson* as a major poetic world. Besides *The Maximus Poems* and the poems that did not find a place in that epic structure, there are the essays and letters which propose the necessary poetic and record the struggle to find it. Olson's poetics are argumentative about the way we stand in the world and how we belong to it (stance and ethos). I wish to emphasize the word "world" for reasons that I hope will become clear.

---

* So George Butterick, Curator of the Olson Archives, University of Connecticut, remarked when we were considering one of Charles Olson's mythological notations in the margins of Whitehead's *Process and Reality:* i.e. "iotunns for iotunns" in the margin of the chapter on "Propositions" (II.IX.VII). Iotunn is the Norse word for giant. Permission to quote unpublished material from the Olson Archives has been granted me by the University of Connecticut which holds the copyrights.

† [Russell] is writing about painting and sculpture. I have expanded his meaning to include literature and poetry.

For Olson, as for any poet, the poetry is primary, but this poetic places before us the argued ground both of practice and of worldview. Poets have repeatedly in this century turned philosophers, so to speak, in order to argue the value of poetry and its practice within the disturbed meanings of our time. These arguments are fascinating because they have everything to do with the poet's sense of reality in which imagery is entangled with thought. Often, they reflect Pound's sense of "make it new" or the modernist notion that this century and its art are simultaneously the end of something and the beginning of something else, a new consciousness, and so forth. It is not one argument or another for or against tradition, nor is it the complex renewal of the imaginary which our arts witness, for, as I take it, the enlightened mind does not undervalue the imaginary, which is the most striking matter of these poetics; what is laid out before us finally is the fundamental struggle for the nature of the real. And this, in my view, is a spiritual struggle, both philosophical and poetic. Old spiritual forms, along with positivisms and materialisms, which "held" the real together have come loose. This is a cliché of our recognitions and condition. But we need only look at the energy of the struggle in philosophy and poetry to make it alive and central to our private and public lives. We need not, I think, at this point be trapped by that view of which Geoffrey Hartman writes:

> Artistic form and aesthetic illusion are today treated as ideologies to be exposed and demystified—this has long been true on the Continent, where Marxism is part of the intellectual milieu, but it is becoming true also of America. (*Beyond Formalism* 358)

The reality of Marxism remains, as it began, the other face of Hegel. To put it unphilosophically, the practice of either of these nineteenth-century prophecies in the twentieth century maintains one side of a dualism, on both sides of which the profound place of the aesthetic, understood as the reach of our "perceptual faith" (Merleau-Ponty's phrase) in human life is short-circuited. Marxism is an instrument, and an excellent one, for social analysis and the understanding of the problems of necessity for large social bodies, and, perhaps, when the wreckage of its twentieth-century practice has been cleared away, it may become an instrument for the founding of social justice. In the meantime, the problem of reality—what do we mean by the real? Part of what is meant is a valuation that includes the world of earth and sky. In the greatest poetry, ancient or modern, the sense of the real is certainly not limited to that other terrifying face of humanism, necessity, an abstract word for the very real limit and terror of poverty and deprivation.[*] The pleasures of art, of philosophy, and of

---

[*] Here, I am reflecting on some of Hannah Arendt's arguments in *On Revolution*.

science are joined to us insofar as we are freed from necessity. In Europe and North America, where necessity, as yet, does not widely rule, we have the curiosity that mercantilism controls form, and art, philosophy and science do not belong to the daily round.* Yet they are, indeed, the elements of a reality, if we try to put one together. (I have in mind Hannah Arendt's moving sense of the possible "recovery of the public world.")[1] I think the fundamental problem here is a "scientism" of the real, from which, in my reading, the gift of Whitehead's searching thought, as corrective, was to allow us to escape: that is, to see and work whatever real we can manage differently. It is this broad, general, rumoured sense of Whitehead, summed up in his word "process," that I believe brings him so forcefully into American poetics. Of that "demystification," which I am here identifying with a scientism of another order, we need to take mind. René Girard writes:

> The cultural heritage of humanity is regarded with suspicion. Its only interest lies in its "demystification." . . .
>
> Humanity, we are told, has fallen victim to a vast mystification unrecognized until now. This is cultural nihilism, and it is often associated with a fetishistic cult of science. Because we have discovered the "original sin" of human thought, we think ourselves free of it. What is now needed is a radically different mode of thought, a new science that will allow us to appreciate the absurdity of all previous thinking. And because this lie was until recently immune from detection, the new scientific approach must be altogether unconnected with the past. Inevitably, it will take the shape of a unique discovery by some inspired being who has little in common with ordinary mortals, or even with his own past. In severing the cord that attached us to the matrix of all mythic thought, this liberator of humanity will have delivered us from dark ancestral falsehood and led us into the luminous world of truth. Our hard and pure science is to be the result of a *coupure épistémologique*, an epistemological revolution that is totally unexpected and for which we are entirely unprepared. (*Violence* 233)

This he names "scientific angelism" (233). It is an apocalypse of the objective or of a generalized humanity which can be seen as an objectivity. It is also a disguised superstition.

What I have noticed in the poetry and poetics of the most important poets is that they are arguing, weaving, and composing a cosmology and an epistemology. Over and over again. There is no epistemological cut-off or gash in our deepest natures, nor in our engagement with life. Nor is the ambition of what is known short on its desire for cosmos. It is this structuring, large and deep in the nature

---

* Take note of Jean Clay, *Modern Art, 1890–1918*, on "art's radical effacement" (23).

of things, that still thrills us in Hesiod's struggle for the sense of it. Such concern, because it does tie to experience, is central to the historical role of poet and poetry. I am not denigrating the song of poetry, for the sense of self is always a part of poetry and reality, and so one sings. But repeatedly in the history of poetry, we find ourselves returning to epic structures and the bases of epic in the shape, size and feel of the world,[2] cosmos, I suggest that great poetry is always after the world—it is a spiritual chase—and that it has never been, in the old, outworn sense, simply subjective or personal. Of course, Whitehead's subjective principle, his theory of prehensions, and his notion of the ingression to the real do not leave the subjective to itself alone. It is this aspect of poetic experience, its yen for largeness and fullness, that has brought poetry throughout its history into close proximity with the modes of theogony and theology, with science in its deepest concerns, and with philosophies which propose a world. The density of meaning in the texts has increased for us, as the gods, that wondrous vocabulary of the world, fall, but not without a trace, and the autonomous mind has had to re-pose itself. We may, then, sit in this corner of things to understand the way in which Whitehead enters so commandingly into Olson's poetic world.

I have arranged my essay to include copious quotation. My reason is that I have found in talking about Olson and teaching his poetry, singular assertion is not enough. And certainly, where his relation to Whitehead is concerned, there will be disparate views. The world of twentieth-century thought involves a huge companionship. I have tried to put together some pieces of that companionship here.

I. WHITEHEAD AND OLSON

Whitehead's sense of reality as process, which stands to correct both materialism and idealism in their command over us, does not enter upon our thought and imaginations unprepared for. Hugh Kenner in his discussion of the importance to Ezra Pound of Fenollosa's "The Chinese Written Character as a Medium for Poetry" notices the depth of preparation for such a view:

> The Descartes who (Boileau complained) had "cut the throat" of poetry, and the Locke who made poetry a diversion of relaxed or enfeebled minds, lived among learned men [. . . who thought] of words naming things, and words as many as there were things, and language a taxonomy of static things, with many an "is" but ideally no verb. And it was just such notions . . . that Ernest Fenollosa, encouraged by ideograms, set out to refute, on behalf of "the language of science which is the language of poetry." (Pound Era 224–25)

In a letter of 1916, before the essay was printed in 1919, Pound states his interest: "'All nouns come from verbs.' To the primitive man, a thing only is what it *does*. That is Fenollosa, but I think the theory a very good one for poets to go by" (Pound, *Letters* 82). It is of singular importance that among poets the effort to regain a world-view is also a search for a different stance in language. Olson will make a similar move by attention to the Hopi language in Benjamin Whorf's studies (*Special View* 24).* And it fascinates me that when I turn to science, I find the physicist David Bohm in his cosmology undertaking the same search:

> The subject-verb-object structure of language, along with its world view, tends to impose itself very strongly in our speech, even in those cases in which some attention would reveal its evident inappropriateness. . . .
> Is it not possible for the syntax and grammatical form of language to be changed so as to give a basic role to the verb rather than the noun? (29)

This involves, I think, a renewed sense of literature, particularly poetry, in which the work of an active, undistanced language goes on, a parataxis.

I note Whitehead's currency in these contemporary cosmological concerns, in Bohm, in Ruth Nanda Anshen's beautiful essay "Convergence," and in Bernard Lovell's *Emerging Cosmology*.† Lovell closes his book with this quotation from Whitehead:

> "There is no parting from your own shadow. To experience this faith is to know that in being ourselves we are more than ourselves: to know that our experience, dim and fragmentary as it is, yet sounds the utmost depths of reality: to know that detached details merely in order to be themselves demand that they should find themselves in a system of things: to know that this system includes the harmony of logical rationality, and the harmony of aesthetic achievement: to know that, while the harmony of logic lies upon the universe as an iron necessity, the aesthetic harmony stands before it as a living ideal moulding the general flux in its broken progress towards finer, subtler issues." (Lovell 197)

This wonderful voice, guiding science and, as we shall see, entering into poetry, draws attention to what is most to be attended to in art—if I may cadge some phrases from a scholar of Melville, Olson's first master—"the mode of his engagement with life, the capacity to the deep-diving literary imagination to plunge to the bottom of human experience and to find there what is funded as ontolog-

---

* Olson asks that we read Benjamin Whorf, "An American Indian Model of the Universe," *International Journal of American Linguistics* 16, no. 2 (April 1950).

† Ruth Nanda Anshen's essay is the statement of purpose for the series "Convergence," of which Lovell's book is one volume. The Whitehead quotation is from *Science and the Modern World* (23–24).

ical possiblity" (Sherrill 238). Funded by Olson and Whitehead on this occasion. But it is Kenner's point that reality as process was prepared for in Emerson's "organicism" to bring us by affinity to "Whitehead and Darwin and Frazer, and Gestaltists and field physicists, and the synergism of Buckminster Fuller," to "organisms not systems," to "process and change and resemblance and continuity."

> And behind that effort? Behind it, preparing for it, a chain of philosophers, a chain which "leads back through Hegel, Lotse, Schelling and Herder to Leibnitz (as Whitehead constantly recognized), and then it seems to disappear": seems to disappear because we are looking for European predecessors, and Leibnitz was indebted to China. So runs Joseph Needham's remarkable hypothesis, which attributes European organicism, via Leibnitz' Jesuit friends of the China Mission, to neo-Confucian Li and the school of Chu Hsi. (Kenner 231)

Kenner is surely right to point to the history of this receptivity, however much modern relativity theory, interpreted by Whitehead, placed a premium on process. Olson, modern as he is, is also New England. He had that ground. In an old-fashioned American education, Emerson was simply among the books on the family shelves. In terms of poetry and process, Olson's first debts are to Pound's Fenollosa and Confucianism and, then, to William Carlos Williams's early interest in science, reflected in his poetry, as a means to gain objectivity and emotional accuracy.* Mike Weaver has finely drawn these concerns together in his discussion of science and poetry in Williams's early work. There, we find out that Williams requested a copy of C. P. Steinmetz's book on relativity in 1926 (Weaver 47), and that he was given a copy of Whitehead's *Science and the Modern World* in December, 1926 (48). Williams wrote in that copy: "Finished reading it at sea, Sept. 26, 1927—A milestone surely in my career, should I have the force and imagination to go on with my work" (Weaver 48 n.2). Because Whitehead's science of reality influences stance and, thereby, form in so powerful a poet as Williams, it is fair to say that the currency of Whitehead in poetry has something like a date just there.

Among Olson's books, now collected in the Charles Olson Archives at the University of Connecticut Library at Storrs, only two of Whitehead's titles turn up: *Process and Reality: An Essay in Cosmology* and *The Aims of Education and Other Essays* (Butterick, "Olson's Reading" 88).† This tells us only so much: that certain ti-

---

* See Robert von Hallberg, *Charles Olson: The Scholar's Art* (235 n. 47).

† Olson purchased the copy of *Process and Reality* now in the Olson Archives early in 1957 (Cambridge University Press, 1929). If one is trying to follow Olson in his interest in Whitehead, it is important to have that edition. The New York Macmillan edition of the same year is differently paged and, in at least one important instance, lacks a Whitehead note.

tles remained in his library, others did not, and that his personal collection is not the record of the breadth of his reading. Charles Boer in his fine memoir of Olson's last months in Connecticut recalls an evening's conversation on Whitehead. His narration is addressed to Olson himself:

> The Wesleyan University undergraduate curriculum in your day had been revamped along "general education" lines and Whitehead's book, published in your freshman year at Wesleyan, became one of the core texts in this curriculum. Its "philosophy of organism," its "subjectivist principle," and especially its scientifically minded efforts to offer a cosmology for the twentieth century, were facets of Whitehead's thinking that remained with you throughout your life. (Boer 108)

Olson was an undergraduate at Wesleyan 1928–1932, and he received his M.A. there in 1933 (Butterick, *Guide* lx). He was later to continue graduate studies at Harvard. Boer's descriptive terms for Whitehead's book seem more suitable to *Process and Reality* than to any other title, though all the elements noted are concerns present in *Science and the Modern World* which would be the likely book for an undergraduate programme. The latter was first published in 1925 and the former in 1929. The conversation, Thanksgiving Day, 1969, here remembered, may well have contained some fusion of the two books, since *Process and Reality* tends to drink up and, then, clarify the vocabulary of the earlier book.

In a lecture at Black Mountain College, dated 1956, Olson describes and dates his take on Whitehead:

> I am the more persuaded of the importance and use of Whitehead's thought that I did not know his work—except in snatches and by rumor, including the disappointment of a dinner and evening with him when I was 25 and he was what, 75!—until last year. So it comes out like those violets of Bolyai Senior on all sides when men are needed, that we possess a body of thinking of the order of Whitehead's to catch us up where we wouldn't poke our hearts in and to intensify our own thought just where it does poke. He is a sort of an Aquinas, the man. He did make a Summa of three centuries, and cast his system as a net of Speculative Philosophy so that it goes at least as far as Plato. And his advantage over either Plato or Aquinas is the advantage we share: that the error of matter was removed in exactly these last three centuries. I quote Whitehead:
>
> > "The dominance of the *scalar* physical quantity, inertia, in the Newtonian physics obscured the recognition of the truth that all fundamental quantities are *vector* and not scalar."
> >   (Scalar, you will recall, is an undirected quantity, while vector is a directed magnitude as of a force or a velocity.)

So one gets the restoration of Heraclitus' flux translated as, All things are vectors. Or put it, All that matters moves! And one is out into a space of facts and forms as fresh as our own sense of our own existence. (Quoted in Charters, *Olson/Melville* 84–85)

This lecture was "*preceded and followed*" by study sessions on *Process and Reality* (Charters 84).* Doubtless, it comes as a shock to find the mathematical vocabulary of Whitehead so quickly translated into "existence." This is characteristic of Olson's use of Whitehead, a kind of translation throughout, beginning with his considered reading of him in 1955. Such translation is founded in Whitehead's own method, as Paul Christensen points out:

> The breadth and comprehension of Whitehead's metaphysical thesis in *Process and Reality* suggested to Olson another manifestation of the new will to cohere. Whitehead proposed to explain through his philosophy of organism how all the evolving forms of the totality are tending toward some final harmonious order which, he argued, will be the material embodiment of God. . . . The movement toward harmony is not directed from any outside force acting upon the chaos; it is occurring through the success of its own accidental combinations. . . .
>
> It is not this thesis by itself that stimulates Olson; rather it is the very grandeur of the act of Whitehead as he "takes thought" on his own perceptions. His speculation is that the bewildering prehensive activities of all levels of matter do have a goal, and he speculates boldly on what the goal might be. Part of Whitehead's argument has to do with the precise formative event in nature; to explain how it is that some entities receive formation and others deny it, he ascribes to any entity or formal group stages of "feeling." Olson finds this explanation the most compelling feature of Whitehead's book. (63–64)

This well-judged summary brings us a long way into a sense of Olson's response to the philosopher, but we should remember that, for Whitehead, the universe was incomplete and in process. And so it stood for Olson. I shall return to the stages of "feeling" in a moment.

What strikes me most in the passage from the Olson lecture is the predominant sense of freshness of view and stance—"out into a space of facts and forms as fresh as" (Charters 85). The violets, seen in his own neighborhood, are remarkable. Sherman Paul, who has written a beautiful, insightful book on Olson, has elegantly gathered together the pieces of Olson's use of the image of a violet or a bunch of them: in this passage, he writes, "Whitehead's thought is a violet" (100), and he notes Olson's violets in the dance-essay, *Apollonius of Tyana*, "'how men spring up, when they are needed, like violets, on all sides, in the spring, when winter has been too long'" (Paul, *Olson's Push* 99–100). Fi-

* The text of the lecture quoted here is included in Ann Charters's "Postscript," in *Olson/Melville: A Study in Affinity* (84–90), copyright by The Charles Olson Estate.

nally, he draws our attention to Olson's first use of the image in a poem of 1950, "The Story of an Olson, and Bad Thing," in which "Olson associates the fragrance of violets with blood and the smell of life—with birth" (100). In the same context, Paul marvelously reminds us of a parallel instance of such a freshening of view in William Carlos Williams's poem, "St. Francis Einstein of the Daffodils, *On the first visit of Professor Einstein to the United States in spring of* 1921" (Paul, *Olson's Push* 100–101), wherein

> Einstein, tall as a violet
> in the lattice-arbor corner
> as tall as
> a blossomy peartree
> > (Williams, *Collected*
> > *Earlier Poems* 379–80)

A fresh worldview, then, indebted to science by way of Einstein and Whitehead, neither otherworldly nor transcendent to life, is what is at stake. And further, the imaginary, the thought given by way of image is not denigrated but made dynamic in the perceptual field. That field is large, relational, in the sense of operative,[3] and alive. This aspect of the translation of science into poetry leads to an enormous change in the formal mode of a poem. William Carlos Williams entitled his lecture at the University of Washington in 1948 "The Poem as a Field of Action." Therein, we find this statement:

> How can we accept Einstein's theory of relativity, affecting our very conception of the heavens about us of which poets write so much, without incorporating its essential fact—the relativity of measurements—into our own category of activity: the poem. Do we think we stand outside the universe? Or that the Church of England does? Relativity applies to everything, like love, if it applies to anything in the world. (*Selected Essays* 283)

Olson's *Maximus Poems* extend into an enormous field of attentions, in which we find the poet in the guise of himself and his renewed, enlarged human figuration, Maximus, in the composition of the poem, attentive. Paul Christensen describes the look and feel of the poems in just such terms:

> . . . the unfinished, in-process look of the pages, the large leaves, the workbook appearance express the nature of this poetic composition. The poems are the partially stated connections between objects in the Gloucester field; they are "soundings" or, for that matter, the "field notes" of its metaphysical and cosmological exploration. The infinite potentiality and complexity of the field make any one effort at best a fragment of understanding; and the final books are just this, the partial filling in of a vast totality. (139)

Olson's direct uses of Whitehead's thought by way of reference, borrowing, and quotation can be traced to *Process and Reality* and to *Adventures in Ideas.** George Butterick points out that Whitehead's "philosophy of process underlies *The Maximus Poems*," that, in one important instance, he names the philosopher "'my great master and the companion of my poems,'" and that the meeting of the two men, referred to in Olson's lecture, occurred in Cambridge in 1938 (*Guide* 358). And, out of his familiarity with the entire Archive, he notes: "The copy of *Process and Reality* [Olson] acquired in February 1957 is one of the most heavily marked and annotated volumes in his library" (*Guide* 358–59).

Reading through Olson's copy is an intellectual delight. There is the complexity and profundity of Whitehead's thought, often in fine prose, and then there is the layered record of Olson's pouring over the text to find the use of it. Inside covers, back and front, flyleaves and title page, all are heavily written over in pencil and ink of various colors, mainly blue and red, offering a kind of personal index of passages and of ideas Whitehead sparked. The first flyleaf contains a dated record of Olson's repeated readings, including those which preceded his purchase of this copy: "1st read sprg 55/ again sprg 56/ now spring 57/ 3rd [4th?] spring-White/head 58," and above these entries, "now 1964," and to the side, "Jan 3, 1966." On the inside cover the notation "Sept. 11th 1969." Other dates turn up in the margins of the text, sometimes to date the place where he started rereading or to date a specific passage as it took on particular significance. The text itself, frequently underlined, contains remarks, exclamations, phrases copied from the text—a kind of memory device, I take it—reflections, schematizations and mythological notes now and again, which extend the text into image. All in all, a record of the richest kind of reading. On the title page, Olson sketches a chronology: beside Whitehead's name, "born 1861 / (Yeats born 1865)/Charles Peirce born 1839 22 years only younger!/(H. Adams 1830/Wm James 1842–3 years." Where the title page identifies Whitehead as Professor of Philosophy in Harvard University, Olson writes "(date of this?)," then, having found out, "1924." And where the title page identifies *Process and Reality* as "The Gifford Lectures delivered in the <u>University of Edinburgh</u> during the session <u>1927–1928</u>" (Olson's underlining), he notes: "I was 16–17, & in Europe that summer." At the bottom of the page is added "[D. H.] Lawrence 1885/24 years younger/than W'h/came to US/when?" The date of Lawrence's coming to the U.S. is not filled in; it was, of course, in 1922. This chronology relates to Olson's violets and it is interesting because, in it, Olson seems to have tried to tie

---

* Butterick has searched these out and noted them in *The Journal of the Olson Archives*, no. 6 (fall 1976), entry under Whitehead.

together the modern English writers who most interested him, Yeats and Lawrence, with Whitehead and his English background. He then places Whitehead in the American philosophical tradition. It is noteworthy that Olson chooses Peirce, a physicist and founder of pragmatism (the term was current by 1878). As for the mass of the notations, it is not possible accurately to date them according to one reading or another, unless Olson has done so himself. The notations do seem to lead in two directions, one toward an understanding of Whitehead's argument and the other toward the use of the material. When we enter upon the use of Whitehead, I do not find the relationship between the two men systematic, but rather companionable, as Olson himself said, and creative.

This move away from a systematic relationship to Whitehead's philosophy of organism should be noted by the reader, and is, indeed, pointed out by Olson himself in the 1956 lecture:

> In the pleasure of these substantiations of Whitehead I should like myself to gather up in a basket—or all it will take is a hand—my own pre-propositions to a knowledge of his thought. And it might be interesting to someone else in this sense, that, like violets we are a bunch!
>
> It comes down to fact and form. A writer, I dare say, goes by words. That is, they are facts. And forms. Simultaneously. And a writer may be such simply that he takes an attitude towards this double power of word: he believes it is enough to unlock anything. Words occur to him as substances—as entities, in fact as actual entities. My words were *space, myth, fact, object*. And they were globs. Yet I believed in them enough to try to reduce them to sense. I knew they were vector and in *Ishmael* [Olson's first book, *Call me Ishmael*, 1947, scholarly on Melville and directive to his own work] treated them as such, but they didn't, for me, get rid of scalar inertia. Whitehead, it turns out, would say that I was stuck in the second of the three stages in the process of feeling:
>
> > "The second stage is governed by the private ideal . . . whereby the many feelings, derivatively felt as alien (the first stage of a response, the mere reception of the actual world), are transformed into a unity of aesthetic appreciation immediately felt as private." [Olson's parentheses]
>
> I cannot urge on you enough to remind you that these stubborn globs one sticks by, and is stuck with, are valid, at the same time that I urge you, one day, to recognize them as "losses" of the vector force in exactly the sense in which Whitehead goes on to characterize this second stage further:
>
> > "This (the second stage described above) is the incoming of 'appetition,' which in its higher exemplifications we term 'vision.' In the language of physical science, the 'scalar' form overwhelms the original 'vector' form; the origins become subordinate to the individual experience. The vector form is not lost, but is submerged as the foundation of the scalar superstructure."
>
> So they sat for me, space   myth   fact   object. (Charters 85–86)

This lecture is marked by its introductory character from the initial statement on coming to know Whitehead's thought to, as we shall see, the poet's admonition which effectively distinguishes between the poetic and the philosophical intention. But, first, I want to draw attention to the passages from Whitehead, which Olson introduces here. They are from the chapter on "Process" (II.X.III 2 1 2–1 3), better than halfway through the argument of *Process and Reality*. Olson's purpose, then, appears to be to move directly to the "process of feeling" (II.X.III 2 1 2) and to emphasize it. It is striking that, knowledgeable in mathematics himself, he continues to maintain Whitehead's mathematical vocabulary. Olson is here approaching the problem of a language that will hold on to reality as process. As it turns out, the solution will be found, not simply in the words, but in the form as well. Where one may have missed the point of Olson's earlier definitions of scalar and vector, which were strictly dictionary definitions, it may be useful, with Whitehead's sense of "the foundation of the scalar superstructure" (II.X.III 2 1 2) in mind, to emphasize that the scalar is "a quantity fully described by a number" and a vector is "a complex entity representative of a directed magnitude, as of a force or a velocity."* Translated, as Olson appears to do, the one is complete form, say, the subjective poet of the old humanism, the other is coming into form by attention. The emphasis is upon prehensive activity. By maintaining Whitehead's vocabulary of the physical sciences, Olson accomplishes two things: he places human nature in the physical, like Whitehead's actual occasions or actual entity—in this instance Whitehead is discussing both— and he shifts the attention to the vector, "the original 'vector' form," "the origins" (II.X.III 2 1 2). This is important to Olson because origin, beginning, and renewal are finally the true subjects of his poems, and such regard transforms the finitude of modern humanism with its despair and terrorisms. He was to search for active form, rather than the referential kind which he reads as entrapment in present cultural conditions. A dead duck, if I may so express myself.

From the passages quoted by Olson, Whitehead turns to a further consideration of the "second stage [of feeling]," which makes the issue even clearer: " . . . the reason why the origins are not lost in the private emotion is that there is no element in the universe capable of pure privacy"—"to be 'something' is 'to have the potentiality for acquiring real unity with other entities'" [this is the third metaphysical principle]—"Thus 'emotion' is 'emotional feeling'; and 'what is felt' is the presupposed vector situation"—"scalar quantities are constructs derivative from vector quantities" (II.X.III 2 1 2). Whitehead, then, makes one of those brilliant adjustments in his argument:

---

* These definitions and Olson's earlier definitions are taken from the same source: *Webster's Collegiate Dictionary*, 5th ed., Abridgement of Webster's *New International Dictionary*, 2d ed. (Merriam, 1 9 4 5).

In more familiar language, this principle can be expressed by the statement that the notion of "passing on" is more fundamental than that of a private individual fact. In the abstract language here adopted for metaphysical statement, "passing on" becomes "creativity," in the dictionary sense of the verb *creare*, "to bring forth, beget, produce." Thus, according to the third principle, no entity can be divorced from the notion of creativity. An entity is at least a particular form capable of infusing its own particularity into creativity. An actual entity, or a phase of an actual entity, is more than that; but, at least, it is that. (II.X.III 212–13)

Thus, without abstraction, we may read the physical and mental entity as coming into form by process, a flowing from its origins.

Because I want the reader to gain a sense of the long-hand of Olson's effort, I will continue to select a few passages from Whitehead. This chapter on "process," in which the three stages of feeling are described, opens with a consideration of the "flux of things": "That 'all things flow' is the first vague generalization which the unsystematized, barely analysed, intuition of man has produced" (II.X.I 208). It is there, Whitehead tells us, in the Psalms, for philosophy in Heraclitus, and "in all stages of civilization" in poetry:

> Without doubt, if we are to go back to that ultimate, integral experience, unwarped by the sophistications of theory, that experience whose elucidation is the final aim of philosophy, the flux of things is one ultimate generalization around which we must weave our philosophical system. (II.X.I 208)

It is at such a point as this that we may begin to understand what I have called Olson's translation of Whitehead. And it is certainly more than a simplification. This "ultimate, integral experience," which is a kind of continuance of feeling, is then distinguished from the "rival and antithetical" notion:

> I cannot at the moment recall one immortal phrase which expresses it with the same completeness as that with which the alternative notion has been rendered by Heraclitus. This other notion dwells on permanences of things—the solid earth, the mountains, the stones, the Egyptian Pyramids, the spirit of man, God. (II.X.I 208)

The ensuing discussion brings face to face "the metaphysics of 'substance,'" which Olson repeatedly in conversation with me, 1957–1959, argued that we must change, and "the metaphysics of 'flux,'" "the static spiritual world" and a "fluent world" (II.X.I 209). I cannot emphasize enough the importance of the disclosure here, as it is argued in modern terms. It is the "static spiritual world," even when it is psychologized in an identity rather than in a fluent individuation, that is dead in the modern cultural condition.

Olson's 1956 lecture is in great part a record of the way in which Whitehead's thought entered into his as both corrective and companion. He uses it as an occasion to reflect back on his own work. "Space as such of course I opened *Ishmael* with. . . . I behaved better in *Ishmael* than I knew. Even, for example, to jamming in the other two terms as well as myth and space, hammering object and fact as powers of the composition." He connects this with words out of a dream:

of rhythm is image
of image is knowing
of knowing there is
a construct
     (Charters 87)

and he draws our attention to Whitehead's sense of a "'blind perceptivity' of the other physical occasions of the actual world" (Charters 87). He had "stumbled and was stumbling" on those four words as they would direct the lifetime of his work. The problem was the vectorial, the fluency of the world. In the same section of Whitehead, where he remarks on Bergson's "charge that the human intellect 'spatializes the universe,' that is to say, that <u>it tends to ignore the fluency,</u> and to analyze the world in terms of static categories," Olson underlines and dates it 1959 (II.X.I 209). Still at it, three years after the 1956 lecture. The problem was to make space alive in time by image. That would, of course, mean myth.

Olson consistently translates Whitehead's philosophy of organism and its magnificent "vision" of process back into his own acts as poet of perception and intelligence. This means that in such use of Whitehead's thought, the poet Olson steps back from the systematic, abstract nature of the metaphysical task.*

It is actually form that I am seeking to draw out of the thought—to seize a tradition out of the live air, or something, the Bejewelled Man once said—the thought which, I have suggested, and Whitehead has the system to demonstrate, man is now possessed of after the last three centuries once again. (I suppose because I am a mythologist and least of all a philosopher I stress that last phrase, once again. The seasons of man also recur, even if it will be some time before we know them as deliberately as we do those of nature. . . .) (Charters 87)

Whitehead's rereading—a corrective, in Olson's mind—of three centuries of philosophy in Descartes, Locke, Hume, Kant and, by implication, Hegel, had

---

* I am not unaware of William A. Christian's sense of "presystematic," "systematic," and "postsystematic" types of discourse in Whitehead. This layering of argument is one of the pleasures of reading Whitehead, but they remain aspects of an explanatory discourse, whereas Olson wishes to remain closer to the flux itself. See Christian, "Whitehead's Explanation of the Past" in George L. Kline, ed., *Alfred North Whitehead: Essays on His Philosophy* (93–101).

been necessary to prepare for the three stages of feeling in process. Mythology in this context suggests a pre-systematic language, imaged, natural and fundamental to the feeling mind, Whitehead's "the 'process' inherent in the fact of being a mind" (II.VI.IV 151). Olson then moves to tie down his difference:

> . That is, I am not aware that many men's acts of form yet tap the total change of stance or posture (postulate or premise) of which Whitehead's "philosophy of organism" is one completed exemplification. Mind you, be careful here. Remember the violets. A philosophy, even of his order, or because of his order, a philosophy, just because it is a wind-up, it does seek, as he says, to be so water-tight that, "at the end, insofar as the enterprise has been successful, there should be no problem of space-time, or of epistemology, or of causality, left over for discussion," form, in the sense in which one means it as of creations, can have no life as such a system. It is like the moon, without air. Or a mother. It has had to be like Whitehead has to find God as wisdom to be, "a tender care that nothing be lost." The creation of form by man could hardly let this statement of his operative growth cover him just because he is not God, and his third stage of feeling— "the satisfaction," Whitehead calls it—can only assert itself, even as a "completed unity of operation," in a new actual entity. In other words has to go back to the vectors of which it is a proof. Taking off from the thought one can define an act of art as a vector which, having become private and thus acquired vision, ploughs the vision back by way of primordial things. Only thus can it have consequence. It cannot, by taking up consequence, into itself. (Charters 88)

Olson terms the condition a "return to object" and he returns art to the "contest" (Charters 88). "I had already," he writes, "practiced the principle of the particular when [Robert] Creeley offered me the formulation form is never more than an extension of content (sign he too was one of Whitehead's violets!)" (Charters 89).

The implication is clear: that the contest—"variance, dissension, contention, dissonance"—belongs to the poetic task and is the companion of that other task, the philosophical (Charters 88). The contest is suggestive of the theory of prehensions. I am reminded of an earlier passage in Whitehead, where Olson underlines "[a]ny instance of experience is dipolar" (I.III.IV 36). The word *dipolar*, which will have continuous relevance for Olson, is encircled and a line drawn to the bottom of the page, where Whitehead is slightly reworded for emphasis: "Wh's cosmological silence repudiates the assumption that the basic elements of experience are to be described, nota, in one, or all, of the three ingredients, viz:/consciousness, thought/sense perception." Olson concludes with a definition of form as tensions, "primordial fluency" and "a consequent one":

> And each makes up the matter: the objective immortality of actual occasions requires the primordial permanence of form, whereby the creative advance ever

re-establishes itself endowed with initial creation of the history of one's self. (Charters 90)

The sudden appearance of "one's self" in this context may seem abrupt. But Olson is here calling forward certain fundamental aspects of Whitehead's thought, keyed by the use of the philosopher's terminology. The issue of creativity is central. As Donald Sherburne has helped me to understand, "*Creativity* is one of three notions involved in what Whitehead calls the Category of the Ultimate; this category expresses the general principle presupposed by all other aspects of the philosophy of organism. . . . The other two notions involved are *many* and *one*" (Sherburne 218). The return to the objective, for which Olson argues, has equally in the process to account for the one. I recall an extraordinary passage from Whitehead:

> But creativity is always found under conditions, and described as conditioned. The non-temporal act of all-inclusive unfettered valuation is at once a creature of creativity and a condition for creativity. It shares this double character with all creatures. By reason of its character as a creature, always in concrescence and never in the past, it receives a reaction from the world; this reaction is its consequent nature. It is here termed "God"; because the contemplation of our natures, as enjoying real feeling derived from the timeless source of all order, acquires that "subjective form" of refreshment and companionship at which religions aim. (I.III.I 31–32)

And so it is also with poetry in which a world-view is at stake. Olson's sense of "creative advance" seems to reflect a passage in "The Theory of Feelings":

> . . . the process of integration, which lies at the very heart of the concrescence, is the urge imposed on the concrescent unity of that universe by the three Categories of Subjective Unity, of Objective Identity, and of Objective Diversity. The oneness of the universe and the oneness of each element in the universe, repeat themselves to the crack of doom in the creative advance from creature to creature, each creature including in itself the whole of history and exemplifying the self-identity of things and their mutual diversities. (III.I.VII 228)

To enter this creativity—"'Creativity' is the universal of universals characterizing ultimate matter of fact" (I.II.II 21)—was, indeed, to enter upon the process of world-view itself.

With many a quotation, I have endeavoured to dramatize the two languages of these men in order to avoid the critical flattening of Whitehead into his broadest generalizations or of Olson into a simplified or incorrect relation to Whitehead. When we come to one of Olson's last statements involving Whitehead, the reader will, perhaps, understand the reason I have been at such pains.

The spiritual edge in Olson reached for Whitehead. At the top of a page in the "Preface" to *Process and Reality*, Olson writes: "aim: a complete cosmology (a cosmology of the 20th century, to succeed the two previous ones: Plato's Timaeus, & the 17th century." In a series of lectures, which followed upon the lecture we have been considering, published as *The Special View of History, Notes from Black Mountain, 1956*, he brilliantly continues the translation of Whitehead into his own terms. Though closely related to the philosophy of organism throughout, these lectures are not on Whitehead in the introductory manner of the earlier lecture. The purpose of the lectures is to outline a "new humanism" that discovers "Actual Willful Man," obedient to the real and potentially heroic. The figuration of the heroic belongs to the depths of poetic imagination, its archaic nature, for heroes belong to "the <u>becoming</u>, the <u>perishing</u>, and the <u>objective immortalities</u> of <u>those things which jointly constitute *stubborn fact*</u>" (PR, Preface xiv; Olson's underlining, Whitehead's italics). Olson describes the "attempt" of these lectures:

> . . . to supply you with what I don't think has had to be faced before, perhaps because the humanism of the Renaissance was sufficient until a few years ago, even if it had run down by Keats' day. The anti-humanism which I have dubbed Hegelian has been made the most the poet's enemy. It is only recently, we might say, in which a pro-humanistic possibility has emerged. (*SV* 35)

Two epigraphs open the argument: Heraclitus's "Man is estranged from that with which he is most familiar" and a passage from Keats's famous letter on "Negative Capability," "when man is capable of being in uncertainties, Mysteries, doubts, without any irritable reaching after fact or reason" (*Special View* 14). These become pointers in Olson's effort to enter upon a measured humanity within the process of things. In practice, this becomes a reversal of our condition, both "backward and outside" our present cultural condition. Sherman Paul has best discussed this active part of Olson's poetics:

> This was Olson's advice to students in the Greek tutorial when they confronted Homer and the other great writers who appeared later in the fifth century B.C.: "take both backwards and outside em, not get caught in that culture trap of taking them forwards, as tho all that we are depends on em." He himself went back to the Sumerians and Hittites and outside to the Mayans, thereby escaping the "Western Box" in which he felt Pound was trapped.[4] (28)

Where in *The Special View*, with its play on Einstein's title, he [Olson] argues the change, in the poetry he effectively pursues it. One may lose track of this if one does not understand the dynamics of the thought and stance his method of backwards and outside proposes. This he summarizes in his "impression that man

lost something just about 500 B.C. and only got it back just about 1905 A.D."
(*Special View* 15). Thus, Olson goes backward to a turning point as he saw it:
Heraclitus who died in 481 B.C. and the loss of the familiar. In "A Compre-
hension," written in 1966,[5] he clarified: " . . . the 'attack' by Plato on *poets &
poetry* already has asserted itself in fragments 57, 40 & 41 of Heraclitus, dating
say 505 when he was in his 40s or at around 480 when in his 60s. . . . " It is
useful to remember these fragments, which Olson was studying in G. S. Kirk's
Heraclitus: The Cosmic Fragments:

> 13: Teacher of the most men is Hesiod: they are sure he knows very many things,
> who continually failed to recognize day and night: for they are one [. . .]. [In the
> *Theogony*, 123 ff., Night is mother of Day] (Kirk 155)
> 14: Learning of many things does not teach sense . . . (386)
> 15: for Wisdom is one thing: to be skilled in true judgement, how all things are
> steered through all. . . . (386)

Olson is proposing to date the loss of the sense of reality as process at that point.
At the other end, the date 1905 A.D., positing a time when we could begin to
return to it, is likely to mean Einstein, for that is the date of Einstein's, in his
own eyes, "very revolutionary" paper on light. Thus, Olson is also suggesting
a turning-point in Whitehead's thought. He writes:

> And that the stance which yields the possibility of acts which are allowably his-
> toric, in other words produce, have to be negatively capable in Keats' sense that
> they have to be, they have to be uncertain.
> Or what we would call today relative. It will be seen within [these lectures]
> how thoroughly I take it Whitehead has written the metaphysic of the reality we
> have acquired, and because I don't know that yet the best minds realize how thor-
> oughly the absolute or ideal has been tucked back into where it belongs—where
> it got out of, in the 5th century B.C. and thereafter—I call attention to Whitehead's
> analysis of the Consequent as the relative of relatives, and that the Primordial—
> the absolute—is prospective, that events are absolute only because they have a fu-
> ture, not from any past. (*Special View* 16)

This introductory notice of Whitehead excellently summarizes a living sense
of the relational. Olson was then to draw out the implications for a "measured"
human will. The uncertainty in the process becomes the most difficult part to
learn, for it is identified with love. Lest the word love seem soft or too human,
I point out that the "backwards and outside" movement of information, made
dynamic in relation to present cultural conditions, becomes in the vast world
of *The Maximus Poems* a methodology for a return to that with which we are most
familiar. The passage just quoted appears also to be drawing upon the extraor-

dinary last chapter of *Process and Reality*, "God and the World," where Whitehead writes:

> Thus the consequent nature of God is composed of a multiplicity of elements with individual self-realization. It is just as much a <u>multiplicity as it is a unity</u>; it is just as much one immediate fact as it is an unresting advance beyond itself. Thus the actuality of God must also be understood as a multiplicity of actual components in process of creation. <u>This is God in his function of the kingdom of heaven</u>. (V. II.VII 350; Olson's underlining)

Olson draws a line from the underlined word *multiplicity* to the bottom of the page and writes: "love etc." He did not let go unnoticed Whitehead's account of evil in this consequent world. Among other notations, he underlined this sentence: "<u>The nature of evil is that the characters of things are mutually obstructive</u>" (V.I.IV 340). Out of the companionship of the Blakean John Clarke, Olson's attention in his last years was drawn to the greatest poet of this vision of the creation as both "the Prolific and the Devouring," William Blake. Whitehead, we recall, returns us to "a complex structure of harmony" (V.I.IV 340).

It is one of the curiosities and discomforts of conversation and of lecturing, when one is involved in the presentation of, say, Dante or Giotto or Michelangelo that one meets embarrassment, even hostility, before the contents among so many people. It is necessary for them to relearn the old, natural calendar of the tradition. Many have fallen into time, so to speak, and seem unable to go forwards or backwards. We should remember that Olson's work and his use of Whitehead grow out of the meaning of the Second World War and be reminded of Pound's words out of the First World War:

> There died a myriad
> And of the best, among them,
> For an old bitch gone in the teeth,
> For a botched civilization.
>
> ("Hugh Selwyn Mauberley,"
Personae 191)

History, for Olson, will not be the history of those powers, as we usually understand them, but "history as primordial and prospective" (*Special View* 16). History, then, taken out of the hands of power, becomes the "function in any one of us" (*Special View* 18), embodied intellectually and emotionally. The self, invoked here as an element of the-beginning-again, is not the "one [of] power," but rather, "the self as center and circumference" (*Special View* 45). Behind which is Olson's definition of will:

"Will is the innate voluntarism of to live. Will is the infinitive of being." (*Special View* 44)

This "WILL" includes an obedience within the process, the renewed sense of subject and object, and leads to art as the "order of man," a principle close to Whitehead's sense of "selection," which is fundamental to the act of prehension. Olson:

> If order is not the world—and the world hasn't been the most interesting image of order since 1904, when Einstein showed the beauty of the Kosmos and one then does pass on, looking for more—then *order is man*. And one can define the present (it does need to be noticed that the present is *post* the Modern) as the search for order as man himself is the image of same. Whitehead, then, makes sense in proposing a philosophy of organism. (*Special View* 47; original emphasis)

This crucial sense of the possibility of a turn is present to Olson's work throughout, spectacularly so, in the reversals of backwards and outward, in order to renew place, one's own earth and cosmos. The most extraordinary reversal is argued in *The Special View*: "History is the practice of space in time. Time is the vertical or tenser and it can be for a man, of a man, precisely defined" (27). Or, as he said in conversation and elsewhere, "Time is the life of space."

When Olson translates this into poetry, the poem-structure is not simply a system of metaphors for the philosophical reversal, but a record of the dynamic as it is practiced. Since I am continuing my sense of the necessary companionship in twentieth century thought, I turn to Don Byrd, one of Olson's most sensitive readers, for a description of this:

> The three stages of feeling which Olson derives from Whitehead . . . can be usefully recalled. The poem [*Maximus: Volume III*] is taking its turn into the third stage. He says: "The first is that in which the multiples of anything crowd in on the individual; the second is that most individual stage when he or she seeks to impose his or her own order on the multiples; and the third is the stage called satisfaction, in which the true order is seen to be the confrontation of two interchanging forces which can be called God and the World" (*History* 50). The first and second stages of feeling are obviously the dominant modes of experience in the first and second volumes respectively. The paradox of the third volume is that the end of the personal process is a denial of the personal. The form which begins to emerge excludes every perfection but its own. *The Maximus Poems, Volume III* is perhaps the first religious poem to have been written since the seventeenth century. Of course, an abundance of poetry has been cast in the dilemma of belief or has asserted a belief which the poet wished he had, but no one has so successfully established himself in his own being that he becomes an agent of "two interchanging forces which can be called God and the World." "I believe in religion," Max-

imus says, "not magic or science I believe in / society as religious both man and society as religious" (*Maximus III,* 55). The God which appears in the *Maximus,* however, is "fully physical" (*Maximus III,* 13). It is the God which Whitehead describes "as the lure for feeling, the eternal urge of desire" [PR V.II.II]. He is not a final cause or creator but a principle of continuation which is no sooner manifest than it becomes a new beginning. (169)

Olson's own words for this, preparing for the work of it in 1956, are:

> We were able, I take it, to establish a cosmology *without letting God in* as creator in the old sense, in the old static sense of the universe. I believe we are equally enabled today to establish a mythology *without letting God in* as a primordial nature in the old static sense, but only an image of Primordial Nature in the prospective sense of the absolute as that which is included in the relative. (*Special View* 55; original emphasis)

Interpretation, with its lingering positivism and its confused urge towards materialism, too often ignores the fundamental religious temper of poetic thought. It is not the embarrassment of outworn ways, but simply the way things belong together in the largest sense of such intuitions. Olson takes careful note of Whitehead's remarks on secularization, which are not to be understood in the contemporary sense of a wipe-out, with underlining and doubled arrows in the margins:

> The secularization of the concept of God's functions in the world is at least as urgent a requisite of thought as is the secularization of other elements in experience. The concept of God is certainly one essential element in religious feeling. But the converse is not true; the concept of religious feeling is not an essential element in the concept of God's function in the universe. (II.IX.VIII 207; Olson's underlining)

This active thought not only moves Olson's cosmology near to Whitehead's, keeping in mind the latter's moving remarks on the tragic consequences of the "'unmoved mover'" in Christianity and Mohammedanism (V.II.I 342), but also reopens the mythological language of poetic cosmology, as a language of the depth of things inside us (*Special View* 53).

I have, by way of carefully ordered quotation, insisted upon the companionable—with the bread of—in this essay because there is another reading of the meeting of these two minds.* Robert von Hallberg in his study, *Charles Olson: The Scholar's Art,* chooses to measure Olson against what appears to be a more sys-

---

* My colleague, Rob Dunham, a Coleridge and Keats man, drew my attention to the etymology of the word companion—with bread.

tematic aspect of Whitehead. He argues that Olson's "humanistic notion of order is not quite faithful to Whitehead" (115). And he cites a passage from Whitehead on higher organisms and their types of order:

> "It is the mark of a high-grade organism to eliminate, by negative prehension, the irrelevant accidents in its environment, and <u>to elicit massive attention to every variety of systematic order</u>. . . . In this way the organism in question suppresses the mere multiplicity of things, and designs its own contrasts. The canons of art are merely the expression, in specialized forms, of the requisites for depth of experience" [IV.IV.III]. When he read this passage Olson wrote in the margin: "The egotism of creation!" But the egotism was more Olson's than Whitehead's. (von Hallberg 115; Olson's underlining added)

This is an important moment of preparation in von Hallberg's argument, because, for all the memorable readings he gives us of individual poems, this alleged Olsonian egotism will lead to a dismissal of the dynamic structure of "feeling" in the whole of The Maximus Poems. Maximus IV, V, VI, and Volume III become a mere ego-centrism. What Olson did, indeed, write above the section heading and running into the margin is: "The egotism of creation is:" and he draws two lines across the text to the word "order." Thus, we are to read: "The egotism of creation is: order." Surely, this is recognition of the prehensive activity of order with its "subjective aim." And as one reflects on the mass of Whitehead's argument, the notation also calls forward the Cartesian separation of mind and matter that Whitehead has struggled to heal. Then, von Hallberg continues: "When Olson suggests that Whitehead's philosophy of organism is based on man as the image of order in the world, he is standing Whitehead on his head in order to define what Olson looked forward to as 'another humanism.' . . . Order, for Whitehead, is process, and the process begins with the atom, not with man" (115). This is astonishing, for surely Whitehead begins with the depths of his own perception and then moves to the deeps where the atom is found.

I want first to say that Olson does not argue man as the image of order, but rather the new man who will have the measured image of order within by way of thought and art. The phrase "another humanism" (Selected Writings 93) is taken from Olson's major text of the outward dynamic, outward of the "Western Box," The Mayan Letters. The Special View, which is also reflected upon in von Hallberg's context, ends with a chapter called "Enantiodromia, or 'the laws'; A METHODOLOGY," the running course of standing up against or with things, and an "Outline" which includes the re-posed subject-object relations (Special View 57–61). Which is where we find "Actual Willful Man" (Special View 61) who acts. Dr. Von Hallberg cites an important passage in Whitehead in order to argue that Olson "takes the diametrically opposite path":

> The philosophy of organism abolishes the detached mind. Mental activity is one of the modes of feeling belonging to all actual entities in some degree, but only amounting to conscious intellectuality in some actual entities. (von Hallberg 115, PR II.I.VI, 56; Olson's underlining added)

Olson draws a line from this passage to the bottom of the page and writes, "Touché (like T S E! 1961)." A few lines further along in *Process and Reality*, Olson is attentive to the continuation of Whitehead's argument:

> This is the problem of the solidarity of the universe [Olson writes in the margin, "Wow!"]. The classical doctrines of universals and particulars, of subject and predicate, of individual substances not present in other individual substances, of the externality of relations, alike render this problem incapable of solution. The answer given by the organic philosophy is the doctrine of prehensions, involved in concrescent integrations, and terminating in a definite, complex unity of feeling. To be actual must mean that all actual things are alike objects. (II.I.VI 56; Olson's underlining)

From the underlined word *objects*, Olson draws a line to the bottom of the page and writes: "The end of the subject-object thing—Wow." What goes wrong in von Hallberg's summary view of Whitehead is his underestimation of the importance of the activity of prehension for Whitehead and for Olson as demonstrated in his use and adaptation of the three stages of feeling. Further, he ignores the radical importance of the "subjective principle." Such distortion by generalization, a result of what I have earlier called singular assertion, is one good reason I have arranged my essay by way of careful quotation—perhaps another time to give an overview. This is a problem of methodology. It is important to understand that Whitehead's "'democracy' of actual entities," to quote von Hallberg again, does not wipe out person but resituates such an entity (125). Thus, we return once more to the problem of "actual willful man." Where Whitehead writes, "the actual entity, in virtue of being *what* it is, is also *where* it is" (II.I.VII 59, Whitehead's italics), Olson draws a line from the underlined phrase "what it is" and writes in the margin, "because of who it is! (1961)." At the top of the page, he has written: " . . . taxonomy is false object because no 'real' in [the?] many eternal objects χαω *Tartaros*." We remember that "Prehensions are not atomic; they can be divided into other prehensions and combined into other prehensions" (III.I.XII 235).

With χαω and Tartaros we enter upon Olson's translation of a Whiteheadian cosmology into mythology, which is to say into a cosmogony. His spelling in Greek letters of the word chaos is interesting; it appears to combine the Greek form kháos with the Indo-European root ghǝw, meaning hollow. Apart from anything else, this spelling and etymology effectively distance us from the sloppy

English notion of chaos as confusion. Tartaros in the *Iliad* is as far below Hades as the Heavens are above the Earth. These two great archaic imaginings of the depths take us back into the depth where the orders of the human imagination begin and end. An extended example of the way Olson works such translation is found outlined across two pages in *Process and Reality* at the end of the chapter on "Propositions" (II. IX.VIII 207). He writes:

<pre>
                    from the <u>induction</u>
              (ground for a probability judgment)
             the statistical—is <u>The Actual World</u>
       <u>status</u>   locus   throwndown ˙ scattered
                                        (strewn)
                                             pavement
                                             (ground)
           I
          (the world) /
                            1.) the tePAS
        II   (God) _____   _____
              the non-statistical (for such a judgment):
              the graduated 'intensive relevances'
                 <u>appetitions</u>   (starting
                              with   G   (χαω)
              constituting the primordial nature of God
                 thus some 'novelty'
                       (otherwise none——
                          & without it . . .
     [opposite page]   the <u>condition</u> is
              hunger—stretching, straining (intensive relevances)
              <u>Mouth</u>*
</pre>

Here, the translation outlines an image of the world as it moves from those sections in which Whitehead analyzes the statistical and non-statistical ground for probability judgments. Whitehead discusses the non-statistical ground, which depends upon the theory of prehensions: "The principle of the graduated 'intensive relevance' of eternal objects to the primary physical data of experience expresses a real fact." He argues "the prehension by every creature of the graduated order of appetitions constituting the primordial nature of God" and the other side of the inductive and statistical, "an intuition of probability" for the origin of novelty, which, as "non-statistical judgments," "lie at a far lower level of experience than do the religious emotions." Just there, we come upon the passage already quoted on "[t]he secularization of the concept of God's func-

---

* I must thank George Butterick for helping to decipher this notation.

tions in the world" (II.IX.VIII 207). Olson was not superstitious. This is not a transcendentalism, nor is it an idealism. Olson was after the depth of the world to which, as I have said, we all respond, though the modern public culture refuses to think of it. It is a moving story of the real that Olson is preparing here. Whitehead argues, and Olson underlines, that "<u>statistical theory entirely fails</u> to provide" for the judgment of novelty (II.IX.VIII 207). It is well to remember the definition of novelty: "'<u>Creativity' is the principle of novelty</u>. An actual occasion is a novel entity diverse from any entity in the 'many' which it unifies" (I.II.II 21; Olson's underlining, original emphasis). Without that individuation within the process, valuation would be lost, and, as Olson writes, "without it" dot, dot, dot. He moves in this outline to the imagination of permanence and change with the human actor within it. "The condition is hunger," "mouth," and I note that the hunger—the appetition, to use Whitehead's more abstract term—is of both body and mind. Meaning in this sense is an aspect of desire. The mythological, the story, begins at the ground, locus, region, where the world begins for any one of us. With the wonderful Greek, epic word TePas, Olson begins. He transliterates the word except for the Greek "rho." It has a double meaning which I take to be important here: a sign, a wonder, the Latin *portentum* or *prodigium*, as the dictionary tells us, used in Homer for the heavenly constellations as signs and in other sources in a concrete sense, a monster, descriptive of the Gorgon's head, Typhoëus and Cerberus. Olson's use of the word in this context is of considerable complexity which I can only briefly suggest. It appears twice-over with its definition as "monster or giant" alongside Whitehead's discussion of the suppressed premise of inductive reasoning which is of limited knowledge (II.IX.VI 203–5). And then in this outline, some few pages later. As we open here into the mythological, the sense of the world, of cosmos, becomes overwhelming and archaic. When Olson draws God into the process, as χαω, we come upon a renewed cosmogony. The outline becomes a curious map of the epic structure of *The Maximus Poems*. It is striking that this notation, which the poems turn into a tale, enters upon a fundamental concern of ancient epic, out of *Gilgamesh* and Hesiod, the ground of knowing, epistemology. The muses were once a vocabulary for this and for a cosmology that belongs to the depths of feeling.

Olson is a careful and poised modern mind, but with this interest in the archaic he follows through on an intuition that has colored the arts of our century. The archaic may be understood as a pre-rational language of being in love with the earth and the heavens, but in its telling in the twentieth century, it is also post-rational.* That is, a discipline of feeling outside what the rational is

---

* This point is implied in Sherman Paul, in Don Byrd's important reading of the poem-structure of *Maximus*, and see especially Charles Altieri, "From Symbolist Thought to Immanence: The Ground of Postmodern American Poetics," in *Boundary* 2 (spring 1973): 605–41.

tied to. In "Letter to Elaine Feinstein," Olson writes: "I find the contemporary substitution of society for the cosmos captive and deathly" (*Human Universe* 97). The archaic is not a primitivism, but a freshness which has been beautifully described by Guy Davenport:

> We have recovered in anthropology and archaeology the truth that primitive man lives in a world totally alive, a world in which one talks to bears and reindeer, like the Laplanders, or to Coyote, the sun and moon, like the plains Indians.
>
> In the seventeenth century we discovered that a drop of water is alive, in the eighteenth century that all of nature is alive in its discrete particles, in the nineteenth century that these particles are all dancing a constant dance (the Brownian movement), and the twentieth century discovered that nothing at all is dead, that the material of existence is so many little solar systems of light mush, or as Einstein said, " . . . every clod of earth, every feather, every speck of dust is a prodigious reservoir of entrapped energy." (*Geography* 26–27)

This energy in the depth of things may be subsumed abstractly; it can be learned, taught, imaged and so felt in poetry. It is not unrelated to religion, that means of controlling the unmeasured violence that is part of ourselves. In *The Special View* Olson writes:

> For the loss of the city-state is now calculable, that man has had restored to him, since 1875, of a unit of place and time to make up for it. . . . He has this traction or friction innately: he either gets his time and place out of himself or via that trope of himself he calls God, and it is the vertu of history as it can now be understood that it restores God as well as locality, and in so doing rids us of two other phonies of discourse, the infinite and eternal which diluted Him in distracting man from that with which he is necessarily most familiar—what he is. (25–26)

The moral of the story is that we must not take what we mean by the aesthetic too narrowly; it is, of course, beauty, but beauty unfinished in context with place and time. Surely, this struggle for the real in Whitehead and in Olson to find a coherence is a modern triumph. It is also an obedience to the real. My mind leaps to that characteristic in Sophocles' thought when it is not read as tragedy; that word is too misjudged by us. I am thinking of Oedipus at Colonus disappearing into the earth and of Herakles' recognition of the coherence in *The Women of Trachis*.

II. ON POETICS

One of Olson's most important statements on the nature of the poem is found written at the bottom of a page in *Process and Reality* (IV.II.IV 300–301). It is a passage from Whitehead on the definition of a "complete locus," which can only be read in terms of the physical sciences. Whitehead:

> The inside of a region, its volume, has a complete boundedness denied to the extensive potentiality external to it. The boundedness applies both to the spatial and the temporal aspects of extension. Wherever there is ambiguity as to the contrast of boundedness between inside and outside, there is no proper region.*

And Olson:

> The inside of a poem, its volume, has a complete boundedness denied to the extensive potentiality external to it. The boundedness applies both to the spatial and temporal aspects of extension. Whenever there is ambiguity as to the contrast of boundedness between inside & outside, there is no proper poem.

This part of *Process and Reality*, which involves us in non-Euclidian geometry among other things, held considerable interest for Olson because it argues and augments our "extensive connection" (IV.II.I 294) to the "geometry of the world." For the unphilosophical and for the non-physicist, one of the pleasures of Whitehead's text is in the shifting quality of his vocabulary. Though one may follow with care the vocabulary which describes "the physical and geometrical theory of nature," Whitehead returns again and again to our experience of the cosmos. Whitehead begins the discussion of this part of his book by discussing "ways of 'dividing' the satisfaction of an actual entity into component feelings" (IV.I.I 283). And we suddenly remember the definition of satisfaction in an earlier chapter (II.I.III 44): "The actual entity terminates its becoming in <u>one complex feeling</u> involving a completely determinate bond with every item in the universe, the bond being either a positive or a negative prehension. This termination is the 'satisfaction' of the actual entity." Olson underlines "one complex feeling." Where Whitehead is discussing the genetic process, which "presupposes the entire quantum," Olson underlines and in the margin refers us far back in *Process and Reality* to Whitehead's citation of William James. The James passage should be recalled:

> Either your experience is of no content, of no change, or it is of a perceptible amount of content or change. Your acquaintance with reality grows literally by buds or drops of perception. Intellectually and on reflection you can divide these into components, but as immediately given, <u>they come totally or not at all</u>. (II.II.II 68; Olson's underlining)

---

* The 1929 Macmillan edition of *Process and Reality* includes this explanatory note by Whitehead at the end of the book (546) under the heading "Corrigenda" (for p. 459); it appears at the bottom of p. 301 in the 1978 Corrected Edition (The Free Press), edited by Griffin and Sherburne.

Returning to the section under discussion, Olson stops over this: "The quantum is that standpoint in the extensive continuum which is consonant with the subjective aim in its original derivation from God. Here 'God' is that actuality in the world, in virtue of which there is physical 'law'" (IV.I.I 283; Olson's underlining). It is important to emphasize that the subjective aim is the "inherence of the subject in the Process" (III.I.V 224), which Donald Sherburne further clarifies: "Process doesn't presuppose a subject; rather, the subject emerges from the process" (Sherburne 244). The inherence of the subject in the process is fundamental to Olson's sense of himself in The Maximus Poems. We have Olson and the figuration of Maximus in the poems. George Butterick, citing Olson's own words in his essay, "The Gate and the Center," writes: "Maximus is the 'size man can be once more capable of, once the turn of the flow of his energies that I speak of as the WILL TO COHERE is admitted, and its energies taken up'" (Guide xxviii–xxix).

In Whitehead's chapter on "Strains," Olson once again adapts Whitehead's vocabulary to the concerns of poetry. Here he draws attention to his sense of poetry as contest:

> The poem established by geometric contents the possibility of "rests," a physical content, in order of space, or "quantitative" verse. In the previous discourse it was all flow (song), bec'z there was no "strain locus." Thus the "flow" was without the character of "flow" (song without song). (Written in PR IV.IV.V; Olson's underlining)

III. THREE PIECES FROM CHARLES OLSON

A Later Note on
Letter #15

In English the poetics became meubles—furniture—
thereafter (after 1630

& Descartes was the value

until Whitehead, who cleared out the gunk
by getting the universe in (as against man alone

& that concept of history (not Herodotus's
which was a verb, to find out for yourself:

'istorin, which makes any one's acts a finding out for him or her
self, in other words restores the traum: that we act somewhere

at least by seizure, that the objective (example Thucidides, or
the latest finest tape-recorder, or any form of record on the spot

—live television or what—is a lie

as against what we know went on, the dream: the dream being
self-action with Whitehead's important corollary: that no event

is not penetrated, in intersection or collision with, an eternal
event

    The poetics of such a situation
are yet to be found out

January 15, 1962
(*Maximus Poems* 249)

This is the opening poem in *Maximus V.* Olson calls it a note, referring back to an
earlier letter on American poetics in the first volume of *Maximus.* It has already
been noted that Olson's poem-structure allows for such openess in finding a new
structure. I take the choice of the German word for dream to be Olson's way of
removing the poetic softness that has come to envelop that word in English and
possibly of allowing us to hear the sense of "trauma" in order to remind us that
poetry is not easy—that it emerges from contest. The word also means vision
in German and it may hold within it a salute to Jung whom Olson studied with
care alongside his repeated readings of *Process and Reality.* There is evidence among
his notations that Olson was trying to relate Jung's interpretation of dreams to
Whitehead. At the end of the chapter on "The Ideal Opposites," Whitehead is
discussing the final opposites of his cosmology, "joy and sorrow, good and evil,
disjunction and conjunction . . . the many in one," ending in "God and the
World" (V.I.IV 341). Whitehead gives to the opposites "a certain ultimate di-
rectness of intuition," except for God and the World, which "introduce the note
of <u>interpretation</u>" (V.I.IV 341). Olson underlines and down the page, he writes:
"Wow, of Jung / says on the interpretation of dreams / M, D, R, p. 310." He adds
the date June 23, 1969. The book is, of course, *Memories, Dreams, Reflections,* wherein
we find Jung writing: "Mathematics goes to great pains to create expressions for
relationships which pass empirical comprehensions. In much the same way, it
is all-important for a disciplined imagination to build up images of intangibles
by logical principles and on the basis of empirical data, that is, on the evidence
of dreams" (Jung 310). Olson may also have in mind a passage from William
Carlos Williams's essay, "The Poem as a Field of Action":

> . . . let me remind you here to keep in your minds the term reality as contrasted
> with phantasy and to tell you that the *subject matter* of the poem is always phantasy—
> what is wished for, realized in the "dream" of the poem—but that the structure
> confronts something else. (*Selected Essays* 281)

Olson would probably not have used the word *phantasy.* In this poem, the self-
action is then attached to "an eternal." Whitehead's proper term would be "eter-

nal object," God in the world. This brings me to think that Olson is reflecting on earlier works by Whitehead in which, Donald Sherburne points out, the notion of event is central (Sherburne 222). But then Olson has returned to his own situation in which the "intersection or collision" would be an event. He ends, movingly, reflecting on the work of his poem of which "The poetics [as practice] of such a situation / are yet to be found out" (*Maximus Poems* 249).

history as time
    alchemy of
slain kings roots
    planets
"through time and exact definition"
    (explicitness and
analogy like to like

the Lake Van Measure
    I reject nothing. I accept it all (though
    there on rejected. What man's senses of
    examples—the demonstrative categories of
    employment which have all descended into the
    organization—of Time for plutocratic
    purposes and the result is the Americans are
    simply examples of the 7 Deadly sins) One
    means rather smelling entirely different—
    both a fantastic sweetened possible difference
    development, inner powers and
    explanations. The spiritual is all in Whitehead's
    simplest of all statements: Measurement is
    most possible throughout the system. That is
    what I mean. That what I feel all inside.
    That is what is love.
        Charles, Saturday morning
        December 13th
        LXIX*

This is a note drawn from a flyleaf of John Philip Cohane's *The Key*, which Olson had been given as a gift. An unorthodox book on ancient migrations, which links ancient civilizations by way of etymology, the gift was well chosen. It meets

* Note made by Olson, p. 134, in John Philip Cohane, *The Key* (Crown, 1969). The passage is also quoted in Boer 134, where I first saw it.

Olson's fascination with global migration, the history of place, but the text appears to have gone unread during those last few weeks. Instead, all over the inside cover, flyleaves and title page are notes that approach poems. In this lovely testament and tribute, I think the only difficulty is with "Lake Van Measure," which turns up several times in Olson's work. George Butterick has straightened the matter out for us. Lake Van is in far eastern Turkey and is the site of the Armenian cruciform church at Achthaman. The "Measure" is an "Ideal Scale," also called "Armenian," as Butterick tells us, "in the general sense of 'northern,' or non-Greek, non-classical," which Olson drew from Josef Strzygowski's *Origin of Christian Church Art* (Guide 687).* There, Olson found that Christianity in the early years included Semites and Iranians, as Butterick notes, "neither East nor West in the modern sense. . . . " (Guide 583) This is another piece of Olson's complex effort to escape the "Western Box." Butterick further notes that Olson took the "church of Achthaman, on Lake Van, built 904–938 A.D. . . . [to] summarize the achievement of non-Western art" and he quotes Olson: "for an American the Northern condition at this point is more interesting than any Mediterranean" (Guide 687). In this testament, then, Lake Van Measure, which was prepared for in *The Maximus Poems*, becomes a code phrase for a new measure of man outside the present Western condition. Then, in what is a fine tribute, Olson attaches that measure to Whitehead's sense of measurement. This takes us back to the chapter "Measurement" in *Process and Reality* where among many underlinings and notations, Olson circles "Measurement is now possible throughout the extensive continuum" (IV.V.V 332). This chapter, argued in terms of "mathematical relations involved in presentational immediacy" (IV.V.III 326), is once again translated by Olson into the spiritual human order. "There is a systematic framework," Whitehead writes, "permeating all relevant fact" (IV.V.III 327). The human being and poet, entering that process among "enduring objects—electrons, protons, molecules, material bodies—at once sustain that order and arise out of it. The mathematical relations involved in presentational immediacy thus belong equally to the world perceived and to the nature of the percipient. They are, at the same time, public fact and private experience" (IV.V.III 326). I am reminded here that "Experience realizes itself as an element in what is everlasting" (II.VII.III 163). At the end of the chapter on "Measurement," the argument is summarized:

> That perception in the mode of presentational immediacy solely depends upon the "withness" of the "body," and only exhibits the external contemporary world

---

* Butterick, *Guide*, entries under Lake Van and Armenian. Butterick's scholarship is an invaluable aid to readers of Olson.

<u>in respect to its systematic geometrical relationship to the "body."</u> (IV.V.VI 333; Olson's underlining)

Beneath this, Olson writes: "sta." With Olson's propensity to turn to etymology in order to make a word in the language move again, this is easily understood. It is the Indo-European base "sta" of the word *stand*. To stand in the process—that is to say, in the vertical of one's acts. It is also the root in Olson's important word *stance*, as a good dictionary tells us: in such words as status, state, circumstance, constant, instant, destiny, exist (Onions, *Oxford* "stand"). Lovely. So, Olson builds the measure of ourselves within the process to stand against the wreckage which the human order has become. A few pages later in *Process and Reality*, Whitehead brings up the "contrivances for stunting humanity" and remarks:

> It belongs to the goodness of the world, that its settled order should deal tenderly with the faint discordant light of the dawn of another age. Also order, as it sinks into the background before new conditions, has its requirements. The old dominance should be transformed into the firm foundation, upon which new feelings arise, drawing their intensities from delicacies of contrast between system and freshness. (V.I.III 339)

In the margin, Olson writes: "The mercy of."

This essay has endeavoured to show the "work" of translating a metaphysics back into poetry, there to retie us to the real. I began with violets. Let me close with Olson's poppies.

> When do poppies bloom I ask myself, stopping again
> to look in Mrs. Frontiero's yard, beside her house on
> this side from Birdseyes (or what was once Cunningham
> & Thompson's and is now O'Donnell-Usen's) to see if
> I have missed them, flaked out and dry-like like
> Dennison's Crepe. And what I found was dark buds
> like cigars, and standing up and my question is
> when, then, will those blossoms more lotuses to the
> West than lotuses wave like paper and petal by petal
> seem more powerful than any thing except the Universe
> itself, they are so animate-inanimate and dry-beauty not
> any shove, or sit there poppies blow as crepe
> paper. And in Mrs. Frontiero's yard annually I
> expect them as the King of the Earth must have
> Penelope, awaiting her return, love lies
> so delicately on the pillow as this one flower,
> petal and petal, carries nothing

into or out of the World   so threatening
were those cigar-stub cups just now, & I <u>know</u>
how quickly, and paper-like, absorbent
and krinkled paper, the poppy itself will, when here,
go again and the stalks stay like onion plants oh
come, poppy, when will you bloom?

                The Fort
                June 15th [Wednesday]
                XLVI

        (From *The Maximus Poems: Volume III* 550)

                                      1983

"Mind Canaries" [1]

Many of us have difficulty when first challenged by an exhibition such as this. Some ask, "What is it?" And others, "What does it mean?" Along with earlier work, the show comprises a ten-year labor—interrogative and creative—begun in 1976: a sequence of collages, in which, as the artist says, "everything comes from the real." That aspect of collage—one of its marvels insists upon the relationship of chance to meaning—is not against imagination, but it is against stereotypical imagination. Collage points to the materiality of its means which are, as Apollinaire noted, "already steeped in humanity" (quoted in Elderfield 71). The "real" here includes photographs, artworks, odd pieces of paper, things found in the lane behind Dikeakos's studio, strands and spools of thread, coiled, wrinkled and pressed kitchen foil, and so forth—things scattered, sometimes haphazardly dropped, other times carefully assembled, become a labyrinth of meaning, as if the left hand had drawn wrongly what the right hand had meant, or *vice versa*. I notice more than once in the sequence the effort "to bust out," as the artist would say, of the labyrinth, the puzzle, the confusion, in order to organize what the works are most sensitive to: the disorder of public and private meaning in our lives.

This desire to be on top of things, even abstractly, is particularly noticeable in the first triptych, *Praxis Makes Perfect*. The Icarus theme of human flight, introduced at the beginning of the sequence in *Explorer I* and in *Poster Ikaria*, becomes a failed transcendence. The subject, Icarus practising for his flight, is one composition changing three times, "constructivist exercises," as the artist explained in conversation, but that practise is also a play of headstands, semispheres, Otto Lilienthal's glider,[2] squares within squares, which brings us back to the labyrinth of the Daedalus-Icarus story and the failure to transcend. These "exercises" are only momentarily self-referential in their foregrounding of an ancient Greek myth, a tale of Dikeakos's ethnic background, which is also an astonishing paradigm of our own civilization with its fragmented transcendentalism of religion and reason. This problem of a human relationship to space, whether of earth or sky, haunts the entire sequence from the space-ship qualities of the Duchamp-Kiesler *Explorer I* to the final collages which present the changing face of Vancouver, *Three Muses in Distress* and *Terminal City* (1986)—I note especially the photograph of Joe David's sculpture of his people's traditional welcoming figure, its hands now dropped to each side, the gesture that once greeted the visitor, the white man, gone. Beginning with Duchamp, then—to whose place in Dikeakos's thought I will return later—the problem of space is fundamental to the meaning of these works. In *Poster Ikaria*, it is a matter of drifting, soaring, floating; in *Praxis Makes Perfect*, this becomes change, flux, entropy—one composition changing three times, but composed by gravity. Thus, again, we are back in the labyrinth designed by Daedalus, and from which he and his son, Icarus, were to escape by means of artistic wings. One implication is that the question is put to art itself: just what can it give us of a world-image, given that the traditional Hebraic-Christian cosmology and ethos are insufficient? The arts have long worked with the crisis of meaning in the Western tradition, only now and again at ease with its idealism or its materialism. If anything identifies twentieth-century art as set apart from the past, it is a full consciousness—sometimes regretful and nostalgic—of this crisis. Every contemporary artist enters this condition, and I am particularly interested in what Dikeakos does with it, whose use of myth and ancient gods is not nostalgic or simply literary. Instead, there are extraordinary elements of disappearance and absence in his work. It is this that many a viewer, including a part of myself, wishes not to understand.

Now, to return to the question, "What is it?" Collages that have been photographed (photography, that realistic illusion and closure of meaning that was thought to improve on painting), enlarged, and then painted, an act that returns these works to painting. The artist chose photographic oils of the kind that were used, before color photography, to tint the portrait or the scene "realistically"—the lips scarlet, the eyes blue, the cheeks flushed, the tree greener than most. Dikeakos's colors are startling—at times festive, a circus of intensity, glitter and gilt; or harsh and dramatic, as in a wonderfully drawn comic strip, say, Flash Gordon; or lyric with lavenders and gentle violets, greens and blues. Now and again, the brightness suggests the colors of Greek statues, as if we had found them unworn, with the white and creamy marble freshly painted—the gaud of color. These collage-paintings are in the mainstream of twentieth-century concern, and not simply because they quote by way of photography and shape (constructivism) and involve us in Dikeakos's long meditation on the work of Duchamp.

And to return to the question, "What does it mean?" One must first imagine an activity of meaning that does not satisfy with resolution or stasis, because there is no traditional meaning that answers to twentieth-century violence and injustice. Our thoughtlessness of the way in which all of Western tradition is implicated in the events of the twentieth century—that the Western search for wholeness, completion, and order has within it the potentiality of the practise of Nazism or Stalinism or Maoism or Campocheanism or Cubanism can hardly be explained as the work of singular madmen (and it is clear that however corrupt Castro is in terms of freedom, he is not a madman). In the past—and now with continuing hangovers—we have tried to take art out of the politico-social commotion and privilege it in order to leave material concerns to the politicians—few of whom are even speakable. This left art to engage an ideality, but ideality is exactly that aspect of reality that has failed, whether we mean the Platonic, the Cartesian, the Hegelian or the Marxian variety. Or a failure within art itself suggested that it was only a matter of self-expression—which leads me to ask just how many private and personal ownerships, whines, griefs, jokes and joys does one want written on the public wall? The writing on the wall (see Daniel V. 5 or Timothy Findley's *Famous Last Words*) is always prophetic. John Russell, writing in 1981, makes the point clearly:

> It is difficult to think of today's world in terms other than those of crisis and emergency. What is at stake is the survival of the earth as a place fit to live on, and of the human race as something that will bear scrutiny. It was not in conditions such as these that the masters of early modern art grew to manhood; and a certain sympathetic indulgence should, I think, be accorded to those who aspire to be their successors. "What can we know for certain?" is a question which has haunted modern art ever since it was first posed by Cézanne. If it has lately been answered primarily in terms of art's own nature—if art, in other words, has aspired primarily to define itself—the lesson in self-knowledge which we can draw from it is nonetheless valid for being metaphorical. . . . Art is there to make sense of the world, and it should surprise nobody if over the last 50 years this has become progressively more difficult. In 1930, when Max Ernst made his *Voice of the Holy Father*, many of the secrets of our century were still intact. To open the book of the future was a perilous act: one to be watched, as it is watched in that little picture, with every symptom of dismay. (404–5)

The predominant concern of art has always been with world-image, public meaning, and the human condition. These elements are central to Dikeakos's concerns, as they are to most of his peers. I suspect that there is an unwillingness on the part of many viewers to read for these elements, because it is more reassuring to look for a personal centre. It is part of our cultural deprivation that whole ranges of human consciousness have fallen into a privatized self. The failure to know modern art and the current retreat from it further displace and sentimentalize the past. The contemporary artist, then, hasn't a chance of being understood by a large public, because his or hers is an imagination in dialogue with the triumphs and faults of modernism. Christos Dikeakos's show is a splendid occasion to turn back and really think about Duchamp and to come forward to understand this artist's contemporary mind. I must imagine chance which is comprised of time, event and condition in contrast to traditional illusionism, abstraction, ideality or immortality. The thought that is art is operational in both the small and the large, the private and the public, because it does not define the self as closed into itself, but in relation to an outside of persons, society, politics, and cosmos. I do not want this to be confused with contemporary apocalyptics—that haunting millennarianism that wishes desperately for an end of time or history, and that ends in a despotism of spirit or matter. Dikeakos presents the relational condition of the present. He has thoughtfully considered Hans Arp's sense of chance:

> Chance opened up perceptions to me, immediate spiritual insights. Intuition led me to revere the law of chance as the highest and deepest of laws, the law that rises from the fundament. An insignificant word might become a deadly thunderbolt. One little sound might destroy the earth. One little sound might create a new universe. ("Dada" 294)

"The law that rises from the fundament." We have called this non-sense and "experimentation" against traditional sense and order. And yet the cultural disorder around us grows apace, and becomes a maze. We must, it seems to me, imagine again, which is exactly the task of the artist. The devastation of the Western sense of order, of "reality," of the transcendental forces us to imagine that God, ourselves and the world are incomplete—a matter of continuous creation.

I think one aspect that troubles viewers is that such art disturbs our traditional anthropocentrism. The displacement of the earth from the centre of the universe (Copernicus and Galileo) was amended by a magnificent vision of the dignity of man (Pico), which twentieth-century experience has made problematic. Heinz R. Pagels has recently discussed the various ways in which we understand ourselves: *homo sapiens*, "the person who follows reason alone"; *homo spiritualis*, persons who "believe in a cosmic consciousness or God"; *homo faber*, "the builder or fabricator" . . . "who moves the modern world"; *homo ludens*, "the one who plays," and the most undervalued (*Perfect Symmetry* 363, 365–67). Pagels comments: "One characteristic I notice in highly creative individuals is their liberation from social and conceptual stereotypes—they create their own exploration of reality, even their own forms of culture. They are radically open-minded, and play and humour, among the highest attributes of cultural life, are the key to this openness" (367). In Dikeakos's work, there is play and humour in the interchange of photography and painting; in the colors often; and ambiguously in the imagery of wings, one up and one down on a figure whose entire effort is to fly. I would only add to Pagels's fanfare of ourselves, each of whom has a different discourse of the real, homo necans, the man who kills, because certain aspects of Dikeakos's work forces me to think of that aspect of ourselves also.*

Perhaps we are concerned by chance, but I note that the insufficiency of our traditional meanings has a long history. I think of one strong transgressive voice:

> Some Hebrew scholars and writers assert that between the sky and the earth, or rather half in one and half in the other, there lives a certain wild rooster, whose feet rest on the earth and whose crest and beak touch the sky. In addition to such peculiarities of his as can be read in those authors, this giant rooster has the use of reason; or, indeed, like a parrot, it has been taught by I know not whom to utter words in the manner of men. In fact, a song entitled "Scir detarnegòl bara letzafra," that is to say, "Morning Song of the Great Wild Rooster," written in Hebrew script and in a language mixed with Chaldean, Targumic, Rabbinic, Cabalistic, and Talmudic, was found in an ancient parchment. (Leopardi 371)

So begins Leopardi's Song, a marvel of laughter, unhappiness and critical depth. As the poet "translates," the Rooster sings:

> Up, mortals, awake! The day is born again; truth returns to earth, and empty images depart. Arise; take up again the burden of life; return from the false to the real world! (373)

But the real, to which the Rooster calls us, takes the form of a "profound quiet"— "no activity whatever":

> . . . no lowing of oxen in the meadows, no roar of wild beasts in the forests, no singing of birds in the air . . . no voice, no movement arose in any place but that of waters, winds, and storms; then the universe would indeed be useless; but would there perhaps be in it a lesser quantity of happiness or a larger amount of misery than there is now? I ask you, O Sun. . . . (373)

This extraordinary imagination of materiality—which is to say, mortality—is unrelenting: Leopardi, writing in 1824, one splendid voice among others that haunt our thought. It is Leopardi, or, rather, the Great Wild Rooster, who by "words

---

* See Walter Burket, *Homo Necans: The Anthropology of Ancient Greek Sacrificial Ritual and Myth*; Georges Bataille, *Visions of Excess*, the essay on "The Sacred"; and René Girard, *Violence and the Sacred*.

in the manner of men," as his English translator notes, "loses himself in the vision of the disappearance of the entire cosmos" (Cecchetti 10). This is not nihilism or simple negativity or psychological depression; nor is it to be understood by any of the easy dismissive terms that one might think up. It is, instead, the true "power of negative thinking," in which lies, illusions, worn-out meanings, superficialities are questioned in order to enter upon the contest which defines the real in art and thought. In one of his dialogues, Leopardi is blunt concerning belief and method, which are, of course, activities of truth:

> I praise and exalt those beliefs, though untrue, which produce noble actions and thoughts . . . those beautiful and happy images, which, though empty, make life worthwhile, the natural illusions of the mind. (Leopardi, quoted in Cecchetti 16)

—the truth being, as Kafka noticed, "difficult to speak . . . , for although there is only one truth, it is alive and therefore has a live and changing face" (quoted in Arendt, *Dark Times* 28). And earlier than Leopardi, I think of Dante who also fell from orthodoxy, led, as he was, through Hell, Purgatory and Paradise, not by the Church, but by Virgil and Beatrice, who were, be it noted, not invented. I want also to remember that for Dante, as one scholar has recently noted, "hope is a scandalous dimension of history" (Mazzotta 13).

"The disappearance of the entire cosmos." It is exactly in this context that I wish to place Dikeakos's work. His long sequence repeatedly suggests the disappearance or absence of workable and decent human order. I am not thinking only of the threat of nuclear war, however much that informs this imagination of disappearance. Dikeakos moves in the great tradition of modernism first to discover, or, rather uncover, what is disappearing—that is, the imaginative relation of things. Then, of course, his whole imaginative effort—at once, accusative, subversive and transgressive—is to point to potential vitalities. His use of mythological figures is a case in point: they are images of archaic vitalities, the physical and mental personifications in which human nature participates, either to be overwhelmed or to become men and women of achievement. Again, John Russell comes to mind in his book *The Meanings of Modern Art*, which he tells us was "built upon two beliefs":

> One is that in art, as in the sciences, ours is one of the big centuries. The other is that the history of art, if properly set out, is the history of everything. (9)

And he continues:

> When art is made new, we are made new with it. We have a sense of solidarity with our own time, and of psychic energies shared and redoubled, which is

just about the most satisfying thing that life has to offer. "If that is possible," we say to ourselves, "then everything is possible"; a new phase in the history of human awareness has been opened up, just as it was opened up when people first read Dante, or first heard Bach's 48 preludes and fugues, or first learned from *Hamlet* and *King Lear* that the complexities and contradictions of human nature could be spelled out on the stage.

This being so, it is a great exasperation to come face to face with new art and not make anything of it. Stared down by something that we don't like, don't understand and can't believe in, we feel personally affronted, as if our identity as reasonably alert and responsive human beings had been called into question. We ought to be having a good time, and we aren't. (13)

We aren't, because disappearance and absence are uncomfortable insights.

I have insisted upon an ongoing disappearance of our traditional world-image and upon my sense that this is fundamental to Dikeakos's concerns. In 1957, in a lecture entitled "The Creative Act," Marcel Duchamp, committing another transgression, argued the importance of the spectator:

> All in all, the creative act is not performed by the artist alone; the spectator brings the work in contact with the external world by deciphering and interpreting its inner qualifications and thus adds his contribution to the creative act. (113)

This proposition extends that aspect of Duchamp's art that transgressed, even refused, the privileged illusionism of traditional art and insisted upon art's entanglement with other discourses, philosophical, linguistic, literary and scientific. A further implication is that of an art which is both personal and collective—to date, an impossibility. Yet the artists themselves—and in this instance, Dikeakos—refuse the old romanticized image of the lonely artist. Considering the same problem in relation to poetry, Octavio Paz reminds us of Benjamin Péret's "reservation": *the practice of collective poetry is conceivable only in a world free from any oppression, in which poetic thought again becomes as natural for man as water and sleep* (Bow 256; original emphasis). (We need only change the words poetry and poetic to remain in our present context.) The spectator, however, as Paz notes, remains "the real repository of the work, who re-creates it and gives it its final meaning" (Bow 256). But if the spectator refuses and turns away, as seems to be the case in the currency of artistic conservatism, what then? Again, I believe this is due to public thoughtlessness of the disappearance and absence of a world-image.

Octavio Paz has discussed this most usefully and he reminds us that such extraordinary loss at the edge of an affirmation has happened before:

> In antiquity the universe had one form and one center; its movement was governed by a cyclical rhythm and that rhythmical figure was for centuries the arche-

type of the city, the laws, and the works. The political order and the order of the poem [of art], public festivals and private rites—and even discord and the transgressions of the universal rule—were manifestations of the cosmic rhythm. Later, the figure of the world widened: space became infinite or transfinite; the Platonic year turned into a linear, unending succession; and stars ceased to be the image of cosmic harmony. The center of the world was displaced and God, ideas, and essences disappeared. We were alone. The figure of the universe changed and man's idea of himself changed; nevertheless, the worlds did not cease to be the world nor man men. Everything was a whole. *Now space expands and breaks apart; time becomes discontinuous; and the world, the whole, explodes into splinters.* Dispersion of man, wandering in a space that is also dispersed, wandering in his own dispersion. In a universe that breaks up and separates from itself, a whole that has ceased to be thinkable except as absence or a collection of heterogeneous fragments, the self also breaks apart. Not that it has lost reality or that we regard it as an illusion. On the contrary, its very dispersion multiplies and strengthens it. It has lost cohesion and has ceased to have a center, but each particle is conceived as a unique self, more closed and clinging to itself than the former self. Dispersion is not plurality, but repetition: always the same self that blindly combats another blind self. Propagation, pullulation of the identical. (239–40; emphasis added)

Dikeakos's work proposes to exhibit such change as a condition of thought and imagination, while at the same time he quarrels with the "pullulation of the identical." Thus, the use of splinters in a splintering of forms, now and again spines, as in the human form or architectural elements that suggest temples falling or reforming in order to exist in space-time.

Yet, the spectator—some part of each of us—remains in the current cultural wipe-out, endangered more than ever by the thoughtlessness and unawareness of technological propaganda. There is nothing wrong with technology *per se*, so long as we know that it is merely an extension of the "blind self"—the human will without intelligence of its own violence. Paz continues to be relevant to my effort to explain our context:

If the world, as image, disappears, a new reality covers the whole earth. Technology is a reality so powerfully real—visible, palpable, audible, ubiquitous—that the real reality has ceased to be natural or supernatural: industry is our landscape, our heaven and our hell. A Mayan temple, a medieval cathedral, or a baroque palace were something more than monuments: sensible points of space and time, privileged observatories from which man could contemplate the world and the transworld as a totality. Their orientation corresponded to a symbolic vision of the universe; the form and arrangement of their parts opened a plural perspective, a veritable crossing of visual paths: upward and downward, toward the four points of the compass. Total view of the totality. Those works were not only a vision of the world, but they were made in its image: they were a representation of the shape of the universe, its copy or its symbol. Technology comes between us and the world, it closes every prospect from view: beyond its geometries of iron, glass, or aluminum there is exactly nothing, except the unknown, the region of the formless that is not yet transformed by man.

Technology is neither an image nor a vision of the world: it is not an image because its aim is not to represent or reproduce reality; it is not a vision because it does not conceive the world as shape but as something more or less malleable to the human will. For technology, the world presents itself as resistance, not as archetype: it has reality, not shape. That reality cannot be reduced to any image and is, literally, unimaginable. The ultimate purpose of ancient knowledge was the contemplation of reality, either sensible presence or ideal form; technological knowledge aspires to substitute a universe of machinery for the real reality. The artifacts and utensils of the past existed in space, which is radically altered by modern machinery. Space is not only populated by machines that tend toward automatism or are already automatons, but it is a field of forces, a knot of energies and relations—something very different from that more or less stable expanse or area of the former cosmologies and philosophies. . . .

The constructions of technology—factories, airports, power plants, and other grandiose establishments—are absolutely real but they are not presences; they do not represent: they are signs of action and not images of the world. (Bow 241–42)

I have quoted at length because these issues seem to me central to our understanding of contemporary art and, on this occasion, to our reading of Dikeakos's collage-sequence.

If it be accepted that our increasingly technological culture pushes us toward the "unknown" and the "formless," then it is exactly this that contemporary art must address, since its care no longer floats in the transcendent or curls around the old humanism. Paz again:

Erected on the formless like the signs of technology and, like them, in search of a ceaselessly elusive meaning, the poem [the collage-painting] is an empty space but one charged with imminence. It is not yet presence: it is a swarm of signs that seek their meaning and whose only meaning is that they are a search.

The consciousness of history seemed to be modern man's great attainment. That consciousness has been transformed into a question about the meaning of history, a question without an answer. Technology is not an answer. If it were, it would be a negative one: the invention of weapons for total annihilation interdicts every hypothesis or theory about the meaning of history and the supposed reason inherent in the movements and struggles of nations and classes. But let us suppose that those weapons had not been invented or that the powers possessing them decided to destroy them: technical thought, lone survivor of the philosophies of the past, would not be able to tell us anything about the future either. Technology can foresee these or those changes and, up to a certain point, construct future realities. In this sense technology can produce the future. None

of these marvels will answer the only question that man asks himself as histori-
cal being and, I must add, as man: the why and wherefore of changes. This ques-
tion already contains, in the germ, an idea of man and an image of the world.
(Bow 243)

Yet, Paz insists that "We have ceased to recognize ourselves in the future" (244).

> The loss of the image of the future, Ortega y Gasset said, implies a mutilation
> of the past. So it is: everything that once seemed loaded with meaning now ap-
> pears before our eyes as a series of efforts and creations that are a non-sense. The
> loss of meaning affects the two halves of the sphere, death and life: death has the
> sense that our living gives it; and the ultimate meaning of our living is being life
> in relation to death. Technology can tell us nothing about all this. (Bow 244)

But art undertakes to do so.

Dikeakos's work is widely engaging in its entanglement and collage of dis-
courses: artistic, mythological, scientific and philosophical. I notice the constant
tease of meaning that is yet—for me, spectator that I am—close to non-sense,
that principle that plays inside all contemporary meaning. Max Ernst was to say
of collage: "'It seems to me that one can say that collage is a hypersensitive and
rigorously true instrument, like a seismograph, capable of registering the exact
quantity of possibilities for human happiness in each epoch'" (quoted in Bre-
ton, What Is Surrealism 363). Master collagist himself, he does not there mention
the "illicit amourous tie" of happiness and terror so often figured in his collages
(see Une Semaine de Bonté)—and that I, in turn, note here in the work of Christos
Dikeakos. For the latter, that terror is both the disappearance of the world-image
and the non-sense of ourselves. This is a realm of feeling that cannot exactly en-
ter discourse. As Hannah Arendt remarked in Men in Dark Times, "Whatever can-
not become the object of discourse—the truly sublime, the truly horrible or the
uncanny—may find a human voice through which to sound into the world, but
it is not exactly human" (25).[3] This is also the realm of feeling on the "border-
land between reason and unreason," where humour dances, as G. K. Chesterton
noted in relation to Lewis Carroll's non-sense and which I wish to place in this
context in order to suggest the kind of terror I find in Dikeakos. Two stanzas
from Carroll's great non-sense epic, The Hunting of the Snark:

> I engage with the Snark—every night after
> dark—
> In a dreamy delirious fight:
> I serve it with greens in those shadowy scenes,
> And I use it for striking a light;

But if ever I meet with a Boojum, that day,
    In a moment (of this I am sure),
I shall softly and suddenly vanish away—
    And the notion I cannot endure!
                                    ("The Baker's Tale" 32)[4]

Martin Gardner, in his wonderful *Annotated Snark*, catches precisely what I am trying to catch in Dikeakos:

> This is the great search motif of the poem, the quest for an ultimate good. But this motif is submerged in a stronger motif, the dread, the agonizing dread, of ultimate failure. The Boojum is more than death. It is the end of all searching. It is final, absolute extinction. . . . In a literal sense, Carroll's Boojum means nothing at all. It is the void, the great blank emptiness out of which we miraculously emerged; by which we will ultimately be devoured; through which the absurd galaxies spiral and drift endlessly on their nonsense voyage from nowhere to nowhere. (10)
>
> Paul Goodman's novel *The Grand Piano* (1941) closes with its hero, Horatio Alger, wiring an explosive to the piano key of B flat . . . just below the center of the keyboard. The idea is to play a composition in which the tones cluster around the death note, never touching it, but always calling for it as a resolution.
> This is, of course, precisely the wild demonic music that the U.S. and the U.S.S.R. have been playing, and in which other, less skillful muscians are joining. It is this background music that gives to Lewis Carroll's poem, when it is read today, a new dimension of anxiety. ("Introduction" 10, 11)

No wonder that André Breton's first surrealist manifesto (1924) claimed Carroll for modern thought, and no surprise that Louis Aragon translated the poem (however unsatisfactorily), *La Chasse au Snark* (1929).

I gaze again, wandering among the pieces of Dikeakos's work, from its beginning in the tinted *Ikaria: Poem = Espace, Explorer I* (1976–84); to *Explorer I and Explorer II* (1979–84); to *Medusa Mirror* (1985); to *Medusa Hair* (1985); to *Context of Medusa: Explorer III* (1986), with its mock-temple façade, decorated with biological problems, its doors open for entrance or exit, and two life-size children, Perseus Emmanuel Dikeakos and Perseus George Dikeakos, artists dressed as warriors, standing before them. This antepenultimate piece seems to bring the curling, turning, entangling sense and non-sense to full measure. For all the charm of the children, the centre cannot be the old humanism, so much in question. Indeed, there can be no centre: this work, as the artist has said, is "multi-thematic," made of many discourses of the real, which at times collapse helplessly into one another; yet, those discourses also describe with clarity the realms of love and strife, which interpenetratingly shape our condition, culturally and individually.

FIG. 1. Christos Dikeakos, *Context of Medusa: Explorer III*, 1985. Hand-colored photograph and collage, 278 × 380 cm. Reproduced courtesy of the artist.

FIG. 2. Christos Dikeakos, *Ikaria; Poster*, 1985. Hand-colored photograph and collage, 165 × 115 cm. Reproduced courtesy of the artist.

Let us stop over some of the details of this *Temple* (I will return to consider *Explorer I* in a moment): we see the backs of two persons with smallpox; interchanging figures of death and sleep; at the centre, a collage within the collage of the Lebanese Civil War; hands whose gestures suggest benediction, but parts of these hands are missing; diseased tongues stick out of the terror. Within this overwhelming gathering of terror, we see—and must look at—Medusa, the "cunning" Gorgon. As the artist remarked to me in conversation, these wild and fierce elements do exist at the edge of existence. The two boys are placed here in confrontation with these mysterious forces which undo life. Joseph Campbell is useful in this context:

> In the legend of Medusa . . . [,] though it is told from the point of view of the classic Olympian patriarchal system, the older message can be heard. The hair of Medusa, Queen of Gorgons, was of hissing serpents; the look of her eyes turned men to stone. Perseus slew her by device and escaped with her head in his wallet, which Athene then affixed to her shield. But from the Gorgon's severed neck the winged steed Pegasus sprang forth, who had been begotten by the god Poseidon and now is hitched before the chariot of Zeus. And through the ministry of Athene, Asclepius, the god of healing, secured the blood from the veins of Medusa, both from her left side and from her right. With the former he slays, but with the latter he cures and brings back to life.
>
> Thus in Medusa the same two powers coexisted as in the black goddess Kali of India, who with her right hand bestows boons and in her left holds a raised sword. Kali gives birth to all beings of the universe, yet her tongue is lolling long and red to lick up their living blood. She wears a necklace of skulls; her kilt is of severed arms and legs. She is Black Time, both the life and the death of all beings, the womb and tomb of the world: the primal, one and only, ultimate reality of nature, of whom the gods themselves are but the functioning agents. (25–26)

I would say that the gods are the functioning vocabulary of that ultimate reality. The confrontation with all those forces that undo life—social, economic, political, psycho-physical and biological—is necessarily felt by us, and such is Dikeakos's sense of the "fundament." So, the kids look straight at you, young as the Hellenes who named the Gorgons, and alive to penetrate great illusion and great awfulness. Of course, the judgment is no longer God's, but our own upon our own works. Wars and injustice, on the other side of our biological chances, are no longer God's judgment; rather, they are a matter of our own processes. The trouble is that we have to do with an art that has to do with the unrepresentable.

I want now to return to the beginning of this collage-sequence: to the *Kiesler-Duchamp* and to *Explorer I*. The first of these is a photocopy of Frederick J. Kiesler's photo-montage entitled *Les Larves d'Imagie d'Henri Robert Marcel Duchamp: M.D. emeritus* for *chronic diseases of the Arts*—the word *Larves* carries both its biological meaning and the Latin for ghost, spectre, mask; and the word *Imagie* combines the words image and magic. Kiesler's black and white montage is a triptych which, he explains in a note, "when unfolded represents three walls of Duchamp's studio on 14th Street in New York." It is also, closed and open, a dense and clever homage to the life and work of Duchamp up to 1945, when it was published in the Marcel Duchamp issue of *View*: two cut-out flaps on the left and the right may be folded inward and interlocked over the figure of Duchamp, thus transforming the centre of the triptych into a "vision" of the *Large Glass* (*The Bride Stripped Bare by Her Bachelors, Even*), which Duchamp left "finally unfinished" in 1923.* On the right volet of the open triptych, Kiesler writes "POEME ESPACE dédié à H(ieronymous) Duchamp," and signs his name. It is a little masterwork itself, the three walls joining in a concave of space, floating on the traffic of New York and disappearing in wavy lines on the left and the right. Christos Dikeakos has simply taken the Duchamp studio of the open triptych, tinted it gently with dawn colors, and signed his name at the left with the date 1976. This act compounds the find that Duchamp is for him as a painter with both Duchamp's own act of signing ready-mades and Kiesler's assembling of his homage. The act of painting this photograph, which is also a collage, is a first principle of Dikeakos's work, which as I've already noted, returns the whole project to painting; the colors are reminiscent of Duchamp's gentle colors in the *Large Glass* with the added imaginative touch of the blues, as if one had looked through the "Glass"—as one can in Philadelphia. And Dikeakos's coloring also tends further to spatialize the work of Kiesler. Even Kiesler's quick reference to Hieronymous Bosch in the dedication vibrates in Dikeakos, whose interest in the great triptychs is of long standing—*The Garden of Earthly Delights* (Madrid), *The Hay Wain* (Madrid) and *The Temptation of St. Anthony* (Lisbon). The riddle of them is demanding, and their density of meaning suggests that this painter, who died in 1516—one step ahead of the Reformation, so to speak—and who could paint within the tradition, had to depart from convention in order to say something radical and critical. I think particularly of *The Garden of Earthly Delights*: open, the left volet presents the garden of Eden; the central panel, an intense and continuous paradise; the right volet, Hell and the loss of earthly delights, especially terrifying in the figuration of the hell of the muscians. The whole panorama is informed by an affirmation of bodily delights. In fact, the body had to be reclaimed from original sin and the dog-

---

* See *View: The Modern Magazine*, "Marcel Duchamp Number," ser. 5, no. 1 (March 1945): 24: Kiesler lists in detail the elements in the work. Note that the photograph of New York streets on the page following the folded triptych, above an advertisement for the Pierre Matisse Gallery, is part of the triptych.

FIG. 3. Christos Dikeakos, *Ikaria: Poem = Espace, Explorer I*, 1976–1984. Hand-colored photograph and collage, 122 × 175 cm. Collection of Brian and Karen de Beck. Reproduced courtesy of the artist.

matics which so denigrated it. Closed, the volets represent an unfinished universe, the third day of creation. Wilhelm Fränger comments:

> while night is fading into dawn, and the sea brings forth from its womb the disc of the earth, while rock and soil become alive with vegetation, and plant-life changes into animal-life, torrents of rain are about to fall from the highest heaven to fertilize Paradise, the navel of the earth . . . (43)

so that Adam may appear. For us, whatever has happened to Adam, it is difficult to say. For now, I want only to point to Dikeakos's interest in radical and critical re-visioning, and to his repeated use of triptych and diptych forms in the sequence. It is interesting that Kiesler and Dikeakos share this original source. Though Bosch's Adamic beliefs cannot be forwarded, his use of extraordinary means can.

Explorer I is again Kiesler, colored and enlarged. The collage of beautiful details begins: perhaps the most important are the wings and the labyrinth. We enter the puzzle or the space-ship of the artist. Duchamp is seen as an explorer of unknown arts in a continuous space, an endless room. Dikeakos's entrance with color and collage begins the narrative of sequence. The wings, as I have already noted, are suggestive over and over again of our effort and failure to transcend contemporary conditions. Here, they are also poetic emblems of the artist's effort to envision a world-image. The labyrinth, its fine intricacy suggestive of Duchamp's chessboard, brings forward the first artist, the mythic Daedalus. Thus, by a thread, so to speak—important for getting through the labyrinth—collage of elements brings together Duchamp, Daedalus and his son Icarus, and Dikeakos to enter the continuous, contemporary puzzle of art: what it is doing and what it can do. Icarus, as the artist has stated, becomes "an extended metaphor of man's unlimited imaginary boundaries versus his physical and moral limitations" (Dikeakos, conversation). The theme of the first artist begins the mythic structure of the sequence, which is later pushed back to the third millennium B.C. with the photograph of the Cycladic harper—a Homer before Homer, from a once flourishing culture located on rocky islands between the coasts of what is now Greece and Turkey. Myth in these works is astonishing and unsentimental, a kind of retrieval system by way of collage, which reaches into the archaic of human nature. This is, of course, a modernist concern that has been much misunderstood. The effort to find a way in art has repeatedly returned to the history of human consciousness, and, by way of myth, to that which overwhelms us. The play—or should I say plight?—of myth in Dikeakos—Apollo, Zeus, Hera, Eros, Sphinx, Morpheus or Thanatos—tends to re-open each of the realms that they command into a largeness, not necessarily beyond human nature, which is not under the control of the human will. If the concern is marriage or death or knowledge, the play of meaning is both large and small in meaning: *Speedy Apollo Pizza* is a case in point; the gods become a pantheon of pizza-makers, and Apollo's name is given by way of an advertisement for a Greek plumbing company. I have, I believe, suggested enough to leave another spectator to make his or her own reading.

I want, however, to say a little about the presence of Duchamp here in *Explorer I* and of the consequences for all of these collage-paintings. This involves us in the central affirmation of Dikeakos's work. We still need some guidance where Duchamp is concerned, and, as it happens, we do have three splendid guides in André Breton, Robert Lebel, and Octavio Paz.[*] Breton, writing of the *Large Glass* [*La Mariée mise a nu par ses célibataires, même (Le Grand Verre, 1915–23)*] in his essay "Lighthouse of the Bride," reflects: "No work of art seems to me, up

---

[*] See André Breton, "Lighthouse of the Bride," in *View* (6–9), reprinted in Robert Lebel (still the best place to begin), *Marcel Duchamp* (New York: Grove Press, 1959).

to this day, to have given as equitable scope to rational and the irrational as *La Mariée mise à nu.* . . . It is wonderful to see how intact it manages to keep its power of anticipation. And one should keep it luminously erect, to guide future ships on a civilization which is ending" (9). This predication of a "civilization which is ending" is, of course, surrealist dogma, but it should not, for all that, be dismissed—Breton is too important a thinker ever to be dismissed. I have tried in this essay to indicate that this is the concern of a wide current of modern and contemporary art—what I called the insufficiency of our traditional meaning in the face of twentieth-century experience. It is not apocalyptic— that moment once and for all—and the depth of this experience of disappearance is unrepresentable, posed as it is between the past and a future which is unknown—a blank. Since it is my purpose to consider Duchamp in the context of contemporary Dikeakos, it is well to keep in mind Jean-François Lyotard's remarks on the "postmodern artist and writer":

> . . . the text he writes, the work he produces are not in principle governed by preestablished rules, and they cannot be judged according to a determining judgment, by applying familiar categories to the text or the work. Those rules and categories are what the work of art itself is looking for. . . .
> Finally, it must be clear that it is our business not to supply reality but to invent allusions to the conceivable which cannot be presented. (*Postmodern Condition* 81)

This is also applicable to Duchamp's work in which a number of important artists and writers have found a "lighthouse."

The use of the term *postmodern* is interesting in this context because, though it is much misunderstood and theoretically shaky, it does indeed point to the necessary, ongoing dialogue with modernism that artists at the end of the twentieth century have undertaken. It is a mistake of both modernism and postmodernism that some of its participants propose a being beyond the past, as with the former, or a being beyond the modern, as with the latter. An informed, radical and critical dialogue is what is required. Sadly, few have worked from a profound knowledge of modernism itself, so that some aspects of postmodernism result in a positivism of language and the sign that is simply another dead end.

For the present occasion, I will adapt the shorthand of Octavio Paz, whose book on Marcel Duchamp seems to me a major document of contemporary thought, to read something of this dialogue:

> Picasso has rendered our century visible to us; Duchamp has shown us that all the arts, including the visual, are born and come to an end in an area that is invisible. Against the lucidity of instinct he opposes the instinct for lucidity: the invisible is not obscure or mysterious, it is transparent. . . . The rapid parallel I have drawn

is not an invidious comparison. Both of them, like all real artists, and not exclud-
ing the so-called minor artists, are incomparable. I have linked their names be-
cause it seems to me that each of them has in his own way succeeded in defining
our age: the former by what he affirms, by his *discoveries*; the latter by what he negates,
by his *explorations*. I don't know if they are the "greatest" painters of the first half
of the century. I don't know what the word "greatest" means when applied to an
artist. (*Duchamp* 3–4; ellipsis original, emphasis added)

Paz highlights the most important characteristics of Duchamp's art, which seem
to me directly relevant to our reading of Dikeakos's collage-paintings. The re-
lationship is not simply formal. Duchamp is first of all a "painter of *ideas*," one
who "never yielded to the fallacy of thinking of painting as a purely manual
and visual art" (*Duchamp* 5). With Dikeakos, however strongly his collage tech-
nique draws our attention to the materiality of his means, the work also begins
with idea, negation and exploration. I note the repeated appearance in these
paintings of studies of eye movements (perspective changing) and of Eadweard
Muybridge's photographic studies of human and animal movement,[5] which
Dikeakos, in turn, connects with the myths of Icarus and Pegasus. All these may,
then, be even further extended by collage relation to other, only apparently,
disparate elements—carefully, thoughtfully leading us into a kind of general
irony. But the darkness in Dikeakos is too profound for the irony to hold still;
thus, the negative "exploration" turns on itself and becomes a recognition or
a series of recognitions of a nameless and unrepresentable condition. And this,
we must recognize, is a kind of affirmation.

Making History (1981–84) is, perhaps, the clearest example in which the dis-
appearing temple-shape contains reflections on Greece since the Second World
War. This occurs in time levels: the Fascist occupation of Greece, followed
by the displacement of democratic government by military regimes, the latter
complicated by the fact that the "news" of these events comes through Cana-
dian sources, the C.B.C., and the *Vancouver Sun*. Indeed, the *Sun* could, within a few
days of one another, run a headline on the imposition of martial law in Greece
and a piece on how nice it is to visit that country. Such topicals are laid along-
side others in Greece itself: Greek TV with its "logo," the Phoenix, and a shot
of the dictatorial George Papadopoulos—even a Greek cartoon for children;
then, above and in the middle, Muybridge's man and horse in procession, which
brings forward the processions of the Parthenon frieze; and in the lower panel,
Muybridge, a rocking horse, and surely our thought of the Trojan horse.

The images of the destruction of the Polytechnik School in Athens and the
resulting student uprising, which turns the Greek people against the Army and
the Junta, brings us forward in time to the important memorialized date, Novem-
ber 17, 1973, when it was clear that, as the artist says, "the youths and children

created a contagious and public revolution" (Dikeakos, conversation). Middle-aged Greeks and parents had not forgotten the plight of the children during the Civil War, and, in sympathy, they joined the rebellion. Finally, even the soldiers refused to obey commands to fire. These become centrifugal signals of the end of the Papadopoulos regime. Underneath the image of a donkey, a caption, dated Feb. 5, 1984, states that "the former Greek dictator George Papadopoulos, 63 years old, serving a life sentence for leading the 1967 coup that overthrew democracy for 7 years, has been declared leader of the new right-wing political group and may try to run for election to the European Parliament." The irony here that is also a blank of meaning has a verbal source: Stratis Haviaras's brilliant novel, The Heroic Age (1984), about a band of homeless children caught in the Civil War which devastated Greece after the Second World War. Dikeakos has said of this novel that it "talks about that aspect of the children at the edge of existence" (Dikeakos, conversation) which the artist wishes to contextualize. And so he has in the very subject of the piece: paralogia, Greek for crazy, and alogos, without reason. Suddenly, one notices the image of the Cycladic harper, who returns again and again in these explorations, an emblem of the archaic vitalities that gave us Homer sometime before 700 B.C. I have, unfortunately, simplified the rush of collisions in this collage-painting, but I hope that what I have done does suggest what Paz calls, in Duchamp, "meta-irony": "It is an irony that destroys its own negation and, hence, returns in the affirmative" (Duchamp 6).

Dikeakos's verbal sources are, of course, very different from Duchamp's. Yet, through Duchamp's incorporation of his own verbal sources—say, Mallarmé—an artist, such as Dikeakos, who has so thoughtfully meditated on Duchamp's work, becomes, to a considerable degree, a participant in those ideas. It is an error to read either Duchamp or Dikeakos as simply literary, the error of those who think of painting as only manual or retinal. Paz brilliantly notices that the "slow movement of the woman machine" (Nude Descending a Staircase, 1912) is

> an echo or an answer to that solemn moment in which Igitur abandons his room forever and goes step by step down the stairs which lead him to the crypt of his ancestors[.] In both cases there is a rupture and a descent into a zone of silence. There the solitary spirit will be confronted with the absolute and its mask, chance. (Duchamp 6)

I note, then, the descent in Dikeakos and the chance that is the condition of his subject.

Duchamp is there at the beginning of this collage-sequence—and fascinatingly present throughout—because he represents, more than any other artist, the "break with traditional conceptions of art"—out of necessity, as I have argued. It is this break with which many contemporary artists continue to work because it is both a "breaking out" and a "breaking into." Paz notices Duchamp's triple experiment, his *physiques amusantes*: "'a straight thread one meter long falls from a height of one meter onto a horizontal plane and, twisting *as it pleases*, gives us a new model for the unit of length,'" in Duchamp's words (*Duchamp* 14). Repeated three times, these are then preserved in a croquet box as "canned chance." Paz comments that this instance, other experiments and notes

> have the aim of rendering useless our notion of left and right, here and there, East and West. If the center is in a state of permanent seism [shaking as in an earthquake], if the ancient notion of solid matter and clear distinct reason disappear and give place to indetermination, the result is general *disorientation*. (*Duchamp* 14, 16)

The idea is that our condition is a kind of "permanent seism."

This is one implication of that aspect of Duchamp's work that is wrongly called "anti-art," the ready-mades such as *The Fountain* and *The Snow Shovel*, so smartly signed by the artist. Paz comments:

> The Readymade does not postulate a new value: it is a jibe at what we call valuable. It is criticism in action: a kick at the work of art ensconced on its pedestal of adjectives. The act of criticism unfolds in two stages. The first belongs to the realm of hygiene, intellectual cleanliness—the Readymade is a criticism of taste; the second is an attack on the idea of the work of art. (*Duchamp* 22)

This seems to me important to our understanding of Duchamp's place in Dikeakos's exhibition: he is part of an intellectual honesty that is also an effort to return art to its place in public thought. Further, it must be understood that Duchamp's "criticism" of art is also a return to the oldest tradition of art—before it lost its meaning by becoming *objets d'art*, only an aspect of the mercantilism that controls us. Paz insists that the *Large Glass* "continues, in its own way, the great tradition of Western painting" (*Duchamp* 73), and he quotes Duchamp's remarkable statement to that effect:

> "It was my intention not to make a painting for the eyes, but a painting in which the tubes of color were a means and not an end in themselves. The fact that this kind of painting is called literary doesn't bother me; the word 'literature' has a very vague meaning and I don't think it is adequate. . . . There is a great difference between a painting that is only directed toward the retina and a painting that goes beyond the retinal impression—a painting that uses the tubes of color as a springboard to go further. This was the case with the religious painters of the Renaissance. The tubes of color didn't interest them. What they were interested in was to express their idea of divinity, in one form or another. With a different intention and for other ends, I took the same concept: pure painting doesn't

interest me either in itself or as a goal to pursue. My goal is different, is a combination or, at any rate, an expression that only gray matter can produce." (*Duchamp* 73–74)

Our public meaning, now more than ever, is invisible, a blank to be filled, an unknown, because it involves us in a more profound knowledge of ourselves, our processes and the cosmos. We are also involved in a "radical skepticism," open and accepting of the unknown, that moves like a shadow through Dikeakos's work (*Duchamp* 35).

He has given over ten years to work with this chance of things:

Chance is only one of the manifestations of a master plan that goes far beyond us. About this plan we know nothing, or next to nothing, except its power over us. (Paz, *Duchamp* 35–36)

We have, then, to do with an art that begins with a meditation on Duchamp, especially the *Large Glass*—that "delay" and exploration of meaning. Even the butterfly images that begin to enter *Explorer I*, like disembodied wings trying to escape through the skylight on the left, picks up the "ventilator mixer" (see Duchamp's notes on *Glass*)[6] of the seventh parasol of the Sieve, which has the shape of a butterfly (the lower, male section of the *Glass*). "Bedazzlement," "metamorphosis," changing forms, "disorientation," the labyrinth—all of them terms that apply to Paz's reading of Duchamp—are at work in Dikeakos in his playing out of the "unknown dimension," which he has made his own. It is necessary to say that we are not, in any sense, entering upon another metaphysics. Dikeakos handles metaphysics as an absence or silence. Paz notes that one critic interpreted a similar characteristic in Duchamp as atheism:

From the point of view of Christian tradition, his verdict is correct. But our believers and our atheists belong to one and the same family: the former affirm the existence of a single God, a personal Creator; the latter deny it. The negation of the latter makes sense only in the context of the Judeo-Christian monotheistic concept of God. As soon as it abandons these grounds, the discussion loses interest and turns into a quarrel inside a sect. In reality our atheism is antitheism. For a Buddhist atheist, Western atheism is only a negative and exasperated form of our monotheism. Duchamp has declared quite rightly on a number of occasions that "the genesis of the *Glass* is exterior to any religious or antireligious preoccupation." (In this context the word "religion" refers to Christianity. The rites and beliefs of the East, for the most part, don't constitute what we would call a "religion": this term should be applied only in the West.) Duchamp expresses himself even more clearly in a letter to Breton: "I don't accept discussions about the existence of God on the terms of *popular metaphysics*, which means that the word "atheist" as opposed to "believer," doesn't even interest me. . . . For me there is something else that is different from *yes, no* or from *indifferent*—for example: *absence of investigation in this area.*" (*Duchamp* 69–70; original ellipsis and emphasis)

A term only to be applied in the West. I have quoted at length this important consideration because it is central to the continuing change in our sense of a world-image. The investigation is, however, also continuing to be undertaken. We are inside that which is to be imagined.

I do not mind that such long quotations tend to make my essay look like an anthology. Paz, in my experience here, is not well enough known, and Duchamp involves an argument. I have, with Paz's companionship, made an argument that is meant to inform our reading of Dikeakos. I want to bear this statement of Duchamp's meaning in mind, as I, as spectator, attempt to read Dikeakos's collage-paintings:

> The history of modern painting, from the Renaissance to our own times, could be described as the gradual transformation of the work of art into an artistic object: a transition from *vision* to the *perceptible thing*. The Readymades were a criticism both of taste and of the object. The *Large Glass* is the last genuinely meaningful work of the West; it is meaningful because by assuming the traditional meaning of painting, which is absent from retinal art, it dissolves it in a circular process and in this way affirms it. With it our tradition comes to an end. Or, rather, the painting of the future will have to begin with it and by confronting it, if painting has a future or the future a painting. (Paz, *Duchamp* 84; original emphasis)

Both form and space are open. We work, as Paz suggests, with an "absence of meaning and the necessity of meaning" (*Duchamp* 80)—not by physical possession, but by way of a vision and a possibility that are honest—in "a world that has not yet taken shape." This is, so far as I am able to express it—with all the assistance I have drawn from Paz and a few others—the "spirit of the age."

But we are in a period that appears to be going backward, evidence of which can be found among artists and spectators alike. Lyotard calls our attention to this and makes a "demand":

> This is a period of slackening—I refer to the color of the times. From every direction we are being urged to put an end to experimentation, in the arts and elsewhere. I have read an art historian who extols realism and is militant for the advent of a new subjectivity. I have read an art critic who packages and sells "Transavantgardism" in the marketplace of painting. I have read that under the name of postmodernism, architects are getting rid of the Bauhaus project, throwing out the baby of experimentation with the bathwater of functionalism. I have read that a new philosopher is discovering what he drolly calls Judaeo-Christianism, and intends by it to put an end to the impiety which we are supposed to have spread. (*Postmodern Condition* 71)

Examples could be multiplied of what can only be backward glances. Lyotard concludes with his "demand":

> Under the general demand for slackening and for appeasement, we can hear the mutterings of the desire for a return of terror, for the realization of the fantasy to seize reality. The answer is: Let us wage a war on totality; let us be witness to the unpresentable; let us activate the differences and save the honor of the name. (82)[7]

With this I wish to return the spectator to my earlier concern in this essay with Dikeakos's bits and pieces, edges, threads, and intertwining discourses.

I wish to close these remarks on the extraordinary "delay" of our world-image, as I find it in Dikeakos's work, with what seems to me a brilliant evocation of what we are trying to imagine. Michel Serres, in his collection of essays, entitled *Hermes*, on our contemporary sense of literature, science and philosophy— thus, to name the Greek god of crossways and boundaries—gives us a sense of what we are approaching:

> The realms of the subjective and of the objective are no longer at odds. The observer as object, the subject as the observed, are affected by a division more stable and potent than their antique separation: they are both order *and* disorder. From this moment on, I do not need to know who or what the first dispatcher is: whatever it is, it is an island in an ocean of noise, just like me, no matter where I am. It is the genetic information, the molecules or crystals of the world, the interior, as one used to say, or the exterior—none of this is important any longer. A macromolecule, or any given crystallized solid, or the system of the world, or ultimately what I call "me"—we are all in the same boat. All dispatchers and all receivers are structured similarly. *It is no longer incomprehensible that the world is comprehensible.* The real produces the conditions and the means for its self-knowledge. The "rational" is a tiny island of reality, a rare summit, exceptional, as miraculous as the complex system that produces it, by a slow conquest of the surf's randomness along the coast. All knowledge is bordered by that about which we have no information.
>
> It is no longer necessary to maintain the distinction between introspective knowledge, or "deep" knowledge, and objective knowledge. There is only one type of knowledge and it is always linked to an observer, an observer submerged in a system or in its proximity. And this observer is structured exactly like what he observes. His position changes only the relationship between noise and information, but he himself never effaces these two stable presences. There is no more separation between the subject, on the one hand, and the object on the other (an instance of clarity and an instance of shadow). This separation makes everything inexplicable and unreal. Instead, each term of the traditional subject-object dichotomy is itself split by something like a geographical divide (in the same way as am I, who speak and write today): noise, disorder, and chaos on one side; complexity, arrangement, and distribution on the other. Nothing distinguishes me ontologically from a crystal, a plant, an animal, or the order of the world; we are drifting together

toward the noise and the black depths of the universe, and our diverse systemic complexions are flowing up the entropic stream, toward the solar origin, itself adrift. Knowledge is at most the reversal of drifting, that strange conversion of times, always paid for by additional drift; but this is complexity itself, which was once called being. Virtually stable turbulence within the flow. To be or to know from now on will be translated by: see the islands, rare or fortunate, the work of chance or of necessity. (*Hermes* 82–83)[8]

1986

"My Vocabulary
Did This to Me"[1]

I sat worrying about these notes today . . . and I think I'll repeat my first reflection—and that is that if I live long enough, I expect to enter an era of Post-toasties—definitely non-Christian.

Now this conference, coming together in panels on Jack Spicer's *context* last night, and his *vocabulary* tonight (so divided, I take it, only for convenience)—I turn them around: vocabulary in context—and turn them around again: context in vocabulary. That is, the intelligence of context is vocabulary, and syntax—whether hypotactic, the author imperiously in charge of the sentence; or paratactic, the author *perhaps* democratically among things. The intelligence of context is vocabulary and syntax, as everyone knows who has truly dealt with Modernism and whatever it is that has followed from Modernism to correct the practice of it—that is, the practice of Modernism.

Now I have to be a little bit anecdotal to go back to the context in 1945–1950, Berkeley. I came there *really*, quite frankly, dressed as Hiawatha. Jack Spicer, who actually is a great deal ahead of me most of the time, came dressed as a detective, including trenchcoat and umbrella. Jack, unlike myself, had a foot in this century. Now the point I'm trying to get to is that I think in "my vocabulary did this to me," the vocabulary has a great deal to do with the information from which one comes, and for myself I literally came out of *that* material. Jack had one foot—as far as I understood him—*one* foot in the twentieth century by *way* of his father. His father had an I.W.W. background and some knowledge, therefrom, of Emma Goldman and Rosa Luxembourg[2]—heroines in Jack's mind. He never forgave his mother for forcing his father to settle down, on account, of course, of his own birth. His father went then to manage a hotel in Los Angeles. Somehow *never* to forgive one's own birth.

When Duncan turned up in 1946, from my point of view, *he* began to drag us into the twentieth century. Why, he'd been to New York! [laughter] He'd met the Surrealists! He knew *View*[3] magazine. I mean *all* that sophistication. But I'm also serious, that it was a total opening into a vocabulary, so that when the magazine edited by George Leite began to appear, called *Circle*[4] magazine, one had *some* chance of understanding what it was about. There were of course then gatherings of people. I call many of them *guides*, and the one that I particularly want to remember as a guide is Rosario Jimeniz, who was the Greek tutor for both Robert Duncan and myself. But she was, for this occasion, especially important because she was the first teacher of García Lorca. We had a counter-University because the danger of Universities is that they *love* the *power* of whatever discourse they decide upon, whether its sociologism, psychologism, or anthropologism—and all of those *dirty* words when they become power systems. When we were in Berkeley there was no possibility of studying the twentieth century at the University of California, Berkeley. None. And so as a consequence Robert Duncan's place at Throckmorton began that possibility with a reading of *Finnegans Wake*—which I must say was a bit of a problem. And of course Rosario gave the García Lorca *marvelously* that evening—unforgettable. Now my point is that vocabulary in that context can only be understood in terms of the way we *get into* the century, where we have to work. And it seems to be one of the great crimes of the century that so few come into the twentieth century at all. One of the few things I've learned in twenty academic years is that almost always the twentieth century—as experience, as creative work, as effort, as *terribly mistaken*—is not present, not even if wars are present, let alone the information of its artists. And that's a little sad, considering the fact that there you are all over again, another eighteen-year-old Spicer or an eighteen-year-old Blaser or whatever, having to face the first characteristics of Modernism—let's not worry about *Post-Modernism* yet—the first characteristics of Modernism—which, as Lyotard has pointed out, began in *conflict*, in opposition, in a kind of de-construction, long before Post-Modernism pre-empted that word. The word, of course, does belong to Mallarmé. Not that he used it, but it belongs there, that is where the information comes from, to *de-construct*. In Mallarmé it means that God has been fought and put away. The content of the word "God"—and it has a content—the content of the word "God" as Melville said, "If you pull him out of the sky you will find him in the street."[5] What we know is that we now find Him/Her in the street, and there's no improvement either. So, the end of what Modernism gave us was—and this is what you have to be introduced to—the end of four hundred years of Western artistic intelligence, out of which came the materiality of language—one, indeed, as I think of it, one of our greatest gifts, but a hard one to accept because it comes in the form of a Trojan Horse. And, of course, we have the materiality of painting in which you can't get the words to hold on to things with the language. You can't, with painting, do anything but get paint on your nose. And, of course, also atonal music, so that we were able to move *against* Wagner, which is to say against humanistic perspective and against resolving finalities of all kinds. "*My vocabulary did this to me.*"

Let me read a few poems by Spicer, and I think it may become clear why it is that I am after this subject. I am adapting from the so-called "a/theologian"[6] a schema, a scheme of discourses in which we read them in just a four, to simplify matters: God, Self, History, and Book. It doesn't take much imagination to know that those four large generalizations of *kinds* of discourses are so interrelated that, if you disturb one of them, all the others shift. And it was perhaps one of the most disastrous aspects of the 1940's—a psychology of the self and of identity. There is that wonderful book by Edith Cobb, the student of Margaret Mead's, called *The Ecology of Imagination*, in which she looked at autobiographies by fifteen hundred brilliant people of achievement, and she went back to Margaret Mead and said "this is very peculiar. None of them say they're looking for themselves—they're looking for a *world* in which to find themselves."[7] And so out came what was a beautiful essay. It's now a memorial book out of Columbia. Anyway, a poem or two from Jack. *The Holy Grail.* And I chose to go to the Galahad passage because Galahad *got* the Grail:

The Grail was merely a cannibal pot
Where some were served and some were not
This Galahad thinks.

The Grail was mainly the upper air
Where men don't fuck and women don't stare
This Galahad thinks.

The Grail's alive as a starling at dawn
That shatters the earth with her noisy song
This Galahad thinks.

But the Grail is there. Like a red balloon
It carries him with it up past the moon
Poor Galahad thinks.

Blood in the stars and food on the ground
The only connection that ever was found
Is what rich Galahad thinks.

(Collected Books 208)

And the last of those poems:

The Grail is as common as rats or seaweed
Not lost but misplaced.
Someone searching for a letter that he knows is around the
   house
And finding it, no better for the letter.
The grail-country damp now from a heavy rain
And growing pumpkins or artichokes or cabbage or whatever
   they used to grow before they started worrying about the
   weather. Man
Has finally no place to go but upward: Galahad's
Testament.

(Collected Books 209)

Now, he moves . . .—this actually, in documents you see the Grail stories from childhood and all that, but when Jack read *The Holy Grail* in Boston—and this is in one of those Vancouver lectures—he asked anyone who'd read Jessie Weston's *From Ritual to Romance* (and I presume he meant her Holy Grail book as well) to leave the room.[8] [Laughter] Now I think that was an excellent suggestion. We've had Jessie Weston's arguments about the nature of the Grail which are very derivative—interesting, but very derivative from Sir James Frazer's *The Golden Bough*: the argument that they are stories, the Grail stories are stories of nature worship, essentially. This is an interesting issue because Spicer came to be most interested at the time he was writing *The Holy Grail* in a book by a woman named Helen Adolf called *Visio Pacis*, "Vision Peace." *Visio Pacis* is an astonishing book. She opens it by saying, now come on, we've searched for the Grail, we've gone all through Celtic mythology, we've taken it into heaven knows what nature worship and you know what really happened is that Jerusalem fell, and all the Western mind lacked its . . . Christo. And the poets, as is their wont, she argues, began to construct this story of the Grail. Now I don't have time tonight to take up the *very* difficult consequences of Quest stories, but I'm drawing attention here to that constant haunting quality that matters of the sacred have for us. It seems to me a mistake to dismiss this *matter*—and I use the word *matter* underlined with consideration—in the name of the societal, or in the name of what was a handy vocabulary, or that it was the only vocabulary that we poor souls knew. The sacred, in my view, is a central problem of the modern condition. And, as a consequence, when we watch it at work in poets I think we need to pay special attention to the way in which that vocabulary works. We have then, in my view, the sacred as a central problem of Modernism. We have that set against the materiality of the language. We have that to set against Jack Spicer's notion of the poetry of dictation. Now the poetry of dictation . . . Ron Silliman, in a previous essay, so marvelously pointed out the way in which Spicer insists upon keeping his language attached to the psychological, and I want that in mind because I want to come back to what it means to insist . . . [Tape breaks off]

The poetry of dictation. It begins, as Spicer well knew, with Dante. It is Dante who chooses to be a dictated poetry that is dictated by the love that moves the world. Dante had the marvelous advantage of believing that love and intellect belonged to the same dynamic character that made the world move round and round. He had, in addition, for his dictation—and Spicer once said he did not invent Beatrice, that is the first thing to remember about Dante (though later on of course he becomes the first writer of science fiction and Spicer likes to be a little hostile to some of the gifts he takes from people)—but Dante had a magnificent range of reference; that is to say his word for all of the utter literalism of image that he believed in in lifting us up into Paradise by changes in the level of the light imagery, he had always the referent, the signifier, the word signified, and he had it.

Now by the time that Jack comes to read Blake he really is very impatient with the prophetic poems—and they are indeed difficult, with their Zoas, so carefully correcting that awful translation from King James of the "beast" around the throne of God—I actually don't think it's bad because one of those beasts is man, and so consequently a translation of man as we know him in the twentieth century, isn't bad as "beast"—but the word in Greek, in the New Testament Greek, is, of course, well Blake uses Zoa from zoology—these are living beings. Now Jack understood the contrariety—the contraries that bring us two states of the human soul from innocence and experience—but he never did go work through the prophetic poems. Blake says, of course, that vision—that word that is being so punished by some of the very ignorant deconstruction going on—visionary is in the human breast, where also, of course, God, if there is one, is there. Now when Jack comes to work on dictation, his closest mentor is Yeats, and Yeats is an early discovery—it's a discovery of this period '45 to '50. Now Yeats is very interesting. Yeats misunderstood Blake, and did a marvelous edition of Blake full of that misunderstanding, so that one can go back and just trace it neatly—and also a very changed sense of symbol. But the curiosity about Yeats is that he required the mediumistic work of his wife, and then he systematized all of this in a book that fascinated Jack, A Vision. And then when one reads the marvel of that lifetime of work, Yeats never gets vision. Yeats does not have, finally, the imago mundi that he so desired.

So we are left with the most extraordinary little history of dictation, where Spicer then takes it and uses it as the other poets of dictation had done, and that is to insist that it not be drunk in, up into the dominating discourses of the time. So that if you set up language as outside you—which Spicer implies, that it is *out there*—you turn it over; of course it's possibly very dangerous because you give it to the Other, and Spicer does this at times, I think we can identify it. But you also have re-posited the position of language, and it was a very important thing to do out of the 1940's, when language quite definitely belonged to *you*: "that's my language and I speak *me* in it!" Now this sense of language leads to the worst kind of poetry, and we have a century of it. Spicer blamed it all on poor Dylan Thomas. In fact, he blamed all of *New York* on Dylan Thomas!

Now what is missing is a discourse of cosmos, and this is the reason I'm drawing attention to this element of the sacred in Spicer, that a discourse of cosmos is an important one. The ancient arts, well, we do have vestiges of it, certainly in Spicer, *traces* of it, however you wish to approach it—but a discourse of cosmos is there in Spicer among other discourses. Now I don't want to be misunderstood, and I chose an entire passage to explain to you that I'm not talking *abracadabra*. I am not arguing that our critical minds and our readers' minds rush back to supernaturalism, to religion and so and so forth. I've *read* Edward Said, I'm not *dumb*. So will that be quite adequate for Edward Said and his . . . ?

Now many of us are involved in reading poets *against* the Parmenidean principle of the identity of thought and being. This is fundamental. And that haunts us, that fundamental notion: the identity of thought and being. In Spicer thought and being are *not* identical. The vocabulary and the discourse of cosmos make that clear. We need what a marvelous man, a man who introduces a very interesting book by Michel de Certeau called *Heterologies*—I haven't liked the title *Heterologies* very much because we have so many ideologies and so on, the notion of that—but [Wlad] Godzich, the man introducing him, makes clear that we read what he calls the "countervailing" tradition all the time.[9] The leaders of these, of course, are Nietzsche, Heidegger, Bataille, Blanchot, Derrida. Fundamental here is the question of the Other—in Spicer's language, the Unknown, the Outside, and so forth. Our tradition sees the Other, in Michel de Certeau's words, as a *threat*, to be reduced[10]—the Other as the realm of the dead, as in Galahad. A proposition, then: we cannot appropriate the Other, even as a realm of knowledge. Proposition: there is no autonomy of poetic knowledge—it is a discourse among others, but a very real one. Nevertheless, as Levinas has said, we are involved in the *lived* experience of the Other.[11] Proposition: that is, the reason that we cannot, as writers, simply turn poetry *over* to language—to adapt de Certeau's point again—it is unlike language (literature), unlike language which, as an object of knowledge, is a construct of philosophers and linguists; whereas poetic language—along with all the other discourses—constitutes "forms of active social interactions and practice." That is a quotation from de

Certeau.[12] Thus, the importance of community in Spicer, and his *negativity* within that community: the use of *black magic*, so to speak: misogyny, anti-semitic remarks, blasephemy, The Magic Workshop. (I would love to do that to all of you, I even thought of it. I thought well we'll just ask everyone in this audience to write a *blasphemy*. I wonder how many of us even know what to blaspheme.) All to charge the community up. These are, of course, these negations are all admissions of the fact that the small, specialized community—and there *was* no other for poetry and there *is* no other now—the small specialized community was not what he wanted. "No one listens to poetry."[13] Certainly true in the imageless, technological society that now governs us. Proposition, again out of de Certeau: "Literature is *not* a special mode of language, but a part of language, a mode of language, a discourse of the sacred"[14]—as in the *homophrosyne*, a word in Greek which means "agreement," "harmony." *That* is of course the central issue of Odysseus, the periplus of Odysseus. When, for example, Penelope is about to give up that weaving that she does and undoes and she's about to give up, she *washes* her weaving and it shines like the sun and the moon (Book 24).[15] You have a man here who understands this so much better than I do (Norman Austin, *Archery on the Dark Side of the Moon*).

These new methods of reading that sometimes lead us into marvels of a changed intelligence—linguistic, structural, deconstructionist—rich and challenging as they are, become dangerous when they become hegemonic, and to my reading thereby *ahistorical*. The materiality of language can be turned into an ahistorical system easily by limp wrist or limp mind. The elements of the sexual, the discourse of the Other, the otherness of language in Jack's work cannot be set aside. They date back to the beginning of modernity, what de Certeau calls "the mystic speech"[16] of the sixteenth and seventeenth centuries. This would mean that we took Jack's vocabulary—dangerous as it became to himself—that we took it and gave it its historical information; that he did indeed know the work of St. Theresa of Avila. In fact, the diamond is, in part, in that poem (the two I've quoted), is informed by St. Theresa. St. Theresa of Avila, her crystal palace; St. John of the Cross, his love poems; St. Ignatius of Loyola, often mentioned by Spicer; and, of course, the special study he made of John Donne. These belong to Spicer's knowledge, his vocabulary, etc. They inform his work. This informs his vocabulary, also. "[A] new mode of discourse freed from dogmatic redundancy" (*Heterologies* 87) is the way in which de Certeau describes the extraordinary work of those figures in the sixteenth and seventeenth centuries. They worked from the humiliation of the Christian tradition, in which the power of the discourse in the Christian tradition had been broken, and in that way they escaped the dogmatic redundancy. But they worked from the disintegration of a sacred model and, of course, the disintegration of the institution, the institutionality of meaning. Proposition: whatever the content of the word "God," those contents needing form are outside[17]—Spicer's "Outside"—of the institutions of meaning. With Modernism's extraordinary tendency to privilege, without thinking, *reason* over these other matters, then you *bet* they're outside. They're certainly outside the Universities.

These sources of vocabulary which haunt us in amazing ways are further founded in—and again I recommend de Certeau's study of them–1) an "insufficiency of . . . knowledge in the face of a disaster in the system of reference" (*Heterologies* 86); founded 2) in knowledge for them—that it must give up textual authority. We get de Certeau's phrase, "'wild' voices"[18] (*Heterologies* 87)—Spicer's "ghosts." We get Merleau-Ponty's lovely phrase, "wild logos,"[19] which I have always in my mind attached to the way in which "Logos" becomes "Lowghosts."[20] And, of course, further vocabulary founded in a dissociation of cosmic language and the divine speaker—that they are separated. That is, the ambition to totalize becomes a dismembered macrocosm. It is perhaps one of my prejudices that macrocosm is a common desire. Spicer's vocabulary and syntax increasingly, book by book, refuse the ego of the speech act—that here and now, that speech act, that here and now, the presence in the world that utterance alone makes possible—a point de Certeau again makes in the context.[21] I think rightly so that refusal, but also dangerously so because the "I" . . . and if I move to "Graphemics" in *Language*:

> I am I—both script i and cursive i. Rolled into one rug, one
> grapheme from whose colors stem, phonemes, morphemes,
> unusual birds. Even—if you put a dot or a dash with it:
> syntactic structures.
> In between
> The spaces on a paper the letters grow like palm-trees in a cold
> wind
> I—
> lands of thought within thought within thought. Those cold
> spaces.
> I within I within i etc.
>
> (*Language, Collected Books* 242)

The "I" is an empty form that simply announces the speaker. In de Certeau's words: "a 'siteless site'" (I love the pun), "a 'siteless site' related to the fragility of social position"—and poets, certainly, are always in a fragile social position—"a 'siteless site' related to the fragility of social position or the uncertainty of institutional referents" (*Heterologies* 90). He, de Certeau, is writing of mystic speech. Thus, in the uncertainty of the real, the exercise of language.

The desire of Spicer's work is enormous, and the absence central to his wandering meaning *does*, as with his forebears, render that range of desire readable. How *shitty* the world is, we all know, as he presumed he and Ginsberg knew. "How shitty the world is."[22] I put alongside this his remark to Don Allen in 1956, when he was leaving New York to come to Boston: "I have nothing but poetry," which, in New York, they took to be a very pitiful position. That is to say, *I place my stake in language*. But given our social and political condition—that of the entire twentieth century, but particularly of the Spicer period and continuing—the disarray of our knowledge, the acknowledged difficulty of our love life, it is a "language which has no property." Spicer's language has no property. The pure word, this notion of pure word attaches to a language that has no property. This is not the English misreading of Mallarmé at all, and we must be careful of it (in fact, Mallarmé is not at all found in an English reading of him). And so without property his beloved language—or so it is to me—takes the form of the lack and the desire of the Other. I'll stop there.

I've built up some paradigms of the problems of these new ways of reading in which we are caught, and they're very interesting, because we're actually caught in what is a battle between Greek and Hebraic attitudes towards the *text*, and it's a marvel of knowledge. I will only recommend to you Susan Handelman's wonderful book, *The Slayers of Moses*, and suggest that you pay particular attention to the section on Derrida's writing, from *Of Grammatology* onward.[23] And I think it's a very important passage, to know *what kind of text* we're taken back to. It is further important to know that the two out of all these people that I admire most, Derrida and Foucault, make themselves amazingly immortal. We absolutely *can't do* what they want us to do after they die. Derrida is still alive so we're safe for a while. Anyway, thank you very much.

1986

Infinite Worlds
The Poetry of Louis Dudek

Introduction

Can anything be done to sew the earth together?
Dudek to Raymond Souster, 1951[1]

*It is not merely knowledge of technique, or skill, it is intelligence
and knowledge of life, of the whole of it, beauty, heaven, hell,
sarcasm, every kind of whirlwind of force and emotion.*
Ezra Pound on Wyndham Lewis, 1916 (*Letters* 122)

The first quotation is the big question that Louis Dudek
put to his friend, the poet Raymond Souster, in 1951, and to himself, in one
way or another, throughout his life-work in poems, essays, lectures, and schol-
arship.* The epigraph from one of Ezra Pound's letters came to my attention
by way of Dudek's thoughtful, measured presentation of Pound on CBC Radio
in 1957.† Repeatedly, as I read through Dudek's work, more than forty years
of his intellectual and artistic engagement, Pound's words came to mind. They
amount to a summary recognition, in the early years of modernism, of the whirl-
wind of meaning that is characteristic of consequential, twentieth-century
writers—Wyndham Lewis being, then, Pound's case in point—and of the mod-
ern project in which Louis Dudek holds an important place. They struck me as

---

* Louis Dudek, from a letter to Raymond Souster, October 11, 1951, ms. in the collection of
Lakehead University Library. Cited in Frank Davey, *Louis Dudek & Raymond Souster* (39).

† Ezra Pound, from a letter to John Quinn, March 10, 1916, in *The Letters of Ezra Pound*, ed. D. D.
Paige (74). Cited in Louis Dudek, CBC Broadcast "The Letters of Ezra Pound," the full text of the
broadcast printed in Louis Dudek, ed., *Dk / Some Letters of Ezra Pound*.

equally descriptive of qualities that I so much admire in Dudek. "*Poetry is my language,*" he writes: "*I go out / on a whirling wind, / an explorer's cry in my ears*" (*En México* 43, 78). Precision and invention of technique develop out of the narrative of his deepest concerns to give us some of the most extraordinary long-poems in the modern canon. I notice his insistence that knowledge of the past be tied intelligently to the present, his use of an approachable language to support his care for the quality of ordinary life, his enveloping devotion to social justice and the civilization that could be based on it. Thus, he has to weave the ugliness of our time in among the threads and yarns of sarcasm, beauty, heaven and hell that compose his art.

His most recent long-poem is *Continuation I* (1981), which will, as its title indicates, continue and will not, as I understand it, stop until the poet does. In response to questions submitted to him by George Bowering, Frank Davey, Steve McCaffery, and bp Nichol—among whom he stands as a contemporary in poetic vitality—he comments tellingly on that poem:

> . . . an effort to live it through, think it through. Gaily to reconcile the opposites, juggle the trivia sometimes in a trance-like meditation, knock the sticks and stones together, low and high, in order to define the human state, and to prove that the great thing exists. (The fact that you drop, like Hopkins' skylark, from time to time, to the bottom of the cage—
> Or wring the barriers in bursts of fear and rage
> —is all part of it.) (*Texts & Essays* 12)

The practice of his poetry, which fascinates from the first poems to the latest, has led him into a flowing, radiant form. "The open-ended structure," he explains, "corresponds to an open-minded problem" (*Texts & Essays* 12).

In his poetry, this correspondence between structure (form) and the problem of contemporary meaning often poses the lyric voice with all its lovely sights and sounds alongside Dudek's fierce arguments for the quality of life—"to prove that the great thing exists" (*Texts & Essays* 12).

This is not to say that Dudek does not write fine lyrics—they are there in abundance, like lines on a map—but the compass by which we navigate in a work covering so many years seems always to point to the largest concerns. The open-mindedness of this work—not to be missed by over emphasis on Dudek's polemics which can certainly shake a reader up—is an inheritance, directly engaged, from that whirlwind of meaning which identifies the modern project in art, philosophy and science. Dudek's work belongs to that project; that is its argument and that is one measure of its size. The "open-minded problem" (*Texts & Essays* 12), which he shares with his great contemporaries and which is characteristic of what is now called post-modernism, is, in the very practice of openness, a correction of those aspects of modernism that thought to solve the order of things by authoritarian structures, political and social—always a concern, to name only the most obvious of our forebears, in Yeats, Pound, and Eliot. All of post-modernism, in contrast to the current reaction against modernism, can be understood in terms of this correction. With Louis Dudek, we come upon one of the distinguished voices of it. He is persistently democratic, though this is not always understood because his determined sense that a knowledge of the past civilizes the present has brought with it charges of elitism. Most of those who use that term should drop it. They are unwitting levelers who leave cultural consciousness ever more vulnerable to the on-going substitution of commercialization and mercantilism for a shared reality. With Dudek, the charge is hardly apposite, skipping, as it does, over the "open-minded problem" that is the issue of his work and ignoring his opposition to that dangerous substitution throughout. It comes up in the poetry again and again. Dudek is Canada's most important—that is to say, consequential—modern voice.

I am not original in this recognition. From over the years, reflections and remarks by Wynne Francis, Dorothy Livesay, Douglas Barbour, Michael Gnarowski, Ralph Gustafson, bp Nichol, and Frank Davey float in the air as I read this work and lead me to it. For example, Michael Gnarowski sketches the quality of mind that tests the reader:

> Always, the mind roams, restless, testing, and curious. The sum total becomes a study of our age; the experience is that of a man who always took the risk of decision, saying what he knew, loud and clear, and, if necessary, ugly. . . . ("Preface" ix)

As accurate to the poetry as it is to the prose. And Frank Davey, from the perspective of his extensive study of this major work, makes Dudek's "centrality to Canadian poetry" clear, however much he is likely to be found contentious, kicking and roaring, in the midst:

> His work binds Smith, Scott, and Klein to the writing of the present generation. It links Canadian writing to the great modernist descent from Joyce, Pound, Eliot, and Williams. It holds McLuhan's examination of the mid-twentieth-century technology tightly to the context of the modernist struggle to achieve value and meaning despite the overwhelming dedication to commodity of the culture at large. Dudek is a successor to Pound, standing unshadowed in the company of Bunting, Olson, and Spicer. [I hear Dudek roar in response to Olson and, I think, to Spicer as well.] His long poems, the first major modernist poems in Canadian literature, open up formal possibilities which are later to dominate important work by Marlatt, Bowering, Nichol, Lee, and Kroetsch. As Wynne Francis has noted, Dudek is

also the first 'man of letters' in Canada, the first to follow Arnold and Pound in combining poetry, criticism, polemic editing, and cultural criticism into one multi-faceted cultural vision.* ("Introduction," *Texts & Essays* 7)

Unshadowed Dudek is among those important writers by whom we may wish to measure him. Indeed, he claims, rightly, a certain measure himself, as in this *cri du coeur* from *Continuation I*:

> We've lost the battle
> against stupidity, vulgarity
> Lost it, Messrs Joyce, Yeats, Eliot, Pound etc. (42)

I shall return to his relationship with Pound, which is the most direct and critical, later.

It is his own viewpoint, his own modernity, more than any single influence, that brings Dudek's poetic task and his profound concern with contemporary cultural problems to meet in lyric care, in analysis and polemic, in meditation, and, sometimes, in collision. I think of his intellectual force in the context to which it belongs, side by side with the intellectual energies of Marshall McLuhan, Northrop Frye, George Grant, and George Whalley, all of them cultural modernists and international in scope. In their Canadian association—in spite of their great differences—they make of our thoughts about art not the standard sophistry, but a philosophical command post of attentions. As I read Dudek in this context, I also find something of a boxing match whenever he responds to either McLuhan or Frye.

The close rein he keeps on McLuhan's technology, already noted by Frank Davey, is especially significant, given the human will at the core of it, which increasingly appears to be unintelligent about its own nature. (In this, E. J. Pratt's voice also becomes one of admonishment.) Dudek opposes McLuhan's technology as an "'extension of the senses'" and as "'altering the ratio of the senses'" (Dudek, *Technology* 11). The answer, he tells us, is to be found in "the gravitational pull of human nature" (*Technology* 16). In other words, McLuhan (H. A. Innis's "emergence of a new civilization" is subsumed here) verges on irreality. Nevertheless, "technology does shape culture" (*Technology* 7):

> Our primal needs, energies, and passions are laid down in the inheritance by which we have survived. It is only the mode of their fulfillment that can be shaped by technology. (*Technology* 10)

---

* The reference is to Wynne Francis, "A Critic of Life: Louis Dudek as a Man of Letters."

"The inheritance by which we have survived" (*Technology* 10) is not displaced or outmoded by technological optimism, merely forgotten. One curious characteristic of modernism is that it argues a progression beyond our inheritance and a human nature beyond anything that our inheritance tells us. Thereby, we may enter unprepared into the many 'isms of reality—sociologism and scientism, all sorts of apocalyptics. On the grand scale, one hears the propositions: an end-of-history or a *coupure épistémologique*. Superstitions in many guises. When this ideology of progress—so very different from the ceremony of passage characteristic of the mentality of poetry—joins with what is far more fundamental to modernism, the heightened sense of an on-going break with the past, the enfolding of the past by the present dissipates. The great poets have opposed this dissipation. I think of Joyce's turning to a primordiality of language and human nature in *Finnegans Wake* and of Pound's renewal of an ancient sense of the sacred and the human place in it, whereby "le paradis n'est pas artificiel" (Canto LXXVI, *Cantos* 480). And, of course, of Dudek in his continuous poem:

> And the indifference of the world to God, God
> > (by God today we mean poetry)
> which is reflection, upon death, reality . . .
> . . .
> Died an atheist, came back a Christian
> > Went through the car-wash?
> Back from the beyond.
> > (Continuation I 48, 49)

The poets have recognized that the break with the past involves us in a secularization of both man and God, which has nothing to do with profanation. The major poets move, perforce, to work with the broken hierarchies of reality, social, political, and religious. The reality that, then, opens to the mind of the poet does not easily or persuasively reorder itself in defined terms, whether of humanism (technological), of scientism (positivistic), or of social system (capitalistic or communist). Thus, Dudek's phrase, "by God we mean poetry" is neither a religious nor anti-religious statement. But it does have to do with the work of meaning and with an open reality in which the human record is all we have to go on. When we come upon him quarreling with McLuhan, the contest has to do with what Dudek sees as a closure of reality into a humanism or, in the context of another argument, into "anthropocentrism." So much of our scurrying about is linked in the subtlest ways to technological optimism that opposition is necessary. We need not be pessimistic about technology, as Dudek notices; the point is to correct the thoughtlessness of such optimism and

to know about "murder with Muzak" (*Continuation I* 49)—the cultural depriva-
tion. Throughout Dudek's work, one finds an insistence upon the viability of
consciousness—the ability to think it through—and a constant care for "the
gravitational pull of human nature."

In his wonderful long-poem *Atlantis* (1967), travelling again and just "leav-
ing Naples," Dudek writes: "*Poesie: Esercizi spirituali*" (42). The spiritual exercise
then becomes a frontier:

> Canadians are retarded at the frontier,
>   as Italy is retarded in the past
> . . .
> But only those at the centre feel
> the pressures and thrusts that make imagination real.
> (43)

I am, happily, never sure, as I read, whether the real of imagination is our nec-
essary fiction or a wondrous quality of mind in the nature of things. Both, I
suppose, as I follow Dudek's reassembly of our imaginative need. Given this
stand in his world, I am not surprised to find him boxing with Northrop Frye.
But some readers might think first of those areas in which they could have been
companions. For example, Frye's considerate social concern, which he has never
ceased trying to integrate with his aesthetics:

> No discussion of beauty can confine itself to the formal relations of the isolated
> work of art; it must consider, too, the participation of the work of art in the vi-
> sion of the goal of social effort, the idea of complete and classless civilization
> (*Anatomy of Criticism* 348);

and

> . . . we may notice that the real basis for the opposition of artist and society is the
> fact that not merely communications media and public relations, but the whole
> structure of society itself, is an anti-art, an old and worn-out creation that needs
> to be created anew. (*Modern Century* 86)

There is also Frye's useful critique of McLuhan's "determinism" among "the
latest of the illusions of progress" (*Modern Century* 39).

Notwithstanding this aspect of Frye's modern viewpoint, Dudek uncovers
the problematic of poetic thinking and of the practice of poetry in an aesthetic
of archetypes. The key essay is "Northrop Frye's Untenable Position,"[2] which
Dudek published in his own magazine, *Delta*, in 1963. The occasion is his read-
ing of Frye's *The Educated Imagination* (1963), but the "aggravation" expressed

in this essay leads us back to that "grammar of mythic form," *Anatomy of Criticism* (1957) (Dudek, *Selected Essays* 175). Dudek begins with full acknowledgement of "Frye saying excellent things, making positive humanistic affirmations about literature," then turns quickly to a selection of statements, which, in the manner endemic to most systematic criticism, condescend to poets, writers and literature (*Selected Essays* 175). They also contradict Dudek's thoroughly modernistic claim that the arts play an important role in whatever reality we may know:

> "Art, on the other hand, begins with the world we construct, not with the world we see. . . ."
>
> "Literature doesn't evolve or improve or progress."
>
> "And you certainly wouldn't turn to contemporary poets for guidance or leadership in the twentieth-century world."
>
> " . . . writers are often rather simple people . . . "
>
> " . . . in literature, it isn't what you say but how it's said that's important. . . . "
>
> " . . . there is really no such thing as self-expression in literature. . . . "
>
> "The imagination in literature has no such test to meet. You don't relate it directly to life or reality. . . . "
>
> " . . . literature is really a refuge or escape from life, a self-contained world . . . a world of play or make-believe. . . . "
>
> " . . . literature, the laboratory where myths themselves are studied . . . " (Quoted in Dudek, *Selected Essays* 175–76)

These are, indeed, cut to the bone of contention. The usual fineness of Frye's prose is not allowed to lead us around them.

Dudek's strategy is not, I think, unfair, and his stake in this enterprise is great. Frye's distanced view of writer and writing—doubtless fully aware of its Platonic aegis ("mathematics and myth")—derives from the fundamental problem with temporality in his theory of structure and form. And this is exactly Dudek's point. Time is, of course, the poet's thought, however metaphorical and imaged, as it moves into form; it is the life of his form. So that, for a modern poet like Dudek, form is alive.[3] When the poem is there, it can be understood as an affective space, not merely as words on the page or a surface called language. Recently, Dudek wrote about the situation of his long-poems that "it is the position of hanging suspended in pure space between the order of the past and the possible order of the future. And hence the long meditative poem" ("Beyond Autobiography" 111). Time and space, Kantian or Einsteinian, are not often talked about in our response to poetry, but every "ideal reader"[4] knows the work of them in the perceptual field of the poem. Time, one notes, is the essential problem of the modernist sense of cultural breakage and change. Time is the modernist Dudek's fated subject and emphasis, folding and unfolding in the long-poems—three out of four are travel poems—in a sea of discovery. In *Atlantis*, for example, I come upon these lines, disturbing in their contemporary recognition:

> Actually, I've never liked Plato (any more than travel)
> and wouldn't versify his prose.
>
> Change is all we ever know, not bullion.
> But all that great change is nothing still.
>
> What is it moves? Since it is true—*E pur si muove!*
>
> Rome doesn't know, and Plato never knew.
>
> Here's the beginning, with Galileo, a new ignorance
> —is what I want to say. (39–40)

Plato's permanence set in contrast to the contemporary mind which endlessly travels and which is not always entirely comfortable; change made to contradict bullion, our substitute for reality; the fine use of the word still, adjective and adverb, motionless and always, which is repeated in the Italian phrase, "And still it moves" (in Dante, it would be the Love that moves desire and will, the sun and the stars)—Dudek's time is one, like that of most of us, in which the universal is missing, whether in agreement or vision, an ignorance. Frye's theory of mythic archetypes is meant to redeem the universal in literature, expressed as a kind of "spatialized pattern" to which all literature belongs and by which everyone may understand it.

Some years ago, Geoffrey Hartman drew attention to this and to Frye's part in a "movement to democratize criticism" by way of a "universality" (25), and he commented on what appears to be an "evasion of . . . temporality" (33). Hartman remarks on Frye's "extroversion of archetypes" (27) and the possibility of a "technological result" (29)—too often, in hands other than Frye's, a banal tracing of themes. We are reminded:

> If the Bible had not been unchained by Gutenberg and the Reformers, and if this liberation had not continued until the gods sat as books in our libraries, the kind of analysis Frye calls archetypal might not have come about.

For there is no mystery about archetypes. The archetype is simply the typical at the highest power of literary generalization.* (Hartman, *Beyond Formalism* 29)

The "typical" becomes the "universal" and thus saves literature from privacy and élitism. But the typical here is merely human (to my reading a closure of reality); and the quality of otherness—of persons, things, and a world as big as the cosmos—about which the great poets have worried most, tends to fray the typical.

The poet Dudek's response is harsh:

> Perhaps these [Frye's] statements irritate me because they are contrary to everything I myself practice and believe. . . . The first faulty premise in what I consider to be Professor Frye's untenable critical position is this attempt to relegate the content of literature to the status of irrelevant "convention." It is an echo of Plato's Book X, and it follows a familiar and well-beaten path to a position of theological dogmatism. . . .
>
> But if critics are the ones we should listen to rather than the great poets, what is it the critics extract from literature? Strange to say, it is not the *best* that has been thought and said: it is not an eclectic judgment such as an intelligent and sensitive reader might reach after much travelling in the realms of gold. No, it is not anything that the poet himself may have found by effort and conviction; it is something that "descended" upon him, and that exits [*sic*] apart from him—the universal "mythology" of literature. . . . [T]hus the poet becomes significant to the critic, as one possessed by a Platonic reality over and above the rational and sensible consciousness of man, but he is not himself a useful thinker. (*Selected Essays* 176–77)

He/she is only a piece in "the archetypal plan" (*Selected Essays* 177). The word *Platonic* is a covering-term; for Frye, the archetypes are largely, in the modern vocabulary, subconscious to the poet, but in the consciousness of the systematic critic, they promise yet another version of a Marxist-Hegelian, classless uni-

---

* My understanding of Northrop Frye's critical "system" has long been influenced by Hartman's reading of it in this book: that is, his delineation of the implications of the "system" has stood up over the years, not surprisingly. I should note, however, that my first response to Frye in the fifties was one of liberation—from the "new criticism" and I. A. Richards—which is still an aspect of Frye's place in a movement "beyond formalism." This first response was based upon the gift for readers of Blake in *Fearful Symmetry* (1947). The implications of the "system," which Dudek takes up, follow from later developments in Frye's work. That the issue is fundamentally one of secularization seems to me clear. Here, too, in the context of discussing Frye in *Beyond Formalism*, Hartman is suggestive: "The secular is the sacred integrated, rather than degraded or displaced" (22). For those interested in modern poets like Dudek, this "integration" is worth attention.

versalism. It should be noted that Dudek is not attacking abstract or conceptual thought. He insists here, as he does in the poetry, on "rational and sensible consciousness" and "useful" thinking, which clearly imply a revaluation of poetic thinking. In modern thought, Heidegger and Merleau-Ponty are remarkable for their arguments to establish a language not of wholeness and system, but of operations and meaning—and both revalue poetic thinking. The counter-movement is accompanied by positivisms of the real,[5] and Dudek quarrels with the wholeness of the claim to, in his words, "the ultimate truth of creation" (*Selected Essays* 177–78). His most trenchant reply comes years later in an essay of 1977:

> With Frye, all the meaning is to be found in the poet, or elsewhere than right there on the page. . . . I do not want to look for such an abstract of unity, nor for any single meaning; I want multiplicity, and actuality, and a forever-expanding field of unpredictable useful meanings.* (*Selected Essays* 369–70)

Dudek's responses to Frye's position, wherein archetypes tend to be spatialized elsewhere and the poet's time is denuded, are always full of tension. They represent a contemporary battle over the nature of poetry—its relation to reality and hard-won meaning—and by means of them Dudek also contradicts the long tradition, philosophical and scientific, which denies the work of reality in poetry.

Our thinkers, the poets among them, are an embattled crew. When I think of Dudek's cultural criticism—never apart from his concerns in the poetry—*Literature and the Press* (1960) and *Technology and Culture* (1979), I also think of George Grant's *Technology and Empire* (1969), from which I draw this passage to stand alongside Dudek, for all their differences:

> . . . as our liberal horizons fade in the winter of nihilism, and as the dominating amongst us see themselves within no horizon except their own creating of the world, the pure will to technology (whether personal or public) more and more gives sole content to that creating. In the official intellectual community this process has been called "the end of ideology." What this phrase flatteringly covers is the closing down of willing to all content except the desire to make the future by mastery, and the closing down of all thinking which transcends calculation. Within the practical liberalism of our past, techniques could be set within some context other than themselves—even if that context was shallow. We now move towards the position where technological progress becomes itself the sole context within which all that is other to it must attempt to be present. (40)

---

* Louis Dudek, "The Psychology of Literature," in *Selected Essays and Criticism* (367–70). See also his elegant, thoughtful essay, "The Bible as Fugue: Theme and Variations," on Northrop Frye's *The Great Code: The Bible and Literature*.

The vulnerability of the modern "open situation" to frantic closures of all kinds—totalitarianisms, consumerism, technology, ultimately the trivialization of human consciousness—must be thought through with the help of every companion we can find. Grant uncovers a "closing down." Dudek argues a multiplicity of meaning, which does not exclude, in Frank Davey's words, his "yearnings for the traditional, the well-crafted and the civilized," though he is himself never formally traditional (*Louis Dudek & Raymond Souster* 174).

In the row with technology, in the scrap with Frye, Dudek is, as I've said, quarreling for a reality, one for which his poems work. George Whalley's loving and generous sense of poetry, in *Poetic Process* (1953), comes to meet Dudek:

> A poem is inexhaustible to analysis because it terminates in "a vision of reality." Reality is a matter of relationships; *we cannot refer a particular poem simply to "reality," because reality is not a determinate entity. Reality is the great unknown and unknowable.* We are constantly in quest of it, yet we can never fully know it and certainly we cannot possess it; the best we can hope for is to preserve our capacity for encountering reality in some of its aspects. (235; original emphasis)

For Whalley, too, there had to be, as long ago as 1958, a quarrel with Frye's reality:

> I feel personal regret at not finding this book [*Anatomy of Criticism*], in its speculative and synoptic aspects, satisfactory. So much of it is brilliant, memorable, stimulating; the writing is superb and there is much excellent criticism. Yet so much of it is perverse, ingenious, desolate; at crucial points gaining rhetorical speed and assuming a sharp edge to seek safety in irony, as though desire were in perpetual conflict with vision.* (*Studies* 43)

"Reality is a matter of relationships," I repeat, and vision also is a matter of relationships with the smallest and greatest things we can take into the mind— that is, if vision is understood as something more than a "tyranny of the eye." I believe it is relationship that Dudek is writing about in the depths of his composition. Recently, in a striking, parenthetic reflection, he tells us:

> (I am groping, I suppose, toward a religious vision—"There is more than man, we all know it"—in contrast, say, to Northrop Frye's totally anthropocentric vision.) (*Texts & Essays* 14)

We must not stumble over the word "religious." That, too, is a matter of relationship. In a splendid section of *Atlantis*, he writes:

---

* Whalley's essay, "Frye's *Anatomy of Criticism*," first appeared in *Tamarak Review*, no. 8 (1958).

The gods are not behind it all, they are in front of it (55)

so, to redefine our sense of the word and make it almost Lucretian.

In 1954, Dudek published the first of his long, meditative poems, Europe. It is, by turns, irritating, expedient, and strangely moving. The Dudek here is a man from Montréal coming to terms with Europe, as if for the first time. The sea is new, grand, and encompassing. But Europe—this reader has the impression that whole centuries of European art and poetics have come crashing down around us, English, French, Italian, and Greek. The voice is often harsh, judgmental, or disappointed. The sea between Europe and Canada seems to fold the mystery of change in its waves and foam:

And I would not be surprised if the sea made Time
in which to build and to destroy
as it builds these waves and indolently breaks them,
        or if the whole fiction
of living were only a coil in her curvature
        of immense imagination. (18)

The sea as imagination also implies an imagination at sea in the immensity of that reality which is Dudek's concern. On the point of return,

The mountains of Gaspé doze, reclining,
        in the air vacant as morning.
At home, there will be faces full of this daylight,
        blank maybe, but beautiful.
Getting started is never easy.
We have work to do.
        Europe is behind us
                America before us. (139)

and the poem closes, the poet heading for the work of his poems, the tone that of a manifesto.

In 1958 came the second of the long-poems, En México, a marvel of detail, image, and rhythm. Reflections on the life of form guide his weaving:

Form is the visible part of being.
We know, the logic of its adaptations—
a signature of individuality,
                an integrity,
the end of perfect resolution—
but not the inner stir.

Rest. Rest in that great affair. (75)

> Therefore art is everything
> but not as we imagined.
> Art is the way of life. (75–76)

But, for Dudek, there is no rest—at least, not in his work.

I have already noted that three of these meditations are travel poems. In the same way that the sea becomes a metaphor of an "immense imagination," of the desire of the mind to have a relationship to such immensity, travel becomes a metaphor of our situation in it. The third of these radiating long-poems appeared in 1967, *Atlantis*:

> Of voyages: there was Ulysses' voyage,
> and Cortez, the great adventurers.
>
> But even suburban dwellers
> voyage, though they commute, eat toast, get their magazines on time.
> . . . .
> There are infinite worlds: green lights,
>   highway lines, homes,
> power stations and industrial domes. (3, 4)

On the one hand, we always have Dudek's admirable, insistent care for the ordinary and the everyday, on the other, *Atlantis* becomes the "true home" we cannot reach. At one point, aboard ship, he imagines he has passed over it. Dudek's reality folds over us again, harsh and beautiful, as deep as the "wherever" of *Atlantis*, and home is as far away as that island of intelligence.

The first run of the great meditative poem, *Continuation*, was published in 1981, a weaving so alive that it will, as I noted, stop only with the author, and not in a closure of form. This narrative—and it is narrative for all the appearance of fragmentation—unlike the previous long-poems, does not follow the path of a literal journey. In this one, the mind darts, travelling through the poetic effort of the whole century and gauging his own part in it. But the tone is more urgent than ever before. Having entered upon that "immense reality,"—that is, into an uncharted freedom—

> The problem was elementary:
> Learn to use your freedom
> without destroying yourself or the others
>
> It was to redeem reality that we wanted it
> and now the reality has failed us.
>
>   (*Continuation* I 42)

I have already quoted the *cri du coeur* from this poem, the battle lost. I cannot agree that it is

> Lost to the Beats, the Beatles, the Activists, the McLunatics
> To Pop & Op & "multiple media",
> > to "total environment"
> To psychedelia & Flower Power,
> > the New Left, SDU, CEGEP, UGEQ, & MAUT
> Lost to the new barbarians
> > without a scrap of poetry worth a pin. (42)

I think Dudek sees these as thoughtless of, or participants in, the ersatz reality we cultivate. (We forget what the word *culture* actually means, the metaphor buried in abstraction.) The presence of the Left in this passage seems odd, unless we remember that the Left, old and new, has always had trouble fitting the arts into their purely social reality—a socialist realism until the end of history. The problem is with the definition of barbarians. Louis Dudek has paid a high price for this among readers who trip over his aversion to such as these and ignore the daring project he has undertaken. They understand him to be reactionary, which is to say that they misunderstand him. One thing he is after in this passage is the prevalent confusion of art as functional thinking with entertainment. Psychedelia and flower power contradict his faith in the tradition of the rational mind. Certain styles of art seem to be run by the market. All these tumbled together with political aggression upon art make up, to my mind, the pieces of a jigsaw puzzle that cannot be put together except in the light of his whole poetic project.

Dudek is more often an excellent guide through the sources of barbarism— the bourgeois dead end from which modernism begins; the consumerism that claims reality by ownership; an anthropocentric view that closes into itself meaninglessly; the continuing, political postponement of a true commitment to social justice; the way poetry disappears in public thought. The poems reflect these problems many times over. Troubling considerations of fame sometimes enter this poem by a poet who is central to anglo-Montréal culture, as well as Canadian modernism, and who has never trucked with major publishing institutions which establish fame. That, I take it, is an aspect of his independent stance. The urgency returns again and again in *Continuation I*:

> I mean what the prophets always said,
> > turn your face against vanity, turn from your "false gods"
>
> The media, spreading their shit music,
> > shit talk, shit advertising

flowing with simple lukewarm consistency
> through the long hot afternoon
Voices of vanity, incurable vanity,
> of triviality,
become the real, the commonplace, the everyday! (48)

I cannot turn away from this; rather, I feel that I, too, must know it for what it is—cultural triviality. And one rightly thinks of Pound: "it is not man / Made courage, or made order, or made grace, / Pull down thy vanity, I say pull down" (Canto LXXXI, *Cantos* 541). Dudek makes us see the triviality that may become our coverlet.

The key seems to be the size of reality and the use of poetry in our being there:

Beyond a few sentences, in our lives, there is nothing

But what did you expect—
> the poem to write itself?
or to start a hurricane?

Not really, only a language
to contain the essentials that matter, in all the flux of illusion
Pebbles, that shine through the cobbled grey
> that emerge, in time's liquid flow
as diaphanous heaven

And the viscosity of things
How it all hangs together
> hiding whatever it is it hides.

> (Continuation I 11)

The wonderful, lengthening lines and the affecting repetition of "it." Dudek never confuses poetry with reality. In a short poem, "Fragment of Continuum," he tells us: "the poem is not the real thing / is not made of the real / It is another thing":

Like nature's doughnut machine
> making the atoms
The key to identity and   order.
> (Infinite Worlds 213)

Our nature, that is, is to work the atoms of the mind's music, words, in a composition of identity and order against triviality.

Dudek's short poems and lyrics lead us into the long meditations on reality, unknown and unowned as it is, by moments, by argument, by anger and laughter, and by celebration and exuberance. Near midway in his career, following *Europe* and *En México*, in 1959, he published "Functional Poetry: A Proposal," which I have included in this selection because it is a manifesto of what he was doing and of what he will continue to do in poetry:

> "Think of all the poems that have been written—"
> No poems have yet been written! . . .
> Written! They have been too much written.
> But thought . . . the poems that are thought . . .
>   thought itself—
>   (Infinite Worlds 126)

This brings us directly into the cultural paradox of contemporary poetry: that it is not merely a subjectivity as in popular understanding and in some educated traditions, but a kind of thinking. The burden of "A Proposal" is quickly stated:

> For some time now (since Whitman? since Lawrence?)
> poets have been experimenting with
>   new subject matter, new forms
> in the effort to break through an impasse.
>   (Infinite Worlds 126)

The impasse derives from our sense of substantiality that "became fossilized in decadent metre and form" and from the "neglect (the push / of society in other directions) [which] threatens poetry / with virtual extinction." Thus,

> The problem, it seems to me, is simply
> the loss of ground to prose over   the centuries
> in the subject matter of poetry
>   (Infinite Worlds 126)

What is obviously a prose reflection is forced into rhythmic pattern, which is an aspect of the irony and aggression of this "Proposal": "Write whatever you write (for print, or letters) / not as prose, but as rhythmic poetry / (you will find the way)" (Infinite Worlds 131). In other words, just take the subject matter back, all the content of thought that the lyric personal voice gives up. This is one key to Dudek's poetics, "some form of improvised rhythmed speech / which is divided and shaped / by the run-on and end-stop system / of notation" (132). From this, Dudek develops the electric periodicity of his thought movements in the poems. If the thought of the world is taken over by commercialism and so disappears as mere commodity with a price on it, the poem says so and brings the world back in a "whirlwind." If the thought of the world is taken over by science and so seems beyond us, the poems brings the world back by thinking of relationships and death. One catches the desire for the epic voice in Dudek, in the midst of the cultural wreckage around us, but he leads us to his tale by rather unusual means. His poetry insists upon "exposition and discourse," and has more in common with Dryden and Pope—"an overt effort to rescue / poetry from sofa-stuffing rhetoric. . . . / and carry it over into prose/meaning!" 129)—and Byron than that of most moderns:

> Cut the poetry, they said
> at all costs, and get the lucid
> rational mind
> on our side
> Byron
> was the last poet (except in Canada, some up to 1860)
> who defended the rational design. (129)

This "rational design" may be taken as the worked-for construct at stake in Dudek's poetry.

He does not fulfill the proposal to write everything in rhythmic form. His own prose is excellent, often elegant. But the argument with prose goes on throughout his work. And it is true that if we give up Dudek's work, or that of any important poet, entirely to its lyric moments, we have also given up the function of a major poetry. The challenge to prose and to subjectivity are fundamental concerns of Pound's "A Few Don'ts" in 1913, and of the whole Imagist effort to clean things up. The best known statement of the challenge is found in a letter from Pound to Harriet Monroe in 1915: "Poetry must be *as well written as prose*" (*Letters* 91; original emphasis). Even clearer and more public in 1913:

> I think this sort of clear presentation is of the noblest traditions of our craft. It is surely the scourge of fools. It is what may be called the "prose tradition" of poetry, and by this I mean that it is a practice of speech common to good prose and good verse alike.*

Dudek is in this tradition which tests the function of words in society, "insisting," as Herbert Schneidau has remarked of Pound, "that form follow[s] func-

---

* Ezra Pound, "The Approach to Paris," in *New Age*, XIII (1913), cited in Herbert H. Schneidau, *Ezra Pound: The Image and the Real* (24–25)—by far the best discussion of the "prose tradition" in poetry that I know.

tion": "At many crucial places in his poetics Pound showed his native American respect for function, once defining great art as 'maximum efficiency of expression'" (*Ezra Pound* 178). Respect for function is American in Pound; it is entirely Canadian in Dudek. This sense that form follows function helps us understand Dudek's formal means, as well as such events in his life as his sharp-edged coming to terms with Europe. Combined with that part of him that belongs to the "prose tradition" of poetry, a style develops, even more frequently than in Pound, which gathers in epigrams and aphorisms. No anthology of them should overlook him. They are so characteristic of the mind at work in the poems that they spilled over into a book of their own, which Dudek published in 1975.*

I began this introduction with recognition of Dudek's part in the modern project, a kind of re-formation of relations among person, things, and world. I want to extend that by calling attention to what seems to me an important event in the Canadian, literary world: Dudek's annotated edition of Ezra Pound's letters to him, *Dk / Some Letters of Ezra Pound* (1974), from 1949 through 1967. There, the record is kept of Dudek's personal efforts to argue for Pound's release from St. Elizabeths Hospital and of his part in the important fourth issue of *CIV/n* (carrying Pound's shorthand for Civilization as its title), which supported the case for release without, in any way, becoming "Poundling." These Canadian arguments were capped by Dudek's polished presentation of Pound by way of his letters on CBC, September 4, 1957, the complete text of which is included in *Dk*. After twelve years, Pound's release was ordered on April 18, 1958. Dudek's is one of the distinguished voices that helped bring it about. His judgment:

> He was a very great poet. The greatest in our time. Even when he wrote ranting poetry and prose, even in confusion and disorder of mind, his words had more glory, more of that spontaneous electric energy that is from our deepest uncharted core, than any other poet of the modern age. (*Dk / Some Letters* 143)

But Pound's agendum in the letters to Dudek, unlike those presented on CBC, is often political—some of it elicited by Dudek's probing of the unfortunate side of Pound's thought. As one reads, it becomes clear that Pound wanted to enter the Canadian literary scene by way of the leading edge of its small presses and magazines, those of Dudek and his associates foremost among them. Pound's extremism in this period is simply and determinedly blocked by Dudek's humanity and commitment to a very different ordering of the real. Annotating a letter of July 5, 1950, Dudek writes:

* Louis Dudek, *Epigrams*. Montreal: DC Books, 1975.

My own political views were leftist and strongly democratic. I was convinced at this time, and for many years afterwards—as in the main I still am—that Pound was an American radical in the democratic tradition, passionately concerned with social justice and also with the heritage of human civilization, certainly not a reactionary or conventional "Fascist." (Dk / Some Letters 46)

This can be argued, and will be, in order to find some balanced response to the mind and art of Ezra Pound, but the point that I wish to make clear is that Dudek can share only the radical tradition, which for him is entirely democratic. Whatever else Pound's politics desired, his move toward a totalitarian vision is a characteristic of modernism now under necessary and severe correction. I have already said that Dudek's is an important voice in that correction.

Pound and Dudek share an anguished sense of our cultural deprivation. The CBC presentation cites this passage from one of Pound's letters, which might be Dudek himself writing:

I mean all that is left is exiled, driven in catacombs, exists in the isolated individual, who occasionally meets one other with a scrap of it concealed in his person or his study. (Dk / Some Letters 127)

The difficulty is that Dudek enters upon a condition even more radically suspended. He denies the totalitarian answers of modernism, knowing that they participate in the terror of our time. I think he would agree that it is "not our business to supply reality"[6]—certainly not in totality.* In a stunningly good series of lectures he gave on CBC's *Ideas* in 1966, *The First Person in Literature*, he tells us:

Our problem is the radical absence of any valid grounds for universality. . . . But the liberation from the gods, and the liberation of the individual self, to face alone the great issues of existence—working always for this time and this place, this self, to find the hidden meaning of all things—that is the great adventure. It's not a dark prospect, but an infinite horizon of possibilities, for those who are strong enough to bear it. And for the great majority of modern artists it is still the only road. (First Person 67, 68)

Dudek's subject is this radical absence. The "infinite horizon of possibilities" shapes and reshapes in his continuous form.

Radical absence also informs the term by which some have dubbed him, "social realist"—not to be confused with socialist realism, one of the many ownerships of the real (Gnarowski viii). Social relations are certainly impli-

* I adapt a phrase from Jean-François Lyotard, *The Postmodern Condition* (81).

cated in cultural trivialization. Dudek at work brings us passages such as these: on "Reality in the Arts and Education" at the University of Prince Edward Island, in 1971,

> In the end we must ask, "What is the world really like? What is reality?" Reality in the full sense, the true nature of things, is not thinkable in trivial terms. The infinite articulation of particles and energies in nature, apparently aimless and hazardlike, out of which nevertheless emerge trees and stones, and purling streams, flowers, creatures, birds . . . men, women, and children . . . is really too much for a plodding, commonplace mind! The incredible complexity of organisms, the variety and identity of their being, life; the inconceivable intricacy of the mind and brain; the power of love, and all emotions; the mystery of death, or non-being— how could this be trivial? The nature of the creation, in which we inexplicably subsist, for a time—in which we actually *are*, alive!—is beyond our conception or understanding; but it is nothing trivial; it *is* incomprehensible, unutterable, magnificent. We should have no fear that anything as deep and immeasurable as this—is trivial. (*Technology* 50)

And responding to questions by his fellow poets in 1981,

> I cannot imagine a great poem that goes against the social good; and I cannot imagine a good political or cultural order that denies the primacy of art. . . .
> . . . In the face of reality, which is a turmoil of heaven and hell, there can only be anguish, and often helplessness. My transcendental optimism does not apply to the real issues of the world: there you either do or die. And you certainly die. Therefore I am willing to accept minor irritations (most of the time) and I try to live without being too much aware of the greater horror of the real. The bird in the teeth of the cat does not rejoice over the universe; but the bird in the tree maybe does. For some time you must be able to be that bird in the tree; there are lots of them there. (*Texts & Essays* 27–28)

Dudek has been called opinionated. True, at times, and I have not curtailed opinions with which I disagree. I stop over the remarks on the thought of William Carlos Williams and Marianne Moore, for example, in "Functional Poetry." Was this a necessary shaking off of other poetics in order to gain his own? A clearing away, at the time (1959), in order to assert his own thought? Then, I reread the beautiful elegy, "For William Carlos Williams," among the poems of *Zembla's Rocks* (1986), "when we were just getting / the whiplash of your New Measure" (50), which I have included near the end of this selection. In his criticism, Dudek has always kept a sharp watch over the important poetics of our time and challenged many of them, including those of his early associates, Irving Layton and Raymond Souster. He is especially harsh in his dismissal of Charles Olson and Robert Creeley as fragmentary and lacking a hold on the "rational design," which strikes me as misreading. Perhaps, with a purpose. His own use of fragmentation is certainly differently suspended within the tale he's telling. There is something at stake in Dudek's opinions, and I think it has to do with poetic power. Pound is one thing, "a great musician of the mind," as John Tytell calls him—a resister who "challenged the state,"[7] and, I would add, the state of affairs (320). And, as a great figure in the western-wide, modernist project, he is not, for Dudek, an aspect of "Americanism." Nor is Whitman who is of considerable importance to Dudek's poetics (though I think he and I share some sadness in thinking of Whitman's "democratic vistas" these days). Of course, Olson and Creeley do not represent "Americanism" either, but they are poetic "powers," close in time to Dudek. They do not, it seems, work that "immense reality" as he would have it in his own time and place. Though he carefully stands apart from the usual arguments of nationalism—among his epigrams, "Nationalism is the collective egoism of mediocrities" (Epigrams 12)—I think a Canadian vision is working its way in the poems, Canada, so to speak, in the midst of that "immense reality." I think of H. D. Forbe's remarks in Canadian Political Thought—because they seem to me to relate to Dudek's independence—on the "pervasive Americanism" of Canadians:

> . . . our tendency to see ourselves through American eyes. This tendency is a natural consequence of American power and can be seen for what it is only by those who neither rage against that power nor bend to its demands. (xii)

Louis Dudek would not look through other eyes in this work which actually begins when "Europe is behind us / America before us" (Europe 139). America is not Americanism.

So, I turn to the praises—lauds—of En México, to the changeling's love of Europe in Atlantis, to the terrible ironies of Continuation I, to the expanses to be worked in Ideas for Poetry, to the short poems from Zembla's Rocks, which take us more gently from cosmology in the old sense to cosmology in the new—in order to follow the mind's work in this poetry. My selection, while suffering all the discontents of cutting out—especially with the long-poems—is meant to follow the development of his work and to put his size and that of his reality in full view. I miss what has had to be left out. I undertook this selection in celebration of what is "there on the page." I've met Louis Dudek only once. I was waiting with Sharon Thesen on a street corner in Montreal for him to join us at lunch. I thought I saw a tall, walking loneliness coming toward us. Which surprised me, because he belongs to a numerous company of men and women who try to "think it through." Now, I am waiting for Continuation II.[8]

1988

The "Elf" of It

Robert Duncan's drawings in ink, pencil and crayon are, for me, a marvelous dimension of his *poiesis* that would make a world. They please and delight the mind's eye with that quality of addition to, not illustration of, his writing, just where I may be left breathless by Duncan's working sense of the boundlessness of language. They represent figurations that are other than himself, other than the writing, and if one looks closely at the energy of the lines he's drawn, they flow, so to speak, from his handwriting. They are, of course, also, a reflection of his long devotion to the painter's art in which I catch the quicknesses of Matisse, of Cocteau, of Picasso, of Jess, and often, of the drawings in childhood books. Whether they fall in place beside one poem or another, or float free on the walls of disparate rooms, they attend like borderguards[1] and enter the ransom of his poems. Some of the drawings imagine a hierarch, who, it seems, frequents our thought, whether we will or not, like those I watch on my study walls, when I look up from writing this: one in ink, a crowned figure with two eyes, one above and forward of the other, two natures looking out from this handmade greeting card, the crown touched with gold ink, a cape of red crayon, the nervously drawn hand the head rests on looks like Duncan's; and another head, in pencil, of imperious mien, one sharp eye looking straight at me, the other gazing elsewhere, as if the head were also in profile—like to the sometimes strangeness of Duncan's eyes—this time wearing a Phrygian cap that is also the liberty cap of the revolving mind—one of Duncan's guises, perhaps. They are not simply himself, but aspects of his thought—these haunting hierarchs.

Now, I look at a crayon which is in familiar conversation with Picasso, the style playing in Duncan's mind, pieces of recognition of another hieratic head, male or female, multiphasic in its which-ways, perhaps Egyptian, drawn together and broken up by colors—blue, several shades of green, red, magenta, a prominent blue ear outlined in black, one eye grey with a blue iris, and well above the eye of another face, which is magenta with a blue iris, and the left side of the Pharaonic headdress is a teal-green turning to shadows, on the right violet shadowed and underlayed by grey—reminiscent of the shadowy tinge which is so often remarkable in the colors of the painter Jess, his companion in life and art. I turn to a small framed field of color patches, rectangled, this time to think of Mondrian, but it is other than Mondrian in its mixed colors— and to a piece of an unrealized project on woven grass-paper, which was to be wallpaper for a whole room, twisting smokey colors of stove-top, homemade crayons, this, I like to think, in response to the rooms and furniture Jess mag- ically painted in their first years of house-imagining.

Duncan seemed to me always to love drawing—it belongs to first imagining and to first making, but during the 1950s his drawings appear more often at the margins, so to speak, of his writing; they range, bearing bits of story, laughing within themselves or grieving, some of the fairy sort at the edge of the West, cats, bus riders, coffee pot, cups, the Enamored Mage, "a lovely early god," a figure thinking, a reader reading. I skim them as I remember them. Beginning in 1951, Robert and Jess, as circumstances led them, put together one house- hold after another until they were able to settle in; each time, a visitor would be startled and drawn in by the imaginary conversation among the "things" of the house. Within this, Duncan's drawings, having become another dimension of his *poiesis*—one of them shows the pen that has just drawn his own hand—enter into close converse with Jess's art. This is not a matter of the one being adjunc- tive to the other; rather, I am thinking of the mystery of artistic relationship. The indispensable first map of the profundity of Jess's art in its own right is to be found in Duncan's "Iconographical Extensions," his introduction of Jess's beautiful book *Translations* (Black Sparrow Press, 1971). There, Duncan writes:

> Where Jess allies himself clearly with the grand masters of phantasmal nonsense that arise in the nineteenth century in the genius of the Romantic Movement— with Edward Lear and Lewis Carroll, as, in his translation of the *Galgenlieder* he al- lied himself with Christian Morgenstern—the modality of the picture is every- where problematic. It is essential that the figure is absolutely what it appears: it is pictorial, but it is not only pictorial, it is a happening of the painting, but it is also an element in the mode of the picture as rebus. It belongs to a playful nonsense, but this play, like the play in *Alice in Wonderland,* has everywhere a momentous hal- lucinatory aura. (vi)

This passage does not, of course, cover the vast structure of imagination that comes to be in Jess's work in painting, collage, made-things, and poems, but

I am after the "happening" in the work, the "problematic" which is content without solution, and the sense of "rebus," which they share in their varying recognitions. This is made clear, when, further along in this essay of 1971, Duncan writes:

> Living with Jess's work for more than twenty years—it was 1950 when we first met, and we have lived together since the beginning of 1951—my own work and thought have grown intimately with his, and, just as writing here of his work I find myself coming into realizations of elements of my own poetics that have been born in contemplations of paintings and paste-ups, so passages come to mind . . . from my work, that seem to speak for his intent. (xiii)

A household of imagination. The imagination of a household. In the late 1950s, in their house in Stinson Beach, a large, handmade scrapbook lay to hand for the visitor as for themselves—a good part of it clipped extravagantly from Skira art-books, then rearranged on a combinative principle that was their own—which amounted to the historical consciousness of art rewoven, not for its history, but for its conversation about the particulars and the immensities of our concern. And the intensities of this household could hook a rug, as we find when Duncan describes the one he made in the poem "Upon Taking Hold":

> this is the hookd rug workd in rich color
> > the red, blue, ochre,
> > violet, emerald, azure,
> > the black, pink, rose,
> > oyster white, the orange . . .
> this is the orange measurement of the lines
> > as I design them.
>
> The joys of the household are fates that command us.
> > (*Letters*, "iii: Upon Taking Hold")[2]

That is to say that one does imagine a house as part and parcel of being at home in the world—how large it is and simultaneously domestic—homemade. Some years ago, Denis Donoghue commented that "we have not grown so accustomed to the creative power of imagination as to think it common, in the nature of the human case, like knowledge or reason" (62). The "grand design" of Robert Duncan's work is out of and among the marvels of common things—the body, transformation of the beloved, colors and sounds of things, *frissons* of what moves around us, events of form in the writing—leading the reader toward those commands which are re-echoing commonly. The penultimate stanza of his last book, *Ground Work II*, comes to mind:

"I have given you a cat in the dark," the voice said.
Everything changed in what has always been there
at work in the Ground: the two titles
                    "Before the War," and now, "In the Dark"
underwrite the grand design.   The magic
                    has always been there,   the magnetic purr
                    run over me, the feel as of cat's fur
charging the refusal to feel.   That black stone,
                    now I see, has its electric familiar. (90)

We are then, in this work, familiar with, readers of—what shall I call it?—the largeness of being at home.

For this occasion, I especially want to think over the series of drawings that Duncan named "The Ideal Reader" and the book *Letters* (Jonathan Williams, *Jargon* 14, 1958, poems from 1952–1956) in which five of the first appeared. Two additional drawings of this imagined reader along with those in *Letters* appear later in the beautiful edition of *A Selection of 65 Drawings from One Drawing-book, 1952–1956* (Black Sparrow Press, 1970). Thus, all seven belong to the working-time of the poems in *Letters*. Here, the ideal reader is she, an ultimate other to this author, and the flowing lines of the drawings of her belong to childhood, to folklore, to children's books. She is also at the beginning of reading and represents a primary notion that language and its implication in the world are amazingly other than one is. She is the one who reads to herself, to the poet, and to you and me, just where, one thinks, nurturing compounds its busyness with language and reaches out. In these drawings, she always wears a hat, a garden hat of wide brim, hiding her face, whether she is inside or outside the house. We glimpse her face in profile in two of the drawings, otherwise she is not known, someone elsewhere, wearing a gown or smock of another time, a figure who reads before the poet himself could read and who is there reading after he has left his work, the idea of a reader.

I follow the drawings in sequence, following the numbering Duncan gave the Black Sparrow edition: she sits by a stream, reading a page of musical notes without staffs, sound loose on the page; she moves to the garden where she stands attending flowers with a watering pot; next, we see her walking and hardly distinguishable among the other shapes, as if from above, as a bird would from its nest high in a tree—but is it fall?—the leaves seem to be flying about and her shape is very like those of the leaves; then, she's sitting up in bed reading a book, the title on the spine reads "Flowers of the Field," and the art nouveau lines of the bed twist alive, the bedpost knobby like a tree trunk, and this time her hat is a flower, trimmed with flowers, hiding her face, the reading Flowers; now, she sits by a table, draped with an intricate shawl of eyelet shapes, on it a pitcher and curious art nouveau vase or lamp displaying two swimming forms, each with an *ocellus*, through which the crown of her striated hat can be seen, her head bent toward an unseen book; she is outdoors, seated by a tree, a bird singing on a branch, in the distance at a juncture of flowing line, the ball of a shaped tree of, perhaps, roses, and the ideal reader's hat is this time a cluster of flowers repeating in shape the flower-tree in the distance; finally, she is sitting in one of those chairs that seem alive, Queen Anne touched by art nouveau, her hat dressier with its high, dented crown, ribboned, as if she were going out, but she is wearing an apron and she holds on her lap a staring cat. This is, I take it, the "electric familiar" of childhood that will reach us as language does, in George Steiner's words, for "[t]he gravity and constancy at the heart of major forms" (*Real Presences* 225).

The book *Letters*, which, as I've noted, is joined with these drawings of "The Ideal Reader," is pivotal—a friend calls it "uncompromising"—in Duncan's work. His preface opens with an epigraph in German from Christian Morgenstern's *Stufen—Steps* (1992): *Ich habe keine Tiefe, als meinen unaufhörlichen Trieb zur Tiefe*—I have no depth, other than my ceaseless drive toward the depths. Morgenstern is already in place here in the language field by way of remarks by Duncan that I have already quoted. Again, I think of Jess's way of working his versions of the *Gallowsongs / Galgenlieder* (1905) in words, "divinitive not definitive" (dedication page), he tells us, and in startling drawings. In another place, I'm told that "Morgenstern said about man's unthinking use of language: 'I don't want to see man shipwrecked, but he should be conscious of the fact that he's sailing on the high seas'" (Jess, quoted in Max Knight 6–7). But I must stop here to say that this, as the consciousness of our language changes, has always been the concern of women, too, and we find full acknowledgement in a poem in this book, "At the End of a Period," apparently describing one of the drawings:

> An imaginary woman reads by her lamplight, inclining her head slightly, listening to the words as I write them: we are there, as the poem comes into existence— she and I—losing ourselves in the otherness of what is written. I too then am imaginary. The sirens that I just heard I mention, she hears them as I do. (*Letters* "xi: At the End of a Period")

So, reading *Letters*, the preface, carrying the title "Nests," begins:

> It is an intensity of excitement which compels a man to work out a designd feeling that variously arrives at stations on three levels: the presence in the imagination in which the speech "comes," a mortality out of immortal letters; the evident manifestation or trace we in the xxth century worship as Art and declare immor-

tal; and the return, the dwelling of the imagination in speech. So that powers and forms gather in the mind where it feeds on any written thing. (i)

My attention is drawn to this claim of the imaginative mind, with all its Blakean and Coleridgean resonances, among others, of a tradition out of the Renaissance, to a language that works with the largeness of cosmos, with the uncanniness of our condition, with the mortality that is the interface of "immortal letters." The old word for this is the sublime, in Hannah Arendt's sense, that it is not exactly human but we know it, one by one.[3] I am calling it here, in order to avoid chimerical highnesses, being-at-home-in-the-world, which may be for a different author, say, Artaud, a not-being-at-home-at-all. Duncan pauses in his preface to write:

> Artaud is torn apart by actual excitations which are intolerable to his imagination and to his material. . . . The writing he has left is evidence of the area of endurance. And Artaud's 'charge' is higher, in an entirely other category, than the charge at which I work. (*Letters* ii)

Both voices and the "texts" they leave us belong to our condition in language, for, as Hannah Arendt reflected on Walter Benjamin and the "dark times" we try to forget:

> Any period to which its own past has become as questionable as it has to us must eventually come up against the phenomenon of language, for in it the past is contained ineradicably, thwarting all attempts to get rid of it once and for all. (*Dark Times* 204)

This wondering about language, the hold of it, the WHAT it lets go of in disbelief, is a wonder of our twentieth-century minds. I, one among many, try to think through the "crisis of authorship" that "accompanies the crisis of life"— Bakhtin's terms[4]—that are abroad, not simply in academe, but in our whole culture, which confuses itself. These practices of "aesthetic outsideness," the perceptual and apprehensive field of our meaning, and of "ethical outsideness (moral, social, political, practical-life outsideness)" break out together for reformation and place the "self" in thunderous straits (Bakhtin, *Art and Answerability* 206). Bakhtin helps us to think about this in essays from 1919–1924, which have only recently been available to us; even so, given our contemporary distress in reading, one of his editors finds it necessary to warn us that the essays come to us "At a time when 'the author' has long been presumed dead, and when the words 'hero' and 'aesthetics' have a certain anachronistic ring to them" (Holquist ix). Bakhtin writes:

Inner infinitude breaks into the open and finds no repose; life is intensely principled. (*Art and Answerability* 206)

So, I would place Duncan's major forms among changing perspectives that were not his own—and polemically so in his "re-visioning."

Language-letters—"immortal letters"—how tense many a contemporary reader becomes in relation to this sense of words, as his/her experience with language falls into history or a no-where of ourselves, on the one hand, transparent, on the other a slumgullion: these *Letters* of Duncan's kinship with tradition reach out. This kinship may, indeed, propose a sacred language that is behind us, that we may return to. That is certainly in the tension of his language, but there is never a closed book. Thus, this tension of his language is also, through and through, a twentieth-century experience of language as "older and other"[5] than one is, and so, beyond one's ownership. In fact, I would say that theorists of philosophical and scientific language have come into this experience by way of the poets since Mallarmé, the best of them bending their heads in acknowledgement. Duncan's concern with the vastness of our condition cannot be dismissed as merely "religious," for that is never mere, as can be seen in the contemporary, often dangerous, resurgence of it. Duncan's language seems always to work from an immediate creative principle incipient in words and syntax and from what I take to be a Whiteheadian proposition—not initially derived from *Process and Reality*: that God is incomplete in the creation among things, "prehensions," as the philosopher would say, or "concrete facts of relatedness."[6] Duncan is "protestant"—his own word for that side of himself, with the accent on the second syllable, thus to take the word away from the institutionalized versions of such modernity. And, to my mind, the process of Duncan's work moves in the midst of our secularizations, so little understood that I take to heart the point Geoffrey Hartman made some years ago:

The secular is the sacred integrated, rather than degraded or displaced. (*Beyond Formalism* 22)

And there are continuous depths toward which each life drives, so the poet Duncan insists. "*Pli selon pli*," he writes in 1970, adapting this resonant phrase from Mallarmé's "Remémoration d'Amis belges"[7] for his essay on Jess's work, fold by fold, insightful words that I may adapt again to his own:

. . . translation leads to and from translation. But there are not established orders here, every order in the order of another order appears significantly disordered ("Iconographical Extensions" ii)

Translations of our materialities, large and small—toward relations among things—a "work in progress," as in Mallarmé's hope of the book, or in Joyce's "a long the / riverrun, past Eve and Adam's"[8] or, again, in "the hymn of connections" of Boulez's own *Pli selon pli*, ongoing.[9] In this search for a "new language" and a "new syntax," I think a spiritual disclosure is being worked. The word "spiritual" bites at our heels—in our arts, in our culture, and in the disturbing voices of our culture-mongers.

From the perspective of the postmodern reader-writer who is entangled in the new consciousness of language as an ultimate materiality of our twentieth-century condition—informed and overwhelmed by brutal "hegemonies" from which we would depart—often, let it be said, translated by recent "language-poets" into brilliant poetic practices—"spirit" may only elicit disbelief. That is, I think, the condition of our belief, and it is not as simple as traditional atheism makes out. Within this new language-consciousness, we come upon the notion that literary language is just another discourse among many. But it is never "just" anything of the sort, for that is to give literary discourse, accepting the currency of the term, over entirely to the ideologies we would know, measure, and hope to correct. That is also to forget the fundamental oppositional nature of the arts, most particularly trenchant in twentieth-century art. We have had enough of formulated art and of socialist realism, even of the capitalist variety; they are the "shoring up" of whatever institution empowers them—"at the very moment when its vulnerability becomes apparent" (Godzich xx). I adapt to my purposes here Wlad Godzich's remarks in his "Foreword" to Michel de Certeau's eye-opening book *Heterologies: Discourse on the Other*:

> The quality that is recognized in literature, he seems to think, does not come from the fact that it is a special mode of language, but rather from the fact that it is a part of language, a mode of language use, that is a discourse. Unlike language, which, as an object of knowledge, is a construct of philosophers and linguists, discourses constitute forms of actual social interaction and practice. As such, they are not irrational, but they are subject to the pulls and pressures of the situations in which they are used as well as to the weights of their own tradition. They must always handle the complex interplay of that which is of the order of representation and the nonrepresentable part which is just as much constitutive of them, their own other. (xx)

The other of the small things and of the immensity of being at home in the world—in Duncan's book *Letters*—teases the reader's mind.

Allow me a moment more on the postmodern reader, who is in her/his own way an Ideal Reader: what are we to make of Duncan's view of "the evident manifestation or trace we in the xxth century worship as Art and declare immortal"? (*Letters* i). On one level this is the transcendental claim of art, itself as language or discourse apart, that we know so well from the Romantics or, at least, a certain reading of them. Duncan once said, sometime in the 1950s, that John Livingston Lowes's *The Road to Xanadu* was his Bible. There, one finds "the shaping spirit"[10] wandering his/her map of the depths that the Enlightenment thought to reason. The trouble is that such reason is also a cosmology and a definition of God that is only *afterthought*—Epimetheus of the flames life takes up. The generous reasons of human nature that the Enlightenment proposed are generalized hope of our goodness and of our societal best-wishes, vulnerable from the start, and their disarray becomes more and more apparent in the twentieth century of ourselves. Modern and postmodern thought inherit the Romantic interrogation of human nature—what can be found there and what can be salvaged from the tradition is one way of reading *The Rime of the Ancient Mariner* and Coleridge's turn to a philosophy and theology and to poetic silence. The work of *poiesis* does gather in a storm from there. Still, one of the greatest challenges of postmodernity is that aspect of it that brings us to a surface of language whose referent has "passed away" and is to be found. Amidst the death of the author and dying hierarchies of meaning. A "wild-logos,"[11] to adapt Merleau-Ponty's term, among us. Here, the writer among the artists keeps watch over the wildness. Here, I have used the word depth, drawing it from Duncan's epigraph from Morgenstern's *Steps,* in order to catch—metaphorically, at least—something the surface of language hides. The depths brim in the cup of our language. Religions and the sacred languages of them are both historically a gift and a dirty trick of those depths in the continuous language about that which dies and that which appears not to. At the depths of the human effort to *mean*. In the midst of postmodernity, we come upon the notion of "outside thought" in Foucault, one of its finest thinkers and as a writer, the most brilliant: "'one may assume that it was born of that tradition of mystic thinking which, from the time of Pseudo-Dionysus, has prowled the borderlands of Christianity'" (quoted in de Certeau 182). (One must remember that Christianity became the reason of things for centuries.) Michel de Certeau in Chapter 12 of his *Heterologies,* "The Black Sun of Language," gives considered attention to Foucault's "outside thought," of which I'll cite only a part:

> Those who cling to continuity think they can escape death by taking refuge in the fiction of a permanence that is real. Those who box themselves inside the solid walls of the discontinuous systems believe they can keep death an external problem, confined to the absurd event that brings an end to a particular order; they avoid the problem posed by the system of order itself, a problem which first appears in the image of the internal "limit." For the sixteenth century, it was the

other world, either divine or demonic; for the seventeenth, "non-being," bestial or imaginary; for the nineteenth, the "inside" dimension (the past, force, dreams).

Internal finitude struggles against the structurings that try to overcome it, and provides the arena for the defense of the same, or self-identity. Alterity always reappears, and in a fundamental way, in the very nature of language. (181)[*]

We may read Duncan's *Letters* and his assertion of "immortal letters" and "Immortal Art" in many ways. We may account for his sources—classical, biblical, Hermetic, and stretching in the years of his work. We may read him as "traditional," as he himself sometimes claimed. But he is, to my reading, always on the borderlands of "outside thought," thus, a protestant and an adventurer in the continuous depths, which are discontinuities:

> The glamorous tyranny of religion, of science, of democracy, of industry, of capitalism, surrounds us, feeds us, protects us. (*Letters*, Preface iii)

And those who have "joind the Legions of the Dead":

> Their gasses flow from the sarcophagi of our belief to infect history. All dead bodies radiate prayers, ancestral emanations to insure the continuity of semen, of blood, of spirit. . . .
>
> I embrace the heated clouds of the past. Thoth and the enormous Imperator Mundi of the frescoes at Tahull stain my souvenirs; luminosities gather from the monthly disorders of Mary. . . .

> It is not expression nor creation that I seek; but my inventions are addressd to an adventure. The medium of words. In the orders of the actual and in the orders of the fantastic, a world—worlds are constantly reveald thru mediums of the arts. A life then, or lives. (*Letters*, Preface iii–iv)

> Lists of imaginary sounds I mean sound signs I mean things
> designd in themselves I mean boundary marks I mean a
> bounding memorizations I mean a memorial rising I mean
> a con glomerations without rising
>
> > (*Letters*, " i: For A Muse Meant" n.p.).

> 1. The streets. Of the mind. Whose gangs
> of who in the whom of avenues   hooing
> passd?   They wrote parts of color.
> Each as the Anthropos
> swallowing himself in continual likeness.
> Who?   Who?
>
> . . . .

---

[*] De Certeau cites the Foucault passage from "La Pensée du Dehors," in *Critique*, 229 (1966), 525.

Old Mother Anthropos
refuses to face her hour's mirror.
You know her.   She lives in the shoe
     that fits her.
Who.   Who. She hears in the mountain
  (a gangster voice in a street to come).
Knows what to do. Who. Who.
Knows in the too many of her.
        What   to   do.
      (*Letters,* "iv: First Invention on the Theme of the Adam" n.p.)

It were a good thing to begin a book with Blake's beginning: HEAR THE VOICE
OF THE BARD! for it is the imagination who listens then—but the Bard is the voice
of the listener, who hears, sees, the ancient trees, the Holy Word walking there,
crying. (*Letters,* "vi: Figures of Speech" n.p.)

I've offered these quotations—pieces, which, unfortunately, loosen the wonder-
ful shaping process of the book *Letters*—in order to suggest the claim of Dun-
can's poetic practice on our intelligence in language. In poem XXIX:

Changing Trains
               for languages. Everything ours
is burden. Even declared, cleard; weighs so much; encum-
bers us as we go. Unable to carry a sentence thru.
    So we checkd the statement thru to its period. To ride
along with it word less. Only to make our claim at the end.
At the ultimate station of our meaning we mean to stop.
With no burden. But there is a burden to the sentence—
even when translated for us—that we do not understand,
and we worry then that our burden will not wait for us.
. . . .
    Here at the border change. Change languages. The
customs inspects casually for contraband. But our declara-
tion is true: we have come thru with nothing. About which,
a guilt gathers. We are not sure even of this.
            (*Letters,* "xxix: Changing Trains")

I do not know another poem that better describes our condition in language
for the reader who first steps into modernity—that is one of our problems, so
few step there until he or she is given a chance to take art as differing some-
what from tiddlywinks. Having stepped there, many a one trips over post-
modernity. Let's for this occasion, in uneasy abbreviation of the matter, take
postmodernism to be pieces of the jigsaw puzzle that the arts came to call "open
form." Philosophy is at it; the arts have been at it.

In this openness of relations, the self of the reader, as of the poet, is at stake, defended and formulaic, perhaps, or in a condition of letting-go into relations that traditional systems do not call to mind. Duncan, reading and writing, enters the charge of modernity, which is reflected upon in Letter I, as "a con glomerations":

> the addition of the un
> plannd for interruption:
> a flavor stinking coffee
> (how to brew another cup
> in that Marianne Moore –
> E. P. – Williams – H. D. – Stein –
> Zukofsky – Stevens – Perse –
> surrealist – dada – staind
> pot)   by yrs R. D.
> (Letters, "i: For A Muse Meant")

I note that Eliot, who had returned to traditional cosmology and, thereby, gained a strange tranquility in his writing-reading, is absent—no longer grounds in this brewing pot. In a late essay, published in 1985, we find Duncan reading Edmond Jabès:

> Oh yes, I can read; the words on the page and their phonetic transcriptions, and the theories of voice, I can read. But this voice on these voices I must hear in an infatuation. This is the language of the "Other," whose ultimate lure is the language of an other "me." Close then to the very voice or mode of Poetry, for I know in the courses of my work the voice is in one sense more me than I am, in another sense is an "I" beyond me. ("Delirium" 209)

> This delirium of finding meanings beyond meaning is initial in The Book of Questions. The work, Jabès observes, is the tributary not of the writer as such but of the reader. In the very act of writing his "authenticity," the writer, if he reads, faces not what he meant or thought to mean but what the words begin to mean. In this writing from the first, this overture, we are led to read as a writer reads who searches the writing for a revelation or prophecy of self that comes into being only through the word—or so it seemed at first, but we find that this word comes into existence by number and letter below the lexiconic level. ("Delirium" 225)

Thus, Duncan reminds this reader of what we have entered upon, as in Letter XXX of 1956:

> . . . the whirlpools of glamor that rise from the unrestraind powers of daily words. . . . For all who enter that kingdom hear a glamor and see a ruin–out of themselves. (Letters, "xxx: The Language of Love")

And so, Ideal Reader, to whom these remarks are addressed—in my childhood or yours, in my maturity or yours—I'll close with some reflections on the self so poised. Robert Duncan is one of the founders of American art and thought—that is to say, such thought and its newness requires continuous refounding. His beloved Emerson is one key to his work, wherein a self becomes another Self among things. Another fine reader of Emerson comes to mind here; in his reflections on two of Emerson's commanding essays, "Self-Reliance" and "Circles," a "dazzling complication," Richard Poirier writes:

> The "self" can rely only on those workings which in turn reveal it; its identity can therefore never be fixed or solidified. As he will say in "Circles," "There is no outside, no inclosing wall, no circumference to us." (*Renewal of Literature* 196)

I, for one, turn round and round in this complexity—thinking over the whole of Duncan's work. I come upon his essays in *Fictive Certainties*, and one of them, "The Self in Postmodern Poetry," particularly sparkles for this occasion:

> The idea of "self" has been with me for a very long time, certainly longer than the idea of "modern," though, born in 1919, my childhood was in the 1920's, the "modern" period. . . . I know only too well the disappointment of finding myself adolescent in the Depression years that ended all thought of the "modern," and still to come the Permanent War Economy in which the euphoria of the 1920's and the mystique of being "modern" was swept away in the Age of Anxiety and the Beginning of Rage. "Modern," for me, is present in my work as a nostalgia for a world long gone, and "postmodern" is a term used, I understand, to discuss even my work, but it is not a term of my own proposition. (219)

Yet, Duncan guided others into the "working orders" of modern and of contemporary art, and he leaves a brilliant record of his tracking. There is, in this passage a staccato thought of what our quaking century has swept away. The essay continues:

> I would not want, in any case, to contend with what postmodern means or does not mean as a possible definition of a period in the history of ideas. What I can do here is simply explore how the idea of "self" relates to my personal development as a poet. But here (for poetry is, as Mallarmé long ago reminded us, written with words, not ideas) I mean how I hear or read the word "self" to mean. (219)

I am struck by the degree to which Duncan belongs to this very contemporary concern—that is, thinking of Mallarmé, many a he or she of writing and reading comes into a materiality of language and the search for a largeness, a glamor of form, other than the very human, twentieth-century disappointment in the human record of itself. Duncan's language amounts to a hard push—to a boundary—to an edge. And there, the self is poised, perhaps shaken:

> The Great Writers, as my parents thought of them, had an authority that was due in their minds to something called Genius and its inspiration by spirits of the dead masters. They lost themselves, theirselves, in their work. Here "self" disappears and "work" appears. Our lives, it was my parents' persuasion, were written in a book, "on the other side," and they, in turn received messages "from the other side" in automatic writing, a received text. Shakespeare, Emerson and Whitman, they thought to be mediums in such a way. In the place of theirselves, a Self, the poet, spoke. But the embodiment of that voice was in the Work, Itself. (Fictive Certainties 225)

This passage brings to attention an inherited sense of language—its sacredness, yes, and its spirituality—an otherness. It was an entrance to language for the poet Robert Duncan, and it may be an entrance for any one of our haunted minds. It is the contemporary sense of this otherness that has shifted, bringing into question the "Logos of history and Scripture." "God, self, history, and book are," it is said, "are . . . bound in an intricate relationship in which each mirrors the other. No single concept can be changed without altering all of the others" (Taylor 7).[12] I suggest a rewriting that modernity and its afterwords are in the midst of. And the self returns—sometimes hapless, sometimes fortunate— in the work of translating these changing relations.

Duncan continues in this essay:

> Today, in 1979, reading that essay ["Self-Reliance"], I find again how Emersonian my spirit is. All of experience seems my trust fund to me; I must cultivate the mistrust that alone can give contrast and the needed inner tension for vital interest. In this, I stand almost heretically disposed to Olson's insistence on Melville's sense of inner catastrophe against the Emersonian bliss. But, if there is bliss acknowledged in Emerson, I read my Emerson dark. (Fictive Certainties 226)

I cannot stop here to comment on the many dissonances in poetic practice; I'll let Duncan notice them again in a moment. Further in his essay, he quotes Emerson on "the reason of self-distrust":

> "Who is the Trustee? What is the aboriginal Self, on which a universal reliance may be grounded? . . . The inquiry leads us to that source at once the essence of genius, of virtue, and of life, which we call Spontaneity or Instinct. We denote this primary wisdom as Intuition, whilst all later teachings are tuitions. . . . We first share life by which things exist and afterwards see them as appearances in nature and forget that have we shared their cause. Here is the fountain of action and of thought." (Fictive Certainties 226–27)

And Duncan comments:

As Emerson concludes this passage he seems to speak directly for the poetic practice of open form, for the importance of whatever happens in the course of writing as revelation—not from an unconscious, but from a spiritual world. In this am I "modern"? Am I "postmodern"? I am, in any event, Emersonian. (227)

A tuition—a word out of Latin which means to watch and to guard. Open form, in which Duncan worked, is one of the great gifts of American poetry, as the work of it came to be among things. Our contemporary sense of the spiritual, as of the Book, is shifty in our relation to the self of the writer-reader, so it is well to look into the *work of language* in this openness—that finds form not as a stop or a rest, but a movement among things.

The Ideal Reader and Duncan, who lose themselves in reading, find in his/her "dark reading" of Emerson a principle that Richard Poirier calls "writing off the self":*

> What we have before us . . . is evidence that human beings can exercise a capacity to wish themselves radically other than what they are, to wish themselves evacuated from those "arrangements of knowledge." It is possible to do this, furthermore, without the comfort of either religion or of the so-called false needs produced by the conditions from which human beings are, it is hoped, to be released. Thus, while Nietzsche and Foucault are far more concerned with cultural than with individual evaporations, the very extremity of their position enables us to come to a new appreciation of the more local and personal acts of self-disposal in, say, Emerson or Thoreau, Pater or Ruskin, Lawrence or Stevens, aspects which have been ignored or suppressed in the interests of accommodating everything they say to the overall humanistic tendencies necessarily exhibited in their work and in the work of their interpreters. (*Renewal of Literature* 196)

Out of his re-reading of Emerson, Duncan recognizes this curious "capacity" to be "radically other":

> What I would point out in my work as one of its underlying currents is the weaving of a figure unweaving, an art of unsaying what it says, of saying what it would not say. I want to catch myself out. If I mistrust "my" trust, I am yet thruout even simple, whole-hearted and trusting in my mistrust. I trust in my mistrust some trust. I've but to twist and to turn to let it show. Back of the "Self," which was but a rime, I want to see the mercurial genius of language, the "Elf" who comes when I lose myself in reading the workings of language in the water. (*Fictive Certainties* 231–32)

> The Self, with a capital S, this Atman, Breath, Brahma, that moves in the word to sound I so love I also would undo the idea of, let it go. The theme increases in recent years, and back of it hovers the dissolution of the physical chemical universe

---

* See Richard Poirier's brilliant chapter in *The Renewal of Literature*, "Writing Off the Self."

which I take to be the very spiritual ground and the body of our being. Something more than Death or Inertia comes as a lure in this "Letting go." (*Fictive Certainties* 233)

I want to leave this as it is—in Duncan's words.

I've said that I think of Duncan as one of the founders of our thought and its *poiesis*, and I have noticed one aspect of his refounding our "intellectual inheritance" in Emerson. As I struggle to draw up a map, another brilliant refounder comes to mind, Stanley Cavell:

> More or less obviously, in writers from Blake to Hegel to Thoreau and Nietzsche, the working through of secularization requires the constructing of a mythology to rival that of Christianity, which in practice means to reinterpret Christianity, bone by bone. But nothing is obvious about "secularization," especially not whether in a given case it looks like, as one might call it, eternalization. The progressive dissociation of spirit and nature (hence the possible disappearance of both) is more commonly thought of, I believe, in spatial terms rather than in these temporal terms, i.e., as a process of the progressive internalization of human interests. The guiding thought in either case is that each is a function of the other, that these are sides of some progressing bilateralization of the human, entailing some further fearful symmetries. (*Claim* 471–72)

These reflections are made in the context of discussing "the concept of the exhaustion of the medium of art," which has a long history from the eighteenth century on. He thinks of John Stuart Mill—between Bentham and Coleridge, so to speak—and comments that "no later writer can be free" of such thought, that "no later man or woman can be" (473). So, we come into what Cavell, writing on Thoreau in his book *In Quest of the Ordinary*, calls "ecstatic and fantastic opportunities" (185) of mind—and we come "to see the reader as fantastic" too (184).

In his "Notes on Grossinger's *Solar Journal: Oecological Sections*" (1970), Duncan gives a language-map of a refounding, to which I would only add Poe:

> In writing on *Maximus* in 1954 I worked out from a quote of Emerson's *Hamatraya*, with the sense that when it was realized how deeply I was Emersonian and in turn when our vision of our genius was enlarged to see how Emerson and Melville, Hawthorne (central to an understanding of Spicer and Robin Blaser), Emily Dickinson (Creeley, Eigner), and Whitman—how these five form a constellation—then the full promise of our rebirth in Poetry would be released. (n.p.)

And, therein, please find, Ideal Reader, many houses and much dissonance in the practice of poetry, keeping, of course, the "Elf" of it in your mind.

14 January 1992

Preface to the Early Poems
of Robert Duncan

What do I want to say about Robert Duncan's early poems? Waiting for the morning news, waiting to write an answer to my own question, I hear on the radio that someone who's read Joyce's *Ulysses* could win a Chevrolet, because practically nobody has: "Do you know what it means? Write us. Frankly, we haven't a clue." The broadcaster is, I suppose, competent from his window on things—that is, as they may be. Still, I'm grateful for his meddling even before I reach to turn him off. He's led me, willy-nilly, back to 1946, to a donut shop on Telegraph Avenue, and into a conversation with Duncan on Joyce, whom I'd only begun to read.[1] Some months later, Duncan would gather a group of us to read *Finnegans Wake* with him; he read aloud, and we, frightened and enchanted by the language, pooled whatever our youth had of knowledge and experience to get through one passage and then another, joyously.

But the morning that I've been led back to, Duncan spread out on our table, between our coffee cups and chocolate donuts, two pages of a densely annotated outline. Preliminary thoughts, he said, of a novel he had in mind. He talked about it—or, rather, inside it—*Ulysses*, on this occasion, the primer of his thought—of the vastness of a single day, of the size of lives and loves, venturous consequences. I think I thought, "Gee whiz!"—an awkward way of expressing to myself my astonishment in the face of his language and his weaving of it. He did not write that novel. Instead, we meet his practice in poetry—the tale he tells of himself and of our selves in language. This is the poet who, during the time of those early poems, 1946–1956, could say of the way he worked:

> I make poetry as other men make war or make love or
> make states or revolutions: to exercise my faculties at large.[2]

And that is not magniloquence, for so, I believe, his readers find him in these poems—at work in our language.

We meet him here in love, strikingly romantic in the glamours of language, headed for the "expanding structure" of his work.

> Beauty is a bright and terrible disk.
> It is the light of our inward heaven
> and the light of the heaven which we walk.
>
> (*Years* 82)

These lines from the poem "Heavenly City, Earthly City" startle. The reader likely thinks of Keats famous difficult line, "Beauty is truth, truth beauty," which Duncan read as an "ecstatic moment," or even, as Duncan did, transformatively, among his last poems (*Ground Work I*, 1984), of George Herbert's two poems, titled "Jordan" (1633). One of them begins:

> *Who sayes that fictions onely and false hair*
> *Become a verse? Is there in truth no beautie?*
> *Is all good structure in a winding stair?*
>
> (*GW I* 76)

The old word for this is the sublime. All modernity is troubled by the sublime which overwhelms us—beautiful, ugly, or monstrous—and some call it romantic, passing by. "In the dark of my manhood the flamey self / leaps" (*Years* 82). I would not have this romanticism mistaken. As Stanley Cavell has said of the Romantics who Duncan read with love and care for their imagination,

> . . . both the wish for the exceptional and for the every day are foci of romanticism. One can think of romanticism as the discovery that the everyday is an exceptional achievement. Call it the achievement of the human. (*Claim* 463)

And according to Duncan's work, that human nature is indeterminate.

In 1966, on the poems written during the years 1950–1953 and gathered in *A Book of Resemblances*, Duncan reflects, as if he were writing them over again:

> In our immediate oceanic being, we can seem to our examining conscious view all but hopelessly lost in a medium at once overpowering and vague, too huge to be true. . . . As we near the language itself (the poem had presented itself as a welling up of words or waters that was yet a well in its fullness, eternal and motionless), we see it as an ocean that is at work at its own boundaries we feel as the revealed contours of the poem we, being the ocean, would shape. . . .
>
> The rage of Love appeard to me to be a convulsion of the sea, driven by storm winds or shaken by upheavals of the under earth, itself an ocean of molten rock

and fire. War, love, and the poem, shaped history as expressions of the deepest forces and cleavings (adherences and divisions) of Man's hidden nature. (Book of Resemblances vii)

A figuration among these poems insists upon an appearance on my prefatory page:

The man with his lion under the shed of wars
sheds his belief as if he sheds tears.
The sound of the words waits—
a barbarian host at the borderline of sense.
. . . .
The borderlines of sense in the morning light
are naked as a line of poetry in a war.[3]

"The Song of the Borderguard." This nakedness in language—the way a poem appears useless unless in the world—seems to me a bravery in language on behalf of our fundamental circumstances. But what, we may ask, of that lion in our minds that would have deeds to his/her credit?

I draw upon the notes on lions, which Duncan published as part of his statement on poetics for Don Allen's The New American Poetry, 1945–1960:

The Christians thought of the lion as Christ the King: because the lion was a terrible power and at the same time a beast of great beauty.

For me, the Lion is the Child, the unfettered intellect that knows in his nobility none of the convictions and dogmas which human mind inflicts itself with— what is the human desire to humiliate even its own being?

For me, the Lion is the sexual appetite that knows no contradiction within itself. (405)

Amidst rumors of "the demise of imagination," which would preempt the correction of modernism that is a primary motivation of our arts since 1945, there is no replacement for this imagination of ourselves.

In celebrating these poems—recognitions that began when Jack Spicer, having met Duncan at an evening with Kenneth Rexroth's "anarchist-pacifist" literary group, brought me three of the "Berkeley Poems" in typescript, early in 1946—I think back to the days that are midway in our cultural experience of this century. And I weigh the conditions young writers in the Berkeley context then entered upon by the historical depths into which the medievalist Ernst Kantorowicz led us—so alive and worlding in Duncan's stunning "Venice Poem"[4]— and by Hannah Arendt's fearful, contemporary clarity. We discovered The Origins of Totalitarianism when she taught at Berkeley in 1955. In the 1950 preface to

that book, she argues that "human dignity needs a new guarantee"(ix) and con-
cludes: "The subterranean stream of Western History has finally come to the
surface and usurped the dignity of our tradition. This is the reality in which we
live" (ix).[5] I copy this out now with the same grief I felt when first I read it.
"It would make sense to ask whether someone may be soul-blind," Stanley Cavell
says, writing on the monstrous among us (*Claim* 378). This, I mean to say, is
the underground of writing wherever that tradition strays—even in America.
Drafted in 1941, Duncan writes a poem from barracks: "The guns / are new
devices in the mind for absolutes, excite a curious art" ("A Spring Memoran-
dum," *Years* 16). The answering mind is in the "open form" and "open uni-
verse" towards which we read in the "expanding structure" of Duncan's work.

Just here, a travelling poem from the vindicative book, *Letters: Poems 1953–1956*,
should be brought forward, lest any reader miss its prophecy for his and our
work in language:

> Changing Trains
>   for languages. Everything ours
> is burden. Even declared, cleard; weighs so much; encum-
> bers us as we go. Unable to carry a sentence thru.
>   So we checkd the statement thru to its period. To ride
> along with it word less. Only to make our claim at the end.
> At the ultimate station of our meaning we mean to stop.
> With no burden. But there is a burden to the sentence—
> even when translated for us—that we do not understand,
> and we worry then that our burden will not wait for us.
>   It is carrying too much, because we loved it all, packd
> it and would transport it, if we must be transported; because
> stones, handsome apparel, books, designs—anything—
> attracted us.
>   Here at the border change. Change languages. The
> customs inspects casually for contraband. But our declara-
> tion is true: we have come thru with nothing. About which,
> a guilt gathers. We are not sure even of this. (xxix)[6]

I read Duncan as a participant in American consciousness of itself and in the
democratic conscience of which it dreams. Elsewhere, I've claimed that he is a
founder of American thought in art,[7] because thinking in art needs now to be
refounded. In the laughter and fun of his "comic masque," *Faust Foutu*, we can-
not find our way—will it never end?—and the characters gripe about it. We
do come upon an exuberant bodyness that, a voice says, "I may retrieve my
immortal image from all perfection." And another voice says, "Could there be
perpetual play in playing where even perfections of form were played out. This

is what I designd, a play in which terror was playful" (71). Though both Marlowe and Goethe will haunt us as we read, the one with damnation, the other with a surprising, saving grace, Duncan's masque, for all its extravagant language, owes more to Gertrude Stein's *Doctor Faustus Lights the Lights*—in which the dog says, "Thank you"—than to our first and second Fausts. When Duncan tries his imagination with Stein, as in *Writing Writing*, the fascinating poems strain at the "tranquility"—his word for something comfortable, yet strange, in her language, as she works with the materiality of words and opens the syntax of them. Her "nonconformity," seen as a re-founding, comes to us through Emerson's self-reliance, as does Duncan's—against "blindman's buff."

I have used the term "expanding structure" more than once. It is Duncan's, when, thinking over his earliest poems, he accepted them and their "disturbing poetics" into his works. Charles Watts,[8] hearing me use it of Duncan one day recently on the telephone, said it suggests something "alive, light, tensile, and permissible." The imagination of structure. In an essay of 1982, "Towards an Open Universe"—keynotes that help us read this structure—Duncan imagines his first day, January 7, 1919, "the hour before dawn, in the depth of winter at the end of a war," and amazingly the window, the room, the furniture, the planets and the stars becoming invisible with daylight:

> The imagination of this cosmos is as immediate to me as the imagination of my household or my self, for I have taken my being in what I know of the sun and of the magnitude of the cosmos, as I have taken my being in what I know of domestic things. (*Fictive Certainties* 76)

This keeping in mind of the large and the particular of our relations is what may be called soul-making—in Emerson's "thousand-eyed present," any day. Emerson writes in "Self-Reliance": "This one fact the world hates, that the soul *becomes*" (*Works*, Vol. V: 50). In "The Method of Nature," Emerson takes up the "wholeness we admire in the order of the world": "Its smoothness is the smoothness of the pitch of the cataract. Its permanence is a perpetual inchoation" (*Works*, Vol. V: 185). Duncan, in his splendid essay of 1983, "The Self in Postmodern Poetry," attends this passage from "Self-Reliance":

> We first share the life by which things exist and afterwards see them as appearances in nature and forget that we have shared their cause. Here is the fountain of action and the fountain of thought. (*Works*, Vol. V: 46)

Duncan comments and questions:

> . . . he seems to speak directly for the poetic practice of open form, for the importance of whatever happens in the course of writing as relevation—not from

an unconscious, but from the spiritual world. In this am I "modern"? Am I "post-modern"? I am, in any event, Emersonian. (*Fictive Certainties* 227)

Now, as I want to reply to those questions, I'm reminded of this by Sherman Paul:

> Poetry is soul-making, the poet's work, Duncan's, H.D.'s, Olson's, necessary to the human history called Poetry because the story is one of survival, of the "evolution of forms in which life survives." And *that*, as Duncan tells it, is the great story of modernism and postmodernism. (*Lost America* 177)

We are in the midst of rethinking—re-imagining—spirituality. And we are, if we stop over the matter of it coming in to form, alive in politics, in the social, in the religion, and approaching the "communal commitment" Duncan worked to envision.

Along with this thinking/writing—wherein Duncan has led us again to Emerson, or, perhaps, for the first time, as America seems to be losing the works of its own mind—the reader might like, as I do, to let this bit of Emerson's "Lecture on the Times" play in his/her mind:

> What we are? and Whither we tend? We do not wish to be deceived. Here we drift, like white sail across the wild ocean, now bright on the wave, now darkling in the trough of the sea;—but from what port did we sail? Who knows? Or to what port are we bound? Who knows? There is no one to tell us but such poor weather-tossed mariners as ourselves, whom we speak as we pass, or who have hoisted some signal, or floated to us some letter in a bottle from far. But what know they more than we? They also found themselves on this wondrous sea. (*Works*, Vol. III: 69)

Duncan's work is much concerned with being-at-home. Simple as that—yet, Odyssean.

"Whence comes this shift of the reader's gaze, upon the disappearance of the writer?" Claude Lefort asks in a context where poetry and philosophy meet, astonishing one another in operational language ("Editor's Foreword" xiii). "The work from which the writer has withdrawn has become a work among others, a part of our cultural milieu, and contributes to situate us in relation to it, since it finds its meaning only within the horizons of that culture and thus renders it present to us while drawing for us a singular figure of it" (xiii). I think this over and over, and so, place it here on the bounding line of Duncan's poems.

30 June 1992

"Here Lies the Woodpecker
Who Was Zeus"

This essay on Mary Butts's *Armed with Madness* (1928) will, I fear, appear to be more an anthology than a commentary. My reasons are that her work is little know, few libraries have her twelve published volumes, and even the little that is written about her is hard to come by and confusing. I have chosen, therefore, to quote extensively and carefully. Her work belongs to the youth of twentieth-century writing, and the creative energy of it helps in the imagination of ourselves. An essay-story, then.

Mary Butts's reputation began with the publication of a volume of stories, *Speed the Plough*, in 1923. Her curious sense of the magic of personal meaning—the game of the possibility of a meaningful life—was there at the center of those first stories. Ford Madox Ford's "Purposes," announcing the *Transatlantic Review* in 1923, included Mary Butts along with H.G. Wells, Conrad, Joyce, cummings, Pound, Eliot, Mina Loy, and Robert McAlmon. Among these, she is striking and remains so. In the history of the magazine *Pagany* (Boston, 1929–1933), put together by its original editor, Richard Johns, and Stephen Halpert in 1969, I find this statement with its strange lack of any sense of the passage of time:

> Johns' original intention was to limit his contributors to those who, whatever their ethnic background, were essentially Americans. One dictionary definition of native, "belonging to, or natural to, by reason of the circumstances of one's birth," would certainly include such writers as Ezra Pound, Gertrude Stein, Mary Butts, and Emanuel Carnevali, who despite their present expatriate status were born and bred in this country. (xxix)* (Halpert 17, 20)

---

* Later in *A Return to Pagany*, Stephen Halpert cites Richard Johns to the effect that "'the exquisite *Armed with Madness*'" has "'introduced her [Butts] to a select audience in this country'" (41).

Doubtless, this is simply confused writing—the point being the original inten-
tion. (Mary Butts died in 1937, and Gertrude Stein in 1946.) Here, the editor of
Pagany: A Native Quarterly, taking its start and title from William Carlos Williams's
A Voyage to Pagany (1928, but also a reminiscence of 1924)—joined by his
collaborator—manages thirty-six years after the demise of his famous journal still
to consider the quintessentially English Mary Butts of London, Dorset and Corn-
wall an American. This seems to have been part of her fate, for, as far as I can tell,
it is in America that her reputation continued, avant-garde—now, I suppose the
word is underground—and firm. Nevertheless, that original view, reflected upon
by Johns and Halpert in *A Return to Pagany*, gives us a measure of her reputation in
the twenties. Kenneth Rexroth wrote in his introduction to that volume:

> Many of them are now unjustly forgotten. They believed and hoped that the arts
> would be the instrument of a fundamental revolution of the human sensibility as
> such. They believed that the word or the pictorial image could be used to subvert
> the dead syntax by which human self-alienation had been grafted into the very
> structure of the brain and nervous system. They believed that The Revolution of
> the Word would liberate a new life meaning for man and sweep away dead shells
> from which meaning had been exhausted or had turned malignant. (Halpert xiv)

In preparation for that introduction, dated April 21, 1969, Rexroth read through
a complete file of *Pagany*: "As I looked through it, it was just like Proust's Made-
leine" (xiii). This youth of the twentieth-century literary effort included Mary
Butts.

Williams's narrative of his year in Pagany—a tricky name for all of Europe—
spent there at the behest of Pound, brings him back to America to search, as
the New Directions book-blurb puts it, for "what is genuinely poetic at home"
(*Voyage to Pagany*, back cover). What followed was, of course, *In the American Grain*
(1925). It is useful to remember the final scene in *A Voyage to Pagany*:

> America, he began again haltingly, is hard to know.
> Yes, she answered, because she had made him serious so that he must speak his
> mind or say nothing.
> I think it is useful to us, he continued, because it is near savagery. In Europe,
> you are so far from it that maybe you will have to die first before you will live
> again.—But Dev was not such a fool.—Europe, I do not know, he corrected him-
> self, I am seeing a few superficial moments only.
> But he had a quick pupil.—That is enough, replied Fräulein von J. I see now
> what I saw at the beginning. You are a savage, not quite civilized—you have Amer-
> ica and we have not. You have that, yes, it is something.
> It is very difficult, said Dev. I am not a typical American. We have few natives
> left but they would not know me—

You are holding on to something, she said.

It is very difficult, Dev went on—something very likely to be lost, this is what—
So he took out the flint arrowhead he had in his pocket and showed it to her.

She was impressed. She held it hard in her hand as if to keep its impression there, felt the point, the edge, tried it, turned it over.

Yes, she said, I have seen the same thing from our own fields, more finished work—but it is very far, very far. No one believes it is real. But this you carry in your coat? It is very strange. Where did you find it?

In a corn-field in Virginia, there are many of them there. . . .

Moving to rejoin Frau M. they saw that it was getting on into the afternoon and that they must be stepping along if they would be back in Rome by nightfall.

You believe in America like a church, mused Fräulein von J. almost to herself.

Dev did not think so.

Do you believe then that the church is an enemy to your belief?

Yes.

She looked away.

Oh come on, said Dev, let's get out of this. (*Voyage to Pagany* 265–66, 267)

I have quoted so much in order to set Williams's "nativist" position which *Pagany* adopted, never, rightly, excluding the expatriates. Williams's quarrel with the "Europeanism" of Pound and Eliot became fundamental to his imagination. His insistence upon the return of language to a sense of place and to the rhythm and imagery of that place—which is a ground rather than a sky for being—defines the major effort of the modern writer and is a triumph of twentieth-century writing. And this gives us a clue to Mary Butts's place among these writers: the rhythm, imagery, and magic of her Dorset and Cornwall are dazzling—another grounding of imagination.

A "Manifesto" by William Carlos Williams appears in the first issue of *Pagany*:

"The ghosts so confidently laid by Francis Bacon and his followers are again walking in the laboratory as well as beside the man in the street," the scientific age is drawing to a close. Bizarre derivations multiply about us, mystifying and untrue as—an automatic revolver. To what shall the mind turn for that with which to rehabilitate our thought and our lives? To the word, a meaning hardly distinguishable from that of place, in whose great, virtuous and at present little realized potency we hereby manifest our belief. (Scott Buchanan, *Poetry and Mathematics*, p. 18) (Quoted in Halpert 50)

The statement reflects Williams's profound interest in modern science, particularly in relativity theory and its implications for a relational imagination. His intention here is not anti-scientific, but rather he means to pick up the changed relation to an objective reality, which is implied, and Williams early recognized the fact. A relational imagination then, rightly, turns to language "to rehabilitate our thought and our lives." As Robert Duncan puts it in another context, "Most importantly it is the word that carries with it the life-consciousness to be, the adventuring biological reality" (Introduction to *Divine Mystery* xxviii). Immediately following Williams's manifesto in the original issue of *Pagany*, is Mary Butts's story, "The House-party," dedicated to Jean Cocteau. This is a finely subtle, "politely sensual"—in the manner of the time—story about homosexual young men, accurate with a Jamesian kind of suggestiveness. But in Halpert-Johns's history of Pagany, this story is said to "[epitomize] the amoral living of some of the wealthy English and American expatriates on the Continent." "In contrast," they continue, "Margery Latimer . . . searched the souls of simple-living Midwest American characters" (Halpert 43). The problem of Mary Butts's reputation may well begin with this kind of careless, fearful comparison:

> Throughout the first two years of *Pagany* Johns had given Mary Butts' decadent sparkle a full display. By the time the fourth issue was ready to be printed, Johns knew he would no longer accept further contributions from her so that space might be available for newer and lesser-known writers, who, in his opinion, had something more vital to say. Somehow in her shorter than usual story, "Green," there seemed to blow a tempering wind through one of the untypically English country houses which generally housed an amorous imbroglio. Now Mary Butts was writing with tartness, almost as if she felt there might be a healthy future for a young couple in the heterosexuality of marriage, cleansed of the emotional friendships of other young men for the husband and the influence of a conniving, mantic mother. . . .
>
> Mary Butts was always brilliant, and Johns was pleased to have had the opportunity to publish her works. . . . But this sign of good health on a generally fevered cheek was new and promising. One of her stories finally looked forward toward a balanced living, . . . an apt swan song for Mary Butts. (Halpert 335–36)

One should not, perhaps, be too harsh in retrospect, but it is disappointing to find this stated in this way in 1969. The charge of decadence involves a moral imperative which defines life by exclusion, and I hasten to add, it has the effect of denying the search for a poetics of life that was the fundamental concern of many of *Pagany*'s writers.

This denial and the editorial changes consequent upon it are reflected in *Pagany* after the October–December, 1931, issue:

> The phasing out of Mary Butts and the introduction of John Cheever indicated that *Pagany*'s fourth issue for 1931 was one of transition, a final encore for a number of writers, yet far too subtle for the reader to notice. (Halpert 337)

Faulkner's homosexual story, "Divorce in Naples," was rejected as "commonplace." "Twittering birds" such as Charles Henri Ford and Parker Tyler were out. Gertrude Stein's "nonsensical couplets had begun to pall" (Halpert 337). Johns himself had been troubled by the reception given his own tentative, defensive exploration (all fiction!) of a homosexual theme in his story "Solstice" (vol. 1, no. 4), which was clearly influenced by Mary Butts in its handling of unstated relations and in one instance, by her archetypal use of classical divinities to describe character—"a Cybele for young men to learn from" (Johns, quoted in Halpert 187). Pound himself was not making sense to Johns. Pound's essay "The First Year of 'Pagany' and The Possibility of Criteria" (vol. 1, no. 1, 1931) with its instructions and its remarks on "Mr. Eliot's fatigue" and "M. Cocteau's adventures" had not apparently instructed Richard Johns (Pound, quoted in Halpert 233). The remaining three issues of *Pagany* are memorable for, among other things, Cocteau's "The Laic Mystery" translated by Olga Rudge, Katherine Anne Porter's "Banquet for October," parts of Williams's *White Mule*, and Zukofsky's "'A'—First Movement," but the adventure of the magazine was over. It began to follow another direction in modern American letters. Still, one notices that H. D. sent "Electra-Orestes" for the April–June, 1932, issue, accompanied by a letter in praise of the magazine, which closes: "You have been fortunate too, to have Mary Butts' exquisite stories" (quoted in Halpert 444).

The turn in Mary Butts's reputation is nearly incomprehensible. In America, it is tied to a "decadence" already spotted in Richard Johns. Elsewhere, I've taken note of the false note in her British reputation as that is reflected in the spite and meanness of spirit of Douglas Goldring in his autobiographical *South Lodge* (1943), published six years after her death (see this volume, 166–70). The tale of that relationship is the business of a biographer—one can only hope for a competent one with a mind as subtle and charmed as Mary Butts's. Her finest collection of short stories, *Several Occasions* (1932), is dedicated to Goldring. Suspicion begins there. The dedication tells us that he had once recognized something, and he tells us as much in an earlier autobiography, *Odd Man Out* (1935). But his own art could not openly praise the beauty of men as hers did, nor could he approach the adventure of the sacred which is her greatest concern. Biographical interest in Mary Butts will be trapped by the merely reductive if the sacred is not traced—tracked—in her work. That vitality I call the sacred begins with her childhood memories of Blake's paintings on the wall and his illuminated books on the shelves of a wondrous library that had come to the family through Blake's friend Thomas Butts. I suggest that Mary Butts's reputation, like that of H. D., suffered because of the complexity of the sacred in her twentieth-century mind, heart, and work.

The adventure of the sacred is then the large issue in Mary Butts's work to which I wish to call attention. The realism of many of her stories is a record of the way lives flow into and out of this adventure. But it was the adventure itself which drew Mary Butts's attention in her most important works. And that adventure is entirely marked by the condition of the sacred in the modern world. It is this, I think, that drew, in turn, the attention of Pound and H. D.—her careful probing of the problem of it. This does not contradict her stand alongside Williams's "Manifesto." Nor is she contradictory, if we read her carefully, to Williams's interest in Einstein—"St. Francis Einstein of the Daffodils, *On the first visit of Professor Einstein to the United States in the spring of* 1921"[1]—or to his fascination with Alfred North Whitehead's *Science and the Modern World* after first reading it in 1927. Both are concerned with the elemental, the ultimate, and the cosmos, which have to do with ground and place—so we are taught first by Hesiod, Oedipus at Colonus, and Lucretius. Theirs are two different ways of writing to a similar condition. Where Williams looked to science—post-Baconian and Newtonian—where he found the ghosts and so settled on the word and a newly posed language, a writer like Mary Butts sets up the contemporary with all its dazzle, free sexuality, sense and nonsense, and finding the ghosts also, she turns to the archaic. And so it is, I assume, with one writer after another that the loosened, embattled relation to meaning, as that condition informs any meaningful life, turns up the ghosts—.

I want now to turn to Mary Butts's *Armed with Madness:*

In the house, in which they could not afford to live, it was unpleasantly quiet. Marvelously noisy, but the noises let through silence. The noises were jays, bustling and screeching in the wood, a hay-cutter, clattering and sending up waves of scent, substantial as sea-waves, filling the long rooms as the tide fills a blow-hole, but without roar or release. The third noise was the light wind, rising off the diamond-blue sea. The sea lay three parts round the house, invisible because of the wood. The wood rose from its cliff-point in a single tree, and spread out inland, in a fan to enclose the house. Outside the verandah, a small lawn had been hollowed, from which the wood could be seen as it swept up, hurrying with squirrels, into a group of immense ilex, beech and oak. The lawn was stuck with yuccas and tree-fuchsias, dripping season in, season out, with bells the color of blood.

Once the house was passed, the wood gave it up, enclosed it decently, fenced a paddock, and the slip of dark life melted into the endless turf-miles which ran up a great down into the sky.

The silence let through by the jays, the hay-cutter, and the breeze, was a complicated production of stone rooms, the natural silence of empty grass, and the equivocal, personal silence of the wood. Not many nerves could stand it. People who had come for a week had been known to leave next day. The people who had the house were interested in the wood and its silence. When it got worse, after dark or at mid-day, they said it was tuning-up. When a gale came up-Channel shrieking like a mad harp, they said they were watching a visible fight with the silence in the wood.

A large gramophone stood with its mouth open on the verandah flags. They had been playing to the wood after lunch, to appease it and to keep their dancing in hand. (*Armed with Madness* 1–2)

Most striking in this passage which opens *Armed with Madness* is the silence, mysterious and unexplained. Its "tuning-up" proposes a primordial relation of sound and silence, even as the wit and magic of the gramophone stops us, first with laughter, then with a sense of the lives of those who play out the story to come. It is characteristic of Mary Butts's fiction that she adapts an older principle of narrative—somewhat akin to Greek drama in which the character is there for the sake of the action and not *vice versa*, or so Aristotle insisted that we understand the fact of the event in tragedy, which even in his time, following upon Plato's insistence that meaning was transcendent and abstract, needed to be straightened out.[*] Mary Butts's sense that a tale is told of human characters inside an action both older and other than themselves[2] challenges that other sense of the novel in which character is interesting in and for itself. As a result of this different narrative technique, each character in a Butts novel remains a sketch poised within a realism of the elemental and mysterious. (That there is such a realism—that we are capable of it—Keats taught us long ago.) The expected psychological centre is displaced in such a way that, as in *Armed with Madness*, one is not always sure who is in charge of the narration which slips from one to another—the author included—allowing motivation and insight to wander.

The wood surrounding the house is old and sacred—that is to say, nurturing life-sanctities—very like the sacred wood of Butts's poem "Corfe" (addressed to Corfe Castle in Dorset), which Louis Zukofsky published in *An "Objectivists" Anthology* in 1932:

But when I remember you Corfe, I remember Delphi
Because your history also is a mystery of God.
. . . .
Very sweet is the Sacred Wood
In the gold clearing, in the mustard patch;
But at night comes a change
Like a gold ball thrown out
And a black ball thrown in
(Not sunset behind Tyneham Cap

* Brilliantly discussed in John Jones, *On Aristotle and Greek Tragedy* (15 ff.).

On a night without a moon.)
But a shift of potencies
Like a black ball thrown in
And a gold ball thrown out
And the players are princes
Of the turf and the weed
And the wind-moulded trees
And the hazel thicket
And the red blackberry thorn.

Never trust a hemlock
An inch above your mouth.
An ice-green hemlock
Is a lover
In the wood.
Now every way the wind blows this sweetie goes
In the south
Where goes the leaf of the rose
And the evergreen tree. (36–37)[3]

The poem gives us a concentrated image of the magic of the wood that is a re-
curring interest in Mary Butts's work—here the night brings a "shift of poten-
cies" represented by the reversed imagery of the gold and black balls, as though
one could catch the potencies in a game, all leading to the storied and threat-
ening hemlock become a lover.

Then, in the house, we meet the main characters: first Scylla and her brother
Felix, and a strong, down-to-earth fellow, Ross, "a rare plant," who shares the
house with them. An American, Dudley Carston, comes for a visit, the outsider
to be tested. These four are joined by Clarence and Picus, two men who share
a cottage some distance away and who have come to stay in the house because,
we are told, their well is low and polluted. One woman, five men, and Scylla's
and Felix's old nurse who acts as house-keeper and general comforter. Noth-
ing is ever told in the novel about the sexual relationship between Clarence and
Picus, but we come to see the anguish and care of it as it falls apart, incapable
of withstanding the test of the game that is played out in their lives. Scylla in
the end wins the love of Picus. Clarence ends in madness and defeat, carving a
punch bowl for Scylla. Felix escapes to Paris where he discovers Boris, a young,
penniless, White-Russian prince whom he brings back to the house in the
woods. Again, nothing is said about their relationship, though we understand
enough. (Incidentally, it is Boris who prepares the plot for Butts's novel to fol-
low Armed with Madness, Death of Felicity Taverner, 1932).

Stated thus baldly, everything is lost except the tension, the possibilities, and a suggestiveness. These are not decadent, but serious and complex young lives. In Mary Butts's world, for whatever reason, male homosexuality is not a matter of decadence, but, rather, of the way lives turn. Boris, who appears near the end of *Armed with Madness* and whose first appearance in her work is in *Imaginary Letters* (dated 1924, published in 1928) is a case in point. *Imaginary Letters* begins Mary Butts's major work in fiction, though it appears very close to her life, and may be autobiographical. Here we meet Boris who will not stay still. Goldring tells us that Mary Butts had a special sympathy for these Russians, princes who had lost a world and were down and out in Paris. Boris is beautiful, underhanded, unstable, lost, homosexual, and unavailable.[4] It is Boris, more fully imagined, who commits murder—mind you, as a gift—to save the land from a real estate development, parking lots and tourists in *Felicity Taverner*. In *Imaginary Letters*, we find the first care that brought him into her art, and there also we find anger that is womanly, direct and puzzled. He somehow starts the imaginary process. Boris, she writes, leads us "a pretty dance." "Capricious, selfish, insensitive." "Lecherous, drunken, bold and chaste" (10). The qualities build in the first pages—someone shapeless and changing. "He arouses equally unconquerable affection and despair" (10). "A monster of vanity and pride" (10). "He is cruel, devoted, jealous" (10), this "black and green boy" (59). The words create this figure, whom, in kind, most of us meet sometime in our lives. Protean love. He or she may be only ourselves, a desire, or perhaps that figure is out there, as Mary Butts says, "the cause of art in others" (9).

But, to return to *Armed with Madness*, the plot is not as simple as an outline of its interpersonal relations suggests. Picus and Clarence bring with them to the house in the wood a cup which they have discovered in their well—Felix, trying to help them, fished it out with a spear. The Grail, we guess immediately— "that mirage, symbol, archetype of unity and integrity that appeared to seers of the Middle Ages" (Adolf 1)—"around 1180, when the Latin Kingdom of Jerusalem was seen to totter," first with alarm and then spiritual defeat "in 1187, when Jerusalem fell" (Adolf 11). In Mary Butts, the Grail is stunningly there and not there simultaneously, symbolic of a possible meaning and of a meaninglessness, neither of which conditions is privileged in the characters' lives. This profound symbol of spiritual fulfillment has returned again and again to modern letters, most brilliantly, I think, in Jack Spicer's *The Holy Grail*, but, then, Spicer was himself indebted to Mary Butts. Later in the novel, we find out that Picus has stolen the cup from his father, an antiquarian of some reputation, and that he planted it in the well and arranged for Felix to use a spear when trying to clear the well. The characters are, all of them, then caught up in an enactment of an old pattern. The interplay—the magic that meaning is, when it is love and a task of lives—among one woman and five men is a tale of a possible Grail. We never know whether the cup is simply a jade cup, an old altar vessel, an ashtray as it is once used in the novel, a spitting-cup, so used by Picus's father's mistress before her death, as the old man cruelly tells us, a poison-cup out of the East—jade is said to detect poison—or the Sanc-Grail. It is, of course, all of these in one way or another. In this way, Mary Butts tests the symbol and pursues her imaginative investigation of the condition of the sacred in our century.

The lives of Scylla and the five men around her shape a spiritual condition that is both frightening and, in the words of the novel, an "enormous lark"—like our own lives. "There was," she wrote, "something in their lives spoiled and inconclusive like the Grail story" (91). And this remark by the youngest of the characters, Felix, which he addresses to Ross, seems especially harsh:

> You're looking for something. I'm not. And I hope when you get it, you'll like it. Looking for the Sanc-Grail. It's always same story. The Golden Fleece or the philosopher's stone, or perpetual motion, or Atlantis or the lost tribes or God. All ways of walking into the same trap. (121)

Certainly, this is a very modern attitude toward the old unicity, but the trap is also sexuality, and Felix speaks his own young fear, confusion, and innocence. What he is looking for he does not yet know. The "trap" in Mary Butts is inchoate and personal, and it always leads to the puzzle of larger meaning.

Early in the novel, when Scylla and Ross are discussing the arrival of their American visitor, the narrator comments:

> "Give him a good time and see what happens." That was her part of their hospitality, whose rewards were varied and irregular. None of them, with perhaps the exception of Felix, could understand a good time that was not based on flashes of illumination, exercises of the senses. . . .
>
> Something long and white came up behind them out of the sea. An extra wave washed Felix a ledge higher. "Thank you," he said and skipped across. (5)

A "pleasant memory" unites them, and

> they became a triple figure, like Hecate the witch, amused, imaginative. They put on their things: Felix' pretty clothes, Ross's rough ones, the girl, her delicate strong dress. With their arms round her shoulders, they crossed the rocks and went up the cliff-path, and through the wood to the house. (6)

The deft touches, the careful realism—all colored by the sudden simile of the witch, Hecate—begins a strange suggestiveness that will take us into the magic and witchery of their lives.

Strange suggestions accumulate throughout the novel. Early on, the reader stops over the name Scylla:

> They called her Scylla from her name Drusilla, altering it because they said she was sometimes a witch and sometimes a bitch. (4)

Exactly, but the name also returns us to Greek lore—initially, to *The Odyssey* (12.235) where we find this mighty daughter of Crataeïs, who lived in a cavern along the straits of Sicily, the rending, mangling, troubling face of the sea. Drusilla, on the other hand, returns us to the Acts of the Apostles (24:24) wherein St. Paul defends himself and his belief in Christ so strongly that he frightens the procurator Felix and his wife Drusilla, the daughter of Herod Agrippa I and sister of Herod Agrippa II. This curious method sets up layers in Butts's story of some very ordinary characters who are to become extraordinary through the serious game of their lives. The novelist appears to work by association and she expects us to. Here, the point is a lightly brushed blend of ancient and Christian heritage carried by contemporary people, if only in their names. Later in the novel, she will call this "the Freud game"—what do you remember of this or that. We need only let our minds play over the elements which the story brings together by association—ancient, Christian, and modern, noting especially the easily and almost sportively associated Scylla and Hecate, leading finally to a further association of love with violence and madness. Only at the end of the novel will we realize that we have been warned from the outset of a possible violence in this pursuit of the love-game which in Mary Butts is always an aspect of the sacred.

This is, perhaps, because the sacred, however we define it, is a power over one, such as love is. One may fail in entering upon the sacred or one may come through into an intelligence. At the beginning of the novel we have seen Poseidon momentarily, or perhaps we missed him: "Something long and white came up behind them out of the sea" (6). A good source book, such as Morford's and Lenardon's *Classical Mythology*, will help me to summarize the depth of association that, I believe, Mary Butts wishes us to have. We should remember that Poseidon, god of the sea, is "violent in his loves." The god

> made advances to Scylla, the daughter of Phorcys and Hecate. Amphitrite was jealous and threw magic herbs into Scylla's bathing place. Thus Scylla was transformed into a terrifying monster, encircled with a ring of dogs' heads. (89)

They remind us that

> Ovid (*Met.* 13.917–68; 14.1–71) tells us this same story about Glaucus, a mortal who was transformed into a sea-god. It was he who fell in love with Scylla; when

he was rejected, he turned to the sorceress Circe for help. But Circe fell in love with him and in her jealousy poisoned the waters of Scylla's bathing place. (Morford 89 n.)

And Hecate, the triple-figured—here amused and imaginative—descended from the Titans, who has her house in the depths of things,

> is a goddess of roads in general and crossroads in particular, the latter being considered the center of ghostly activities, particularly in the dead of night. Thus the goddess developed a terrifying aspect; triple-faced statues depicted the three manifestations of her multiple character as a deity of the moon: Selene in heaven, Artemis on earth, and Hecate in the realm of Hades. . . . How different is the usual depiction of Artemis, young, vigorous, wholesome, and beautiful! (Morford 126–27)

We also remember that Circe, a daughter of the Sun, is the aunt of Medea. So, the associations play around Mary Butts's novel. Violence, sexual frustration, and sexual transformation all lie in wait in this book. Irradiative associations inform the realism of the characters' young lives.

Throughout the novel there are introspective moments in which the narrator of the moment mulls his or her personal stake in this. Here, for example, Scylla goes to meet their American visitor in Starn, while Ross and Felix go picking mushrooms.

> It was all very well. She had told Felix to collect mushrooms and not allow Ross to experiment. He could get them in Ogham meads—What was she worried about? Money, of course, and love affairs; the important, unimportant things. Hitherto God had fed his sparrows, and as good fish had come out of the sea. But everywhere there was a sense of broken continuity, a dis-ease. The end of an age, the beginning of another. Revaluation of values. Phrases that meant something if you could mean them. The meaning of meaning? Discovery of a new value, a different way of apprehending everything. She wished the earth would not suddenly look fragile, as if it was going to start shifting about. . . . There was something wrong with all of them, or with their world. A moment missed, a moment to come. Or not coming. Or either or both. Shove it off on the war; but that did not help.
>
> Only Ross was all right—He never wanted anything that he did not get. Life had given it up and paid over Ross' stakes, because once his strong appetites were satisfied, he did not want anything in human life at all. It was something to eat and drink, to embrace and paint. Apart from that, he knew something that she was only growing conscious of. And wouldn't tell. Not he—laughed at her for not knowing, and for wanting to know.
>
> Felix was quite different. Felix was scared. Fear made him brittle and angry and unjust. Without faith.
>
> Faith was necessary for the knowledge of God. Only, there were fifty good rea-

sons for supporting the non-existence of God. Besides, no one wanted to believe
that any more. That was the point. And it was a shame for those two men to make
her go all that way through a valley, while they were grubbing about in the wind.
(*Armed with Madness* 10–11)

This haunted passage, ending in the strictly personal, is exact in its description
of the modern predicament—the missed meaning of tradition, the loss and the
change.

Scylla meets the American, Carston, rents a car and brings him back to the
house in the woods. Meanwhile, Ross and Felix have interrupted their mush-
room hunting to visit Clarence and Picus, which, as we have already noted,
brings all four back to the house in the wood. The following passage allows us
to watch the visitor size up the main characters.

> That was the situation for him, as he listened, translating, to the story Felix
> had to tell. Felix said that Ross and he had been to a place called Gault, and he'd
> sung to it. Presumably a dangerous place. They had then decided to call on dis-
> tant friends, who might or might not be inhabiting a cottage on a place called
> Tollerdown. Anyhow, supposing they were not there, a rare species of hawk
> known as a honey-buzzard might be observed in the vicinity. On arriving they
> had found their friends (Scylla seemed to be the only woman in the group, a point
> for reflection) in difficulties owing to their well, shrunk by the drought, yield-
> ing nothing but dead hedgehogs. A digression on the use of soda-water to make
> tea. An excursion down the well to clean out the hedgehogs had led to a discov-
> ery. An odd cup of some greenish stone had been found, rather like pea-soup car-
> nelian. The state of the well had necessitated the transfer of Picus and Clarence
> for an indefinite stay. "You're done in this country if your well gives out. Wait
> till ours does." Carston was not interested. This might interfere with his making
> love to Scylla, which he had decided was to be his expression of a successful visit.
> Unless he found out how to use it.
>
> Then Ross produced the cup suddenly, out of his pocket, and handed it round.
> Carston said:
>
> "That means nothing to me."
>
> "Been cut by hand," said Felix. "Is there a kind of opaque flint glass? Keltic
> twiddles, I think, very worn round the rim."
>
> A good deal was told Carston, casually, about Kelts and Saxons and Romans and
> early Christianity; things completely over so far as he knew—Not that they talked
> about what he hadn't heard. Only they talked as if there was no time, no progress,
> no morality. He knew, of course, that there was no progress, and no morality.
>
> Then Ross said, roughly and softly, as though he was loving something:
>
> "The thing was that we fished it out with a spear."
>
> Scylla said: "Ross, that's odd."
>
> Clarence fidgeted attentively. Felix stared, and Carston saw the boy's tricky bril-
> liant eyes light up. Picus was grave, a man so tall and thin he seemed to go on for

ever. Unnaturally supple, he had seen him pick up something behind him as if it had been in front. He tried to think what a spear had to do with it.

Felix said, sharply:

"Good old Freud."

"Idiot!" said Ross, and turned away furious and contemptuous.

"It seems to me," said Scylla, "that people had to start some way of thinking of things. What they saw once they'd learned to think might be quite different from the things they'd learned on."

Then, to Carston, she said that odd things were always happening, and old patterns repeated themselves. That it was sometimes alarming when they did, and Freud very useful in the case of irrational fear. Very true, too, when there had been a row, and no one could feel what was just or what was not. Always look out for the suppressed wish that's taken the wrong turning. But that what had happened to-day was objective and odd.

Carston said:

"I think I'll have to ask you to explain a little more than that."

But Ross had turned round again. "I'm awfully sorry," he said. The insolent insincerity was not meant to be lost on Carston, but it was. "Put it down to the solstice or the heat."

"Tell us the news," said Felix. "We couldn't get back without our tea. Ross believes in perspiration. I don't."

Carston had come with elaborations of the best gossip. They listened to him— rather too attentively, he thought. At the same time there was something that spoiled his effects. It was the place, the faintly lit room mixing with the starlight outside. A shallow little green dish was lying among the glasses. Might have been made out of star-material. The woman had called it a diversion, but they weren't going to let him play. He began suddenly to dislike them, wish to humiliate them. Far too troubled to think how to do it.

Even Ross saw there was something wrong when he left them and went up to bed.

But this Carston had seen. Four ways of saying the woman good-night. Ross nodded to her. Felix embraced her. Clarence kissed her gallantly, with a flourish indicating affectionate indifference to their difference of sex. Picus, busy with a siphon, crooked his fore-finger at her across the room. (19–22)

The next day, following up on this astonishing and annoying event of the cup and the confusing responses to it, Carston turns to Felix for information:

"Tell me more about your friends."

"Picus is Clarence's 'old man of the sea' only he's young. Clarence doesn't know it. Scylla says I'm hers. He only does one or two small things like whistling, but he does them perfectly. Riding and blowing birds' eggs. You saw how powerful his body is, but he's like a bird. Off in a flash. Hence the name. Picus was the Woodpecker.

"Clarence fights for him and with him. What he fights for, I don't know. Clarence is quite all right. A bit insincere, because he's afraid. And what he's afraid of, I don't know." (24–25)

The passage tells the reader a great deal in spite of its being limited by Felix's innocence. We need to remember the "old man of the sea" in the *Arabian Nights* and that he climbed on Sinbad's back and, then, refused to get off after having been carried across a stream. Finally, Sinbad made him drunk and shook him off. In *Armed with Madness*, Scylla breaks the pattern of dependence which holds the two men together.

> Carston could only say: "Tell me more."
> "Scylla's a different egg. If there is anything wrong about my sister, it's every-thing. I've said the word 'fear' at least ten times lately. This time it's my own." He horrified Carston—he was like a desperate butterfly, angry, petulant and white.—"It's she at one end, and Picus at the other, who get me going. It's because she wants everything to happen to its last possibility. That's how she gets kick out of life. Once a thing's got going, she'll understand it and manage it. And enjoy it. She'll never tone it down. Sort of woman who'd have mothered the house of Atreus, and though I owe her everything, it's wasted on me. She'll enjoy—"
> "What will she enjoy?"
> "What will happen out of what happened yesterday. Don't you see? That in-fernal Picus is a psychic if there ever was one. Or if there is such a thing."
> "Does she believe in that?"
> "Believing doesn't trouble her. Only what is going to happen. She doesn't cre-ate situations. She broods them and they hatch. And the birds come home to roost. Some mighty queer birds. Truth isn't everyone's breakfast egg. She isn't happy till it's hatched. Calls it knowing where you are. I wish I knew where I was—"
> (25–26)

I have stopped over the associative nature of Mary Butts's use of names, and it is necessary to do so again: "Picus was the Woodpecker," as Felix has told us. This is the first mention in the novel of the peculiar provenance of this char-acter's name. He is "like a bird"—"Off in a flash"—"Hence the name" (25). Carston lets the matter pass. We know picus is one of the birds used in augury (Plautus)—a woodpecker, and we may remember Picus, son of Saturn, king of the aborigines of pre-Latin Italy and prophet who for spurning Circe was turned into a woodpecker (Ovid and Virgil). Such archaic elements require at-tention because they color the characterization and inform the imagery.

Carston then continues to ask about Scylla whom he considers his primary interest until the Grail involves him also.

> Carston revised his ideas again about Scylla as a lover. He could only say: "But what can she and your friend Picus make out of what happened yesterday, anyhow?"
> "Don't you see? It was fishing it out of the well with that old spear—they always went together."

"What went with what?"

"The cup of the Sanc-Grail, of course, It and the spear, they always hunted in couples. You've heard of it. All sexual symbolism. I wish I hadn't."

"Does sexual symbolism get you?" It would be news if it did.

"I should worry. But the Sanc-Grail was a very funny thing. People used to think it was a shallow greenish dish. And the cup's a shallow, greenish dish. Those well-shafts on the downs might be any age. So might it. Tollerdown had a bad reputation, and I never heard of the Sanc-Grail doing anyone any good. With that moron Picus behind it, and that demon, my sister, in front of it."

Carston took stock of several things: what he remembered of the Grail story, the possibility of anyone behaving as if it had happened, and what that implied in human character. Felix's youth.

He said at last:

"Don't tell me your sister is superstitious."

"Not she. Better if she was. She'd read it up and do processions and things. It might be like that. But with her it won't get its home comforts. It will get vision."

On the last four words he changed, and Carston saw the sister in the brother, in the elegant, frightened boy now explaining that what he wanted was not vision, but fashionable routine. (26–27)

Such conversations not only delineate the quick changes of personality that fascinate Mary Butts—here, Felix's resistance to sexuality, his own and that of others, and Carston's slowly increasing awareness—they also forward the contemporary tension of the sacred as it belongs to imaginative life.

This tension increases as it is enacted by the characters—some of them named for ancient and archaic sanctities—and as they respond to their memories of medieval English Grail stories. Two scenes seem especially important. Ross goes up a hill to paint:

Then he whistled as he drew, out of tune, but as though he was loving something. No nonsense about being the thing he loved, but like a lover, aware of the presence of what he loved everywhere. (31)

Just so much is given us to suggest the special knowledge that had earlier eluded Scylla. Suddenly,

There was a hard, explosive sound. Several mixed noises. A bird tore out of a thicket and crossed an open space, indirectly, frantically, and disappeared. He imitated its call and burst out laughing. "Woodpecker up to his tricks again." Then he went back to his work, straining his eyes. (31–32)

We do not know that Picus of the novel is responsible, nor do we ever find out, but we do know that the Latin *picus* was a trickster. In addition, this is a kind of warning—mysteriously understood by Ross—well before we find out that Picus has tricked them all, for it is Picus who arranges to bring the spear and the cup together when Felix goes down into the well.

In the second scene, a doctor has come to check on Picus's health.

> The doctor said:
> "Shew me the cup you got out of the well." And when he had looked at it: "The luck of the country's with you. I'm glad to find a few roman pots. It isn't glass at all, too heavy. I think it's jade. It may have been set once. I tell you, it might have been the cup of a chalice." Intelligent interest. Carston felt quite friendly now towards the thing. The others were giving polite attention. Five people at once thinking about a spear. No, six. He was.
> "One has time to remember things, shooting about this country in a Ford. Do you know it makes me think of what I remember of the cup of the Sanc-Grail?"
> Picus said, meekly: "What was that?"
> Carston thought: 'How was that camp, or wasn't it? Would one of them pick up the challenge? Of course, it was a challenge.' Ross said: "That's a long story," but Scylla leaned forward, excited, and said: "The best way to get that story out is for everyone to say what he thinks or feels or remembers. The Freud game really. Start, Felix!"
> "Tennyson," said Felix.
> "Oh, my dear," said Clarence, "those awful pre-Raphaelite pictures put me off it long ago."
> Ross said: "A mass said at Corbenic."
> "Wagner," said the doctor.
> "A girl carrying it," said Carston, staring at Scylla and trying to play.
> Scylla said: "*Quod inferius sicut superius est.*"
> Picus said: "You haven't told me much."
> "Second round," said Scylla,—"people enlarge on what they said before."
> "I said Tennyson," said Felix, "because I hate the Keltic twilight. And nearly all its works. I hate it because it's a false way of telling about something that exists. No, a messy way. Responsible for the world's worst art. Now and then it nearly comes off. Milton left it alone, and I don't blame him. Tennyson made it idiotic with his temperance knights. Fixed it, too, enough for parody. Killed the unstated thing which I don't mind telling you scares me."
> Clarence said: "I agree with Felix. I can't stand bad drawing."
> Ross said: "At Corbenic, wherever that was, there was a different mass. It may have been the real thing."
> The doctor said: "Parsival is like a great religious service to me."
> Carston, embarrassed at his turn coming, saw their pained faces. He said: "I supposed the girl who carried it was the female spirit of life."
> Scylla said: "I quote again: 'Here lies the Woodpecker who *was Zeus*.'"
> "Thank you," said Picus. (37–39)

All the elements of the narrative are brought together almost violently in this exchange, whether or not the reader thinks that Scylla has taken the part of trickster. A certain amount of confusion is the result for both the characters and the reader, but I want to point out that this is part of the operational magic of the book—a concurrence and competition of layers of meaning. The history of the modern Grail is reflected from Tennyson to Wagner. Each character, except for Picus who is slyly noncommittal, expresses some tentative relation to the original spirituality that the Grail represented. The doctor's taste is for the dramatic and ritualistic in religious matters, but we know so little about him that we can only trust his curiosity about the cup and try to measure his love of Wagner's *Parsifal*. The words "a great religious service" (38) seem carefully chosen, though the service is hardly to be considered conventional. In contrast, Ross's suggestion that there was once a "real" mass—presumably with reference to transubstantiation—expresses contemporary loss. The doctor effectively brings the most important modern imagination of the Grail story—"'like a belated inheritance,'" in Pierre Boulez' words—into the novel (quoted in Gregor-Dellin 447). (*Parsifal* was first performed in 1882.) Again, I believe we need to stop—this time over Wagner's overwhelming presence in modern thought about the Grail. The doctor may represent the ordinary Wagnerite since he appears to hold the mistaken view that *Parsifal* is Christian. The knights of the Grail have been greatly modified when compared to those of Wagner's principal source, Wolfram von Eschenbach's thirteenth-century *Parzival*, and, as Martin Gregor-Dellin has noted, "the Grail itself has been divested of its Eucharistic function" (448). The doctor's remarks may simply reflect a modern sentiment for religion or a religious aestheticism. Still, I cannot help but think of Nietzsche's surprising recognition of the *Parsifal* Prelude: "Supreme psychological assurance with regard to what is intended to be said, expressed, *communicated*. . . . Such things exist in *Dante*, but nowhere else. Did ever a painter portray so melancholy a loving gaze as Wagner does with the final accents of his prelude?" (Gregor-Dellin 457; original emphasis).

Carston's view is perhaps the most twentieth-century and anthropological. Clarence, who will be driven mad in his helplessness, unlike Felix with whom he says he agrees, is attached to the merely stylish and mannered, a voice out of the twenties that could dismiss in the name of a newer, more geometric art, pre-Raphaelite, *art nouveau* and symbolist alike. Felix, with characteristic emotional energy, points to a profound aspect of all the Grail legends that whatever they were about was unstated—"Killed the unstated thing"—which leads to the modern arguments about Keltic [sic] sources and vegetation myths.

Scylla's responses are more gamesome and complex, in part because she has a clear motive—the winning of Picus. Her point is to push the edge, as Felix has warned us. Her first rather imperious and priestly sounding remark is a quotation from the most important of alchemical texts, the *Tabula Smaragdina*, the Emerald Table of Hermes Trismegistus. The complete quotation reads in translation:

> What is below is like that which is above, and what is above is like that which is below, to accomplish the miracles of one thing.*

It is striking that Scylla quotes from the Latin in which the text comes down to us—(the original text was probably Greek and may date back to the first or second centuries of the Christian era).† And it is remarkable that Scylla quotes only one half of this famous formula: "What is below (inferius) is like that which is above (superius)." In so doing, she does not complete the alchemical formulation of the unity of all things; instead, she leaves the other characters and the reader with a fundamental statement of correspondence, understood, so to speak, from below whatever spiritual or transcendent is above. Scylla's phrase brings into the novel the ambiance of the Hermetic tradition—"a magical attitude to life." Titus Burckhardt, an engaged scholar of this tradition, remarks:

> The perspective of Hermetism proceeds from the view that the universe (or macrocosm) and man (or the microcosm) correspond to one another as reflections; whatever there is in the one, must also in some manner be present in the other. This correspondence may best be understood by reducing it to the mutual relationship of subject and object, of knower and known. The world, as object, appears in the mirror of the human subject. (34)‡

In Frances Yates's words, "the famous *Emerald Table*, the bible of the alchemists . . . gives in a mysteriously compact form the philosophy of the All and the One" (*Giordano Bruno* 150). But the tradition was not originally philosophical, however we abstract it; rather, it was a perceptual practice by way of image, metaphor and symbol. With this magical attitude in mind, one begins to reread some of the characters: Ross's love, which we have already noted, for example, probably represents an aspect of this view, and we return to Felix's remark that his sister would "read it up and do processions and things," leading to "vision"

---

* This translation printed in John Read, *Prelude to Chemistry* (54). The translation is reprinted from G. F. Rodwell, *The Birth of Chemistry* (1874). Mary Butts is likely to have known A. E. Waite's *The Hermetic Museum, Restored and Enlarged* (1893, 2 vols).

† See John Read, *Prelude to Chemistry* (51–55) for a summary of the *Emerald Table*, its importance and the arguments about its age.

‡ See also James Webb's *The Flight from Reason: The Age of the Irrational* (125), perhaps useful, but spoiled throughout by an unexamined privileging of Reason and no apparent understanding of the psychology of this undertaking.

(27)—whatever that may turn out to be. Vision in Mary Butts's work repeatedly leads to a *dynamics* of experience, conflictual, creative, and harsh, rather than comfortable.

The novelist would have been fully cognizant of the controversy surrounding the lore of the *Hermetica* and of the occult tradition that derives from it, not only alchemy, but Cabbala, Tarot, Rosicrucianism, astrology, magic, theosophy, and the various texts of the mystery religions, Egyptian, Eleusinian, and Gnostic. What is often considered the "muck" of "religious back-waters." This disreputation sets aside the true imaginative value of such sources. She, born in 1890, like her peers, inherited the turmoil of belief and disbelief of the nineteenth century along with its literature and scholars. One thinks immediately of A. E. Waite's *Lives of the Alchemical Philosophers* (1888) and *The Hermetic and Alchemical Writings of Aureolus Philippus Theophrastus Bombast, of Hohenheim, called Paracelsus the Great* (1894), of J. Ferguson's *Bibliotheca Chemica* (1906), and of G. R. S. Mead's *Thrice-Greatest Hermes* (1906)—perhaps also E. A. Wallis Budge's *The Gods of the Egyptians* (1904)—to name only the most obvious whose influence remains current among those whose concern is with the lore of the human mind and imagination.* Such studies come into the play of imagination because they represent an anthropology faced with the direct imagination of a cosmos which is not a doctrine, an objectification, or abstraction. Such thought is always by way of protest against definition and determination, whether social or religious—Robert Duncan's "unregenerate archaic subscriptions" ("Introduction," *Divine Mystery* xv). Duncan, discussing Allen Upward, writes of a time when "religion and childhood phantasy—the Christ and the Wizard King—are seen anew in the light of comparative folklore and the new anthropology."

> Anthropology, even as it presented itself in late nineteenth-century thought as having the grown-up authority of a science, was also a development of the early nineteenth-century Romantic Vision of Man with its poetic and spiritualizing revaluations both of the Christian enthusiasms of the Seventeenth Century and of the Classical rationalism of the Eighteenth Century Enlightenment. Man—it was to be the persuasion of the new Sciences of Man—in his religions, even as in his dreams and in his romances and phantastic fictions, was everywhere at work to create at once a Self-Reality and a World-Reality. ("Introduction," *Divine Mystery* xv)

After Isaac Casaubon in 1614 dated the *Hermetica*—"though there may have been a man called Hermes Trismegistus of hoary antiquity, the *Hermetica* cannot

---

* See Kenneth Rexroth's measured introductions to G. R. S. Mead's *Fragments of a Faith Forgotten* and to A. E. Waite's *The Holy Kabbalah*, both reissued by University Books, 1960.

have been written by any such person"—academic reason made the subject increasingly disreputable.* The battle for "reality"—first seen to be crucial in the poetry of William Blake—was given over to objectivity. Though the Hermetic tradition continued to be voiced, out of the Renaissance, well into our own century, the ability to understand this ancient and modern imagination of reality came increasingly to be more "occult"—"embarrassing," Auden said of this side of Yeats's work—until even the reputations of the scholars of it, such as Mead and Waite, were deprecated.† Mary Butts joins her peers in the use of this material—Yeats, Pound, and H. D. are the most obvious. (We should also, I think, recall such figures as A. R. Orage and especially Allen Upward whose work she is likely to have known.) She also had a strong interest in most things French and had lived in Paris, which suggests that she may have known the work of Sâr Péladan (1858–1918), such as his odd and cranky Le Secret du Troubadour which Pound had reviewed in 1906.‡ I also note that Péladan had himself established an Ordre de la Rose Croix du Temple et du Sanct Graal. Thus the combination of the Hermetic tradition with the Holy Grail was not unprecedented, but there is another precursor closer to home and to the new anthropology that we will consider shortly.

The lore of this multifarious tradition should be better known and acknowledged for what it is: a continuous activity of direct participation in the divine—the old sacred of the world that did not objectify reality or leave personal experience to a lonely, singular subjectivity. Its central concern is the activity of subject and object in the largest terms—cosmological and epistemological, which are not pretensions of art but fundamental to art. Mary Butts chooses the magical aspect of this old tradition—in personal lives to disturb and transform any singular dullness, and in a sense of the world to know that it is alive—so the gramophone plays to the wood. This "disreputable" side of Mary Butts's work is not simply nonsense. Her sense of magic is skillful at the same time that it is modernly tentative. In an essay of 1932, she writes:

> Magic has not yet been properly defined. In its practice it is, of course, very largely primitive science, misunderstandings by false analogy of the way things work, of natural law. But behind that there seems to remain a very peculiar kind of awareness, an awareness modified and sometimes lost by people whose life has been

* Quoted and commented on in Yates (Giordano Bruno 170).
† For the important opposition of such thought to Victorian values, see Samuel B. Hynes, The Edwardian Turn of Mind, especially his chapter "Science, Seers, and Sex." I am greatly indebted to this study, as will appear later in the essay.
‡ See Leon Surette, A Light from Eleusis (34 ff.), for an interesting discussion of this in relation to Pound.

passed in towns. It is most difficult to describe. It has something to do with a sense of the invisible, the non-existent in a scientific sense, relations between things of a different order: the moon and a stone, the sea and a piece of wood, women and fish. (*Traps* 25)

In other words, the imagination and character of difference—what I have called a relational imagination which will have profound consequences in twentieth-century art.

This "awareness" is fundamental to a cultural conflict that continues into the present, involving the use and abuse of the human imagination. Blake is the first and greatest warrior of this conflict. His "mental fight" first clearly draws attention to the issue—that subject and object must meet, and it is in art that such a meeting is possible. Blake himself chose Newton to represent the contraction of reality—"Single vision & Newton's sleep."[5] But the contraction goes back to the quarrel with the Hermetic tradition, as Frances Yates's distinguished studies inform us.

> In his eagerness to establish a purely objective view of nature as a mechanism, in his enthusiasm for pure mathematics as the only safe tool for objective enquiry, Descartes was left with the problem of mind somewhat embarrassingly on his hands. He provisionally solved the problem in a very crude way, by his so-called dualism, "one world consisting of a huge mathematical machine, extended in space; and another world consisting of unextended thinking spirits. And whatever is not mathematical or depends at all on the activity of thinking substance . . . belongs with the latter." Descartes even assigns an actual place in the body, the conarion or part of the brain, to this "thinking substance" which has to deal with everything which is not part of the vast external machine. This strangely inadequate way of dealing with mind did not long remain unquestioned and since Descartes' day many philosophers and thinkers have struggled with the problem of knowledge, of epistemology, of the relation between mind and matter. Nevertheless, this bad start of the problem of knowledge has never been quite made up. About the external world, man has discovered ever more and more. About his own mind, why he can reflect nature in it and deal with nature in it in this amazing way, he has made much less progress.
>
> Why was Descartes so contemptuous, even one might think, so afraid of the *mens* that he wanted to park it carefully by itself, out of the way of the mechanical universe and mathematics? Might not this be because of the struggle of his world to emerge from "Hermes Trismegistus" . . . and all that he stood for? The basic difference between the attitude of the magician to the world and the attitude of the scientist to the world is that the former wants to draw the world into himself, whilst the scientist does just the opposite, he externalizes and impersonalises the world by a movement of will in an entirely opposite direction to that described in the Hermetic writings, the whole emphasis of which is precisely on the reflec-

tion of the world in the *mens*. Whether as religious experience or as magic, the Hermetic attitude to the world has this internal quality.

Hence, may it not be supposed, when mechanics and mathematics took over from animism and magic, it was this internalisation, this intimate connection of the *mens* with the world, which had to be avoided at all costs. And hence, it may be suggested, through the necessity for this strong reaction, the mistake arose of allowing the problem of mind to fall so completely out of step and so far behind the problem of matter in the external world and how it works. Thus, from the point of view of the history of the problem of mind and of why it has become such a problem through the neglect of it at the beginning of the modern period, "Hermes Trismegistus" and his history is important. . . . In any case we ought to know the history of what they discarded, if only to understand the motives which lay behind the triumph of mechanism. And that history uncovers the roots of the change which came over man when his mind was no longer integrated into the divine life of the universe. In the company of "Hermes Trismegistus" one treads the borderlands between magic and religion, magic and science, magic and art or poetry or music. It was in those elusive realms that the man of the Renaissance dwelt, and the seventeenth century lost some clue to the personality of that *magnum miraculum*. (Giordano Bruno 454–55)

I have quoted at length this summary view both because it helps to clarify my own argument and because I believe the disreputation of this material may have tended to put Yates's work aside also.

In the four years between *Armed with Madness* and her essay *Traps for Unbelievers* (1932), it is clear that Mary Butts continued to study the magical and religious aspects of her concern, but with the new anthropology in hand. This essay is a major statement of her modern view: "The word Religion, with its vast connotations, is working its way into the category of the shame-making or obscene" (*Traps* 12):

> But with all this discarding, man, whether he likes it or not, whether he thinks about it or not, has been forced back (and that was the last thing he bargained for) onto the final, inescapable, and implacable question: "Is there anything there or not? Anything at all? Or has the whole vast various structure been built out of nothing but my misunderstandings of phenomena and my suppressed wishes? (*Traps* 13)

One notices the characteristic, modernist concern with the loss of the old definition of being, the old metaphysical or God, but with that I wish to return to the magic of her imagination.

The "Freud game" passage in which Scylla insistently affirms the alchemical-magical tradition when faced with a possible Grail is rich in implication. In so doing, she proposes an interpretation of the Grail, that it is—in the words of the latter essay, adapting a vocabulary from the new anthropology—the "Mana" or "virtus" of things:

> What a man or a woman will, if put to it, have no nonsense about, is the question of the "virtus" common and proper to both, their virility, courage, the source of each of their separate virtues. The best name for it is "Mana," the word which science has taken from the Polynesians; that which gives a man or a woman potency in every act or situation. (*Traps* 40)

The Grail, then, of the novel—"the unstated thing"—has to do with energy, act, and intelligence.

> Where a modern might ask: "What is it?" the medieval mind asked: "What must it have been?" No sacred object was conceivable outside of Christianity; therefore the search was for a known Christian relic with which it could be identified. By no later than 1200 two conflicting explanations had been advanced. One claimed that it was the cup with which Joseph of Arimethea caught the blood of Christ as it flowed down from His crucified body; in which case, the lance of the story was the lance of the soldier Longinus who pierced the side of the crucified Christ. The second claimed that it was the cup with which Jesus instituted the Eucharist at the Last Supper, and it was this second explanation which was to prevail among writers after 1225 or so. Meanwhile there was the confusing word "graal." Around 1200, the monk Helinandus of Beauvais sought in vain for a Christian tradition of the Grail, but his statements affirm the existence in Old French of a common noun "graal." It signified, he said, "a broad, deep dish," a kind of platter, and was derived from Latin "gradalis" or "gradale" because such dishes were "pleasing" (grata) to guests! (Mustard and Passage, Introduction to *Parzival* xl–xli)

And so the unstated—even unstateable—is the issue for the modern mind. In *Armed with Madness*, Carston questions Scylla directly, rather than Felix:

> "And the new name for all this is our subconscious minds. And between Freud and Aquinas, I've managed to tell you about it completely wrong. For another of its names is intellectual beauty, and another, the peace of God."
>
> "D'you believe in God?"
>
> "I don't know. All we do know is what happens to faith based on catch-as-catch-can visions."
>
> "Weren't all religions based on that?"
>
> "They were, and look at them! But now you see why we felt we were being laughed at, dangerously, when we lifted that cup out of a well on the point of a spear?"
>
> Carston pulled himself together. "What did you mean by the other thing: 'Here lies the Woodpecker who was Zeus'?"

"A little poetry, a little witchery, a little joke. It's the same thing as I said before. Now I'll tell you something worse than what I said before.

"Along with faith fit for people like us, and good taste which are where morals end, there is no goodwill left anywhere in the world. Which started to go first, or if they all went together, or which pushed the other out, I don't know. I've an idea that something else, a principle we haven't named yet, got rid of the lot."

Beginnings for an erotic conversation. (41–42)

This last sentence is, of course, Carston's wry sense of the canny conversation with Scylla. Carston, as a character, always presents a near stereotype of the American who has lost all memory of the past: he belongs to the new, the direct, the simply sexual, until late in the novel; it is he who resolves as much of the Grail trick as is possible, a true modern Grail knight in that he asks the right questions.

Though Carston asks those questions, Scylla's answers on one level merely tease—"a joke," perhaps. (I think of a quotation Butts uses elsewhere: "Mais comme tu taquines éternité"[Armed with Madness 81].) On another level, her remarks turn about the darkness of modern meaning—God become the unstated thing. She is sharp, bitter, and troubled, much as she was in her ruminations on the way to meet Carston.

Scylla has subtly shown her understanding of the whole business in her emphasis on "below" in the quotation from the Emerald Table. She has, if we could only follow—and she wants that possibility to be difficult and mysterious—indicated that the high mystery of the Grail is here at work among them, dangerously and laughingly; with the erudite reference to Picus the Woodpecker, she has, while mystifying everybody except Picus, tipped him off to the fact that she knows he is the trickster. Carston continues to question her:

"Stay a minute. Maybe it's because I have no memories, but I don't see where the fun comes in."

"Don't you call it fun to watch how violently, strangely and in character people will behave? Watch Ross, watch Clarence. Watch me." He was watching her. (43)

Seriousness and laughter interplay in Mary Butts, even cruelly. But Carston's necessary question leads back to "Here lies the Woodpecker who was Zeus." With those words, bird-magic enters the layered meaning of the novel, and such magic leads directly to a chapter in Jane Harrison's Themis (1912, 2d ed. 1927), a brilliant example of the new anthropology and of the new reading of the ancient world. There the mysterious phrase as cited in Suidas, is given and translated: ἐνθάδε κεῖται θανών . . . Πῆκος ὁ καὶ Ζεύς

—Here lies dead the Woodpecker who also is Zeus. (Harrison, Themis 109)

Scylla's version is carefully edited, removing the word "dead" and changing the tense to the past. The original suggests an ancient mythic event in which Zeus displaces or assimilates an indigenous Picus. The quotation has obviously been adapted to the magic of the narrative. Picus "lies" both because he is present and, in the tradition of Picus, the magician and trickster, he is lying in the matter of the cup. Picus who "was" Zeus is now the Picus of their own lives, setting off the recurring pattern of the search for the Grail.

Jane Harrison's discussion of Picus occurs in the chapter on magic, and she begins with a consideration of the word itself: "The word (μαγεία) from which our word magic is derived, was, among the Greeks of classical days, never really at home" (75). Yet, she notes that "the first dialogue that bears the name of Alcibiades" contains a surprising definition of the term. Of the four Persian "Royal paedagogues" chosen for their virtues—the "wisest teaches the magic (μαγείαν) of Zoroaster" (75). And it is Socrates who surprises when he explains: "the art of the magician is the service (θεραπεία) of the gods" (75). Harrison remarks that "in primitive days in Greece, as in Persia, magic had to do, if not with divinities (θεοί), yet at least with things divine, with sanctities (Τὰ θεῖα)" (76). She reminds us of Picus in Aristophanes (The Birds 480), in Vergil (Aeneid VII.170 ff.), and in Ovid (Metamorphoses XIV.6 and Fasti III). "Picus and Faunus are not regular dei like Jove, they are numina, spirits, genii, a bird spirit and a wood-spirit; like the Tree-King who watched over the Golden Bough, they haunt the dark groves" (Harrison 106–7). Her argument that there existed sanctities before the anthropomorphic gods of sacrifice, suits Mary Butts's sense that we have returned to sanctities, personal and natural, unnamed things. Harrison concludes her remarks on indigenous Picus:

> Finally Picus enshrines a beautiful lost faith, the faith that birds and beasts had mana other and sometimes stronger than the mana of man. The notion that by watching a bird you can divine the weather is preceded by the far more primitive notion that the bird by his mana actually makes the weather, makes and brings the rain, the thunder, the sunshine and the spring. Beasts and birds in their silent, aloof, goings, in the perfection of their limited doings are mysterious still and wonderful. We speak of zoomorphic or theriomorphic or ornithomorphic gods, but again we misuse language. Birds are not, never were, gods: there is no definite bird-cult, but there are an infinite number of bird-sanctities. (Themis 110)

Picus, she argues, can be seen in Ovid to have been preempted by the thunderer Zeus, but the name becomes a title of Zeus. The history of the curious Greek phrase which Scylla adapts to her purposes is complex:

> Picus himself, according to the Byzantine syncretizers, knew that he was really Zeus. "When he had handed over the western part of his kingdom he died at the age of

120, and when he was dying he gave orders that his body should be deposited in the island of Crete, and that there should be an inscription:

'Here lies dead the Woodpecker who also is Zeus.'" (*Themis* 109)

Crete is, of course, Zeus's ancient birthplace, indicating that the Greeks had never lost their sense that their gods were born of the earth. One can hear Mary Butts's laughter and feel her delight in the wildness of this history of the divine. She then prepares it again, through Scylla, in *Armed with Madness*.

Jane Harrison's work leads us, in turn, to another great example of the new anthropology, A. B. Cook's *Zeus: A Study of Ancient Religion* (1914). Cook comments at length on the strange history of the phrase Πίκος ὁ καί Ζεύς which cannot be traced beyond the second century—a "wild farrago" of world history put together by Byzantine chroniclers. But Cook notes:

> In weighing . . . various hypotheses we must not lose sight of the fact that Zeus is constantly said to have been buried in Crete. Now the Idaean Cave has yielded a *tympanon* of the ninth or eighth century B.C., which represents the youthful Zeus or Zagreus in definitely Assyrian guise. . . . Moreover, we have seen reason to surmise that at *Hagia Triada* the soul of the prince embodying this deity took the form of a jay (*pica*)—a bird whose bright plumage suggested comparison with the woodpecker (picus). . . . It is, then, conceivable that the phrase Πίκος ὁ καί Ζεύς finds its ultimate explanation in an actual Cretan cult, and that this cult was known, at least by tradition, to the chronographer who first tacked the history of Rome on to that of Assyria. When Euelpides in Aristoph. av. 480 spoke of Zeus as "soon destined to restore the sceptre to the Woodpecker," it was no mere flight of fancy but a genuine piece of folk-belief. (697)

Indeed, it is Cook who begins the investigation of the phrase by calling attention to it in 1903, to be followed by Jane Harrison in 1912, W. R. Halliday's *Greek Divination* (1913), and J. Rendel Harris's *Picus Who Is Also Zeus* (1916). It is fascinating to trace the fun of what Mary Butts is likely to have read and then to note the serious side of her interest in archaic awareness.

The key to the violent combination of *Emerald Table*, Grail and ancient bird-magic, with which all these associations began, is, I believe, to be found in the work of still another scholar. Jessie Weston's studies of the Arthurian cycle may all have been important to Mary Butts's imagination, but it is *From Ritual to Romance* (1920) that seems particularly suggestive. This book draws upon a large range of the new scholarship, so important to twentieth-century writers, including direct reference to Sir James Frazer, Franz Cumont Anrich, Jane Harrison, G. R. S. Mead, and Sir Gilbert Murray. Especially important is Harrison's commentary on a Cretan Hymn of the Kouretes, which is addressed to Zeus as a

"Full-Grown Youth" (Themis 11) not to the "most unreasonable and ungovernable of the Olympians." This is, of course, "Zeus of the birth-cave" (5) whose nature seems so strange to those who know only the later strata of myth in which Kornian Zeus is an overpowering sky-deity. In Harrison, this example becomes striking evidence for an older, archaic sanctity that is part of an original relation to nature (Themis 6). Ms. Weston's use of this to approach the "secret of the Grail"[6] is complex in that her ultimate endeavor is to trace all mystery religions back to such archaic vitalities. In so doing, she searches out the earliest Christian material available to her, what she called the "Naassene Document"— and here she draws upon G. R. S. Mead who analyzed and translated the document in Thrice-Greatest Hermes. His chapter on "The Myth of Man in the Mysteries" takes up this document, which Hippolytus (c. 222 A.D.) incorporates into his Refutation, and argues that it is a palimpsest: "an original Pagan source," a "working over of this source by a jewish mystic of the time of Philo" (1 century B.C.), and a "subsequent working over, with additions, by a Christian Gnostic (Naassene), in the middle of the second century A.D."[7]—all this edited by the arch-enemy of the Gnostics, Hippolytus. Ms. Weston is especially impressed by Mead's summary remarks: "'The claim of these Gnostics was practically that Christianity, or rather the Good News of the Christ, was precisely the consummation of the inner doctrine of the Mystery-institutions of all the nations: the end of them all was the revelation of the mystery of Man'" (quoted in Weston 153). Drawing from this and from Frazer and Harrison, among others who sought archaic human nature, Weston concludes her famous argument: "The Grail story is not du fond en comble the product of imagination, literary or popular. At its root lies the record, more or less distorted, of an ancient Ritual, having for its ultimate object the initiation into the secret of the sources of Life, physical and spiritual" (191).[*] However much we are disinclined to turn to Weston nowadays for an "explanation" of the Grail story—she seems so unaware of the place of narrative and imagination in thought and of the sheer energy of language—her book was startling in its day for good reason. Mary Butts had only to follow her own bent in the imaginative use of this scholarship to set about a novel in which "the unstated thing" would become active in contemporary terms. "Old patterns repeat themselves," one character tells us, and we may note that they are sometimes dangerously new.

Mary Butts was twenty when Roger Fry's first post-impressionist show opened in London—that is, when modernism first came to England, of which Virginia

---

[*] For lack of space, I can here only refer the reader to Henry and Renée Kahane, The Krater and the Grail: Hermetic Sources of the Parzival.

Woolf, looking back in 1924, would say in a lecture at Cambridge: "on or about December, 1910 human character changed." "Think how little we know about character—think how little we know about art."* Cézanne, Van Gogh, Gauguin, Matisse, Picasso, Redon, Signac, Seurat were a storm for the English mind. For Mary Butts, behind this was the commotion of Victorian and Edwardian change, held together by what Samuel Hynes calls "established orders" until 1914–1918:

> As it was, the trauma of 1914–1918 ended the garden party as swiftly and rudely as a shower of hail or a four-letter word. It did so most dramatically within the fighting forces, though only after a good deal of bloody fumbling; but it also ended the more gracious aspects of the age. After the war there was never again so much money in the hands of the wellborn. (Hynes 13)

With the established orders weakened what was left to responsible minds was the inheritance of change that the Victorians had left them:

> Victoria's reign had been a triumphant Age of Science; advances in geology, biology, and physics had not only affected the way men thought about their physical environment but had altered men's ideas of their relation to that environment— had brought, that is, a new cosmology and a new conception of the nature of change. It had been a scientific revolution, and, as is often true of revolutions, the revolutionaries in their moment of victory saw only their successes and not the new problems that success had created. (Hynes 132–33)

This revolution with its resultant new cosmology also required a new anthropology, bits and pieces of which I have been considering. Most of this anthropology goes unnoticed now by a later non-classical, more "scientific" and structuralist anthropology. And, it should be noted, cosmology, new or old—not simply a detached logic of epistemology—is a fundamental activity of art, even if it is understood as self-expression. A new cosmology was the issue and remains so for the twentieth century.

One gets a charming view of this matter from Virginia Woolf's essay "The Cosmos," a review of *The Journals of Thomas Cobden-Sanderson, 1879–1922*, which she wrote in 1926:

> "'And what is Cosmos, Mr. Sanderson?' asks Sister Edith. 'What is the meaning of the word?' And then I go off like a rocket and explode in the stars in the empyrean."

---

* Cited and the exhibition discussed in Hynes (325), taken from Virginia Woolf's "Mr. Bennett and Mrs. Brown"—"a paper read to the Heretics, Cambridge, on May 18, 1924"—published in *The Captain's Death Bed and Other Essays* (91).

These two volumes are full of the sparks that fell from that constantly recurring explosion. For Mr. Cobden-Sanderson was always trying to explain to somebody— it might be Professor Tyndall ("I gave him my own view of human destiny, namely, the ultimate coalescence of the human intellect in knowledge with its other self, the Universe"), it might be Mr. Churchill, it might be a strange lady whose motor-car had broken down on the road near Malvern—what the word Cosmos meant. (*Captain's Death Bed* 82)

. . . we are left asking, with Sister Edith: "But, Mr. Sanderson, how does one 'fly to the great Rhythm'? What is the extraordinary ring of harmony within harmony that encircles us; what reason is there to suppose that a mountain wishes us well or that a lake has a profound moral meaning to impart? What, in short, does the word Cosmos mean?" Whereupon the rocket explodes, and the red and gold showers descend, and we look on with sympathy, but feel a little chill about the feet and not very clear as to the direction of the road. (*Captain's Death Bed* 84)

"My idea was magnificent; the act was ridiculous," he said. "Besides," he reflected, "nothing was explicable." And perhaps he was right. (*Captain's Death Bed* 86)

As Hynes observes, "Victorian science may have made metaphysics obsolete [still the work of our contemporary deconstructionists] but it had not destroyed men's metaphysical itch, and much of what one might generally call Edwardian science is concerned with the problem of restoring metaphysics to the human world" (134).

One effect of the new sciences, including the new anthropology, was that it implied and required a new psychology. We have seen Mary Butts, through Scylla and Felix, fooling around with Freud, which is not to say that she was not also serious. But the recognition of Freud came late to England, in fact, not until the War put his work to the proof.[*] Mary Butts was, thus, in the thick of the matter as she was writing. Nevertheless, she had available to her in her youth, the extraordinary work of Edward Carpenter and Havelock Ellis, which has a history of its own. As Samuel Hynes notes: "One field of scientific investigation in particular seemed to offer an escape from Darwinism—the field of mental events. . . . Psychology . . . became in late-Victorian and Edwardian times the liberating movement in science, as the suffrage movement was in social relations, and socialism was in politics; and as such it attracted many of the same people" (138–39). We need to remember, in this context, that the Society for Psychical Research was founded in 1882, later to count both Freud and Jung as honorary members, and that the first English psychological journal, the British

---

[*] I wish to emphasize the usefulness of Hynes's discussion of this in the chapter already noted, "Science, Seers, and Sex" (132–71).

Journal of Psychology, begins in 1904, which, Hynes observes, withdrew from speculation "about the nature of sex"—"Edwardian England's principal contribution to modern psychology" (Hynes 148). The acceptance of Freud in America came even later, and what Butts's editor Johns did not know and could not understand was the fact that something else was at work in her milieu. She may have known Carpenter's pamphlets of the nineties: for example, *Woman and her place in a free society* and *Homogenic Love and its place in a free society* (1896), but the influence of his *Love's Coming of Age* (1906) she can hardly have missed. The something else at work is likely, in part, to have been derived from Carpenter: "he sought human freedom, and when he wrote about sex it was about the sexual implications of the whole liberation of men" (Hynes 151). His is the first voice of this in the English speaking world—except, once again, Blake. Carpenter's is also the first defense of homosexuality. There was also Havelock Ellis's great work in seven volumes, *Studies in the Psychology of Sex* (1897–1928). Ellis, with whom H. D. would work, sums up his own sense of his achievement:

> I had done mankind a service which mankind needed, and which, it seemed, I alone was fitted to do. I had helped to make the world, and to make the world in the only way that it can be made, the interior way, by liberating the human spirit. (quoted in Hynes 159)

However their contribution to later psychology is judged, they were pioneers and prophets who had spoken to one part of Mary Butts's life and art.

In order to clarify the interplay of all these intellectual and spiritual concerns in Mary Butts's work and before I turn to the final scene of *Armed with Madness*, I want to draw attention to a few passages in the essay of 1932, *Traps for Unbelievers*:

> Jung has something to say about the value, the possibly unexhausted value, of classic religious symbolism and myth. It used to be fashionable to think that they had survived because of the motifs they supplied to the arts; we know now that it is more true to say that it was the quality of the belief which produced the works, and that each religion gets the art it deserves.
> What sort of religion was it? . . . Then came the rise of anthropology and the science of comparative religions, and we have learned how to take fresh stock, compare Zeus with Jehovah, Aphrodite with Ashtaroth, and the pair of them with the Virgin; re-state Athene as a "functional daimon," as a vegetation spirit, as a totem, as a Luck; as an owl, as a feminist, as a wish-fulfillment; compare Orpheus and Osiris as Saviours, and both with Christ. It was a re-examination of extraordinary possibilities and value. Its exaggeration came from a desire to be primitive

at all costs, to scour the cults and ceremonies for traces of totem-worship and fetish, for cannibalism and human sacrifice, for orgies and black magic, for exogamy and endogamy, and all the "gay science" of the anthropologist. (*Traps* 35–36)

Her critical mind goes over and over these new disciplines, never sentimental and never at rest.

So far as christian [sic] theology is concerned, it is all a question of date. We are still only emerging from its forms, the bones of them sticking up all about us, still dripping wet from that sea; and determined, or presumably determined, to get dry as soon as possible. Like all lately rejected things, about which we feel self-conscious, Christianity is going through a period of tabu, of being one of the things which are not done. (*Traps* 33)

And she continues:

So it would seem that the Gods, who for two thousand years have survived the organised forces of Christianity, are about to descend into a final twilight with their conqueror. As we have seen, they have not, like Christianity, become tabu, merely more and more symbolic, and what is more at the moment, artistically suspect. (*Traps* 37)

We need only note, in this regard, her sensitivity, accurately outlined, to the growing positivism of scholarly thought and intellectual tradition.

Much of her concern seems involved in an analysis of the twentieth century's translation of Renaissance humanism into a modern humanism of closure and its escape-hatch, power. Immediately following upon the remarks above comes one of Mary Butts's most prophetic and incisive admonitions:

But the God to look out for is the God who does not put up a fight. His successes may not be spectacular, he has no hell up his sleeve, nor even much of a heaven. He is himself, for what he is worth. Take him or leave him, he makes no protest. Takes himself off, manifests himself in other ways, is called by another name. Until one is suddenly aware of him again, that his departure has been a feint, a trick that has been played on one by oneself. (*Traps* 37–38)

This is, I repeat, 1932, and this magical mind seems capable of reading European ideologies, including what was to happen to Communist practice, in a glass darkly. (Yeats's "Second Coming" which appears to go on coming is dated 1920.) And who or what is this trickster that turns out to be ourselves?

These Gods, "to whom a doubtful philosopher can pray, . . . as to so many radiant and heart-searching hypotheses," are no more and no less than so many descriptions man has made of himself. Descriptions that cover the ground pretty fully, the "subtle knot" retied, thread by thread. Man as an animal, as a prince, as a saviour, as a lover, as a phallos, as a warrior, as an artist, as a "magic," a flash of the hidden forces in nature. The subdivisions are often exceedingly delicate. Put together it is difficult to find one aspect of human nature or occupation or desire which is not personated. And always, as Professor Murray points out, the trivial or base, the obscene or irrational, the mysterious or the merely obscure and tiresome elements, are subordinated and kept within bounds. Which is, after all, what man likes to think about himself and do with himself. (*Traps* 39)

This is not exactly the euhemerism that the Sicilian came up with around 300 B.C. because it is Man who is deified in this argument, not an historical person or event, and it is Man who burst out of the nineteenth century to find only Himself. Some few pages later, she returns to her point of departure and to the magic of the meaning she wove into her work:

We have seen the universal discredit of christian [sic] monotheism. In an age of violent transition and discovery its old weakness has appeared again, its insufficient insistence on the wild, enchanting, incalculable force in nature, the mana of things, the non-moral, beautiful, subtle energy in man and in everything else, on which the virtue of everything depends. (*Traps* 47)

"We are," she concludes,

back in the historical situation which Nietzsche described of a people "for whom God is dead, and for whom no baby-god is yet lying in his cradle." Back where we were at Alexander's death, with an instinct that is more than an instinct, a habit of life and a necessity for us, unsatisfied. Back in the blind and primitive assertion of that instinct; running after Luck and awaiting Destiny, or indulging ourselves in an orgy of mana, stripped of the morals and even of the tabus which once made it serviceable. Or, if we must specialise, back with certain people of the Hellenistic Age, in "chic" cults of the least of other men's divinities. . . .

In common with the Christian, the classic mind at its best insisted that, though it was possible for the divine and the human to mix, "man is not God and it is no use pretending that he is." . . . Something not very far off the deification of man is on us now, not, or not yet, of the kings and millionaires, but, and again, and this is primitive, of the conspicuous young men and women, our sexually desirable ones, whose nature it is to wax and wane and be replaced. Our Year-in-Year-out spirits, *eniautoi daimones*, "whose beauty is no stronger than a flower."

Human nature was not meant for that strain. The star-dust at Hollywood is full of dead stars. For the potency of the human god wanes, and his end is horror; rebirth, but for their human nature, terror. That is a story told in the Gospels as well as in *The Golden Bough*. (*Traps* 49–51)

One catches the translation of Frazer and Harrison into contemporary terms without Harrison's "beautiful lost faith" (*Themis* 110) and a direction of vision very different from D. H. Lawrence's discovery of "blood-knowledge" in Frazer's *Totemism and Exogamy* (*Letters to Russell*). Nor does she here express herself as a companion of Bloomsbury, "the formulators," as Hynes puts it, "of that religion of art, intelligence, and human relationships that was born in Edwardian London and died in the Second World War" (Hynes 154). She had, however, some respect from Virginia Woolf, for, having submitted an unnamed manuscript, she was invited to tea with Mrs. Woolf on Sunday, 29 October, 1922 (*Diary*, Vol. II: 209). It is also interesting to note that Virginia Woolf apparently intended to publish what must have been *Armed with Madness*, but rejected it for financial reasons: "Novels are the great bloodsuckers" (*Diary*, Vol. III: 150). In her *Diary* from which this information comes, Woolf seems interested in Mary Butts, but her judgment is clearly colored by William Plomer's friend and Mary's brother, Anthony Butts. The entry for March 18, 1932, quotes him: "'I cannot say anything of my sister—She is a bad woman—pretentious—I can see no merit in her books—pretentious. She corrupts young men. They are always committing suicide. She now has married Gabriel Atkins—without any character. They were given 25 decanters for their wedding.'" And Mrs. Woolf comments: "Tony is ashamed of Mary, who thus defiles the Butts blood" (Vol. IV: 84). Many of these details are simply repeated by Goldring in *South Lodge*.

It is also notable in these passages from *Traps for Unbelievers* that they are preparation for her last two novels, *The Macedonian* (1933) and *Scenes from the Life of Cleopatra* (1935), which begin to track that "historical situation" by way of a life of Alexander, well founded on historical sources, and a feminist defense of the personality of Cleopatra who, of course, came to her position in Egypt as one result of the Macedonian's imperialism. Without biographical information, one can't be sure which came first, the essay or *The Macedonian*, since the preface to the latter is dated August, 1931. Still, I wish to say that her work is all of a piece, a deeply probing interrogation of an historical situation, which never ignores the "fun" that is part of the answer. *The Macedonian* closes with the death of Alexander, having delicately interwoven the characteristics of the public and private man:

> And Demosthenes was soon to say: "Alexander is not dead, for if he were, the whole earth would smell his body."
> But in the Serapeum, a priest sang:
> . . . .
> "I praise him for his wars and quickness:
> "I praise him for his patience and far-seeing:
> "I praise him for his solitude and beauty:
> "I praise him for Clitus and Hephaestion:

"I praise him for the fleet and the phalanx:
"I praise him for Tyre and Alexandria:
"I praise him for Arbela and Gedrosia:
"I praise him for the East and the West.
"I praise him that he is Alexander: and more than Alexander: and less.
"I praise the Earth that she has restored to herself Alexander the Macedonian, son of Philip the Macedonian—being so nobly named—

"That on her breast lies there
he of the fairest-rare-
hyacinth-curled hair,
of the world famed." (Macedonian 209–10)

This finely imagined hymn is no simple praise of the heroic; instead it is addressed to Earth who receives him and ends with the deft, personal touch of the "hyacinth-curled hair" reminding us of the boy from whose blood sprang the iris of that name, marked αιαι, "alas, alas!" (Mary Butts carefully credits not only Murray on Greek religion, but also Harrison's *Prolegomena to the Study of Greek Religion* and *Themis* for helping to tell this tale.) We are also to remember the long tradition that in 324, Alexander "officially" requested the Greek cities to recognize him as a god and another tradition that Alexander believed in his own divinity. The novel is a study of the man Alexander and that edge of power which we have called "gods" and which so tempted him in Persia and Egypt— a range of energy very like what Mary Butts calls the virtue of things.

Near the end of *Traps for Unbelievers*, we come upon another aspect of the intelligence of her work, which she drew from Nietzsche. This may already have been noted in *Armed with Madness* where, in Scylla's meditation as she goes to meet Carston at Starn, we come upon the phrases "Revaluation of values" and "Discovery of a new value, a different way of apprehending everything" (10). A Nietzschean concern, for Mary Butts, is not pretentious—though it might seem so to society writers such as her brother, Plomer, and Goldring—nor does it set her apart; rather, it firmly places her in the context of the most important English effort to come to terms with the change that marks the end of the nineteenth century and the beginning of the twentieth. The modern philosopher, *par excellence*, had long been part of English literary thought during her lifetime, for, in the words of one writer at the turn of the century, Nietzsche made possible "a new habitation for the imagination of man" (Thatcher 80).* The first English translations of Nietzsche were of aphorisms and began in New

* John Davidson, cited in David S. Thatcher (80), *Nietzsche in England, 1890–1914*, a valuable discussion (53–91).

York in 1889 and in London in 1891.* After overcoming obstacles, machinations and delays, the editor, Oscar Levy, published *The Complete Works of Friedrich Nietzsche*, the final eighteenth volume in 1913. This important event meant that the young writers of the day had the texts at hand and would no longer be dependent upon such popular, poisonous introductions as Max Nordau's *Degeneration*, first published in English in 1895, "coincident" with Oscar Wilde's trials, and reprinted in a "Popular Ed." in 1913 and 1920—a thoroughly reactionary view which appears to have had profound consequences for both popular and literary understanding. David Thatcher's indispensible study, *Nietzsche in England*, 1890–1914, discusses this in detail for the first time. He notes that Wilde, in Nordau's book, "finds himself in the distinguished company of the pre-Raphaelites, Whitman, Gautier, Baudelaire, Maeterlinck, Tolstoy, Ibsen, Wagner, Zola, Nietzsche, and almost everybody of artistic account in the late nineteenth century, the writers, in fact, whom Havelock Ellis had praised in *The New Spirit* (1890)" (27). Behind this reaction, then, we have, as already noted, the recognitions of Havelock Ellis and Edward Carpenter—both strongly literary—who present the beginnings of a renewed, revalued literary psychology. And central to this psychology is Nietzsche whose "transvaluation of values" both implies and argues a changed psychological ground. Thatcher draws attention to the way in which this problem is slipped over in such studies as John A. Lester's *Journey Through Despair, 1880–1914: Transformations in British Literary Culture* (1968):

> This was, Lester maintains, a time of confusion and bewilderment, of disillusion and malaise; the transition from materialistic determinism to a world of chance and change involved "the urgent and pained necessity of a 'transvaluation of all values,' to keep man's imaginative life alive under conditions which seemed unlivable." (Thatcher 3)

But, for all the weight here upon that famous phrase, Nietzsche, in Lester's discussion, becomes one of the symptoms rather than harbinger and guide. That literary minds took up the imagination of an indeterminate human nature, founded in change and chance—among them Mary Butts—both before and after the meeting with Nietzsche is a major aspect of the profound meditation of twentieth-century thought. Thatcher cites two important passages from Nietzsche on this transvaluation, both of them available to the enquiring Mary Butts:

---

* Helen Watterson in *Century Magazine* (New York, May 1889) and John Davidson in *Speaker* (London, 1891), noted and discussed by Thatcher (22).

These weeks I have employed in "transvaluing values."—You understand this trope?—After all, the alchemist is the most deserving kind of man there is! I mean the man who makes of what is base and despised something valuable, even gold. He alone confers wealth, the others merely give change. My problem this time is rather a curious one: I have asked myself what hitherto has been best hated, feared, despised by mankind—and of that and nothing else I have made my "gold" (Letter to Brandes, May 23, 1888, London, 1914). (Thatcher 84)

and Nietzsche's definition of the "transvaluation of values,"

an emancipation from all moral values, in a saying of yea, and in an attitude of trust, to all that which hitherto has been forbidden, despised, and damned. (Thatcher 85 n.)

This issue of values, which involves a psychology, a practice and an imaginative structure, has been painful to think about for decades. Mary Butts, like many of her peers, seems to have simplified the problematic of "crossing over" inferred in the prefix "trans." The term "revaluation" is common in discussions of Nietzsche then and now. In *Traps for Unbelievers*, she, like Yeats in "The Second Coming," seems to have stopped over the moment of terror—a necessary moment, I think, in all such thought and one in which one notices the constant interweaving of cultural condition and imagination in twentieth-century art.

Having been reminded by Thatcher of Havelock Ellis's judgment that Nietzsche was "'one of the greatest spiritual forces which have appeared since Goethe'" (101), I turn back, briefly, to brushstroke the strength of Nietzsche's presence in English literary thought. Phyllis Grosskurth's recent biography of Ellis (1980) notices that his judgment of Nietzsche is largely based on early work, which is true, but it is hardly likely, setting aside *The Will to Power* and *Ecce Home*, that *Thus Spoke Zarathustra* "had nothing to say to him" (209), given, as she also notices, that his "reality" is "based on a biological structure" (208). This opening, more likely through Freud than Ellis, will have an extraordinary history in modern letters by way of Charles Olson, Robert Duncan, and Michael McClure. Nietzsche has, indeed, been difficult to come to terms with, in large part because of the fascist preemption of his work, which translated what is first a psychological condition and then a problem of meaning on every level of the human structure—Mary Butts's "historical situation"—into a monstrosity—her "terror." Only recently has a new effort been made to understand his influence on the modern imagination in such studies as Otto Bohlmann's *Yeats and Nietzsche* (1982), Ofelia Schutte's *Beyond Nihilism* (1984), and fundamentally, whether one is deconstructionist or not, Gilles Deleuze's *Nietzsche and Philosophy* (French, 1962; English, 1983). Deleuze:

> The sense of Nietzsche's philosophy is that multiplicity, becoming and chance
> are objects of pure affirmation. The affirmation of multiplicity is the speculative
> proposition, just as the joy of diversity is the practical proposition. (197)

The speculative character of modern art, especially writing, is often under-estimated and undervalued. For Mary Butts and many another young writer, Nietzsche, in Thatcher's words, "was the philosopher à la mode in England between 1909 and 1913" (42). This influence grew dramatically with the appointment of A. R. Orage as co-editor of New Age in 1907—a socialist journal, one notes, and a factor in the hopes of the time. He was the author then of three books which have seldom been gauged, except by Thatcher, for their place in the modern imagination: Friedrich Nietzsche: The Dionysian Spirit of the Age (1906); Nietzsche in Outline and Aphorism (1907); and Consciousness: Animal, Human, and Superman (1907)—this last one, for us startlingly published by the Theosophical Publishing Co. of London. With his appointment to the New Age, he carried these concerns into the currency of periodical publication. Thatcher adds this up: "From May, 1907, until the end of 1913—a period of five and a half years— Nietzsche's name is hardly absent from the pages of the New Age" (235).

I think of the extraordinary range of public and private concern represented by the New Age and of its authors, particularly Ezra Pound. There, one finds, to name only one instance, Pound's "I Gather the Limbs of Osiris," a series of essays on his "New Method of Scholarship," a method of "luminous detail," 1911–1912. Pound's "Obituary: A. R. Orage" (1934) and "In the Wounds (Memoriam A. R. Orage)" (1935) remember the importance of New Age to his welfare, but his praise of Orage himself is mainly subsumed under their companionship in Douglasite economic reform. In the latter, Pound writes: "I had no interest in Orage's mysticism and am unqualified to define it. I was thankful he had it simply because it kept him in action."* There can be no doubt that Pound's sense of process is the contrary of Orage's "mysticism," but, though I have no time to bear it out here, a bridge can be made by way of Allen Upward's The Divine Mystery which Pound read as "a history of the development of human intelligence" (Selected Prose 403). It is important, I think, to our understanding of Mary Butts's compounded elements in Armed with Madness to notice— Orage as our example—the connection between hermetical beliefs and Nietzsche, especially in the proposition of "Übermensch," best translated by Thatcher's "Beyond-Man."[8] That is to say, beyond the manhood so confused, determined and despairing that the arts had undertaken, along with Nietzsche, to answer

---

* Both are reprinted in Pound's Selected Prose, 1909–1965, ed. William Cookson—this quotation p. 446.

with an undetermined imagination of human nature. Thatcher tells us that Orage's interest in Nietzsche began in 1900, following a chance meeting with Holbrook Jackson, "already an avid reader of *The Eagle and the Serpent*" (1898–1903), an early English, Nietzschean journal, and he cites Jackson's memory of what followed:

> We all developed supermania. He wanted a Nietzsche circle in which Plato and Blavatsky, Fabianism and Hinduism, Shaw and Wells and Edward Carpenter should be blended, with Nietzsche as the catalytic. An exciting brew. (221–22)

Such syncretism can be easily criticized, but it does demonstrate both the desperation and the effort of a new meaning. It is also an unprofessional and undisciplined response to the dialectics of Kant and Hegel.

More relevant to our literary interest here is, perhaps, a passage from Orage's *Friedrich Nietzsche: The Dionysian Spirit of the Age*:

> Friedrich Nietzsche is the greatest European event since Goethe. From one end of Europe to the other, wherever his books are read, the discussion in the most intellectual and aristocratically-minded circles turns on the problems raised by him. In Germany and in France his name is the war cry of opposing factions, and before very long his name will be familiar in England. Already half a dozen well-known English writers might be named who owe, if not half their ideas, at least half the courage of their ideas to Nietzsche. Ibsen seems almost mild by the side of him. Emerson, with whom he had much in common, seems strangely cool: William Blake alone among English writers seems to have closely resembled Nietzsche, and he who has read the *Marriage of Heaven and Hell*, and grasped its significance, will have little to learn from the apostle of *Zarathustra*. (Quoted in Thatcher 230–31)

This led in turn to the affirmation of such affinity in *New Age* by its co-editor, Holbrook Jackson (Thatcher 234). It is fair to say that the ability of twentieth-century readers to read Blake begins here. Without the necessary biographical underpinnings, I can only guess and speculate, but based on Mary Butts's autobiography, *The Crystal Cabinet* (1937), covering only her childhood, I can say with some assurance that her attentive sense of the Nietzschean problematic begins with Blake in whose work the issues of becoming, consciousness, and will are given a necessary vision. From Orage and the Nietzscheans, she seems also to have caught hold of a sense of our "historical situation" that Thatcher describes as "a relativist view of history in which all phenomena were interpreted in terms of the conflict of polarities, a philosophy of man which stressed his role as the noble protagonist in the drama of tragic existence" (Thatcher 233). A very ancient view which is reflected in Pound's Ulysses and Malatesta and in Mary Butts's Alexander as well as in the curious trickster quest of *Armed with Madness*, packed as it is with more ordinary-extraordinary personal affairs. On the one hand, as one writer says of Hölderlin,[9] in whose work, like Blake's, so much that we call modernism begins, "a precarious dialogue with the Other—whether this take the form of madness, revolution, or those gods of ancient Greece . . . vanished immediacies," and on the other, the "reinvention of antiquity out of the evidence of wreckage."[*] Blake and Nietzsche share a "consolidation of errors," psychological, social and religious, which "coincides with the revelation" of what they called the truth—that is to say, cultural belonging.[†] We have tended to give up this incredible compounding of theosophy, anthropology, psychology, reinvented antiquity, and Nietzsche consolidation— to leave it unstudied and unimagined—for the Freudian approach to mind, imagination and culture, also hailed by later issues of *New Age*. There are, it seems to me, good reasons to consider both Freud and Nietzsche as consolidators and "physicians of culture." For Mary Butts and many another who lived much longer facing into their work, the truth is a kind of indeterminancy of what we are. It is well to remember that Freud entered the English imagination late, and when he did, it was through this wide-spread interest in "mental events." Samuel Hynes takes note:

> Psychoanalytic ideas had spread more slowly in England than anywhere else in Europe or America. When Freud was made an honorary member of the Society for Psychical Research in 1911, he wrote to Jung that it was "the first sign of interest from dear old England"; the London Psycho-Analytical Society was not founded until two years later, in 1913, and then with only nine members, of whom only four ever practiced. Freud's methods became acceptable to the British medical world only after they had been proved in war-time treatment of shell-shock cases. (164)

What is apparent and of enduring interest is, as Ellis, Carpenter, and Orage had discovered and argued publically with the considerable assistance of Nietsche, art cannot be considered apart from the cultural condition in which it works. In this instance, a loss of cultural meaning, Mary Butts startlingly plays a game of hide-and-seek with such meaning.

---

[*] Richard Siebuth's introduction to *Friedrich Hölderin, Hymns and Fragments* (11 and 33), slightly adapted for my purposes.

[†] The notion of a "consolidation of errors," adapted here, is from Brian Wilke and M. J. Johnson, *Blake's Four Zoas* (141).

Now, out of this labyrinth—necessarily speculative—of her heart and mind (I like her proposal of a speculative imagination), let us turn to the final scenes of *Armed with Madness*. Carston has managed to track down the source of the cup, and Picus produces a document to the effect that it was found in a church in 1881. The Rev. John Norris who could verify this is dead:

> Carston said:
> "Then we get nowhere."
> "Nowhere. Only in ghost-stories, and those not the best, do you get anywhere that way."
> "But what are we going to do with the damned thing? It can't lie about the house like a green eye that doesn't wink. . . . This has been a fool's errand—"
> "I have an idea," said the vicar. "Take it back to Tollerdown and replace it where you found it. If the next drought sends it up in a suspicious manner, well and good. It seems to like wells. And truth, if she prefers to talk, can return to one."
> Carston said: "I like that."
> "Good," said Picus, "learn it to be a toad." (196)

Meanwhile, Clarence has been spitefully informed by a letter from London that Scylla and Picus intend to marry, and Scylla, having found this out, goes to Tollerdown to talk with Clarence:

> Clarence had not seen her. Unshaved, half-dressed, he was trying to torture the body of Picus, the statue he had done of him in clay. He had dragged it out against the quarry wall and pierced it with arrows of sharpened wood, feathered from a gull he had shot overnight.
> Scylla found the door open and went softly in.
> "Clarence, I've come all this way. Can I have tea?"
> He heard the low voice, thought of the gull crying. She saw the bird's half-plucked body, bloody on the floor, and that there were papers torn in strips and little darts. She turned over a fold and saw her own body, and her cry was more like the gull. Bird-alone in the lonely room. Except for a ghost called Clarence, everything was empty. She thought:
> 'Run away: Can't: Where to? It's all empty, and my knees shake. And I'm curious. Curious and furious and only my body is afraid.'
> Clarence wanted to be sure about the bird. He came in slowly, dazed with violence and grief. Bad conscience and fear of making a fool of himself nagged his blazing obsession. He saw Scylla at the door in silhouette, her scarf fluttering off the back of her neck, sweat-darkened curls appliquéd on her forehead, her hat thrown familiarly on a chair, her mouth open.
> "Come and look," he said, and with the fingers of one hand dug into her collarbone, led her through the kitchen into the half-circle of quarry behind.
> She saw Picus in greenish clay, pricked with white feathers. Clarence had made him exactly as he was, a body she had known, for which hers ached.
> "You see," he said, "I only had what I'd made of him to do it to."

There was an arrow through his throat, and his head had not fallen forward.

"You're going down the well, where the cup came—"

"Why, Clarence?"

"Best place for you, my fancy girl. If there's enough water, you'll drown. If there isn't, and I don't think there is, you'll break every bone in your body."

She could run like a lapwing, but he could run faster. She was strong as a tree-cat, but he could tear her in two.

"I came to bring you to Picus. He does not want you to be alone on Toller-down. He is at Tambourne. Lydia sent you a silly letter because" (get his vanity if you can) "she is so in love with you that she's mad."

"And so are you, it seems. Gods! I'm a lucky chap. Unfortunately, Picus doesn't join the harem. He doesn't like me any more.

"Going to marry me, are you? You shall in a way. I mean to follow you down the well."

"Picus is at Tambourne, waiting for you."

"In time he will be here again. My body will fetch him."

"You are the most beautiful man in the world, but you won't be when they get you up out of the well."

He took her other shoulder in his fingers, thrusting them into the muscle-hollow under her neck, hurting her. She forgot him exacting, petulant; remembered him long before, beautiful, merry, inventive, good. And cruel now. Stupid cruelty. Cruelty frightened her. She lied:

"Clarence, I am going to marry Carston"—I teased Lydia—He turned her towards the well.

"There will be one less of you bitches to come into our lives."

"We bear you, and I am no stronger in your hands than that bird. Why did you shoot a gull? It isn't done." Time seemed very precious. Only a thimbleful left. The well very near. The sun turning a little away from them.

"Woodpecker," she shrieked, and flung Clarence off, and ran to the statue. She had been careful not to say that name, and now saw Clarence hurrying to her, the mournful crazy mask splitting, the mouth turning up, the eyes shooting death at her. And Picus, pierced with arrows, smiled down his sweet equivocation. She heard: "That'll do better." He had a cord round his waist. He had cattle-ranched once: that was his lariat. She ran once round the statue. A second later he had thrown her, picked her up half stunned, and tied her against Picus. A black flint had cut her head, a patch of blood began to soak through the moon-fair hair.

Clarence walked back and stood by the kitchen door, fitting an arrow to the string. It ripped the skin on her shoulder and entered the clay. She saw another fly towards her and notch her forearm. Another, and there was a tearing pain below her left breast.

Three instants of pain, set in one of fear. Like a great jewel. Clarence stood by the kitchen door, sharpening an indifferent arrow. She made a supreme effort: not to scream much; not to betray herself. Then a moment of absolute contempt of Clarence. Then of pain. Then, as if she were looking out a window, into a state, a clarté the other side of forgiveness. Not by that route. She fainted. (198–202)

Carston makes his way to Tollerdown to return the cup to the well and so interrupts this violent scene, just as Clarence is preparing another arrow. It is Clarence who is made to drop the cup in the well—"Plop went a noise a very long way below them" (205). This is no novel to bring in the police of social judgments. The next day Clarence cannot remember his actions; he only wishes to carve a punch-bowl for Scylla, but he is led, step following step by Picus, through exactly what he has done, the madness seeming to be a part of himself:

> Of Picus. Of the band he had grown up with. Of war, whose issues he had found too simple. Of their spiritual adventure he had not been equal to. Of the fool he had made of himself. The revenge his death would be. Not stay to be called Judas. *And bring our souls to His high city.*
>
> He took a step to the edge. Scylla jumped off the divan, and with her hand at her side, ran out to him.
>
> "Clarence, come in."
>
> She had hold of him as he had held her. . . .
>
> "Look," she said, and pulled off the handkerchief that tied her shoulder—"and my head is cut and my side. It was partly my fault that Lydia wrote to you. Go on carving while we talk."
>
> He did as she told him. Carston watched them. Like an idyll: a young lover making a present for his sweetheart, sitting on her bed. A harrow of wild geese with their necks out at flight. A border of fish. (218–19)

In the end, Carston takes Clarence away to rest, we are not sure where or for how long. Carston himself is asked to return to the house in the wood:

> "Our house is your house," said Scylla.
>
> "Besides," said Picus, "did you ever enjoy a summer more?"
>
> "Hasn't it been better than a movie? Leave Clarence at Tambourne and come over and look at Felix's find."
>
> In his heart he knew he would not. Though there was continuity in this adventure, a circle like the design on Clarence's maze, a ring near to a magic ring, he knew that nothing would induce him to go back to that poverty and pride, cant and candour, raw flesh and velvet; into that dateless, shiftless, shifting, stable and unstable Heartbreak House. Not for a bit. Off to Paris on his own folk adventure. In his last moments with them, looking at Clarence's bowl, he saw the changes in things.
>
> There had been an apple once. There had been an apple tree. When it gave no more apples, it had made fire, and a slice of its trunk had become a bowl cut out into birds. The bowl unless it was turned into fire again, would stop growing and last for ever. Things that came out of time, and were stopped, could be made over into another sort of time. (220–21)

And, of course, the novel ends with Felix's "find," Boris, the cause of art and magic in others.[10] This return to the magic circle in the wood, to bird-sanctities and metaphors of them that color the characters of Scylla and Picus is youthful and indeterminate of meaning, constantly endangered by violence. In the novel to follow *Armed with Madness, Death of Felicity Taverner*, as I have already noted, Boris takes murder to be a gift, and so implicates all the characters in his lack of understanding. The only figure in *Armed with Madness* who is truly armed is mad in loss and otherwise forgetful. A curious weight in the novel falls on Carston's meditation that "Things that came out of time, and were stopped, could be made over into another sort of time" (221): art, perhaps, but, then, there is the commotion of lives, valued because it is not determined, or, for that matter, material.

I have labored long over what is my own fascination with Mary Butts, and I have insisted that we remember the context and stake of her art because when memory goes, it leaves so many fine things behind. In closing this essay-story, I note that the transformation from determinism to chance and change—a matter of companionship too often goes unnoticed because our sense of what we mean by science changes—brings us into twentieth-century art. It is one of the curiosities of this century that "reality" continues to be pre-empted by objectivity, which leaves us with a loose, even more preemptive subjectivity. Needless to say, this is destructive of imagination and our understanding of it. Closer to the necessary imagination are these remarks of Octavio Paz:

> . . . in extirpating the notion of divinity, rationalism diminished man. It frees us from God but encloses us in an even more rigorous system. The humbled imagination avenges itself, and atrocious fetishes sprout from God's corpse: in Russia and other countries, the divinization of the leader, the cult of the letter of writings, the deification of the party; among us, the idolatry of the self. To be *one's self* is to condemn oneself to mutilation because man is perpetual longing to be another. (Bow 247)

And so it is with Clarence's defeated desire for Picus and with Scylla's successful game to be with him—true also of Carston's departure for Paris and of Felix's finding Boris. We need, somehow, to arrive at such a perspective to understand our art and in this context, to read Mary Butts. Paz continues:

> The revolt of the romantic poets and their heirs was not so much a protest against the exile from God as a search for the lost half, a descent into the region that puts us in communication with the *other*. Therefore they did not find a place in any orthodoxy, and their conversion to this or that faith was never total. Behind Christ or Orpheus, Lucifer or Mary they were seeking that reality of realities we call the divine or the *other*. The situation of the contemporary poets is radically different. Heidegger has expressed it admirably: *We were too late for the gods and too early for being;* and he adds: *whose poem, already begun, is being.* Man is that which is incomplete, al-

though he may be complete in his very incompletion; and therefore he makes poems, images in which he realizes and completes himself without ever completing himself completely. He himself is a poem: he is being always in a perpetual possibility of being completely and thus fulfilling himself in his non-completion. But our historical situation is characterized by the *too late* and the *too early*. Too late: in the tremulous light, the gods, already disappeared, their radiant bodies submerged below the horizon that devours all the mythologies of the past; too early: being, the central experience coming out of our selves to the encounter of its true presence. We are lost among things, our thoughts are circular and we perceive but dimly something, as yet unnamed, that is emerging. (Bow 247–48; original emphasis)

Mary Butts's grail, Felix's "unstated thing," and so on—*

1995

* Mary Butts became unknown because men didn't like women that intelligent—because "closeted" writers like Plomer, Goldring, and Anthony Butts had more style than intellect—because the editor of *Pagany* was out of touch with her real effort—because Bloomsbury was "ignorant" of Nietzsche: he was "practically ignored by almost everyone known by me in the last seventy years, and I cannot remember even a discussion about him" (letter of Leonard Woolf to Thatcher, Oct. 17, 1968, cited by him, *Nietzsche in England* [267])—because literary history gave too much credit to T. E. Hulme, which made the dropping of Nietzsche the easier, and the readership could become the new criticism which often had only the shadow of our art to talk about—because English Departments go on and on in an unintelligence of our cultural situation and the task of it in art—

Bach's Belief

It's a conversation I would have with "you"
"Bach's belief"

George Butterick cites Charles Olson's response to a performance of Pierre Boulez's *Second Sonata* at Black Mountain College, 1951, played by David Tudor:[1]

I hadn't heard anything as interesting as that since I once heard Bach.[2]

This initial recognition and juxtaposition of musical minds—perhaps aided by David Tudor's knowledge of the score and of The Tributes to Bach in the final bars of the Sonata—continued for years—the early intensity of his acknowledgement appears in letters to Robert Creeley and in letters to Cid Corman, as editor of *Origin*.

In "Notes for a University at Venice, California" [1959?], Charles proposes one composer for the curriculum: "if Boulez not available, course solely Bach complete by reproduction, including David Tudor playing same on restored (accurately) harpischord, clavichord & organ as at Bach's date."[3]

In 1967, he phones me from London: "Boulez is in the air. Come on over." I couldn't, so sat listening to Boulez conducting Debussy's *La Mer*, long distance.

In 1968, "A Plan for a Curriculum for the Soul"[4] reads simply "Bach's belief," preceded by "Homer's art" and followed by "Novalis' 'subjects'"—across the page "jazz playing."

Shortly after Charles's death, January 10, 1970, Jack Clarke asked me to undertake Bach's belief, Jack Clarke, who died in 1992, whose beautiful book *From*

Feathers to Iron (1987) is itself a spiritual answer to the commotion of belief. He cites Blake:

> The Lungs, the Heart, the Liver, shrunk away far distant from Man
> And left a little slimy substance floating upon the tides. (*Jerusalem* 2: Plate 49,
> l.17–18)

and says himself that

> Religion gets *even* with the world, but does not complete it (Clarke 211),

that we must

> know with Homer, that home is not a location but a narrative activity (180),

and argues that

> Democracy, even our own, is still based upon the kingship paradigm, however reduced to Hamlet's nutshell. For Americans living after the 19th century, the burden of being "freed from self-obsession," Cioran's urgent imperative, falls to Whitehead's even more "urgent requisite": a secular Theory of God (163),

and posits, philosophically sure footed,

> 1.) Don't take from systems which don't have to do with your experience of otherness . . .
>
> 2.) If you want a text to be a door to the present you must posit the world of its construction . . .
>
> 3.) Only the heat of one's own discarded elements can produce the proper fire . . .
>
> 4.) Otherwise it can become an occasion for speculation or, worse, fundamentalist belief. (xv)[5]

(elucidated in John Thorpe's fine "Prologue" to Jack's book)

Olson, in an interview in Gloucester in 1966, is especially drawn to my attention by Jack Clarke:

> . . . the actual universe as a geography has turned around and is moving toward us, at the very moment that the species thinks it's going out into space. Actually, space is coming home to occupy us—in fact, to re-occupy the earth. . . .
> . . . but when the universe comes in, it declares its limit—which is the principle of creation, not the expansion. That it *defines* space, and also defines time. (*Muthol– ogos* I, 189, 191)

Jack Clarke, then, one of the finest minds among the companions of Olson's work, can be blunt about the project:

> What I'm trying to do is clear poetry of religion. Images bind the mind to the "Wheel of Religion" (*Jerusalem* 3:77,13) directionally moving "west to east, against the current / of Creation." If you have a burning desire to get past the "lyric block" [Olson], then you know you need, not the myth of America, but a way to restore narrative to image. You can't do this by grinding out poems from a broken Sampo [the Mill from the *Kalevala*].[6] Nor can you look to European epic, Virgil to Milton, because after Whitman it's not "ground" anymore, it's all "figure." (Clarke 68)

One would be "clear of religion" and, thus, freed into uncentered relations among things—which may be as big as a cosmos or as small as a pebble—as near and dear as the daily street or a lover who is one's self alive—the spirit of things— belief—our word for whatever that is is very old and comes down to us changed in the effort by a prefix-substitution and with a loss of a final syllable, meaning **to hold dear, to cherish, to trust in**[7]—implying an ethic of otherness—

soul[8]—that mysterious word, contracted by loss of syllables into a single sound and with which Christianity grabs at belief with a muscle-bound hand—originally meant **life itself, animate existence**—such quickness—subsequently made obsolete by crossdressing in immortality—its original sounds **saiwalas** "corresponding formally" to Greek αιολόσ, <u>fleeting</u>, <u>flitting</u> movement—of, say, earth, air, water, and fire—each of them <u>**lief**</u>. And what of that groundless, mere ornamentation— the "figure" to which Jack Clarke calls our attention?—to my mind becoming a terror—of human nature having collapsed into itself, maimed and vicious, whereas it would be a composer of the "good." I value Harold Bloom's *The American Religion* (1992) for its overview of American religious shenanigans, against "our secular origins," especially now that they are being exported with meritorious (look at the Latin) faith and meritricious ornament. They have a composition, not of the "good," but of "Pentecostals directly sent by the Holy Spirit, Catholic nuns and priests, assorted Fundamentalists, and followers of new and still obscure sects." Harold Bloom stops me dead in my tracks, as the saying goes, with this prophecy:

> We are on the verge of being governed by a nationally established religion, an ultimate parody of the American Religion sketched in this book. The Established Church of the South and Southwest, The Southern Baptist Convention, and the burgeoning, soon to be Established Church of the West, The Mormons, are only two components of a multiform alliance that will transform our nation by the year 2000,

under the leadership of a Republican Party that since 1979 has borne the barely secular version of the American Religion. The crusade against abortion will accomplish its aims, against the will of sixty percent of us, through the instrument of a Reagan-Bush Supreme Court, but that may be only the opening triumph of the parodistic American Religion's militancy in the concluding decade of the twentieth century. (270)

Mr. Bloom himself has a gnostic view of the world that, I think, allows him to see this danger clearly: "the emergence of the 'Post-Christian nation,'" wherein one may or may not come upon a parody of ancient, venerable belief in the good and happiness that we ourselves compose.

I return again and again to Geoffrey Hartman's thought that

> The secular is the sacred integrated, rather than degraded or displaced. (Beyond Formalism 22; original emphasis)

Wolfgang Giegerich offers the insight (always a kind of courage) that allows us to see the "figure" for what it has become:

> Christ was not only nailed down at the time of his crucifixion, but to be He who is nailed down to Himself, who is absolutely identified with Himself, indeed, to be the principle of pinpointedness and fixation is his very nature. . . .
> . . . no Pharaoh, no Dali Lama has his divinity as his personal property. On the contrary, he is, precisely because he is the incarnation of a divine person, de-emphasized as the empirical individual that he is and is instead reintegrated into the larger divine reality that he has to embody, and he is relativized [made relational] by its manifold embodiments in previous and future persons. By virtue of the dissemination of the incarnation into each of its many manifestations, his presence is essentially gentle, whereas the entire divinity of Christ is concentrated in the single historical person Jesus of Nazareth as the exclusive focus of History as such, which endows the Christian incarnation with a violent acuteness. Every possible "here" of a theophany or epiphany has once and for all been stuffed into the exclusive historical Jesus so that no actual here and now before or after Him can be the place of a full-fledged epiphany anymore. The "yonder" of that Jesus of Nazareth has swallowed up every possible "here and now." It has deprived Time of its life and soul and seized it. . . . Now there is only one single fulfilled moment (καιρόσ) in all of history, leaving the entire remainder of time essentially (psychologically) empty. ("The Rocket" 71)

And dangerous. The whole effort of human consciousness over millennia goes unthought in this emptiness, for consciousness of how old we are in time is psychologically replenishing.[9]

And the crucifix, as two intersecting coordinate axes, is the symbol of the zero point of Being and of the subordination of Being under a system of coordinates. Long before the number zero had been accepted in mathematics, Christianity had invented the zero as a metaphysical principle. And characteristically enough the mathematical recognition of zero as a number occurred during that age in which the actual realization of Christianity began, namely in the year 1629 (one year after Harvey had discovered the circulation of the blood) and again, only a few years later, by one of the great minds who decisively advanced the realization of Christianity: Descartes (1637). For Descartes provided modern man with the *fundamentum inconcussum*, the ego, that rock on which the modern period could build its house and from which it could unhinge the natural world (the world experienced mythically or imaginally).

Just as in mathematics the zero concept made it possible to break out of the realm of natural (positive) numbers and conquer the worlds of negative, irrational, imaginary and transcendent numbers (for which reason the zero has been termed mathematics' most momentous invention), so the metaphysical zero is the point at which, figuratively speaking, Uncle Sam breaks through the containment in natural (imaginal) reality and into positive reality "out there." (Giegerich 72)

That "unshaken, unshakeable fundament" is, however, oddly limited by Descartes, whose admirable, elegant thought actually parks the *mens* in a parking lot—as Frances Yates noted long ago[10]—out of his curious distrust of it—leaving the mind to us. This ego, excised from Descartes' distinguished labor—a process that he could not intellectually or emotionally leave as an open-ended process of *cogito*—becomes, yes, a rock, and best described as the human Will detached from the will of the cosmos and of othernesses (Whitehead's "prehensions"):[11] a closure into itself; in technology, the human Will that does not recognize itself; in modern Christianity, the self triumphant; the I *AM*, a backside of its own blessing. Thus, the misunderstanding of language and its process in sacred books; thus, the proliferation of contemporary prophets who do not recognize that they are egotistically (viciously) writing their own texts; and thus, our trip to the moon, reading "God's words" from "out there," where we left our "mystic rag" and our garbage. Space, as "out there," beyond, like God, rather than "moving toward us," "coming home to occupy us."

We are perforce inside the paradigms of cultural thought and tradition, now disguised as Christianity, though it is after it and barely clothed in its vocabulary. Mark C. Taylor's astonishing summary of these paradigms comes to mind repeatedly. God, self, history, and book,[12] a shift in meaning and experience in any one of them brings with it turbulence in all the others—a sandculture.

So what then is being sold and exported? I think of the old Puritan consternation: who should receive the wine and bread of communion? Not the sinners, for they could easily be marked and excluded. Ah, the successful who have received God's determining blessing, like a manifest destiny. The contemporary situation translates, repetitively, the one imagination of the order of things into another, which is far removed from the process of imagined meaning, something alive and living, like the soul—and settles for ownership, the individual mask of kingship that would be itself and nothing more. Its ultimate goal is outer space where it may lose itself (a closed meaning), only to reposition it in a heavenly enclosure. There, Star-Trekkers may run into Apollo—over and out. Jean-François Lyotard writes of the contemporary dilemma:

> The experience of the human subject—individual and collective—and the aura that surrounds this experience, are being dissolved into the calculation of profitability, the satisfaction of needs, self-affirmation through success. Even the virtually theological depth of the worker's condition, and of work, that marked the socialist and union movements for over a century, is becoming devalorized, as work becomes a control and manipulation of information. These observations are banal, but what merits attention is the disappearance of the temporal continuum through which the experience of generations used to be transmitted. (*The Inhuman* 105)

Here, the desperate—in the face of the cultural closure of the human effort to compose and disclose meaning—reaffirm their traditional God with His vengeance, which is actually theirs, explicated by the bozos among them. Out there. Out of time, which is otherwise *the life of space*,[13] and our timbrel. I may be intermittently sympathetic, but I feel their coldness and freeze in my tracks, for this God merely blesses the system in which we would, in those terms, impose meaning, undemocratic from His birthright in human thought. We are inside—in the stomach of—a dying paradigm. And the cultural punishment is afoot. Self, history and book unquestioned in this imagined permanence. Ah, absolute, from which we are not absolved. Robert Avens writes in his "Reflections on Wolfgang Giegerich's 'The Burial of the Soul in Technological Civilization'":

> Transcendence, according to Giegerich, should not be conceived literally and metaphysically, but as a quality within reality, as another "style" of reality. The manufactured God is an empirical absolute, an immanent transcendence, a sensibly given non-sensible. It is the technological world—artificial, unnatural—that transcends the natural world. (43–44)

We first experience Transcendence in the very nature of language and of musical notes. So, writes Lyotard in his Introduction to *The Inhuman*:

> And finally, since development is the very thing which takes away the hope of an alternative to the system from both analysis and practice, since the politics which

'we' have inherited from revolutionary modes of thought and actions now turns out to be redundant (whether we find this a cause for joy or a matter to be deplored), the question I am raising here is simply this: what else remains as "politics" except resistance to this inhuman? And what else is left to resist with but the debt which each soul has contracted with the miserable and admirable indetermination from which it was born and does not cease to be born?—which is to say, with the other inhuman?

This debt to childhood is one which we never pay off. But it is enough not to forget it in order to resist it and perhaps, not to be unjust. It is the task of writing, thinking, literature, arts, to venture to bear witness to it. (7)

Civilization is, as the man said, who lost part of it in the twentieth-century melee beyond his childhood, an individual task. *The book becomes books, the notes a generating structure. The restoration of a universal language* is not our destiny. This is not a matter for despair, but rather, for the energy of attention. Nor is it a matter for *nostalgia* in the face of the energy of attention.

Bach's <u>belief</u>, then, placed here within a sketch of the tension the thought draws up as from a well. Belief and the soul have for me (I wish to say "we") no universal language—certainly not that of the Christian ("we" are in a stockade in defense against the viciousness and poverty of its current, television resurgence) or of the so-informed metaphysical traditions. The course is, for me, poignant, from the beginning, the question of its stinging in body and mind even when studying the technical analyses of Bach's scores. Always a "matter" of form reopening, like footsteps. Bach's *belief* then, here in summary—that would be a long, meandering, helpless book.

Bach, for me, becomes a midpoint, midmost in the elegance of musical and religious thought, a beloved mind—of a "state of life," of a "gathering together," of a perusal (in series) of that which, it seems to me, binds men and women these days faster, as if it walked **so** in our streets. Bach is a holdfast in that moving structure I study in order to write and he stands alongside what my mind tries to keep and guard in, say, Hannah Arendt. Take, for example—"once again," I say to myself[14]—this passage from the Preface in the first edition of *The Origins of Totalitarianism,* Summer, 1950, midway in our time:

We can no longer afford to take that which was good in the past and simply call it our heritage, to discard the bad and simply think of it as a dead load which by itself time will bury in oblivion. The subterranean stream of Western history has finally come to the surface and usurped the dignity of our tradition. This is the reality in which we live. And this is why all efforts to escape from the grimness of the present into nostalgia for a still intact past, or into the anticipated oblivion of a better future, are vain. (ix)

The "usurped dignity of our tradition." We stand in this condition and often fall into that usurpation. A repetitious religious tradition can only promise a return to the same usurpation—against which it could not teach or act—was by its own totalitarianisms implicated in it—a horrible transcendence—beyond the food, shelter, clothing and health of its citizens—false, willy-nilly, into usurpation of meaning and a superstitious future.

If I listen to Bach outside this and traditionally as *Bach and the Dance of God*, I could do no better than to draw attention to Wilfrid Mellers's accomplished book of that title:

> Later Renaissance composers, believing more in the validity of human passion, were more concerned with its incarnation through melodic appeal, rhythmic vivacity, instrumental coloring and harmonic tension and relaxation. Early Baroque composers turned such humanly expressive elements into operatic "projection" and, as we have seen, it was partly in this tradition that Bach was trained. Yet, as we've also noted, the heart of his achievement was in combining this maximum awareness of "the pain of consciousness" with the maximum command of an abstract spiritual order—or, in musical terms, the highest density of harmonic tension with the most perfect extension of contrapuntal science. What happens in the music of his last years is not that the human core of his art evaporates but that, no longer "projected," it becomes one with the only science (mathematics) which is exact because it is founded on eternal verities. Pythagoras taught that there is a "mysterious connection between gods and numbers, on which the Science of Arithmacy is based." Pythagoras also called music "an Arithmetic, a science of true numbers," and believed that music was of all human activities closest to mathematical law. Only those tones which are numerically determined according to the harmonic series are music; other sounds are noise. Moreover the harmonic spectrum parallels the movements of astral bodies. Number proceeds from unity; things originate from number: so there can be unity without things, but never things without unity. In this sense the Pythagorean aphorism that "all is number" came to imply the Platonic doctrine of transcendent ideas, and was thus interpreted by the church fathers from Aquinas to Duns Scotus. In Bach's day Leibniz reinterpreted the notion, remarking in 1712 that "musica est exercitum arithmeticae occultum nescientis de numerare animi." Music is a hidden practice of the soul which deals in number without knowing it's so doing; in a confused perception the soul thus achieves that which, in clearer perceptions, it is unable to achieve. "If therefore the soul does not notice that it calculates, it yet senses the effect of its unconscious reckoning, be this as joy over harmony or oppression over discord." This goes to the heart of the matter. Bach's musical mathematics in his last works may be as exact as an exercise in dialectical logic of Leibniz or Spinoza, but it is "truer" in that its intellectual rigour encompasses the total range of human experience. Paradoxically, mathematical abstraction liberates us from the tryanny of fact. As Walter Kaufmann has put it: "In mathematics we experience a taste of freedom; the bondage of accident is broken; the soul is no longer the prisoner of the body; man is as a god." The Swiss mathematician-

philosopher Ferdinand Gonseth (quoted by Kaufmann) makes the same point in stating that "mathematics exists between two complementary poles: one the world of reality, called exterior, the other interior. These two worlds are transcendental, that is, beyond consciousness. They cannot be perceived 'in themselves' but only by the traces which they leave in the field of our consciousness." (258–59)

But "we" are now listening within the usurpation and decadence of that tradition, the dying paradigm. So, what are we listening to in the vast intelligence of Bach's art? I can only answer that I am listening to a *projection of a temporal process*, the life of space, the *meaning in music as the relation of the sounds to one another*. I follow in particular, note by note, made joyful by the multiplicity of voices, complex and seemingly always enlarging. I have in mind *The Pasacaglia and Fugue in C Minor*, c. 1717, 20 variations and the "thema fugatum." Towards the conclusion of the fugue, the momentum increases, heading for a climax in what is called a "neapolitan sixth chord," a complete break—in a flood of sound, "the liberating C major of the ending," "one of the greatest moments in all music." Something extended, expanded, awesome—and, to my ear, open-ended—an expansion of what we can reconstruct of what we knew.

[Jan] Chiapusso writes of Bach's "spiritual reality" (1) and of his remaining in an "Age of Faith" (2), that "he came into painful contact with the new movement of the Enlightenment" in Leipzig (2). His worldview is that of postmedieval Luther, including a "traditional supernaturalism" (2); he did not know Voltaire's work or Newton's "who died one year before Bach created the St. Matthew Passion" (2). In the work of the theological flood, the wavy commotions begin, however: Bach was educated to "the medieval view of himself as the center of the universe" (2), and he did not know the work of Copernicus and Kepler, thus the loss of the "geocentric doctrine" (2). It is true that Bach would write that art is "'only for the Glory of God'" (3). Still, he too would translate the notes into a temporal process true to his time, whether or not he knew Newton only by Zeitgeist.

David B. Greene in his challenging book *Temporal Processes in Beethoven's Music* writes:

> Bach's music is an aural image of Newtonian time. In the Newtonian world-view, the totality of material entities constitutes a universe in the sense that they all operate according to the same laws which exhaustively explain their behavior. . . . . . . the pattern of change is fixed and constant. (7)

And he continues:

> Hearing a performance of Bach's music chugging along to a conclusion that will feel inevitable is, then, like the process of gaining a perspective from which

change is experienced not as vicissitude or as the result of making a decision but as patterned movement. Although different performances of the same piece may project somewhat different patterns, each performance is a process in which there is change, but the change is ordered, and the principle of the order is fixed and unchanging. If the music leads to a perspective from which one recognizes unchanging order and if the contrast of present, past and future necessarily presupposes change, then this perspective stands outside the temporal process. The experience of listening to a Bach movement is the experience of moving through a temporal process to that which endures non-temporally. (10)

"Endurance in non-temporality": precisely that has slipped away, as a soul would in Homer's art. This amounts to a shift in the matter of the self, which is equally a change in form—and consequently in the form of our love of the world. I hear Bach as composition of structures—the notes as "generators of structure" (*Stocktakings* 11) in Boulez's phrase, the life of them more vivid than a cosmology of non-temporality. Bach's magnificence that leaves him standing midmost among us is found in this: that he does not "close an epoch," as the saying goes, that he does not simply look back as if continuing an extraordinary permanence; his element is generative thought.

Olson, apparently inspired by a performance in 1951 of Boulez's *Second Piano Sonata* (composed in 1948), thought to juxtapose these two minds for our study. In an essay Olson seems not to have known, published in the same year that he heard the *Sonata*, Boulez writes:

> At the time of Bach's arrival on the musical scene, tonality is already completely constituted; in Germany, Buxtehude, Pachelbel, Kuhnau are his direct precursors; in Italy, Corelli and above all Vivaldi. Bach adds nothing new to this tool, but he raises it to maximum efficiency. If he retains links with the Renaissance, it is through his taste for complex polyphony rather than through any element of morphology or syntax. He does not live, as Riemann tells us, "in an age of transition," unless one considers—as some are not shy of doing—harmonic functions in themselves as the true flowering of tonality. (This scarcely explains the counterpoint in Mozart and Beethoven; but one can simply describe their efforts as a destructive interruption, and resolve the discontinuity by putting it conveniently into parentheses.) It is precisely because Bach uses a morphology and syntax that are not transitional but firmly established—Rameau's theoretical works are their contemporary codification—that he can give all his attention to the possibilities implied thereby. In some ways we could regard the "48" with its preludes and fugues on the twelve semitones—and indeed Bach's works in general—as a certificate less of conquest than of expansion—one might almost say occupation, if it had not become such a dirty word. For, while the forms which Bach's predecessors used—prelude, fugue, chorale, recitative, air, etc.—display a specifically tonal kind of structuring (in particular the tonic-dominant, dominant-tonic, relations; modulations to rel-

ative and neighboring keys; shifts to the subdominant), Bach perfects and expands this structuring to the point where it can play a decisive part in the stabilizing of musical forms. (*Stocktakings* 6–7)

In the first place, my liking for what his work has contributed to musical architecture will be obvious. (A century of romanticism has distracted us from the problem, and even Debussy is not innocent—far from it!—of this lack of interest.) In Bach, in fact, one can regard the *canons* and *imitations* not simply as technical artifice but as generators of structure: the organ variations on the chorale "Von Himmel Hoch"—the so-called "Mizler Variations"—are the most striking example. The progressive increase in the complexity of the canonic writing, and in the number of real parts, the increasing difficulty of the canons themselves, the process of augmentation—that is the rhythmic progression—and finally the changing disposition of the canons within each variation and their arrangement in *stretto*: all this together defines the architecture of the chorale-variations. We can thus see the rigour and logic with which the variations are linked, thanks solely to the contrapuntal technique and super-imposed structure, whose schema it is possible to abstract.

I should like equally to draw attention to the chorale "Vor Deinem Thron tret' ich hiermit," which Bach dictated a few days before his death. Everybody remarks on its exceptional contrapuntal richness. What has perhaps not been clearly enough said is that the structure of the chorale melody generates the structure of the chorale itself. The chorale consists in effect of four sequences—developments which correspond to the four phrases of the melody. Notice that these four sequences respectively use as contrapuntal material only their own fragment of the figured chorale, and that we are therefore dealing here with a highly specialized developmental procedure, reinforced by the contrapuntal technique: a procedure which rejects all superfluous figures and makes use exclusively—through the multiple resources of counterpoint: *imitation, inversion, augmentation*—of the phrase it is developing; all automatism is excluded. We may sum up by saying that the 'theme' generates both the material of its development and its own architecture, and that the latter derives from the former.

I think I have defined, through these two chorales, what is the most vital thing for us to study in Bach, namely his formal technique, which unites contrapuntal technique and architecture in a positively *uterine* way. The form is essentially variable and comes back into question with each work. (Remember, in this connection, what has already been pointed out many times, that with Bach even fixed forms are presented under extremely varied aspects: for example, no two fugues have exactly the same plan.)

Finally I draw attention to a particularly striking feature of Bach, best described in François Florand's *Jean-Sébastien Bach*:

When it comes to constructing a development, Bach prefers a method which consists in developing the concert of voices without departing from the registers assigned to them at the start, maintaining them as if by force within

the same limits—scarcely more than an octave for each part—and directing
a process which comes entirely from the melodic flow itself, rather like a
river which seems to grow for no apparent reason, not through tributaries,
glaciers, or storms, but solely through the activity of mysterious underground
springs. This is something other than a simple aesthetic of repetition, in the
Oriental or Hindu sense. It is a process peculiar to Bach, which derives from
an internal build-up of energy, or emotional force, to the point where the
author and listener are saturated, and as if intoxicated.

Francois Florand refers again to a dispostion to musical intoxication in Bach: "There
is certainly no need [he adds] to see anything brutal or crude in this. But in the
end there comes a moment when, by dint of turning and returning his motif over
and over, the author's own head seems to turn. *Es schwindelt* . . . And this is the high
point of the work." He defines this musical "vertigo" as "a fermentation within
the polyphony itself." He concludes his analysis by reminding us that this "delir-
ium" of Bach's is "lucid, his intoxication conscious, his renunciations deliberate
and always controlled in the background of his creative awareness by a will and
intellect which never sleep for one second." (*Stocktakings* 11–13)

Perhaps David Tudor helped Charles to hear the Bach in the *Second Sonata*. Cer-
tainly, I needed assistance in hearing those notes, hovering and translated within
a work so "remarkably vehement" (240), as Dominique Jameux puts it. "Apart
from the second movement and the coda to the fourth, an eruptive violence
pervades most of the Sonata" (240). His chapter in *Pierre Boulez* (French, 1984;
English, 1991) on the *Second Sonata* is succinct and invaluable, especially if one is
concerned with Boulez or serialism, for this is his "first truly post-serial work"—
with all the intelligence of serialism transformed. For the purpose of our at-
tention to the presence of Bach, Jameux takes note of

the trill, which in this [first] movement intervenes like a nervous tic, and which
will later be seen as the pre-echo of a figure fundamental to the fourth movement;
. . . from the fourth bar onwards, a well-known cryptogram appears—an anagram
of the letters B A C H, also to be found in the coda to the fourth movement. It
appears at the same time as the first entry of the aforementioned trill. (243)

Bach's presence is continuous after him, so to speak, announcing something—
directional—to one composer after another within their composing means—
perhaps, his genius in variation lets him so stand there—within our culture,
even—as if he were composing his <u>belief</u> again, a complexity of relation to the
world that is never still. Jameux's attention to Boulez's skill in variation is given
in terms that draw my mind to this work—to something like what I think drew
Olson:

With Boulez, variation is not merely a matter of skilled procedures used to modify the appearance of initial material; it is much more an invitation to exploration, adventure and discovery—in other words, to creation. This movement [the second] is a quest for the unknown, an initiatory process, a mystical—even erotic—experience. (250)

And the fourth movement is astonishing—"a progressive and relentless increase in both dynamics and speed" (Jameux 255). The score says "pulverize the sound" (255). I am persuaded that Jameux articulates, in his remarks about the final page of this sonata, so nearly something like David Tudor played in 1951, and Olson heard, that I place them here to be remembered as if we were there—then, now:

Thus, a classical form is seized by an almost expressionistic frenzy, and with a violence that forces submission. The composer here asks for the utmost force, without nuance—demanding a degree of commitment from performer and audience alike, which stretches their respective capacities to the very limit.

At the indication *sans élargir* the discourse breaks off abruptly, and the Coda begins. This final page of total calm serves not only as Coda to the movement but to the Sonata as a whole. The tempo moves from slow to very slow, with minor fluctuations; the dynamic stays between *mezzo-piano* and *pianissimo*, with only the briefest increase to *mezzo-forte*. Two structures are superimposed: the first is formed from an echo of the first four cells from the Fugue, again in a linear succession (bar 1), the second from the omnipresent B A C H figure (which returns no less than six times on this page, up to and including the final cadence) that punctuates the polyphonic apotheosis represented by this Sonata and by serial thinking in general.

It seems relatively insignificant that the four rhythmic motifs announced here constitute a series of twelve notes, since it has no connection with the other series of the Sonata—although the B A C H motif can be traced to the chromatic fragments that form part of each of the series from the second movement. In this encounter between structure and coded narrative we find something akin to the mysterious combination of means that enabled Berg—in his Concerto "To the memory of an angel"—to introduce the component notes of Bach's chorale "Es ist genug" alongside the original series of his own work. It would be impossible to imagine a more eloquent conclusion. (255)

Those who study this Curriculum of the Soul could well start there—to find Bach's <u>belief</u>.

Incommensurability of means remains between the thought in music and the thought in words, even with Bach's sublime and affective interweaving of religion and sacred texts in mind—the *Passions*, the *Mass in B minor*, the *Magnificat*, and something like 200 church cantatas, but, even so, I am confronted by what I take to be the wordless belief of the music I most love: the Pasacaglia (BWV582);[15] the Canonic Variations on "Von Himmel hoch, da komm ich hier" (BWV767); the *Art of the Fugue*, Choral "Vor Deinen Thron Tret ich" (BWV668)—unattended by symbolic assurance. Nor am I unmindful of the importance of euphony in our use of words (having near to hand W. B. Stanford's brilliant, recorded reconstruction of the sound of ancient Greek, "one of the most musical languages ever spoken").[16] And, in recent years, I've turned to Mallarmé to study the implications of music for poetry—what he thought he'd taken back by way of syntactical freedom, therewith, to find Boulez on "the formal implications of poetry and music": "Let us claim for music the right to parentheses and italics . . . , a concept of discontinuous time," a new syntax.

I've already noted that Olson's interests in Boulez can best be traced in his letters. George Butterick, that most valuable man to any attempt to enter upon this curriculum of the soul, gives us the core instances from the letters in his notations for the *Muthologos* collection:

> "I thought I'd flip. I hadn't heard anything as interesting as that since I once heard Bach. The only other piece of music I've heard in my life, practically, was this goddamned Tudor playing the Second Sonata of Boulez" (quoted in Alasdair Clayre, "The Rise and Fall of Black Mountain College," *The Listener*, 27 March 1969, p. 412). Olson had written to Creeley, 4 October 1951: " . . . there is the opposite wish (for me, anyway) there, to remind music of its percussive force (gratuitous, after hearing Boulez 2nd Sonata—what a piece; try to run into this guy, somehow, there, Paris. Or ask him down to visit you: will try to get his address. Jesus: he's our boy. Surely." See also Olson's letter to Cid Corman, 29 August 1953, concerning Boulez (*Letters for Origin*, p. 126): " . . . the composer (to whom I shall inscribe the poem 'Cold Hell'—to his Deuxième Sonate—when—as it wasn't the past time—an inscription is possible). For Boulez is one of the singular men alive. And any thing he says is worth listening to . . . Though all his writing known to me is on composition, yet even that is instructive to the other arts, including writing. And he is so aware of form problems, that he could as well do you, direct, from the base of music, a witty, sharp piece on 'the Creative' as of now."
> In a letter to Donald Sutherland, 21 January 1968, Olson explains his interest in Boulez: "why . . . at an earlier point, I so admired Pierre Boulez's 2nd Sonata was the formalization of the use of chance by a *series* of series into which the accidence was spilled, and *then* used . . . " (217; original ellipses and emphasis)

Just here, my meandering *would* turn toward *Alea*, that cosmos "we" are working, that temporality that art is working.

To Boulez on Alea:

"Towards this supreme conjunction with probability"[1] one certainly cannot go with absolute self-confidence. Here I shall certainly not fail to be accused once again of "dehumanization" . . . the high-sounding ineptitudes one hears on this subject are inexhaustibly monotonous: but they all boil down to a very primitive conception of what we mean by "human." A lazy nostalgia, a taste for (extremely patchy) patchwork, sometimes known as synthesis: this is what the forced "feeling" of these vigilant critics amounts to. I can answer, at the most elementary level, that, far from rejecting or doing away with the performer, I am plugging him back into the creative circuit, after he has for years been told to play the text as "objectively" as possible. What am I saying? That I am actually ending up glorifying the performer! And not some terrifying precise robot-performer, but one who is interested and free in his choices. For the benefit of those who are disturbed by this dynamite at the heart of the work of art, this non-"composing" chance; who argue that human poetics and extra-human chance are sworn enemies, and that their marriage could never yield a positive result, I offer this passage from *Igitur*: "In short where chance is involved in an action, chance always fulfils its own Idea, whether in affirming or denying itself. In the face of its existence, negation and affirmation alike fail. It contains the Absurd—implies it, but latently, while preventing its existence: which permits the Infinite to exist."[2]

Perhaps there is a certain innocence—as well as insolence—in broaching this doubtful topic, but is that not the only way to *define the Infinite?* Such must be the unconfessed aspiration of anyone who rejects simple hedonism and a limited craftsmanship, in a creative world overburdened with humble trickery. Any dilettante would be shattered by the responsibility he evades through such strategems, any worker—horrible[3]—would be destroyed by the inanity, the emptiness of his labours. And in the end, would it not be the one way of killing the Artist?

[1.] "Vers cette conjonction suprême avec la probabilité"; a quotation from Mallarmé's poem "Un coup de des jamais n'abolira le hasard." [SW]

[2.] Mallarmé, OEuvres complètes, p. 441. [SW]

[3.] "tout travailleur—horrible": cf. Rimbaud's letter to Paul Demeny of 15 May 1871: "Que [le Poète] crève dans son bondissement par les choses inouïes et innommables: viendront d'autres horribles travailleurs" (*Oeuvres de Rimbaud*, ed. S. Bernard [2nd edn., Paris, 1960]), 344–50. [SW]

(*Stocktakings* 37–38)

To Olson's 1952 poem "A Toss, for John Cage," in which his annoyance is premonitory of the "distance" that would develop between Cage and Boulez on the issue of chance:

is there yet recorded that other thing which is a duration,
hath frequency, overtone, attack, is serial—
have you got that in, have you caught it,
that which I catch
in your hm?

(*Collected Poems* 272)

To Michel Serres's discussion of the "logic of the note, of any discrete note. From which Leibniz derived the idea that music was indeed the language closest to the universal language, or to the *mathesis universalis*" (*Hermes* 46). And though I have not been able to verify this in Bach's library, Serres tells us that "at Johann Sebastian Bach's death, Leibniz's *De Arte Combinatoria* was discovered at the composer's bedside (which, in return, permits us to read several fugues)" (*Hermes* 46).

To the issue that we are rereading Leibniz, as in Gilles Deleuze's startling book, *The Fold: Leibniz and the Baroque* (French, 1988; English, 1993):

> The question always entails living in the world, but Stockhausen's musical habitat or Dubuffet's plastic habitat do not allow the difference of inside and outside, or public and private, to survive. They identify variation and trajectory, and overtake monadology with a "nomadology." Music has stayed at home; what has changed now is the organization of the home and its nature. We are all still Leibnizian, although accords no longer convey our world or our text. We are discovering new ways of folding, akin to new developments, but we all remain Leibnizian because what always matters is folding, unfolding, refolding. (137)

Try Stockhausen's *Klavierstüke*.

To Ian Hacking on Alea:

> Peirce was the first philosopher completely to internalize the way in which chance had been tamed in the course of the nineteenth century. It is fitting that the further reaches of his metaphysics could also be summed up in my title, 'the taming of chance'. But where my title was metaphorical, in a Peircian summation it would be literal. For Peirce's history of the universe, in which blind Chance stabilizes into approximate Law, is nothing other than the taming of chance.
>
> Is Reason comforted then, does that giantess, metaphysical chance, no longer threaten or offer untold delights? Do we live in a world made safe by statistical laws, the laws of averages writ small upon the tiniest particles of matter? Of course not. Peirce was fond of trios, which he called Firsts, Seconds, and Thirds. "Chance is First, Law is Second, the tendency to take habits is Third." That did not mean that chance is annulled by statistical law, or that the successive throws of the dice engender a world in which we can resume or reassume Hume's comfortable habits. What was First is always so. Even when the dice are cast in circumstances of eternity, as when we contemplate the constellations of the cosmos, or cast in circumstances of complete and personal particularity, as when we seal our own fate, chance pours in at every avenue of sense. We cannot suppose that Peirce saw the 1897 copy of *Cosmopolis* containing the poem by Mallarmé, three years his junior. But he was at one with the thought, "A throw of the dice never will annul chance." (*The Taming of Chance* 215)

To the moments, again and again, in the *modern project* to find a new language
and syntax for relations among things, which slip like a soul into the vastness
of meaning, the chance and *nomadism* of that condition midmost—in, say, Cecil
Taylor:

> Playing Bach, for instance, when I was eight or nine, it became clear that each note
> was a continent, a world in itself, and it deserved to be treated as that;

or Olson's translational lines:

> I believe in God
> as fully physical
> thus the Outer Predmost
> of the World on which we 'hang'
> as though it were wood and our bodies are
> hanging on it
>
>   (*Maximus* 381)

But I'll simply read these lines from *Maximus* III over again

> pre-Testament & Muslim Arabian pre-Phoenician
> holy Idrïs view of lowest Trismegistus
> take anything but one thing only out of
> coffee human being or visit talk or work
> one element of all a low tide night or day
> teaches me is Enoch's view here
> for Fitz Hugh Lane's clumsiness of
> foreground in so many paintings I
> have cut off at my loss & now
> this night regain the virtue of
> in loneliness & in such pain I <u>can't</u>
> lift the bottom of the alemb the gold-
> making juices lie in sounding in the
> striking of the surf & waves while
> off-shore out the Harbor for the 1st
> of all the nights of life I've lived upon,
> around this Harbor I hear also
> even in the fair & clear near round
> & full moon August night the
> Groaner <u>and</u> the Whistling Buoy in their
> soft pelting of the land I love
>   as though I were my love & master Bach
> and say in hymn & prayer
> himself

God festen Berg or Earth Is Shown
Beneath Her Nails tonight

(*Maximus* 594–95)

for now
Robin Blaser

I think therefore I am—Descartes
I am therefore I think—Zukofsky
I walk therefore I am—Deleuze
the poem of it

1995

Love Will Eat the Empire

A Commentary on the Essays of Robin Blaser

MIRIAM NICHOLS

A large collection of essays invites the reader to wander between different points of interest, stopping at favorites, perhaps, or looking up comments on certain themes or writers. Like a gallery, a "collected" offers the pleasures of repetition and difference: same subject, different treatments; different subjects, same author. This commentary is intended as a guided tour. But before beginning my commentary, I want to point out a formal feature of the essays taken as a whole. Blaser typically works in fugal fashion. In the early essays, he introduces key "subjects,"[1] which he then elaborates in the later works, just as the subject of a Bach fugue is explicated in a number of voices and keys, or a Schönbergian tone row through inversion or retrograde manipulation. In "The Fire," for instance, the Memory Theater first appears as a distinguishing image of Blaser's project, but its importance really only begins to show retrospectively, through elaborations in the later pieces. In this process of unfolding, the poet is as much a follower of the poem as is the reader. The real trick of reading Blaser is to take the essays as traversals of a field of attention, oriented to one another as complex acts of thought and memory rather than progressive arguments. This is poet's prose: it shows a mind thinking and a subject unfurling rather than an idea argued.

POETICS

"The Fire" is Blaser's first full statement of poetics. Published first in *Pacific Nation* 2 (1967), the essay was reprinted in *Caterpillar* 12 (1970) and in *The Poetics*

---

1. In a fugue, the "subject" consists of a short melody, usually three or four bars long, repeated and counterpointed in different voices (soprano, alto, tenor, bass) and keys throughout the piece.

of the New American Poetry (1 9 7 3). This foundational piece of Blaser's oeuvre is deceptively brief and simple; in fact, it is a major declaration of poetic independence as well as a tightly compressed manifesto on issues of chronic concern: the significance and function of poetry, the public role of the poet, and the puzzlements of genre post-the-modern. "I am thirty years old before I begin even tentatively to accept the title of poet," Blaser writes.

> In San Francisco, I was tied to two other poets, Jack Spicer and Robert Duncan, who, it was my superstition, wrote my poems for me. When that notion became sentimental, I dropped it and became another poet. I have worked since 1 9 5 5 to find a line which will hold what I see and hear, and which will tie a reader to the poems, not to me. This fascination precedes my great debt to Charles Olson. (9)

This is a move-over statement, although Blaser leaves it to the reader to extrapolate his differences from Spicer and Olson, and he says nothing here of the quarrel with Robert Duncan that occasioned "The Fire." I want to stop over this quarrel for a moment, though the story has been told before,[2] because it brings out Blaser's distinctiveness and opens up the larger issues of his project in poetry. In 1 9 6 5 Blaser had published translations of Gérard de Nerval's *Les Chimères*. Duncan responded critically, to the point of producing his own translations as a corrective to Blaser's. The resulting argument, made bitter for Blaser by former closeness and by Duncan's status as the senior poet, is partly recorded in a special issue of *Poetry/Audit* (1 9 6 7), where Duncan published his Nerval and reproduced letters that passed between him and Blaser about the poems. Duncan's main objection is that Blaser ruined the symbolic structure of Nerval's poems by omitting the occult because he, Blaser, could not bring those elements of Nerval over into his own experience of the world. Duncan argues that "Blaser as an artist aims at signature or style" (49), while he, a self-described derivative poet, seeks participation in the virtual community of poets, living and dead. In the letters, he challenges Blaser to articulate a position:

> "I have been inarticulate in joining you in that 'tradition,'" you write. Of course. For to articulate at all is to bring into action all the definitions of differences, one from the other; to articulate the terms of a poetic theory is to raise a challenge in Poetry. Had you offered an explicit poetics, I would not have had to project from the implicit poetics of your work so entirely. The maturity of an art demands an awareness in terms of theory as well as practice. (*Poetry/Audit* 6 1)

Blaser responded to this foray by writing an essay in which the personalism to which Duncan had objected ("signature or style") appears as one pole of a

---

2. See my entry on Blaser in *The Dictionary of Literary Biography* (6 3).

personal-cosmic pair. The story of Orpheus that Blaser claims as his central metaphor in "The Fire" holds an image of the decentered self in the torn and scattered body of the singer. Out of that decentering—out of the loss of naive, prereflexive consciousness—the self emerges as an other. The personal-cosmic pair that kicks off "The Fire" and structures the essay in both form and content returns many times in the public-private, inside-outside, self-other pairings of later essays. These pairs are not identical to the binaries so handily deconstructed by poststructuralists and again by postcolonial proponents of hybridity. What polarity means in the context of Blaser's essays and poems is a Möbius-like relationship between the perceiving self and the world. The "flowing boundary" ("Image-Nation 9," *Holy Forest*), as Blaser calls it, is a twisting of inside and outside into porous, mobile forms. Here is one answer to Duncan: the personal is never *merely* so.

Another answer can be found in Blaser's conception of the communal as an array of particularized persons and events that cannot be represented through archetypes. If the communal seems to be missing at first in the "polar logic"[3] of "The Fire," it is missing as that which is to be reimagined rather than assumed. The emergence of social heterogeneity as an unignorable fact of the postmodern condition meant to Blaser that poets who take as their prime task the saying of a common world have to account for difference. Here is the larger issue of the quarrel with Duncan. In Duncan's writings, historical life incarnates an evolving language of archetypes. To take a well-known example, the poem "Uprising," about the Vietnam War, presents a political event as an instantiation of mythic evil: President Richard Nixon, in perpetuating the misery of war, manifests certain aspects of Satan. Myth finds its actuality in history and history its meaning in the evolution of myth. Like a DNA code, cultural archetypes evolve through repeated embodiment. Social heterogeneity is epiphenomenal in relation to this more primary continuity of human cultures. In contrast, Olson makes history come first and myth emerge from the minutiae of actual, historical events, the little "'istorins'" that may achieve projective size or not. The shape of the human universe is to be arrived at inductively rather than deduced from a mythical past: this is open form. Blaser is closer to Olson on this point, but in "The Fire," he chooses memory over history as a way to reconceive the common. A foundational image for Blaser's poetics, the term "Memory Theater" comes from Frances Yates's account of a classical and Renaissance memnonic device in her *Art of Memory*. The theater was an imaginary "box

---

3. The phrase "'polar logic' of experience" comes from "The Practice of Outside" (*Collected Books* 277) where Blaser uses it to describe Spicer's poetics, but the same logic is everywhere evident in his own practice.

with tiers, where the initiate would take the place of the stage and look out on the tiers, which in an ordinary theater would hold the audience—here there are images upon images, so that a man could hold the whole world in view" ("The Fire" 9–10). Memory so constructed is a very special view of history, a lowercase version of both history and myth, in fact, that insists on the singularity of the poet's voice rather than its allegorical or archetypal potential. The Nerval episode, then, was more than a spat. It was symptomatic of a disagreement over the determining power of tradition and a consequent disagreement over the nature of the common. If the past is formally authoritative, the future may be largely determined. However, if the past can be treated as selectively citable as Walter Benjamin had proposed,[4] then chance comes into play and the future opens to possibilities beyond those of the dominant cultural paradigms.

In "Particles" (1969), Blaser restates this argument for particularity in political terms. Most arts that claim political significance, unless they are anarchist, turn on the construction of collective subjects, whether the terms of definition be nation, class, race, gender, sex, or some other political signifier. Through ideology critique, a politicized art can expose as interested social construction whatever the dominant powers (also definable through class, race, gender, etc.) seek to pass off as "reality" or "necessity," and it can insist on the potential of the collective to be otherwise. This, to my understanding, is the most common meaning of public art: it is an art that exposes social injustice. But while Blaser acknowledges the fundamental importance of this task, he follows Hannah Arendt in distinguishing between the social and political faces of public life.[5]

4. On Walter Benjamin's view of history, I have in mind this passage from Hannah Arendt's introduction to Benjamin's *Illuminations*. The passage comes from a section of her essay subtitled "The Pearl Diver," and the image is precise to the notion of diving into the past for what treasure one can find. Arendt writes:

Insofar as the past has been transmitted as tradition, it possesses authority; insofar as authority presents itself historically, it becomes tradition. Walter Benjamin knew that the break in tradition and the loss of authority which occurred in his lifetime were irreparable, and he concluded that he had to discover new ways of dealing with the past. In this he became a master when he discovered that the transmissibility of the past had been replaced by its citability and that in place of its authority there had arisen a strange power to settle down, piecemeal, in the present and to deprive it of "peace of mind," the mindless peace of complacency. (38)

5. Arendt's supporters, as well as her critics, stumble over this distinction between the social and political. For a small sampling of such responses, see the transcript of the 1972 conference at York University held in Arendt's honor. The transcript is included in a collection of essays on Arendt, titled *Hannah Arendt: The Recovery of the Public World*, edited by Melvyn A. Hill (301–99). For a more sympathetic reworking of the social-political distinction, see Seyla Benhabib, *The Reluctant Modernism of Hannah Arendt*. I have discussed this issue in relation to Blaser's use of Arendt at greater length in my essay "Reading Robin Blaser" in *Even on Sunday*.

In Arendt's political writings, the social pertains to distributive justice, whereas the political has to do with creative acts of public self-fashioning. For Blaser, the political aspect of public life as Arendt defines it is a point of intersection between politics and the arts:

> Now, it is objected that the particularity of modern poetry, its concern with deeds, thoughts, place, make it private and irrelevant. This is not so much ignorance as it is disrespect for particularity. Which is to say that men share not their place, their time, and those invisible activities called emotions,—to which poets give permanence—, but only generality. That poem is about love, the man says. And it is forgotten that love does not exist, even in thought, without its particularity. I love one, and with the peculiar virtue words have of attaching sound to the name I give away, each man can grasp that love. ("Particles" 22)

From a certain perspective, poetic disclosure of the particular such as Blaser describes it here does exactly what politicized art is usually expected to do: it exposes what ideology hides. But Blaser goes about this task by dissolving collective identities back into their "particles" rather than turning them into political signifiers. The main thought is that collective social naming represses a more profound complexity of personal thought and feeling that it is the poet's special province to reveal. The democratic community—and radical, participatory democracy is the regulating concept of "Particles"—is the political form that best corresponds to the heterogeneity of its constituents. Hence a community of "ones" who share their differences rather than a collective identity.

In proposing this community of "particles," Blaser implies a shift in the social function of the poet from sayer of the tribe to practitioner of an "outside," where "outside" means the *plentitude* of history—the uncountable number of stories in excess of the few paradigms that count for real. But there is a compromise here: what Blaser gains in open futurity has to be paid for in loss of scale. Poets may disclose this other world of countermemory outside the dominant one but *only* in the singular. Whatever exemplary force the poet's tropes may have will accrue in retrospect, through the affective power of the work to draw a community of readers into the poems and, from there, to a world of mutual concerns. When it is the manifold world that is to be held in common, rather than a set of archetypes or exemplary perspectives, poets may solicit public response and challenge official stories, but they cannot represent others, and the risk is obscurity. Like the ghosts of the ancient underworld, the voices in the language must vie for the blood of the living if they are to speak beyond their moment. They must be remembered into the present.

In "The Stadium of the Mirror," Blaser extends the question of public form to aesthetic and psychological terms rather than explicitly political ones, but this essay is apposite to "Particles" in the idea that "the thought of totals [is] the original totalitarianism" ("Stadium" 34). The essay opens with the lovely statement that "form is alive, not a completion of the heart or mind," and goes on to reprise the argument for particularity over the archetypal:

> The movement back of the great poets is not to a tradition—a golden time or wisdom behind us that places thought in the past and kills it—but it is toward a reopening of words—towards the violence and dynamism of Language—the work of it is in Pound's return to Homer, Egypt, Na-Khi and in Olson's ultimate return to Pleistocene,—his curriculum. A beginning again with everything. This reopening of words lets us see their solidifications—the crystals FORMing in the work—(a crust, akin to *cruor*—blood, *Kryos*—icy-cold, a coagulation that is the "external expression of a definite internal structure." (31)

The image of "crystals FORMing" through a process of coagulation shows Blaser's kinship with Olson and Whitehead on formal matters. In *Process and Reality*, Whitehead's aim had been to explain novelty in the universe. He does this by supposing a process of selection and recombination through which entities form themselves by taking in, or not, components of their environment, much as atoms recombine to create new material forms. In Whitehead's terms, every "actual entity"[6] is a datum for every other, to be positively or negatively selected. Adapted as a metaphor of self-making or poem-making, the "philosophy of organism" positions creative agency alongside chance and circumstance in the ongoing "creative advance" of the cosmos (Whitehead's terms): selection and recombination become the method and means by which a self or a poem comes to presence.

In "The Stadium of the Mirror," this account of form as recombination works alongside Blaser's reading of poststructuralist theory as it had begun to emerge in the 1970s. The title of the essay comes from Jacques Lacan's *le stade du miroir*, "translated for the metaphor" Blaser says. In Lacan's *Écrits*, the mirror stage is that point of psychic development when the child mistakes the unity of its specular image for psychic wholeness. Analogously, the mirror stage of poetry takes poetic speech for unmediated expression, and a good part of Blaser's effort in this essay goes to shatter that illusion. Reflexivity, then, is an important step in the argument, and Blaser cites Lacan, Merleau-Ponty, and Foucault as supports

---

6. For a useful glossary of Whitehead's terms, see Donald Sherburne's *A Key to Whitehead's Process and Reality* (205–48). An "actual entity" is not a thing but a process. Sherburne explains:

> Like the atoms of Democritus they are microcosmic entities, aggregates of which, termed *societies* or *nexus*, form the macrocosmic entities of our everyday experience—trees, houses, people. But whereas the atoms of Democritus are inert, imperishable, material stuff, Whitehead's actual entities are vital, transient "drops of experience, complex and interdependent." (205)

for a self-conscious, "operational language" for poetry (36). But it is Blaser's difference from these theorists that is more remarkable than his agreement with the broad lines of their thought. In a move that would set him at odds with many who turned to language in the 1970s and 1980s, Blaser acknowledges the derivative nature of conscious experience, but then refocuses on it rather than the mediating systems that shape it. "Poetry always has to do with consciousness" (29), he says. Lacan, Foucault, and even Merleau-Ponty take the various determinants of perception as their objects of investigation—the unconscious, the "discursive formations" that structure an epoch, or the nature of perception. In contrast, Blaser writes reflexivity as *affect*, and this brings him back to polarity. Language experienced as consciousness is polar to language understood as formal system. The crucial distinction is between what must be undergone and what can be known—between experience and knowledge. To delegitimize the former in the name of the latter is to make a category mistake.

The significance of Blaser's affective rendering of reflexivity is that the lyric "I"—the authorial voice—does not die as it did so famously for poststructuralists, nor does it get stuck in naive self-expression or "mirror stage" speech. Rather it is disjunctive in relation to its mediating ground, a recombinant that does not reduce to the sum of its social and linguistic components. "[I]magination," Blaser writes in "The Fire," "is more a power to take in and hold than it is a power of making-up" (7), a power, then, of remembering. Twisting into another version of the Memory Theater, the stadium of the mirror holds as much of otherness as the poet can see and bear. Hence the welter of disjunctive, polarized pairs: language and silence (26), the visible and the invisible (28), absence and presence (29), the body and the mind (29), the known and the unknown (30), the thought and the unthought (35), and language and experience (36). These pairs make explicit the polar logic nascent in "The Fire" and reiterate the creative play of the Memory Theater. If in "Particles" Blaser positions the self as one among others, in "Stadium" he places the others inside the self.

This thought of others, in its most radical form, spills into Blaser's long investigation of the sacred as both a limit concept and a significant dimension of experience: this is the capitalized Other of "The Stadium of the Mirror." The Other relativizes historical worlds—that is really its formal function in that work, where it hinders the "thought of totals" (34)—but it also opens onto the unknown and unthought as inescapable Others of experience. When "Stadium" was written, this kind of language positioned Blaser contrarily in relation to other discourses afoot. In its suspicion of consciousness, Continental theory was oddly bedfellowed with scientific and technological empiricism, which had already delegitimized experience by rendering the bare senses obsolete as organs of knowing.[7] In "Poetry and Positivisms," Blaser addresses contemporary skepticism as it implies a dismissal of poetry and the discourses of the sacred. This is a long essay, dense with quotations from a formidable chorus of voices that Blaser has assembled in defense of poetry—Blake, Rilke, Mallarmé, René Girard, Susan Handelman, and Herbert Schneidau, to name a few. His argument hinges on the claim that skepticism is a form of positivism and as such a superstition. From Herbert Schneidau's *Sacred Discontent*:

> "Positivism is discourse containing an implicit assumption that we have an easily accessible standard of 'external reality' against which to measure any of our utterances. Usually it tends to assume, also, that only the thinking of the most recent epoch (variously defined) has been usefully guided by the application of this standard, and that all previous discourse is tainted with superstition." ("Positivisms" 61)

In the name of reality, positivism discredits the discourses of affect. But as Blaser then asks, where is this naked reality?

Written at the end of the 1980s, "Poetry and Positivisms" includes deconstruction in the critique of positivism for its refusal of experience. Blaser handles the epistemological challenge in several ways. First, through Wlad Godzich, he distinguishes between discourses that "constitute forms of actual social interaction and practice" and language as "a construct of philosophers and linguists" ("Positivisms" 42)—between a mode of language use and an account of how being is produced in language. Second, he draws on Susan Handelman's discussion of Greek versus Hebraic epistemologies to claim the Hebraic for poetry. In the passage Blaser cites, Handelman says that *davar* means both "thing" and "word" in Hebrew:

> [T]he name, indeed, is the real referent of the thing, its essential character—not the reverse, as in Greek thought. One does not pass beyond the name as an arbitrary sign towards a non verbal vision of the thing, but *rather from the thing to the word, which*

---

7. See Giorgio Agamben's review of the history of experience in *Infancy and History: Essays on the Destruction of Experience* (1993). Agamben opens this collection with the statement that "the question of experience can be approached nowadays only with an acknowledgement that it is no longer accessible to us" (13). In chapter 2, he begins by saying that "the expropriation of experience was implicit in the founding project of modern science" (17). Agamben also notes that philosophers underwrote this event:

> The distinction between logical truth and truths of sufficient reason (which Leibniz formulates thus: "When we expect the sun to rise tomorrow we are acting as empiricists because it has always been so until today. The astronomer alone can judge with sufficient reason") subsequently sanctions this condemnation [of experience]. (17)

creates, characterizes, and sustains it. Hence, *davar* is not simply thing but also *action, efficacious act, event, matter, process.* ("Positivisms" 43; Handelman's emphasis)

Handelman here claims a constructivist epistemology for the Hebraic that is congenial to Blaser's sense of form as continually emerging out of an indefinite sensuous and historical plentitude.

Blaser's argument against positivism is thus twofold. The Handelman section can be taken to mean that no sort of knowledge actually meets the demand for certainty implied in skeptical philosophy. A citation from Jean-François Lyotard's *Postmodern Condition* underlines the point that "'science and industry are no more free of the suspicion which concerns reality than are art and writing'" ("Positivisms" 46). At base, this is an old quarrel between poetry and philosophy, with the poets coming down for the rhetoricity of the idea as opposed to its fixing in metaphysical concepts. The second facet of Blaser's argument addresses the relationship between poetry and knowledge, elaborating on "The Stadium of the Mirror." "Our poetic context," Blaser says, "involves relation to an unknown, not a knowledge or method of it" (54). This important comment positions poetry as *relation-to* rather than *knowledge-about*. In a passage linking Hegel's view of language as abstractable signage and "the Marxist attitude toward the literary text as ideology or propaganda—language as a system of ideas with which to push the 'real' around" (58), Blaser argues "the poetic point of view, [that] this is a negation of language in the particular" (59). Poetic language is "'relation, an activity, both intellectual and emotional'":

> The terms are not necessarily religious, but, rather, belief, disbelief, and unbelief to be gauged by the sense, which Olson pointed out long ago, that all method is belief. Silence, the Word and the Sacred, then, in one's own experience, while noting that one's own experience is always a reduction, a corner of a very large room. (48)

The two components of the argument cross in this little passage: (1) the special purview of poetic discourse is not knowledge but affect ("an activity, both intellectual and emotional"); and (2) the knowledge claimed by other discourses is also situated, and their methods constitute belief ("all method is belief"). But while Blaser takes the poet's part against that of the philosopher, he also urges a polylogical relationship among the various disciplines. As he says in the above passage, "one's own experience is always a reduction." There is no going back to the naive equating of experience with knowledge. Better, then, a fruitful tension between poetic affection and philosophical truth, poetic particularity and practical politics, perceptual experience and empirical experiment—better an ongoing argument.

The whole push of "The Recovery of the Public World" (1993) is to encourage fruitful tensions between the discourses and to argue a "multi-dimensional and multi-logical" worldview. The two big intellectual challenges to poetry since the 1950s have come from politics and philosophy. "Particles" lays out the basis of Blaser's response to the reproach that a poetry of "particles" is politically irrelevant; "Poetry and Positivism" responds to the epistemological argument against perception common in the deconstructive decades. These two lines of response come together in "The Recovery of the Public World." Here Blaser says that realpolitik "passes in the currency of accommodations and powers," requiring pragmatic give-and-take. It does not translate easily into poetic vision, as poetry does not translate well into institutional policy. The core of the political argument in "Recovery" is thus close to that of "Particles," although the later essay is much longer and more intricately developed. It begins, however, with the same Arendtian distinction between the social and political.

> The social has to do with the problems of large numbers of people: food, shelter, clothing, sanitation—in a word necessity. To solve necessity, we draw together in reasoning, logic, and syntax—a discourse concerning these needs. This, it seems to me, is reality enough for social discourse to claim. Ideologies of social reality are built on this basis, and then in a little-understood and decadent Platonic fashion, whichever ideology is said to comprise reality. Only for the mass subjected to such ideology, out of which, as I've said, every man and woman drops repeatedly, even hourly, certainly daily. I am simplifying, indeed, but I have so stated this matter of social reality in order to insist that socio-economic reality, profound as it is, is not all of reality. ("Recovery" 66)

Blaser's comment that persons repeatedly drop out of single frameworks underlines his earlier point in "Particles" that collective naming cannot hold the complexity of its constituent members. Names, in fact, turn out to be processes ("the crystals FORMing") or relational networks rather than substantives. In this essay, the term humanism is made to open up to its labyrinthine past as Blaser meditates on what the humanities have been, are, and might be, and what they can and cannot do as public discourses. The pragmatic and often prescriptive world of social life and realpolitik represses complexity for the sake of action and utility. The aesthetic discourses, however, dwell on the complexity of human relations, and at their limit, they can render the finite infinite in its potential to recombine and become. "The discourses of the arts and of the sacred have to do with the othernesses of the world, of being in the world," Blaser writes. "Otherness is the fandango itself and not the fanfaronade we have thought it—the flow of persons, places, things and cosmos in relation" (83). This remark moves right back to "The Fire," where Blaser defines the serial poem as "the story of persons, events, activities, images, which tell the tale of the spirit." The trick is not to expect expediency from poetry. In "Afterthoughts," a brief concluding essay in the *Cultural Policy* collection in which "Recovery" was first published, Blaser writes that "the arts do not very often teach boys and girls to be good, but they do teach the undulating way toward meaning" (92).

That poetry has long lost prestige to philosophy, science, and the social sciences lies in the fact that it remains to the side of what contemporary cultures are able to recognize as compelling: it cannot command consent by claiming empirical reality, philosophical truth or historical verisimilitude, nor can it translate easily into institutional forms or even entertain so effectively as visual and popular media. Yet the decorum that is the special business of the poet—the manner in which we stand in the world, our disposition to others, our flexibility and range in the sorts of relations we are capable of, our awareness of affective investments and beliefs—has every sort of social, political, and environmental consequence. In "The Irreparable," the latest of the poetics essays, completed in August 2003, Blaser responds to world events, from the September 11, 2001, suicide bombing of New York to the American war with Iraq of 2003. This essay sets a life's worth of poetics to work in the world, and the first lesson is parataxis:

> The statement I drive the car is much less interesting than what the car is doing. A key, silver-silk, gas, burns, gears, motion, outer parts, wheels, hubs, spokes, fellies, tires, Fortuna, distances: I drive. Perhaps Amor hitches a ride. The first example is arranged according to hypotaxis, the "subordinative expression" of what is going on in the sentence—I'm in charge. The second is arranged according to a kind of parataxis, one thing beside another without "expression of their syntactic relation."
>
> Now, let us consider this current, world-wide war with its stunned vocabulary of sorrow (September 11) mixed with appetites for vengeance, oil, and money, and try to find the soldier who's been sent there. First off, we run into a manipulation of language that is meant to shape a herd, an amalgamated voice, answered from the other side by a violent refusal to be subordinated. . . . Then the appropriation of this war and its leaders to God, verified predominantly in English, needs to be reminded that the words *god* and *good* are not etymologically related. So, what of the one who stands and sleeps alongside things, even you and me? Inside all of this? This war with its eyes out. *Air clear, hot in the sand, zing, scream, blood, terror, a man, a woman, a child, a whatnot: I shot.* (99)

The contemporary lack of imagination for relational complexity, dangerously expressed in the hardening of oppositional stances, finds radical expression in violence. Once more, we are back to the reductive horrors that Olson confronted half a century ago in "The Resistance": humanity rendered into so much "fat for soap." The thought of totals. And again we have a poet telling us that a language stripped of the attention poetry brings to the particular becomes a useful tool in the justification of the brutal reductions of actual war.

"The Irreparable" turns around and around the writings of Giorgio Agamben, as he explores the historical destruction of experience and urges redefinition of "the transcendental in terms of its relation with language" (Infancy 4). Blaser's linkage of these meditations of Agamben's with realpolitik and the poet's role in it all reprises the key arguments of the poetics essays in the context of contemporary urgencies: if we lose experience to the positivisms and language to an outmoded physics or metaphysics, we lose the ability to imagine ourselves, others, and our relations to them creatively. Relational thinking stops dead on "default," and the historical record suggests that this position has signified too often a will to dominate and reduce the other. In Agamben's writings, the "irreparable" means the being-thus of being—irreducible particularity and necessary contingency. This is how language gives us transcendence: as that which is not contained by its concept. So Blaser quotes Agamben's comments in The Coming Community: "Seeing something simply in its being-thus—irreparable, but not for that reason necessary; thus, but not for that reason contingent—is love. At the point you perceive the irreparability of the world, at that point it is transcendent" ("Irreparable" 109–10). This is the kind of love that Blaser had written of decades earlier in "Particles," posed here against the erasures of war and economic aggression. Adorno's provocative comment that art "gives voice to what ideology hides" (39) cuts two ways. It may be taken to mean ideology critique practiced as the unmasking of "spirit that is specifically false" (39)—culture debunked as partisan—but it can also mean the disclosure of particularities that other discourses—political, social, scientific, or philosophical—are not structured to reveal—"a form of reaction to the reification of the world," as Adorno says so succinctly (40), and a reclamation of the creative power to install a different reality. As Blaser's "Irreparable" implies, the poet's effort after that different reality is now about "the survival of complexity" (Lyotard, The Inhuman 7).

COMMENTARIES

The remainder of the essays in this collection are commentaries on an eclectic mix that includes the poets Jack Spicer, Charles Olson, Robert Duncan, George Bowering, and Louis Dudek; the novelist Mary Butts; the visual artist Christos Dikeakos; and J. S. Bach. Because of the continuities between some of these pieces, I have grouped them here thematically rather than chronologically. The pieces on Spicer, Olson, and Duncan, for instance, circle themes close to the

heart of Blaser's own concerns and importantly extend the work of the poet-
ics essays. These were Blaser's closest early friends in poetry after all, and the
commentaries flow out of that intimacy. The essays on Bowering and Dudek,
both written as editor's introductions to collections of poems, reveal recogni-
tions of shared poetic ground, but they also speak to Canadian nationalism, a
cultural attitude from which Blaser's critical reception in Canada has suffered.[8]
The remaining commentaries are occasional pieces, prepared by request. Mary
Butts has been a longtime favorite of Blaser's because of her idiosyncratic style,
her undeserved obscurity, her empathy for homosexual men, and perhaps, a
little, her red hair, but she is also a companion writer in Blaser's exploration of
the sacred. The "Afterword" on Butts was written to accompany Talonbooks'
1979 reissue of *Imaginary Letters*, and "'Here Lies the Woodpecker Who Was Zeus'"
was requested by Christopher Wagstaff for a 1995 collection of essays on Butts.
"'Mind Canaries'" was originally a catalogue piece commissioned by the Van-
couver Art Gallery for a 1986 feature showing of Christos Dikeakos's collages
that included a tribute to Marcel Duchamp. Blaser's commentary takes the show
into a meditation on chance, technology, and the arts. This essay is curiously
apposite to "Bach's Belief," although the two pieces are separated by content
and chronology. Blaser juxtaposes Bach to Pierre Boulez, focusing on the aleatoric
in music, so chance is a theme in both pieces. The 1995 Bach essay answers to
an old friendship with Charles Olson. Olson had conceived of the *Curriculum of
the Soul*, a series of poetic investigations on various topics to be carried out, and
after his death, Jack Clarke took over the project, publishing the series in pam-
phlet form, piece by piece, through the Institute for Further Studies (Canton,
New York). Clarke asked Blaser to take on "Bach's belief."

As the lineup shows, Blaser does not define himself as an academic critic, al-
though his treatment of his subjects demonstrates devoted scholarship. Instead,
he writes out of kinship rather than the professional need to cover a field, and
his method of reading is to contextualize rather than to explicate or critique.
This way of writing literary commentary is consistent with the project Blaser
lays out in "The Fire." There he says that the poet can no longer begin with a
discrete self and move outward to discover a world that is already there but
must instead make a world in which a self can be found—a comment that refers
to the decentering of the self, or better, the polarity of self and world that con-
stitutes what Blaser and others of his generation called a cosmos. It follows that
to find another poet, it will be necessary to construct his or her world. Thus be-
gins "The Practice of Outside":

8. For many years, the "critical reception" of Blaser in Canada was simply silence. See my dis-
cussion in "Reading Robin Blaser," *Even on Sunday* (25–29).

At first this essay was short and simple—about Jack. But that became a reduction which every twist and turn of the work denied—a biography without the world the poet earned or a split between the man and the work which drank him up and left him behind. . . . My essay then became watchful of the context of the poetry and of the composing "real" that is Jack's concern. (113)

In the commentary that follows, Blaser situates Spicer in an intricate poetic and philosophical territory. The main through-line, however, is Spicer's radical polarity and "devotion towards the real" (113) as practiced through a poetics of dictation. With training in post-Saussurian linguistics (Edward Sapir, Benjamin Lee Whorf), Spicer had a keen awareness of the power of language to shape consciousness, but for him, as for Blaser, it was the affect rather than the science of linguistics that was the poet's business. A poetry of dictation that takes as its operative metaphor the receiving of messages from Martians makes strong theater of the linguist's recognition that real presences are alien to the mechanics of consciousness. In *After Lorca*, Spicer had wanted a poetry that could hold onto "real objects"—"The lemon to be a lemon that the reader could cut or squeeze or taste" (*Collected Books* 33). But instead of lemons or—more to the point—the flesh of that "very tall blond boy / Who ate all of my potato-chips at the Red Lizard" [*Collected Books* 333]), there were only words. Hence Spicer's version of the "practice of outside": Spicer made language point to a "real" that it cannot actually display. Given over to desire for immediacy, Spicerean polarity is more extreme than is Blaser's Möbius version because Spicer's demand for authenticity can really only be met by climbing outside consciousness itself. The illogic of this desire, of course, points to death.

What "The Practice of Outside" adds to the argument for polarity in "The Stadium of the Mirror" is a much more developed wresting of intellectual territory away from philosophy.[9] The repetitions and sometimes tortured language register this struggle: "I am here entering that combat for language which was Jack's," Blaser writes. "And I'm having a hell of a time with the description of the process which he performed. I feel my language thicken and become more abstract" (131). To get away from the abstract, Blaser turns to other poets. Mallarmé is key:

9. See Peter Middleton's "An Elegy for Theory" on Blaser's "The Practice of Outside" as a poetic performance and alternative to the poststructuralist management of reflexivity. Middleton argues that "Blaser almost paints us into the same corner as the poststructuralists when he says we are inside language, but then opens a door by saying that this interior is itself a performance, and like certain rituals, there are only performers within its ambit" (202). It is the poet's performance in language that gets us out of the poststructuralist suspension of experience Middleton says—a point with which I agree.

> The extraordinary nature of language is that it attaches to the prior, to the before one, and to the after one. It is determinedly polar to one's presence in it. If our visibility falls out of language, the language comes back to talk by itself. For such extravagance, see Mallarmé's *Un Coup de Dés* and Jack's *Language*—"Sable arrested a fine comb," a computer language, a language speaking by itself. Such a language may seem obscure because it is double—that is, holds a duplicity. ("Outside" 130)

The vocabulary of this passage lingers on the affective dimension of reflexivity. Along with Mallarmé, Poe, Artaud, and Duchamp are predecessors, all of them known for the high drama of their encounters with what can only be experienced—as opposed to conceptualized—as Other. Poe wrestled with death, Mallarmé with language; Artaud confronted madness and the unconscious, and Duchamp, chance. Blaser adds Vico to the list, for his treatment of poetry as primary relational thought, self to the otherness of the world (140), and Coleridge for his "polar logic":

> Coleridge's argument then in a few phrases: "polarity is dynamic, not abstract"— "a living and generative interpenetration"—"where logical opposites are contradictory, polar opposites are generative of each other"—"the apprehension of polarity is itself the basic act of imagination"—it is not a matter of "a picture of bodies already formed." (142)

The poetic territory indicated by these poets gives Blaser a ground onto which theory can be pulled. Most often, Merleau-Ponty and Foucault are the recruits. Blaser had already taken the term *wild logos* from Merleau-Ponty in "The Stadium of the Mirror" to name a language untethered from instrumental usage. In "The Practice of Outside," the chiasm (from Merleau-Ponty's *The Visible and Invisible*) serves as another description of polarity: "binding and . . . entangling with the essential unknown that is part of the life of the known" (134). To notice, however, is that the epistemology of the chiasm[10]—the "primacy of perception" and its embeddedness in the "flesh" of the world—is not Blaser's primary concern because he reads Merleau-Ponty for relational possibilities rather than truth. Foucault is similarly treated. From *The Order of Things*, Blaser takes Foucault's discussion of the "'disappearance of discourse'" ("Outside" 135) as a support for the reflexive, operational language he had argued in "Stadium" and Foucault's "'man and the unthought'" as a description of the experience of otherness (137)—polarity, again. What was of most interest for academic readers of these philosophers during the 1980s—namely, their epistemologies—is pointedly not

---

10. See Merleau-Ponty's *The Visible and the Invisible* for a discussion of perception as chiasmatic, especially the chapter titled "The Intertwining—The Chiasm" (130–55).

the issue here. The derivative nature of perception, after all, had already come to Blaser through the poets: it was not news. What concerns him—and the Spicer he constructs in the course of this essay—is what reflexivity might *mean* to all of us here who must live with it in this disenchanted world.

That the turn to language could mean suspicion of relational thought and contempt for experience, a focus on social interpellation, and the death of the author is entirely contrary to Blaser's own "practice of outside." In a stunning move, Blaser brings the essay to its dénouement with a real death scene that counters, without ever saying so directly, the Barthesean one. By this, I do not mean to suggest that the scene is contrived, but however faithful to Blaser's re-memory it may be, it is *also* an act of mourning and a replay of Spicer's poetic at its most savage:

> I return to the scene in the hospital, the alcoholic ward of the San Francisco General Hospital one afternoon during the two weeks he was there before he died. I have already said his speech was a garble. He could manage a name once in a while. Otherwise there were long-runs of nonsense sounds. No words, no sentences. That afternoon, there were something like a dozen friends around his bed, when it became clear that he wished to say something to me. By some magic I can't explain, everyone left to let it be between us. It was odd because I didn't ask them to leave and Jack couldn't be understood. Their affection simply accounted for something inexplicable. Jack struggled to tie his speech to words. I leaned over and asked him to repeat a word at a time. I would, I said, discover the pattern. Suddenly, he wrenched his body up from the pillow and said,
>
> *My vocabulary did this to me. Your love will let you go on.*
>
> The strain was so great that he shat into the plastic bag they'd wrapped him in. He blushed and I saw the shock on his face. That funny apology he always made for his body. ("Outside" 163)

The speech is garbled, gone into its sonic components, and the body is dying in a way that differs categorically from the "life" or "death" of linguistic and social systems. "We make up a different language for poetry / And for the heart—ungrammatical" (*Collected Books* 233), Spicer had said in *Language*. Now the non-sense of the "real" he had summoned as a poet really arrives, unbidden. And yet it is the remaining self-consciousness ("he blushed and I saw the shock") that paradoxically makes the death meaningful and engages us in mourning. Born alongside consciousness, death springs to life through the process of individuation that makes of it an Other rather than simply an elemental component of species becoming or atomic motion. Death performed as aporia[11] indexes a difference between the existent and its mediating ground

---

11. See Derrida's discussion of death in *Aporias*, especially pp. 36–37, where he turns to the relationship between language and death "as such": "Consequently, death refuses itself as such to

that cannot be displayed, and this is behind Spicer's courting of it in poetry: the "Princess" of *Heads of the Town up to the Aether*,[12] for instance, is an obvious emblem of death's allure.

Coming at the end of this big essay, the hospital scene stands Barthes on his head. The body can die—it can stop performing its words—even though the text and the author (he, she, I, or we) cannot. Cruelly, death does better what language does poorly: it points to the aliveness and unrepeatability of a unique presence "saying / something / as it goes" (Creeley, *Selected Poems* 123). The distinction between lived experience that cannot not be felt as presence and absence and the social *tĕchne* that produces that experience is one that Spicer had performed repeatedly. Now, in Blaser's narrative, he performs it again. "*Your love will let you go on.*" The second half of the message says that love is the other face of death. Love and mourning bear witness to the particular: both say "this one and no other"; both ask, childlike and insistent, after meaning and presence; both are a-rationally "outside" the languages of analysis rather than irrationally opposed—"outside" causal chains, logical argument, empirical experiment, or collective naming and therefore "outside" what counts as knowledge. There is no definitive answer to the "why" of love—why this one and not that—just as there is no way to consciously undergo or to articulate the *as such* of death. Blaser simply lets Montaigne do the answering with a Gallic shrug: "If you ask me why I loved him—'par ce que c'estoit luy; par ce que c'estoit moy'" (163).

I have not included Blaser's talks and other prose in this collection of essays, and "'My Vocabulary Did This to Me'" properly belongs to a collected prose, but it is so useful an addition to "Outside" that I have included it. "'Vocabulary'" was originally prepared for a 1986 Spicer conference in San Francisco and published in a special conference issue of *Acts*. It picks up where the essay leaves off, with an explication of the term *outside*. It means that the poet has "re-posited the position of language," Blaser says, and this "was a very important thing to do out of the 1940's, when language quite definitely belonged to *you*: 'that's my language and I speak *me* in it!'" (258).

Fundamental here is the question of the Other—in Spicer's language the Unknown, the Outside, and so forth. Our tradition sees the Other, in Michel de Certeau's words,

---

testimony and thereby marks even what refuses its *as such* both to language and to what exceeds language, it is there that any border between the animal and the Dasein of speaking man would become unassignable" (37). From a poet's perspective, death indexes an empirical liveness that language cannot reveal.

12. Spicer takes much of the imagery for the first section of *Heads of the Town* from Jean Cocteau's film *Orpheus*. In the film, Orpheus forsakes his living Eurydice for the dark and imperious Death. It is really for her, the "Princess," that he journeys to Hell rather than to rescue his wife.

as a threat, to be reduced—the Other as the realm of the dead, as in Galahad [Spicer's Grail poems]. A proposition, then: we cannot appropriate the Other, even as a realm of knowledge. Proposition: there is no autonomy of poetic knowledge—it is a discourse among others, but a very real one. Nevertheless, as Levinas has said, we are involved in the lived experience of the Other. Proposition: that is, the reason that we cannot, as writers, simply turn poetry over to language—to adapt de Certeau's point again—it is unlike language (literature), unlike language which, as an object of knowledge, is a construct of philosophers and linguists; whereas poetic language—along with all the other discourses—constitutes "forms of active social interaction and practice." ("'Vocabulary'" 258)

This passage clarifies the double-sided argument in "Outside" against both naive and deconstructive views of language. "'My Vocabulary'" came at a time when the prestige of theory and language poetry were at their zenith, and the timing makes Blaser's comments all the more pointed. To make matters more interesting, Ron Silliman sat beside Blaser at the conference table and offered a talk with the same title. Silliman was the man of the hour, the poet whose *New Sentence* and *American Tree* anthology had done much to articulate the new turn to language of the poetic avant-garde in the 1970s and 1980s. He saw, of course, a precedent in Spicer's recognition of the formal properties of language. In this context, Blaser's capitalized "Other" is provocative. We cannot "turn poetry *over* to language," Blaser says, because it (poetry) is a mode of "'active social interaction'" (258). For Blaser, the problem with both ideology critique and deconstruction is that neither acknowledges sufficiently its own stance: "These new methods of reading that sometimes lead us into marvels of a changed intelligence—linguistic, structural, deconstructionist—rich and challenging as they are, become dangerous when they become hegemonic, and to my reading thereby *ahistorical*" (259). The argument here, later developed in "Poetry and Positivism" and "The Recovery of the Public World," says that no theory can achieve exteriority (foundational status) on all the others, abolish its outside, or eliminate experience as an unavoidable rubric for organizing the world because none can shake free of historical specificity.

In "The Violets" (1983), Blaser plays out this argument for historical thinking in a meditation on Olson and Whitehead. I find the specificity of this essay is most sharply illustrated in his disagreement with Robert von Hallberg over Olson's use of *Process and Reality*. In *The Scholar's Art*, von Hallberg had argued that Olson inverts Whitehead by making man, rather than the atom, the image of order. In a passage Blaser quotes, von Hallberg says:

> "When Olson suggests that Whitehead's philosophy of organism is based on man as the image of order in the world, he is standing Whitehead on his head in order to define what Olson looked forward to as 'another humanism' (*Selected Works* 93).

Order, for Whitehead, is process, and the process begins with the atom, not with man." ("Violets" 217; von Hallberg's emphasis)

Blaser comments: "This is astonishing, for surely Whitehead begins with the depths of his own perception and then moves to the deeps where the atom is found" (217). The disagreement stems from von Hallberg's grounding of Whitehead in scientific thought: "The whole point of Whitehead's system— which attempts to reconcile humanistic and scientific thought—is that the order attained by each atom is only quantitatively different from the order of man's experience, and for this reason Whitehead begins with modern scientific analyses of the atom and works outward to man. . . . Olson takes the diametrically opposite path when he tries to define what distinguishes man from the rest of the natural world" (von Hallberg 115). Von Hallberg's reading of Whitehead and Olson is entirely reasonable if we take "modern scientific analyses" as a starting place. Olson indeed begins from a "diametrically opposite path" because he positions science within historical and anthropological boundaries: there is no "rest of the natural world" beyond the human universe because the latter is all we can know. From this point of view, Olson's "humanism" is a refusal to distinguish subjective from objective modes of knowing, and this Olson claims to share with Whitehead. The question neither Blaser nor von Hallberg addresses is whether Whitehead's cosmology could actually stand up as "scientific analysis" in the usual sense of the term. For Blaser, this is not an issue, because Whitehead is to be read for the relations he makes available for experience rather than empirical validity or rigor of logic. If we read Whitehead for the latter, surely the *analogy* between the behavior of matter at the atomic level and the behavior of complex, conscious organisms would give pause.

But there is another element in von Hallberg's comment that raises a crucial question in this Blaser-Olson-Whitehead conversation. Von Hallberg's uneasiness may be grounded in the feeling that the poet should be responsive to some measure of truth or value beyond personal whimsy—that the subjective-objective distinction has at least conditional validity. In another section of "The Violets," Blaser touches on this question. If measure is not objective and if the human will, as Olson defined it, is the "'innate voluntarism of to live,'" neither good nor ill in itself ("Violets" 215),[13] then how might we speak of measure?

13. To my ear, this is Spinoza via Whitehead, as apprehended by Olson. See Spinoza's *Ethics* for "*conatus*": "Everything, in so far as it is in itself, endeavours to persist in its own being" (136, III:iv). And on good and evil:

We call a thing good or evil, when it is of service or the reverse in preserving our being (IV. Deff. i. and ii.), that is (III.vii), when it increases or diminishes, helps or hinders, our power

Whitehead had said that "perception in the mode of presentational immediacy [conscious awareness of the world] solely depends upon the 'withness' of the 'body,' and only exhibits the external contemporary world in respect to its systematic geometrical relationship to the 'body'" ("Violets" 226–27). The underlining is Olson's, Blaser tells us. And then:

> Beneath this, Olson writes: "sta." . . . It is the Indo-European base "sta" of the word stand. To stand in the process—that is to say, in the vertical of one's acts. It is also the root in Olson's important word stance, as a good dictionary tells us: in such words as status, state, circumstance, constant, instant, destiny, exist. (227)

"Stançe," as Blaser glosses it here, emphasizes the primacy of being-with (mit-sein here modifies the Heideggerian Dasein) for embodied consciousness. Measure then becomes how one ex-ists, how one turns toward the world, with what decorum or lack thereof—how one relates. On the question of evil that must surely come of this definition, Blaser notes Olson's underlining of this passage in Whitehead: "'The nature of evil is that the characters of things are mutually obstructive'" ("Violets" 214). I think this is where Olson's der weg points in two disjunctive directions: the social and cosmic. The individual tragedies that come of "mutual obstruction" may draw some toward the pursuit of social justice and utilitarian goals such as the greatest good for the greatest number. But these social measures are not necessarily coincident with the cosmic good as Whitehead imagines it, as the maximization of complexity,[14] or with the poet's feeling for

---

> of activity. Thus, in so far as we perceive that a thing affects us with pleasure or pain, we call it good or evil; wherefore the knowledge of good and evil is nothing else but the idea of the pleasure or pain, which necessarily follows from that pleasurable or painful emotion (II. xxii). (195, IV: viii)

Whitehead acknowledges Spinoza when he notes that the cosmos in its becoming is causa sui and its own reason for being (Sherburne 30–31).

14. In the same passage from which Olson and Blaser select the statement on evil, Whitehead writes:

> The evil of the world is that those elements which are translucent so far as transmission is concerned, in themselves are of slight weight; and that those elements with individual weight, by their discord, impose upon vivid immediacy the obligation that it fade into night. "He giveth his beloved—sleep." (PR V.IV. 518, 341)

If I read Whitehead correctly, he is suggesting that some actual entities may serve as enablers for others. An ecosystem may illustrate the point. The maximum complexity and best health of the system might well be served by the death or diminishment of certain members. But what makes good sense as ecology or cosmology cannot, in this instance, serve as social policy.

In another context, Jane Harrison makes a similar point in Themis, her study of the social origins of the Greek fables. This was a book that Olson knew well. Harrison writes:

> To any rational thinker it is at once clear that Dike, Natural Order, and Themis, Social Order, are not the same, nay even they are not mother and daughter; they stand at the two poles

relational intricacy and potential for meaning. Such aesthetic imperatives are closer to those of natural law, with its implied sacrifice of individual species members, than to social management, and this should be a cautionary to the reader. Whiteheadean cosmicity does not translate well into sociology or moral precept, just as poetry does not translate well into institutional policy, and to read it this way— or to read it as science—is not just to reduce the work to ungenerous critique but also to miss its potential to produce meaning as the mode of relational thought.

In "Apollonius of Tyana," Olson had written that "'men spring up, when they are needed, like violets, on all sides, in the spring, when winter has been too long'" ("Violets" 203). Blaser begins with violets and concludes with poppies from *Maximus III*, "'so animate-inanimate and dry-beauty'" ("Violets" 227). "The Violets" remembers a flowering between poets and makes of its act of attention an offering and bouquet. When Blaser turns to Robert Duncan, the tone is rather more arch. "The 'Elf' of It" is a careful essay with no obvious trace of past disagreements but a mischievous one nonetheless.

Blaser begins by claiming the domestic for Duncan, a "household of imagination" ("'Elf '" 285) that opens outward to "the largeness of being at home" (286). As Duncan's readers know well, the trope is appropriate. Home and hearth are complex, enduring emblems in Duncan's work, as evidenced in the lovely *Passages* series that begins with "Tribal Memories." From the flickering campfire of the prehistoric to "the hearth stone, the lamp light, / the heart of the matter where the / house is held" the project is to recount the human story (*Bending the Bow* 9). In "'Elf,'" Blaser lets the *heimlich* slowly open outward. From *Letters* (1958) and *A Selection of 65 Drawings from one drawing-book, 1952–1956*, he fastens on a series called *The Ideal Reader*, which consists of art nouveau drawings of a woman in a large flowered hat. She is an "ultimate other to this author," Blaser writes: "the flowing lines of drawings of her belong to childhood, to folklore, to children's books. She is also at the beginning of reading and represents a primary notion that language and its implication in the world are amazingly other than one is" (286). The childlike quality of the Reader and the flowers of her hat tie her to the garden and hence the homely, but she is also an "other." Her gender sets up a tension with Duncan's homoerotics, and her face is always turned away or hidden under the hat, so she carries the *unheimlich* with her as

---

remote and even alien. Natural Law is from the beginning; from the first pulse of life, nay even before the beginning of that specialized movement which we know as life, it rules over what we call the inorganic. Social Order, morality, "goodness" is not in nature at the outset; it only appears with "man her last work." (534)

I am suggesting here that both Olson and Whitehead are better read as cosmologists rather than sociologists; they give us a process of self-fashioning that aims for relational complexity rather than moral goodness.

well. She is "Her-Without-Bounds," at the edge of the poet's home fire, just beyond his seeing and saying (*Bending the Bow* 9), and she is also as near as his own skin. Duncan made reading and writing interchangeable processes and thus himself took on the role of Ideal Reader, creatively misreading in order to bring the cultural archive to life and new generative possibility.

Through the Reader, then, Blaser sets up a play between the familiar and strange that serves as both text and subtext. It speaks directly to Duncan's poetic practice but also to Blaser's relationship with him. Once a familiar of Duncan's household, Blaser was pushed to play the stranger after the *Chimères* episode. In the *Poetry/Audit* correspondence, Duncan writes:

> If I had taken your "translations" as separate from Nerval and separate from my own work, I would have been cut off indeed from the syncretism in Poetry I seek, from what makes the Hellenistic syncretism in religion so fascinating: the structure containing its contraries. . . .
>
> The principle I found in Whitehead's *Process and Reality* that the intellect seeks to transform conflicting elements into contrasting elements could never be set into action if elements were conceived of as things in themselves complete. So, I see my creative imagination raising a war in things in order to come into the world of opposites and contraries, to hear that clash of arms in the cosmos that haunted Yeats—so that Heraklitus and Boehme see a strife at the heart of the Divine Creative Will Itself. (61)

Here is the polarized cultural territory Blaser also inhabits, but in quite a different manner. Twenty-five years later in "'Elf,'" he characterizes Duncan as "protestant"—protesting—"with the accent on the second syllable, thus to take the word away from the institutionalized versions of such modernity" ("'Elf'" 289). He does not bother to add that over the years he has translated his own Catholic background into poetry as "companionability." The companionable expresses a sacramental attitude toward cosmic being-with: the poet takes the world in "with bread" (Skeat: L. *com*, together; *panis*, bread). In contrast, there are Duncan's battle tropes: the "clash of arms" or "man's fulfillment in order and strife."[15]

This contrariety that Blaser sets up, ostensibly in Duncan's own work and more covertly between himself and his old companion, is beautifully modulated through a quotation from Michel de Certeau's commentary on Foucault's "La Pensée du Dehors." The passage that Blaser cites is from de Certeau's "The Black Sun of Language" in *Heterologies*, where de Certeau discusses Foucault's contention that the "outside" is intrinsic to language and culture. The Foucauldian point is that "A truth spoken by the organization of a culture . . . escapes its

15. See Duncan's essay, "Man's Fulfillment in Order and Strife," in *Fictive Certainties* (111–41).

own collaborators" (181). Future generations or heterological others misread a culture into new meanings. According to Foucault, these unaccounted for readings that wait beyond the occasion and self-articulation of a culture constitute its "unthought," its "outside." This passage from Foucault and de Certeau extends the meaning of the Ideal Reader, as it subtly positions Blaser and Duncan as each other's readers and "outsides." It also slyly references Blaser's championing of Spicer—over Duncan—in "The Practice of Outside."

"'Elf'" concludes with Emerson's "Circles"[16] and a final pirouette on the *topos* of the familiar-strange. In "Circles," Emerson had envisioned a self always becoming-other. Duncan repeatedly claimed Emerson as a predecessor, and in a passage Blaser quotes, he comments on the Emersonian dynamism as a component in his own work:

> "What I would point out in my work as one of its underlying currents is the weaving of a figure unweaving, an art of unsaying what it says. . . . Back of the 'Self,' which was but a rime, I want to see the mercurial genius of language, the 'Elf' who comes when I lose myself in reading the workings of language in the water." ("'Elf'" 297)

This passage from "The Self in Postmodern Poetry" yields Blaser a title, but it may imply the "unsaying" of an old quarrel too. Duncan and Blaser both relented late in the friendship, but without giving up much poetic territory. There is nothing in Blaser's essay that is not entirely faithful to Duncan's project as Duncan himself described it, and yet the whole is elvishly contrary. In his last line, Blaser calls on an Ideal Reader beyond both of them to enter the "language-map" of their shared poetic territory:

> And, therein, please find, Ideal Reader, many houses and much dissonance in the practice of poetry, keeping, of course, the "Elf" of it in your mind. (298)

The essays on Spicer, Olson, and Duncan recognize Blaser's oldest kin; the Canadian essays on George Bowering and Louis Dudek establish newer affiliations and comment importantly on a literary history of the cross-border exchange between the West Coast TISH poets and the New Americans in the early 1960s. TISH, a poetry newsletter first edited by Frank Davey, George Bowering, Lionel Kearns, Fred Wah, David Dawson, and James Reid from 1961 to 1963,[17]

---

16. For a more extended commentary on Duncan and Emerson, see Blaser's "Preface to the Early Poems of Robert Duncan."

17. TISH was published until 1969 but under various editors (including Daphne Marlatt and Dan MacLeod at different times). However, the first nineteen issues published by the original col-

initiated a Canadian translation of Black Mountain poetics into local circumstance while its editors were still students at the University of British Columbia. The brash, manifesto-like tone of the newsletter caused a stir at the time, so much so that its principals are sometimes still referred to as TISH poets. Moreover, the long, influential careers of Davey, Bowering, and Wah have extended the reach of TISH beyond its historical moment and contributed significantly to the making of a Canadian postmodern. Bowering, for instance, has recently been honored as the first parliamentary poet laureate of Canada. In the 1960s and 1970s, however, the association with Black Mountain was controversial, even damning in some eyes,[18] for writers and academics intent on establishing national distinctiveness and building a contemporary Canadian canon. As the resident "New American," Blaser was included in a controversy that once bubbled around TISH and has since colored his critical reception in Canada. In the essays on Bowering and Dudek, he outlines two broad lines in Canadian poetics, one congenial to his kind of postmodernism and the other not.

"George Bowering's Plain Song" gives us a poet aligned with Hemingway, James T. Farrell, and Frederick Philip Grove in his realism, but Blaser notes that Bowering also credits "Kenneth Rexroth, Kenneth Patchen and William Carlos Williams with a part in his finding his own voice" ("Plain Song" 185). From Williams, for instance, Bowering takes a localism that turns him toward the "'sticks and stones' of his own condition" (186) in the sleepy interior towns of British Columbia before the coming of the tourists and the cappuccino bars. Staying home meant the strenuous exercising of the poetic faculties—sight, sound, and intellect—against ready-made ways of seeing that were rooted in traditions from elsewhere. Literary Toronto, with its British heritage, was Bowering's antagonist, symbolic of a cultural establishment that had no room for western homeboys. As Blaser comments, "Bowering has been blamed for this first language [the "plain song" of place]; it is said to be American in a critical rejection of what this poet is and what he witnesses" (186).

Although sometimes described in geographic terms as a regional, east-west difference, the "deep division in Canadian poetic concern" ("Plain Song" 187) between a practice derived from local experience and one bound up with a particular literary canon comes from conflicting treatments of the cultural her-

---

lective have had the most enduring impact. These issues have been collected and published as a book, TISH No. 1–19 (Vancouver: Talonbooks, 1975), under Frank Davey's editorship. Davey's introductory essay gives the history of early TISH (7–11).

18. See, for instance, Poetry and the Colonized Mind: Tish by Keith Richardson and the preface by Robin Mathews. For a more sympathetic view of TISH, see The Writing Life, edited by C. H. Gervais. Both works were published in 1976.

itage. "The distinction to be noted," Blaser says, "is between what used to be called a 'high art' and language which stood apart from circumstance and another art which is intimate with circumstance" (187). The question is similar to the old one of the Duncan quarrel: do cultural traditions stand behind us as determining archetypes, or can poets draw form out of the "'darkness of the lived instant'" (182)? Blaser traces the Canadian version of this debate back to the 1940s and two competing constructions of CanLit by A. J. M. Smith and John Sutherland:

> Louis Dudek and Michael Gnarowski have noted that for Sutherland, "The 'modern' school was not 'metaphysical' or 'cosmopolitan,'" as A. J. M. Smith had argued, "but essentially local and particular." Eli Mandel summarizes: Sutherland " . . . simply identified 'cosmopolitan' with British poetry and consequently with social reaction. . . . Smith is constructing a rationale for his own poetry and the poetry of A. M. Klein, F. R. Scott, and Leo Kennedy; Sutherland, for Irving Layton, Louis Dudek, and Raymond Souster." (187)

Layton, Dudek, and Souster are Bowering's immediate predecessors, in Blaser's view, because they have "stood for qualities of the imagination that have backed Bowering up" (191). These fiery lines from Irving Layton illustrate the "qualities" in question:

> Each day the world must be created anew. Otherwise the symbolic volcano is forgotten and people build their lives out of slag. More, they spread the heresy that the universe is composed only of slag, the more impudent among them—the so-called "cultured"—displaying proudly the ash flecks on the lapels of their grey flannel suits. ("Plain Song" 190)

Layton is ruder and cruder than Blaser, but Blaser's manner of including this passage implies approval.

In the Bowering essay, Blaser praises Dudek as of "extraordinary importance" for his large meditative poems "on the dark of the modern condition" (190). When he turns to Dudek some years later, as editor of the collected poems, *Infinite Worlds*, he puts him in the company of modernists such as Yeats, Pound, or Eliot who, in responding to the disembedding of prereflexive modes of life, took up "the work of reality in poetry" (271). But the "work of reality," Blaser contends, is just what poetry has been denied, particularly by traditionalists in Canadian literature. In an argument parallel to that of the Bowering essay, Blaser takes up Dudek's own disagreement with Northrop Frye (*Anatomy of Criticism*) on the archetypal. This version of the argument, with Frye and Dudek at the center, fleshes out the implications of the archetypal view of culture as opposed to a particularized one. In a passage Blaser cites, Dudek make the moves:

No, it [what critics want to extract from literature] is not anything that the poet himself may have found by effort and conviction; it is something that "descended" upon him, and that exists apart from him—the universal "mythology" of literature. . . . Thus the poet becomes significant to the critic, as one possessed by a Platonic reality over and above the rational and sensible consciousness of man, but he is not himself a useful thinker." (270)

A passage from George Whalley restates and summarizes the core argument.

A poem is inexhaustible in analysis because it terminates in "a vision of reality." Reality is a matter of relationships; *we cannot refer a particular poem simply to "reality," because reality is not a determinate entity. Reality is the great unknown and unknowable.* We are constantly in quest of it, yet we can never fully know it and certainly we cannot possess it; the best we can hope for is to preserve our capacity to encounter reality in some of its aspects. (*Infinite* 272; Blaser's emphasis)

The malleability of the real, and hence the degree to which it can be shaped, is at the heart of Blaser's investigations in poetics. In the context of these Canadian essays, the indeterminacy (and hence creative power) Blaser is after translates as hostility to collective identities, including nationalism in the Canadian context. The problem with nationalism from Blaser's perspective is that it is another form of collective naming and as such reduces the complexity of its constituents and replaces the plentitude of history with a few paradigmatic narratives. Hence the manifesto-like tone of the brief essay "out of the velvet," a poetics piece that attacks the "isms"—nationalism in particular—and which should be read as an addendum to the Canadian commentaries.

Nationalism, however, is a volatile construct that can shift meanings from one context to the next. While it may signify the erasure of its constituent "particles," it can also be used in various struggles for self-determination. In Canada, nationalism has meant, for instance, federal protection of literary publishing in order to encourage indigenous writers, just as it has also meant the diminishment of regional and ethnic voices in favor of a "Canadian" identity that is actually specific to central Canada. There is a complicated argument to be made here, beyond the present occasion, and it is perhaps a limit in his thinking of nationalism that Blaser sees only the repressive side of it.

When it comes to heterodoxies as opposed to orthodoxies, however, Blaser is always receptive. The essays on Mary Butts pick up a shared interest in the esoteric sacred, treated by both Butts and Blaser as a rich dimension of perceptual experience. In the brief "Afterword" (1979) to Talonbooks' reissue of Butts's *Imaginary Letters*, Blaser first positions Butts among prominent moderns: her social milieu included Evelyn Waugh, Rebecca West, G. B. Stern, and Ford Maddox Ford (167); professionally she appeared in leading journals such as the *Transatlantic Review* with H. G. Wells, Conrad, Joyce, Cummings, Pound, Eliot, Mina Loy, and Robert McAlmon (167). He then turns to Butts's interest in magic and the occult, tangled as it was in the irregular living to be had in a demimonde of artists, occultists, and homosexuals. On the latter, Blaser writes that "She understood their [gay men's] distance from women, the underworld of their thought, even to madness" (166). In the much longer essay on Butts, "'Here Lies the Woodpecker Who Was Zeus'" (1995), the sacred, the magical, and the homosexual converge in yet another version of the "practice of outside."

The "'Woodpecker Who Was Zeus'" (1995) begins like the "Afterword," by establishing Butts's place among the moderns, but Blaser quickly moves to what he reads as the major issue of the work, the "adventure of the sacred" (309). The essay is mostly about *Armed with Madness*, a novel with five male characters, two of whom are a homosexual couple and one female character. All six end up in a house flanked by a numinous sea and forest and the novel concerns the relations between them as these unfold over the finding of a jade cup that may or may not be the Sanc-Grail. In the process of responding to the cup and to each other, the characters unravel the sacred back to a "dynamics of experience" (324). The "'muck'" of the occult leads to "an anthropology faced with the direct imagination of a cosmos which is not a doctrine, an objectification, or abstraction" (324). Blaser's title tells the story. It comes from a comment by Scylla, the female character, but Blaser traces it back to Jane Harrison's *Themis* and a chapter on *numina* or spirits like Picus (the woodpecker) and Faunus who existed as "sanctities" of nature before the "anthropomorphic gods of sacrifice" (330). Like most mythic histories, this one is syncretic, but the key idea Harrison retrieves is the relationship with nature symbolized by figures like Picus who is not a god but a bird with "*mana*": in Harrison's words, "Picus enshrines a beautiful lost faith, the faith that birds and beasts had *mana* other and sometimes stronger than the *mana* of man" (quoted in "'Woodpecker'" 330). Butts juxtaposes this exploration of human-nonhuman relatedness—back through the tangled web of the hermetic tradition to a pre-human Zeus—to the psychological descent of the character Clarence into madness. Clarence is Picus's homosexual partner in the novel and when Clarence is informed by a malicious letter that Scylla intends to marry Picus, he attacks her violently, later claiming to remember nothing. This final episode, as Blaser interprets it, suggests a "defeated desire" to possess the god (348)—to hypostatize a *mana* that is really an ungraspable power. Wild *mana* is inseparable from the primordial cosmicity the novel asks us to imagine: it implies the possibility to emerge, to become. The lure of the sacred is that it is a place, or condition of the imagination, that holds onto this power to be, a place where something—anything—might emerge or arrive. It is a place, then, of de-reification and creative renewal. At the end of the essay, Blaser writes: "It is one of the curiosities of this century that 'reality' continues to be pre-empted by objectivity, which leaves us with a loose, even more preemptive subjectivity. Needless to say, this is destructive of our imagination and our understanding of it" (348). To remember Butts, whose "disreputable" forays into magic may have contributed to the critical forgetting of her, is also to remember the "youth" of modernism in the twentieth century that moved us, Blaser says, from the remnants of metaphysical determination to an investigation of "chance and change" (348).

In "'Mind Canaries'" (1987), chance and technology—chance and will—are the dominant themes. Christos Dikeakos's large collages, displayed in a major show at the Vancouver Art Gallery, February 1 to March 16, 1986, reference the artist's Greek heritage in broken images of the gods and figures from myth combined with images from urban spaces, body parts, kitchen foil, thread, cut-up words, torn bits of crossword puzzles, and so on. Some of the collages have been photographed and then hand-painted with photographic oils. One of the major pieces of the show, called Explorer I, is a tinted photocopy of Frederick J. Kiesler's photo-montage of Duchamp in his studio. The Kiesler consists of a folding triptych representing the three walls of Duchamp's studio. Dikeakos has painted the unfolded triptych, dated the piece, and signed his name. The gesture is a tribute to Duchamp's ready-mades. Blaser comments:

> Christos Dikeakos's show is a splendid occasion to turn back and really think about Duchamp and to come forward to understand this artist's contemporary mind. I must imagine chance which is comprised of time, event and condition in contrast to traditional illusionism, abstraction, ideality or immortality. The thought that is art is operational, in both the small and the large, the private and the public, because it does not define the self as closed into itself, but in relation to an outside of persons, society, politics and cosmos. . . . Dikeakos presents the relational condition of the present. (232)

Contrary to chance—pulling in the opposite direction toward predictability and control—is technology. Referencing Octavio Paz, Blaser says that technology gives us the world as an obstruction to be overcome rather than a shape in which to live. Hence in an era dominated by it, we move "toward the 'unknown' and the 'formless'" (237)—matter as lump to be moved or molded by the will (or, I would add, problem to be solved rather than form to be created). In the Kiesler-Dikeakos collage, Duchamp is pictured in a room that opens to outer space, implying conquest of the unknown. Keisler has given him wings and Blaser reads these as "suggestive over and over again of our effort and failure to transcend contemporary conditions" and "poetic emblems of the artist's effort to envision a world-image" (244). In the context of the show, the wings also reference Daedalus and Icarus, a myth that links technology and hubris. In Dikeakos's words, the Icarus story is "'an extended metaphor of man's unlimited imaginary boundaries versus his physical and moral limitations'" ("'Mind Canaries'" 244).

Explorer I handles technology in a manner parallel to Blaser's own method of working through selection and recombination. If technology gives us a world without image—a world that expresses the human will unaware of itself—Dikeakos's collages not only depict that condition, but touch it by returning the photo-collages to painting through the tinting of them. The hand is distanced from its work in photography and, in the found object, from the tēchne that originally created the object, but tinting draws both photograph and mass-produced object in closer to the body. Tinting indexes the artist's hand in the traces of a handiwork, an effect reinforced by the image of hands collaged in a piece called Ikaria; Poster (1985). The effect is to place the body back in among the relics and shards of an ancient world order and the techno-urban landscapes that have replaced it, back where chance and circumstance modulate the will as represented by technology. That placement constitutes a reach for relationship—placement always does—and hence a gesture toward the absent world-image: world as shape. In an essay published alongside Blaser's in the catalogue for the show, the curator, Scott Watson, draws attention to the relationship between the cosmetic and the cosmic that makes this point. He writes of the tinted pieces that "the addition of color has become the act of painting 'reduced' to its ancient cosmetic function, which was to bring order and adornment to nature. (Cosmetic, from the Greek verb kosmeo; to order, arrange, adorn. The noun is kosmos; order, ornament, the world or universe, mankind as we use the world)" (Watson 13). This gesture to the cosmic through the cosmetic shows the contemporary pathos and labor of art in the tension between the delicacy and liveness of the color, the touching it references, and the world-mess that is to be so adorned.

In a later essay, "Bach's Belief" (1995), Blaser returns to chance as a theme. Pierre Boulez was inspired by Bach and wrote about him; Olson was impressed by Boulez after hearing a performance of the Second Piano Sonata in 1951 and thought to "juxtapose these two minds [Bach and Boulez] for our study" ("Bach" 359). Blaser's essay pulls together commentaries on Bach, including that of Boulez; commentaries on Boulez; and philosophical meditations on the baroque, including Michel Serres's linking of Bach and Leibniz, and Deleuze's treatment of the baroque in The Fold. In Bach, Blaser hears a "projection of a temporal process, the life of space, the meaning in music as the relation of the sounds to one another" (358; Blaser's emphasis). Like Leibniz's cosmology, Bach's counterpoint gives us endless, open-ended variation within a world that is internally consistent because it is grounded in a transcendence that holds the whole together. Inside this divine world-space, however, the notes are "'generators of structure'" ("Bach" 359; Boulez's phrase) that endlessly restate, complicate, and renew the life of the whole. Boulez, however, inhabits a post-Newtonian, decentered universe open to the incommensurable, the aleatoric eruption. The *Second Sonata* that caught Olson's attention turns on the anagram B A C H, but now theme and variation become "'exploration, adventure and discovery'" ("Bach" 362), and a "'classical form is seized by an almost expressionistic frenzy'" ("Bach" 362). The difference between Bach and B A C H is comparable to that which Deleuze describes in *The Fold* between a monadology and a nomadology. The former consists of the serial elaboration of a single world; the latter allows for divergent series or worlds.[19] What was crucial for Olson in Boulez "'was the formalization of the use of chance by a *series* of series into which accidence was spilled, and *then* used'" ("Bach" 363). Blaser adds to this Olson comment: "Just here, my meandering *would* turn toward *Alea*, that cosmos 'we' are working, that temporality that art is working" (363). Chance, time, circumstance, and creative agency—these are the elements of a poetic imagination that conceives the world as creative cosmicity or relational network rather than archetype or material lump; they are coordinates of the "operational language" Blaser has wished for poetry.

I think Blaser's essays leave us with a number of possibilities and propositions. First, they make a case for poetry as a significant discourse among others and reclaim for present use the aesthetic in its root sense of perceptual experience. The polemical energy of them is directed toward three major objections to the aesthetic that have come out in various forms over the past fifty years: a poetics based on perception is (1) epistemologically naive; (2) merely self-expressive, solipsistic; or (3) politically irrelevant.[20] Blaser responds to the epistemological challenge with the argument against positivism. The second question of self-

19. See Deleuze in *The Fold*, especially chap. 9, pp. 121–37, where he turns to music.

20. The epistemological challenge goes back to the structuralist/poststructuralist critique of phenomenology, which I take as sufficiently elaborated.

On the charge that a poetry of perception is *merely* self-expressive, see for a summary Hank Lazer's essay, "Criticism and the Crisis in American Poetry," in *Opposing Poetries* (1: 6–36). Lazer's topic is "workshop" poetry, or what Charles Bernstein has called "'official verse culture'" (Lazer 27). This is a poetry of sensibility—of authentic moments presented in well-crafted verse. Lazer's essay dates from 1986 in its original publication, and it is meant to promote the language writing then very new for many readers. In my view, however, the workshop poem is still a force in "official verse culture." Blaser's effort after experience is *not* to be confused with a reach for expression of this kind. The repeated insistence on polarity says that the personal does get into the poem but never

expression he meets by *performing* the personal as always also worldly—a singular perspective on a sharable world. To the reproach that subject-centered poetries are politically conservative, he offers an alternative form of ideology critique as the undoing of collective identities into their "particles." These are defenses of the aesthetic that ask us to make space for it among the other discourses, not to erase them. The other component of these essays, however, bears on what we gain from doing so. Blaser's position here is that perceptual judgment—let's call it imagination as defined in "The Fire" ("the power to take in and hold")—is the operative faculty when we look for meaning and reality. I pair these terms because the reality we live is inextricable from the meanings we assign to persons, places, things, and events. Meaning is civil artifice, mode of life, decorum—all belonging to relational thought. If, as Blaser claims, this is the special domain of the poet, then we might well turn to the poet for an art of real life. That poets and most of the rest of us have lost the power to arrange anything in the actual—that the public world has been displaced by the market and the dazzle of new technologies that seem to have more to do with the will than with the imagination or judgment—says that it is not only the ownership of wealth that is at issue in the new global order of the twenty-first century but that of reality as well.

I have said that poetry does not translate well into social institutions, not, at least, in those parts of the world where the grip on the absolute has loosened. The early postmoderns responded to the antifoundational world with a reach for the creative power to shape the real. The point was to open the open, and thus to set up a dialogue with other discourses and institutions that must, pragmatically, close. From the poetic point of view, this opening was a way of democratizing power, because it says that no one owns the real—that what counts for reality comes out of the busyness of our being together. If ever the real were, utopically, to be democratized in this way, the solicitous role Blaser gives to poetry might then become more than urgent opposition to the bad language of official media culture or the "financial surface" of things. It might even, one can imagine, blossom into a discourse of continual refreshment, possibility, and joy as one of the many languages of *humanitas*. The idea seems quaint, I know, so dis-

---

by itself and never as psychological authenticity. To repeat the proposition of "The Fire" and the Memory Theater, the poem is a singular perspective on a public domain, hard-won by attention to the world in its many dimensions—not a magic moment.

The political challenge to the aesthetic has come in forms ranging from Marxist critiques of the modern-postmodern as ideology (Raymond Williams, Terry Eagleton, or Fredric Jameson for the best known) to the postcolonial to art journals such as Toronto's *Fuse* that simply assume art can be treated as a form of political intervention.

tant are we from it in this era of thick media and commercial domination. But Hannah Arendt argued long ago in *The Origins of Totalitarianism* that even a fascist regime cannot, finally, suppress the sheer many-ness and incalculability of its constituents.[21] The community of those who refuse representation, who disidentify, who are not predictable—who have nothing in common, to use Alphonso Lingis's phrase[22]—is full of lives and stories that go on unsaid beneath the official representations of them. This fullness of history remains a potential source of renewal and Blaser's oeuvre is a passionate call for and to it.

Reading through the Duncan catalogue in which Blaser published "The 'Elf' of It," I stumbled over Christopher Wagstaff's citation of these lines from Duncan's "Hero Song": "Love . . . / will eat away the empire / until chaos remains" (Wagstaff 16). I thought of that distant and embarrassing sixties slogan, "All you need is love," taken from a Beatles' song, and the contempt that subculture has provoked since as it seemingly petered out into triviality, self-interest, and impotence against the "hard" economic "facts" of the "real" world. But in 1969, in "Particles," Blaser talked a hard kind of love that meant a commitment to complexity and the whole difficult effort to really see the intricacy and dynamism of the world. "Esstoneish me," Spicer had said back then (*Collected Books* 178). And from another corner of what I conjure now as an imaginary room, Olson in *Maximus* I, for the contrariety: "What weeds / as an explanation / leaves out, is / that chaos / is not our condition" (*Maximus* I: 96, p.100). Then Blaser, much later:

we've met, it turns out, in the labour of form, a cultural
largeness talking to itself   its memory damaged   its past
not there   and its future Nietzschean . . .
                                    ("Bits of a Book," *Holy Forest*)

Thus to leave Blaser in conversation, and us too.

21. I have in mind Arendt's comments on the subversive nature of "incalculability" under totalitarian regimes.

It is in the nature of totalitarian regimes to demand unlimited power. Such power can only be secured if literally all men, without a single exception, are reliably dominated in every aspect of their life. In the realm of foreign affairs new neutral territories must constantly be subjugated, while at home ever-new human groups must be mastered in expanding concentration camps, or, when circumstances require, liquidated to make room for others. The question of opposition is unimportant both in foreign and domestic affairs. Any neutrality, indeed any spontaneously given friendship, is from the standpoint of totalitarian domination just as dangerous as open hostility, precisely because spontaneity as such, with its incalculability, is the greatest of all obstacles to total domination over man. (*Origins of Totalitarianism* 456)

22. The phrase comes from the title of Lingis's book, *The Community of Those Who Have Nothing in Common*.

CHRONOLOGY

This chronology was compiled with the assistance of Robin Blaser, David Farwell, Kevin Killian, Stan Persky, Peter and Meredith Quartermain, Ellen Tallman, and Scott Watson, December 2005.

1925   Born Robin Francis Blaser, May 18, in Denver, Colorado (middle name in honor of St. Francis Xavier, 1506–52), son of Ina Mae McCready and Robert Augustus Blaser. Blaser was conceived before his parents married, and Ina Mae passed ten weeks of her pregnancy in the care of a generous couple at 1545 South Emerson, Denver, arranged by her mother, Sophia Nichols McCready, and Sister Seraphina and Sister Mary Madalena, teachers at the Sacred Heart Academy, Ogden, Utah, where she had been at school. At the time of Blaser's birth, his mother was nineteen years old and his father twenty-four. Immediately after their marriage, they moved to Blaser, Idaho, where the Blasers had a farm and Sophia Nichols worked as a telegrapher for the Union Pacific Railroad. During Blaser's childhood, the family moved from one small railroad town to another in Idaho, searching for work: Blaser, Wapi, Kimama, Dietrich, Orchard. According to the latest *Rand McNally Atlas*, Blaser, Idaho, has no population.

1927   Brother Irvin Augustus ("Gus") born April 5.

1928   Sister Dorothy Hope, born April 15.

1931   Attended grammar school at Dietrich and Twin Falls, Idaho.

1937   Brother Harold James ("Jimmy") born August 23.

1939   Attended Twin Falls High School. Memorable teachers included Bernice Babcock (Latin), Helen Minier (biology), Bernard Martyn (physics), Mercedes Paul (English), Florence Rees (theater), and Thelma Tolefson (geometry, algebra, trigonometry). Blaser was cast as Lord Fancourt Babberly in *Charley's Aunt* by Brandon Thomas). He also studied with Monsignor O'Toole and Father Henry Ackerman for a possible life in the priesthood and Mme. Larson for private weekly French lessons.

1943	Graduated from high school. Received a fellowship for summer study at North-western University in Evanston, Illinois. The criticism of an instructor there, Mrs. Arpan, prompted Blaser to destroy all his early poems. "Too derivative of Walt Whitman," she said. (Walt Whitman was Blaser's primary discovery during his time at Northwestern.)
1944	Attended the College of Idaho at Caldwell, fall and spring terms, 1944. In addition to his regular courses, Blaser taught French to three faculty children. Joined a weekly Brahms group. Played the role of Beverly Carlton, the "Noel Coward part" in *The Man Who Came to Dinner* by Moss Hart and George Kaufman.
	Left Idaho in fall 1944 to attend the University of California, Berkeley, drawn there by correspondence with two Twin Falls friends ahead of him by one year, Tom Jones and Frances Schweickhardt. Arrived by bus and was met by Jones and Schweickhardt. Stayed at the Hotel Durant in Berkeley and attended Euripides' *Trojan Women* on his first day.
	Found an apartment on Channing Way.
c.1945 –46	Was introduced to Jack Spicer by Spicer's musician friend Gene Wahl. At an Anarchist meeting—Wednesday nights at the Workman's Circle on Steiner Street in San Francisco—Spicer became acquainted with Robert Duncan and brought three of his poems to Blaser. This initiated a Duncan-Blaser-Spicer companionship in poetry that was to be crucial for all three.
	At the Circle, Blaser, Spicer, and Duncan also met Ellen Tallman, who would later become instrumental in bringing all three to Vancouver and would remain Blaser's lifelong friend. In 1946 Ellen was an eighteen-year-old music student at Mills College in Oakland. With her best friend, Marthe Larsen, later to be Marthe Rexroth, she attended the Wednesday meetings where Kenneth Rexroth was a key organizer of the Anarcho-Pacifist Libertarian Circle. As Tallman recalls, "During this period right after World War II, pacifism remained one of the major issues at our meetings." The group was interested in exploring "'viable alternative forms of *voluntary* organization" as opposed to "order . . . from above" ("My Stories" 1).
	These years also marked the beginning of the "Berkeley Renaissance," a literary scene in which Blaser, along with Spicer and Duncan, would become a key participant (see Ellingham and Killian's biography of Spicer, *Poet Be Like God*, especially chap. 1, for a detailed description). A key event (c. 1946–47) was Duncan's weekly evenings of off-campus readings at 2029 Hearst Street, a house that he shared with Hugh and Janie O'Neill. The soirées were conducted by Duncan, Rosario Jiminez, and many knowledgeable others to study moderns who were not being taught on campus or who were, from the Blaser-Duncan-Spicer perspective, incompetently taught. Duncan held a series of readings of *Finnegans Wake* (1939) and Rosario Jiminez taught García Lorca. Blaser recalls that reading Mallarmé was a "special gift of these evenings." Here began Blaser's ties to Mallarmé and Spicer's to García Lorca. The evenings also included group readings of Yeats, Rilke, Pound, H.D., and Eliot.

At the university, memorable professors were Josephine Miles (Romantics, Shakespeare), and Ernst Kantorowicz (French, German, Latin and Greek, Byzantine history, English constitutional history, medieval studies, thirteenth century, Dante). Kantorowicz, legendary at Berkeley for his intellect, scholarship, and charisma, would become an important intellectual influence for Blaser, Spicer, and Duncan—even for their poetry.

Sophia Nichols supported the Berkeley venture financially, but as the studies continued, Blaser chose to earn his way by working in the library under a Mrs. Monahan and at the Campus Textbook Exchange.

c. 1947   Met James Felts, a student of biochemistry at Berkeley who would become his partner for seventeen years, and moved with him to 2520 Ridge Road. Formed important and lasting friendships with Robert Berg (a librarian at San Francisco State University Library), Donald Allen (later editor of the now-famous anthology, *The New American Poetry*, 1960), and Jess Collins ("Jess"), the painter and collagist who would become Duncan's life partner.

c. 1952   Began graduate studies with a doctoral project on the poetic drama from Wordsworth's *The Borderers* to Hardy's *The Dynasts* and Yeats. In a 1999 interview with Miriam Nichols (*Even on Sunday*), Blaser said of his topic that it was "far too big for any one Ph.D. dissertation, but it made for splendid reading. And I took all of my exams, language exams and stuff and so on and so forth, and then just dipped out. Mark Schorer was then head of the department, and I went in to tell him I just had to leave. Irving Howe had written a thing in *Partisan Review* on conformity ["This Age of Conformity," *Partisan Review* 21, no. 1 (January–February 1954)]—this was the 50s, you know—and I believed every word of it. That's the way I felt too" (354).

1955   Left Berkeley with an M.A. and an M.L.S. Accepted a position in the Widener Library at Harvard University as assistant librarian in cataloging (1955–59), under Susan Haskins, head of cataloging. One of Blaser's most important assignments during these years at the Widener was to assemble a bibliography and display of American philosophy from its beginnings to the contemporary—Jonathan Edwards to Alfred North Whitehead.

c. 1956   Lived with James Felts (employed at Tufts in biochemistry) at 42 Kirkland Street, Cambridge, Massachusetts, and wrote "The Boston Poems." Joined a Boston literary scene that included the experimental poets Joe Dunn, John Wieners, Steve Jonas, and Jack Spicer. Spicer had tried New York but did not like it; Blaser then helped him to find a position in the Rare Book Room of the Boston Public Library. During trips to New York, Blaser met John Ashbery and Frank O'Hara.

1957   Began correspondence with Charles Olson. Blaser wrote to Olson in April 1957, protesting what he heard as Olson's dismissal of Dante. Olson's quick reply (May 3, 1957) came in a long, dense letter: "these masterpieces of what you will understand if I call old form, are too important for you to lose in any welter: until that welter say has blown you up, broken yr door off" ("Charles

Olson–Robin Blaser Correspondence," in *Minutes* 16). Blaser and Don Allen met Olson at the Tavern, in Gloucester, Massachusetts, a "white weatherboarded frame building" (*Minutes* 5) close to the beach. "When we arrive," Blaser writes, "Olson is waiting for Don Allen and me at a small table in The Tavern bar. We'd barely settled when Olson turned to me and asked, 'Who is Matilda?' It took me some time to find my bearings. We were, it turned out, in the midst of Dante—Purgatorio, Cantos XXVIII & XXVIX" ("Introduction to Olson-Blaser Correspondence," in *Minutes* 11).

1959   Left the Widener to tour Europe, July 14, on the *Nova Scotia*, a ship of the Furness Line. Arrived in Liverpool, England, July 28. After a month in London, Blaser traveled to Paris and met with Ashbery. He completed the trip with visits to Venice, Rome, and Florence.

Returned by ship from Brest, France, to New York, c. September, to stay with Donald Allen and discuss *The New American Poetry* anthology. From there, Blaser returned to San Francisco. Felts hated Boston and had already accepted a position at the School of Medicine, University of California, Berkeley, in 1958. Blaser joined him after the European trip and the two moved into a Baker Street apartment.

Worked in a bookstore and began to write *Cups*.

c. 1960   Wrote "The Park" and "The Faerie Queene." "The Park" would appear in *Locus Solus* 3 and 4, edited by John Ashbery, and again later in the *A Controversy of Poets* (1965), edited by Paris Leary and Robert Kelly. Excerpts from "The Faerie Queene" were also included in *Controversy*. A selection of Blaser's poems appeared in Donald Allen's landmark anthology, *The New American Poetry*.

At this time, Spicer was holding weekly Sunday reading groups with Jim Herndon and Landis Everson on dictation and the serial poem that Blaser sometimes attended.

1962   Accepted a position as a librarian in acquisitions at San Francisco State College (1962–65).

Wrote *The Moth Poem* and began *Image-Nations* 1–4.

Grandmother Sophia Nichols Auer died, August 11.

At about this time, Blaser was given $3,000 by a female admirer to act as a cultural guide on a proposed tour of Paris. When he discovered her interest in the adventure was not limited to culture, he turned her down. She insisted, however, that he keep the money, so he agreed to use it to open an art gallery. The Peacock Gallery opened in a house on Union Street in San Francisco that Blaser had rented and redecorated. The first show—paintings on every wall, even in the kitchen—featured the local artists Tom Field, Jess, Robert Duncan, Harry Jacobus, Fran Herndon, Paul Alexander, and others. As Blaser recalls, he did not sell a thing and could not afford to keep the gallery open for long. However, he bought many of the pieces himself, and that work now forms the core of his art collection.

Starred in a production of Robert Duncan's play, *Adam's Way*, performed at the Tape Music Center, along with Helen Adam, Tom Field, Paul Alexander, Ida Hodes, and Lew and Deneen Peckinpah Brown. At this point Spicer and Duncan were not getting along, and to bedevil Duncan, some of the boys in Spicer's North Beach circle, Stan Persky and George Stanley in this case, picketed the production with signs reading "'Fuck Duncan, Fuck Jess, Fuck Chi-Chi [Blaser]'" (Ellingham and Killian 239–40).

1962 –63   The Vancouver Festival of the Arts (1962) and the Vancouver Poetry Conference (1963) at the University of British Columbia (UBC) hosted Charles Olson, Robert Duncan, Robert Creeley, Denise Levertov, Margaret Avison, Allen Ginsberg, and many more.

These events, in addition to many off-campus readings and lectures, came about through the mentoring of Warren and Ellen Tallman, who had moved to Vancouver and were both teaching at UBC. Out of the UBC vortex came an important strand of the postmodern for Canadian poets (*TISH* magazine was initiated by Tallman's students, Frank Davey, George Bowering, Jamie Reid, Fred Wah, and David Dawson, after a Duncan visit in 1961), and the energy thus created was a factor in Blaser's decicision to immigrate to Vancouver in 1966. Some of those young UBC students—George Bowering and Daphne Marlatt, for instance—have since become lasting friends.

1963   The relationship with Jim Felts began to break up. Blaser moved to 24 Allen Street on Russian Hill in San Francisco and became romantically involved with Stan Persky.

1963 –64   Translated Gérard de Nerval's *Les Chimères*. Berkeley friendships became strained. Spicer was drinking heavily, and he and Duncan were not speaking. Blaser was caught in the middle. On completion of the translations, Duncan reacted negatively. Blaser and Duncan quarreled seriously over this.

1964   *The Moth Poem* was published by White Rabbit Press in San Francisco. White Rabbit was conceived by Spicer and founded by Joe Dunn in 1957. By 1964 the artist Graham Mackintosh had taken over, assisted by Stan Persky. Persky was also editing the magazine *Open Space*, to which Blaser, Spicer, and Duncan contributed, leading to some Open Space books, printed by Mackintosh.

Blaser began a series of poems that would later be collected in *The Holy Forest* as *Charms* (1964–68).

1965   First trip to Vancouver, in the company of Jack Spicer and Stan Persky. Blaser, Spicer, and Persky read together c. spring 1965 at the New Design Gallery.

In summer Blaser participated in the Berkeley Poetry Conference, San Francisco, an important gathering of poets that included Robert Duncan, Jack Spicer, Gary Snyder, Charles Olson, Edward Dorn, Allen Ginsberg, and Robert Creeley.

Les Chimères was published by Persky's Open Space in San Francisco.

Spicer died in the alcoholic ward of San Francisco General Hospital on August 17. Blaser was his executor.

1966	Accepted the offer of a teaching position at Simon Fraser, Burnaby, British Columbia (1966–86), a newly established university already acquiring a reputation for faculty radicalism. Blaser moved into a house at 4570 West First Avenue in Point Grey with Stan Persky, but the relationship ended in 1968. The two have since remained close friends.
1967	Duncan published his own translation of *Les Chimères* in *Poetry/Audit*, along with letters between him and Blaser over the poetics of translation.
	Blaser wrote "The Fire," a first major statement of poetics that implicitly responded to Duncan's critique of *Les Chimères*, and read it for the first time in San Francisco, at the San Francisco Museum of Modern Art, 401 Van Ness Avenue.
	Worked on *Image-Nations 5*. Along with "The Fire," this poem responded to Duncan's critique and countered Duncan's "Up Rising."
	Launched a literary journal called *Pacific Nation*. In a 1966 letter to Charles Olson, he wrote: "The shitiest [sic] thing about this San Francisco scene is that we've been cut off from discourse except among ourselves, and I wanted *The Pacific Republic* [first idea for a title] to open up" ("Charles Olson–Robin Blaser Correspondence," in *Minutes* 16). Among the contributors to the journal were Jim Herndon, Gerry Gilbert, Richard Brautigan, Karen Tallman, George Stanley, Charles Olson, Antonin Artaud, Gladys Hindmarch, Allen Ginsberg, Paul Alexander, Keith Jones, and Jess [Collins]. On the editorial page of the first issue (in which Blaser's "The Fire" received its first publication), there was this statement of intent: "I wish to put together an imaginary nation. It is my belief that no other nation is possible, or rather, I believe that authors who count take responsibility for a map which is addressed to travellers of the earth, the world, and the spirit. Each issue is composed as a map of this land and this glory. Images of our cities and of our politics must join our poetry. I want a nation in which discourse is active and scholarship is understood as it should be, the mode of our understanding and the ground of our derivations" (3). Unfortunately, the new professor at Simon Fraser University was asked to take on extra teaching duties just as the journal was getting established and found he could not attend to it. After a much-delayed second issue that Persky helped to bring out, the journal folded in 1969.
1969	Wrote "Particles" for a conference on poetry and politics at UBC and published the article in *Pacific Nation* 2 (1969).
	Blaser's lectures at SFU on the moderns and romantics were becoming legendary and drew audiences beyond the university's student body.
c. 1969 –70	Moved to a house on Bellevue Avenue in the Dundarave neighborhood of West Vancouver with Colin Stuart, a promising young poet.
1971	First "Great Companion" poem on Pindar. Began work on *The Collected Books of Jack Spicer* and "The Practice of Outside," published in 1975.
c. 1972 –73	After the short-lived Stuart relationship, Blaser met Scott Watson through Stan Persky at a poetry reading. Watson was a student in an experimental liberal arts program at UBC ("Arts 1"), where he studied with Ellen Tallman. Through the common friendship with Ellen, Scott and Robin began to "hang

out." Tallman remembers, for instance, a trip to Cold Mountain with Wendy Barrett, Scott, and Robin in the early 1970s (pers. com., January 6, 2005). (Cold Mountain Institute was a center for psychotherapy and personal growth, located on Cortez Island off the British Columbian coast. Blaser sometimes participated in the center's activities and contributed Tarot readings.)

Watson and Blaser lived together for only about two years, but they have since remained friends. As Watson recalls, Blaser was working on the Spicer *Collected Books* and "The Practice of Outside" during this time (pers. com., December 23, 2004). Watson is now an associate professor of fine arts at UBC and curator of UBC's Belkin Gallery.

c. 1973 –74 Met David Farwell, who would become his life partner. Then a student of the classics at UBC, Farwell has since become a counselor at St. Paul's Hospital. Blaser and Farwell moved to a house on Trafalgar Street in Vancouver's Kitsilano quarter, which they shared with the artists Ardele Lister and Bill Jones. The house was a large, gracious up-down duplex in a neighborhood that was once the heart of Vancouver's flower power and is now one of the city's most beautiful and sought after areas, close to Point Gray and Kitsilano ("Kits") beach.

1974 Published *Image-Nations 1–12* and *The Stadium of the Mirror* with Ferry Press, London. Recorded *Astonishments*, a literary autobiography on audiotape. The tapes were made at the home of Warren Tallman, with a small circle of interested Vancouver writers: Angela Bowering, Dwight Gardiner, Martina Kuharic, Daphne Marlatt, and Warren Tallman. They are now housed in the Contemporary Literature Collection at Simon Fraser.

Began poems later gathered as *Streams I* in *The Holy Forest* (1993).

Became a Canadian citizen but retained dual U.S. citizenship.

1977 With Ellen Tallman, Blaser bought the Trafalgar Street house. Ellen and Warren had separated at this point, and Ellen was living with Wendy Barrett. The new arrangement turned out to be permanent. Blaser and Farwell continue to share the duplex with Ellen and her present partner, Sarah Kennedy.

1978 Father, Robert Augustus Blaser, dies April 20.

Wrote the afterword to Mary Butts's *Imaginary Letters*, published in Vancouver by Talonbooks in 1979.

1979 Began the series that would be published by Talonbooks in 1981 as *Syntax*.

1980 Edited *Particular Accidents: George Bowering, a Selected Poems*, and wrote the introduction, "George Bowering's Plain Song."

1981 Began work on the poems that would be collected in 1988 as *Pell Mell*.

1983 Wrote "The Violets," a long essay on Olson's reading of Alfred North Whitehead's *Process and Reality*, which was published first in *Process Studies*, a Whitehead journal, and then reprinted in *Line*, a journal of modern and postmodern writing, edited by Blaser's colleague at Simon Fraser, Roy Miki.

c. 1984 –86 Wrote "Mind Canaries," a catalogue essay for a show of Christos Dikeakos's collages at the Vancouver Art Gallery. Began poems that would be gathered as

Streams II, 1986–91. Edited *Art and Reality: A Casebook of Concern* with Robert Dunham, a Romantics professor, SFU colleague, and close friend.

Wrote "No Matter," an introduction to a collection of poems by Luis Posse, *Free the Shadows* (Talonbooks, 1986). When Posse, a onetime partner of Rob Dunham's, died of AIDS in 1984, Dunham selected the poems for *Shadows*. The epigraph reads "*I am building / a flotilla / of poems / to attack / english.*"

Took early retirement from Simon Fraser University in 1986.

Delivered "'My Vocabulary Did This to Me'" at a Spicer conference in San Francisco, June 20, 1986. The talk was published with other conference papers in *Acts* 6 (1987). Blaser was on a panel with Ron Silliman, whose talk was also titled "'My Vocabulary Did This to Me.'"

1986
–88

Edited Louis Dudek's *Infinite Worlds: Collected Poems* and wrote the introduction.

Wrote "Poetry and Positivisms" for publication in *Silence, the Word and the Sacred*, edited by E. D. Blodgett and H. G. Coward.

Pell Mell, an important book in Blaser's oeuvre, was released by Talonbooks in 1988.

Robert Duncan died of kidney failure. Blaser wrote the "Great Companion" poem in memoriam.

1990

Began poems gathered as *Exody* in 1993.

Rob Dunham died of AIDS. As his executor, Blaser managed the estate.

1991
–93

Wrote "The 'Elf' of It," a catalogue essay for Christopher Wagstaff's two-part exhibition of Duncan's drawings at the University Art Museum and Pacific Film Archive, February 9–April 12, 1992, and the Bancroft Library, February 9–May 30, 1992, University of California, Berkeley.

Mother, Ina Mae McCready Blaser, died on Febuary 25, 1992.

Wrote "The Recovery of the Public World" and "Among Afterthoughts on This Occasion," both of which would appear in *Reflections on Cultural Policy, Past, Present and Future*, a collection Blaser coedited with Evan Alderson (SFU) and Harold Coward (University of Calgary).

The Holy Forest, edited by Stan Persky and Michael Ondaatje, with an introduction by Robert Creeley, was published by Coach House Press, Toronto (1993). This first edition of the *Collected Poems* gathered the various serials in one volume for the first time.

1994

Delivered a keynote address at the tenth anniversary of the Kootenay School of Writing. The address was titled "Thinking about Irreparables" and marked the beginning of a long meditation on irreparability as presented in the philosophy of Giorgio Agamben. The address was transcribed from tape and published in *Raddle Moon* 18 (2000).

1995

Published "Preface to the Early Poems of Robert Duncan" and "'Here Lies the Woodpecker Who Was Zeus'" for *The Sacred Quest*, a collection of essays on Mary Butts, edited by Christopher Wagstaff.

Published *Bach's Belief* for the series *Curriculum of the Soul*, conceived by Olson before his death and carried forward by the poet and scholar John (Jack) Clarke through the Institute for Further Studies.

"The Recovery of the Public World: A Conference on the Poetry and Poetics of Robin Blaser" was held at the Emily Carr College of Art and Design, June 1–4 June. Organized by Edward Byrne, Charles Watts, Tom McGauley, Karen Tallman, Brian De Beck, Christos Dikeakos, Miriam Nichols, and many volunteers, the conference attracted scholars from Canada, the United States, New Zealand, and the United Kingdom. Conference papers were later edited by Charles Watts and Edward Byrne for publication by Talonbooks in 1999 (*The Recovery of the Public World*).

First visit to the Naropa University Summer Writing Program as a guest poet and lecturer.

Seventieth birthday celebration in summer at the University of California, Davis.

1996   In November, the SubVoicive Poetry collective, headed by Nicholas Johnson of Etruscan Press and the Five Towns Festival, invited Blaser to read in London (Three Cups Pub), Stoke-on-Trent, and at Preston, with Edward Dorn. On this same trip, the poet and scholar Peter Middleton (University of Southampton) hosted him at the John Hansard Gallery, where he read with Lee Harwood and Wendy Mulford.

1997   Presented "Great Companion: Dante Alighieri" as a keynote address for a conference on the influence of Dante in North America, held in April at Universita "G.D'Annunzio," Chieti-Pescara, Italy, organized by Annalisa Goldoni.

1999   Wrote "out of the velvet—the denim—the straw of my mind" for a collection of poetics statements edited by Charles Bernstein for the journal *Boundary* 2.

Second visit to the Naropa University summer program where he recorded a panel discussion with Robert Creeley and Michael Ondaatje, published in *Civil Disobedience: Poetics and Politics in Action*, edited by Anne Waldman and Lisa Birman (2004).

2000   In collaboration with the British composer Sir Harrison Birtwistle, wrote the libretto for an opera, *The Last Supper*. Jointly commissioned by the Staatsoper and Glyndebourne Touring Opera Company, the opera opened at the Staatsoper in Berlin on April 8 and at Glyndebourne in September. Blaser attended both openings. *The Last Supper* was also performed at the Royal Festival Hall in London and broadcast in full by the BBC.

Read at the Cambridge Conference of Contemporary Poetry, April 28–30. A new poem for the reading, "Pentimento," was published in *The Cambridge Conference of Contemporary Poetry Review* (2000).

San Francisco Poetry Centre, seventy-fifth birthday celebration and reading, May 18.

Third visit to Naropa, June 9–15; his course was titled "What Do Poets Do?"

2001	Brother Jimmy (Harold James) died April 14.
	Invited speaker at International Festival of Poetry at Coimbra, Portugal, May 27–30.
	Fourth trip to Naropa, June 25–July 1, for a segment of the Summer Writing Program titled "Politics of Identity/Gender/Queer Theory."
2002	Revised ongoing work on irreparability for a talk at Temple University, Philadelphia, to be delivered as part of an October writer-in-residency.
	Wanders, an exchange of poems between Blaser and Meredith Quartermain, was published by Nomados Press.
	Launched *Even on Sunday*, a collection of essays and archival materials concerning his poetics, with readings at the Western Front, Vancouver, B.C., on October 18 and at the University of Maine, Orono, October 24. The Orono event was part of the New Writing Series organized for the fall, sponsored by the English department at the University of Maine and the National Poetry Foundation. Blaser read with Robert Creeley.
2003	"The Irreparable" became an essay. The piece now positioned Blaser's poetics in the context of world events following the September 11, 2001, attack on the World Trade Center in New York and the subsequent "war on terror" launched by U.S. president George W. Bush. It was published immediately as a chapbook by Nomados Press in Vancouver.
	Jess Collins died.
2004	With David Farwell, Blaser flew to Granada, Spain, in April to research a new "Image-Nation" poem. Granada is the last place, Blaser says, where Jews, Christians, and Muslims lived together in a civilized fashion.
	Fifth visit to Naropa, June 21–27, for a segment of the Summer Writing Program titled "Translation and Intercultural Literary Arts."
2005	Awarded the Order of Canada in a ceremony at Rideau Hall, Ottawa, June 10. This award recognizes outstanding lifetime achievement and contribution to a community.
	Delivered talk on "The Irreparable" in New York at Poet's House, 72 Spring Street, October 4, and gave a poetry reading with Etel Adnan at St. Mark's Church-in-the-Bowery, October 5. Read at Evergreen State College, Olympia, Washington, October 17. Participated in the "Poetry Bash," Granville Island, Vancouver, an evening of readings sponsored by the Vancouver Writers Festival, October 22.
	The Vancouver composer David MacIntyre set a selection of Blaser's recent lyrics to music, and these were performed at Heritage Hall, Vancouver, November 2, in an event billed as "Radio Songs: 12 songs for 3 singers, a cappella." The evening was sponsored by the Canada Music Fund and the School for Contemporary Arts at Simon Fraser University.

Blaser, Idaho, 1922.

Ina Mae McCready Blaser,
c. 1925; Robin Blaser's
mother.

Sophia Nichols,
Robin Blaser's grandmother.

Robin Blaser
at age three,
1928.

Robin Blaser, c. 1935–37.

Water tower in Orchard,
Idaho, 1936.

Robin Blaser playing
Sir Fancourt Babberly
in *Charley's Aunt*, Twin
Falls High School,
1943.

Robin Blaser at the
University of California,
Berkeley, c. 1948.

James Felts.

Robin Blaser
in sweater tuxedo,
c. 1973–74.

David Farwell (left) with Robin Blaser, 2004.

Robin Blaser and statue of Seneca,
Granada, Spain, 2004. Photograph
courtesy of David Farwell.

EDITOR'S NOTES

Where a note opens with a quotation enclosed in quotation marks followed by a colon, I am quoting Robin Blaser quoting someone else. Where a note opens with a quotation not enclosed in quotation marks, I am quoting Blaser.

THE FIRE

This essay was first published in *Pacific Nation* 1 (1967): 19–30, ed. Robin Blaser; and *Caterpillar* 12 (July 1970): 15–23; reprinted in *The Poetics of the New American Poetry*, ed. Donald Allen and Warren Tallman (New York: Grove Press, 1973), pp. 235–50.

1. Ebbe Borregaard joined the Spicer, Blaser, Duncan circle at Berkeley in 1957, when he signed up for Jack Spicer's "Poetry as Magic" workshop. In *Poet Be Like God*, his biography of Spicer, Kevin Killian introduces Borregaard this way:

> One of the first to sign up [for Spicer's workshop] was Ebbe Borregaard, already famous in a minor way as a poet runaway. His mother had appealed to the newspaper of San Francisco to help them find their missing son. Labeled "the Beatnik Boy" to his chagrin, he was triumphantly declared found, his picture appearing on the front page of the papers. Borregaard had served in Korea and had stumbled onto Black Mountain College in literally its last days— its last three or four days, showing up on the doorstep just as the College was being sold. Now the painter Tom Field dragged him to the Public Library and presented him to Spicer as a kind of gift. (82)

Borregaard later became a regular at the Sunday poetry readings and discussions in Joe and Carolyn Dunn's apartment which were to follow the Magic workshop.

2. Blaser first read "The Fire" at the San Francisco Museum of Modern Art, 401 Van Ness Avenue.

3. "The test of poetry is the range of pleasure it affords as sight, sound, and intellection" (Zukofsky, *Test of Poetry* vii).

4. Fire is *Blase-r*'s signature element and it is a recurrent trope in the collected serial poems: *The Holy Forest* is a forest on fire. In a passage that brings out the significance of fire as an emblem of creative transformation, Blaser writes in "Image-Nation 15 (the lacquer house":

> *after the fire in the lacquer house,*
> the point is transformation of the theme—
> enjoinment and departure—like

the Christmas trees, stripped of all
adornment, burned on Locarno Beach . . .

5. Stan Persky became a regular in the Spicer poetry circle in the late 1950s, when, as a teenager, he arrived in San Francisco from Chicago with the U.S. Navy. Persky had read Kerouac and Ginsberg and first joined the beat scene. However, after meeting George Stanley, Persky began to attend Sunday readings with Spicer and soon became involved in Spicer's North Beach circle, editing a literary magazine, M, with Lewis Ellingham and Gail Chugg in 1962 and later his own *Open Space* journal. Blaser's romantic involvement with Persky ended a seventeen-year relationship between Blaser and Jim Felts, and in 1965, when Blaser moved to Vancouver, British Columbia, Persky went with him. Although Blaser and Persky only lived together until 1968, Persky settled permanently in Vancouver, and the two have remained close friends. Persky is a writer of fiction (gay-themed) and political commentary. His publications include *The House That Jack Built* (1980), on civic politics in Vancouver; *Buddies: Meditations on Desire* (1989); *Fantasy Government* (1989), on provincial politics in B.C.; *Mixed Media, Mixed Messages* (1991); *Then We Take Berlin: Stories from the Other Side of Europe* (1995); and *The Autobiography of a Tattoo* (1997). With John Dixon he coauthored *On Kiddie Porn: Sexual Representation, Free Speech and the Robin Sharpe Case* (2001). He is a prolific book reviewer and columnist on social and cultural issues and writes from both Vancouver and Berlin. He currently teaches philosophy at Capilano College in North Vancouver.

6. "What we describe as imagination . . . '': As Blaser says, he has adapted this quotation: it is "so much to my purpose, slightly re-worded, that I won't give the author credit: it is in that meeting entirely mine." This becomes a way of using quotations in the earlier essays as part of a poetic performance that places the poet's voice among many others.

7. The two "strangely structured" books by Thoreau are *Walden* and *A Week on the Concord and Merrimack Rivers.*

8. Blaser here refers to Henry Adams's *Mont-Saint-Michel and Chartres.*

9. The "scholarly book" by Josephine Miles could be either *The Continuity of Poetic Language: Studies in English Poetry from the 1540's to the 1940's* (1951) or *The Continuity of Poetic Language: The Primary Language of Poetry, 1540's–1940's* (1965).

10. These lines open Book I of Ovid's *Metamorphosis,* Loeb Classical edition, trans. Frank Jastus Miller (3). Blaser has adapted Miller's translation and recast it as poetry. The Latin is original to the Loeb edition.

11. Edith Cobb:

Using various forms of so-called projective methods and play techniques (in particular modified versions of the Lowenfeld World-Play Technique and the Thematic Apperception Test, accompanied by a continual reference to the Rorschach categories of Form, Color, Motion, Time and Space, Animal and Human Response), I became acutely aware that what a child wanted to do most of all was to make a world in which to find a place to discover a self. This ordering reverses the general position that self-exploration produces a knowledge of the world. Furthermore, while observing the passionate world-making behavior of the child when he is given plastic materials and working dimensions which are manageable and in proportion to his need, accompanied by a population of toys, fauna and flora, and artifacts that do duty as "figures of speech" in the rhetoric of play, I have been made keenly aware of those processes which the genius in particular in later life seeks to recall. (540)

12. Margaret Mead: In *Continuities in Cultural Evolution* (the Terry Lectures), Mead writes that "The work of Edith Cobb suggests that human beings need to perceive and re-create internally and expressively what they perceive of the universe in which they are growing—they have in fact a 'cosmic sense'" (320). She makes the same point in very similar language in her introduction to the book-length version of Cobb's *The Ecology of the Imagination* (8), a publication that postdates "The Fire" by ten years. However, I have not found the phrasing that Blaser cites here.

13. Frank Speck:

> The generalized concept of the form of the earth, which is termed tsi·tɔtci·'nau, "our world, universe" (Mistassini), appears to be that it is shaped like a hill and floats on water. Ques-tioning fails to evoke the belief that it rests upon the carapace of the tortoise or that it is the carapace itself, as is believed by the Algonkian southward. It was stated by a Mistassini in-formant (Charley Metowe'cic) while discussing the matter, that the earth's form comes to be known only from the testimony of a person about to die. In the vision that comes at this time the mind can view the universe and sees all around the earth as it rises above the water. And he feels it rocking! (58)

14. The idea that a poet's vision is only completed at death is to be found in Mal-larmé's "Au tombeau d'Edgar Poe": "Tel qu'en lui-même enfin l'éternité le change, / Le poëte suscite avec un hymne nu / Son siècle épouvanté de n'avoir pas connu / Que la mort s'exaltait dans cette voix étrange" (*Oeuvres complètes* 128).

15. The key family members to whom Blaser refers are as follows:

Paternal

Father: Robert Augustus Blaser, b. 20 July 1902, d. 20 April 1978.

Grandfather: Augustus Frederick Blaser, b. 6 October 1872, d. 10 June 1954; mar-ried to Minnie C. Blaser, b. 7 June 1880, d. 4 July 1942. Grandfather Blaser was the "French" relation, but despite his stories about being the lost Dauphin, he was of Swiss origin.

Maternal

Mother: Ina Mae McCready Blaser, b. 6 June 1905, d. 25 February 1992.

Grandmother: Sophia Nichols Van Aukin McCready Auer, b. 12 May 1876, d. 11 Au-gust 1962; married first to a Van Aukin who disappeared into Canada and then to Simon Auer, b. 1869, d. 1935. Blaser never met Van Aukin, but the German grand-father, Auer, was a member of his childhood household.

Great-grandmother: Ina Mae Johnson, b. 1854, d. 1939, secretary to Brigham Young.

Great-uncle, brother to Ina Mae Johnson: Mitchell R. Johnson, b. 1867, d. 1939, "Uncle Mitch" of *Cups*.

These are the relations that are most vivid and significant to Blaser. Among them, Grand-mother Sophia Nichols stands out in personal memory, in the poetry, and in *Astonishments*, a series of autobiographical audiotapes Blaser made in 1974. She lived with the family in Idaho, during Blaser's childhood years, and in *Astonishments*, Blaser recalls her encouragement and kindness. She also financed Blaser's education at Berkeley. For a poetic account of family life in Idaho, see *Cups*, "Sophia Nichols" and "Image-Nation 24 ('oh, pshaw,'" all in *The Holy Forest*.

16. See *Cups* and "Image-Nation 24" for poetic references to the Idaho of Blaser's childhood (*Holy Forest*).

17. Step-grandfather Auer, second husband of Sophia Nichols.

18. "two other poets": The two were Jack Spicer and Robert Duncan. See also "The Medium" from *The Moth Poem*, where these lines carry the plot of *The Holy Forest*:

> . . . the story is of a man
> who lost his way in the holy wood
>
> because the way had never been taken without
> at least two friends, one on each side[.]

19. Blaser dates his independence as a poet from 1955, when he left Berkeley to accept a librarian's position in the Widener Library at Harvard University. *The Boston Poems*, 1956–58, are the earliest collection he preserves, although he has been writing poetry since adolescence. In the *Astonishments* audiotapes, Blaser tells of destroying his early writings. Before moving to Berkeley, he attended Northwestern University for a season, and an instructor there criticized his poems for being too Whitmanic. "Mrs. Arpan" was the guilty one; she turns up as the "wife of a sailor" in "The Literalist," the first of the *Moth* poems.

20. Arthur Brodeur was a philologist and professor of Anglo-Saxon in the English department at Berkeley. Both Blaser and Jack Spicer took his course and, because of it, went on to take a full-year course on the history of the German language. Brodeur's publications include *The Art of Beowulf* (1959).

21. Frances A. Yates, *The Art of Memory* (1966). The passage in Yates is as follows:

> The Leibnizian monads, when they are human souls having memory, have as their chief function the representation or reflection of the universe of which they are living mirrors— a conception with which the reader of this book will be thoroughly familiar. (388)

22. Yates describes the Memory Theater of Giullio Camillo (b. circa 1480) in a chapter of *The Art of Memory* (129–72). Her description of the "box with tiers" is quoted from Erasmus's *Epistolae* (Yates 131–32). Viglius Zuichemus, a friend of Erasmus, had reported the phenomenon. Yates tells us that the images in the Theater were of planetary gods.

23. The italicized phrases are from Frances Yates's description of the memory system of Giordano Bruno in *The Art of Memory*. On concentric wheels that Yates says make up a memnonic device of "appalling complexity" (212), Bruno inscribes images deriving from "ancient Egyptian star-lore" (213). Taurus is "(1) a man ploughing (2) a man bearing a key (3) a man holding a serpent and a spear" (213). Saturn is "A man with a stag's head on a dragon, with an owl which is eating a snake in his right hand" (214).

24. For the poetics issues of the *Chimères* translations and the quarrel between Blaser and Duncan, see my commentary in this volume.

25. The original of this poem is available in Gérard de Nerval, *Oeuvres* (30).

26. The "present war" is the Vietnam War.

PARTICLES

This essay was prepared for the Arts Council Symposium on Art and Politics, held at the University of British Columbia in 1967, and published in *Pacific Nation* 2 (February 1969): 27–42. *Pacific Nation* was a poetics journal that Blaser conceived and edited. However, he published only two issues (1967 and 1969) because, as he explains now, his teaching duties at Simon Fraser were unusually onerous at that time.

1. At Berkeley, Blaser studied medieval political theology with Ernst Kantorowicz who was then teaching material that would be published as *The King's Two Bodies: A Study of Medieval Political Theory* (1957). In *Astonishments* (1974), he again recalls Kantorowicz's significance as the teacher who offered a historical sensibility. Of particular importance was Kantorowicz's treatment of Dante. Kantorowicz found in Dante a satisfying response to the overlapping claims of pope and emperor, arguing that Dante referred each to the perfections of his realm. Hannah Arendt's distinction between the private and the public, the social and the political, bears a formal resemblance to Kantorowicz's dividing of the sacred and the secular.

2. See also Blaser's citations of Arendt in "The Recovery of the Public World" (1993). As the date on this later essay indicates, Arendt has continued to inform Blaser's thinking on politics. Crucially, Blaser accepts Arendt's distinction between necessity and freedom, and this distinction informs poems and essays that do not include direct references to Arendt. Consider this passage from "The Violets" (1983):

> Marxism is an instrument, and an excellent one, for social analysis and the understanding of the problems of necessity for large social bodies, and, perhaps, when the wreckage of its twentieth century practice has been cleared away, it may become an instrument for the founding of social justice. In the meantime, the problem of reality—what do we mean by the real? Part of what is meant is a valuation that includes the world of earth and sky. (197)

3. On the pages Blaser cites, John Harrison's comments on the "hardness" of Yeats's verse are as follows:

> What Yeats, Pound, Lewis and Eliot wanted in literature was bareness, hard intellectual approach ruled by the authority of strict literary principles. They rejected the humanist tradition in literature, and in society, the democratic, humanitarian tradition. The same principles governed their social criticism as their literary criticism, and led them to support the fascist cause, either directly, as Pound and Lewis did, or indirectly, as Yeats and Eliot did. (33)

> The attitude, feeling, style, rhythm, metaphors all merge in Yeats's later poetry to produce some of the most intellectual, authoritarian, passionate and, as far as texture goes, the hardest poetry ever written. It has what Hulme called a desire for precision, austerity and bareness in literature. (57)

> In his later verse, Yeats uses hard, predominantly monosyllabic words, corresponding to the individual pieces of a mosaic. (58)

4. Charles Olson, "This Is Yeats Speaking," in *The Human Universe and Other Essays*, ed. Donald Allen, p. 102; cited below as *Human Universe*. Olson's prose is now more readily available in *The Collected Prose of Charles Olson*, ed. Donald Allen and Benjamin Friedlander; cited below as *Collected Prose*. The Yeats citation is on p. 144 in the *Collected Prose*.

5. Novalis was a pseudonym for Georg Friedrich Philipp Hardenberg (1772–1801). The quotation here is as cited in Fischer (60).

6. *Marat/Sade* (dir. Peter Brook; dist. Festival Films, 1966, and United Artists, 1967). This is the film adaptation of the Royal Shakespeare Company production of the Peter Weiss play, which was also directed by Peter Brook. The full title of the play is *The Persecution and Assassination of Jean-Paul Marat Sade as Performed by the Inmates of the Asylum of Charenton under the Direction of Monsieur de Sade.*

7. The quotation ("God is 'only society transfigured and symbolically expressed'"), as Blaser's endnote says, comes from Sheldon Wolin's *Politics and Vision* (362). Wolin is quoting, however, and he credits Émile Durkheim with the phrase: *The Elementary Forms of Religious Life*, trans. J. W. Swain (London: Allen and Unwin, 1915), pp. 16–17, 437. (Wolin's page references cover several paraphrases and citations.)

8. The phrase "process of image" comes from "The Human Universe" (*Human Universe* 10; *Collected Prose* 162), but "rhythm of it" does not appear in the original exactly as Blaser phrases it. Clearly, however, he has in mind the passage from "Human Universe" where Olson is talking about the kinetics of life and art:

> The process of image (to be more exact about transposition than the "soul" allows or than the analysts do with their tricky "symbol-maker") cannot be understood by separation from the stuff it works on. Here again, as throughout experience, the law remains, form is not isolated from content. The error of all other metaphysic is descriptive, is the profound error that Heisenberg had the intelligence to admit in his principle that a thing can be measured in its mass only by arbitrarily assuming a stopping of its motion, or its motion only by neglecting, for the moment of the measuring, its mass. And either way, you are failing to get what you are after—so far as a human being goes, his life. There is only one thing you can do about kinetic, re-enact it. Which is why the man said, he who possesses rhythm possesses the universe. And why art is the only twin life has—its only valid metaphysic. (*Human Universe* 10; *Collected Prose* 162)

9. Blaser has adapted the phrases he cites here from Olson. In the original:

> He [Shakespeare] isn't picking up his objects (words), despite one hand is tied behind his back, either for their music or image. He gets both by going in further to the word as meaning and thing, and, mixing the governing human title and experience (which prompts him to bother with words at all), his effect is the equivalent of his act: . . . We are in the presence of the only truth which the real can have, its own undisclosed because not apparent character. ("Quantity," *Human Universe* 93–94; *Collected Prose* 282)

10. "disinterested use of language": Blaser has said in conversation that the phrase has no single source. He puts it in quotation marks as an Arnoldian description of poetic language in the nineteenth century. For instance, Matthew Arnold defines literary criticism as "*a disinterested endeavor to learn and propagate the best that is known and thought in the world*" ("The Function of Criticism" 42; original emphasis).

11. "Let me bring this to a close . . . ": Walt Whitman, "Repondez." Blaser gives no citation, but the poem can be found in various anthologies.

THE STADIUM OF THE MIRROR

This essay was originally published at the back of the chapbook titled *Image-Nations 1–12 and The Stadium of the Mirror* (London: Ferry Press, 1974), pp. 51–64.

1. Dante Alighieri, *The Divine Comedy*, 3 vols., trans. Charles S. Singleton. The phrase "those who have lost the good of the intellect" is from vol. 1, *Inferno*, Canto III (25). Virgil is describing the inhabitants of hell.

2. The names are alive, out of jars: This line references H. D.'s *Trilogy*, which is full of jars: "Genius in the jar / which the Fisherman finds" (10); stars are "little jars of that indisputable // and absolute Healer, Apothecary" (33); "the heart's alabaster" (39); and "a jar too circumscribed, // a little too porous to contain the out-flowing / of water-about-to-be-changed-to-wine" (42). As well, a significant segment of the poem centers on Mary Magdalene's gift to Christ of ointment in an "alabaster jar" (129) as a powerful regenerative emblem.

"The e of Eros closes and reopens the rose": A fugitive line. Blaser remembers it as coming from H. D., but I have yet to find it there. A search of Robert Duncan's *H. D. Book* also failed to reveal this line.

3. "I am not, there where I am the plaything of my thought . . ." : Jacques Lacan, *Language of the Self*, reprinted under the title, *Speech and Language in Psychoanalysis*:

> Je ne suis pas, là où je suis le jouet de ma pensée; je pense à ce que je suis, là où je ne pense pas penser. [I am not, there where I am the plaything of my thought; I think about what I am, there where I do not think that I am thinking (that is, at the level of the unconscious).] (183)

The English translation in brackets is Anthony Wilden's and the passage occurs in his commentary, "Lacan and the Discourse of the Other," which follows his translation of Lacan in *The Language of the Self* or *Speech and Language in Psychoanalysis*. On the above passage, Wilden comments as follows:

> In essence, then, for Lacan, the conscious cogito is supplemented by an unconscious subject who may be the subject saying "I think" or "I am," but never both at once, since the question of the subject's being is posed at the level of the unconscious. (183)

4. Merleau-Ponty elaborates on the chiasm in *The Visible and the Invisible* (1968). See, in particular, the chapter "The Chiasm" (130–55) and the note of the same name (214–15) in the "Working Notes" published with *The Visible and the Invisible*.

> The chiasm is not only a me other exchange (the messages he receives reach me, the messages I receive reach him), it is also an exchange between me and the world, between the phenomenal body and the "objective" body, between the perceiving and the perceived: what begins as a thing ends as consciousness of the thing, what begins as a "state of consciousness" ends as a thing. (215)

5. The italicized phrases come from Claude Lefort's introduction to *The Visible and Invisible*:

The wild-logos
the reversability of experience and language (xxx)
neither experience not language is a reality that
will suffice to itself alone (xxx)
two aspects of the reversability which is ultimate
truth (xxix, 155)
there is no frontier between language and world (xxx)
A wild-logos   to recognize the movement that
prevents the fixing of the meaning of the thing,

visible or invisible, and makes arise indefinitely,
beyond the present given, the latent content of the
world (xxxii)

6. Victor Hugo, *William Shakespeare* (Paris: Nelson Editeurs, n.d.). Blaser took the passage as cited in Gwendolyn Bays, *The Orphic Vision: Seer Poets from Novalis to Rimbaud* (1964) (116–17).

7. Aristotle, *Poetics*, trans. A. E. Wardman and J. L. Creed (410–31). Section 8 is relevant to Blaser's comment that Greek tragedy is an imitation of an action, not a character study. According to Aristotle:

> A plot is not a unity, as some think, as the result of being concerned with one man. Many undefined things happen to an individual, some of which add up to no unity at all; similarly one individual can commit many actions, which do not make a single unified action. . . .
>   The plot . . . should be one, just as in other arts of imitation there is a unified imitation of one thing. Since it is an imitation of action, it should be about one whole action. (419)

8. G. W. F. Hegel, from the preface to the *Phenomenology of Spirit*. Hegel is discussing the "evanescent" as essential to the True. In the Clarendon Press edition translated by A. V. Miller (the edition Blaser keeps in his home library), the passage reads as follows:

> Appearance is the arising and passing away that does not itself arise and pass away, but is "in itself" [i.e. subsists intrinsically], and constitutes the actuality and the movement of the life of truth. The True is thus the Bacchanalian revel in which no member is not drunk; yet because each member collapses as soon as he drops out, the revel is just as much transparent and simple repose. (27)

9. "We are never in possession of ourselves, yet passion is ourselves": This sentence is an adaptation of a passage in Merleau-Ponty's essay "Reading Montaigne" in *Signs*, trans. Richard C. McCleary (1964):

> The critique of passions does not deprive them of their value if it is carried to the point of showing that we are never in possession of ourselves and that passion is ourselves. At this moment, reasons for doubting become reasons for believing. The only effect of our whole critique is to make our passions and opinions more precious by making us see that they are our only recourse, and that we do not understand our own selves by dreaming of something different. (206)

10. Serge Leclaire, quoted in the editor's notes to *Speech and Language in Psychoanalysis*, ed. and trans. Anthony Wilden (1968). In the original, the passage reads as follows:

> If we imagine experience to be a sort of tissue, that is, taking the word literally, like a piece of cloth made of intersecting threads, we can say that repression would be represented in it by a snag or rip of some sort, perhaps even a large rent, but always something that can be darned or rewoven, whereas foreclusion [*Verwerfung*] would be a sort of 'original hole,' never capable of finding its own substance again since it had never been anything other than 'hole-substance'; this hole can be filled, but never more than imperfectly, only be a 'patch,' to take up the Freudian term [already cited]. (98; original emphasis and brackets)

11. Hannah Arendt, "On Humanity in Dark Times: Thoughts about Lessing," in *Men in Dark Times* (1955):

. . . the world is not humane just because it is made by human beings, and it does not become humane just because the human voice sounds in it, but only when it has become the object of discourse. However much we are affected by the things of the world, however deeply they may stir and stimulate us, they become human for us only when we can discuss them with our fellows. Whatever cannot become the object of discourse—the truly sublime, the truly horrible or the uncanny—may find a human voice through which to sound into the world, but it is not exactly human. We humanize what is going on in the world and in ourselves only by speaking of it, and in the course of speaking of it we learn to be human. (24–25)

12. Walter W. Skeat, *A Concise Etymological Dictionary of the English Language* (1963):

Consider. (F.–L.) O.F. *considerer*, L. *considerare*, to consider, orig. to contemplate the stars (Festus).— L. *con-* (*cum*), together; *sider*, for **sides-*, stem of *sidus*, a star. (108)

Disaster. (F.–L.) M.F. *desastre*, "a disaster, misfortune"; Cot. Lit. "ill-fortune." —O.F. *des-*, for L. *dis-*, with a sinister or bad sense; and M.F. *astre*, a star, planet, also destiny, fortune, from L. *astrum*, a star. (144)

13. "mysticism which means nothing to anybody": The phrase comes from an early review. Blaser is pleased to have forgotten the source.

14. Skeat gives the etymologies of *crust* and *crystal* as follows:

Crust. (F.–L.) O.F. *crouste* (F. *croûte*). —L. *crusta*, crust of bread. Cf. Gk. *kryos*, frost; see Crystal. Der. *crust-y*, hard like a crust, stubborn, harshly curt (of people). (122)

Crystal. (F.–L.– Gk.) Formerly *cristal*. —O.F. *cristal*. —L. *crystallum*, crystal, –Gk. *krystallos*, ice, crystal.—Gk. *krystainein*, to freeze. —Gk. *kryos*, frost. (122)

The phrase "external expression of a definite internal structure" seems to take language from the *Oxford English Dictionary*, where the relevant definition of *crystal* reads as follows:

5. (Chem. & Min.) Aggregation of molecules with definite internal structure and external form of solid enclosed by symmetrically arranged plane faces, solid with regular arrangement of atoms, etc.

15. Michel Foucault, *The Archaeology of Knowledge* & *The Discourse on Language*, trans. A. M. Sheridan Smith (1972):

I know how irritating it can be to treat discourses in terms not of the gentle, silent, intimate consciousness that is expressed in them, but of an obscure set of anonymous rules. How unpleasant it is to reveal the limitations and necessities of a practice where one is used to seeing, in all its pure transparency, the expression of genius and freedom. (210)

16. "Half under its breath, amid the murmuring of things": The language of this undocumented citation suggests Merleau-Ponty, as does the context in Blaser's essay.

17. "a speaking that *lodges within my own speech*": Blaser may have in mind a passage like this one in Foucault's *Order of Things*:

How can he [Man] be the subject of a language that for thousands of years has been formed without him, a language whose organization escapes him, whose meaning sleeps an almost invincible sleep in the words he momentarily activates by means of discourse, and within which he is obliged, from the very outset, to lodge his speech and thought, as though they were doing no more than animate, for a brief period, one segment of that web of innumerable possibilities. (323)

18. Jacques Lacan, *Speech and Language in Psychoanalysis:*

For, however neglected by our interest—and for good reason—*le Mot d' Esprit et l'Inconscient* remains the most unchallengeable of his [Freud's] works because it is the most transparent, in which the effect of the unconscious is demonstrated to us in its most subtle confines. And the face which it reveals to us is that of the spirit in the ambiguity conferred on it by Language, where the other side of its regalian power is the *"pointe"* by which the whole of its order is annihilated in an instant—the *pointe*, in fact, where its creative activity unveils its absolute gratuitousness, where its domination over the Real is expressed in the challenge of non-sense, where humour, in the malicious grace of the *esprit libre*, symbolizes a Truth that has not said its last word. (33)

19. Merleau-Ponty suggests that the mind is the body's invisibility in *The Visible and the Invisible:*

The mind is in no objective site, and yet it is invested in a site which it rejoins by its environs, which it circumvents, as my locality for myself is the point that all the vanishing lines of my landscape designate to me, and which is itself *invisible.* (222)

20. The Curtius that Blaser cites in the original text is Ernst Robert Curtius, *European Literature and the Latin Middle Ages*, trans. Willard R. Trask (1953). However, a search of this volume has not yielded the phrase in question: *"The language regards the guilty man as he who it was."* The italics indicate that Blaser may be quoting from memory.

21. The etymologies in Skeat are as follows:

Courage. (F.–L.) F. *courage*, O.F. *corage*; formed with suffix *–age* (L.–*aticum*) from O.F. *cor*, heart.— L. *cor*, heart. Der. encourage

Syntax. (F.–L.–Gk.) F. *syntaxe.*—L. *syntaxis.*—Gk. *syntaxis*, arrangement; hence, arrangement of words.—Gk. *syn*, together; *taxis*, order, from *tassein*, to arrange.

Ecstasy. (F.–L.–Gk.) O.F. *extasie* (H.)—Late L. *ecstasis*, a trance.—Gk. *ekstasis*, displacement; also, a trance.—Gk. *ek*, out; *stasis*, a standing, allied to *histemi*, I stand.

22. Alexander Mourelatos, *The Route of Parmenides: A Study of Word, Image and Argument in the Fragments* (1970) (3).

23. This explication of transcendence derives from Merleau-Ponty's "On the Phenomenology of Language" in *Signs*, trans. Richard C. McCleary:

When I speak or understand, I experience that presence of others in myself or of myself in others which is the stumbling-block of the theory of intersubjectivity, I experience that presence of what is represented which is the stumbling-block of the theory of time, and I finally understand what is meant by Husserl's enigmatic statement, "Transcendental subjectivity is intersubjectivity." To the extent that what I say has meaning, I am a different "other" for myself when I am speaking; and to the extent that I understand, I no longer know who is speaking and who is listening. (97)

24. "operational Language": See Merleau-Ponty on the "operative language" in *The Visible and Invisible:*

Why not admit that, just as the musical notation is a *facsimile* made after the event, an abstract portrait of the musical entity, language as a system of explicit relations between signs and signified, sounds and meaning, is a result and a product of the operative language in which sense and sound are in the same relationship as the "little phrase" and the five notes found in it afterwards? This does not mean that musical notation and grammar and linguistics and the "ideas of the intelligence"—which are acquired, available, honorary ideas—are useless, or that, as Leibniz said, the donkey that goes straight to the fodder knows as much about the properties of a straight line as we do; it means that the system of objective relations, the acquired ideas, are themselves caught up in something like a second life and perception, which make the mathematician go straight to entities no one has yet seen, make the *operative* language and algorithm make use of a second visibility, and make ideas be the other side of language and calculus. (153)

See also Lingis, "Translator's Preface," in *The Visible and Invisible* (liii).

25. "*le stade du miroir*": The phrase occurs throughout Lacan's writings and is the subject of the essay, "The Mirror Stage as Formative of the Function of the I as Revealed in Psychoanalytic Experience," now included in *Écrits*, trans. Alan Sheridan (1977) (1–7). In his commentary on *Speech and Language in Psychoanalysis*, Anthony Wilden writes:

> The "mirror phase" derives its name from the importance of mirror relationships in childhood. The significance of children's attempts to appropriate or control their own image in a mirror . . . is that their actions are symptomatic of these deeper relationships. Through his perception of the image of another human being, the child discovers a form (*Gestalt*), a corporeal unity, which is lacking to him at this particular stage of his development. Noting the physiological evidence for the maturing of the cortex after birth—which Freud sought to relate to the genesis of the ego—Lacan interprets the child's fascination with the other's image as an anticipation of his maturing to a future point of corporeal unity by identifying himself with this image. Although there are certain difficulties in Lacan's expression of his views on this extremely significant phase of childhood, the central concept is clear: this primordial experience is symptomatic of what makes the *moi* an Imaginary construct. The ego is an *Idealich*, another self, and the *stade du miroir* is the source of all later identifications. (160)

Blaser's translation of the French *le stade* (stadium, stage) as "stadium" carries the sound of the original, but it also may include by connotation the multiple points of view afforded by a stadium and therefore imply a refracting of the Imaginary egoic self of psychoanalysis. "Stadium" might also recall for us Frances Yates's Memory Theater, cited by Blaser in "The Fire." The effect of these connotations is to complicate specular identity, to imagine the mirror-self multiplied, alienated, or perhaps even shattered. Broken mirrors and broken glass recur in Blaser's early poetry, well before "The Stadium" essay of 1974. For instance, in *The Faerie Queene* sequence (1961), see "So"; and in the *Charms* series (1964–68), see "Aphrodite of the Leaves," "Bottom's Dream," and "The Finder," all included in *The Holy Forest*. The images of broken mirror and glass in these poems point back to Blaser's comment in "The Fire": "It is precisely in the image of the scattered body and mind of Orpheus that I place whatever I know about the poetic process— that scattering is a living reflection of the world" (9).

26. Jack Spicer's inescapable diamond in the Runcible Mountains, which has bases and players inside it. Blaser refers to Spicer's "Seven Poems for the Vancouver Festival: 1": "Start with a baseball diamond high / In the Runcible Mountain wilderness" (*Collected Books* 259). The diamond is a recurring image in Spicer's poems, and as this poem shows, Spicer liked to combine the physical properties of the gem (purity, hardness,

colorlessness, refraction of light, everlastingness) with the punning possibilities of the word: baseball diamond and dia-mond or double world. The diamond is actually a cipher of the human condition—the human "city" as Spicer has it in this poem. It is the play of the game of life (a Kantian purposiveness without purpose); the unanswerable desire for love, immortality, unmediated expression (the diamond as emblem of romance, durability, and purity), and form that has an external "crust" and yet remains dynamic (being as both substance and process, noun and verb, or "wave and particle" as Spicer says [Collected Books 234]). This latter sense is the one that Blaser emphasizes: "his greatest gift was to know this instability. . . ."

27. See also Blaser's citation of Shelley's Triumph of Life in "Lake of Souls" (Holy Forest).

28. See Richard Holmes's Shelley biography, Shelley: The Pursuit (1976), for examples of these stories.

[Shelley] talked to her [Mary Shelley] calmly in the morning about the many other visions he had been seeing lately. The only one Mary records was another meeting with himself. " . . . He had seen the figure of himself which met him as he walked on the terrace & said to him—'How long do you mean to be content?'" It was of course his Zoroastrian double. (727)

29. On the "instability of words" such as "gods, loves, lives," Blaser has this to say in Astonishments, tapes made in 1974, the same year in which Image-Nations 1–12 and The Stadium of the Mirror was published by the Ferry Press:

The word "soul" and the word "God," "ghost," a whole series of these, they're all broken words. They've fallen because they belong to a hierarchy of some kind, a world vision. The world vision fell, the words are still there and they float and haunt us, "ghost" in particular. . . . And one notices that the moment that the words dump out of their images, the hierarchy had the image of God as the old bearded daddy in the sky, a fully humanized figure, the soul with the very definite range of—well, there are even images attached to the nature of the soul. . . . As they fall down, the words all re-open and they re-open into their contents. One notices immediately that the moment that you know that the unknown is at the very edge of the known, and you can take the known to be you at whatever limit you're in at the moment—the unknown, that the moment you've hit that, you've also hit one of the contents that was inside the word "god." ("Excerpts" from Astonishments, Even on Sunday 294)

30. Louis Althusser and Etienne Balibar, Reading Capital (1997), trans. Ben Brewster:

We have now reached the point we had to reach in order to discover from it the reason for this oversight where a sighting is concerned: we must completely reorganize the idea we have of knowledge, we must abandon the mirror myths of immediate vision and reading, and conceive knowledge as a production. (24)

Here Althusser argues that classical economics mistook its object (labor) for something already there when in fact it had produced that object ("What political economy does not see is not a pre-existing object which it could have seen but did not see—but an object which is produced itself in its operation of knowledge and which did not pre-exist" [24]). Althusser contends that Marx recognized this "oversight" for what it was (original emphasis).

31. Gerede: See Martin Heidegger, Being and Time, trans. John Macquarrie and Edward

Robinson (1962), esp. p. 212 on *passing the word along* (original emphasis). By "idle talk," Heidegger refers to talk that closes off Being in its primordial aspect—talk that stages the ontic rather than the ontological.

On Lacanian *parole vide* and its relationship to *Gerede*, Wilden comments:

Gerede ("idle talk")—which is not intended as disparaging in Heidegger as the *parole vide* is disparaging in Lacan—is explicated as "a discoursing which has lost its primary relationship-of-Being towards the existent talked about, or else has never achieved such a relationship." . . . [T]here is a significant and less technical expression of Heidegger's views quoted by Jean Reboul in his "Jacques Lacan et les fondements de la psychanalyse" (1962) . . . : "Man behaves as if he were the creator and master of Language, whereas on the contrary, it is Language which is and remains his sovereign. . . . For in the proper sense of these terms, it is Language which speaks. Man speaks insofar as he replies to Language by listening to what it says to him. Language makes us a sign and it is Language which, first and last, conducts us in this way towards the being of a thing." (201–2)

32. Charlie Chan: This film character was created first by the novelist Earl Derr Biggers and featured in Fox films during the 1930s and 1940s. Charlie was a detective with the Honolulu Police Department and traveled the world solving crimes. In this effort he was hampered to comic effect by his wannabe-detective sons (referred to as #1 son and #2 son); the formulaic plots had him solving mysteries despite their blundering interference. Charlie was also known for his Chinese proverbs. In retrospect, the character exemplified a racial stereotype, and he was played by Caucasian actors: Warner Oland was Charlie Chan until Oland's death in 1938; Sidney Toler picked up the role until 1947, followed by Roland Winters. After World War II, Monogram took over the Chan series from Fox but with little success, and the series went under in the late 1940s (www.charliechan .net). The saying Blaser puts in Chan's mouth here, however, is his own adaptation from the Heraclitean fragments ("it is impossible to step into the same river twice").

33. Merleau-Ponty, *The Visible and Invisible*:

With one sole movement it ["sensoriality"] imposes itself as particular and ceases to be visible as particular. (217–18)

Alphonso Lingis, in his "Translator's Preface" in *The Visible and Invisible*, contextualizes this passage with a comment on serial music:

Serial music, Merleau-Ponty points out (p. 218), discovers the ability of any tone in a series to function as an individual sounded in a field and as the dominant, the field tone, the level at which the melody plays. (xlix–l)

34. "Meaning is a kind of movement": Merleau-Ponty. A fugitive line. The sense of the phrase is apposite to the passages I cited in note 33 above.

35. In *Astonishments*, Blaser recalls reading Mallarmé during his student years at Berkeley. The idea that language can go on speaking without the speaker comes up in passages such as Mallarme's "Crisis in Poetry": "The pure work implies the disappearance of the poet as speaker, yielding his initiative to words, which are mobilized by the shock of their difference" (*Selected Poetry and Prose* 75).

36. Merleau-Ponty, *The Visible and Invisible*:

The taking possession of the world of silence, such as the description of the human body effects it, is no longer this world of silence, it is the world articulated, elevated to the *Wesen*, spoken. . . . Can this rending characteristic of reflection (which, wishing to return to itself, *leaves itself*) come to an end? There would be needed a silence that envelops the speech anew, after one has come to recognize that speech enveloped the alleged silence of the psychological coincidence. What will this silence be? As the reduction finally is not for Husserl a transcendental immanence, but the disclosing of the *Weltthesis*, this silence will *not be the contrary* of language. (179)

37. "discloses a world-thesis": Merleau-Ponty; see note 37 above.

38. "dissimulation of our inherence in the world, history and language": Lefort, "Editor's Foreword":

Finally we must traverse again the route of reflection which is that of modern philosophy—at whose term all the problems appear solved, since thought doubles now the perceptual life over its whole extension and bears into it the principle for a discrimination between the true and the false, the real and the imaginary—and see in what conditions this "solution" is reached, at the cost of what mutilation our situation is converted into a simple object of knowledge, our body into a thing like any other, perception into the thought of perceiving, speech into pure signification, by what artifices the philosopher succeeds in dissimulating to himself his inherence in the world, in history, and in language. (xxv)

Blaser adapts the last part of this sentence.

39. Blaser adapts this phrase from Lefort:

Thus, in the first drafts for an introduction, he [Merleau-Ponty] started with the observation that we cannot find an origin in God, in nature, or in man, that such attempts converge in the myth of a total explication of the world, of a complete adequation between thought and being, which nowise takes into account our insertion in the being of which we speak; that, moreover, this myth no longer sustains any fruitful research in our time, and that to dissipate it is not to fall back into scepticism and irrationalism but is to know for the first time the truth of our situation. (xxv–xxvi)

40. "freedom from the sense of root": This phrase derives from Lefort:

Kafka already said that the things presented themselves to him "not by their roots, but by some point or other situated toward the middle of them." He doubtless said it to express his distress, but the philosopher who frees himself from the myth of the "root" resolutely accepts being situated in this midst and having to start from this "some point or other." (xxvi)

41. Michel Foucault, *The Order of Things* (1970). In the chapter "Man and His Doubles," Foucault argues that the end of unselfconscious representation has meant that "Man" can no longer appropriate his origins as an object of knowledge. Modern, reflexive man is coeval with "the unconscious, and the forms of the unthought":

Man has not been able to describe himself as a configuration in the *episteme* without thought at the same time discovering, both in itself and outside itself, at its borders yet also in its very warp and woof, an element of darkness, an apparently inert density in which it is embedded, an unthought which it contains entirely, yet in which it is also caught. (326)

42. "in the interior labyrinth where the frontiers of the visible fade": This phrase comes from Lefort, "Editor's Foreword," and follows immediately from the comment on Kafka cited in note 40 above:

This restraint ["being situated in this midst" rather than at an origin] is the sign of his [the philosopher's] attachment, and it is because he submits to it that the hope is given him of progressing from one domain to another, in the interior labyrinth where the frontiers of the visible fade, where every question about nature leads to a question about history, every question of this kind to a question about the philosophy of nature or of history, every question about being to a question about language. (xxvi)

43. "an installation": Lefort, "Editor's Foreword,":

It is not a matter of clearing our ruins in order to lay a new foundation; it is rather a matter of recognizing that, whatever we may say about being, we inhabit it with our whole selves, our labor of expression is still an installation in it, finally our interrogation is, for the same reason, without origin and without termination, since our questions always arise from older questions and since no answer can dissipate the mystery of our relation with being. (xxvi)

44. "the grammatical could come to fruition in the heart of what is alone": A fugitive line that Blaser attributes to Claude Lévi-Strauss, without further documentation.

45. "we must ground the notion of the Other with a big O as being the ground of the deployment of the word": Lacan, as cited in Anthony Wilden's notes to Speech and Language (114).

46. "It must be posited that, as a facet of an animal at the mercy of Language, man's desire is desire of the Other": Lacan, as cited in Wilden's notes to Speech and Language (114).

47. "zero-phoneme": See Wilden's endnotes and commentary in "Lacan and the Discourse of the Other," in Speech and Language (128, 220): "the zero-phoneme is one whose function is simply to be opposed to all other phonemes, without entailing any constant phonetic or differential value in itself" (128).

48. The reference is to Charles Olson's Special View of History. As Olson phrases the idea, "Belief, of course, is the same thing as methodology" (42).

49. "The ultimate of my languages or yours—or the culture's—is missing": This notion comes from Mallarmé:

Languages are imperfect in that although there are many, the supreme one is lacking: thinking is to write without accessories, or whispering, but since the immortal word is still tacit, the diversity of tongues on the earth keeps everyone from uttering the word which would be otherwise in one unique rendering, truth itself in its substance. (Selected Poetry and Prose 75)

50. "spoken rather than speaking": Jacques Lacan, "The Function of Language in Psychoanalysis," in Speech and Language in Psychoanalysis:

. . . the question of Language does not remain entirely within the domain of the convolutions in which its use is reflected in the individual.

> We are the hollow men
> We are the stuffed men
> Leaning together
> Headpiece filled with straw. Alas!

and so on.

The resemblance between this situation and the alienation of madness insofar as the formula given above is authentic—that is, that here the subject is spoken rather than speaking—is obviously the result of the exigency, presupposed by psychoanalysis, that there be a true Word. (45)

51. "The Magus Zoroaster, my dead child, / Met his own image walking in the garden": These lines are from Percy Bysshe Shelley's *Prometheus Unbound* (1.192–93).

52. ". . . it is enough to have seen in the recent [myxomatosis] epidemic a blinded rabbit in the middle of a road, lifting the emptiness of his vision changed into a look toward the setting sun: he was human to the point of the tragic" (Lacan, *Speech and Language* 43).

53. "perilous act": Foucault, *Order of Things*:

> Even before prescribing, suggesting a future, saying what must be done, even before exhorting or merely sounding an alarm, thought, at the level of its existence, in its very dawning, is in itself an action— a perilous act. (328)

54. "All true language is thought and so reverses into experience." Compare Lefort, in his foreword to *The Visible and the Invisible*:

> That chance seals the book on ultimate truth, that the book, still far from the term it aimed at, yet closes on a thought that is its prefiguration—in this the reader will not fail to see a sign— the trace of an admonition, as it were, that the work, in the absence of the man, was able to receive. But this sign could not make us forget the meaning, and we must also recognize that what is said here, at the last moment, clarifies the problem of the philosophical work— of the work in general, and of this one we are reading. For in it is disclosed the reversibility of experience and language. It is because it brings or claims to bring the task of expression to its furthest limits, because it wishes to gather up the truth of experience such as it is before it is put into words, and, simultaneously, because it wishes to concentrate and exhaust in it all the powers of speech, that it discovers the impossibility of remaining in either intention, sees its movement reverse itself in both directions, and is finally obliged to declare this indetermination, which constitutes its existence. (xxix–xxx)

55. "profound kinship of language with the world": Foucault, *Order of Things*:

> . . . in the sixteenth century, one asked oneself how it was possible to know that a sign did in fact designate what it signified; from the seventeenth century, one began to ask how a sign could be linked to what it signified. A question to which the Classical period was to reply by the analysis of meaning and signification. But given the fact itself, language was never to be anything more than a particular case of representation (for the Classics) or of signification (for us). The profound kinship of language with the world was thus dissolved. (42–43)

56. "Who is speaking?": Foucault, *Order of Things*:

> For Nietzsche, it was not a matter of knowing what good and evil were in themselves, but of who was being designated, or rather *who was speaking* when one said *Agathos* to designate oneself and *Deilos* to designate others. For it is there, in the *holder* of the discourse and, more profoundly still, in the *possessor* of the word, that language is gathered together in its entirety. To the Nietzchean question: "Who is speaking?", Mallarmé replies—and constantly reverts to that reply— by saying that what is speaking is, in its solitude, in its fragile vibration, in its nothingness, the word itself—not the meaning of the word, but its enigmatic and precarious being. (305)

57. "intentionless and non-communicative utterances of a world": A fugitive line that Blaser attributes to Hannah Arendt.

58. "*cross our celestial legs in the celestial grass*": Herman Melville, in a letter to Hawthorne, June 1851:

> If ever, my dear Hawthorne, in the eternal times that are to come, you and I shall sit down in Paradise, in some little shady corner by ourselves; and if we shall by any means be able to smuggle a basket of champagne there (I won't believe in a Temperance Heaven), and if we shall then cross our celestial legs in the celestial grass that is forever tropical, and strike our glasses and our heads together, till both musically ring in concert,—then, O my dear fellow-mortal, how shall we pleasantly discourse of all the things manifold which now so distress us,—when all the earth shall be but a reminiscence, yea, its final dissolution an antiquity. (*Correspondence* 191–92)

59. "*ungraspable phantom of life that is the key to it all*": Melville, chap. 1 in *Moby-Dick*:

> Why is almost every robust healthy boy with a robust healthy soul in him, at some time or other crazy to go to sea? Why upon your first voyage as passenger, did you yourself feel such a mystical vibration, when first told that you and your ship were now out of sight of land? Why did the old Persians hold the sea holy? Why did the Greeks give it a separate deity, and make him the own brother of Jove? Surely all this is not without meaning. And still deeper the meaning of that story of Narcissus, who because he could not grasp the tormenting, mild image he saw in the fountain, plunged into it and was drowned. But that same image, we ourselves see in all rivers and oceans. It is the image of the ungraspable phantom of life; and this is the key to it all. (5–6)

60. Colin Stuart, a poet and personal friend of Blaser's.

61. "*in these great times . . .* ": The outbreak of World War I caused the humanist and pacifist Karl Kraus to deliver an address against it and the political forces that brought it about, on 19 November in Vienna. The address is titled "In These Great Times":

In these

great times

which I knew when they were this small; which will become small again, provided they have time left for it; and which, because in the realm of organic growth no such transformation is possible, we had better call fat times and, truly, hard times as well; in these times in which things are happening that could not be imagined and in which what can no longer be imagined must happen, for if one could imagine it, it would not happen; in these serious times which have died laughing at the thought that they might become serious; which, surprised by their own tragedy, are reaching for diversion and, catching themselves red-handed, are groping for words; in these loud times which boom with the horrible symphony of actions which produce reports and of reports which cause actions: in these times you should not expect any words of my own from me—none but these words which barely manage to prevent silence from being misinterpreted. (70)

62. "*flesh composed of suns   how can that be?*": Robert Browning, "Parleying with Certain People," as quoted in Lacan, *Speech and Language*:

> "Flesh composed of suns. How can such be?" exclaim the simple ones. (3)

Blaser has adapted the line.

POETRY AND POSITIVISMS

This essay was first published in *Silence, the Word and the Sacred*, ed. E. D. Blodgett and H. G. Coward (Waterloo: Wilfrid Laurier University Press for the Calgary Institute for the Humanities, 1989), pp. 21–50. The book gathers essays presented at a conference sponsored by the Calgary Institute for the Humanities, in Calgary, Alberta, 2–5 October 1986.

1. In a sentence preceeding his endnotes to "Poetry and Positivism" as they appear in *Silence, the Word and the Sacred*, Blaser attributes the phrase "'spiritual ketchup'" to Geoffrey Hartman.

2. Wallace Stevens's poem, "Esthétique du mal," is available in various collections. It was originally published in *Transport to Summer* and can be found in *The Collected Poems of Wallace Stevens* (313–26). For the passages Blaser cites, page references in the *Collected Poems* are 314, 315, 319.

3. "Map is not territory": Alfred Korzybski, *General Semantics Seminar 1937: Olivet College Lectures*. The phrase occurs throughout Lecture 2 (17–31) in this collection as a key point of the seminar and in various places in the other lectures. In Lecture 2:

> PREMISES: 1. Map *is not* territory
>
> 2. Map *is not all* of the territory
>
> 3. Map is *self-reflexive* (28; original emphasis)

The nonidentity of map (language) and territory (the real) is also crucial to Jack Spicer (see Spicer's poem, "The Territory Is Not the Map," in *Heads of the Town up to the Aether* [*Collected Books* 122]). As a component of Blaser's poetics it turns up in "The Stadium of the Mirror" in the idea that language (map) and experience (territory) are polarities.

4. "discourse of cosmos": Michel de Certeau uses the phrase in the essay "Mystic Speech," in *Heterologies: Discourse on the Other*:

> The autographical I is the (empty) space in which the discourse of subjectivity and individuality is constructed. It is defined on the basis of a signifier as a (proper) name, ab-solute, un-bound from the world which no longer supports it, and as the reciprocal term of God, ab-solute, un-bound from the world He no longer supported as his language. This the *mythos* (that which founds speech) our civilization substitutes for the discourse of the cosmos; it is a "full" discourse spoken/produced by its speaker. (94)

5. "the confines of the lyric voice and sensibility": A fugitive quotation. Blaser gives no source.

6. Blaser references Wlad Godzich's foreword to de Certeau's *Heterologies* for this line, but I have been unable to find it there.

7. In Godzich's context, the phrase refers to Lévinas:

> The most consistent denouncer of the Gnostic position in our day has been the French philosopher and Talmudic scholar Emmanuel Lévinas, who, in a work that spans nearly fifty years, has rigorously argued for a notion of truth that is at considerable odds with the dominant rationalist one, a notion that relies upon the category—or, more accurately within the Lévinasian framework, upon the lived experience—of the other. (xv–xvi)

Blaser takes the phrase "lived experience . . . of the other" for poets.

8. See Blaser's "Luck Unluck One Luck" from *Streams I* in *The Holy Forest* for a poetic treatment of *"fortune, infortune, fortune."*

9. "all method is belief": Blaser refers to this idea of Charles Olson's in a number of essays, including "The Stadium of the Mirror" and "The Recovery of the Public World." It comes from *The Special View of History*: "Belief, of course, is the same thing as methodology" (42).

10. For another treatment of the Nicene Creed, see Blaser's "lake of souls (reading notes)," from *Syntax*, in *The Holy Forest*.

11. For a fuller description of Blaser's years at Berkeley and companionship with Spicer and Duncan, see "Excerpts from *Astonishments*" (275–347) and "Interview with Robin Blaser" (349–92) in *Even on Sunday*, ed. Miriam Nichols.

12. This passage from Arendt is a favorite. Blaser cites it in "The Recovery of the Public World" and lifts phrases from it for his libretto, *The Last Supper* (5).

13. In the edition of Mallarmé that Blaser cites—the *Selected Poetry and Prose*, edited by Mary Ann Caws—*grimoire* appears in this passage already translated as "book of spells" (91).

14. "pseudepigraphical Daniel; apocryphal Maccabees": These are books of the Old Testament *Apocrypha*. James H. Charlesworth, in his commentary *The Old Testament Pseudepigrapha & The New Testament*, says of these texts:

> Along with other experts I am convinced that a definition of "Pseudepigrapha" is not possible; one can only describe its contours. Thus, I would define the Old Testament Pseudepigrapha as ancient documents composed by Jews (and sometimes by Christians or expanded by them) that date from approximately 250 B.C.E. to about 200 C.E. . . . Usually, they are attributed to Old Testament figures like Adam, Enoch, Abraham, Isaac, Jacob, Joseph, Moses, David, Solomon, Isaiah, Jeremiah, Baruch, and Ezra. While modern research has shown that such attribution is pseudepigraphical (that is, inaccurately attributed to Adam or other prominent persons in the Bible), the ancient authors (and their communities) believed in the sacredness of these writings. Many Jews most likely assumed that the work derived ultimately (perhaps through dreams or visions) from the person to whom it was attributed. . . . Pseudepigraphical attribution is thus typical of so-called extracanonical and intracanonical works—but one must be careful not to give the impression that we can talk about a closed "canon" before 70 C.E. (xi–xii)

The pseudepigraphical additions to the biblical Book of Daniel as well as the books of the Maccabees are available in various editions as *The Apocrypha*.

15. Blaser does not cite the source in Mallarmé, but the phrase "se percevoir, simple, infiniment sur la terre" comes from "Bucolique," a prose piece that can be found in various anthologies, including Mallarmé's *Oeuvres complètes II* (2003). It is the last phrase in a very long sentence that reads as follows:

> Combien, véritablement, une capitale, où s'exaspère le present, restreint, dehors, la portée de ce miasme . . . il ne traverse pas l'atmosphère de quinze lieues, au-dessus d'herbes et de feuilles . . . nul intérêt ne rappellerait sur le coup—combien de la forteresse construite, par les gens, exprès, contre leur magnificence comme la répand la nature, sauf un recours à la musique dont le haut fourneau transmutatoire chôme, ces mois—je dis combien, sur les remparts, tonne, peu loin, le canon de l'actualité: que le bruit puisse cesser à une si faible distance pour qui coupe, en imagination, une flûte où nouer sa joie selon divers motifs celui, surtout, de se percevoir, simple, infiniment sur la terre. (256)

An English version postdating Blaser's essay is included in *Mallarmé in Prose*, edited by Mary Ann Caws (the editor Blaser favors) and translated by Jill Anderson. For comparison:

> How little does the sound emanate in the fortress deliberately constructed by people as a barrier against nature's magnificence, unless one has recourse to music whose high, transmutative furnace is extinguished during these months. I say how little, on the ramparts, does the cannon of our contemporary period thunder forth: the noise ceasing at such a short distance for the person who, in his imagination, cuts a flute for himself out of a reed, with which to consummate his bliss according to various motifs, in particular that of perceiving himself as ingenuous, in infinite union with the earth. (141–42)

16. "welling fountain of the middle": This phrase occurs in various forms in Hermann Broch's *Death of Virgil*, in the last chapter of the book, titled "Air—The Homecoming," where the dying Virgil is contemplating the cosmos as a form of plant life. Broch's sentences are typically too long to quote in full, but the following excerpts show the sense of the phrase:

> . . . now the fountain of the middle was growing and extending itself upward and downward, welling with liquid elements, having become transparent in conjunction with its own incipient light, stretching upward and downwards, coming into planthood, scarcely a shaft now, far rather a transparent tree branching out with the sun-echo in its rooty depths, caught into a gleaming inscrutability of plant-and-star growth, and at this point it was sheerly unperceivable whether there was still a borderline between plant and star, whether star and plant were not already touching in the archetype, star-echo and plant-echo enmeshed and intergrown in each other, merged together into that mirrored depth where the firmament above and that below touched and dissolved the boundaries of the other and flowed together to form the orb of the world. (472)

> The boundary of plant-life had been reached, the amplitude of growth covered space after space, covered sky after sky, enveloping the starry abundance; the welling, glowing, life-giving fountain of the middle was dried up and dissolved into cool light; the climax was past. And this universe of plants, as if exhausted from the enormous effort of its attack, breathless after its final flare-up, breathed itself out in a sighing silence. (475)

17. "reconstitution of the whole relation of mind and of poem to the world": This phrase refers back to the long quotation from Hazard Adams on Mallarmé (*Philosophy of the Literary Symbolic* 139).

THE RECOVERY OF THE PUBLIC WORLD

This essay was first published in *Reflections on Cultural Policy Past, Present and Future*, ed. Evan Alderson, Robin Blaser, and Harold Coward (Waterloo: Wilfrid Laurier University Press for the Calgary Institute for the Humanities, 1993), pp. 17–38.

1. "The Recovery of the Public World," as Blaser says, is a title taken from a collection of essays on Hannah Arendt: *Hannah Arendt: The Recovery of the Public World*, ed. Melvyn A. Hill (New York: St. Martin's Press, 1979). The phrase refers to Arendt's lifelong meditation on the Greek *polis* as a space for public self-fashioning. Confusingly, the same title was used for a 1995 conference on Blaser, held at the Emily Carr College of Art and Design in Vancouver, and for the publication of conference essays: *The Recovery of the Public*

World: Essays on Poetics in Honour of Robin Blaser, ed. Charles Watts and Edward Byrne (Vancouver: Talonbooks, 1999). In relation to Blaser, the title may thus refer to four separate occasions: the Hill collection on Arendt (an important book for Blaser), the Blaser conference, the Watts-Byrne collection of conference materials, and the essay at hand.

2. This sentence and the one preceeding condense arguments from Arendt's *Human Condition* and *On Revolution*. In *The Human Condition*, see the chapter "Labor" (71–117) where Arendt takes issue with Marx's interpretation of work. In *On Revolution*, in the chapter titled "The Social Question" (59–114), Arendt argues that the French Revolution brought into the public sphere *les malheureux* and then foundered on social problems that had to do with need rather than political freedom. Here is a brief excerpt from this argument in *On Revolution*:

> All rulership has its original and its most legitimate source in man's wish to emancipate himself from life's necessity, and men achieved such liberation by means of violence, by forcing others to bear the burden of life for them. This was the core of slavery, and it is only the rise of technology, and not the rise of modern political ideas as such, which has refuted the old and terrible truth that only violence and rule over others could make some men free. Nothing, we might say today, could be more obsolete than to attempt to liberate mankind from poverty by political means; nothing could be more futile and more dangerous. For the violence which occurs between men who are emancipated from necessity is different from, less terrifying, though often not less cruel, than the primordial violence with which man pits himself against necessity, and which appeared in the full daylight of political, historically recorded events for the first time in the modern age. The result was that necessity invaded the political realm, the only realm where men can be truly free. (114)

3. Blaser takes the idea that "method has all the characteristics of a belief system" from Charles Olson's *Special View of History*. (See "The Stadium of the Mirror," note 48: "Belief, of course, is the same thing as methodology" [*Special View* 42].) This notion is important to Blaser's poetics and it turns up in "The Stadium of the Mirror" (35) and "Poetry and Positivism" (48) as well as "The Recovery of the Public World" (69).

4. The Austrian physicist Erwin Schrödinger (1887–1961) won a Nobel Prize for his theory of wave mechanics, which describes the behavior of electrons. Both Schrödinger and Heisenberg were significant to Blaser's early companions for the new vision of matter they offered. That matter could be both wave and particle delighted Olson in *The Special View of History*, for instance, where it becomes evidence of the dynamism and indeterminacy of things (Olson cites Heisenberg's Uncertainty Principle in *Special View* [39]). See also Spicer's poem in *Language*, "Morphemics" section: "Lew, you and I know how love and death matter / Matter as wave and particle—twins / At the same business" (*Collected Books* 234).

5. "Ah, humanity!": This phrase is uttered by the lawyer who narrates Melville's tale, "Bartleby the Scrivener" and who is unable to comprehend Bartleby's refusal ("I prefer not to") of the commercial world of Wall Street (*Selected Tales* 131).

6. Blaser is quoting accurately from Kantorowicz. However, the Wicksteed translation of Dante's *De Monarchia* that Blaser cites earlier reads as follows:

> That unutterable providence, then, has set two ends before man to be contemplated by him; the blessedness, to wit, of this life, which consists in the exercise of his proper power and

is figured by the terrestrial paradise, and the blessedness of eternal life, which consists in the fruition of the divine aspect, to which his proper power may not ascend unless assisted by the divine light. And this blessedness is given to be understood by the celestial paradise. (277)

7. In Lewis Carroll's nonsense poem, "The Hunting of the Snark," the snark becomes a boojum. See Blaser's comments on this poem in "The Practice of Outside": it was, Blaser says, a favorite of Spicer's.

8. See Blaser's citation of René Girard on scientism or "scientific angelism" at the beginning of "The Violets" (198). The reference is to Girard's *Violence and the Sacred*.

9. The *Globe and Mail* is a Toronto-based newspaper that presents itself as a national, Canadian voice.

10. And flights of angels see thee to thy restlessness: The parody of Horatio's farewell to Hamlet ("Now cracks a noble heart. Good night sweet prince. / And flights of angels sing thee to thy rest" [V.ii.360]) should bring to mind the last scene of the tragedy, when the entire royal family has been poisoned. Blaser's alteration of "rest" to "restlessness" may suggest the restlessness of the Ghost who initiates the action of the play when he tells Hamlet of the King's wrongdoing. The voices Blaser evokes throughout the essay as well as the list of texts in this last paragraph (the *Mahābhārata*, the *Ṛgveda*, Gilgamesh, the *Odyssey*) serve as Ghosts to a culture that, Blaser says in his introductory paragraph, has "murder[ed] . . . human nature."

AMONG AFTERTHOUGHTS ON THIS OCCASION

This essay was first published in *Reflections on Cultural Policy: Past, Present and Future*, ed. Evan Alderson, Robin Blaser, and Harold Coward (Waterloo: Wilfrid Laurier University Press for the Calgary Institute for the Humanities, 1993), pp. 183–90.

1. "This occasion": In the foreword to *Reflections on Cultural Policy*, Harold Coward describes the project that issued in this essay collection:

This volume is the result produced by a research network of scholars who set out to examine the history and development of cultural policies throughout the Classical, Medieval, Renaissance, Romantic, Modern and Postmodern periods. The aim of the project was to examine the roles various worldviews have played in generating the cultural policies of particular periods in the Western world. The [Calgary] Humanities Institute formed a network of scholars from the Humanities and Social Sciences to undertake this task in 1987. In 1988 they were brought to the Institute for several days in September for the purpose of testing out first drafts of their chapters on each other and within the hearing of an invited group of arts administrators, cultural trustees, researchers and educators. The presence of this latter group (the "curriculum group" as we called them) ensured a continual integration between the theoretical and applied aspects in the discussion of the draft chapters. The chapters presented in this volume were revised following the critical discussions described above. (vii)

2. "Evan Alderson's introduction": See *Reflections on Cultural Policy* (1–16). Alderson was a colleague of Blaser's at Simon Fraser University and a founding director of the School for the Contemporary Arts there. He taught interdisciplinary art history and theory in the School before moving to direct the university's Graduate Liberal Studies Program.

3. homes on the range: See Blaser's poem "'home, home on the range'":

'words alone'   yeah   now it's the confrontation with words,
then it's a creation with words   ordinary and
sublime relations   *of the rime you meant to*
come to   a.m. aureole and blue, blue thought all day (*Holy Forest*)

4. Jean Clay, *Modern Art*. The full sentence reads as follows:

Nor does anything exclude the fact that in Western societies, characterized by an extreme specialization in the division of labor and by a mercantilism that controls distribution and hence form, these attributes result little by little in art's radical effacement. (23)

5. Blaser adapts the phrase from Hans Mayer's *Outsiders*. It occurs in Mayer's introductory essay titled "What Are Outsiders? A Note for the American Edition," in a passage where Mayer argues that everyone has become an outsider. The passage is significant to Blaser beyond the present reference in "Among Afterthoughts." See, for instance, his citations from Mayer in the important poem, "Even on Sunday" (*Holy Forest*), written for the Gay Games in Vancouver, 1990.

Mayer:

It becomes more and more difficult, as I see my experiences since the completion of this book in 1975, to distinguish at all any more between outsiders and majorities. Everything can be turned around, so that the historical process that I attempted to sketch must perhaps be understood as the path from the intentional to the existential outsider that then ends with a virtual outsiderdom for everyone, of whatever origin, skin color, language, or tradition.

In all of this there becomes manifest in contradictory fashion both the recantation of the bourgeois Enlightenment and its frightening fulfillment. Again and again in the nineteenth century significant critics of the bourgeoisie yearned for a return to prebourgeois conditions. The consequences of an egalitarian Enlightenment became recognizable in peoples' turning to precisely that which appeared to them *not* as equal and similar but as incomparable: their town and their landscape, their linguistic usage and their origins. It was a process with which we are acquainted today to a far greater extent. (xix–xx)

OUT OF THE VELVET—
THE DENIM—THE STRAW OF MY MIND

This essay was first published in *99 Poets/1999: An International Poetics Symposium, boundary 2* 26, no. 1 (spring 1999): 52–53, a special issued edited by Charles Bernstein.

1. Amos Oz (b. 1939) is an Israeli novelist and peace activist. Author of more than eighteen books in Hebrew and hundreds of articles on the Israeli-Arab conflict, Oz has been active in the Israeli Peace Movement since 1967 and a leading figure in Peace Now, founded in 1977. His writings have been translated into many languages.

2. Christopher Hitchens (b. 1949) is a British-born journalist and prolific author, known for his wit and contrary views (he has criticized Henry Kissinger, Bill Clinton, and Mother Theresa). For the past twenty years, he has been based in Washington, D.C., where he has become an acknowledged expert on American politics and culture. A correspondent for the *Nation* for twenty years, he is an editor at *Harpers* and reviews for the *Times Literary Supplement* and the *New York Times Book Review*. He also writes for *Vanity Fair*.

3. Maya Lin (b. 1959) is a Chinese American architect. At the age of twenty-one she designed the Vietnam Veterans' Memorial in Washington, D.C. (1982), a monument that was at first controversial and then celebrated.

4. the elf of his or her language: Blaser's phrasing recalls "The 'Elf' of It" and his essay on Duncan. The context of this comment in "out of the velvet"—that the poet "hasn't a chance at being apolitical, even if the elf of his or her language wishes to be"—may remind us of the quarrel between Denise Levertov and Duncan over poetry and politics: Duncan argued that Levertov's political engagement was detrimental to her poetry.

5. See "The Recovery of the Public World" and the opening paragraphs of "The Violets" for Blaser's Arendtian commentary on social justice.

6. Francis Fukuyama: Blaser refers to Fukuyama's *The End of History and the Last Man* (1992). See also "Even on Sunday" in *The Holy Forest* for another protestation of Fukuyama.

7. "the lack of meaning in our time and the lack of a world at the centre of meanings we try to impose": Blaser attributes the phrase to Jean-Luc Nancy. It is a dust jacket synopsis of Nancy's *The Sense of the World*.

8. "existentially given": See "Even on Sunday" for a telling passage on the social abuse of the "existential given":

and Hans Mayer notes the tying and untying that confines things:
At the height of the Victorian era, the Bible is once again, as in Cromwell's
time, . . . the spiritual and social foundation of everyday life—O, the once-
again in which we trust—*Declaration is made in the Bible of what is*
proper for woman and what is not. The Bible depicts that which God punished
in Sodom. St. Paul only confirmed the curse one's mind may have a
certain affinity with Christopher Marlowe's, if it is true, as his room-mate
Thomas Kyd tells us, that he thought the apostle Paul a swindler—
who taught a curdled godhead and a curdling view of the *existential*
given—and the black milk of it is blasphemy, so to revile existence

(Holy Forest)

THE IRREPARABLE

This work was published by Nomados Press, Vancouver, in 2003.

1. The phrase, "the immeasurable distance between love and language," comes from an anonymous, back cover paragraph on the paperback edition of Cixous's *Book of Promethea*:

In writing *Le Livre de Promethea* Hélène Cixous set for herself the task of bridging the immeasurable distance between love and language. She describes a love between two women in its totality, experienced as both physical presence and a sense of infinity.

2. See also Blaser's citation of this passage from Flaubert on matter and accompanying commentary in "Interview," *Even on Sunday* (387).

3. This image of Blaser as a small boy reading the big Doré edition of Dante also comes up in "The Hunger of Sound" (*Holy Forest*) and in "Excerpts from *Astonishments*" (*Even on Sunday* 281).

4. as if by chance: the phrase is also the title of one of Blaser's poems, "As If by Chance" (*Holy Forest*).

THE PRACTICE OF OUTSIDE

This essay was first published in Jack Spicer, *The Collected Books of Jack Spicer*, ed. Robin Blaser (1975; reprint, Santa Barbara: Black Sparrow, 1980), pp. 269–329.

1. I have added page references from *The Collected Books of Jack Spicer* for Blaser's many citations of Spicer throughout this essay.

This poem beginning "Heros eat soup" refers to the Mock Turtle's poem in Lewis Carroll's *Alice in Wonderland*:

Beautiful Soup, so rich and green,
Waiting in a hot tureen!
Who for such dainties would not
  stoop?
Soup of the evening, beautiful Soup!
Soup of the evening, beautiful Soup!

  Beau—ootiful Soo—oop!
  Beau—ootiful Soo—oop!
Soo—oop of the e—e—evening,
Beautiful, beautiful Soup!

(Carroll 141)

2. "the serial poem": See Spicer's "Vancouver Lecture 2," now published in *The House That Jack Built: The Collected Lectures of Jack Spicer* (1998), ed. Peter Gizzi (52–96).

3. Spicer, "Vancouver Lecture 1," in *Caterpillar* 12 (176–78) and *The House That Jack Built* (5–8). When Blaser wrote "The Practice of Outside," the first "Vancouver Lecture" had been transcribed from audiotapes, edited by Colin Stuart and Stan Persky, and published in the small press journal, *Caterpillar* 12. A transcript (unpublished) of the other two taped lectures was in Blaser's possession. Blaser takes his quotations from *Caterpillar*, the unpublished transcript, and the tapes themselves. Peter Gizzi, in his edition of Spicer's "Vancouver Lectures" (*The House That Jack Built*) retranscribed all the tapes and his version of "Lecture 1" differs in many details from the *Caterpillar* transcript and from the bits of the other "Lectures" that appear in Blaser's citations. (See Gizzi's description of his edition of the tapes in the preface to *House* [xiv]). I have kept the quotations as Blaser cited them, but where applicable I have cross-referenced the page numbers of "Lecture 1" with Gizzi's edition, since the latter is now the only accessible published version of the "Lectures."

4. "low-ghost": The phrase comes from Spicer's "A Textbook of Poetry" in *Heads of the Town up to the Aether*:

"Esstoneish me," the words say that hide behind my alarm
clock or my dresser drawer or my pillow. "Etonnez moi," even
the Word says.

  It is up to us to astonish them and Him. To draw forth
answers deep from the caverns of objects or from the Word
Himself. Whatever that is.

Whatever That is is not a play on words but a play between
words, meaning come down to hang on a little cross for a while.
In play.

And the stony words that are left down with us greet him
mutely almost rudely casting their own shadows. For example,
the shadow the cross cast.

No, now he is the Lowghost when He is pinned down to
words. (178)

5. "compound of the visible and invisible": Alphonso Lingis, "Translator's Preface,"
in Merleau-Ponty's *The Visible and Invisible*:

Empiricism was a sort of disbelief in the things, an underestimation of the coherence of the
things. The sensible thing is not simply a "wandering troop of sensations"; it holds together
of itself and can be recognized when it returns. Intellectualism is the recognition of this im-
manent unity of the things: the constituent moments of the thing are not simply contin-
gently contiguous to one another; they are internally, intentionally, or meaningfully related
to one another. Only thus can sensuous data announce or manifest a thing—or, at least, that
internal principle, that essence, by which it is one thing and by which it is recognizable. . . .
But can we really *understand* this conjuncture? How is this compound of the visible and the
invisible possible, without undetermining all our positive conceptions of what it means to
be visible and what it means to be invisible? (xli; original emphasis)

6. Spicer, "Vancouver Lecture 2," in *The House That Jack Built* (85). The interlocutor who
"accuses" Spicer of being "more interested in truth than in poetry" was Elliott Gose,
then a professor in the Department of English at the University of British Columbia.

7. Spicer, "Vancouver Lecture 2," in *The House That Jack Built*:

I think it [*The Holy Grail*] goes into more the human condition in relation to the divine, tak-
ing the human just like "Textbook" took the divine in relation to the human. (67–68)

8. Ghosts occur periodically in "A Textbook of Poetry." For instance in #18:

When the gas exploded the ghosts disappeared. There was
merely a city of chittering human beings. (177)

Or in #21:

Hold to the future. With firm hands. The future of each
afterlife, of each ghost, of each word that is about to be
mentioned. (179)

There is also, importantly, the "lowghost" or logos (see note 4 above)

9. With this comment, Blaser refers indirectly to Robert Duncan's remarks on the
"ghostly" in *Poetry/Audit* (1967). These comments were part of the *Chimères* argument,
since Blaser aligned his Nerval translations with the translation theory Spicer had put
forward in *After Lorca*. Here is Duncan:

A FOOTNOTE:

ghost. Throughout his translation Blaser replaces "**esprit,**" "spirit" or "mind," and "**âme,**"
"soul," by the word "ghost"—here clearly associated with "the dead," which Blaser imports
into Nerval's poetry out of the poetry of Jack Spicer. . . .

[Duncan then gives etymologies for *spirit* and soul] in contrast to the word "ghost":

"Although the word is known only in West Germanic languages (in all of which it is found with substantially identical meaning) it appears to be of pre-Teutonic formation" with the meanings listed "to rage, to terrify, to tear to pieces" and related to the word "ghastly": "the kind of horror related to the sight of death or carnage." Which I take to refer to the fury or wrath (wraith) of a person. In the world of Nerval's belief, the esoteric cult of the Kabbala, this effluvia of the decaying body, this corpse-gas, was particularly distinguished from the divine breath and the living spark. It is a serious criticism of Spicer's creation in poetry that he believed in ghosts and remained sceptic of and even antagonistic to life forces. (*Poetry/Audit* 59)

10. On the reversibility of language and experience, see Blaser's comments in "The Stadium of the Mirror" (30) and the passage from Claude Lefort's "Editor's Foreword" to Merleau-Ponty's *The Visible and the Invisible*, cited in my note 54 to "The Stadium of the Mirror."

11. "wild-meaning" (Merleau-Ponty, *Visible* 155); "wild-logos" (Lingis, "Translator's Preface" liii); "birth of meaning" (Merleau-Ponty, *Visible* 155). These terms are also important to Blaser's "Stadium of the Mirror."

12. "infinitely small vocabulary": Spicer, *After Lorca*:

A really perfect poem (no one yet has written one) could be perfectly translated by a person who did not know one word of the language it was written in. A really perfect poem has an infinitely small vocabulary. (*Collected Books* 25)

13. Spicer, "Vancouver Lecture 2":

And you have to go into a serial poem not knowing what the hell you're doing. That's the first thing. You have to be tricked into it. It has to be some path that you've never seen on a map before and so forth. (*House* 52)

14. I have not been able to find the phrase "what must be thought" in Foucault, but the sense of Blaser's allusion to "what has been under or outside our discourse" can be found in Foucault's discussion of the thought and the unthought in "Man and His Doubles," a chapter in *The Order of Things* (303–43). In this chapter Foucault argues that self-reflexive thought cannot grasp its own a priori grounds and will therefore always be accompanied by an "unthought" or "non-thought":

Man is a mode of being which accommodates that dimension—always open, never finally delimited, yet constantly traversed—which extends from a part of himself not reflected in a cogito to the act of thought by which he apprehends that part; and which, in the inverse direction, extends from that pure apprehension to the empirical clutter, the chaotic accumulation of contents, the weight of experiences constantly eluding themselves, the whole silent horizon of what is posited in the sandy stretches of non-thought. (322–23)

15. See note 10 above.

16. a "transparency" of descriptions and relations: On the transparency of language, Foucault writes:

The critical elevation of language, which was a compensation for its subsidence within the object, implied that it had been brought nearer both to an act of knowing, pure of all words, and to the unconscious element in our discourse. It had to be either made transparent to the forms of knowledge, or thrust down into the contents of the unconscious. This certainly explains the nineteenth century's double advance, on the one hand towards formalism in thought and on the other towards the discovery of the unconscious—towards Russell and Freud. (*Order* 299)

17. "recommencement of perception": An adaptation of Merleau-Ponty:

The dialectic become *thesis* (statement) is no longer dialectical ("embalmed" dialectic). This is not for the profit of a *Grund* of which one could not say anything. The failure of the thesis, its (dialectical) reversal discloses the Source of theses, the physico-historical *Lebenswelt*, to which we have to return   To recommence perception, *Einfühlung*, and in particular speech, and not to eschew them. We know simply that, if it is to remain dialectical, speech can no longer be statement, *Satz*, it must be thinking speech, without reference to a *Sachverhalt*, speaking (*parole*) and not language (*langage*). (*Visible* 175; original emphasis)

18. Spicer's *Heads of the Town* is structured like the *Divine Comedy,* as a hell, purgatory, and heaven. See "Vancouver Lecture 1":

This "Textbook of Poetry" is the third part of the HEADS OF THE TOWN UP TO THE AETHER, which is a complicated book, it's all one book. . . . The three books in this, the "Homage to Creeley," "The Fake Novel of the Life of Arthur Rimbaud," and finally, "The Textbook of Poetry," all do connect and they connect in very important ways, but I think that the only thing reading it separately I have to tell you is, that in a sense the first book, the "Homage to Creeley" was on the analogy of Dante's Inferno. The second book, "The Fake Novel about the Life of Arthur Rimbaud" was analogous to Purgatorio, and "The Textbook of Poetry" is analogous to Paradiso. (*Caterpillar* 186; *House* 18)

19. "not the same as the dead": Blaser attributes this phrase to Spicer, "Vancouver Lecture 3," but it does not appear in Gizzi's edition.

20. Ezra Pound, "Canto XC." The Latin citation is in the epigraph:

Animus humanus amor non est,
sed ab ipso amor procedit, et
ideo seipso non diligit, sed amore
    qui seipso procedit. (605)

Blaser does not give the source of the translation he uses in "The Practice of Outside," but it is not Pound's version. At the end of "Canto XC":

Not love but that love flows from it
ex animo
& cannot ergo delight in itself
but only in the love flowing from it. (609)

21. The diamond in Spicer's *Book of Magazine Verse* is a baseball diamond, a dia-mond or double world, and gem. It is the first poem of the sequence "Seven Poems for the Vancouver Festival" (259). See note 26 to "The Stadium of the Mirror."

22. "recommence the perception": See note 17 above.

23. "exhibition of world": R. E. Palmer, discussing Martin Heidegger in Palmer's *Hermeneutics* (160).

24. "have the ground cut from under us": The phrase reads "have cut the ground from under us" in Spicer, "Love Poems #1," from *Language*:

Do the flowers change as I touch your skin?
They are merely buttercups. No sign of death in them. They die
    and you know by their death that it is no longer summer.
    Baseball season.
Actually
I don't remember ever touching your back when there were
    flowers (buttercups and dandelions there) waiting to die.
    The end of summer
The baseball season finished. The
Bumble-bee there cruising over a few poor flowers.
They have cut the ground from under us. The touch
Of your hands on my back. The Giants
Winning 93 games
Is as impossible
In spirit
As the grass we might walk on. (225)

25. "ceremony of his book": Foucault: "Mallarmé was constantly effacing himself from his own language, to the point of not wishing to figure in it except as an executant in a pure ceremony of the Book in which the discourse would compose itself" (*Order* 306).

26. "installation": See Claude Lefort, "Editor's Foreword," in Merleau-Ponty's *The Visible and Invisible* (xxvi), and my note 43 to "The Stadium of the Mirror." See also Blaser's quotations from this "Foreword" in "The Stadium of the Mirror."

27. the dictation will be true and false: Blaser attributes this idea to Spicer, in "Vancouver Lecture 3," but there is no phrase corresponding to it there. In Blaser's series, *The Park* (1960), however, "True and false" are "two sparrows, / chittering" (*Holy Forest*).

28. "operative language": Blaser adapts the idea of an "operative language" from Merleau-Ponty, *The Visible and Invisible* (153). See also Alphonso Lingis's "Translator's Preface" (liii) and my note 24 to "The Stadium of the Mirror."

29. This language is then "'open upon'": This description of the "operative language" comes from Lingis's "Translator's Preface": "This language 'is open upon the things, called forth by the voices of silence, and continues an effort of articulation which is the Being of every being'" (liii). Lingis is citing Merleau-Ponty from *The Visible and Invisible* (126–27).

30. Blaser refers to Giambattista Vico's argument in *The New Science* (*Scienza nuova*, Naples, 1744), Book 2, "Poetic Wisdom," where Vico proposes that perceptual experience ("poetry") is primary to the forming of civil societies (109–297). On Heidegger's sense that we "end" with poetry, Blaser may have in mind the essay ". . . Poetically Man Dwells . . . " (original ellipses) in *Poetry, Language, Thought*: "The poetic is the basic capacity for human dwelling" (228).

31. Here is an example of "Artaud's special language" from the *Artaud Anthology*:

no ezer
e nabo
numiniama
et niamini
maniaminia
    uma (218)

Compare Spicer's "Martian" from "Vancouver Lecture 1": "y yum-bekionshtyk un yk shutd ick mudit taek unponslya?" (*Caterpillar* 182) or "hyem beggedy skreet um ik schudt merdit tek umpolsya. Ishne betronya temp? Gah. Kushnee pad ta" (*House* 12). The two versions are transcriptions of the same "Martian."

32. "the furniture in the room": Spicer, "Vancouver Lecture 1":

> Now, Creeley talks about poems following the dictation of language. It seems to me that's nonsense. Language is part of the furniture in the room. Language isn't anything of itself. It's something which is in the mind of the host that the parasite (the poem) is invading. (*Caterpillar* 179; *House* 9)

33. Ezra Pound, "Canto CXVI" (*Cantos* 795); Charles Olson, "La Chute" (*Collected Poems* 82); Spicer, "Seven Poems for the Vancouver Festival," #1 (*Collected Books* 259).

34. This passage is from Olson's review of Eric Havelock's *Preface to Plato*, now available in *Collected Prose*, ed. Donald Allen and Benjamin Friedlander (357, 358). Blaser's original endnote references the review as published in *Niagara Frontier Review* (summer 1964): 43–44.

35. "intertwining": see Merleau-Ponty's chapter "The Intertwining—the Chiasm" in *The Visible and Invisible* (130–55).

36. "Nobody listens to poetry": Spicer's phrase is "No one listens to poetry," from "Thing Language" in *Language* (*Collected Books* 217).

37. For a description of Spicer's Magic Workshop, see "Toward a Community of Poets: The Magic Workshop Questionnaire" in the "Poems and Documents" section of *The Collected Books of Jack Spicer* (353–60). See also Kevin Killian's account of the workshop in *Poet Be Like God* (79–98).

38. "a finitude which is radically other": Blaser draws this phrase from Foucault's *Order of Things*, quoting, however, without ellipses. The relevant passage in *Order* is as follows:

> At the foundation of all empirical positivities, and of everything that can indicate itself as a concrete limitation of man's existence, we discover a finitude—which is in a sense the same: it is marked by the spatiality of the body, the yawning of desire, and the time of language; and yet it is radically other; in this sense, the limitation is expressed not as a determination imposed upon man from outside (because he has a nature or a history), but as a fundamental finitude which rests on nothing but its own existence as fact, and opens upon the positivity of all concrete limitation. (315)

39. "exhibition of the world": See note 23 above.

40. who is speaking: Foucault, *Order of Things* (305). Foucault identifies the question as "Nietzschean." See also Blaser's use of the question in "The Stadium of the Mirror" and my note 56 to that essay.

41. In the first of these citations on the death of God, Michaud is citing Mallarmé's "Letter to Henri Cazalis (May 14, 1867)" (Michaud 47). The context of the second citation is as follows:

> It has already been pointed out that Mallarmé had lost his faith while pondering "Hérodiade." . . . At the end of this courageous quest, after all appearances were dissolved, there remained only Nothingness, Emptiness, the "Nothing which is truth." This "crushing thought" left room for nothing but despair.

It was just at this moment that Hegel revealed to Mallarmé that *Nothingness was not an end but a point of departure.* (53; original emphasis)

42. This is an edge of thought and it is perilous: See Foucault, Order of Things, on thought as "a perilous act" (328). See also Blaser's citation of this passage in "The Stadium of the Mirror" and my note 53 to that essay.

43. Camponigri:

The fable is the inner and constitutive form of the poetic "logos" and it derives from the time structure of the poetic character. Indeed, the basic sense of "logos," Vico suggests, is fable or myth, while fable, in turn, is properly defined as "true narration." By the fable, as the inner or mental word, the poetic consciousness recounts to itself the significance of the poetic character which it has evoked or created. The essence of this mode of recounting, the narrative, is its time-structure, the before and after of the events which it recounts, because the poetic character is a time-structure. It is only thus, consequently, that its significance can be indicated. The significance of the figure of Jove, for example, in its first reference as the poetic character of the heavens imagined as a vast body incorporating sensate spirit is to re-count the actions of that principle. The significance of Jove is thus indicated by the narra-tion of the acts attributed to him. (178–79)

44. "flowing boundary": This is a phrase Blaser repeats in a number of contexts. See, for instance, his use of it in "Image-Nation 9 (half and half" (Holy Forest).

45. See note 6 above. Here is the exchange in "Vancouver Lecture 2" as Gizzi records it, on truth versus message:

EG [Elliott Gose]: I hate to sort of throw your attack at me back at you, but it seems to me that maybe you're more interested in truth than in poetry. It would seem to me that the per-son who's interested in poetry is interested in language first of all. And he may be interested in truth, or finding something secondly. Whereas I really think that you're interested in find-ing truth first, and that poetry is secondary.

JS [Jack Spicer]: I'm interested in being a conveyor of messages, whether they're the truth or not. There's no reason to suppose that a message necessarily because it's conveyed from an outside source to a poet is true. As far as not being interested in language, it's probably because I'm a professional linguist. (House 85)

46. "The batter is the Martian, spook, or ghost": Spicer, "Vancouver Lecture 3":

The batter is the green Martian, the ghost, the spook, whatever, and it depends entirely on the batter and also on the pitcher, whether he pitches a screw ball or something like that which a catcher can't ordinarily catch, or has to have big gloves to catch and so forth. (House 125)

47. See Duncan's comments on "spirit" and "ghost" in Audit/Poetry, note 9 above.

48. the Event of the real: Alfred North Whitehead, Process and Reality. Donald Sherburne's assemblage of Whitehead's comments on the Event is helpful:

In Process and Reality an event "is a nexus of actual occasions interrelated in some determinate fashion in some extensive quantum: it is either a nexus in its formal completeness, or it is an objectified nexus. . . . An actual occasion is the limiting type of an event with only one member. . . . For example, a molecule is a historic route of actual occasions; and such a route is an 'event.'" (Sherburne 222–23)

49. See Spicer, "Poetry and Politics" (*House* 152–72). The whole lecture is relevant, but Blaser's point is made particularly in comments like this one:

> I mean you're not going to be able to do a good goddamn thing about Vietnam—that's absolutely out—because President Johnson is not terribly interested in whether intellectuals like Vietnam or not. As a matter of fact, I imagine he thinks whenever an intellectual says something about Vietnam, that it's a very good thing for him. (*House* 153)

50. "mosaics of the same elemental particles . . . ": The passage comes from Barnett Lincoln's *The Universe and Dr. Einstein* (1957):

> Man's inescapable impasse is that he himself is part of the world he seeks to explore; his body and proud brain are mosaics of the same elemental particles that compose the dark, drifting dust clouds of interstellar space; he is, in the final analysis, merely an ephemeral conformation of the primordial space-time field. (115)

51. "no longer speaks of identity but of correspondence": This is not Spicer's phrase, but the relevant Spicer comments on correspondence come in *After Lorca*: "Things do not connect; they correspond. That is what makes it possible for a poet to translate real objects, to bring them across language as easily as he can bring them across time" (*Collected Books* 33).

52. "Mela, Mela peto / In medio flumine": These lines are from "Orpheus after Eurydice," now published with Spicer's early poems in *One Night Stand & Other Poems* (20).

53. George Stanley was a participant in Spicer's Magic Workshop (Spicer had chosen 15 of the 50 applicants). In *Poet Be Like God*, Kevin Killian notes that Stanley had written poetry during his first college year at Salt Lake City and later in the army. As a sophomore at Berkeley, Stanley found his way to The Place in North Beach and met Spicer through Joe Dunn, to whom he had shown a poem (Ellingham and Killian 81–83). Stanley became active in Spicer's circle in North Beach and then moved north to Vancouver with Blaser and Persky in the 1960s. He is now an established poet and teaches at Capilano College in North Vancouver.

54. See also Blaser's comments on love in "The Violets":

> This introductory notice of Whitehead [in Olson's *Special View of History*] excellently summarizes a living sense of the relational. Olson was then to draw out the implications for a "measured" human will. The uncertainty in the process becomes the most difficult part to learn, for it is identified with love. Lest the word love seem soft or too human, I point out that the "backwards and outward" movement of information, made dynamic in relation to present cultural conditions, becomes in the vast world of *The Maximus Poems* a methodology for a return to that with which we are most familiar. (213)

55. "Die Moorsoldaten" was written by Johann Esser and Wolfgang Langhoff, with music by Rudi Goguel. The German original of the song is readily available on the Internet (http://viadrina.euv-frankfurt-o.de/~juso-hsg/lieder/moorsoldaten/moor.htm). It differs from Blaser's transcription in certain details of spelling, and Blaser has omitted verses 2–4.

56. Ezra Pound, "Canto LXXVI":

> Le paradis n'est pas artificiel,
>   l'enfer non plus.
>
>   (*Cantos* 460)

57. Jean Doresse attributes the book title, *The Heads of the Town up to the Aether*, to the Peratae sect of the Egyptian Gnostics. (The Gnostic sects competed with Christianity in the first centuries after Christ until they were eventually suppressed by orthodox Christians as heretical.) On *Heads of the Town*, Doresse writes:

> It seems to have been, essentially, a description and enumeration of the powers of the lower heavens. . . . According to the Peratae, "the universe is composed of the Father, the Son and of Matter. Each of these *three* principles possesses within itself an infinity of powers. Between Matter and the Father resides the Son—Word and Spirit—a median principle always in movement, either toward the immobile Father or towards Matter, which is moved." (50)

58. The line from Poe's *Marginalia* is "Indefiniteness is an element of the true music." The Spicer poem Blaser here refers to is "Improvisations on a Sentence by Poe":

> "Indefiniteness is an element of the true music."
> The grand concord of what
> Does not stoop to definition. . . .
>
> (*Collected Books* 69)

59. Michel de Montaigne, "De L'Amitié" (*Essais*, Livre 1, 236).
In the Penguin edition, these lines from "On Friendship" are translated as follows:

> If I were pressed to say why I love him, I feel that my only reply could be: "Because it was he, because it was I." (*Essays* 97)

See also the poem "untranslatable reason" in *Pell Mell* (from *The Holy Forest*) where Blaser repeats this passage.

IMAGINARY LETTERS BY MARY BUTTS

This essay appeared as the afterword in Mary Butts, *Imaginary Letters* (Vancouver: Talonbooks, 1979), pp. 61–80.

1. "Brightness falls from the air": This line recurs again in the title of the short story "Brightness Falls" from the *Selected Stories* (203–17).

2. Goldring's account of the occult symbols on the floor of Cecil Maitland's bedroom is in *South Lodge*:

> Everything to do with esoteric religion and its practitioners, everything to do with Magic—black or white—had a peculiar fascination for Cecil, in spite of the fact that he was naturally skeptical and like most Scots, hard-headed. As a boy, scarcely out of his teens, he had attended a Black Mass in Edinburgh, and found it a dull performance. When I first met him he had for some time past been indulging—in his big basement-bedroom at Belsize Park Gardens—in various experiments for the raising of devils. Pentagons and magic circles were chalked on the floor. (158–59)

Goldring mentions the Butts-Maitland visit to "a noted Mage" (148) earlier in this same chapter, titled "Mary and Cecil" (*South Lodge* 147–64).

3. In the original version of this essay, Blaser does not give page references or documentation for the citations. The page references I have inserted for the quotations from Alistair Crowley's *Confessions* come from a 1989 reprint, edited by John Symonds and Kenneth Grant. The text, however, reads the same as it does in Blaser's essay.

4. As Goldring puts it, "Neither Cecil nor I had ever been able to cure Mary of her passion for befriending odd persons of apparently aristocratic origin. Prince _____ was the worst of a long series of similar protégés" (*South Lodge* 153). The context of this remark is Goldring's story of a predinner absinthe at the Butts and Maitland residence, during which pleasantry Maitland turns the latest "Prince," a domestic nuisance apparently, out of doors (*South Lodge* 153–54).

5. The "Lettres Imaginaire" are more readily available in the 1992 edition of Mary Butts's *From Altar to Chimney-Piece: Selected Stories*. The lines Blaser quotes appear on pp. 170–71 of that edition. The text is identical to Blaser's citation.

GEORGE BOWERING'S PLAIN SONG

This essay first appeared as the introduction to *Particular Accidents, Selected Poems / George Bowering*, ed. Robin Blaser (Vancouver: Talonbooks, 1980), pp. 9–28.

1. Form, then, in this practice is alive: see also Blaser's discussion of form in "The Stadium of the Mirror," beginning with the statement, "Form is alive, not a completion of the heart or of the mind."

2. In *Particular Accidents*, this line from "The Descent" is on p. 40. However, the poem is also available in the more recent *George Bowering Selected Poems, 1961–1992*, ed. Roy Miki (6–12).

3. the otherness of language, *older and other than ourselves:* See "The Stadium of the Mirror" for elaboration on the concept and the italicized phrase (34).

4. The writer and teacher Robin Mathews has long been a passionate defender of Canadian autonomy and an antagonist of Bowering's and the TISH poets. Among Mathews's publications on what he sees as American cultural imperialism and shameful Canadian complicity are the following: *The Struggle for Canadian Universities, a Dossier* (1969); *Canadian Literature: Surrender or Revolution* (1978); *Canadian Identity: Major Forces Shaping the Life of a People* (1988); *The Treason of the Intellectuals: English Canada in the Post-Modern Period* (1995). Mathews is, to my knowledge, the most outspoken among critics who read Bowering and other TISH writers as Americans in disguise. Hence Bowering's digs at "Sparrow" in *A Short, Sad Book*. Blaser refers to Bowering's comment that robins migrate and sparrows never leave. Blaser, of course, is a "robin" who migrated. In *A Short Sad Book*, one of the ironies of the Sparrow references is that Mathews, the most nationalistic of Bowering's critics, received some of his education in the United States, at Ohio State University.

5. "Mars" was originally published in *Genève*; it is also included in *Particular Accidents* (93). *The Sensible* (1972) is a chapbook.

6. "Grandfather": This poem, dating from 1962, has been much anthologized. It is to be found in *Particular Accidents* (30–31) and in such anthologies as *Fifteen Canadian Poets*, edited by Gary Geddes and Phyllis Bruce, a standard teaching collection of contemporary Canadian poetry that has gone through several editions, each one larger than the last—hence *Fifteen Canadian Poets Plus Five* and *Fifteen Canadian Poets Times Two*.

7. "sticks and stones": The phrase is taken from an early Bowering collection, *Sticks and Stones*, published with a preface by Robert Creeley and drawings by Gordon Payne by Tishbooks in 1963 and reissued by Talonbooks in 1989.

8. The young man, born in Penticton in 1935, would inevitably think he had to make "it" out of whole cloth: Like a few other young men, perhaps? In "The Practice of Outside," Blaser writes, "Out there [in Berkeley], as Duncan once said, we made a poetry up out of wholecloth" (in Spicer, *Collected Books* 324).

9. "Desert Elm" (1973) is a poem in ten parts, published in *The Catch* (1976) (103–12). These lines are from section VIII (110). Sections of the poem also appear in various later collections.

10. "trying to find out where you are—not a literary device": Blaser has adapted this line from Bowering's comments in the *Out-Posts* interview:

> The word that we used all the time was "locus," which we liked partly because it came out of Olson, partly because it didn't say setting, it didn't say place, it didn't say landscape, it didn't say all those things that are literary devices. Every time you use one of those terms you posit a person who is saying, OK, now how can I organize all this into a literary work. But if you say locus, it implies trying to find out where you are. It implies, I'm trying to locate myself. (Bayard and David 79)

11. In this passage from the introduction to *TISH* 1–19 (Talonbooks' 1979 reprint of the first nineteen issues of *TISH*), Davey is paraphrasing Warren Tallman's essay, "When a New Music Is Heard the Walls of the City Tremble" (published in *TISH* 3). Blaser elides the reference to Tallman. Davey's original reads as follows:

> Tallman's essay also makes clear that in the overall tradition of Canadian poetry TISH and its poets belong to the "universist" line of Lampman, Carman, W. W. E. Ross, Klein, Souster, Layton and Purdy, rather than to the humanist and rationalist one of Goldsmith, Sangster, Pratt, Smith, F. R. Scott, Finch, LePan, Reaney, Mandel and Gustafson. (10)

12. These lines are from Margaret Avison's "Perspective." Blaser cites the poem but not the book or page number. The poem is perhaps most easily available now in Avison's 1991 *Selected Poems* (3).

13. Warren Tallman's essay, "The Wonder Merchants: Modernist Poetry in Vancouver in the 1960s," is a seminal description of TISH and Black Mountain in 1960s Vancouver. Tallman was a professor in the Department of English at the University of British Columbia and a key figure in bringing New American poets to Vancouver. The TISH poets were initially his students, and it was Warren and Ellen Tallman who organized the visits of Robert Duncan that sparked the creation of the TISH newsletter (see Frank Davey's introduction to *TISH* 1–19 for the narrative). The Tallmans were also instrumental in organizing the Vancouver Poetry Conference of 1963, which brought many key New Americans to the city (Olson, Creeley, Duncan, Levertov, and Ginsberg, among others).

14. Bowering's book on Purdy is simply called *Al Purdy* (1970); the essay on Avison is "Margaret Avison's Imitation of Christ the Artist," in *Canadian Literature* (1972).

THE VIOLETS

This essay first appeared in *Process Studies* 13, no. 1 (spring 1983): 8–37; reprint, *Line* 2 (fall 1983): 61–103.

For the many citations from *Process and Reality* in this essay, I have added page numbers to the part, chapter, and section numbers from the "Corrected Edition" for convenience of reference. However, as Blaser's notes make clear, Olson was using the 1929 Cambridge University Press edition, which is paginated differently. The version of "The Violets" published in *Process Studies* differs in some details from that in *Line*: for this collection, the text from *Line* has been used as it is a slightly fuller version.

1. "recovery of the public world": See my note 1 to "The Recovery of the Public World" on the occurrence of this phrase in Blaser's work.

2. Blaser's references to the epic here may remind us that the postmodern long poem blends the epic and lyric genres. In my view, the serial poem, as Olson and Blaser practice it, situates the lyric voice in its historical context. Unlike ancient epic, it personalizes and diminishes the epic voice; unlike the romantic lyric, it lets history into the poem, repositioning the personal in a public (historical) context.

3. On Blaser's use of the word *operative*, see "The Stadium of the Mirror" and my note 24 to that essay. The term comes up in "The Practice of Outside" as well, where it is informed by Alphonso Lingis's introduction to Merleau-Ponty's *The Visible and Invisible* as well as Merleau-Ponty's own use of it. Lingis writes that Merleau-Ponty had planned a text that would

> explore the divergencies, the disequilibriums, the reverberations back over itself that initiate and animate speech. It would explore not the cultivated language that employs a system of explicit relations between signs and meanings, but the operative language, that of literature, of poetry, of conversation, and of philosophy, which possesses meaning less than it is possessed by it, does not speak of it, but speaks it, or speaks *according to it*, or lets it speak and be spoken within us, breaks through our present. (liii)

In this passage, Lingis uses phrases from Merleau-Ponty's discussion of speech in *The Visible and Invisible* (118).

4. The Olson phrases in Sherman Paul's citation come from *Olson: The Journal of the Charles Olson Archives* #2 (45).

5. Blaser himself first published Olson's "A comprehension (a measure, that" in *Pacific Nation* 1 (June 1967): 42–44. This piece of Olson's is now more readily available in *The Collected Prose*, edited by Donald Allen and Benjamin Friedlander. (361–63).

"MIND CANARIES"

This essay first appeared in *Christos Dikeakos* (Vancouver: Vancouver Art Gallery, 1986), pp. 17–36, a catalogue for an exhibition of the work of Christos Dikeakos, curated by Scott Watson for the Vancouver Art Gallery, 1 February–16 March 1986. The catalogue includes an essay by Watson, "The Legend of Icarus: From Subversion to Transgression," as well as Blaser's "Mind Canaries."

1. "Mind Canaries": The title of this essay came out of a conversation between Chris Dikeakos and Robin Blaser about the exhibition. Dikeakos had compared his works to the canaries formerly used to test the safety of underground mines; the birds would be sent down mine shafts to determine whether the air was toxic or not. Analogously, Dikeakos's collages are *mind* canaries that test the intelligence of and check for toxicities in contemporary culture.

2. Otto Lilienthal (1848–96), a mechanical engineer from Anklam, Germany, invented gliders and flying machines that were precursors to the Wright brothers' first airplane. Lilianthal launched his first glider in 1891.

3. This passage from Hannah Arendt is one that Blaser turns to often. For example, see "The Stadium of the Mirror" (30) for a paraphrase and a different context.

4. See Blaser's comments on "The Hunting of the Snark" in "The Practice of Outside" (151). The poem was especially important to Jack Spicer.

5. The reference is to Eadweard Muybridge's *Complete Human and Animal Locomotion*.

6. Duchamp's notes on the Glass have been published in *Marcel Duchamp, Notes*, trans. and arranged by Paul Matisse (1983).

7. For another use of this passage from Lyotard, see "Poetry and Positivisms" (48).

8. See Blaser's use of the Serres passage "Nothing distinguishes me ontologically from a crystal, a plant, an animal, or the order of the world: we are drifting together toward the noise and the black depths of the universe" at the beginning of "Image-Nation 25 (Exody" (*Holy Forest*).

"MY VOCABULARY DID THIS TO ME"

This essay first appeared in *Acts: A Journal of New Writing* 6: *A Book of Correspondences for Jack Spicer*, ed. David Levi Strauss and Benjamin Hollander (1987): 98–105.

"'My Vocabulary'" was transcribed from a talk given at the Jack Spicer Conference at New College of California on 20 June 1986. As a published talk, "'My Vocabulary'" really belongs in a "collected prose" rather than here in the *Collected Essays*. However, as I say in my commentary at the end of this collection, I have included it here because it complements and explicates "The Practice of Outside," one of Blaser's most significant essays.

1. See "The Practice of Outside" for the narrative of Spicer's death and the origin of this title.

2. I.W.W.: Industrial Workers of the World, a pan-American labor union organization, had its founding convention in 1905 in Chicago. The Wobblies, as they were called, stood for workers' rights and fair working conditions. During World War I, the IWW lost support for language that sounded too inflammatory in the context of the times and for its championing of immigrants and minorities. In the last year of war, the U.S. government seized records and jailed union leaders for potential subversion, effectively breaking the union. Although the IWW had surges in membership during the Great Depression and the 1960s and although it continues to exist, it has not recovered its earlier power.

Emma Goldman (1869–1940), a Lithuanian-born anarchist activist, worked as a seamstress in a corset factory in Chicago. Her political work included the promotion of free workers' cooperatives and women's rights, including birth control and unmarried love. From 1908 to 1916 she published "Mother Earth," an anarchist newletter. She was arrested in 1919 for antidraft activities and deported to Russia, where she first supported and then critiqued the Bolshevik Revolution.

Rosa Luxembourg (1871–1919), a Polish-born political radical, was active in the German Social Democatic Party (SPD) and the Russian Revolution of 1905. She founded the Spartacists, a revolutionary faction of the SPD and from this group a Communist Party. She was arrested and executed in Germany for her political activities.

3. *View* magazine, 1940–47, a quarterly from New York, was edited by Charles Henri Ford. The magazine counted among its contributors André Breton, Henry Miller, Randall Jarrell, Man Ray, Marcel Duchamp, Wallace Stevens, Marc Chagall, Max Jacob, Jorge Luis Borges, Jean-Paul Sartre, René Char, Albert Camus, Picasso, Brancusi, Paul Goodman, and many more.

4. *Circle* magazine, c. 1944–46, was based in Berkeley, California, and edited by George Leite and Bern Porter. An editorial frontispiece in the first issue (*Circle* 1, no. 1 [1944]) announces the magazine as "West Coast," with a mandate to publish local work. Contributors to that first issue included Henry Miller, Philip Lamantia, and Josephine Miles. Miles was a professor at Berkeley and an important teacher for Blaser, Spicer, and Duncan.

5. "If you pull him out of the sky you will find him in the street": Herman Melville, letter to Nathaniel Hawthorne, c. 16 April 1851, Pittsfield. The line is slightly misquoted. In the *Letters*, the passage reads as follows:

> We incline to think that the Problem of the Universe is like the Freemason's mighty secret, so terrible to all children. It turns out, at last, to consist in a triangle, a mallet, and an apron,—nothing more! We incline to think that God cannot explain His own secrets, and that He would like a little information upon certain points Himself. We mortals astonish Him as much as He us. But it is this *Being* of the matter; there lies the knot with which we choke ourselves. As soon as you say *Me*, a *God*, a *Nature*, so soon you jump off from your stool and hang from the beam. Yes, that word is the hangman. Take God out of the dictionary, and you would have Him in the street. (*Letters* 125)

6. Mark C. Taylor is the "a/theologian." Blaser refers to a passage in *Erring: A Postmodern A/Theology*: "God, self, history, and book are, thus, bound in an intricate relationship in which each mirrors the other. No single concept can be changed without altering all of the others" (7).

7. See my notes 11 on Edith Cobb and 12 on Margaret Mead and Cobb to "The Fire." The passage Blaser refers to is not in Cobb's *Ecology of the Imagination* but in an article titled "The Ecology of Imagination in Childhood," *Daedalus* (summer 1959): 540.

8. The Spicer comment is in the second "Vancouver Lecture," transcribed in *The House That Jack Built* (ed. Peter Gizzi): "If you don't know what happened in the search for the Grail and all of that, presumably if the poem's good enough, it won't matter. And if you've read Jessie Weston, you might as well leave the room" (57).

9. the countervailing tradition: Wlad Godzich, "Foreword," in de Certeau's *Heterologies*, p. viii.

10. The language here comes from Godzich: "Western thought has always thematized the other as a threat to be reduced, as a potential same-to-be, a not-yet-same" ("Foreword" xiii).

11. The phrase "lived experience of the Other," comes from Godzich, not directly from Levinas: "The most consistent denouncer of the gnostic position in our day has been the French philosopher and Talmudic scholar Emmanuel Lévinas, who, in a work

that spans nearly fifty years, has rigorously argued for a notion of truth that is at considerable odds with the dominant rationalist one, a notion that relies upon the category—or, more accurately within the Lévinasian framework, upon the lived experience—of the other" ("Foreword" xv–xvi).

12. The phrase "forms of active social interactions and practice" references Godzich: "Unlike language, which, as an object of knowledge, is a construct of philosophers and linguists, discourses constitute forms of actual social interaction and practice" ("Foreword" xx).

13. "No one listens to poetry": This line comes in Spicer's "Thing Language," from the series *Language* (1964):

> This ocean, humiliating in its disguises
> Tougher than anything.
> No one listens to poetry. The ocean
> Does not mean to be listened to. A drop
> Or a crash of water. It means
> Nothing.
> It
> Is bread and butter
> Pepper and salt. The death
> That young men hope for. Aimlessly
> It pounds the shore. White and aimless signals. No
> One listens to poetry.

(Collected Books 217)

14. "Literature is not a special mode of language, but a part of language, a mode of language, a discourse of the sacred": This sentence sounds very much like an adaptation of Godzich rather than de Certeau: "The quality that is recognized in literature, he [de Certeau] seems to think, does not come from the fact that it is a special mode of language, but rather from the fact that it is a part of language, a mode of language use, that is a discourse" ("Foreword" xx).

15. Blaser does not give a citation for this reference to *The Odyssey*, Book 24, but in the Russell Fitzgerald translation, it reads as follows:

> So every day she wove on the great loom—
> but every night by torchlight she unwove it,
> and so for three years she deceived the Akhaians.
> But when the seasons brought the fourth around,
> as long months waned, and the slow days were spent,
> one of her maids, who knew the secret, told us.
> We found her unraveling the splendid shroud,
> and then she had to finish willy nilly—
> finish, and show the big loom woven tight
> from beam to beam with cloth. She washed the shrouding
> clean as sun or moonlight. (449)

16. "the mystic speech": See Michel de Certeau's essay, "Mystic Speech" in *Heterologies* (80–100).

17. content of the word "God": See Blaser's comments on the content of this word in "Excerpts from *Astonishments*," in *Even on Sunday*, cited in my note 29 to "Stadium of the Mirror."

See also my discussion of this passage and of the sacral element in Blaser's poetics in "Spilling the Names of God: Robin Blaser's *The Last Supper*," Mosaic 36, no. 2 (June 2003): 163–78.

18. "'wild voices'": De Certeau is referring to the mystic tradition: "A field of knowledge takes leave of its textural 'authorities' to turn to the exegesis of 'wild' voices. Innumerable biographies of poor 'girls' or 'enlightened illiterates' were produced, and constitute an important part of the spiritual literature of the time" (*Heterologies* 87).

19. "wild logos": See my note 11 to "The Practice of Outside." The "wild logos" is from Merleau-Ponty's *The Visible and the Invisible*.

20. "Lowghosts": See my note 4 to "The Practice of Outside" on this word of Spicer's.

21. De Certeau makes this argument in "Mystic Speech" where he says that "the 'I' speaks the language of the other" (*Heterologies* 93).

22. "How shitty the world is": This is Spicer in #10 of "Ten Poems for Downbeat" (*The Book of Magazine Verse*), addressing Allen Ginsberg:

> At least we both know how shitty the world is. You wearing a
> beard as a mask to disguise it. I wearing my tired smile. I
> don't see how you do it. One hundred thousand university
> students marching with you. Toward
> A necessity which is not love but is a name.
>
> (*Collected Books* 267)

23. See Blaser's "Poetry and Positivisms" in this collection for a discussion of Susan Handelman's *Slayers of Moses* and her treatment of deconstruction.

INFINITE WORLDS

This essay first appeared in *Infinite Worlds: The Poetry of Louis Dudek*, ed. Robin Blaser (Montréal: Véhicule Press, 1988), pp. 7–29.

1. "Can anything be done to sew the earth together?": This line is quoted in Frank Davey's *Louis Dudek & Raymond Souster* (39).

2. "Northrop Frye's Untenable Position" is now more readily available in Dudek's *Selected Essays and Criticism* (175–79).

3. form is alive: This phrase directly repeats a line in "The Stadium of the Mirror": "Form is alive, not a completion of the heart of the mind" (27).

4. "ideal reader": See Blaser's essay on Duncan, "The 'Elf' of It," which features Duncan's series of drawings titled "The Ideal Reader." See also my remarks on the same in the concluding commentary to this collection.

5. See Blaser's "Poetry and Positivisms" for a full and polemical discussion of modern positivisms.

6. As Blaser's footnote indicates, the quoted phrase is an adaptation of Jean-François Lyotard. In *The Postmodern Condition*, Lyotard writes:

Finally, it must be clear that it is our business not to supply reality but to invent allusions to the conceivable which cannot be presented. (81)

7. The relevant passage in John Tytell's *Ezra Pound: The Solitary Volcano* reads as follows:

And Pound's resistance, though born of blind folly and a stubborn sort of self-righteousness, was tragic because it caused a man of great sensibility, a great musician of the mind, to suffer great pain. Suffering itself is a private matter; tragedy is something that can touch us all. Pound, in his challenge to the state, had made himself a public man, an archetype of the rebel artist, and his pain was a matter that people would continue to consider. (320)

8. *Continuation II* was released in 1990 by Véhicule Press (Montréal).

THE "ELF" OF IT

This essay first appeared in *Robert Duncan: Drawings and Decorated Books*, ed. Christopher Wagstaff (Berkeley: Rose Books, 1992), pp. 21–28, 44–53, a catalogue for a two-part exhibition at the University Art Museum and Pacific Film Archive, 9 February–12 April 1992, and the Bancroft Library, 9 February–30 May 1992, University of California, Berkeley, curated by Christopher Wagstaff. The discontinuous page numbering for Blaser's essay accommodates reproductions of Duncan's drawings.

1. "borderguards": A reference to Duncan's "Song of the Borderguard," a chapbook originally published at Black Mountain by the Black Mountain Graphics Workshop. The poem "Song of the Borderguard" also appears in *A Book of Resemblances: Poems: 1950–1953* (20–22) and is included in the 1997 *Selected Poems*, edited by Robert Bertholf (27–28). In this poem, "The sound of words waits— / a barbarian host at the borderline of sense" (*Selected Poems* 27). The poet is the one who stands between sense and non-sense.

2. The poem "Upon Taking Hold," from *Letters*, is also available in the *Selected Poems*, edited by Bertholf, 1997 (43–45). The *Letters* poems are arranged by lowercase roman numerals instead of page numbers. I have cited them in the text in this fashion: "iii: Upon Taking Hold."

3. The reference is to a passage from Arendt in the essay on Lessing in *Men in Dark Times* (25). See Blaser's use of it in "The Stadium of the Mirror" and my note 11 to that essay.

4. Blaser has adapted these phrases from Bakhtin's *Art and Answerability*:

The crisis of life, in distinction to the crisis of authorship (although the former often accompanies the latter), consists in populating life with literary heroes, in life's falling away from its absolute future, in the transformation of life into a tragedy without a chorus and without an author. (206)

5. language as "older and other": Blaser explicates this idea in "The Stadium of the Mirror" (34).

6. The phrases from Whitehead come from *Process and Reality* I.II.II (p. 22 in the corrected edition). "Prehensions, or Concrete Facts of Relatedness," constitute one of Whitehead's eight categories of existence.

7. *pli selon pli*: The phrase comes from Mallarmé's poem "Rémemoration d'amis belges":

Á des heures et sans que tel soufflé l'émeuve
Toute la vétusté presque couleur encens

Comme furtive d'elle et visible je sens
Que se dévêt pli selon pli la pierre veuve

(*Oeuvres complètes* I 32)

"Folding" is of particular significance to Blaser, as it comes to him in Mallarmé and much later in Gilles Deleuze's *The Fold*. On Blaser's text as a Deleuzean "*poiesis* of origami" (McCaffery 378) see Steve McCaffery's essay, "Blaser's Deleuzean Folds," in *The Recovery of the Public World* (1999).

8. The phrase from Joyce is the first in *Finnegans Wake*:: "riverrun, past Eve and Adam's, from swerve of shore to bend of bay, brings us by a commodius vicus of recirculation back to Howth Castle and Environs" (3).

9. I have not been able to find the phrase "hymn of connections," but Pierre Boulez's *Pli selon Pli*, a musical work in five movements, was mapped in 1958–59 and realized between 1958 and 1961. The piece sets to music three poems by Mallarmé: "Le vierge, le vivace et le bel aujourd'hui," about a swan stuck in ice and unable to fly; "Une dentelle s'abolit," a poem of disappearances and absence, a hollow mandolin, a room without a bed; and "A la nue accablante tu," about a shipwreck. (See note 7 above for the source of the title.) Joan Peyser, in a book on Boulez that Blaser used in his teaching at Simon Fraser, notes the following:

> Boulez took his title *Pli Selon Pli* ("Fold by Fold"), from another of Mallarmé's poems in which the poet describes how the dissolving mist gradually reveals the city of Bruges. "In the same way," Boulez writes in program notes to his Columbia recording, "as the five pieces unfold, they reveal, fold by fold, a portrait of Mallarmé." (*Boulez* 143)

10. Blaser may have in mind the "informing spirit" in John Livingston Lowes's *The Road to Xanadu*:

> And it is the precisely the incredible *olla-podrida* as it is which I am anxious, before going farther, to set forth: confusion at its worst confounded, as the elemental stuff of poetry—its "*materies . . . et corpora prima*"—waiting only for the informing spirit which broods over chaos to draw it (in Milton's rendering of the magnificient Lucretian phrase) into "precincts of light." (6–7; original ellipsis and emphasis)

11. "wild logos": See "The Stadium of the Mirror" (28) and "The Practice of Outside" (119) where Blaser makes broader use of this term of Merleau-Ponty's.

12. This passage from Mark C. Taylor is a favorite. See "Poetry and Positivism" (56), "Among Afterthoughts" (94), "'Elf,'" and "'My Vocabulary'" (255).

PREFACE TO THE EARLY
POEMS OF ROBERT DUNCAN

This preface, published as a chapbook of nine pages (Toronto: Shuffaloff Books, 1995), includes the following note on the copyright page: "This essay was originally written for the first volume of *The Collected Works of Robert Duncan*, to be published by the University of California Press. Because of a revised plan for the edition, it could not be included. It has appeared in a previous version in *A Symposium of the Imagination: Robert Duncan in Word and Image* published by the Poetry/Rare Books Collection, University Libraries, State University of New York at Buffalo." Shuffaloff Books is a small Toronto-based press; its books are distributed by Small Press Distribution.

1. See Blaser's account of Duncan's introduction to Joyce in "Excerpts from Astonishments," *Even on Sunday* (316–22).

2. Robert Duncan: "I make poetry as other men make war or make love." In the chapbook publication of the preface, Blaser cites "The Artist's View," no. 5, 1953, for these lines with no page number. Duncan republished this piece as "Pages from a Notebook" for his "Statement on Poetics" in *The New American Poetry*, where the cited lines appear on p. 407.

3. See note 1 in "The 'Elf' of It" for publication data on "The Song of the Borderguard."

4. *The Venice Poem* has been published as a chapbook of twenty-seven pages ([Sidney, Australia]: Prism, 1975).

5. This passage from Arendt's *Origin of Totalitarianism* also appears in "The Recovery of the Public World" (82), "Poetry and Positivism" (52), "Bach's Belief" (356), and the "Prologue" to the libretto of *The Last Supper* (5).

6. See also Blaser's citation and commentary on this passage from *Letters* in "The 'Elf' of It" (293), included in this collection.

7. In "The 'Elf' of It," Blaser writes: "Robert Duncan is one of the founders of American art and thought—that is to say, such thought in its newness requires continuous refounding. His beloved Emerson is one key to his work, wherein a self becomes another Self among things" (295).

8. Charles Watts was the curator of Special Collections in the Bennett Library at Simon Fraser University and a part of the Vancouver literary scene for many years. His meticulous attention to postmodern and contemporary poetry did much to establish the collection. A Pound scholar, Watts was a former student and longtime friend of Blaser's and a key organizer of the 1995 Blaser conference at Emily College of Art and Design in Vancouver. With Edward Byrne, he edited the proceedings of that conference, now published as *The Recovery of the Public World* (Talonbooks, 1999). His death from cancer in 1998 was untimely.

"HERE LIES THE
WOODPECKER WHO WAS ZEUS"

This essay first appeared in *A Sacred Quest: The Life and Writings of Mary Butts*, ed. Christopher Wagstaff (Kingston, N.Y.: McPherson, 1995), pp. 159–222. However, the essay got its start as a talk for a conference on Butts at the University of California, Davis, 23 and 24 February 1984, organized by Christopher Wagstaff. Other participants included Robert Duncan, Robert Byington, Kenneth Irby, and Barbara Wagstaff.

"'Here Lies the Woodpecker Who Was Zeus'" has been cited and remarked by Laura Marcus in an article titled "Playing the Sacred Game" in the *Times Literary Supplement* (24 August 2001): 3–4. Marcus was reviewing a reissue of Butts's *Armed with Madness* by Penguin as well as Nathalie Blondel's biography of Butts, *Mary Butts: Scenes from the Life: A Biography* (New York: McPherson, 2001). This issue of the *TLS* features a reproduction of a portrait of Butts on the cover with the caption "Mysterious Mary Butts."

1. William Carlos Williams's poem, "St Francis Einstein of the Daffodils" is available in various collections. In Williams's *Selected Poems*, it is on pp. 75–77.

2. See Blaser's comments in "The Stadium of the Mirror" on character as existing for an action rather than vice versa and on language as "older and other" than ourselves.

3. The poem "Corfe" is cited in full at the end of Blaser's afterword to the *Imaginary Letters*. It was originally included in Louis Zukofsky's The "Objectivists" Anthology, 1932 (37–39).

4. See the description of Butts's character, Boris, in Blaser's afterword, where Boris is "underhanded, unstable, lost, homosexual, unavailable" (173).

5. William Blake, "Letter to Thomas Butts," 22 November 1802 (*Letters* 46).

6. "The Secret of the Grail" is a chapter title of Jesse Weston's *From Ritual to Romance* (137–63). The page numbers I have cited for Weston's book in these notes and in the body of Blaser's essay are from the 1957 Doubleday reprint of the original Cambridge University Press publication. Blaser's page numbers in the essay as published in *A Sacred Quest* are from a 1941 Peter Smith (New York) printing of Weston that I have not been able to find. Except for the page numbers, the Doubleday text is identical to the one Blaser uses.

7. Blaser is quoting Jesse Weston's paraphrase of Mead's "three stages" of the Naassene document (*Ritual to Romance* 152). Mead's own phrasing differs slightly. He writes of the Naassene Document that it "was worked over by a Jewish Hellenistic mystic J., whose general ideas and method of exegesis are exactly paralleled by those of Philo. . . . J. again was overwritten by C., a Christian Gnostic . . . who claimed that he and his were the true realisers or all that had gone before" (*Thrice-Greatest Hermes* 134).

8. I have not found the phrase "Beyond-Man" in Thatcher, but the sense of it is there in passages like this one:

> It is clear from three theosophical lectures [A. R.] Orage gave, later published as *Consciousness: Animal, Human, and Superman* (1907), that he was preoccupied with one key problem: "Is it possible for the human to transcend the human? Can man become more than man? May he enter the one ocean of consciousness from which the myriad streams of particular modes of consciousness flow?" (*Nietzsche in England* 221)

9. As Blaser's note says, the author is Richard Sieburth, writing in his introduction to Holderlin's *Hymns and Fragments*:

> Hölderlin's entire oeuvre pursues a precarious dialogue with the Other— whether this take the form of madness, revolution, or those gods of ancient Greece whose vanished immediacies are celebrated in his eary elegies and odes. (11)

> Voleny's *Les ruines, ou méditations sur les révolutions des empires* (1791) supplied Hölderlin (and later Byron and Shelley) with the topos: the modern imagination invents itself (and thereby reinvents antiquity) out of the wreckage; it has only fragments to shore against its ruins. (33)

10. Boris is the "the cause of art in others": This unmarked line is from Butts's *Imaginary Letters* (9).

BACH'S BELIEF

This essay is number 10 of *A Curriculum of the Soul*, a series conceived by Charles Olson and assembled by John [Jack] Clarke. After Olson's death in 1970, Clarke asked a number of poets to each take on one item of Olson's curriculum. Blaser's "assignment" was to research Bach's belief. In the original chapbook form (Canton, N.Y.: Glover Publishing for the Institute of Further Studies, 1995), this essay is laid out like a collage, with spaces dividing sections of the text in some cases rather than paragraph indents. I have preserved that form here.

1. David Tudor (1926–) is a legendary performer of avant-garde music and a composer in his own right. His 17 December 1950 performance of Pierre Boulez's *Deuxième Sonate pour Piano* in New York pioneered Boulez in the United States. In the 1950s, Tudor was a music instructor and pianist-in-residence at Black Mountain College in North Carolina, where Olson was Rector. He became a close associate of John Cage's during this period and worked as well with the Merce Cunningham dance troupe.

2. *I hadn't heard anything as interesting as that since I once heard Bach:* Butterick cites this remark of Olson's in his *Guide to the Maximus Poems* (726). Blaser has added the italics.

3. "Notes for a University at Venice, California," can be found in *Olson: The Journal of the Charles Olson Archives* 2 (fall 1974): 66. However, Butterick cites the passage Blaser quotes in the *Guide* (726).

4. "A Plan for a Curriculum for the Soul": The "plan" is included on the inside covers, front and back, of Blaser's chapbook, *Bach's Belief,* taken from the Charles Olson Archives at the University of Connecticut at Storrs. It has been published in the *Magazine of Further Studies*, no. 5 (1968), State University of New York, Buffalo.

5. These phrases Blaser cites are not numbered in the original. They occur in Thorpe's "Prologue" as a citation from Clarke's lectures in the following format:

> You apply textual pressure by using at least 5 different analogues simultaneously . . . Don't take from systems which don't have to do with your experience of otherness . . . If you want a text to be a door to the present you must posit the world of its construction . . . Only the heat of one's own discarded elements can produce the proper fire . . . Otherwise it can become an occasion for speculation or, worse, fundamentalist belief. (xv; original ellipses)

6. The *Kalevala* is an epic poem of Finland. See Elias Lönnrot's compilation of *The Kalevala*, recently translated by Keith Bosley (1999).

In the first section of *From Feathers to Iron*, Jack Clarke takes the concept of a "Sampo" from the *Kalevala*, defining it as "'the setting and scansions of time'" (26). He interprets this to mean the rhythm of a given cosmology. A "Sampo" can run down, at which point the *Kalevala* poets advise that "the only thing to do is make it into a harp, string it and sing songs of sadness at its passing and songs of joy heralding the new" (27).

7. Blaser uses *The Oxford Dictionary of English Etymology* (1966) in his home library, although he also uses Walter W. Skeat's *A Concise Etymological Dictionary of the English Language* (1963) in "The Stadium of the Mirror."

8. See "Image-Nation 10 (marriage clothes" for a poetic treatment of the etymology of "soul."

9. consciousness of how old we are in time: See also "The Recovery of the Public World": "'We need to know how old we are. We need to trace the consciousness of that ageing. In order to gain an attitude that knows how to take care and preserve and admire the things of the world'" (86).

10. Frances Yates on Descartes:

Why was Descartes so contemptuous, even one might think, so afraid of the *mens* that he wanted to park it by itself, out of the way of the mechanical universe and mathematics? Might not this be because of the struggle of his world to emerge from "Hermes Trismegistus" . . . and all that he stood for? The basic difference between the attitude of the magician to the world and the attitude of the scientist to the world is that the former wants to draw the world into himself, whilst the scientist does just the opposite, he externalises and impersonalises the world by a movement of the will in an entirely opposite direction to that described in the Hermetic writings, the whole emphasis of which is precisely on the reflection of the world in the *mens*. (*Giordano Bruno* 454)

See also Blaser's use of this passage in "'Here Lies the Woodpecker Who Was Zeus'" (326–27).

11. Whitehead's "prehensions": This is Whitehead's word for the manner in which actual entities take each other in. In Donald Sherburne's selective glossary of Whiteheadean terms: "'Prehensions are the vehicles by which one actual entity becomes objectified in another' . . . ; they 'are vectors'; for they feel what is *there* and transform it into what is *here*" [PR 133]. And Sherburne: "Prehensions are what an actual entity is composed of: 'The first analysis of an actual entity, into its most concrete elements, discloses it to be a concrescence of prehensions, which have originated in its process of becoming' [PR 35]" (*Key to Whitehead's Process and Reality* 235).

12. Mark C. Taylor: "God, self, history, and book are, thus, bound in an intricate relationship in which each mirrors the other. No single concept can be changed without altering all of the others. As a result of this thorough interdependence, the news of the death of God cannot really reach our ears until its reverberations are traced in the notions of self, history and book" (7).

13. Out of time, which is otherwise *the life of space* . . . : Compare Olson in *The Special View of History*: "History is the practice of space in time" (27).

14. Blaser turns to this passage from Arendt on numerous occasions. See my note 5 to "Preface to the Early Poems of Robert Duncan."

15. BVM: a numbering system for Bach's musical works.

16. W. B. Stanford's book is titled *The Sound of Greek: Studies in Greek Theory and Practice of Euphony* (1967).

BIBLIOGRAPHY

WORKS CITED

Adams, Hazard. *Philosophy of the Literary Symbolic.* Tallahassee: University Press of Florida, 1983.

Adams, Henry. *Mont-Saint-Michel and Chartres.* 1905; Boston: Houghton Mifflin, 1963.

Adolf, Helen. *Visio Pacis: Holy City and Grail.* Philadelphia: Pennsylvania State University Press, 1960.

Adorno, Theodor W. "On Lyric Poetry and Society." *Notes to Literature.* Vol. 1. Trans. Shierry Weber Nicholsen. New York: Columbia University Press, 1991. 37–54.

Agamben, Giorgio. *The Coming Community.* Trans. Michael Hardt. Minneapolis: University of Minnesota Press, 1993.

————. *Infancy and History: Essays on the Destruction of Experience.* Trans. Liz Heron. London: Verso, 1993.

————. *Language and Death: The Place of Negativity.* Trans. Karen E. Pinkus with Michael Hardt. Minneapolis: University of Minnesota Press, 1991.

Alighieri, Dante. *The Divine Comedy.* Trans. Charles S. Singleton. Princeton: Princeton University Press, 1970.

————. *De Monarchia. Translation of the Latin Works of Dante Alighieri.* Trans. Philip H. Wicksteed. London: J. M. Dent and Sons, 1940.

Althusser, Louis, and Etienne Balibar. *Reading Capital.* 2d ed. Trans. Ben Brewster. 1970; Old Woking, Surrey: Unwin, Gresham Press, 1977.

Altieri, Charles. "From Symbolist Thought to Immanence: The Ground of Postmodern American Poetics." *Boundary 2* (spring 1973): 605–41.

Anshen, Ruth Nanda. "Convergence." In *Emerging Cosmology,* by Bernard Lovell. New York: Columbia University Press, 1981. 1–11.

Arendt, Hannah. *Between Past and Future.* London and New York: Faber and Faber and Viking, 1961; New York: Viking, 1968 [Viking Compass Edition]; reprint, New York: Penguin Books, 1977, 1993.

————. *The Human Condition*. Chicago: University of Chicago Press, 1958; Garden City, N.Y.: Doubleday, 1959.

————. Introduction. In *Illuminations*, by Walter Benjamin. Trans. Harry Zohn, ed. Hannah Arendt. 1969; New York: Schocken, 1978. 1–55.

————. *The Life of the Mind*. Vols. 1 and 2. New York: Harcourt Brace Jovanovich, 1978.

————. *Men in Dark Times*. Trans. Clara Winston and Richard Winston. San Diego: Harcourt Brace, 1983.

————. *On Revolution*. 1963; New York: Viking, 1965.

————. *The Origins of Totalitarianism*. 1948; 2d ed., Cleveland: World Publishing Co., 1958; San Diego: Harcourt Brace, 1976.

Aristotle. *Poetics*. Trans. A. E. Wardman and J. L. Creed. New York: New American Library/ Mentor, 1963. 410–31.

Arnold, Matthew. "The Function of Criticism." In *The Works of Matthew Arnold*, vol. 3. Essays in Criticism: First Series. London: Macmillan/Smith, Elder and Co., 1903. 1–44.

Arp, Hans. "Dada Was Not a Farce" (1949). Trans. Ralph Manheim. In *The Dada Painters and Poets*, ed. Robert Motherwell. N.p.: Wittenborn, Schultz, 1951; reprint, Boston: G. K. Hall, 1981. 291–95.

Artaud, Antonin. *Artaud Anthology*. 2d ed. Ed. Jack Hirschman. San Francisco: City Lights, 1965.

Auerbach, Erich. "Odysseus' Scar." In *Mimesis*. Trans. Willard R. Trask. Princeton: Princeton University Press, 1968; reprint, 1973. 3–23.

Austin, Norman. *Archery at the Dark of the Moon*. Berkeley: University of California Press, 1975.

Avens, Robert. "Reflections on Wolfgang Giegerich's 'The Burial of the Soul in Technological Civilization.'" Sulfur 20, 7, no. 2 (fall 1987): 34–54.

Avison, Margaret. *Selected Poems*. Toronto: Oxford University Press, 1991.

Bacigalupo, Massimo. *The Formed Trace: The Later Poetry of Ezra Pound*. New York: Columbia University Press, 1980.

Bakhtin, M. M. *Art and Answerability: Early Essays*. Ed. Michael Holquist and Vadim Liapunov, trans. Vadim Liapunov. Austin: University of Texas Press, 1990.

Barfield, Owen. *What Coleridge Thought*. Middletown, Conn.: Wesleyan University Press, 1971.

Barthes, Roland. *Writing Degree Zero*. Trans. Annette Lavers and Colin Smith. Preface by Susan Sontag. New York: Hill and Wang, 1968; reprint, 1980.

Bataille, Georges. *Visions of Excess*. Minneapolis: University of Minnesota Press, 1985.

Bateson, Gregory, and Mary Catherine Bateson. *Angels Fear*. New York: Macmillan, 1987.

Bayard, Caroline, and Jack David, eds. *Out-Posts/Avant-Postes*. Erin, Ont.: Press Porcépic, 1978.

Bays, Gwendolyn. *The Orphic Vision: Seer Poets from Novalis to Rimbaud*. Lincoln: University of Nebraska Press, 1964.

Benhabib, Seyla. *The Reluctant Modernism of Hannah Arendt*. Thousand Oaks, Calif.: Sage, 1996.

Benjamin, Walter. "The Storyteller." In *Illuminations*, ed. Hannah Arendt. New York: Schocken, 1969. 83–109.

Berger, John. "Two Essays by John Berger: Intellectuals." *Brick* 37 (autumn 1989): 36–37.
———. "Where Are We?" *Harper's* (March 2003): 13–17. Reprinted in *Between the Eyes: Essays on Photography and Politics*, by David Levi Strauss. New York: Aperture, 2003. vii–xiv.
Blake, William. *The Complete Poetry and Prose of William Blake*. Rev. ed. Ed. David V. Erdman. Garden City, N.Y.: Anchor Books, 1982.
———. *The Letters of William Blake*. Ed. Geoffrey Keynes. London: Rupert Hart-Davis, 1956.
Blaser, Robin. "Charles Olson–Robin Blaser Correspondence, 1957–1959, with an Introduction by Robin Blaser." Ed. Ralph Maud. *Minutes of the Charles Olson Society*, no. 8 (June 1995): 5–33.
———. "Charles Olson–Robin Blaser Correspondence: White Rabbit Press and *The Pacific Nation*, 1965–1969." Ed. Miriam Nichols. *Minutes of the Charles Olson Society*, no. 49 (March 2003): 9–27.
———. Excerpts from *Astonishments*. *Even on Sunday: Essays, Readings, and Archival Materials on the Poetry and Poetics of Robin Blaser*. Ed. Miriam Nichols. Orono, Me.: National Poetry Foundation. 275–347.
———. *The Holy Forest*. Toronto: Coach House Press, 1993.
———. *The Last Supper*. Libretto. London: Boosey & Hawkes, 2000.
———. "Letter to Charles Olson. 29 April 1957." Charles Olson Papers, University of Connecticut.
Bloom, Harold. *The American Religion: The Emergence of the Post-Christian Nation*. New York: Simon and Schuster, 1992.
Boer, Charles. *Charles Olson in Connecticut*. Chicago: Swallow Press, 1975.
Bohlmann, Otto. *Yeats and Nietzsche: An Exploration of Major Nietzschean Echoes in William Butler Yeats*. New York: Macmillan, 1982.
Bohm, David. *Wholeness and the Implicate Order*. New York: Routledge & Kegan Paul, 1980.
Boulez, Pierre. *Stocktakings from an Apprenticeship*. Collected by Paule Thévenin. Trans. Stephen Walsh. Oxford and New York: Clarendon Press and Oxford University Press, 1991.
Bourassa, André G. *Surrealism and Quebec Literature: History of a Cultural Revolution*. Trans. Mark Czarnecki. Toronto: University of Toronto Press, 1984.
———. *Surréalisme et Littérature Québécoise*. Montréal: L'Etincell, 1977.
Bowering, George. *Al Purdy*. Toronto: Copp Clark, 1970.
———. *Allophanes*. Toronto: Coach House Press, 1976.
———. *Another Mouth*. Toronto: McClelland and Stewart, 1979.
———. *Autobiology*. Georgia Straight Writing Supplement Vancouver Series, no. 7. 1972.
———. "Avison's Imitation of Christ the Artist." *Canadian Literature* 54 (1972): 56–69.
———. *Burning Water*. Don Mills, Ontario: Musson Book Co., 1980.
———. *Curious*. Toronto: Coach House Press, 1973.
———. *Flycatcher and Other Stories*. Ottawa: Oberon Press, 1974.
———. *Genève*. Toronto: Coach House Press, 1971.
———. *George, Vancouver: A Discovery Poem*. Toronto: Weed/Flower Press, 1970.
———. *In the Flesh*. Toronto: McClelland and Stewart, 1974.
———. "Interview." In *Out-Posts/Avant-Postes*, ed. Caroline Bayard and Jack David. Erin, Ont.: Press Porcépic, 1978. 77–106.

————. Interview. "14 Plums." *Capilano Review* 15 (1979): 86–107.

————. *Mirror on the Floor.* Toronto: McClelland and Stewart, 1967.

————. *Particular Accidents: Selected Poems.* Ed. Robin Blaser. Vancouver: Talonbooks, 1980.

————. *The Sensible.* Toronto: Massasauga Editions, 1972.

————. *A Short Sad Book.* Vancouver: Talonbooks, 1977.

————. *Sticks and Stones.* Vancouver: Tishbooks, 1963; Vancouver: Talonbooks, 1989.

————. "That Was Ida Said Miss Stein." *Open Letter.* 2d ser., no 8 (summer 1974): 37–47.

Bowra, Cecil Maurice. *Poetry and Politics, 1900–1960.* Cambridge: Cambridge University Press, 1966.

Breton, André. "Lighthouse of the Bride." *View: The Modern Magazine. Marcel Duchamp Number.* Ser. 5, no. 1 (March 1945): 6–9.

————. *What Is Surrealism: Selected Writings.* Ed. Franklin Rosemont. London: Pluto Press, 1978.

Bridgman, Richard. *Gertrude Stein in Pieces.* Oxford: Oxford University Press, 1970.

Broch, Herman. *The Death of Virgil.* Trans. Jean Starr Untermeyer. San Francisco: North Point, 1983.

Brodeur, Arthur. *The Art of Beowulf.* 1959; reprint, Berkeley: University of California Press, 1960.

Brown, Norman O. *Closing Time.* New York: Random House, 1972.

Burckhardt, Titus. *Alchemy: Science of the Cosmos, Science of the Soul.* London: Stuart and Watkins, 1967.

Burket, Walter. *Homo Necans: The Anthropology of Ancient Greek Sacrificial Ritual and Myth.* Berkeley: University of California Press, 1983.

Butterick, George. "Editor's Notes." In *Muthologos: The Collected Lectures and Interviews,* by Charles Olson. 2 vols. Ed. George Butterick. Bolinas, Calif.: Four Seasons Foundation, 1978. 201–30.

————. *A Guide to the Maximus Poems of Charles Olson.* Berkeley: University of California Press, 1975.

————. "Olson's Reading: A Preliminary Report." *Olson: The Journal of the Charles Olson Archives* 6 (fall 1976): 77–95.

Butts, Mary. *Armed with Madness.* London: Wishart & Co., 1928; reprint, London: Penguin, 2001.

————. *Ashe of Rings.* Paris: Contact Editions, Three Mountains Press, 1925; reprint, London: Wishart, 1933.

————. "Corfe." In *An "Objectivist's" Anthology,* ed. Louis Zukofsky. Le Beausset, France: TO, Publishers, 1932. 36–39.

————. *The Crystal Cabinet: My Childhood at Salterns.* London: Methuen, 1937.

————. *Death of Felicity Taverner.* London: Wishart, 1932.

————. *From Altar to Chimney-Piece: Selected Stories of Mary Butts.* Preface by John Ashbery. New York: McPherson & Co., 1992.

————. *Imaginary Letters.* Vancouver: Talonbooks, 1979.

————. *The Macedonian.* London: W. Heinemann, 1933.

————. *Scenes from the Life of Cleopatra.* London: W. Heinemann, 1935.

————. *Traps for Unbelievers*. London: Desmond Harmsworth, 1932.

Byrd, Don. *Charles Olson's Maximus*. Urbana: University of Illinois Press, 1980.

Byrne, Edward, and Charles Watts, eds. *The Recovery of the Public World*. Vancouver: Talonbooks, 1999.

Campbell, Joseph. *Masks of God: Occidental Mythology*. New York: Viking, 1964.

Caponigri, A. Robert. *Time and Idea: The Theory of History in Giambattista Vico*. London: Routledge & Kegan Paul, 1953; reprint, Notre Dame: University of Notre Dame Press, 1968.

Carroll, Lewis. *The Annotated Alice*. Ed. Martin Gardner. New York: New American Library, 1960.

————. *The Annotated Snark*. Ed. Martin Gardner. New York: Bramhall House, 1962.

————. *The Hunting of the Snark: An Agony in Eight Fits*. London: Macmillan, 1876.

Castoriadis, Cornelius. *Crossroads in the Labyrinth*. Trans. Kate Soper and Martin H. Ryle. Cambridge, Mass.: MIT Press, 1984.

Cavell, Stanley. *The Claim of Reason*. Oxford: Oxford University Press, 1979.

————. *In Quest of the Ordinary: Lines of Skepticism and Romanticism*. Chicago: University of Chicago Press, 1988.

Cecchetti, Giovanni. "Introduction." In *Operette Morali: Essays and Dialogues*, by Gaicomo Leopardi. Trans. Giovanni Cecchetti. Berkeley: University of California Press, 1982. 1–18.

Certeau, Michel de. *Heterologies: Discourse on the Other*. Theory and History of Literature, vol. 17. Trans. Brian Massumi. Minneapolis: University of Minnesota Press, 1985.

————. *The Practice of Everyday Life*. Trans. Steven F. Rendell. Berkeley: University of California Press, 1984.

Charters, Ann. *Olson/Melville: A Study in Affinity*. Berkeley: Oyez, 1968.

Chiapusso, Jan. *Bach's World*. Bloomington: Indiana University Press, 1968.

Christensen, Paul. *Charles Olson: Call Him Ishmael*. Austin: University of Texas Press, 1979.

Christian, William. "Whitehead's Explanation of the Past." In *Alfred North Whitehead: Essays on His Philosophy*, ed. George L. Kline. Englewood Cliffs, N.J.: Prentice-Hall, 1963. 93–101.

Cixous, Hélène. *The Book of Promethea*. Trans. Betsy Wing. Lincoln: University of Nebraska Press, 1991.

Clarke, John [Jack]. *From Feathers to Iron: A Concourse of World Poetics*. Bolinas, Calif.: Tombouctou Books, 1987.

Clay, Jean. *Modern Art, 1890–1918*. New York: Vendome Press, 1978.

Cobb, Edith. "The Ecology of Imagination in Childhood." *Daedelus*, no. 3 (summer 1959): 537–48.

Cohane, John Philip. *The Key*. London: Crown, 1969.

Coleridge, Samuel Taylor. *Biographia Literaria*. 2 vols. Ed. J. Shawcross. Oxford: Oxford University Press, 1907; reprint, 1967.

————. "On Poesy or Art." In *Biographia Literaria*, by Samuel Coleridge Taylor. Vol. 2. Ed. J. Shawcross. Oxford: Oxford University Press, 1907. 253–63.

Collins, Jess ["Jess"]. *Gallowsongs/Galgenlieder*, by Christian Morgenstern. Versions by Jess. Los Angeles: Black Sparrow, 1970.

Congdon, Lee. "History and Class Consciousness." *World and I* 2, no. 6 (1987): 549–61.

Cook, A. B. *Zeus: A Study of Ancient Religion.* Vol. 2. New York: Biblo and Tannen, 1965.

Corbin, Henry. *Creative Imagination in the Sufism of Ibn 'Arabi.* Princeton: Princeton University Press, 1969.

Creeley, Robert. *The Collected Essays of Robert Creeley.* Berkeley: University of California Press, 1989.

———. *A Quick Graph: Collected Notes and Essays.* Ed. Donald Allen. San Francisco: Four Seasons Foundation, 1970.

———. *Selected Poems.* Berkeley: University of California Press, 1991.

Crowley, Aleister. *Confessions of Aleister Crowley: An Autohagiography.* Ed. John Symonds and Kenneth Grant. London: Arkana, 1989.

———. *Magick in Theory and Practice, by the Master Therion.* Paris: Lecram Press, 1929.

Curtius, Ernst Robert. *European Literature and the Latin Middle Ages.* Trans. Willard R. Trask. New York: Pantheon, 1953.

Davenport, Guy. *The Geography of the Imagination.* San Francisco: North Point, 1981.

Davey, Frank. *From There to Here.* Erin, Ont.: Press Porcépic, 1974.

———. "Introduction." In *Louis Dudek: Texts & Essays. Open Letter.* 4th ser., nos. 8–9 (spring–summer 1981): 7–8.

———. "Introduction." *TISH* 1–19. Ed. Frank Davey. Vancouver: Talonbooks, 1975. 7–11.

———. *Louis Dudek & Raymond Souster.* Vancouver: Douglas & McIntyre, 1980.

Deleuze, Gilles. *The Fold: Leibniz and the Baroque.* Trans. Tom Conley. Minneapolis: University of Minnesota Press, 1993.

———. *Nietzsche and Philosophy.* Trans. Hugh Tomlinson. New York: Columbia University Press, 1983.

Derrida, Jacques. *Aporias.* Trans. Thomas Dutoit, ed. Werner Hamacher and David E. Wellbery. Stanford: Stanford University Press, 1993.

———. *Dissemination.* Trans. with Introduction by Barbara Johnson. Chicago: University of Chicago Press, 1981.

Donoghue, Denis. *Thieves of Fire.* London: Faber and Faber, 1973.

———. *Yeats.* London: Fontana, 1971.

Doolittle, Hilda (H. D.) *Trilogy.* New York: New Directions, 1973.

Doresse, Jean. *The Secret Books of the Egyptian Gnostics: An Introduction to the Gnostic Coptic Manuscripts Discovered at Chenoboskion.* London: Hollis & Carter, 1960.

Draenos, Stan Spyros. "Thinking without a Ground: Hannah Arendt and the Contemporary Situation of Understanding." In *Hannah Arendt: The Recovery of the Public World,* ed. Melvyn A. Hill. New York: St. Martin's Press, 1979. 209–24.

Duchamp, Marcel. "The Creative Act." In *Surrealists on Art,* ed. Lucy R. Lippard. Englewood Cliffs, N.J.: Prentice-Hall, 1970. 112–13.

———. *Marcel Duchamp, Notes.* Trans. and arranged Paul Matisse. Preface Anne d'Harnoncourt. Boston: G. K. Hall, 1983.

Dudek, Louis. *Atlantis.* Montréal: Delta Canada, 1967.

———. "Beyond Autobiography." *Open Letter: Long-liner Conference Issue,* 6th ser., nos. 2–3 (summer–fall 1985): 107–14.

————. "The Bible as Fugue: Theme and Variations." *University of Toronto Quarterly* 52, no. 2 (winter 1982–83): 128–35.

————. *Continuation I*. Montréal: Véhicule Press, 1981.

————. *Continuation II*. Montréal: Véhicule Press, 1990.

————, ed. *Dk/Some Letters of Ezra Pound*. Montréal: DC Books, 1974.

————. *East of the City*. Toronto: Ryerson, 1946.

————. *En México*. With drawings by Zygmunt Turkiewicz. Toronto: Contact Press, 1958.

————. *Epigrams*. Montréal: DC Books, 1975.

————. *Europe*. Toronto: Laocoon (Contact) Press, 1954.

————. *The First Person in Literature*. Arranged by Phyllis Webb and William Young. Toronto: Canadian Broadcasting Corporation, 1967.

————. *Ideas for Poetry*. Montréal: Véhicule Press, 1983.

————. *Infinite Worlds: The Poetry of Louis Dudek*. Ed. Robin Blaser. Montréal: Véhicule Press, 1988.

————. *Louis Dudek: Texts & Essays*. Ed. Frank Davey and bp Nichol. Special Issue. *Open Letter*, 4th ser., nos. 8–9 (spring–summer 1981).

————. *Selected Essays and Criticism*. Ottawa: Tecumseh Press, 1978.

————. *Technology and Culture*. Ottawa: Golden Dog Press, 1979.

————. *Zembla's Rocks*. Montréal: Véhicule Press, 1986.

Dudek, Louis, and Michael Gnarnowski, eds. *The Making of Modern Poetry in Canada*. Toronto: Ryerson Press, 1967.

Duncan, Robert. *A Book of Resemblances: Poems, 1950–1953*. Illus. Jess. New Haven: H. Wenning, 1966.

————. *Bending the Bow*. 1963; New York: New Directions, 1968.

————. "The Delirium of Meaning." In *The Sin of the Book: Edmond Jabès*, ed. Eric Gould. Lincoln: University of Nebraska Press, 1985. 207–26.

————. *Faust Foutu: A Comic Masque*. 2d ed. Barrytown, N.Y.: Station Hill Press, 1985.

————. *Fictive Certainties*. New York: New Directions, 1985.

————. *Ground Work I: Before the War*. New York: New Directions, 1984.

————. *Ground Work II: In the Dark*. New York: New Directions, 1987.

————. "Iconographical Extensions." In *Translations by Jess*. Los Angeles: Black Sparrow Press. 1971. i–xiv.

————. "Introduction." In *The Divine Mystery*, by Allen Upward. Santa Barbara, Calif.: Ross-Erikson, 1976. ix–xxviii.

————. *Letters: Poems, 1953–1956*. Highlands, N.C.: J.Williams, 1958.

————. [Letters to Robin Blaser regarding Nerval's *Les Chimères*, Duncan's translation of *Les Chimères*, and other writings.] *Poetry/Audit* 4, no. 3 (1967): *Robert Duncan*. [Special issue.]

————. *Notes on Grossinger's Solar Journal: Oecological Sections*. Los Angeles: Black Sparrow Press, 1970. Pamphlet.

————. *The Opening of the Field*. New York: Grove Press, 1960.

————. "Pages from a Notebook." In *The New American Poetry*, ed. Donald Allen and Warren Tallman. New York: Grove Press, 1960. 400–407.

----------. *Robert Duncan: Selected Poems*. Rev. and enl. Ed. Robert J. Bertholf. New York: New Directions, 1997.

----------. *The Song of the Borderguard*. Black Mountain, N.C.: Black Mountain Graphics Workshop, n.d.; reprint, *Robert Duncan: Selected Poems*, ed. Robert Bertholf. New York: New Directions, 1997. 27–28.

----------. *The Venice Poem*. [Sidney, Australia]: Prism, 1975.

----------. *Writing Writing: A Composition Book for Madison, 1953: Stein Imitations*. Albuquerque, New Mex.: Sumbooks, 1964.

----------. *The Years as Catches: First Poems (1939–1946)*. 1966; reprint, Berkeley: Oyez, 1977.

Eagleton, Terry. *The Ideology of the Aesthetic*. Oxford: Basil Blackwell, 1990.

Ehrenfeld, David. *The Arrogance of Humanism*. New York: Oxford University Press, 1978.

Elderfield, John. *Kurt Schwitters*. London: Thames and Hudson, 1985.

Ellingham, Lewis, and Kevin Killian. *Poet Be Like God: Jack Spicer and the San Francisco Renaissance*. Hanover, N.H.: Wesleyan University Press, 1998.

Ellis, Havelock. *Studies in the Psychology of Sex*. New York: Random House, 1942.

Emerson, Ralph Waldo. *The Works of Ralph Waldo Emerson*. Vols. 3 and 4. Philadelphia: John D. Morris & Co., 1906.

Empson, William. "Introduction: The Anti-Democratic Intelligentsia." In *The Reactionaries*, by John Harrison. London: Gollancz, 1966. 15–35.

Fischer, Ernst. *The Necessity of Art: A Marxist Approach*. Trans. Anna Bostock. 1963; Harmondsworth: Penguin, 1964.

Flaubert, Gustave. *The Temptation of St. Anthony*. Trans. Kitty Mrosovsky. Harmondsworth: Penguin, 1983.

Flew, Antony, ed. *A Dictionary of Philosophy*. London: Pan Books, 1978; London: Macmillan, 1984.

Forbes, H. D., ed. *Canadian Political Thought*. Toronto: Oxford University Press, 1985.

Ford, Hugh. *A Poet's War: British Poets and the Spanish Civil War*. Philadelphia: University of Pennsylvania Press, 1965.

Foucault, Michel. *The Archaeology of Knowledge & The Discourse on Language*. Trans. A. M. Sheridan Smith. New York: Pantheon/Random House, 1972.

----------. *Madness and Civilization: A History of Insanity in the Age of Reason*. Trans. Richard Howard. 1965; New York: Vintage Books/RandomHouse, 1973.

----------. *The Order of Things*. New York: Random House, 1973.

Francis, Wynne. "A Critic of Life: Louis Dudek as a Man of Letters." *Canadian Literature* 22 (autumn 1964): 5–23.

Fränger, Wilhelm. *The Millennium of Hieronymous Bosch*. Chicago: University of Chicago Press, 1951.

Frye, Northrop. *Anatomy of Criticism*. Princeton: Princeton University Press, 1957.

----------. *The Modern Century*. Toronto: Oxford University Press, 1967.

Fukuyama, Francis. *The End of History and the Last Man*. New York: Avon Books, 1992.

Fuss, Peter. "Hannah Arendt's Conception of Political Community." In *Hannah Arendt: The Recovery of the Public World*, ed. Melvyn A. Hill. New York: St. Martin's Press, 1979. 157–76.

Gardner, Martin. "Giving God a Hand." *New York Review of Books*. 13 Aug. 1987.

———. "Introduction." In *The Annotated Snark*, by Lewis Carroll. New York: Bramhall House, 1962. n.p.

Gass, William H. *Habitations of the Word*. New York: Simon and Schuster, 1985.

Geddes, Gary, and Phyllis Bruce. *Fifteen Canadian Poets Plus Five*. Toronto: Oxford University Press, 1978.

Gervais, C. H., ed. *The Writing Life: Historical & Critical Views of the Tish Movement*. Coatsworth, Ont.: Black Moss Press, 1976.

Giddens, Anthony. *A Contemporary Critique of Historical Marxism*. Berkeley: University of California Press, 1981.

Giedion, S. *The Beginnings of Architecture*. New York: Bollingen Foundation, 1964.

———. *The Eternal Present: The Beginnings of Art*. New York: Bollingen Foundation, 1962.

Giegerich, Wolfgang. "The Rocket and the Launching Base, Or the Leap from the Imaginal into the Outer Space Named 'Reality.'" *Sulfur* 28, vol. 11, no. 1 (spring 1991): 63–78.

Girard, René. *Violence and the Sacred*. Trans. Patrick Gregory. Baltimore: Johns Hopkins University Press, 1977.

Gnarowski, Michael. "Preface." In *Selected Essays and Criticism*, by Louis Dudek. Ottawa: Tecumseh Press, 1978. vii–ix.

Godzich, Wlad. "Foreword." In *Heterologies: Discourse on the Other*, by Michel de Certeau. Trans. Brian Massumi. Minneapolis: University of Minnesota Press, 1986. vii–xxi.

Goldring, Douglas. *Odd Man Out: The Autobiography of a "Propaganda Novelist."* London: Chapman and Hall, 1935.

———. *South Lodge: Reminiscences of Violet Hunt, Ford Madox Ford, and the English Review Circle*. London: Constable, 1943.

Grant, George. *Lament for a Nation: The Defeat of Canadian Nationalism*. Toronto: McClelland and Stewart, 1965.

———. *Technology and Empire*. Toronto: Anansi, 1969.

Greene, David B. *Temporal Processes in Beethoven's Music*. New York: Gordon and Breach, 1982.

Greene, Robert. *The Honorable History of Friar Bacon and Friar Bungay*. In *The Elizabethan Plays*, ed. Edwin Johnston Howard. New York: Ronald Press, 1931. 126–58.

Gregor-Dellin, Martin. *Richard Wagner*. New York: Harcourt Brace Jovanovich, 1983.

Grieve, Thomas. "Displacing the Self: The Progress of Ezra Pound's Pre-Cantos Poetics." Ph.D. diss., Johns Hopkins University, 1986.

Grosskurth, Phyllis. *Havelock Ellis: A Biography*. New York: Alfred A. Knopf, 1980.

Hacking, Ian. *The Taming of Chance*. Cambridge: Cambridge University Press, 1990.

Hainsworth, J. B., ed. *Traditions of Heroic and Epic Poetry*. Vol. 2, *Characteristics and Techniques*. Gen. ed. A. T. Hatto. London: Modern Humanities Research Association, 1989.

Halpert, Stephen, with Richard Johns, eds. *A Return to Pagany: The History, Correspondence, and Selections from a Little Magazine, 1929–1932*. Boston: Beacon Press, 1969.

Handelman, Susan H. *The Slayers of Moses: The Emergence of Rabbinic Interpretation in Modern Literary Theory*. Albany: State University of New York Press, 1982.

Harrison, Jane Ellen. *Epilogomena to the Study of Greek Religion and Themis: A Study of the Social Origins of Greek Religion*. New Hyde Park, N.Y.: University Books, 1962.

Harrison, John R. *The Reactionaries*. London: Gollancz, 1966.

Hartman, Geoffrey. *Beyond Formalism*. New Haven: Yale University Press, 1970.

Harvey, David. *The Condition of Postmodernity*. Oxford: Basil Blackwell, 1989.

Hauser, Arnold. *The Social History of Art*. Vol. 2. Trans. Stanley Godman. London: Routledge & Kegan Paul, 1951.

Haviaras, Stratis. *The Heroic Age*. New York: Simon and Schuster, 1984.

Hegel, G. W. F. *Phenomenology of Spirit*. Trans. A. V. Miller. Oxford: Clarendon Press, 1977.

Heidegger, Martin. *Being and Time*. Trans. John Macquarrie and Edward Robinson. New York: Harper & Row, 1962.

———. *Poetry, Language, Thought*. Trans. Albert Hofstadter. New York: HarperColophon Books, 1971.

Heller, Erich. *The Disinherited Mind*. New York: Harcourt Brace Jovanovich, 1975.

Hill, Melvyn A., ed. *Hannah Arendt: The Recovery of the Public World*. New York: St. Martin's Press, 1979.

Holmes, Richard. *Shelley: The Pursuit*. London: Weidenfeld & Nicolson, 1974; Harmondsworth: Penguin Books, 1987.

Holquist, Michael. "Editor's Introduction." In *Art and Answerability: Early Essays*, by M. M. Bakhtin. Austin: University of Texas Press, 1990.

Homer. *The Odyssey*. Trans. Robert Fitzgerald. Drawings by Hans Erni. Garden City, N.Y.: Doubleday, 1961; reprint, New York: Anchor Books, 1963.

Hume, David. *Hume Selections*. Ed. Charles W. Hendel Jr. New York: Scribner's, 1927.

———. *A Treatise on Human Nature: Hume Selections*. Ed. C. W. Hendel Jr. New York: Scribner's, 1927.

Hung, William. *Tu Fu*. Cambridge, Mass.: Harvard University Press, 1952.

Hynes, Samuel B. *The Edwardian Turn of Mind*. Princeton: Princeton University Press, 1968.

James, Henry. "The Figure in the Carpet." In *The Figure in the Carpet and Other Stories*, ed. Frank Kermode. Harmondsworth: Penguin, 1986. 355–400.

Jameson, Fredric. "Postmodernism and Consumer Society." In *The Anti-Aesthetic: Essays on Postmodern Culture*, ed. Hal Foster. Port Townsend, Wash.: Bay Press, 1983. 111–25.

Jameux, Dominique. *Pierre Boulez*. Paris: Fayard: Fondation SACEM, 1984; English trans. Susan Bradshaw. London: Faber and Faber, 1991.

Jess. *See* Collins, Jess.

Jones, David. *Introducing David Jones*. Ed. John Matthias. London: Faber and Faber, 1980.

Jones, John. *On Aristotle and Greek Tragedy*. London: Chatto & Windus, 1962.

Joyce, James. *Finnegans Wake*. London and New York: Faber and Faber and Viking, 1939; New York: Penguin, 1976.

Jung, C. G. *Memories, Dreams, Reflections*. Ed. Aniela Jaffé, trans. Richard Winston and Clara Winston. 1961; reprint, New York: Random House/Pantheon Books, 1963.

Kahane, Henry, and Renée Kahane. *The Krater and the Grail: Hermetic Sources of the Parzival*. Urbana: University of Illinois Press, 1965.

Kantorowicz, Ernst H. *Kaiser Friedrich der Zweite*. 1936; reprint, Dusseldorf: H. Kupper, 1963. Authorized English version by E. O. Lorimer. *Frederick the Second, 1194–1250*, by Ernst Kantorowicz. New York: F. Ungar, 1967.

————. *The King's Two Bodies: A Study in Medieval Political Theology.* Princeton: Princeton University Press, 1957.

Kearney, Richard. *The Wake of Imagination: Toward a Postmodern Culture.* Minneapolis: University of Minnesota Press, 1988.

Kenner, Hugh. *The Pound Era.* Berkeley: University of California Press, 1971.

Kirk, G. S. *Heraclitus: The Cosmic Fragments.* Cambridge: Cambridge University Press, 1954; reprint, 1962.

Knight, Max. "Introduction." In *The Gallows Songs: Christian Morgenstern's Galgenlieder: A Selection.* Trans. Max Knight. 1963; Berkeley: University of California Press, 1966. 1–12.

Kolakowski, Leszek. *Main Currents of Marxism.* 3 vols. Oxford: Clarendon Press, 1978.

Korzybski, Alfred. *General Semantics Seminar 1937: Olivet College Lectures.* 3d ed. Ed. Homer J. Moore Jr. New York: Institute of General Semantics, 2002.

Kraus, Karl. "In These Great Times." In *In These Great Times,* ed. Harry Zohn. Trans. Joseph Fabry, Max Knight, Karl F. Ross, and Harry Zohn. Montréal: Engendra, 1976. 70–83.

Kristeller, Paul Oskar. *The Renaissance Philosophy of Man.* Ed. Ernst Cassirer, Paul Oskar Kristeller, John Herman Randall, in collaboration with Hans Nachod. Chicago: University of Chicago Press, 1948.

La Barre, Weston. *The Ghost Dance: Origins of Religion.* New York: Dell, 1972.

Lacan, Jacques. *Speech and Language in Psychoanalysis.* Trans. with commentary by Anthony Wilden. Baltimore: Johns Hopkins University Press, 1981.

Layton, Irving. *A Laughter in the Mind.* Highlands, N.C.: J. Williams, 1958.

Lazer, Hank. "Criticism and the Crisis in American Poetry." In *Opposing Poetries.* Vol. 1, *Issues and Institutions.* Evanston: Northwestern University Press, 1996. 6–36.

Lebel, Robert. *Marcel Duchamp.* New York: Grove Press, 1959.

Lefort, Claude. "Editor's Foreword." In *The Visible and the Invisible,* by Maurice Merleau-Ponty. Trans. Alphonso Lingis. Evanston: Northwestern University Press, 1968. xi–xxxiii.

Leopardi, Gaicomo. *Operette Morali: Essays and Dialogues.* Trans. Giovanni Cecchetti. Berkeley: University of California Press, 1982.

Lester, John A. *Journey through Despair, 1880–1914: Transformations in British Literary Culture.* Princeton: Princeton University Press, 1968.

Levi Strauss, David. *Between the Eyes: Essays on Photography and Politics.* Introd. John Berger. New York: Aperture, 2003.

Lincoln, Barnett. *The Universe and Dr. Einstein.* 1948; rev. ed. New York: William Sloane Associates, 1950.

Lingis, Alphonso. *The Community of Those Who Have Nothing in Common.* Bloomington: Indiana University Press, 1994.

————. "Translator's Preface." In *The Visible and Invisible,* by Maurice Merleau-Ponty. Ed. Claude Lefort, trans. Alphonso Lingis. Evanston: Northwestern University Press, 1968. xl–lvi.

Lönnrot, Elias. *The Kalevala: An Epic Poem after Oral Tradition.* Trans. Keith Bosley. Oxford: Oxford University Press, 1999.

Lovell, Bernard. *Emerging Cosmology.* New York: Columbia University Press, 1981.

Lyotard, Jean-François. *The Inhuman: Reflections on Time*. Cambridge: Polity Press, 1991.

———. *The Postmodern Condition: A Report on Knowledge*. Trans. Geoff Bennington and Brian Massumi. Minneapolis: University of Minnesota Press, 1984.

Mallarmé, Stéphane. *Mallarmé in Prose*. Ed. Mary Ann Caws. New York: New Directions, 2001.

———. *Oeuvres complètes I*. Ed. Bertrand Marchal. Paris: Gallimard, 1998.

———. *Oeuvres complètes II*. Ed. Bertrand Marchal. Paris: Gallimard, 2003.

———. *Selected Poetry and Prose*. Ed. Mary Ann Caws. New York: New Directions, 1982.

Mandel, Eli. "Introduction." In *Contexts of Canadian Criticism*, ed. Eli Mandel. Chicago: University of Chicago Press, 1971. 3–25.

Marat/Sade. Dir. Peter Brook. Dist. Festival Films, 1966, and United Artists, 1967.

Mayer, Hans. *Outsiders*. Cambridge, Mass.: MIT Press, 1982.

Mazzotta, Giuseppe. *Dante, Poet of the Desert*. Princeton: Princeton University Press, 1979.

McCaffery, Steve. "Blaser's Deleuzean Folds." In *The Recovery of the Public World*, ed. Charles Watts and Edward Byrne. Vancouver: Talonbooks, 1999. 373–92.

McFadden, David, Bill Schermbrucker, Sharon Thesen, and Paul de Barros. "14 Plums." [Interview with George Bowering.] *Capilano Review* 15 (1979): 86–107.

McLuhan, Marshall. *The Gutenberg Galaxy: The Making of Typographic Man*. Toronto: University of Toronto Press, 1962.

Mead, G. R. S. *Thrice-Greatest Hermes: Studies in Helenistic Theosophy and Gnosis, Being a Translation of the Extant Sermons and Fragments of the Trismegistic Literature, with Prolegomena, Commentaries and Notes by G. R. S. Mead*. Vol. 1. London: John M. Watkins, 1964.

Mead, Margaret. *Continuities in Cultural Evolution*. The Terry Lectures. 1964; reprint, New Haven: Yale University Press, 1965.

———. "Introduction." In *The Ecology of the Imagination*, by Edith Cobb. New York: Columbia University Press, 1977. 1–14.

Mellers, Wilfrid Howard. *Bach and the Dance of God*. London: Faber and Faber, 1980.

Melville, Herman. *Correspondence*. Rev. and augmented from *Letters of Herman Melville* (1960). The Writings of Herman Melville, vol. 14. Exec. ed. Lynn Horth. Evanston and Chicago: Northwestern University Press and the Newberry Library, 1993.

———. *The Letters of Herman Melville*. Ed. Merrill R. Davis and William H. Gilman. New Haven: Yale University Press, 1960.

———. *Moby-Dick or The Whale*. The Works of Herman Melville, vol. 7. Standard Edition. New York: Russell and Russell, 1963.

———. *Selected Tales and Poems*. Ed. Richard Chase. New York: Holt, Rinehart and Winston, 1950.

Merleau-Ponty, Maurice. *Signs*. Trans. Richard C. McCleary. Evanston: Northwestern University Press, 1964.

———. *The Visible and the Invisible*. Ed. Claude Lefort, trans. Alphonso Lingis. Evanston: Northwestern University Press, 1968.

Mesch, Harald. "Robert Creeley's Epistemopathic Path." *Sagetrieb: Robert Creeley Issue* 1, no. 3 (winter 1982): 57–85.

Michaud, G. *Mallarmé*. Trans. Marie Collins and Bertha Humez. New York: New York University Press, 1965.

Middleton, Peter. "An Elegy for Theory: Robin Blaser's Essay, 'The Practice of Outside.'" In *Even on Sunday: Essays, Readings and Archival Materials on the Poetry and Poetics of Robin Blaser*, ed. Miriam Nichols. Orono, Me.: National Poetry Foundation, 2002. 179–206.

Miles, Josephine. *The Continuity of Poetic Language: The Primary Language of Poetry, 1540's–1940's*. New York: Octagon, 1965.

———. *The Continuity of Poetic Language: Studies in English Poetry from the 1540's to the 1940's*. Berkeley: University of California Press, 1951.

Milosz, Czeslaw. *The Land of Ulro*. New York: Farrar, Straus and Giroux, 1984.

Montaigne, Michel de. "De L'Amitié." In *Essais, Livre 1*. Paris: Garnier-Flammarion, 1969. 231–42.

———. *Essays*. Trans. J. M. Cohen. 1958; reprint, Harmondsworth: Penguin, 1981.

Morford, Mark P. O., and Robert J. Lenardon. *Classical Mythology*. New York: McKay, 1971; 2d ed. New York: Longman, 1977; 4th ed. New York: Longman, 1991.

Morgenstern, Christian. *Galgenlieder: A Selection*. Trans. Max Knight. Berkeley: University of California Press, 1966.

Mourelatos, Alexander. *The Route of Parmenides: A Study of Word, Image and Argument in the Fragments*. New Haven: Yale University Press, 1970.

Mustard, Helen M., and Charles E. Passage. "Introduction." In *Parzival*, by Wolfram von Eschenbach. New York: Vintage Books, 1961. vii–lv.

Muybridge, Eadweard. *Muybridge's Complete Human and Animal Locomotion*. Philadelphia: University of Pennsylvania Press, 1887; New York: Dover, 1979.

Nancy, Jean-Luc. *The Inoperative Community*. Ed. Peter Connor. Trans. Peter Connor, Lisa Garbus, Michael Holland, and Simona Sawhney. Minneapolis: University of Minnesota Press, 1991.

———. *The Sense of the World*. Trans. Jeffrey S. Librett. Minneapolis: University of Minnesota Press, 1997.

Nerval, Gérard de. "Aurélia." In *Selected Writings of Gérard de Nerval*. Trans. Geoffrey Wagner. New York: Grove Press, 1957. 111–78.

———. "Le Point Noir." *Poésies. Precedées de Nerval et La Magie Du Souvenir par Jean Richer*. Paris: Union Générale d'Éditions, n.d.

———. *Oeuvres*. Tome Premier. Ed. Henri Lemaitre. Paris: Editions Garnier Frères, n.d.

———. *Selected Writings of Gérard de Nerval*. Trans. Geoffrey Wagner. New York: Grove Press, 1957.

Nichol, bp. *Journal*. Toronto: Coach House Press, 1978.

———. *The Martyrology*. Toronto: Coach House Press, 1977.

Nichols, Miriam. "Introduction: Reading Robin Blaser." In *Even on Sunday: Essays, Readings and Archival Materials on the Poetry and Poetics of Robin Blaser*. Orono, Me.: National Poetry Foundation, 2002. 25–77.

———. "Robin Blaser." In *Dictionary of Literary Biography*. Vol. 165, *American Poets since World War II*. 4th ser. Ed. Joseph Conte. Detroit: Gale Research/Bruccoli Clark Layman, 1996. 57–68.

Nietzsche, Friedrich. *The Complete Works*. Ed. Oscar Levy. New York: Russell & Russell, 1964.

Olson, Charles. *Charles Olson and Ezra Pound: An Encounter at St. Elizabeths*. Ed. Catherine Seelye. New York: Grossman, 1975; reprint, New York: Paragon House, 1991.

———. "Charles Olson–Robin Blaser Correspondence, 1957–1959, with an Introduction by Robin Blaser." Ed. Ralph Maud. *Minutes of the Charles Olson Society*, no. 8 (June 1995): 5–33.

———. "Charles Olson–Robin Blaser Correspondence: White Rabbit Press and *The Pacific Nation*, 1965–1969." Ed. Miriam Nichols. *Minutes of the Charles Olson Society*, no. 49 (March 2003): 9–27.

———. *The Collected Poems of Charles Olson*. Ed. George F. Butterick. Berkeley: University of California Press, 1987.

———. *The Collected Prose of Charles Olson*. Ed. Donald Allen and Benjamin Friedlander. Berkeley: University of California Press, 1997.

———. "A Comprehension, a Measure That." *Pacific Nation* 1 (1967): 42–44; reprinted, *The Collected Prose of Charles Olson*. Ed. Donald Allen and Benjamin Friedlander. Berkeley: University of California Press, 1997. 361–63.

———. *The Human Universe and Other Essays*. Ed. Donald Allen. New York: Grove Press, 1967.

———. "Letter to Robin Blaser, May 3, 1957." *Minutes of the Charles Olson Society: A Special Issue for the Robin Blaser Conference*, no. 8 (June 1965): 15–16.

———. *The Maximus Poems*. Ed. George F. Butterick. Berkeley: University of California Press, 1983.

———. *Muthologos: The Collected Lectures and Interviews*. 2 vols. Ed. George Butterick. Bolinas, Calif.: Four Seasons Foundation, 1978.

———. "Olson in Gloucester, 1966." In *Muthologos: The Collected Lectures and Interviews*. 2 vols. Ed. George Butterick. Bolinas, Calif.: Four Seasons Foundation, 1978. 69–198.

———. *Poetry and Truth*. San Francisco: Four Seasons Foundation, 1971.

———. Review of *Preface to Plato* by Eric Havelock. *Niagara Frontier Review* (summer 1964). Reprinted in *The Collected Prose of Charles Olson*. Ed. Donald Allen and Benjamin Friedlander. Berkeley: University of California Press, 1997. 355–58.

———. *Selected Writings of Charles Olson*. Ed. Robert Creeley. New York: New Directions, 1966.

———. *The Special View of History*. Ed. Ann Charters. Berkeley: Oyez, 1970.

———. "This Is Yeats Speaking." In *The Human Universe and Other Essays*. Ed. Donald Allen. New York: Grove Press, 1967. 99–102. Reprinted in *The Collected Prose of Charles Olson*. Ed. Donald Allen and Benjamin Friedlander. Berkeley: University of California Press, 1997. 141–44.

Ondaatje, Michael. *The Long Poem Anthology*. Toronto: Coach House Press, 1979.

Onions, C. T., ed. *The Oxford Dictionary of English Etymology*. Oxford: Oxford University Press, 1966.

Ovid. *Metamorphoses*. Vol. 1. Loeb Classical Edition. 2d ed. Trans. Frank Jastus Miller. Cambridge, Mass: Harvard University Press, 1921; reprint, 1966.

Oxford Dictionary of English Etymology. Oxford: Clarendon Press, 1966.

Pagels, Heinz R. *Perfect Symmetry: The Search for the Beginning of Time*. New York: Simon and Schuster, 1985.

Palmer, Richard E. *Hermeneutics: Interpretation Theory in Schleiermacher, Dilthey, Heidegger, and Gadamer*. Evanston: Northwestern University Press, 1969.

Paul, Sherman. *The Lost America of Love*. Baton Rouge: Louisiana State University Press, 1981.

————. *Olson's Push: Origin, Black Mountain, and Recent American Poetry*. Baton Rouge: Louisiana State University Press, 1978.

Paz, Octavio. *Marcel Duchamp: Appearance Stripped Bare*. Trans. Rachel Phillips and Donald Gardner. New York: Viking, 1978.

————. *The Bow and the Lyre*. Trans. Ruth L. C. Simms. Austin: University of Texas Press, 1973.

Peyser, Joan. *Boulez: Composer, Conductor, Enigma*. 1976; New York: Schirmer Books/Macmillan, 1978.

Poetry/Audit. Vol. 4, no. 3 (1967). [Special issue on Robert Duncan.]

Poirier, Richard. *The Renewal of Literature: Emersonian Reflections*. New York: Random House, 1987.

Portillo, Luis. "Unamuno's Last Lecture." In *The Golden Horizon*, ed. Cyril Connolly. London: Weidenfeld & Nicolson, 1953. 397–403.

Pound, Ezra. *The Cantos of Ezra Pound*. London: Faber and Faber, 1975.

————. *Ezra Pound, Letters, 1907–1941*. Ed. D. D. Paige. New York: Harcourt Brace, 1950; London: Faber and Faber, 1951.

————. *Selected Prose, 1909–1965*. Ed. William Cookson. New York: New Directions, 1973.

Read, John. *Prelude to Chemistry: An Outline of Alchemy, Its Literature and Relationships*. London: G. Bell, 1936; reprint, Cambridge, Mass.: MIT Press, 1966.

Rexroth, Kenneth. "Introduction." In *The Holy Kabbalah*, by A. E. Waite. New Hyde Park, N.Y.: University Books, 1960. vii–xvi.

————. "Introduction: A Primer of Gnosticism." In *Fragments of a Faith Forgotten: The Gnostics, a Contribution to the Study of the Origins of Christianity*, by G. R. S. Mead. New Hyde Park, N.Y.: University Books, 1960.

Richardson, Keith. *Poetry and the Colonized Mind: Tish*. Oakville, Ont.: Mosaic Press, 1976.

Rilke, Rainer Maria. *Letters of Rainer Maria Rilke*. Vol. 2, 1910–1926. Trans. J. B. Green and M. D. Herter Norton. New York: Norton, 1948.

————. *The Selected Poetry*. Ed. and trans. Stephen Mitchell. New York: Random House, 1982.

Rodwell. G. F. *The Birth of Chemistry*. London: N. p., 1874.

Russell, John. *The Meanings of Modern Art*. New York: Museum of Modern Art and Harper and Row, 1981.

Schneidau, Herbert H. *Ezra Pound: The Image and the Real*. Baton Rouge: Louisiana State University Press, 1969.

————. *Sacred Discontent: The Bible and Western Tradition*. Baton Rouge: Louisiana State University Press, 1976.

Schutte, Ofelia. *Beyond Nihilism: Nietzsche without Masks*. Chicago: University of Chicago Press, 1984.

Scott, William Taussig. "Science: Its Successes, Its Mischiefs, and Its Humanness." *World and I* 2, no. 8 (1987): 624–25.

Serres, Michel. *Hermes: Literature, Science, and Philosophy*. Ed. Josu V. Harari and David F. Bell. Baltimore: Johns Hopkins University Press, 1982.

Shakespeare, William. *The Tragedy of Hamlet, Prince of Denmark. The Riverside Shakespeare.*
Textual ed. G. Blakemore Evans. Boston: Houghton Mifflin, 1974. 1135–97.

Shelach, Oz. "Clause 21." *Harper's* (September 2003): 13–17.

Shelley, Percy Bysshe. *Alastor, or the Spirit of Solitude and Other Poems.* 1886; reprint, New York:
AMS, 1975.

———. *Promethus Unbound.* In *The Selected Poetry and Prose of Percy Bysshe Shelley,* ed. Carlos Baker.
New York: Modern Library/Random House, 1951. 54–130.

Sherburne, Donald, ed. *A Key to Whitehead's Process and Reality.* 1966; Chicago: University of
Chicago Press, 1981.

Sherrill, Rowland A. *The Prophetic Melville: Experience, Transcendence, Tragedy.* Athens: University
of Georgia Press, 1979.

Siebuth, Richard. "Introduction." In *Friedrich Hölderin, Hymns and Fragments,* by Friedrich
Hölderin. Princeton: Princeton University Press, 1984. 3–43.

Silliman, Ron. *The New Sentence.* New York: Roof, 1987.

Skeat, Walter W. *A Concise Etymological Dictionary of the English Language.* New York: Capricorn
Books, 1963.

Smith, Steven B. "What Is Analytical Marxism?" *World and I* 2, no. 6 (1987): 572–83.

Sontag, Susan. *Styles of Radical Will.* New York: Delta, 1978.

Speck, Frank. *Naskapi: The Savage Hunters of the Labrador Peninsula.* Norman: University of Okla-
homa Press, 1935.

Spinoza, Benedict de. *On the Improvement of the Understanding; The Ethics; Correspondence.* Trans.
R. H. M. Elwes. 1955; New York: Dover, n.d.

Spicer, Jack. *The Collected Books of Jack Spicer.* Ed. Robin Blaser. Santa Barbara, Calif.: Black
Sparrow Press, 1980.

———. *The House That Jack Built: The Collected Lectures of Jack Spicer.* Ed. Peter Gizzi. Hanover,
N.H.: Wesleyan University Press, 1998.

———. *One Night Stand and Other Poems.* Ed. Donald Allen. Preface by Robert Duncan. San
Francisco: Grey Fox Press, 1980.

———. "Vancouver Lecture 1." *Caterpillar* 12 (1970): 175–86.

Stanford, W. B. *The Sound of Greek: Studies in the Greek Theory and Practice of Euphony.* Berkeley:
University of California Press, 1967.

Steiner, George. *Real Presences.* Chicago: University of Chicago Press, 1989.

Steiner, Wendy. *Exact Resemblance to Exact Resemblance: The Literary Portraiture of Gertrude Stein.* New
Haven: Yale University Press, 1978.

Stevens, Wallace. *The Collected Poems of Wallace Stevens.* New York: Alfred A. Knopf, 1954;
reprint, 1964.

Strauss, David Levi. *Between the Eyes: Essays on Photography and Politics.* New York: Aperture, 2003.

Surette, Leon. *A Light from Eleusis: A Study of Ezra Pound's Cantos.* Oxford: Clarendon Press; New
York: Oxford University Press, 1979.

Tallman, Ellen. "My Stories with Robert Duncan." Unpublished talk delivered at Stan-
ford University, 8 November 2003.

Tallman, Warren. "The Wonder Merchants: Modernist Poetry in Vancouver in the

1960s." *Godawful Streets of Man.* Special Issue. *Open Letter,* 3d ser., no. 6 (winter 1976–77): 175–207.

Taylor, Mark C. *Erring: A Postmodern Theology.* Chicago: University of Chicago Press, 1984.

Thatcher, David S. *Nietzsche in England, 1890–1914.* Toronto: University of Toronto Press, 1970.

Thoreau, Henry David. "Manifesto on Civil Disobedience." In *The Writings of Henry David Thoreau.* Vol. 4. Boston: Houghton Mifflin, 1906. 356–87.

———. *Walden and Other Writings.* Ed. with Introduction by Brooks Atkinson. 1950; reprint, New York: Modern Library, 1965.

Thorpe, John. "Prologue." In *From Feathers to Iron,* by John [Jack] Clarke. Bolinas, Calif.: Tombouctou Books, 1987. xiii–xx.

Turner, Graham. "The U.S. Empire." *Vancouver Sun,* 16 August 2003, C1–C6.

Tytell, John. *Ezra Pound: The Solitary Volcano.* New York: Doubleday, 1987.

Vico, Giambattista. *The New Science of Giambattista Vico.* Trans. Thomas Goddard Bergin and Max Harold Fisch. 1961; reprint, Ithaca: Cornell University Press, 1986.

View: The Modern Magazine. Ser. 5, no. 1 (March 1945). [Special issue on Marcel Duchamp.] Reprint, Nendeln/Liechtenstein: Kraus Reprint, 1969.

Voegelin, Eric. *From Enlightenment to Revolution.* Ed. John H. Hallowell. Durham, N.C.: Duke University Press, 1975.

von Hallberg, Robert. *Charles Olson: The Scholar's Art.* Cambridge, Mass.: Harvard University Press, 1978.

Wagstaff, Christopher. "An Interior Light: A Note on Robert Duncan's Crayon Drawings." In *Robert Duncan: Drawings and Decorated Books,* ed. Christopher Wagstaff. Berkeley: Rose Books, 1992. 12–18.

Wah, Fred. *Breathin' My Name with a Sigh.* Toronto: Coach House Press, 1979.

Waite, A. E. *The Hermetic Museum, Restored and Enlarged.* 2 vols. London, 1893.

Waldman, Anne, and Lisa Birman, eds. *Civil Disobedience: Poetics and Politics in Action.* Minneapolis: Coffee House Press, 2004.

Watson, Scott. "The Legend of Icarus: From Subversion to Transgression." In *Christos Dikeakos.* Vancouver: Vancouver Art Gallery, 1986. 7–16.

Watterson, Helen. "Paragraphs from the German of Friedrich Nietzsche." *Century Magazine* 38, n.s. 16 (May 1889–October 1889): 160.

Weaver, Mike. *William Carlos Williams: The American Background.* Cambridge: Cambridge University Press, 1971.

Webb, James. *The Flight from Reason: The Age of the Irrational.* London: Macdonald, 1971.

Weston, Jessie. *From Ritual to Romance.* Cambridge: Cambridge University Press, 1920; reprint, Garden City, N.Y.: Doubleday, 1957.

Weyl, H. *Philosophy of Mathematics and Natural Science.* Princeton: Princeton University Press, 1949.

Whalley, George. "Fry's [sic] Anatomy of Criticism." *Tamarack Review* 8 (summer 1958): 92–101.

———. *Poetic Process.* London: Routledge & Kegan Paul, 1953.

———. *Studies in Literature and the Humanities: Innocent of Intent.* London: Macmillan, 1985.

Whitehead, Alfred North. *Process and Reality: An Essay in Cosmology.* New York: Macmillan, 1929; Corrected Ed., ed. David Ray Griffin and Donald W. Sherburne. New York: Macmillan/Free Press; London: Collier Macmillan, 1978.

Whitman, Walt. *Whitman: Selected by Robert Creeley.* Ed. Robert Creeley. Harmondsworth: Penguin Books, 1973.

Whorf, Benjamin Lee. "An American Indian Model of the Universe." *International Journal of American Linguistics* 16, no. 2 (April 1950): 67–72.

Wilden, Anthony. "Lacan and the Discourse of the Other." In *Speech and Language in Psychoanalysis,* by Jacques Lacan. Ed. Anthony Wilden. Baltimore: Johns Hopkins University Press, 1981. 159–311.

Wilke, Brian, and M. J. Johnson. *Blake's Four Zoas.* Cambridge, Mass.: Harvard University Press, 1978.

Williams, William Carlos. *The Great American Novel.* Paris: Three Mountains Press, 1923.

———. *Pictures from Brueghel and Other Poems: Collected Poems, 1950–1962.* New York: New Directions, 1962.

———. *Selected Essays.* New York: Random House, 1954.

———. *A Voyage to Pagany.* New York: New Directions, 1970.

Wolin, Sheldon S. *Politics and Vision.* Boston: Little, Brown, 1960.

Woolf, Virginia. *The Captain's Death Bed and Other Essays.* London: Hogarth Press, 1950; New York: Harcourt, Brace, 1950.

———. *The Diary of Virginia Woolf.* 4 vols. Ed. Anne Oliver Bell. London: Hogarth Press, 1977–84.

Yates, Frances A. *The Art of Memory.* Chicago: University of Chicago Press, 1966.

———. *Giordano Bruno and the Hermetic Tradition.* London: Routledge & Kegan Paul, 1964.

Yeats, William Butler. *A Vision.* Rev. ed. New York: Collier Books/Macmillan, 1966; reprint, 1977.

Zukofsky, Louis. *An "Objectivist's" Anthology.* Le Beausset, France: TO, Publishers, 1932.

———. *A Test of Poetry.* New York: Jargon/Corinth, 1974.

WORKS BY ROBIN BLASER

Poetry

Les Chimères: Translations of Nerval for Fran Herndon. San Francisco: Open Space, 1965. Chapbook.

Cups. San Francisco: Four Seasons Foundation, 1968. Chapbook.

The Faery Queene and The Park. Vancouver: Fissure Books, 1987. Chapbook.

The Holy Forest. Toronto: Coach House Press, 1993.

Image-Nations 1–12 and The Stadium of the Mirror. London: Ferry Press, 1974.

Image-Nations 13 & 14, Luck Unluck Oneluck, Sky-stone, Suddenly, Gathering. North Vancouver: Cobblestone Press, 1974. Chapbook.

The Last Supper. London: Boosey & Hawkes, 2000. Libretto.

The Moth Poem. San Francisco: White Rabbit Press, 1964. Chapbook.

Pell Mell. Toronto: Coach House Press, 1988.

Syntax. Vancouver: Talonbooks, 1983.

Wanders. With Meredith Quartermain. Vancouver: Nomados Press, 2002. Chapbook.

Uncollected Prose

"Excerpts from *Astonishments*." Transcribed and edited by Miriam Nichols. *Even on Sunday: Essays, Readings and Archival Materials on the Poetry and Poetics of Robin Blaser*. Orono, Me.: National Poetry Foundation, 2002. 273–347.

"Hello!" *Sulfur* 37, vol. 15, no. 2 (fall 1995): 84–94. [Talk for "Recovery of the Public World" conference, first delivered 1 June 1995 at Emily Carr College of Art and Design.]

"The Metaphysics of Light." Excerpt from *Astonishments*. Transcribed and edited by Daphne Marlatt. *Capilano Review*, no. 6 (fall 1974): 35–59.

"No Matter." In *Free the Shadows*, by Luis Posse. Vancouver: Talonbooks, 1986. 3–9.

"Thinking about Irreparables." *Raddle Moon* 18 (2000): 92–121. [Talk transcribed from a taped keynote address for the tenth anniversary of the Kootenay School of Writing, 1994.]

Broadsides and Miscellaneous Publications

"Apparators." *A Poetry Folio*. San Francisco: Auerhahn Press, 1964. Broadside.

"Artaud on Nerval." Trans. Robin Blaser and Richard Ross. *Pacific Nation*, no. 1 (1967): 67–78.

"Les Chimères," "The Fire," "The Holy Forest section from *The Holy Forest*," "Pindar's Seventh Olympic Hymn." *Caterpillar* 12 (July 1970): 2–53.

"Cups." *Locus Solus* 1 (winter 1961): 136–51. Ed. James Schuyler. Dans-en-Vercors (Isère), France: Locus Solus Press.

"Five Poems." *No Apologies: A Magazine of Gay Writing* 3 (1984): 89–93. Guest ed. Kevin Killian.

"From Cups, 4" and other poems reprinted from *The Holy Forest*. *Etruscan Reader* 4. South Devonshire, U.K.: Etruscan Books, 1998. 9–58.

"Great Companion: Dante Alighieri." *Testo & Senso* 3 (2000): *Dante: "For Use, Now."* A cura di Annalisa Goldoni e Andrea Mariani. 13–27.

"Harp Trees." Vancouver: Sun Stone House and Cobblestone Press, 1977. Broadside.

"Honestas." Buffalo: Poetry/Rare Book Collection, State University of New York, 1987. Broadside. [Published in conjunction with a Charles Olson Memorial Lecture by Robin Blaser, sponsored by the Gray Chair of Poetry and Letters and the Department of English, State University of New York.]

"The Hunger of Sound." *Junge Amerikanische Lyrik*. Ed. Gregory Corso and Walter Höllerer. Munich: Hanser, 1961.

"Image-Nation 13 (the telephone." Vancouver: Talonbooks, 1975. Broadside.

"Image-Nation 15 (the lacquer house." Vancouver: William Hoffer, 1981.

"Image-Nation 25." *Sodomite Invasion Review*, no. 6 (summer 1994): 24–25.

"Image-Nations 1–5." *Gnomon*, no. 2 (spring 1967): 15–20.

The Irreparable. Vancouver: Nomados Press, 2003. Chapbook.

"Kimm." Prince George, B.C.: Caledonia Writing Series, 1977. Broadside.

"Literary Behaviour": [A report of the Writer's Conference of the University of California, spring semester, 1948/Robin Blaser, chairman]. Berkeley: University of California, 1948. Mimeograph.

"Muses, Dionysus, Eros." Lawrence, Kans.: Tansy Press and Friends of the Kansas University Poetry Collective, 1990. Broadside.

"Nomad." *Sulfur* 37, vol. 15, no. 2 (fall 1995): 117. Reprint, Vancouver: Slug Press, 1995. Broadside.

"Of is the word love without the initial consonant." Vancouver: Slug Press, 1979. Broadside.

"The Park." *Locus Solus* 3–4 (1963): 49–57. Ed. John Ashbery. Dans-en-Vercors (Isère), France: Locus Solus Press.

"The Park," "from The Faerie Queene," "Sophia Nichols." In *A Controversy of Poets,* ed. Paris Leary and Robert Kelly. Garden City, N.Y.: Anchor Books/Doubleday, 1965. 28–37.

"Pentimento." *The Cambridge Conference of Contemporary Poetry Review* (2000): n.p.

"Pindar's Seventh Olympic Hymn." In *Episodes in Five Poetic Traditions,* ed. R. G. Barnes. San Francisco: Chandler, 1972.

"Shipped Shape," "The Truth Is Laughter 18, 19, 20, 21." *West Coast Line* 36, vol. 35, no. 3 (winter 2001–2): 4–6.

A Symposium of the Image: Robert Duncan in Word and Image with a Foreword by Robert J. Bertholf and an Afterword by Robin Blaser. Buffalo: Poetry/Rare Books Collection, State University of New York, 1993. Catalogue of exhibition at the State University of New York, 12 September–31 October 1993.

"Three poems: The flame; Ode for museums, all of them; A story after Blake." Dublin: Oneinkbook Press, 1995.

Tom Field: Paintings from Black Mountain College and the Beat Era. San Francisco: 871 Fine Arts, 1996. Exhibition catalogue for Tom Field Show, 19 September–24 December 1996.

"Tumbleweed." From *Six B.C. Poets* [A series of six broadsides complied by Roy Miki] Vancouver: Talonbooks, 1978. [Issued in portfolio for the B.C. Heritage Poetry Festival, 27 May 1978, sponsored by the Department of English and Continuing Studies, Simon Fraser University.]

The Writings and the World of Mary Butts. Davis: University of California, 1984. [Brochure for "A conference at the University of California Davis, February 23 and 24, 1984, with brief essays by Robin Blaser, Robert Duncan, and Barbara Wagstaff."]

Correspondence

"Charles Olson–Robin Blaser Correspondence, 1957–1959, with an Introduction by Robin Blaser." Ed. Ralph Maud. *Minutes of the Charles Olson Society,* no. 8 (June 1995): 5–33.

"Charles Olson–Robin Blaser Correspondence: White Rabbit Press and *The Pacific Nation,* 1965–1969." Ed. Miriam Nichols. *Minutes of the Charles Olson Society,* no. 49 (March 2003): 9–27.

"A Correspondence." With Lisa Robertson. *Capilano Review* ser. 2, nos. 17–18 (winter–spring 1996): 97–108. [Special issue: *A Festschrift for Robin.*]

Audio and Video Recordings

Astonishments. Rec. Warren Tallman. Vancouver, 1974. 24 audiocassettes. [Autobiographical tapes made over the spring and summer of 1974 at the home of Warren Tallman in Vancouver. In attendance, Warren Tallman, Angela Bowering, Martina Kuharic, Dwight Gardner, and Daphne Marlatt. Housed at Simon Fraser University, Contemporary Literature Collection, W. A. C. Bennett Library.]

"Belief, doubt, and politics." 2 parts. Videocassette. Rec. Boulder, Colo.: Naropa University Summer Writing Program, 1992.

Charles Olson Lectures (Buffalo, 1987). Introduction Robert Creeley.

   Lecture 1, part 1 (46:19); part 2 (38:57): MP3, RealAudio.

   Lecture 2, part 1 (46:09); part 2 (26:00): MP3, RealAudio.

   Lecture 3, part 1 (44:45); part 2 (44:03): MP3, RealAudio.

   January 2, 2005. http://www.writing.upenn.edu/pennsound/x/Blaser-1966.html.

The Holy Forest. Robin Blaser reading with Roy Kiyooka. *Collapse* No. 1 (1995). CD.

"Lecture on Robert Duncan." Buffalo, 1996. (41:02): MP3, RealAudio. 2 January 2005. http://www.writing.upenn.edu/pennsound/x/Blaser-1966.html.

"Poetry Reading" (Buffalo, 1987) (54.04): RealAudio. January 2, 2005. http://www.writing.upenn.edu/pennsound/x/Blaser-1966.html.

The Recovery of the Public World: A Conference and Festival in Honour of Robin Blaser, His Poetry and Poetics: June 1–4, 1995. San Francisco: Cloud House Poetry Archives, 1996. Video- and audiocassettes.

"Relocating the High Lyric Voice." With John Kinsella, Denise Riley, and Iain Sinclair. MP3, RealAudio. BBC Radio, 1994. January 2, 2005. http://www.writing.upenn.edu/pennsound/x/Blaser-1966.html.

Robin Blaser. Dir. and prod. Ralph Maud. Vancouver, 1991. Videocassette.

"Robin Blaser: February 11, 1976." San Francisco: San Francisco State University: Poetry Center and American Poetry Archives. VHS (available).

"Robin Blaser: May 18, 2000." San Francisco: San Francisco State University: Poetry Center and American Poetry Archives. VHS (available).

"Robin Blaser: November 9, 1983." San Francisco: San Francisco State University: Poetry Center and American Poetry Archives. VHS (available).

"Robin Blaser: September 29, 1988." San Francisco: San Francisco State University: Poetry Center and American Poetry Archives. VHS (available).

Robin Blaser/Olson Interview. Dir. Colin Browne. Vancouver: Northwest Imaging, 1999. Videocassette.

"Robin Blaser, reading from Jack Spicer's & his own work: March 9, 1967." San Francisco: San Francisco State University: Poetry Center and American Poetry Archives. Audiocassette.

Robin Blaser, Robert Creeley, Michael Ondaatje Panel Discussion. 2 parts. Rec. Boulder, Colo.: Naropa University Summer Writing Program, 1999. Videocassette.

Works Edited by Robin Blaser

Art and Reality: A Casebook of Concern. Ed. Robin Blaser and Robert Dunham. Vancouver: Talon-books, 1986.

The Collected Books of Jack Spicer. 1975; reprint, Los Angeles: Black Sparrow Press, 1980.

Imaginary Letters. By Mary Butts. Vancouver: Talonbooks, 1979.

Infinite Worlds: The Poetry of Louis Dudek. By Louis Dudek. Montréal: Véhicule Press, 1988.

Pacific Nation 1 and 2. Vancouver, B.C., 1967; 1969 with Stan Persky.

Particular Accidents: Selected Poems. By George Bowering. Vancouver: Talonbooks, 1980.

Reflections on Cultural Policy, Past, Present and Future. Ed. Robin Blaser, Evan Alderson, and Harold Coward. Waterloo: Wilfrid Laurier University Press for the Calgary Institute for the Humanities, 1993.

Interviews

With John Sakkis. *The Poker* 5 (winter 2005): 61–74.

With Miriam Nichols. *Even on Sunday: Essays, Readings and Archival materials on the Poetry and Poetics of Robin Blaser.* Orono, Me.: National Poetry Foundation, 2002. 349–92.

WORKS ABOUT ROBIN BLASER

Books

Byrne, Edward, and Charles Watts, eds. *The Recovery of the Public World.* Vancouver: Talon-books, 1999. [Conference essays from the 1995 "Recovery of the Public World" conference honoring Blaser's seventieth birthday.]

Nichols, Miriam, ed. *Even on Sunday: Essays, Readings and Archival Materials on the Poetry and Poetics of Robin Blaser.* Orono, Me.: National Poetry Foundation, 2002.

Articles

Bernstein, Charles. "Robin on His Own." *West Coast Line* No. 17, vol. 29, no. 2 (fall 1995): 114–21.

Boone, Bruce. "Robin Blaser's New Syntax: Pointing Up Ahead, Behind, Wherever." *No Apologies: A Magazine of Gay Writing* 3 (1984): 94–105. Guest ed. Kevin Killian.

Boughn, Michael. "Bringing Poetry to Opera." *Globe and Mail*, October 4, 2001.

Conte, Joseph. "Seriality and the Contemporary Long Poem." *Sagetrieb* 11 (spring–fall 1992): 35–45.

Creeley, Robert. "For Robin." *Capilano Review*, ser. 2, nos. 17–18 (winter–spring 1966): 44. [Special issue: *A Festshrift for Robin.*]

Cross, Jonathan. "Introduction to *The Last Supper*." CD. Glyndebourne Productions, 2000.

Killian, Kevin. "Blaser Talk." *West Coast Line* No. 17, vol. 29, no. 2 (fall 1995): 126–31.

Marlatt, Daphne. "Erratic/Erotic Narrative: Syntax and Mortality in Robin Blaser's 'Image-Nations.'" *West Coast Line* No. 17, vol. 29, no. 2 (fall 1995): 136–41.

Mossin, Andrew. "In the Shadow of Nerval: Robert Duncan, Robin Blaser, and the Poetics of (Mis)Translation." *Contemporary Literature* 38, no. 4 (winter 1997): 673–704.

———. "Recovering the Public World: Robin Blaser and the Discourses of Subjectivity and Otherness in Image-Nations 1–12." *Sagetrieb* 17, nos. 1–3 (2002): 135–65.

Nichols, Miriam. "Independent Realities: Notes on Robin Blaser's *Pell Mell*." *Sulfur* 27, vol. 15, no. 2 (fall 1990): 222–26.

———. "The Poetics of God: Spilling the Name in Robin Blaser's *The Last Supper*." *Mosaic* 26, no. 2 (June 2003): 163–78.

———. "Robin Blaser." In *Dictionary of Literary Biography*. Vol. 165, *American Poets since World War II*. 4th ser. Ed. Joseph Conte. Detroit: Gale Research/Bruccoli Clark Layman, 1996. 57–68.

———. "Robin Blaser." In *The Literary Encyclopedia*, ed. Robert Clark. http://www.LitEncyc .com. 2004.

———. "Robin Blaser." In *The Reader's Encyclopedia*, ed. William H. New. Toronto: University of Toronto Press, 2002.

———. "Robin Blaser's Poetics of Relation: Thinking without Bannisters." *Sagetrieb* 9 (spring–fall 1990): 121–45.

———. "Robin Blaser's *Syntax*: Performing the Real." *Line* 3 (spring 1983): 64–77.

———. "Three for Public: Steve McCaffery, Nicole Brossard, and Robin Blaser." *Public* 12 (spring 1995): 97–111.

Paul, Sherman. "Serial Poems from Canada." In *Hewing to Experience*. Iowa City: University of Iowa Press, 1989. 37–48.

Persky, Stan. "About Robin Blaser." 2003. *Dooney's Café: A News Service*. December 23, 2004. www.dooneyscafe.com.

Quartermain, Meredith. "Lyric Capability: The Syntax of Robin Blaser." *Capilano Review* ser. 2, no. 41 (fall 2003): 95–102.

Quartermain, Peter. "The Mind as Frying Pan: Robin Blaser's Humor." *Sulfur* 37, vol. 15, no. 2 (fall 1995): 108–16.

Rasula, Jed. "Taking out the Tracks: Robin Blaser's Syncopation." *Sulfur* 37, vol. 15, no. 2 (fall 1995): 95–107.

Watts, Charles. "Foreword." *Sulfur* 37, vol. 15, no. 2 (fall 1995): 81–84.

Webb, Phyllis. "Extract from The Crannies of Matter: Texture in Robin Blaser's Later 'Image- Nations.'" *Capilano Review*, ser. 2, nos. 17–18 (winter–spring 1966): 194–96. [Special issue: *A Festshrift for Robin*.]

———. "Robin Blaser's 'Image-Nations.'" In *Nothing but Brush Strokes, the Writer as Critic V*, ed. Smaro Kamboureli. Edmonton: NeWest Publishers, 1995. 55–73.

ACKNOWLEDGMENTS
OF PERMISSIONS

ROBIN BLASER'S ESSAYS

"Among Afterthoughts on this Occasion." *Reflections on Cultural Policy Past, Present and Future.* Ed. Evan Alderson, Robin Blaser and Harold Coward. Waterloo: The Wilfrid Laurier University Press for the Calgary Institute for the Humanities, 1993. 183–190. Reprinted by permission of Wilfrid Laurier University Press.

"The 'Elf' of It" first appeared in *Robert Duncan: Drawings and Decorated Books.* Ed. Christopher Wagstaff. Berkeley: Rose Books, 1992. 21–53.

"'Here Lies the Woodpecker Who Was Zeus'" first appeared in *A Sacred Quest: The Life and Writings of Mary Butts.* Ed. Christopher Wagstaff. Kingston, New York: Macpherson & Co., 1995. 159–223.

"Introduction." *Infinite Worlds.* By Louis Dudek. Ed. Robin Blaser. Montréal: Véhicule Press, 1988. 7–29. Reprinted by permission of Véhicule Press.

"'Mind Canaries'" first appeared in *Christos Dikeakos.* Vancouver: Vancouver Art Gallery, 1986. 17–36.

"'My Vocabulary Did This To Me'" was first published in *ACTS 6: A Book of Correspondences for Jack Spicer,* ed. David Levi Strauss and Benjamin Hollander (1987): 98–105.

"out of the velvet-the denim-the straw of my mind." *Boundary 2* 26, no. 1 (spring 1999): 52–3. Copyright © 1999, Boundary 2, SUNY-Binghamton. Used by permission of the publisher.

"The Practice of Outside" was first published in *The Collected Books of Jack Spicer.* Ed. Robin Blaser. Santa Rosa: Black Sparrow Press, 1975. 271–329.

"Poetry and Positivisms." *Silence, the Word and the Sacred.* Ed. E. D. Blodgett and Harold Coward. Waterloo: Wilfrid Laurier University Press for The Calgary Institute for the Humanities, 1989. 21–50. Reprinted by permission of Wilfrid Laurier University Press.

"The Recovery of the Public World." *Reflections on Cultural Policy Past, Present and Future.* Ed. Evan Alderson, Robin Blaser, and Harold Coward. Waterloo: The Wilfrid Laurier University Press for the Calgary Institute for the Humanities, 1993. 17–38. Reprinted by permission of Wilfrid Laurier University Press.

"The Violets" was first published in *Process Studies* 13, no. 1 (spring 1983): 3–37, ed. Donald Sherburne.

WORKS QUOTED IN ROBIN BLASER'S ESSAYS

Adams, Hazard. *Philosophy of the Literary Symbolic.* Tallahassee: University Press of Florida, 1983. Copyright © 1983 by the Board of Regents of the State of Florida. Used by permission of the University Press of Florida.

Agamben, Giorgio. *The Coming Community.* Trans. Michael Hardt. Minneapolis: University of Minesota press, 1993. Copyright © 1993 by the Regents of the University of Minnesota. Used by permission of the University of Minnesota Press.

———. *Infancy and History.* Trans. Liz Heron. London: Verso, 1993. Copyright © Giulio Einaudi 1978; translation © Liz Heron 1993 published by Verso 1993. Used by permission of Verso.

Arendt, Hannah. *Between Past and Future.* New York: Viking/Penguin, 1977. Copyright © 1954, 1956, 1957, 1958, 1960, 1961 by Hannah Arendt. Used by permission of Viking Penguin, a division of Penguin Group (USA) Inc.

———. *The Human Condition.* Chicago: University of Chicago Press, 1958. Copyright © 1958 by The University of Chicago. Used by permission of the University of Chicago Press.

———. *Men in Dark Times.* Trans. Clara Winston and Richard Winston. San Diego: Harcourt Brace, 1983. Copyright © 1968 by Hannah Arendt and renewed 1996 by Lotte Kohler, reprinted by permission of Harcourt, Inc.

———. *The Origins of Totalitarianism.* 1948. 2d ed. Cleveland: World Publishing Co., 1958; San Diego: Harcourt Brace, 1976. Copyright © 1973, 1968, 1966, 1958, 1951, 1948 by Hannah Arendt, copyright renewed 2001, 1996, 1994, 1986 by Lotte Kohler, copyright renewed 1979 by Mary McCarthy West, copyright renewed 1976 by Hannah Arendt. Used by permission of Harcourt, Inc.

———. "The Social Question." *On Revolution.* 1963; New York: Viking/Penguin, 1965. 59–114. Copyright © 1963 by Hannah Arendt. Used by permission of Viking Penguin, a division of Penguin Group (USA), Inc.

Boulez, Pierre. *Stocktakings from an Apprenticeship.* Collected by Paule Thévenin. Trans. Stephen Walsh. Oxford and New York: Clarendon Press and Oxford University Press, 1991. Copyright © Clarendon Press 1991. Used by permission of Clarendon Press.

Bowering, George. *In the Flesh.* Toronto: McClelland and Stewart, 1974. Used by permission of the author.

Butts, Mary. *Armed with Madness, Ashe of Rings, The Crystal Cabinet, Death of Felicity Taverner, From Altar to Chimney-Piece: Selected Stories of Mary Butts, Imaginary Letters, The Macedonian, Traps for Unbelievers,* and "Corfe." Passages from the above works used by permission of Camilla Baggs.

Davey, Frank. "Introduction." *Louis Dudek: Texts & Essays.* Open Letter. 4th ser. no. 8–9 (spring-summer 1981): 7–8.

———. "Introduction." *TISH* 1–19. Ed. Frank Davey. Vancouver: Talonbooks, 1975. 7–11.

Passages from above works cited by permission of the author.

Dudek, Louis. *Atlantis, En Mexico, Epigrams, Louis Dudek: Texts & Essays, Selected Essays, Technology and Culture*. Passages from the above works used by permission of Gregory Dudek.

Duncan, Robert. *A Book of Resemblances: Poems 1950–1953*. Illus. Jess. New Haven: H. Wenning, 1966.

———. "The Delirium of Meaning." *The Sin of the Book: Edmond Jabès*. Ed. Eric Gould. Lincoln: University of Nebraska Press, 1985. 207–26.

———. "Iconographical Extensions" Translations by Jess. Los Angeles: Black Sparrow Press, 1971. i–xiv.

———. *Letters: Poems 1953–1956*. Highlands, N.C.: J. Williams, 1958.

———. *Notes on Grossinger's Solar Journal: Oecological Sections*. Los Angeles: Black Sparrow Press, 1970.

———. "Pages from a Notebook." *The New American Poetry*. Ed. Donald Allen and Warren Tallman. New York: Grove Press, 1960. 400–407.

Passages from the above works cited by permission of the Estate.

Duncan, Robert. *Fictive Certainties*. New York: New Directions, 1985. Copyright © 1955, 1956, 1961, 1965, 1966, 1968, 1978, 1983, 1985 by Robert Duncan.

———. *Ground Work I: Before the War*. New York: New Directions, 1984. Copyright © 1968, 1969, 1970, 1971, 1972, 1974, 1975, 1976, 1977, 1982, 1984 by Robert Duncan.

———. *Ground Work II: In the Dark*. New York: New Directions, 1987. Copyright © 1977, 1978, 1979, 1980, 1981, 1982, 1983, 1985, 1987 by Robert Duncan.

———. *The Opening of the Field*. New York: New Directions, 1973. Copyright © by Robert Duncan.

Passages from the above works cited by permission of New Directions Press.

Ehrenfeld, David. *The Arrogance of Humanism* by David Ehrenfeld. New York: Oxford University Press, 1978. Copyright © 1978 Oxford University Press, USA. Used by permission of the Oxford University Press.

Foucault, Michel. *Madness and Civilization: A History of Insanity in the Age of Reason*. Trans. Richard Howard. New York: Vintage Books/Random House, 1973. English Translation copyright © 1965 by Random House, Inc. Originally published in French as *Histoire de la Folie* copyright © 1961 by Librarie Plon. Reprinted by permission of Georges Borchardt, Inc., for Librarie Plon.

———. *The Order of Things*. New York: Random House. Copyright © 1970 by Random House, Inc., New York. Originally published in French as *Les Mots et les Choses*. Copyright © 1966 by Editions Gallimard. Reprinted by permission of Georges Borchardt, Inc., for Editions Gallimard.

Gass, William H. *Habitations of the Word*. New York: Simon and Schuster, 1985. Reprinted by permission of the author.

Handelman, Susan A. *The Slayers of Moses: the Emergence of Rabbinic Interpretation in Modern Literary Theory*. Albany: State University of New York Press, 1982. Copyright © 1982 State University of New York. Used by permission of State University of New York Press.

Hartman, Geoffrey. *Beyond Formalism*. New Haven: Yale University Press, 1970. Reprinted by permission of the author.

Hung, William. *Tu Fu: China's Greatest Poet*. Cambridge, Mass.: Harvard University Press, 1952. 51–52. Copyright © 1952 by the President and Fellows of Harvard College.

Hynes, Samuel B. *The Edwardian Turn of Mind*. Princeton: Princeton University Press, 1968. Used by permission of the author.

Lacan, Jacques. *Speech and Language in Psychoanalysis*. Trans. with introduction and notes by Anthony Wilden. Baltimore: Johns Hopkins University Press, 1981. 33, 45, 160, 183, 201–2. © 1981 by Anthony Wilden. Used by permission of The Johns Hopkins University Press.

Lefort, Claude. "Editor's Foreword." *The Visible and the Invisible*, by Maurice Merleau-Ponty. Trans. Alphonso Lingis. Evanston: Northwestern University Press, 1968. xi–xxxiii. Copyright © 1968 by Northwestern University Press. Used by permission of Northwestern University Press.

Lingis, Alphonso. "Translator's Preface." *The Visible and the Invisible*, by Maurice Merleau-Ponty. Trans. Alphonso Lingis. Evanston: Northwestern University Press, 1968. xl–lvi. Copyright © 1968 by Northwestern University Press. Used by permission of Northwestern University Press.

Lyotard, Jean-François. "Answering the Question: What is Postmodernism." *Innovation/Renovation*, by Ihab Hassan. Madison: University of Wisconsin Press, 1983. 329–41. Copyright © 1983 by the Board of Regents of the University of Wisconsin System. Used by permission of The University of Wisconsin Press.

Merleau-Ponty, Maurice. *Signs*. Trans. Richard C. McCleary. Evanston: Northwestern University Press, 1964. Translation copyright © 1964 by Northwestern University Press. Used by permission.

———. *The Visible and the Invisible*. Ed. Claude Lefort. Trans. Alphonso Lingis. Evanston: Northwestern University Press, 1968. xi–xxxiii. Copyright © 1968 by Northwestern University Press. Used by permission of Northwestern University Press.

Olson, Charles. *The Maximus Poems*. Ed. George F. Butterick. Berkeley: University of California Press, 1983. Used by permission of the University of California Press.

———. *Muthologos: The Collected Lectures and Interviews*. Vol 1. Ed. George Butterick. Bolinas, Calif.: Four Seasons Foundation, 1978. The Charles Olson Papers, Archives and Special Collections, Thomas J. Dodd Research Center, University of Connecticut Libraries. Used by permission.

———. Note on flyleaf of *The Key*. By Philip Cohane. London: Crown, 1969. The Charles Olson Papers, Archives and Special Collections, Thomas J. Dodd Research Center, University of Connecticut Libraries. Used by permission.

———. *The Special View of History*. Ed. Ann Charters. Berkeley: Oyez, 1970. The Charles Olson Papers, Archives & Special Collections, Thomas J. Dodd Research Center, University of Connecticut Libraries. Used by permission.

Paz, Octavio. *The Bow and the Lyre*. Translated by Ruth L.C. Simms. Austin: University of Texas Press, 1973. Copyright © 1956 by Fondo de Cultura Economica. Copyright © 1973 by Octavio Paz. Used by permission of the University of Texas Press.

———. *Marcel Duchamp: Appearance Stripped Bare*. Trans. Rachel Phillips and Donald Gardner. New York: Viking, 1978. English language translation copyright © 1978 by Viking

Penguin Inc. Reprinted from *Marcel Duchamp: Appearance Stripped Bare* by Octavio Paz, published by Seaver Books, New York. Used by permission of Seaver Books.

Portillo, Luis. "Unamuno's Last Lecture." *The Golden Horizon.* Ed. Cyril Connolly. London: Weidenfeld & Nicolson, 1953. An imprint of The Orion Publishing Group. All attempts to trace the copyright holder of this essay were unsuccessful.

Rilke, Rainer Maria. *Letters of Rainer Maria Rilke: 1910 – 1926.* Trans. Jane Bannard Greene and M.D. Herter Norton. New York: Norton, 1948. Copyright 1947, 1948 by W.W. Norton & Company, Inc., renewed © 1975 by M. D. Herter Norton. Used by permission of W.W. Norton & Company, Inc.

———. *The Selected Poetry of Rainier Maria Rilke.* Ed. and Trans. Stephen Mitchell. New York: Random House, 1982. Copyright ©1982 by Stephen Mitchell. Used by permission of Random House, Inc.

Stevens, Wallace. "Esthétique du mal." *The Collected Poems of Wallace Stevens.* New York: Alfred A. Knopf, 1961. 313–26. Copyright © 1954 by Wallace Stevens and renewed 1982 by Holly Stevens. Used by permission of Alfred A. Knopf, a division of Random House, Inc.

Thatcher, David S. *Nietzsche in England, 1890–1913.* Toronto: University of Toronto Press, 1970. Copyright © University of Toronto Press. Used by permission of the University of Toronto Press.

Whitehead, Alfred North. *Process and Reality: An Essay in Cosmology.* New York: Macmillan, 1929; Corrected Ed., ed. David Ray Griffin and Donald W. Sherburne. New York: Macmillan Free Press, 1978. Reprinted by permission of Scribner, an imprint of Simon & Schuster Adult Publishing Group. Copyright © 1929 by The Macmillan Company; copyright renewed © 1957 by Evelyn Whitehead.

Yates, Frances. *Giordano Bruno and the Hermetic Tradition.* London: Routledge & Kegan Paul, 1964. Copyright © 1964 by Frances A. Yates. Used by permission of the University of Chicago Press.

INDEX

Mell, 407, 408, 443n58; "Poetry and Positivisms," xvi, 38, 376–77, 378, 386, 408, 428, 428n1, 431n3, 447n7, 450nn23,5, 453n5; "Practice of Outside, The," xvi, 113, 371n3, 381–84, 382n9, 386, 391, 395, 406, 407, 432n7, 435, 435n3, 438n20, 445n8, 446n3, 447, 447n4, 450n20, 452n11; *Preface to the Early Poems of Robert Duncan*, 299, 391n16, 408; "The Recovery of the Public World," xv, xvi, 64, 85, 198, 372n5, 378–79, 386, 408, 409, 415n2, 429n9, 430, 431nn1,3, 434n5, 446n1, 453n5, 455n9, 456n14; "The Stadium of the Mirror," xii, xvi, 26, 32, 373–76, 377, 382, 383, 407, 416, 421n25, 422n29, 428n3, 429n9, 431n3, 437nn10,11, 438n21, 439n26, 440n40, 441, 444nn1,3, 446n3, 447n3, 450n3, 451nn3,5, 452n11, 453n2, 455n7; *Syntax*, 407, 429n10; "The Violets," xiii, xvi, 196, 202–4, 205, 206, 210, 227, 386–89, 407, 415n2, 432n8, 434n5, 442n54, 445–46; *Wanders*, 410

Blau DuPlessis, Rachel, xi

Blavatsky, Madame (Helena), 343

Blodgett, E. D., 408, 428

Bloom, Harold, *The American Religion*, 352–53

Bloomsbury, 338, 349n

Boehme, Jacob, 390

Boer, Charles, *Charles Olson in Connecticut*, 196, 202, 225n

Bohlmann, Otto, *Yeats and Nietzsche: An Exploration of Major Nietzschean Echoes in William Butler Yeats*, 341

Bohm, David, 200; *Wholeness and the Implicate Order*, 77n

Book of Magazine Verse (Spicer), 53, 114, 117, 123, 125–26, 139, 143, 153–54, 156, 161, 421n26, 438n21, 440n33, 450n22

Book of Music, A (Spicer), 161, 443n58

Book of Promethea, The (Cixous), 99, 434n1

Book of Resemblances (Duncan), 300–301, 451n1

Borregard, Ebbe, 3, 411n1

Bosch, Hieronymous, 243; *The Garden of Earthly Delights*, 242; *The Hay Wain*, 242; *The Temptation of St. Anthony*, 242

Boston Poems, The (Blaser), 403, 414n19

Boulez, Pierre, 322, 350, 381; on Bach, 359–62, 381, 397, 398; and Cage, 364; chance,

363, 397; and Mallarmé, 289, 363, 364, 452n9; *Pli Selon Pli*, 290, 452n9; *Second Piano Sonata*, 350, 359–60, 361, 363, 397, 398, 455n1; serialism of, 361, 362; *Stocktakings*, 359, 364

Boulez: Composer, Conductor, Enigma (Peyser), 452n9

The Bow and the Lyre (Paz), 83, 235–38, 348–9

Bowering, Angela, 407

Bowering, George, xi, 177, 186n, 263, 264, 380, 381, 391, 392–93, 405; *Αλλοφανες*, 182, 194n; *Another Mouth*, 180; *Autobiology*, 182, 183, 185, 194, 195n; *Baseball*, 182; *Burning Water*, 180; *The Catch*, 445n9; and Creeley, 181, 444n7; *Curious*, 182, 191; "The Descent," 178; "Desert Elm," 186, 445n9; *Flycatcher*, 183; *Genève*, 181, 444n5; *George, Vancouver*, 182; "Grandfather," 182, 185, 444n6; *In the Flesh*, 181–82; language, use of, 178–80, 185; literary portraits, 191–92; long poem, 182; on locus, 186, 445n10; lyricism of, 181–82, 186, 193; "Mars," 185; *Mirror on the Floor*, 183; "Moon Shadow," 182; naturalism of, 185, 189; *Particular Accidents*, 444nn5,6; poetics, context of, 185–92; "Radio Jazz," 180, 182; realism of, 185, 190; *The Sensible*, 182, 185, 444n5; *Short Sad Book, A*, 182–85, 444n4; *Sticks and Stones*, 444n7; Williams, influence on, 183, 185, 186, 392

Bowra, Maurice Sir, *Poetry and Politics*, 13

Bradley, F. H., 54

Brautigan, Richard, 406

Breathin' My Name with a Sigh (Wah), 179

Breton, André, 239, 244, 245, 249, 448n3; "Lighthouse of the Bride," 244n; *What is Surrealism*, 238

Bride Stripped Bare by her Bachelors, Even, The (*Large Glass*) (Duchamp), 242, 248–50, 447n6

British Journal of Psychology, 335

Broch, Hermann, *The Death of Virgil*, 60–61, 102, 430n16

Brodeur, Arthur, 9, 414n20

Bruno, Giordano, 142, 152, 414n23

"Bucolique" (*Oeuvres complètes*; Mallarmé), 60, 429n15

Buddha, 86

Buddhism, 162, 249

Budge, E. A. Wallis, *The Gods of the Egyptians*, 324

Bunting, Basil, 264

Burckhardt, Titus, *Alchemy: Science of the Cosmos, Science of the Soul*, 323

Burning *Water* (Bowering), 180

Burroughs, William, 193

Bush, George W., 410

Butterick, George, 196n, 219n, 350; editor's notes to *Muthologos* (Olson), 363; *A Guide to the Maximus Poems of Charles Olson*, 202, 205, 223, 225–26, 226n, 455n2; *Journal of the Charles Olson Archives*, 201, 205n, 455n3

Butts, Anthony, 338, 349n

Butts, Mary, 381, 394; *Armed with Madness*, 164, 165, 168, 169, 304, 310–23, 327–32, 335, 338, 339, 342, 344, 345–48, 395, 453; *Ashe of Rings*, 170, 172–73; archaic, in works of, 310, 320, 324, 332; biography, 165–66, 306, 443n2, 444n4; and Blake, 172; and Cocteau, 167, 308, 309; "Corfe," 174–76, 311–12, 454n3; *Crystal Cabinet*, 164, 165, 166, 167, 169, 172, 343; *Death of Felicity Taverner, The*, 165, 168, 169, 173, 312, 313, 348; grail, in works of, 313, 314, 317–22, 325, 327–30, 345–49, 395; and H.D., 309, 310, 325; hermetic tradition, in works of, 323–29, 332n, 342, 395; homosexuality, relation to, 166, 173–74, 308–9, 313, 335, 381; *Imaginary Letters*, 165, 167, 169, 173, 309, 313, 394, 443, 454n10; *Last Stories*, 173; literary context, 305–10; *The Macedonian*, 167, 338–39; magic, in works of, 166, 168, 169–71, 181, 305, 307, 311–15, 322, 324–31, 336, 337, 347, 395–96, 443n2; modernity of, 307, 394–95; mysticism of, 165, 332, 342; occult, in works of, 167, 170–71, 324–25, 395, 443n2; and Nietzsche, 337, 339–44, 339n, 349n; the Other, in works of, 311, 334, 344, 348, 395; realism of, 310, 311, 314, 316; sacred, in works of, 168, 174, 176, 309–11, 314–15, 320, 325, 328, 381, 394–95, 443n5; *Scenes from the Life of Cleopatra*, 167, 338; *Selected Stories*, 164, 165, 173, 443n1, 444n5; *Several Occasions*, 309; *Speed the Plough*, 166, 167, 305; *Traps for Unbelievers*, 170, 326–28, 335–37, 338, 339, 341; Zeus-Picus (woodpecker), in works of, 319–21, 328–32, 346–48

Butts, Thomas, 172, 309, 454n5

Byrd, Don, *Charles Olson's Maximus*, 215–16, 220n

Byrne, Edward, 409; *The Recovery of the Public World*, 453n8

Byron, George Gordon, Lord, 278, 454n9

Cabbala, 324

Cage, John, 364, 455n1

Calatrava, Santiago, 103

Call Me Ishmael (Olson), 206, 209

Calvin, Jean, 125, 151

Campbell, Joseph, *Masks of God: Occidental Mythology*, 241

Canada: art of, 182, 184; criticism of, 187n, 192; culture of, 193; history of, 182, 183–84; imagination of, 188, 191; literary scene in, 279; modernism of, 192, 264, 275; nationalism of, 193, 282, 381, 394, 444n4; poetry of, 178, 187–90, 264, 392, 444n6, 445n11; postmodernism in, 190, 392–93, 405, 453n8; tradition of, 186, 393; vision of, 282; voice of, 264, 432n9; writing in, 185, 193, 264

Canadian Political Thought (Forbes), 282

Cantos (Pound), 3, 5, 123, 196, 276, 438n20, 442n56

capitalism, 71, 92, 266, 290, 292; global, 97, 104

Caponigri, A., *Time and Idea: The Theory of History in Giambattista Vico*, 140, 441n43

Caproni, Giorgio, "Ritorno," 109

Captain's Deathbed and Other Essays, The (Woolf), 333–34, 333n

Carman, Bliss, 188, 445n11

Carnevali, Emanuel, 305

Carpenter, Edward, 334, 335, 340, 343, 344

Carroll, Lewis, 126, 284; *Alice in Wonderland*, 284, 435n1; *The Hunting of the Snark*, 151, 238–39, 284, 432n7

Cartesian thought: humanism, 77; idealism, 217, 231. *See also* Descartes, René

Casaubon, Isaac, 324

Cassirer, Ernst, *The Renaissance Philosophy of Man*, 71n, 135

Castoriadis, Cornelius, *Crossroads in the Labyrinth*, 42

Castro, Fidel, 231

41, 258–59, 260, 290, 291, 390, 391,
428n4, 450nn18,21; on mystic speech,
259, 260, 428n4, 450nn18,21; *The Practice
of Everyday Life*, 88, 94, 95, 95n

deconstruction, xiii, 41, 87, 254, 257, 259,
334, 450n23; debt to Mallarmé, 88; and
poetry, 192; and positivism, 41, 376,
386. *See also* poststructuralism

Dee, John, 135

Degeneration (Nordau), 340

"De L'Amitié" (*Essais, Livre 1*, Montaigne),
163, 385, 418n9

Deleuze, Gilles, xii, 367; *The Fold*, 365, 397,
398, 398n19, 452n7; *Nietzsche and Phi-
losophy*, 341–2

Delphi, 8; in "Corfe" by Mary Butts, 174, 311

Delta (Dudek), 267

Demeter, 173

democracy, 15, 74, 80, 95, 96, 97, 101, 105,
141, 192, 193, 218, 246–47, 253, 264,
280, 282, 302, 351, 355, 373

De Monarchia (Dante), 72, 73, 74, 431n6

Derrida, Jacques, xii, 258; *Aporias*, 384n11;
Dissemination, 58; and Mallarmé, 58;
Handelman on, 44, 261

Descartes, René, 93, 152, 354, 367; Olson
on, 209, 223; opposition to magic, 326;
and poetry, 199; and science, 101. *See also*
Cartesian thought

"Descent, The" (Bowering), 178

"Desert Elm" (Bowering), 186, 445n9

determinism, 72, 340; McLuhan's, 267;
versus modernism, 348, 396; Pico on,
70; technological, 68

Dewey, John, 72

dialectic, 12, 29, 30, 343, 357; Agamben
on, 100; Blaser, use of, 36; as experience,
117; Marxist, 14, 67; Merleau-Ponty on,
120, 438n17; Olson on, 133; Vico, use
of, 140

Diary of Virginia Woolf, The (Woolf), 338

Dickinson, Emily, 298

dictation: poetics of, 36, 102; tradition of,
152, 257; in Yeats, 115, 247. *See also* Spicer,
Jack

Die Moorsoldaten, 156–57

Dikeakos, Christos, 380, 407, 409, 446n1;
collage-paintings, 229–30, 233, 238,
243–44, 250, 251, 381, 396–97; *Context

of Medusa: Explorer III*, 239, 240; in cultural
context, 234–35, 236, 241–43, 247,
248–50; and Duchamp, 232, 235, 239,
242, 244–50, 381, 396; *Explorer II: The
Story of Ikarus*, 239; *Ikaria: Poem = Espace*,
Explorer I, 229, 230, 239, 241, 243, 244,
249, 396, 396–97; *Ikaria: Poster*, 229, 230,
240, 397; *Making History*, 246; *Medusa Hair*,
239; *Medusa Mirror*, 239; *Medusa Temple*, 241;
Praxis Makes Perfect, 229, 230; *Speedy Apollo
Pizza*, 244; and technology, 237, 396–97;
Terminal Avenue/Terminal City, 230; *The Three
Muses in Distress*, 230

Dionysus, 8–9, 173

"Displacing the Self: The Progress of Ezra
Pound's Pre-Cantos Poetics" (Grieve), 39

Dissemination (Derrida), 58

Divine Comedy, The (Dante), 74, 100, 234,
417n1; Singleton translation of, 417n1

Divine Mystery, The (Upward), 325, 342;
Duncan's introduction to, 324

"Divorce in Naples" (Faulkner), 308

Dk/Some Letters of Ezra Pound (Dudek), 279–80

Doctor Faustus Lights the Lights (Stein), 303

Donne, John, and Spicer, 147, 259

Donoghue, Denis: *Thieves of Fire*, 285; *Yeats*,
141

Doolittle, Hilda (H. D.), 26, 168, 335, 402,
417n2; and Butts, 309, 310, 325

Doré, Gustave, 105

Doresse, Jean, *The Secret Books of the Egyptian
Gnostics*, 160, 443n57

Dorn, Ed, 405

Draenos, Stan Spyros, "Thinking Without a
Ground: Hannah Arendt and Contempo-
rary Situation of Understanding," 83

Dryden, John, and Dudek, 278

dualism: Coleridge on, 142; in Descartes,
326; gnostic, 40, 123; humanist, 77; in
Marxism, 197; Merleau-Ponty on, 143;
in Spicer, 120, 123, 131, 134

Duchamp, Marcel, 235, 448n3; and Breton,
244n; *The Bride Stripped Bare by Her Bachelors,
Even (Large Glass)*, 242, 248–50, 447n6;
and chance, 232, 244, 249, 383; and
Keisler, 241–43, 242n, 396; *Nude Descend-
ing a Staircase*, 247; Paz on, 133, 245–50;
ready-mades, 248, 250, 396; and Spicer,
121, 383. *See also* Dikeakos, Christos

339, 341; and sacred, 84, 194, 310, 313, 314, 327, 328

modernity: and aesthetics, 141; and artists, 280; and canon, 263; and Christianity, 354; and criticism, 141; cultural policy, 432n1; discourse, 62; field theory, 143; grail quest, 322, 329; history, 23, 80; humanism, 69, 70, 71, 73, 75, 207, 336; humanities, 81; imagination, 341, 454n9; literature, 143, 178, 183, 187, 206; and loss of meaning, 327, 329; magic, 325–27; materiality of language, 41; and the modern condition, 165, 187, 190, 208, 256, 293; moderns, 278, 328; positivism, 81, 450n5; predicament of, 317; and poetry, 22, 33, 34, 40, 44, 47, 61, 73, 126, 131, 132, 197, 263, 373; and politics, 21, 143; project of, 82, 86, 93, 262, 263, 279, 282, 366; and public culture, 220; and revolutions, 15, 19, 20, 65, 68; science, 101, 201, 307, 376n7, 387; and sublime, 43, 300; and superstition, 21; and technology, 94, 237; thought of, 88, 139, 237, 239, 271, 291, 424n41, 454n9; tradition of, 186, 190, 317; world, 189

Mohammed, 86, 216

Mondrian, Piet, 284

Monroe, Harriet, 278

Montaigne, Michel de, "De L'Amitié," 163, 385, 418n9

Mont-Saint-Michel and Chartres (Adams), 5, 412n8

"Moon Shadow" (Bowering), 182

Moore, Marianne, 281

Morgenstern, Christian, 287, 291; Galgenlieder: A Selection, 284

Moth Poem, The (Blaser), 12, 404, 405, 414nn18,19

Mouré, Erin, xi

Mozart, Wolfgang Amadeus, 359

music, 84, 125, 164, 239, 327, 350, 356, 357, 358–59, 363, 397, 398n19; aleatoric, 363–65, 381; in Blaser's work, 410; Bowering, 181, 186; in Dudek's work, 275, 276; in Duncan's work, 286; and language, 27, 36, 58, 80, 98, 146, 158, 355, 362, 365, 420n24; and mathematics, 354, 357–58; in Olson's work,

363, 416n9; Orphic, 9, 14; and Plato, 9; and poetry, 363, 429n15; serial, 34, 115, 119, 120n, 255, 362, 364, 423n33; of spheres, 4, 146; in Spicer's work, 146, 158, 161, 443n58; as temporal process, 358. See also Bach, Johann Sebastian; Boulez, Pierre

Muslim, 80, 99, 107, 366

Muthologos (Olson), 351, 363; Butterick's notes on, 363

Muybridge, Eadweard, 447n5

mysticism, 31, 152, 291, 354, 362, 419n13, 454n7. See also Butts, Mary; de Certeau, Michel

"My Stories" (Tallman), 406–7

"'My Vocabulary Did This To Me'" (Blaser), xvi, 163, 253, 255, 384–86, 408, 447, 452n12, 456n12

Nancy, Jean-Luc, 108; The Sense of the World, 434n7

Nashe, Thomas, 168

nationalism, xvi, 96; Canadian, 193, 282, 381, 394. See also Mathews, Robin

naturalism, 185, 186

necessity, 66–67, 71, 130, 136, 197, 372, 378, 431n2

Necessity of Art: A Marxist Approach (Fischer), 14, 17

Needham, Joseph, 201

negative capability. See Keats, John

Nerval, Gérard de, 10–11, 107, 149; Les Chimères, 370, 372, 390, 405, 436n9. See also Blaser, Robin; Duncan, Robert

New Age (Orage), 278n, 342, 343, 344

New American Poetry, The (Allen), xi, xiv, 301, 403, 404, 411, 453n2

New American poets, xi, xiv, 391, 392, 445n13

new criticism, 270n, 349n

New Science of Giambattista Vico, The (Vico), 140, 439n30

New Sentence, The (Silliman), 41n, 386

New Spirit, The (Ellis), 340

New Testament (Bible), 51, 257, 429n14

Newton, Sir Isaac, xii, 202, 326, 358, 398

Nichol, bp, xi, 179, 190, 191, 193, 195n, 263, 264; Journal, 195n; Martyrology, 195n

Nichols, Sophia, 401, 403, 405, 413n15

Pound Era, The (Kenner), 199, 201

Practice of Everyday Life, The (de Certeau), 88, 94, 95, 95n

"Practice of Outside, The" (Blaser), xvi, 113, 371n3, 381–84, 382n9, 386, 391, 395, 406, 407, 432n7, 435, 435n3, 438n20, 445n8, 446n3, 447, 447n4, 450m20

pragmatism, 206. See also Peirce, Charles

Pratt, E. J., 188, 265, 445n11

Praxis Makes Perfect (Dikeakos), 229, 230

Preface to the Early Poems of Robert Duncan (Blaser), 299, 391n16, 408, 452

Prelude to Chemistry: An Outline of Alchemy, Its Literature and Relationships (Read), 323n

pre-Raphaelites, 321, 322, 340

Process and Reality: An Essay in Cosmology (Whitehead), 50, 72–73, 76, 150, 196n, 201n, 201–3, 205, 207, 208, 210–27, 222n, 289, 374, 386–90, 407, 441n48, 445, 451n6, 456n11

"Projective Verse" (Olson), xii, 115

Prolegomena to the Study of Greek Religion (Harrison), 339

Prometheus, 14, 15, 194

Prometheus Unbound (Shelley), 36, 426n31

Prophetic Melville: Experience, Transcendence, Tragedy (Sherrill), 200–201

Protractatus: An Early Version of Tractus Logico-Philosophicus (Wittgenstein), 51n

Proust, Marcel, 306

Psalms, 208

Pseudepigrapha, 59, 429n14

Ptolemy, 69

Purdy, Al, 179, 184, 188, 189, 445nn11,14

Puritanism, 125, 354

Pythagoras, 123, 153, 357

Quartermain, Meredith, 401, 410

Quartermain, Peter, 401

"Radio Jazz" (Bowering), 180, 182

Ray, Man, 448n3

Reactionaries, The (Harrison), 15, 16, 415n3

Read, John, Prelude to Chemistry: An Outline of Alchemy, Its Literature and Relationships, 323n

Reading Capital (Althusser and Balibar), 33, 422n30

real, the: absent, 33; in art, 233–41; capitalist, 97; as composition, xiii, xiv, 4, 25, 27–28, 30, 33, 34, 36, 67, 168, 182, 197–98, 229, 239, 245, 251, 266–70, 372–73, 379–80, 393–96, 399–400; consumerist, 275; destruction of, 101; dispersal of, 236; empirical, 379; as experience, 101; grammars of, 73; in Hebraic tradition, 43–44, 376; imagination of, 77, 101, 134, 268; loss of, 79–80, 191; in media, 87; objective, 307, 348; personal, 78; as poiesis, 57, 59, 394–96, 399–400; positivism of, 42, 44–45, 61–66, 72, 81, 88, 197–98, 354, 376, 377; as postmodern, 46–48, 251; principle of, 79; shared, 264; as social construct, 14, 66, 67, 75, 78, 81–83, 95, 280, 372; socialist (Marxian), 66, 67, 92, 197, 275, 290, 377–78; spiritual, 58, 358; struggle for, 197, 221, 272, 325–26, 416n9; as technology, 83, 236–38, 272; ultimate, 54, 65, 66, 68, 103, 232, 241, 270, 291, 348, 353, 355, 358; uncertainty of, 41, 260; uncharted, 274; wounded, 179, 182. See also Olson, Charles; Spicer, Jack

realism, xiii, 42, 45, 65, 69, 92, 144, 152, 183, 185–86, 190, 230, 238, 250–52, 310, 311, 314, 316, 327, 392

Real Presences (Steiner), 287

Reaney, James, 188, 445n11

"Recovery of the Public World, The," (Blaser), xv, xvi, 64, 85, 198, 372n5, 378–79, 386, 408, 409, 415n2, 429b9, 430, 431nn1,3, 434n5, 446n1, 453n5, 455n9, 456n14

Recovery of the Public World, The (Byrne and Watts, eds.), 453n8

Redon, Odilon, 333

Reed, David, Language (journal), 152

Reflections on Public Policy: Past, Present and Future (Alderson, Blaser, Coward), 408, 430, 432; Alderson's introduction to, 91, 408, 432n2

"Reflections on Wolfgang Giegerich's 'The Burial of the Soul in Technological Civilization'" (Avens), 355

Reid, Jamie, 87, 391, 405

relativism, 75, 77

religion, 40, 46, 48, 65, 68, 72, 82–84,
88, 91, 96, 97, 100, 107–8, 131, 132,
152, 180, 221, 230, 258, 290, 291–92,
297, 322, 335, 344, 352–53, 377; and
aesthetics, 32, 338; American, 352–53;
esoteric, 324–31, 443n2; Greek, 331–32,
339; origins of, 54–55; and poetry, 211,
215–16, 219, 258, 266, 272, 289, 304;
as tradition, 52, 75–77, 82, 230, 248–49,
357. *See also* Christianity; sacred, the
Renaissance, 56, 69–71, 75–76, 80–81, 135,
151, 188, 212, 248, 250, 288, 325, 336,
357, 359, 371, 432n1
Renaissance Philosophy of Man, The (Cassirer), 71n,
135
Renewal of Literature: Emersonian Reflections (Poirier),
295, 297, 297n
Republic, The (Plato), 9, 54, 270
"Resistance, The" (Olson), xii, 379
*Return to Pagany: The History, Correspondence, and
Selections from a Little Magazine, 1929–1932*
(Halpert and Johns), 305, 305n, 306, 307,
308, 309; Rexroth's introduction to, 306
Revelations (Bible), 97
revolution, xv, 16, 356; American, 16, 19–
21, 23–24, 66; and arts/poetry, 136,
143, 299, 306; bourgeois, 81; Chinese,
19: Cuban, 19; epistemological, 198;
French, 19, 59, 66; Greek, 246–7; Marx-
ian, 19, 67–68, 71, 447n2; modern, 15,
20, 65, 344; scientific, 333. *See also* Arendt,
Hannah
Rexroth, Kenneth, 185, 186, 301, 392, 402;
introduction to *Fragments of a Faith Forgotten*
(Mead), 324n; introduction to *The Holy
Kabbalah* (Waite), 324n; introduction to *A
Return to Pagany* (Halpert and Johns), 306
Ṛgveda, 86, 432n10
Richards, I. A., 270n
Richardson, Keith, *Poetry and the Colonized Mind:
Tish*, 392n
Richard Wagner (Gregor-Dellin), 322
Riding, Laura, 168
Riel, Louis, 184
Rilke, Rainer Maria, 39–40, 49, 55–56, 61,
101, 144, 376, 402; *Duino Elegies*, 39–40,
56; *Letters of Rainer Maria Rilke*, 55, 144
"Rilke and Nietzsche with a Discourse on
Thought, Belief and Poetry" (Heller), 56

Rimbaud, Arthur, 107, 131, 151, 159, 364
Rime of the Ancient Mariner, The (Coleridge), 291
"Ritorno" (Caproni), 109
Road to Xanadu, The (Lowes), 291, 452n10
Robbe-Grillet, Alain, 183
"Robert Creeley's Epistemopathic Path"
(Mesch), 51, 51n
Roberts, Oral, 73
"Rocket, The" (Giegerich), 353–54
Rodker, John, 166, 170, 171
Rodwell, G. F., 323n
romanticism, 62, 87, 93, 141, 185, 284,
291, 300, 324, 348, 360, 446n2
Rosicrucianism, 324, 325
Ross, W. W. E., 188, 445n11
Rousseau, Jean Jacques, 21
Rudge, Olga, 309
Ruskin, John, 297
Russell, John, *The Meaning of Modern Art*, 196,
196n, 231, 234

sacred, the, 26, 38–41, 48–50, 53, 55, 61–
62, 65, 72, 78, 80, 83–84, 90, 98, 106,
108, 233, 233n; language, 289, 291, 296,
362; modern question of, 256–59, 266,
270n, 354. *See also* Blaser, Robin; Butts,
Mary; grail; religion; Spicer, Jack
Sacred Discontent (Schneidau), 61–62, 376
Said, Edward, 258; *The World, the Text, and the
Critic*, 40
San Francisco Renaissance, xi, 138, 168,
402, 405, 406, 411n1, 412n5
Sangster, Charles, 188, 445n11
Sapir, Edward, 382
Sâr Péladan, 325
Sartre, Jean Paul, 91, 448n3
Saturn, 10, 319, 414n23
Savage Hunters of the Labrador Peninsula, The (Speck),
6, 413n13
Scenes from the Life of Cleopatra (Butts), 167, 338
Schelling, Friedrich Wilhelm Joseph von,
201
Schneidau, Herbert: *Ezra Pound: The Image and the
Real*, 278–79, 278n; *Sacred Discontent*, 61–
62, 376
Schorer, Mark, 403
Schrödinger, Erwin, 69, 77n, 431n4
Schutte, Ofelia, *Beyond Nihilism: Nietzsche without
Masks*, 341

Heads of the Town up to the Aether, 117–18, 121–22, 139, 146, 147, 159–60, 385, 385n12, 400, 428n3, 435n4, 436n8, 438n18, 443n57; The Holy Grail, 117–18, 136, 139, 145–46, 156–58, 255–56, 313, 436n7; "Imaginary Elegies," 49; Language, 117, 124, 127, 130, 151, 152, 155, 156, 260, 384, 431n4, 438n24, 440n36, 449n13; One Night Stand and Other Poems, 442n52; "Poetry and Politics," 442n49; Vancouver Lectures, 115–19, 132, 256, 435nn2,3, 436nn6,7, 437n13, 438nn18,19, 439n27, 441nn45,46, 448n8

Spinoza, Baruch, 9, 357; On the Improvement of the Understanding: The Ethics, 387n13

Spoils of Poynton, The (James), 168

"Stadium of the Mirror, The" (Blaser), xii, xvi, 26, 32, 373–76, 377, 382, 383, 407, 416, 421n25, 422n29, 428n3, 429n9, 431n3, 437nn10,11, 438n21, 439n26, 440n40, 441, 444nn1,3, 446n3, 447n3, 450n3, 451nn3,5, 452n11, 453n2, 455n7

Stanford, W. B., The Sound of Greek: Studies in Greek Theory and Practice of Euphony, 363, 456n16

Stanley, George, 145, 153, 155, 405, 406, 412n5, 442n53

Stalin, Joseph, 92, 231

Stein, Gertrude, 168, 183, 185, 185n, 191, 294, 305, 306, 309; Doctor Faustus Lights the Lights, 303; A Long Gay Book, 184, 185n

Steiner, George, Real Presences, 287

Steiner, Wendy, Exact Resemblance to Exact Resemblance: The Literary Portraiture of Gertrude Stein, 187

Steinmetz, C. P., 201

Stern, G. B., 167

Stevens, Wallace, 297, 448n3; "Esthétique du mal," 38, 428n2

"St. Francis Einstein of the Daffodils" (Williams), 204, 310

Sticks and Stones (Bowering), 444n7

Stockhausen, Karlheinz, Klavierstüke, 365

Stocktakings (Boulez), 359, 364

"Story of an Olson, and Bad Thing," (Olson), 204

Strauss, David Levi, Between the Eyes: Essays on Photography and Politics, 106

structuralism, 87, 259, 386, 398n20

Strzygowski, Josef, The Origin of Christian Church Art, 226

Stuart, Colin, 406, 427n60, 435n3

Studies in Literature and the Humanities: Innocent of Intent (Whalley), 62–63, 272

Studies in the Psychology of Sex (Ellis), 335

Styles of Radical Will, (Sontag), 178n

sublime, 5, 30, 38, 46–47, 131, 148, 178, 238, 288, 300, 362, 419n11

Surette, Leon, A Light from Eleusis: A Study of Ezra Pound's Cantos, 325n

surrealism, 71, 116, 160, 166, 167, 186, 192, 238–39, 245, 254, 284

Sutherland, John, 187, 393

syntax, 57, 66, 97, 137, 155, 179, 195n, 200, 253, 260, 289–90, 303, 306, 359, 366, 378, 407, 420n20; definition of, 26–27; hypotaxis, 32, 98, 253, 379; parataxis, 32, 97–98, 200, 253, 379

Syntax (Blaser), 407, 429n10

Tallman, Ellen, 401, 402, 405, 445n13; "My Stories," 406–7

Tallman, Karen, 406, 409

Tallman, Warren, 187n, 189, 405, 407, 411, 445n11; "The Wonder Merchants: Modernist Poetry in Vancouver in the 1960s," 189, 445n13

Taming of Chance, The (Hacking), 365

Tarot, 153, 324, 407

Taylor, Cecil, 366

Taylor, Mark C., Erring: A Postmodern A/ Theology, 56, 94, 296, 254, 448n6, 452n12

technology, xv, 46, 61, 78, 94, 355, 375, 399, 431n2; and arts, 236–8, 381, 396–97; Dudek on, 264–66, 269, 271–72; Grant on, 271–72; and humanism, 76; as will, 69, 83, 236–38, 354

Technology and Empire (Grant), 271

Temporal Processes in Beethoven's Music (Greene), 358–59

Temptation of St. Anthony, The (Bosch), 242

Temptation of St. Anthony, The (Flaubert), 105, 434n2

Tennyson, Alfred, 321, 322

Terminal Avenue/ Terminal City, 230

terrorism, 106, 207

Tertullian, 161

Whitman, Walt, 5, 25, 277, 282, 296, 298, 340, 352, 402; "Repondez," 25, 416n11

Wholeness and the Implicate Order (Bohm), 77n

Whorf, Benjamin Lee, 382; "An American Indian Model of the Universe," 200, 200n

Wieners, John, 403

Wilbur, Richard, 143

Wilde, Oscar, 340, 420

Wilden, Anthony, "Lacan and the Discourse of the Other," 35, 417n3, 418n10, 421n25, 423n31, 425n47

wild-logos, 28, 119, 260, 291, 383, 417n5, 437n11

Wilke, Brian, and M. J. Johnson, *Blake's Four Zoas*, 344n

William Carlos Williams: The American Background (Weaver), 201

Williams, Jonathan, 286

Williams, Raymond, 399n20

Williams, William Carlos: Bowering, influence on, 183, 185, 186, 392; Dudek, influence on, 264, 281; *The Great American Novel*, 183; *In the American Grain*, 306; as modernist, 132, 133, 143, 168, 185, 264, 294; Olson, influence on, 196, 201, 204, 224; *Paterson*, 196; *Pictures from Breughel and Other Poems: Collected Poems, 1950–62*, 186; "The Poem as a Field of Action," 204, 224; science, interest in, 201, 307, 310; Spicer, influence on, 132–33; "St. Francis Einstein of the Daffodils," 204, 310; *A Voyage to Pagany*, 306–8, 310; *White Mule*, 309

William Shakespeare (Hugo), 418n6

Will to Power, The (Nietzsche), 341

Wittgenstein, Ludwig, 51, 54, 102; *Pro-tractatus: An Early Version of Tractus Logico-Philosophicus*, 51n

Wolin, Sheldon S., *Politics and Vision*, 21, 21n, 22n, 416n7

Women of Trachis, The (Sophocles), 221

"Wonder Merchants: Modernist Poetry in Vancouver in the 1960s" (Tallman), 189, 445n13

Woolf, Leonard, 349n

Woolf, Virginia: *The Captain's Deathbed and Other Essays*, 333–34, 333n; *The Diary of Virginia Woolf*, 338

Wordsworth, William, 403

World, the Text, and the Critic, The (Said), 40

World War I, 214, 427n61, 447n2

World War II, 214, 246, 247, 338, 402, 423n32

Writing Writing (Duncan), 303

Yates, Francis, 354; *The Art of Memory*, 9–10, 371, 414nn21,22,23, 421n25; *Giordano Bruno*, 323, 325n, 326–27, 456n10

Years as Catches (Duncan), 300, 302

Yeats (Donoghue), 141

Yeats, William Butler, 402, 403; as modernist, xi, 15–16, 39, 141, 193, 264, 265, 325, 336, 341, 390, 393, 415n3; Olson, influence on, 205–6, 415n4; "The Second Coming," 336, 341; Spicer, influence on, 115, 117, 139, 141, 145, 147, 257

Yeats and Nietzsche: An Exploration of Major Nietzschean Echoes in William Butler Yeats, (Bohlmann), 341

Zembla's Rocks (Dudek), 281, 282

Zeus, 156, 241, 244, 305, 319–21, 328–32, 335, 345–48, 395. *See also* Jove

Zeus: A Study of Ancient Religion (Cook), 331

Zola, Emile, 340

Zoroaster, 86, 330, 426

Zukofsky, Louis, 3, 309; *An Objectivist's Anthology*, 167, 174, 311, 454n3; *A Test of Poetry*, 441n3